Environmental Management Readings and Cases

Environmental Management Readings and Cases

Edited by

Michael V. Russo
University of Oregon

HOUGHTON MIFFLIN COMPANY   Boston   New York

Cover design and image: Minko T. Dimov, MinkoImages

Sponsoring Editor: *Kathleen L. Hunter*
Senior Associate Editor: *Susan M. Kahn*
Senior Project Editor: *Fred H. Burns*
Senior Production/Design Coordinator: *Jennifer Waddell*
Senior Manufacturing Coordinator: *Marie Barnes*
Marketing Manager: *Juli Bliss*

Printed in the U.S.A.

Library of Congress Catalog Card Number: 98–72083

ISBN: 0-395-87817-9

123456789-QF–02 01 00 99 98

Contents

● **Preface   ix**

● **Part 1   Perspectives on the Environmental Challenge   1**

　　1   Beyond Greening: Strategies for a Sustainable World   2
　　　　Stuart L. Hart
　　　　　Thinking Globally and Inclusively About Sustainable
　　　　　Business Practices

　　2   Building a New Economy   15
　　　　Lester R. Brown and Jennifer Mitchell
　　　　　Remaining Challenges and Signs of Transition to a
　　　　　Greener Global Economy

● **Part 2   The Institutional Setting of Environmental Issues   37**

　　3   The Land Ethic   40
　　　　Aldo Leopold
　　　　　What Is the Relationship Between Humankind and the Environment?

　　4   Asking How Much Is Enough   51
　　　　Alan Durning
　　　　　A Critical Examination of the Culture of Consumption

　　5   The Tragedy of the Commons   71
　　　　Garrett Hardin
　　　　　The Classic Discussion of Population and Common Resources

　　6   EPA and the Evolution of Federal Regulation   82
　　　　Paul R. Portney
　　　　　Regulation and Economic Models for
　　　　　Meeting Pollution Reduction Goals

　　7   Costs and Benefits   95
　　　　Frances Cairncross
　　　　　How Can Environmental Costs Be Better Captured in Prices?

8   Discounting the Future: Economics and Ethics   107
     Timothy J. Brennan
        A Critical Analysis of the Practice of Discounting
        in Economic Analysis
9   Behind the Scenes: How Policymaking in the European Community,
     Japan, and the United States Affects Global Negotiations   113
     Raymond Vernon
        A Survey of Environmental Policies in the Triad
10   Global Trade and the Environment   133
     Edward Goldsmith
        How International Trade Imperils Environmental Quality
11   Making Trade Work for the Environment   143
     Daniel C. Esty
        How the Environment Can Be Protected Through International Trade

● **Part 3   Managing to Be Environmentally Responsive   153**
12   Strategic Management for a Small Planet   155
     W. Edward Stead and Jean Garner Stead
        Using Environmental Capabilities to Foster Competitive Advantage
13   Corporate Obstacles to Pollution Prevention   170
     Peter Cebon
        How the Sociology of the Workplace Influences Program Success
14   The Emergence of Environmental Partnerships   173
     Frederick J. Long and Matthew B. Arnold
        Creating Dialog and Collaboration with Environmental Groups
15   Consumers with a Conscience   187
     Jacquelyn A. Ottman
        Who Are the Green Consumers?
16   The Next Big Product Opportunity   202
     Jacquelyn A. Ottman
        How Can Businesses Reach Green Consumers?

● **Part 4   Principles of Corporate Ecology   215**
17   Note on Life Cycle Analysis   217
     Susan Svoboda
        A Methodology for Identifying Costs Across the Life of Products
18   An Introduction to Environmental Accounting
     as a Business Management Tool   228
     United States Environmental Protection Agency
        A Tool Kit for Incorporating the Environment
        into Accounting Practice

19   Integrating Environment and Technology: Design for Environment   245
     Braden R. Allenby
          Designing Products with Environmental Impact in Mind
20   Introduction to ISO 14000   256
     Tom Tibor with Ira Feldman
          *An Overview of the International Environmental
          Management System*
21   The Natural Step to Sustainability   267
     Wingspread Journal
          Unifying Scientific Principles with Sustainability

● **Part 5   Environmental Management Cases   273**
22   Bank of America and the Carlsbad Highlands Foreclosure (A)   274
     Anne T. Lawrence
23   Pacific Lumber Company   283
     Michael V. Russo and Cindy Noblitt
24   The International Climate Change Partnership:
     An Industry Association Faces the Climate Change Issue   299
     David L. Levy
25   Acid Rain: The Southern Company   312
     Forest Reinhardt
26   Self (A)   318
     Scott B. Sonenshein, Michael Gorman, and Patricia Werhane
27   Self (B)   323
     Scott B. Sonenshein, Michael Gorman, and Patricia Werhane
28   Deja Shoe (A): Creating the Environmental Footwear Company   327
     Paul Hardy
29   Procter & Gamble Inc.: Downy Enviro-Pak   338
     Janet Lahey, Chris Lane, and Adrian B. Ryans
30   McDonald's Environmental Strategy   344
     Susan Svoboda and Stuart L. Hart
31   The Clamshell Controversy   359
     Susan Svoboda
32   The Procter & Gamble Company: Disposable
     and Reusable Diapers—A Life-Cycle Analysis   370
     Management Institute for Environment and Business
33   DesignTex, Incorporated (A)   374
     Matthew M. Mehalik, Michael E. Gorman, Andrea Larson,
     and Patricia H. Werhane
34   Bayerische Motoren Werke AG   381
     Christopher A. Cummings and Frank den Hond

35   Industrial Products, Inc. (A): Measuring Environmental Performance   406
     Richard Wells
36   Oil in the Ecuadorean Rainforest   415
     Christopher A. Cummings, Barbara L. Marcus, R. Edward Freeman,
     and Jason Lunday
37   Cost Accounting and Hazardous Wastes at Specialty Glass, Inc.   429
     Christopher H. Stinson

Preface

Toward Environmentally Literate Managers

First consider a young child, an infant of roughly twelve months of age. Soon, the child will make a stunning discovery—objects that pass from her view do not disappear entirely. The realization of permanency is critical to the development of the child, forming a key cognitive building block that serves as the foundation of understanding about the surrounding physical world.

Consider now the modern corporation. Together with its corporate competitors and collaborators, in the last stages of the twentieth century, the typical corporation dominates global economic activity. Although its relationships with other economic actors are breathtaking in their complexity, sophistication, and vision, until just recently its relationship with the ecological domain was as simple as that of the infant. Pollutants it emitted while producing goods and services were treated as though they ceased to exist once they vanished into the air, water, and soil. Environmental impacts of the use and disposal of products weren't given a second thought.

Only in the last several decades have corporations attained even an adolescent's awareness of their environmental impacts. This limited state of maturity was largely the result of societal outcries and ensuing political and legal mandates that have prodded corporations to rethink their relationship with the natural environment. No longer could pollution and its social and economic cost be externalized and presumed to disappear. Regulations tightened and a string of high-profile industrial accidents dramatized the need for action.

But while many corporations have viewed environmental stewardship as a worthy goal, others are not meeting the challenge. In fact, on any given day, the *Wall Street Journal* is likely to report that one or more corporations have been targeted for environmental challenges by foreign or domestic governments, activist groups, or one of a host of stakeholders expecting better performance. Somewhat paradoxically, at the same time that critics are voicing concerns, market forces promoting "greener" products are gaining steam, presenting businesses with enormous opportunities, both domestically and globally. The managerial challenge in these uncertain times is indisputable.

Unfortunately, though, corporations often are confounded when they try to answer this challenge for a simple organizational reason: their managers often lack environmental awareness, literacy, and sensitivity. The goal of this book is to address this shortcoming by engaging students in an inquiry that challenges them to step away from their prejudices and ingrained habits and see the world around them through new eyes. So that new ideas can breed action, it also provides them with tools to implement change.

The Motivation for This Collection

Oscar Wilde once said, "When the gods wish to punish us, they answer our prayers." The collection in your hands is the result of initial enthusiasm giving way to unexpected frustration. It was a thrill to have a class on environmental management approved at the University of Oregon's Lundquist College of Business. But finding appropriate reading materials and cases to support the course proved a thorny task. After several years of exasperation, I decided that a textbook including a broad range of readings and cases was the answer. I also felt it would "serve the cause" by creating a coherent teaching tool for instructors interested in the subject but not fully conversant in its very broad literature.

Just as the manufacturing function yields products that meet previously established specifications, the "specs" for this book had to be determined. Here, a key issue was the absence of any standard for what was included in courses and course modules that addressed environmental management. While the lack of standards promotes freedom for individual instructors seeking to fulfill their needs, it seriously complicated the task I faced. So in producing this book, readings and cases were chosen to support 100 percent of the materials necessary for a course module on the topic or 90 percent of the materials necessary for an entire course. In the latter case, the choice was made based on the great diversity in course offerings combined with the need to keep the book's length and cost at a reasonable level. In either case, the collection is intended to provide either all or substantially all of the requirements to support pedagogy in this area. In the case of complete courses on environmental management, instructors will be free to supplement the readings and cases included here with other items chosen due to the special focus of their courses, local or emerging environmental issues, or other specific circumstances.

The Organization of the Collection

In attempting to develop environmentally literate managers, this collection stresses important areas organized in five sections of the book. The first is an appreciation of the problem itself. Here, the term "appreciation" is interpreted broadly. Not only do students need to understand the impact that business activity and economic growth have on the natural world, but they also need to appreciate that the problem has both economic and sociocultural dimensions. For this reason, the collection was structured such that students will have both a practical and a more conceptual appreciation of the relationships between humankind and the natural world.

A second section addresses the institutional setting in which environmental decisions and actions occur. Here again, the area is interpreted broadly, to include readings that touch upon cultural values, as well as institutions such as governments and markets. Two readings with strong ethical components lead this section, so that students are confronted with several of the deeper, value-laden issues that environmental stewardship suggests. We then turn to a discussion of environmental regulation and economics. Here, we discuss how the economic model that dominates world commerce might lead to environmental decay, and how it can be amended through the use of policy and economic tools to protect and even enhance environmental quality. We conclude with a debate on the environment-trade issue, an intellectual flashpoint that has provoked strong and conflicting viewpoints.

The third section of the book focuses specifically on the organizational and strategic challenges of environmental stewardship. Here the strategic imperatives of environmentalism are addressed, and the reader begins to appreciate how organizations can take explicit actions to address their new competitive context.

The fourth section concentrates on skills that managers need as they confront the challenges and opportunities presented by mandates for environmental quality. Thus, given an appreciation of the nature of the challenge and the political and economic infrastructure under which corporations and other organizations act, the prospective manager is ready to examine methods for responding to threats and opportunities in the external context. This section concentrates on providing pragmatic and readily accessible tools for applying principles of environmentally sound techniques to actual business situations. It concludes by taking a step back to consider the ultimate conditions that must be met for sustainability to be a reality.

Sixteen cases are included in the final section of this collection. Each was carefully screened and chosen from a much larger number of candidates. Selection was made on a holistic basis—that is, the entire set of cases was chosen to meet overall criteria. The first criterion was that the cases be well-written and certain to provoke discussion in a classroom setting. The second was that the cases adequately cover the topic areas. The third aspect that was stressed was diversity among the cases, in terms of their settings, extent of numerical analysis, and length. Together, the cases form a coherent set that will breathe further life into the readings that they illustrate and supplement.

Pedagogical Aids

Because courses and modules in environmental management are unstandardized and unique to the instructor, it was a challenge to create supplemental materials that would anticipate and address the needs of various instructors. To meet this challenge, a detailed and extensive *Instructor's Resource Manual* provides in-depth teaching notes for both the readings and the cases. In addition, the manual provides a chart linking the cases to different environmental management subject areas; a chart linking the readings and cases to popular business, government, and society topics; several sample course outlines; and a note about group projects. A set of overhead illustrations that display and outline key points is also available. Together, we hope these tools will give instructors the information and flexibility to plan and execute a course that achieves their goals.

Acknowledgements

Many individuals played a role in bringing this project to reality. I thank the students, faculty, and administration at the University of Oregon for their encouragement as I developed and delivered my Management of Environmental Issues course for several years. All were supportive, involved, and committed to experimentation as the course was built from scratch and rebuilt each year until it was "ready for prime time." As noted, the search for a solid course was one of the motivating forces for this collection.

I thank Houghton Mifflin Company for being entrepreneurial in its approach to this project, and for their understanding that creating this new product meant stepping outside of the traditional bounds of textbook publishing. Special thanks go to Jennifer Speer, Susan Kahn, Kathy Hunter, and Fred Burns for sustaining and gently shaping the final product. I must also thank a number of organizations and people for allowing use of materials they developed, in particular Worldwatch Institute, the National Pollution Prevention Center, and, especially, Rick Bunch and the World Resource Institute's Management Institute for Environment and Business

I am deeply indebted to several outside reviewers who went the extra mile in delivering reviews that ultimately had a profound effect on this collection. Their advice on the choice and organization of the readings and cases enhanced the collection considerably. My gratitude goes to

Ken Baker
Dartmouth College
Brad Brown
University of Virginia
Paul F. Buller
Gonzaga University
Yiorgos Mylonadis
University of Pennsylvania

William A. Ruch
Arizona State University
Mark Sharfman
University of Oklahoma
W. Daniel Svedarsky
University of Minnesota

Final thanks go to my family. Living with a committed environmentalist, my spouse and partner Wendy has always been a source of both challenge and support. As someone outside of the business of management education, she never lost sight of the absolute need for environmental education for all of today's students. And I thank my sons Andy and David, whose presence reminded me of the need for our society to practice sustainability—the notion that we should meet our needs without compromising the ability of future generations to meet theirs.

Michael V. Russo

Part 1

Perspectives on the Environmental Challenge

THE FIRST PART of this book provides background on the nature and magnitude of the environmental challenges facing the planet. Our first reading is "Beyond Greening: Strategies for a Sustainable World," by Stuart L. Hart of the University of North Carolina. It serves as a keynote for the book by tying major international environmental challenges to the need for business to adopt sustainable practices. The solution lies in business strategies that are sustainable not only in a competitive sense, but also in an environmental sense. To build such strategies requires businesses to develop a vision of sustainability, which will act as a road map guiding them toward actions that reduce impacts on the earth, while enhancing the company's long-term viability.

The second reading provides further background on the environmental problems facing the planet and underscores the imperative for change. Written by Lester R. Brown and Jennifer Mitchell of the Worldwatch Institute, "Building a New Economy" surveys a number of critical environmental issues, showing that considerable work remains to be done. However, it also outlines a number of areas in which countries, policy makers, and corporate leaders have taken major initiatives toward sustainability. Nevertheless, Brown and Mitchell underscore the critical need for further leadership in the governmental domain, without which further progress is unlikely.

1

Beyond Greening: Strategies for a Sustainable World
Stuart L. Hart

The environmental revolution has been almost three decades in the making, and it has changed forever how companies do business. In the 1960s and 1970s, corporations were in a state of denial regarding their impact on the environment. Then a series of highly visible ecological problems created a groundswell of support for strict government regulation. In the United States, Lake Erie was dead. In Europe, the Rhine was on fire. In Japan, people were dying of mercury poisoning.

Today many companies have accepted their responsibility to do no harm to the environment. Products and production processes are becoming cleaner; and where such change is under way, the environment is on the mend. In the industrialized nations, more and more companies are "going green" as they realize that they can reduce pollution and increase profits simultaneously. We have come a long way.

But the distance we've traveled will seem small when, in 30 years, we look back at the 1990s. Beyond greening lies an enormous challenge—and an enormous opportunity. The challenge is to develop a *sustainable global economy:* an economy that the planet is capable of

supporting indefinitely. Although we may be approaching ecological recovery in the developed world, the planet as a whole remains on an unsustainable course. Those who think that sustainability is only a matter of pollution control are missing the bigger picture. Even if all the companies in the developed world were to achieve zero emissions by the year 2000, the earth would still be stressed beyond what biologists refer to as its carrying capacity. Increasingly, the scourges of the late twentieth century—depleted farmland, fisheries, and forests; choking urban pollution; poverty; infectious disease; and migration—are spilling over geopolitical borders. The simple fact is this: in meeting our needs, we are destroying the ability of future generations to meet theirs.

The roots of the problem—explosive population growth and rapid economic development in the emerging economies—are political and social issues that exceed the mandate and the capabilities of any corporation. At the same time, corporations are the only organizations with the resources, the technology, the global reach, and, ultimately, the motivation to achieve sustainability.

It is easy to state the case in the negative: faced with impoverished customers, degraded environments, failing political systems, and unraveling societies, it will be increasingly difficult for corporations to do business. But the positive case is even more powerful. The more we learn about the challenges of sustainability, the clearer it is that we are poised at the threshold of a historic moment in which many of the world's industries may be transformed.

To date, the business logic for greening has been largely operational or technical: bottom-up pollution-prevention programs have saved companies billions of dollars. However, few executives realize that environmental opportunities might actually become a major source of *revenue growth*. Greening has been framed in terms of risk reduction, reengineering, or cost cutting. Rarely is greening linked to strategy or technology development, and as a result, most companies fail to recognize opportunities of potentially staggering proportions.

WORLDS IN COLLISION

The achievement of sustainability will mean billions of dollars in products, services, and technologies that barely exist today. Whereas yesterday's businesses were often oblivious to their negative impact on the environment and today's responsible businesses strive for zero impact, tomorrow's businesses must learn to make a positive impact. Increasingly, companies will be selling solutions to the world's environmental problems.

Envisioning tomorrow's businesses, therefore, requires a clear understanding of those problems. To move beyond greening to sustainability, we must first unravel a complex set of global interdependencies. In fact, the global economy is really three different, overlapping economies.

The *market economy* is the familiar world of commerce comprising both the developed nations and the emerging economies.[1] About a billion people—one-sixth of the world's population—live in the developed countries of the market economy. Those affluent societies account for more than 75% of the world's energy and resource consumption and create the bulk of industrial, toxic, and consumer waste. The developed economies thus leave large ecological *footprints*—defined as the amount of land required to meet a typical consumer's needs. (See Exhibit 1, "Ecological Footprints.")

Despite such intense use of energy and materials, however, levels of pollution are relatively low in the developed economies. Three factors

Exhibit 1 ● Ecological Footprints

In the United States, it takes 12.2 acres to supply the average person's basic needs; in the Netherlands, 8 acres; in India, 1 acre. The Dutch ecological footprint covers 15 times the area of the Netherlands, whereas India's footprint exceeds its area by only about 35%. Most strikingly, if the entire world lived like North Americans, it would take three planet Earths to support the present world population.

United States   The Netherlands   India

Source: Donella Meadows, "Our 'Footprints' Are Treading Too Much Earth," *Charleston* (S.C.) *Gazette,* April 1, 1996.

account for this seeming paradox: stringent environmental regulations, the greening of industry, and the relocation of the most polluting activities (such as commodity processing and heavy manufacturing) to the emerging market economies. Thus to some extent the greening of the developed world has been at the expense of the environments in emerging economies. Given the much larger population base in those countries, their rapid industrialization could easily offset the environmental gains made in the developed economies. Consider, for example, that the emerging economies in Asia and Latin America (and now Eastern Europe and the former Soviet Union) have added nearly 2 billion people to the market economy over the past 40 years.

With economic growth comes urbanization. Today one of every three people in the world lives in a city. By 2025, it will be two out of three. Demographers predict that by that year there will be well over 30 megacities with populations exceeding 8 million and more than 500 cities with populations exceeding 1 million. Urbanization on this scale presents enormous infrastructural and environmental challenges.

Because industrialization has focused initially on commodities and heavy manufacturing, cities in many emerging economies suffer from oppressive levels of pollution. Acid rain is a growing problem, especially in places where coal combustion is unregulated. The World Bank estimates that by 2010 there will be more than 1 billion motor vehicles in the world. Concentrated in cities, they will double current levels of energy use, smog precursors, and emissions of greenhouse gas.

The second economy is the *survival economy:* the traditional, village-based way of life found in the rural parts of most developing countries. It is made up of 3 billion people, mainly Africans, Indians, and Chinese who are subsistence oriented and meet their basic needs directly from nature. Demographers generally agree that the world's population, currently growing by about 90 million people per year, will roughly double over the next 40 years. The developing nations will account for 90% of that growth, and most of it will occur in the survival economy.

Owing in part to the rapid expansion of the market economy, existence in the survival economy is becoming increasingly precarious. Extractive industries and infrastructure development have, in many cases, degraded the ecosystems upon which the survival economy depends. Rural populations are driven further into poverty as they compete for scarce natural resources. Women and children now spend on average four to six hours per day searching for fuelwood and four to six hours per week drawing and carrying water. Ironically, those conditions encourage high fertility rates because, in the short run, children help the family to garner needed resources. But in the long run, population growth in the survival economy only reinforces a vicious cycle of resource depletion and poverty.

Short-term survival pressures often force these rapidly growing rural populations into practices that cause long-term damage to forests, soil, and water. When wood becomes scarce, people burn dung for fuel, one of the greatest—and least well-known—environmental hazards in the world today. Contaminated drinking water is an equally grave problem. The World Health Organization estimates that burning dung and drinking contaminated water together cause 8 million deaths per year.

As it becomes more and more difficult to live off the land, millions of desperate people migrate to already overcrowded cities. In China, for example, an estimated 120 million people now roam from city to city, landless and jobless, driven from their villages by deforestation, soil erosion, floods, or droughts. Worldwide, the number of such "environmental refugees" from the survival economy may be as high as 500 million people, and the figure is growing.

The third economy is *nature's economy,* which consists of the natural systems and resources that support the market and the survival economies. Nonrenewable resources, such as oil, metals, and other minerals, are finite. Renewable resources, such as soils and forests, will replenish themselves—as long as their use does not exceed critical thresholds.

Technological innovations have created substitutes for many commonly used nonrenewable resources; for example, optical fiber now replaces copper wire. And in the developed economies, demand for some virgin materials may actually diminish in the decades ahead because of reuse and recycling. Ironically, the greatest threat to sustainable development today is depletion of the world's *renewable* resources.

Forests, soils, water, and fisheries are all being pushed beyond their limits by human population growth and rapid industrial development. Insufficient fresh water may prove to be the most vexing problem in the developing world over the next decade, as agricultural, commercial, and residential uses increase. Water tables are being drawn down at an alarming rate, especially in the most heavily populated nations, such as China and India.

Soil is another resource at risk. More than 10% of the world's topsoil has been seriously eroded. Available cropland and rangeland are shrinking. Existing crop varieties are no longer responding to increased use of fertilizer. As a consequence, per capita world production of both grain and meat peaked and began to decline during the 1980s. Meanwhile, the world's 18 major oceanic fisheries have now reached or actually exceeded their maximum sustainable yields.

By some estimates, humankind now uses more than 40% of the planet's net primary productivity. If, as projected, the population doubles over the next 40 years, we may outcompete most other animal species for food, driving many to extinction. In short, human activity now exceeds sustainability on a global scale. (See Exhibit 2, "Major Challenges to Sustainability.")

As we approach the twenty-first century, the interdependence of the three economic spheres is increasingly evident. In fact, the three economies have become worlds in collision, creating the major social and environmental challenges facing the planet: climate change, pollution, resource depletion, poverty, and inequality.

Consider, for example, that the average American today consumes 17 times more than his or her Mexican counterpart (emerging economy) and hundreds of times more than the average Ethiopian (survival economy). The levels of material and energy consumption in the United States require large quantities of raw materials and commodities, sourced increasingly from the survival economy and produced in emerging economies.

In the survival economy, massive infrastructure development (for example, dams, irrigation projects, highways, mining operations, and power generation projects), often aided by agencies, banks, and corporations in the developed countries, has provided access to raw materials. Unfortunately, such development has often had devastating consequences for nature's economy and has tended to strengthen existing political and economic elites, with little benefit to those in the survival economy.

At the same time, infrastructure development projects have contributed to a global glut of raw materials and hence to a long-term fall in commodity prices. And as commodity prices have fallen relative to the prices of manufactured goods, the currencies of developing countries have weakened and their terms of trade have become less favorable. Their purchasing power declines while their already substantial debt load becomes even larger. The net effect of this dynamic has been the transfer of vast amounts of

Exhibit 2 ● Major Challenges to Sustainability

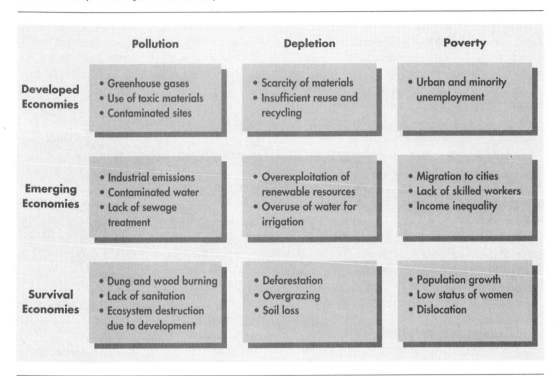

	Pollution	**Depletion**	**Poverty**
Developed Economies	• Greenhouse gases • Use of toxic materials • Contaminated sites	• Scarcity of materials • Insufficient reuse and recycling	• Urban and minority unemployment
Emerging Economies	• Industrial emissions • Contaminated water • Lack of sewage treatment	• Overexploitation of renewable resources • Overuse of water for irrigation	• Migration to cities • Lack of skilled workers • Income inequality
Survival Economies	• Dung and wood burning • Lack of sanitation • Ecosystem destruction due to development	• Deforestation • Overgrazing • Soil loss	• Population growth • Low status of women • Dislocation

wealth (estimated at $40 billion per year since 1985) from developing to developed countries, producing a vicious cycle of resource exploitation and pollution to service mounting debt. Today developing nations have a combined debt of more than $1.2 trillion, equal to nearly half of their collective gross national product.

STRATEGIES FOR A SUSTAINABLE WORLD

Nearly three decades ago, environmentalists such as Paul Ehrlich and Barry Commoner made this simple but powerful observation about sustainable development: the total environmental burden (EB) created by human activity is a function of three factors. They are population (P); af-

fluence (A), which is a proxy for consumption; and technology (T), which is how wealth is created. The product of these three factors determines the total environmental burden. It can be expressed as a formula: $EB = P \times A \times T$.

Achieving sustainability will require stabilizing or reducing the environmental burden. That can be done by decreasing the human population, lowering the level of affluence (consumption), or changing fundamentally the technology used to create wealth. The first option, lowering the human population, does not appear feasible short of draconian political measures or the occurrence of a major public-health crisis that causes mass mortality.

The second option, decreasing the level of

affluence, would only make the problem worse, because poverty and population growth go hand in hand: demographers have long known that birth rates are inversely correlated with level of education and standard of living. Thus stabilizing the human population will require improving the education and economic standing of the world's poor, particularly women of childbearing age. That can be accomplished only by creating wealth on a massive scale. Indeed, it may be necessary to grow the world economy as much as tenfold just to provide basic amenities to a population of 8 billion to 10 billion.

That leaves the third option: changing the technology used to create the goods and services that constitute the world's wealth. Although population and consumption may be societal issues, technology is the business of business.

If economic activity must increase tenfold over what it is today just to provide the bare essentials to a population double its current size, then technology will have to improve twentyfold merely to keep the planet at its current levels of environmental burden. Those who believe that ecological disaster will somehow be averted must also appreciate the commercial implications of such a belief: over the next decade or so, sustainable development will constitute one of the biggest opportunities in the history of commerce.

Nevertheless, as of today few companies have incorporated sustainability into their strategic thinking. Instead, environmental strategy consists largely of piecemeal projects aimed at controlling or preventing pollution. Focusing on sustainability requires putting business strategies to a new test. Taking the entire planet as the context in which they do business, companies must ask whether they are part of the solution to social and environmental problems or part of the problem. Only when a company thinks in those terms can it begin to develop a vision of sustainability—a shaping logic that goes beyond to-day's internal, operational focus on greening to a more external, strategic focus on sustainable development. Such a vision is needed to guide companies through three stages of environmental strategy.

Stage One: Pollution Prevention

The first step for most companies is to make the shift from pollution control to pollution prevention. Pollution control means cleaning up waste after it has been created. Pollution prevention focuses on minimizing or eliminating waste before it is created. Much like total quality management, pollution prevention strategies depend on continuous improvement efforts to reduce waste and energy use. This transformation is driven by a compelling logic: pollution prevention pays. Emerging global standards for environmental management systems (ISO 14,000, for example) also have created strong incentives for companies to develop such capabilities.

Over the past decade, companies have sought to avoid colliding with nature's economy (and incurring the associated added costs) through greening and prevention strategies. Aeroquip Corporation, a $2.5 billion manufacturer of hoses, fittings, and couplings, saw an opportunity here. Like most industrial suppliers, Aeroquip never thought of itself as a provider of environmental solutions. But in 1990, its executives realized that the company's products might be especially valuable in meeting the need to reduce waste and prevent pollution. Aeroquip has generated a $250 million business by focusing its attention on developing products that reduce emissions. As companies in emerging economies realize the competitive benefits of using raw materials and resources more productively, businesses like Aeroquip's will continue to grow.

The emerging economies cannot afford to repeat all the environmental mistakes of Western development. With the sustainability imperative in mind, BASF, the German chemical giant, is helping to design and build chemical industries in China, India, Indonesia, and Malaysia that are less polluting than in the past. By colocating facilities that in the West have been geographically dispersed, BASF is able to create industrial ecosystems in which the waste from one process becomes the raw material for another. Colocation solves a problem common in the West, where recycling waste is often infeasible because transporting it from one site to another is dangerous and costly.

Stage Two: Product Stewardship

Product stewardship focuses on minimizing not only pollution from manufacturing but also all environmental impacts associated with the full life cycle of a product. As companies in stage one move closer to zero emissions, reducing the use of materials and production of waste requires fundamental changes in underlying product and process design.

Design for environment (DFE), a tool for creating products that are easier to recover, reuse, or recycle, is becoming increasingly important. With DFE, all the effects that a product could have on the environment are examined during its design phase. Cradle-to-grave analysis begins and ends outside the boundaries of a company's operations—it includes a full assessment of all inputs to the product and examines how customers use and dispose of it. DFE thus captures a broad range of external perspectives by including technical staff, environmental experts, end customers, and even community representatives in the process. Dow Chemical Company has pioneered the use of a board-level advisory panel of environmental experts and external representatives to aid its product-stewardship efforts.

By reducing materials and energy consumption, DFE can be highly profitable. Consider Xerox Corporation's Asset Recycle Management (ARM) program, which uses leased Xerox copiers as sources of high-quality, low-cost parts and components for new machines. A well-developed infrastructure for taking back leased copiers combined with a sophisticated remanufacturing process allows parts and components to be reconditioned, tested, and then reassembled into "new" machines. Xerox estimates that ARM savings in raw materials, labor, and waste disposal in 1995 alone were in the $300-million to $400-million range. In taking recycling to this level, Xerox has reconceptualized its business. By redefining the product-in-use as part of the company's asset base, Xerox has discovered a way to add value and lower costs. It can continually provide its lease customers with the latest product upgrades, giving them state-of-the-art functionality with minimal environmental impact.

Product stewardship is thus one way to reduce consumption in the developed economies. It may also aid the quest for sustainability because developing nations often try to emulate what they see happening in the developed nations. Properly executed, product stewardship also offers the potential for revenue growth through product differentiation. For example, Dunlop Tire Corporation and Akzo Nobel recently announced a new radial tire that makes use of an aramid fiber belt rather than the conventional steel belt. The new design makes recycling easier because it eliminates the expensive cryogenic crushing required to separate the steel belts from the tire's other materials. Because the new fiber-belt tire is 30% lighter, it dramatically improves gas mileage. Moreover, it is a safer tire because it improves the traction control of antilock braking systems.

The evolution from pollution prevention to product stewardship is now happening in multinational companies such as Dow, DuPont, Monsanto, Xerox, ABB, Philips, and Sony. For example, as part of a large sustainability strategy dubbed A Growing Partnership with Nature, DuPont's agricultural-products business developed a new type of herbicide that has helped

ARACRUZ CELULOSE: A STRATEGY FOR THE SURVIVAL ECONOMY

"Poverty is one of the world's leading polluters," notes Erling Lorentzen, founder and chairman of Aracruz Celulose. The $2 billion Brazilian company is the world's largest producer of eucalyptus pulp. "You can't expect people who don't eat a proper meal to be concerned about the environment."*

From the very start, Aracruz has been built around a vision of sustainable development. Lorentzen understood that building a viable forest-products business in Brazil's impoverished and deforested state of Espirito Santo would require the simultaneous improvement of nature's economy and the survival economy.

First, to restore nature's economy, the company took advantage of a tax incentive for tree planting in the late 1960s and began buying and reforesting cut-over land. By 1992, the company had acquired over 200,000 hectares and planted 130,000 hectares with managed eucalyptus; the rest was restored as conservation land. By reforesting what had become highly degraded land, unsuitable for agriculture, the company addressed a fundamental environmental problem. At the same time, it created a first-rate source of fiber for its pulping operations. Aracruz's forest practices and its ability to clone seedlings have given the company advantages in both cost and quality.

Aracruz has tackled the problem of poverty head-on. Every year, the company gives away millions of eucalyptus seedlings to local farmers. It is a preemptive strategy, aimed at reducing the farmers' need to deplete the natural forests for fuel or lumber. Aracruz also has a long-term commitment to capability building. In the early years, Aracruz was able to hire local people for very low wages because of their desperate situation. But instead of simply exploiting the abundant supply of cheap labor, the company embarked on an aggressive social-investment strategy, spending $125 million to support the creation of hospitals, schools, housing, and a training center for employees. In fact, until recently, Aracruz spent more on its social investments than it did on wages (about $1.20 for every $1 in wages). Since that time, the standard of living has improved dramatically, as has productivity. The company no longer needs to invest so heavily in social infrastructure.

*Marguerite Rigoglioso, "Stewards of the Seventh Generation," *Harvard Business School Bulletin,* April 1996, p. 55.

farmers around the world reduce their annual use of chemicals by more than 45 million pounds. The new Sulfonylurea herbicides have also led to a 1-billion-pound reduction in the amount of chemical waste produced in the manufacture of agricultural chemicals. These herbicides are effective at 1% to 5% of the application rates of traditional chemicals, are nontoxic to animals and nontarget species, and biodegrade in the soil, leaving virtually no residue on crops. Because they require so much less material in their manufacture, they are also highly profitable.

Stage Three: Clean Technology

Companies with their eye on the future can begin to plan for and invest in tomorrow's technologies. The simple fact is that the existing technology base in many industries is not environmentally sustainable. The chemical industry, for example, while having made substantial headway over the past decade in pollution prevention and product stewardship, is still limited by its dependence on the chlorine molecule. (Many organochlorides are toxic or persistent or bioaccumulative.) As long as the industry relies on its historical competencies in chlorine chemistry, it will have trouble making major progress toward sustainability.

Monsanto is one company that is consciously developing new competencies. It is shifting the technology base for its agriculture business from bulk chemicals to biotechnology. It is betting that the bioengineering of crops rather than the application of chemical pesticides or fertilizers represents a sustainable path to increased agricultural yields. . . .

Clean technologies are desperately needed in the emerging economies of Asia. Urban pollution there has reached oppressive levels. But precisely because manufacturing growth is so high—capital stock doubles every six years—there is an unprecedented opportunity to replace current product and process technologies with new, cleaner ones.

Japan's Research Institute for Innovative Technology for the Earth is one of several new research and technology consortia focusing on the development and commercialization of clean technologies for the developing world. Having been provided with funding and staff by the Japanese government and more than 40 corporations, RITE has set forth an ambitious 100-year plan to create the next generation of power technology, which will eliminate or neutralize greenhouse gas emissions.

SUSTAINABILITY VISION

Pollution prevention, product stewardship, and clean technology all move a company toward sustainability. But without a framework to give direction to those activities, their impact will dissipate. A vision of sustainability for an industry or a company is like a road map to the future, showing the way products and services must evolve and what new competencies will be needed to get there. Few companies today have such a road map. Ironically, chemical companies, regarded only a decade ago as the worst environmental villains, are among the few large corporations to have engaged the challenge of sustainable development seriously.

Companies can begin by taking stock of each component of what I call their *sustainability portfolio*. (See Exhibit 3, "The Sustainability Portfolio.") Is there an overarching vision of sustainability that gives direction to the company's activities? To what extent has the company progressed through the three stages of environmental strategy—from pollution prevention to product stewardship to clean technology?

Consider the auto industry. During the 1970s, government regulation of tailpipe emissions forced the industry to focus on pollution control. In the 1980s, the industry began to tackle pollution prevention. Initiatives such as the Corporate Average Fuel Efficiency requirement and the Toxic Release Inventory led auto companies to examine their product designs and manufacturing processes in order to improve fuel economy and lower emissions from their plants.

The 1990s are witnessing the first signs of product stewardship. In Germany, the 1990 "take-back" law required auto manufacturers to

Exhibit 3 ● The Sustainability Portfolio

This simple diagnostic tool can help any company determine whether its strategy is consistent with sustainability. First, assess your company's capability in each of the four quadrants by answering the questions in each box. Then rate yourself on the following scale for each quadrant: 1—nonexistent; 2—emerging; 3—established; or 4—institutionalized.

Most companies will be heavily skewed toward the lower left-hand quadrant, reflecting investment in pollution prevention. However, without investments in future technologies and markets (the upper half of the portfolio), the company's environmental strategy will not meet evolving needs.

Unbalanced portfolios spell trouble: a bottom-heavy portfolio suggests a good position today but future vulnerability. A top-heavy portfolio indicates a vision of sustainability without the operational or analytical skills needed to implement it. A portfolio skewed to the left side of the chart indicates a preoccupation with handling the environmental challenge through internal process improvements and technology-development initiatives. Finally, a portfolio skewed to the right side, although highly open and public, runs the risk of being labeled a "greenwash" because the underlying plant operations and core technology still cause significant environmental harm.

	Internal	**External**
Tomorrow	**Clean Technology** Is the environmental performance of our products limited by our existing competency base? Is there potential to realize major improvements through new technology?	**Sustainability Vision** Does our corporate vision direct us toward the solution of social and environmental problems? Does our vision guide the development of new technologies, markets, products, and processes?
Today	**Pollution Prevention** Where are the most significant waste and emission streams from our current operations? Can we lower costs and risks by eliminating waste at the source or by using it as a useful input?	**Product Stewardship** What are the implications for product design and development if we assume responsibility for a product's entire life cycle? Can we add value or lower costs while simultaneously reducing the impact of our products?

take responsibility for their vehicles at the end of their useful lives. Innovators such as BMW have influenced the design of new cars with their *design for disassembly* efforts. Industry-level consortia such as the Partnership for a New Generation of Vehicles are driven largely by the product stewardship logic of lowering the environmental impact of automobiles throughout their life cycle.

Early attempts to promote clean technology include such initiatives as California's zero-emission vehicle law and the U.N. Climate Change Convention, which ultimately will limit greenhouse gases on a global scale. But early efforts by industry incumbents have been either incremental—for example, natural-gas vehicles—or defensive in nature. Electric-vehicle programs, for instance, have been used to demonstrate the infeasibility of this technology rather than to lead the industry to a fundamentally cleaner technology.

Although the auto industry has made progress, it falls far short of sustainability. For the vast majority of auto companies, pollution prevention and product stewardship are the end of the road. Most auto executives assume that if they close the loop in both production and design, they will have accomplished all the necessary environmental objectives.

But step back and try to imagine a sustainable vision for the industry. Growth in the emerging markets will generate massive transportation needs in the coming decades. Already the rush is on to stake out positions in China, India, and Latin America. But what form will this opportunity take?

Consider the potential impact of automobiles on China alone. Today there are fewer than 1 million cars on the road in China. However, with a population of more than 1 billion, it would take less than 30% market penetration to equal the current size of the U.S. car market (12 million to 15 million units sold per year). Ulti-

mately, China might demand 50 million or more units annually. Because China's energy and transportation infrastructures are still being defined, there is an opportunity to develop a clean technology yielding important environmental and competitive benefits.

Amory Lovins of the Rocky Mountain Institute has demonstrated the feasibility of building *hypercars*—vehicles that are fully recyclable, 20 times more energy efficient, 100 times cleaner, and cheaper than existing cars. These vehicles retain the safety and performance of conventional cars but achieve radical simplification through the use of lightweight, composite materials, fewer parts, virtual prototyping, regenerative braking, and very small, hybrid engines. Hypercars, which are more akin to computers on wheels than to cars with microchips, may render obsolete most of the competencies associated with today's auto manufacturing—for example, metal stamping, tool and die making, and the internal combustion engine.

Assume for a minute that clean technology like the hypercar or Mazda's soon-to-be-released hydrogen rotary engine can be developed for a market such as China's. Now try to envision a transportation infrastructure capable of accommodating so many cars. How long will it take before gridlock and traffic jams force the auto industry to a halt? Sustainability will require new transportation solutions for the needs of emerging economies with huge populations. Will the giants in the auto industry be prepared for such radical change, or will they leave the field to new ventures that are not encumbered by the competencies of the past?

A clear and fully integrated environmental strategy should not only guide competency development, it should also shape the company's relationship to customers, suppliers, other companies, policymakers, and all its stakeholders. Companies can and must change the way customers think by creating preferences for prod-

Exhibit 4 ● Building Sustainable Business Strategies

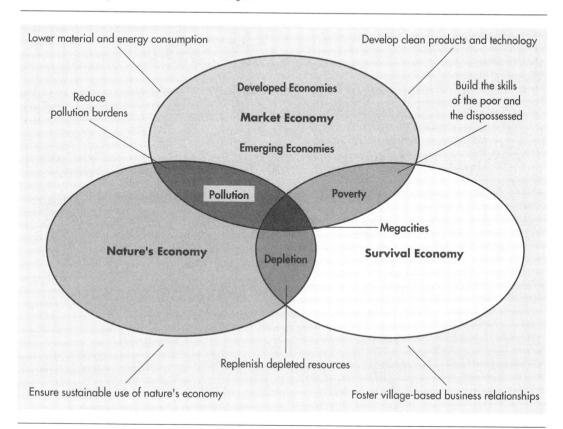

ucts and services consistent with sustainability. Companies must become educators rather than mere marketers of products. (See Exhibit 4, "Building Sustainable Business Strategies.")

For senior executives, embracing the quest for sustainability may well require a leap of faith. Some may feel that the risks associated with investing in unstable and unfamiliar markets outweigh the potential benefits. Others will recognize the power of such a positive mission to galvanize people in their organizations.

Regardless of their opinions on sustainability, executives will not be able to keep their heads in the sand for long. Since 1980, foreign direct investment by multinational corporations has increased from $500 billion to nearly $3 trillion per year. In fact, it now exceeds official development-assistance aid in developing countries. With free trade on the rise, the next decade may see the figure increase by another order of magnitude. The challenges presented by emerging markets in Asia and Latin America demand a new way of conceptualizing business opportunities. The rapid growth in emerging economies cannot be sustained in the face of mounting environmental deterioration, poverty, and resource depletion. In the coming decade, companies will be challenged to develop clean technologies and to implement strategies that drastically reduce the environmental burden in the developing world while simultaneously increasing its wealth and standard of living.

Like it or not, the responsibility for ensuring a sustainable world falls largely on the shoulders of the world's enterprises, the economic engines of the future. Clearly, public policy innovations (at both the national and international levels) and changes in individual consumption patterns will be needed to move toward sustainability.

But corporations can and should lead the way, helping to shape public policy and driving change in consumers' behavior. In the final analysis, it makes good business sense to pursue strategies for a sustainable world.

Notes

1.   The terms *market economy, survival economy,* and *nature's economy* were suggested to me by Vandana Shiva, *Ecology and the Politics of Survival* (New Delhi: United Nations University Press, 1991).

2

Building a New Economy
Lester R. Brown and
Jennifer Mitchell

As the world economy has expanded nearly six-fold since 1950, it has begun to outrun the capacity of the Earth to supply basic goods and services. . . . We forget how large our continually expanding global economy has become relative to the Earth's ecosystem. The annual growth of 4 percent in 1997 seems rather modest, but that one year's additional output of $1.1 trillion exceeded the growth in output during the entire seventeenth century.[1]

Despite the many collisions with the Earth's natural limits, we continue to expand our numbers and raise our consumption levels as though the Earth's capacities were infinite. If the global economy grows at 3 percent a year, it will expand from an output of $29 trillion in 1997 to $57 trillion in 2020, nearly doubling. It will then more than double again by the year 2050, reaching $138 trillion. Yet even in reaching $29 trillion, the economy has already overrun many of the Earth's natural capacities.[2]

Nearly all forms of environmental deterioration—including soil erosion, aquifer depletion, rangeland deterioration, air pollution, and climate change—adversely affect agriculture. Combined with a shrinking backlog of technology available to farmers to raise land productivity,

these are slowing growth in the world grain harvest. Meanwhile, the world demand for grain is expanding at a near-record pace, driven by the addition of 80 million people each year and unprecedented gains in affluence in the developing world, led by China. Despite the recent return to production of idled cropland, world grain stocks have dropped to the lowest level on record, leaving the world just one poor harvest away from potential chaos in world grain markets.[3]

With world water use tripling since midcentury and continuing to expand, water scarcity is threatening economic progress indirectly through its effect on the food supply. Wherever there is irrigation overpumping today there will be irrigation cutbacks tomorrow; cuts in irrigation mean cuts in food production. With nearly half the world's grain produced on irrigated land, this is not good news. If we are facing a future of water scarcity, we are also facing food scarcity. Irrigation water shortages are already raising grain imports in many countries, including Algeria, China, Egypt, India, Iran, Mexico, Pakistan, and Saudi Arabia. In the three years after Saudi Arabia's aquifer began to dry up in 1994, irrigation cutbacks raised the country's net grain imports from 3 million tons to more than 7 million.[4]

As populations outrun their water supplies, there is much talk of conflicts over water. Some analysts note that in regions facing acute water scarcity, such as the Middle East, future wars are more likely to be over water than oil. But the competition for water is moving into world grain markets as countries try to offset irrigation water shortages by expanding grain imports. In this arena, the winners are likely to be those who are financially strongest, not those who are the strongest militarily.[5]

In the absence of a technological breakthrough that can create a quantum jump in output, such as the ones that followed the discovery of fertilizer or the hybridization of corn, the world is likely to be facing higher grain prices. The rise in world grain prices from 1993 to 1997, reversing a long-term trend of decline, may give us a picture of the future. If so, it could lead to instability in Third World cities on a scale that could disrupt global economic progress.[6]

We are already getting some glimpses of what may lie ahead. For example, in the summer of 1996, the government of Jordan—a country suffering from aquifer depletion, higher prices for imported wheat, and a scarcity of foreign exchange—was forced to eliminate its bread subsidy. The resulting bread riots lasted several days and threatened to bring down the government. In 1997, Pakistan—a country of roughly 140 million people—needed to double its wheat imports to 5 million tons but was unable to do so, having exhausted its line of credit. As a result, wheat prices rose and in April long lines formed at bread shops in Karachi, leading to political unrest and sporadic looting in the city.[7]

If the world economy as it is now structured continues to expand, it will eventually destroy its natural support systems and decline. Despite the inescapable logic of this decline-and-collapse scenario, we seem unable to limit our claims on the Earth to a sustainable level. Canadian ecologist William Rees talks about "a world addicted to growth, but in deep denial about the consequences."[8]

The good news is that we know what an environmentally sustainable economy would look like. We have the technologies needed to build such an economy. And we know that the key to getting from here to there lies in restructuring the tax system, decreasing personal and corporate income taxes while increasing taxes on environmentally destructive activities. The challenge is to convince enough people of the need to do this in order to make it happen.

A NEW ECONOMY

While ecologists have long known that the existing economic system is unsustainable, few economists share this knowledge. What kind of system would be ecologically sustainable? The answer is simple—a system whose structure respects the limits, the carrying capacity, of natural systems. A sustainable economy is one powered by renewable energy sources. It is also a reuse/recycle economy. In its structure, it emulates nature, where one organism's waste is another's sustenance.

The ecological principles of sustainability are well established, based on solid science. Just as an aircraft must satisfy the principles of aerodynamics if it is to fly, so must an economy satisfy the principles of ecology if it is to endure. The ecological conditions that need to be satisfied are rather straightforward. Over the long term, carbon emissions cannot exceed carbon dioxide (CO_2) fixation; soil erosion cannot exceed new soil formed through natural processes; the harvest of forest products cannot exceed the sustainable yield of forests; the number of plant and animal species lost cannot exceed the new species formed through evolution; water pumping cannot exceed the sustainable yield of aquifers; the fish catch cannot exceed the sustainable yield of fisheries.

Recognizing the limits of natural systems is often seen as a call for no growth, but the issue is not growth versus no growth. The question is, What kind of growth? And where? Growth based on the use of renewable energy may be able to continue for some time, while that based on fossil fuels is ultimately limited by remaining reserves, but more immediately by potentially unacceptable climate disruption. Similarly, a reuse/recycle economy can grow much larger than a throwaway economy without imposing excessive demands on the Earth's ecosystem. Growth in the information economy puts minimal pressure on the Earth's natural systems, especially compared with heavy industry, a common source of past growth. Within agriculture, huge growth is needed to satisfy future food needs in developing countries but not in industrial ones, where population has stabilized and where diets are already sated with livestock products.

Building such an economy means stabilizing population sooner rather than later and replacing the fossil-fuel-based economy with a solar/hydrogen energy economy. These two key steps—both extraordinarily difficult undertakings—are discussed later in this chapter. If we can do both, many of the other problems the world faces will become manageable.

In mature industrial economies with stable populations, claims on the planet are leveling off. In the European Union (EU), for example, population has stabilized at 380 million. With high incomes, grain consumption per person has plateaued at around 470 kilograms a year. As a result, EU members, now consuming roughly 180 million tons of grain annually, have essentially stabilized their claims on the Earth's agricultural resources—the first region in the world to do so. (See Figure 1.) And, perhaps more important, the region has done this within the limits of its land and water resources, since it is a net exporter of grain.[9]

As noted earlier, one of the keys to an environmentally sustainable future is to convert the existing throwaway economy to a reuse/recycle economy, thus reducing the environmentally disruptive flow of raw materials from mines or forests to smelters and mills, as well as the vast one-way flow of discarded materials to landfills. With a reuse/recycle structure, mature industrial economies with stable populations, such as those in Europe, can operate largely on the

Figure 1. ● Grain Production and Consumption in the European Union, 1961–97

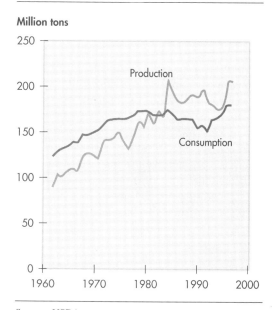

Million tons

Source: USDA

existing stock of steel, aluminum, glass, paper, and other materials already in the economy.

The huge material flows associated with industrialization can be reduced in developing economies if these countries go directly from the preindustrial to the postindustrial stage of development, leapfrogging the intermediate stage. For example, they can invest directly in cellular phones without spending money on millions of miles of telephone lines and poles. Instead of relying on the transportation system to carry a letter to a distant destination, modern technologies can send a facsimile halfway around the world using the global network of satellites. And with computerization, e-mail can replace the fax, eliminating the need even for paper. Similarly, if developing economies bypass the automobile stage of development, going directly to sophisticated public transportation and to bicycles, they can save huge amounts of materials and energy, while providing greater mobility.[10]

The transition from a throwaway economy to a reuse/recycle one is well under way. In the United States, where the steel industry is now dominated by electric-arc steel furnaces that feed on scrap metal, 55 percent of 1996 steel output was from scrap. Abandoned cars are melted down to produce soup cans. When these are discarded, they can be melted down to produce refrigerators. When they wear out, refrigerators can be used to produce automobiles. And so on. A steel industry feeding largely on scrap both minimizes the disruption associated with mining and transporting virgin ore and reduces energy use by some 60 percent.[11]

As industries move from using primarily virgin raw materials to using recycled materials, their geographic distribution changes. The U.S. steel industry, once concentrated in western Pennsylvania, where there was an abundance of both iron ore and coal, is now spread throughout the states. Modern electric-arc minimills scattered across the country often feed entirely on locally available scrap metal to produce steel, and at the same time create local jobs and revenue flows.[12]

Similarly with paper. Instead of cutting trees, paper companies now negotiate long-term contracts with local communities to buy their scrap paper. In the United States, few if any recent paper mills have been built in the heavily forested northwest or in Maine. Instead, they are being built near heavily populated areas where paper use is concentrated. This shift to wastepaper helps bring demands on forests down toward a sustainable level.[13]

The small, densely populated state of New Jersey, for instance, has little forested area and no iron mines. Yet there are 13 paper mills that use only wastepaper and eight steel minimills that rely almost exclusively on scrap. Collectively, these paper plants and steel mills market more

than $1 billion worth of products each year, providing both local jobs and hefty tax revenues.[14]

For communities considering whether to dispose of solid waste by recycling, incinerating, or landfilling, the employment advantages are obvious: for every 150,000 tons of waste, recycling creates nine jobs, incinerating creates two, and landfilling, just one. Within Europe, Germany has been a leader in reducing the amount of packaging used and in recycling packaging waste. In 1996, 80 percent of all packaging in Germany—including glass, paper, plastic, tin plate, and aluminum, totalling some 5.3 million tons—was recycled, greatly reducing pressure on landfills.[15]

Another way to reduce waste is to redesign industrial economies to emulate nature so that one industry's waste becomes another's raw material, a science that is becoming known as industrial ecology. In the industrial zone of Kalundborg in Denmark, a network of materials and energy exchanges among companies has been formed. It involves a wide variety of linkages: the warm water from cooling a power plant is used by a company with fish farms; sludge from the fish farms is sold to a nearby farmer for fertilizer; the fly ash from a power plant is used as a raw material by a cement manufacturer; and surplus yeast from a pharmaceutical plant producing insulin is fed to pigs by local farmers.[16]

The result is a system that emulates nature—a win-win situation. Air pollution is down, water pollution is down, waste is down, and profits are up. A $60-million investment by participating firms in a transport infrastructure to facilitate the exchange of energy and materials has yielded $120 million in revenues and cost savings. At the international level, one effort to assess the potential of such systems is the Zero Emissions Research Initiative at the United Nations University, in Tokyo; it recently expanded into a $12-million research project at the University of Tokyo.[17]

In contrast to the wholesale restructuring of the energy economy needed to make it environmentally sustainable, what is needed in the world food economy is more a change in degree than in kind, partly because the principal transformation required to achieve an acceptable balance between food and people lies outside agriculture. Balancing the food supply/demand equation may now depend more on family planners than on fishers and farmers. Decisions made in ministries of energy about fossil fuel use may have a greater effect on climate and therefore on the food security of the next generation than those made in ministries of agriculture.

But within agriculture, there are also major challenges. Building a sustainable food economy depends on protecting cropland both from soil erosion and from conversion to nonfarm uses. It also means using land and water more efficiently. On soil erosion, the United States is a leader, with the Conservation Reserve Program (CRP) launched in 1985. Among other things, the CRP promotes the conversion of highly erodible cropland into grassland, thus protecting its only sustainable use. Beyond this, U.S. farmers with excessive erosion on their land are denied the benefits of any government programs if they do not adopt conservation tillage practices that reduce losses of soil from erosion below the amount of new soil formed from natural processes.[18]

In a world of food scarcity, land use emerges as a central issue. Cropland is no longer a surplus commodity. Perhaps the best model of successful cropland protection is Japan, whose determination to protect its riceland with land-use zoning can be seen in the thousands of small rice plots within the city boundaries of Tokyo. By tenaciously protecting its riceland, the nation remains self-sufficient in its staple food. While Japan has relied heavily on zoning to protect cropland, a stiff tax on the conversion of crop-

land to nonfarm uses can also be highly effective in protecting the global cropland base. China is encouraging cremation of the dead rather than burial as it tries to save cropland. Viet Nam, like Japan, has turned to regulation, banning the construction of golf courses in order to protect its riceland.[19]

With little new land left to plow anywhere and with Asia sustaining heavy cropland losses as it industrializes, the need to raise land productivity is more pressing than ever. As yield per crop moves toward the physiological limits, further gains will come increasingly from raising the number of crops per year. The challenge to scientists is to breed crop varieties that mature earlier, permitting northern hemisphere countries, for example, to expand the double-cropping of a winter crop such as wheat or barley with a summer crop such as soybeans. Other changes, such as transplanting more crops from seedbeds into the field, shorten the field-growing season, as happens with most of Asia's rice, which is produced from transplanted seedlings.[20]

Aside from stabilizing population, the key to reducing the unsustainable demand on aquifers is to convert the existing systems that supply water to farmers, industries, and urban dwellers either at no cost or at a nominal cost into water markets where users pay the market price for water. Combined with special rates that protect minimum supplies for low-income consumers, water markets such as those now operating in California and Chile can help lower water demand to the sustainable yield of aquifers. Shifting to a market economy for water would automatically create a market for more water-efficient technologies, ranging from irrigation equipment to household appliances.[21]

Reducing water use to a sustainable level means boosting the efficiency with which it is used, emulating the achievements of Israel—the pacesetter in this field. Land productivity has long been a part of our vocabulary, something we measure in yield per hectare. But the term "water productivity" is rarely heard. Until it, too, becomes part of our everyday lexicon, water scarcity will cloud our future. In addition to using more-efficient irrigation techniques, cropping patterns can be adjusted, shifting toward more water-efficient crops as Egypt is doing in shifting land from rice to wheat.[22]

The efficiency of converting grain into animal protein—milk, meat, and eggs—can be enhanced by adopting modern feeding practices, including shifting to nutritionally balanced, formulated rations in developing countries and by everywhere shifting to the more grain-efficient livestock products. Most of the world's beef and mutton is produced with forage from rangeland that is not suitable for plowing. But once rangelands are fully used, as is now the case, then additional output can come only from feedlots. At this point, the ability of chickens to add a pound of body weight with only 2.2 pounds of feed gives them an advantage over cattle, which require some 7 pounds of feed per pound of weight gain. The expected shift from beef to poultry is already under way: poultry overtook beef in 1996. (See Figure 2.)[23]

If grain prices rise rapidly, the world's affluent will start eating less meat, but they are not likely to do so before prices threaten the survival of the world's urban poor. With little idled cropland remaining and the carryover stocks of grain at near-record lows, the grain fed to livestock is the only reserve that can be tapped in a world food emergency. The most efficient way of doing this is to levy a tax on the consumption of livestock products, offsetting it with an income tax cut. Such a step would not solve the food problem, but as a temporary measure it could help avoid politically destabilizing grain price rises, buying additional time to stabilize population. Public education programs on the adverse health effects of excessive consumption of fat-rich livestock products can also help people move down the food chain.

Figure 2. ● World Beef and Poultry Production, 1950–97

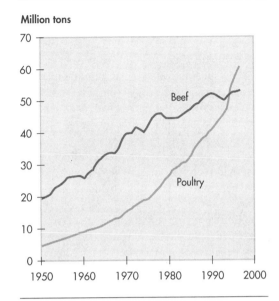

Source: USDA

STABILIZING POPULATION

A sustainable society is a demographically stable one, but today's population is far from that point. The United Nations projects that over the next 50 years world population will reach 9.4 billion—3.6 billion more people than today. Since the population of the industrial world is expected to decline slightly during this period, these 3.6 billion people will be added to the developing world, where natural resources and social services are already in short supply. Even with only modest gains in nutrition, this addition will require a doubling of the world grain harvest and, for irrigation alone, a quantity of water equal to more than 20 Nile Rivers. It will also require hundreds of millions of new classrooms, homes, and jobs.[24]

Nearly 60 percent of the projected population growth is expected to occur in Asia, which will grow from 3.4 billion people in 1995 to more than 5.4 billion in 2050. By then, China's current population of 1.2 billion is expected to exceed 1.5 billion, while India's is projected to soar from 930 million to 1.53 billion. Over this same time period, the population of the Middle East and North Africa is likely to more than double, while that of sub-Saharan Africa will triple. By 2050, Nigeria alone is expected to have 339 million people—more than the entire continent of Africa had 35 years ago.[25]

Stabilizing population is an essential step in arresting the destruction of natural resources and ensuring that the basic needs of all people are met. Thirty-three countries now have stable populations, including Japan and most of those in Europe. (Those with 10 million or more people are listed in Table 1.) These countries—representing 14 percent of world population—provide a solid base for a population stabilization effort. The sooner the remaining countries follow, the better the chance of stabilizing population at a level that the Earth can support.

A comparison of population trends in Bangladesh and Pakistan illustrates the importance of acting now. When Bangladesh was created in a split with Pakistan in 1971, its political leaders made a strong commitment to reduce fertility rates, while the leaders in Islamabad wavered over the need to do so. At that time, the population in each country was roughly 66 million. Today, however, Pakistan has roughly 140 million people, while Bangladesh has some 120 million. By putting family planning programs in place sooner rather than later, Bangladesh not only avoided the addition of nearly 20 million people during this 25-year period, it is projected to have 50 million fewer people than Pakistan does in 2050. (See Figure 3.)[26]

The world now faces a similar choice. The United Nations projects that the number of people on the Earth could reach anywhere from 7.7 billion to 11.1 billion by 2050. Ultimately,

TABLE 1. ● Sixteen Countries With Zero Population Growth, 1997

Country	Annual Rate of Natural Increase (percent)	Midyear Population (million)
Belarus	-0.1	10.4
Belgium	0.1	10.2
Czech Republic	-0.1	10.3
France	0.2	58.6
Germany	-0.2	82.0
Greece	0.1	10.6
Hungary	-0.4	10.3
Italy	0	56.8
Japan	0.2	125.7
Netherlands	0.4	15.6
Poland	0.2	38.6
Romania	-0.3	22.5
Russia	-0.6	147.3
Spain	-0.1	39.1
Ukraine	-0.4	50.4
United Kingdom	0.2	57.6

Source: U.S. Bureau of the Census, *International Data Base,* electronic data base, Suitland, MD, 10 October 1997.

the future size of the population will depend on actions that are taken or not taken today.[27]

The first step in stabilizing population is to remove the physical and social barriers that prevent women from using family planning services. Approximately one third of projected world population growth will be due to unwanted pregnancies that occur because couples still do not have access to the family planning services they desire, according to John Bongaarts of the Population Council. Worldwide, more than 120 million married women, and many more unmarried sexually active adults and teens, fall into this category.[28]

There are several reasons why couples are not planning their families despite their desire for fewer children. In many countries such as

Figure 3. ● Population of Pakistan and Bangladesh, 1950–97, With Projections to 2050

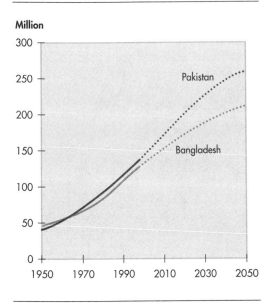

Source: UN

Saudi Arabia and Argentina, government policies restrict access to contraceptives. Geographic accessibility also affects use; in some rural areas of sub-Saharan Africa, it can take two hours or more to reach the nearest contraceptive provider. Furthermore, family planning services can be expensive, many couples lack health care to cover services, and family planning clinics are often underfunded—leaving them short of supplies or understaffed.[29]

Women who want fewer children may also be constrained from using family planning by a lack of knowledge, prevailing cultural and religious values, or the disapproval of family members. In Pakistan, for example, 43 percent of husbands object to family planning. Moreover, as recently as 1989 some 14 countries required a woman to obtain her husband's consent before she could receive any contraceptive services, while 60 required spousal authorization for permanent methods. Although it has been argued that these practices lessen conflicts between spouses and health care personnel, they are serious impediments to a woman's ability to control her fertility.[30]

Information about contraceptives and family planning for young men and women also facilitates the use of birth control. In Thailand, people of all ages have been educated on the importance of family planning. Mechai Viravidaiya, the charismatic founder of the Thai Population and Community Development Association (PCDA), encouraged familiarity with contraceptives through demonstrations, ads, and witty songs. Math teachers even use population-related examples in their classes. As a result of the efforts of Mechai, the PCDA, and the government, the growth of Thailand's population has slowed from more than 3 percent in 1960 to approximately 1 percent today—the same as in the United States.[31]

Access to family planning services, however, will not by itself stabilize population growth. Even if services were available to all who desired them, the population is still expected to increase by some 2.3 billion over the next 50 years. One reason for this is that many couples choose to have large families. John Bongaarts projects that reducing the demand for large families by addressing the underlying social factors that create it could bring population growth in developing countries down another 18 percent. Changing desired family size is of course more difficult for governments to accomplish.[32]

In many developing countries, having lots of children is a matter of survival: children are a vital part of the family economy and a source of security in old age. Institutions such as the Grameen Bank, which specializes in microenterprise loans, are attempting to change this situation by providing credit to well over a million villagers—mostly impoverished women—throughout Bangladesh and other countries. These loans are empowering women, helping to end the cycle of poverty, and thus reducing the need for large families.[33]

Although alleviating poverty is an important goal, rapid economic growth is not a prerequisite for reduced fertility rates. Bangladesh has reduced fertility rates from nearly 7 children per woman in the early 1970s to 3.3 children per woman today despite incomes averaging only around $200 a year. In the struggle to slow population growth, access to family planning services, solid government leadership, and improvement in social conditions are proving to be more important than the growth of a nation's economy.[34]

Reducing infant and child mortality will give parents the confidence to have fewer children. In situations where many children die young, parents often have more children than they want to ensure that some will survive. Children born less than a year and a half apart are twice as likely to die as those born two or more years apart. Educating couples about birth spacing, increasing child immunizations, and improving health care can reduce child mortality.[35]

Education also reduces family size. The education of women in places like the south Indian state of Kerala has given women options beyond childbearing, as well as an alternative source of future security. Furthermore, requiring school attendance for all children lowers their use as laborers while accelerating cultural change. And finally, publicized studies on local carrying capacities and campaigns to raise awareness can help individuals understand the need for smaller families and make the idea of two-child families familiar and acceptable.[36]

Yet even if each couple were to have only two children, population would continue to grow due to the sheer number of young women reaching reproductive age. This third force—called population momentum—accounts for nearly half of projected population growth. It can be lowered by policies that encourage women to delay childbearing, which stretches the time between generations. Delaying childbearing by 2.5 years would reduce population growth by maybe 10 percent over the next 50 years, while delaying it by 5 years would reduce it by perhaps 21 percent.[37]

Raising the legal age of marriage, as Tunisia and China have done, delays childbearing. But policies that educate and empower women have the same result, and are ultimately more effective. The longer girls stay in school, the later they marry and the later they start bearing children. In 23 developing countries, for instance, women with a secondary education married on average four years later than those with no education.[38]

Slowly, governments are realizing the value of investing in population stabilization. One study found that the government of Bangladesh spends $62 to prevent a birth, but saves $615 on social services expenditures for each birth averted—a 10-fold return on investment. Based on the study's estimate, the program prevents 890,000 births annually. The net savings to the government totals $547 million each year, leaving more to invest in education and health care.[39]

At the 1994 International Conference on Population and Development in Cairo, the governments of the world agreed to a 20-year population and reproductive health program. The United Nations estimates that $17 billion a year will be needed for this effort by 2000 and $21.7 billion by 2015. (In both cases, this is less than is spent every two weeks on military expenditures.) Developing countries and countries in transition have agreed to cover two thirds of the price tag, while donor countries have promised to pay the rest—$5.7 billion a year by 2000 and $7.2 billion by 2015.[40]

Unfortunately, while developing countries are on track with their part of the expenditures, donor countries are not. A recent U.N. Population Fund study reports that the assistance of bilateral donors, multilateral agencies and banks, and charitable foundations amounted to only $2 billion in 1995. Although donors' contributions in 1995 were 24 percent more than in 1994, preliminary estimates indicate that contributions declined some 18 percent in 1996. And it is likely that funding levels in 1997 declined even further.[41]

As a result of donor shortfalls following the Cairo conference, the United Nations estimates that an additional 122 million unintended pregnancies will occur by 2000. A little over a third of these unwanted pregnancies will be aborted, and more than half will be considered unintended births. Moreover, an additional 65,000 women will die in childbirth and 844,000 million will suffer chronic or permanent injury from their pregnancies.[42]

Yet "global population problems cannot be put on hold while countries reform their health care, rebuild their inner cities, and reduce . . . budget deficit[s]. Avoiding another world population doubling . . . requires rapid action," notes Sharon Camp, former Vice President of Population Action International. The difference between acting today and putting it off until tomorrow is the difference between a world in which population stabilizes at a level the Earth might be able to support and one where it expands until environmental deterioration disrupts economic progress.[43]

STABILIZING CLIMATE

Evidence that the Earth is getting warmer is building with each passing year. In the 132 years since recordkeeping began in 1866, the 13 warmest years have occurred since 1979. . . . Concern about the effects of climate change comes from many quarters. Aside from the reports of environmental scientists, the global insurance industry—faced with a dramatic surge in weather-related insurance claims—is worried about the increasing intensity and destructiveness of storms. Another source of concern comes from the possible effect on food security,

since agriculture is keyed to a climate system that has been remarkably stable over the 10,000 years since farming began.[44]

Stabilizing climate depends on reestablishing a balance between carbon emissions and nature's capacity to absorb CO_2. There are two principle ways to do this: use energy more efficiently and replace fossil fuels with noncarbon energy sources. Although impressive gains have been made in raising energy efficiency since the oil price shocks of the 1970s, there is still a vast potential for raising it further.

One way to boost the energy efficiency of the global economy is, as noted earlier, to shift from a throw-away economy to a reuse/recycle economy. Another obvious area that needs improvement is the energy-intensive automobile-centered transportation systems of industrial societies, which are extraordinarily inefficient not only in energy use, but in the congestion they produce, which leads to an inefficient use of labor as well. In congested London today, average automobile speed is similar to that of the horse drawn carriages of a century ago. In Bangkok, the typical motorist now spends the equivalent of 44 working days a year sitting in traffic jams.[45]

Two indicators of the human desire for mobility are the sales of bicycles and cars. In 1969, world manufacture of bicycles totaled 25 million and that of automobiles was 23 million. The production of cars, expanding rapidly, was on the verge of overtaking bicycles. But then rising environmental awareness, as evidenced in the first Earth Day in 1970, and the 1973 oil price shock each boosted bicycle production relative to that of automobiles. By 1980, some 62 million bicycles were manufactured compared with 29 million automobiles, an edge of two to one.[46]

A third surge came following the 1978 economic reforms in China as rapidly rising incomes boosted the number of people who could afford bicycles. As bicycle ownership surged in China, so did their production, pushing world output to 105 million in 1988. In 1995, bicycle

Figure 4. ● World Bicycle and Automobile Production, 1950–96

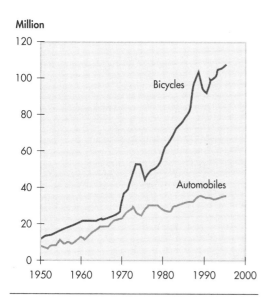

Source: UN, AAMA, DRI/McGraw-Hill

manufacturing totaled 109 million, compared with 36 million automobiles, an advantage of three to one. (See Figure 4.) Many cities, from Amsterdam to Lima, are now actively encouraging the use of bicycles. In the United Kingdom, the government hopes to double 1996 bicycle use by 2002 and then double it again by 2012.[47]

The original attraction of the automobile was its promise of unlimited mobility, something it could deliver when societies were largely rural. But in an urbanized world, there is an inherent incompatibility between the automobile and the city—witness the air pollution, traffic congestion, and urban sprawl now facing the world's cities. In addition, the segment of global society that can afford to buy and operate an automobile is likely to remain small.

The only reasonable alternative to the automobile in urban settings is a combination of state-of-the-art rail passenger-transport systems augmented by other forms of public transportation and bicycles. Whether the goal is mobility, breathable air, the protection of cropland, limits on congestion, or stabilization of climate, the automobile is not the answer. Indeed, these criteria suggest that the bicycle is the transport vehicle of the future. The sooner governments realize that the worldwide dream of a car in every garage is not realistic, the sooner they can get on with building transportation systems that will provide the desired mobility and are environmentally sustainable.

There are many new technologies for raising energy efficiency. One of the most effective is the compact fluorescent light bulb, which provides the same illumination as a traditional incandescent bulb but uses only a fourth as much electricity. Compact fluorescent bulbs in use in 1995 saved the electricity equivalent of the output of 28 large, coal-fired power plants. Although the compact fluorescents cost 10 times as much as incandescents, investing in them is highly profitable because they last much longer and use so little electricity. Worldwide manufacture has increased from 45 million in 1988 to 240 million in 1995. (See Figure 5.) Encouragingly, China has moved to the forefront in the manufacture of these bulbs, relying on them to reduce the need for building coal-fired power plants.[48]

Historically, the world has relied on two sources of renewable energy, firewood and hydropower. Firewood continues to provide cooking fuel for perhaps 2 billion people, most of whom live in Third World villages and cities, while hydropower supplies one fifth of the world's electricity. Future growth in renewables, however, is likely to come from other sources, notably wind power, photovoltaic cells, and solar thermal power plants. Installed wind electric generating capacity worldwide exceeded 7,600 megawatts by 1997. (See Figure 6.) In California, wind farms in Altamont Pass east of San

Figure 5. ● Sales of Compact Fluorescent Bulbs World-wide, 1988–95

Million

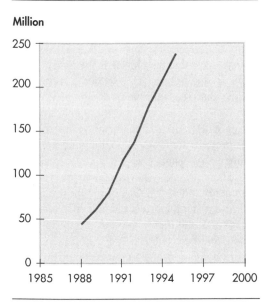

Source: Mills

Figure 6. ● World Wind Energy Generating Capacity, 1980–97

Megawatts

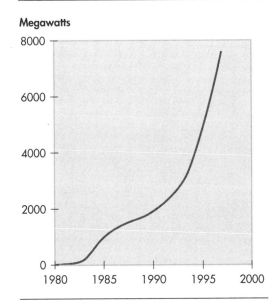

Source: Madsen, Gipe, Rehfeldt

Francisco, in the Tehachapi Pass, and in the desert near Palm Springs now generate enough electricity to satisfy the residential needs of San Francisco.[49]

An inventory of U.S. wind resources by the Department of Energy indicates a vast national potential, with three wind-rich states alone—North Dakota, South Dakota, and Texas—having enough harnessable wind energy to satisfy national electricity needs. A similar inventory in China indicates that the nation could easily double its current electricity generation by harnessing wind energy.[50]

Early leadership in the harnessing of wind energy came from the United States and Denmark. More recently, Germany and India, both rapidly growing wind powers, have forged into the lead. Tomen, a Japanese firm, plans to invest $1.2 billion in the installation of 1,000 large

wind turbines in Europe over the next five years. The world's fastest-growing energy source during the 1990s, wind generation is expanding by 25 percent a year. With the cost continuing to decline as technologies advance and as the scale of turbine manufacturing increases, wind promises to become a major power source.[51]

A second highly promising source of electricity is the photovoltaic cell. This silicon-based technology, which found its first commercial use as the energy source for satellites and space stations, has since become economical for remote sites, including in secluded vacation homes in industrial countries or in remote Third World villages. In many developing countries faced with the cost of both building a centralized power plant and constructing a grid to deliver the electricity from it, it is now cheaper to install photovoltaic cells for individual households. At the end of 1996, some 400,000 homes, mostly in villages, were getting their electricity from photovoltaic cells.[52]

The latest advance, a photovoltaic roofing material, is becoming competitive in buildings already linked to a grid. Japan, a leader in solar cell manufacturing, has announced plans to install 4,600 megawatts of rooftop generating capacity by 2010, an amount equal to the generating capacity of Chile. The United States and several European countries are expected to follow soon with similarly ambitious programs. With this technology, the roof in effect becomes the power plant for the building. In Germany and Switzerland, new office buildings are incorporating photovoltaic cells into the windows in their south-facing facades. A two-way metering system with the local utility enables building owners to sell electricity to the utility when generation is excessive and to buy it back when generation is not sufficient.[53]

As the cost of electricity generated from wind and other renewable sources falls, it will become economical to electrolyze water to produce hydrogen, thus providing a way to both store and transport wind and solar energy. Electricity and hydrogen can together provide energy in all the forms needed to operate a modern economy, whether it be powering computers, fueling cars, or manufacturing steel.

As the energy revolution gains momentum, some of the largest gas and oil companies are beginning to support it. Enron, originally a large Texas-based natural gas company, has made a strong move in the renewables field with its acquisition of Zond, the largest wind power company in the United States, and its investment in Solarex, the second largest U.S. manufacturer of photovoltaic cells.[54]

British Petroleum and Royal Dutch Shell are also investing in renewable energy resources. For example, British Petroleum has announced a major commitment to renewable energy, starting with construction of a $20-million solar-cell manufacturing facility in California. Shell plans to invest more than $500 million in solar cells and sustainable forestry plantations in developing countries to fuel local power plants. Bechtel, one of the world's largest construction firms and a traditional builder of hydroelectric dams and nuclear power plants, is now investing in a jointly owned company to develop decentralized energy sources, including solar and wind. Some governments and some corporations continue to resist the energy revolution, but the question is not whether there will be a revolution, only how rapidly it will unfold.[55]

The transition from a fossil-fuel-based energy economy to a high-efficiency, solar/hydrogen energy economy provides enormous investment and employment opportunities. This energy transition is not something that may happen; it is happening. We can see glimpses of the new climate-stabilizing energy economy in the wind farms in California, the bicycles in Amsterdam, photovoltaic arrays in Third World villages, compact fluorescent light bulbs in China, and photovoltaic rooftops in Japan.

.   .   .

CROSSING POLITICAL THRESHOLDS

Now that we know what an environmentally sustainable economy would look like, do we want it badly enough to make the needed changes? Do we have the political will needed to create a sustainable economy? Do we care enough about the next generation to take the steps now to move off the path of environmental deterioration and eventual economic decline and social disintegration?

The gap between what we need to do to reverse the degradation of the planet and what we are doing widens with each passing year. How do we cross the threshold of political change that will shrink this gap, reversing the trends of environmental degradation that are undermining the economy? Most environment ministers un-

derstand that we are headed for economic decline, but there is not yet enough political support to overcome the vested interests that oppose
changes.

In a landmark 1997 book, Ross Gelbspan,
an investigative reporter for the *Boston Globe,*
documents the efforts of these vested interests to
protect the status quo. He chronicles a disinformation campaign on global warming that is
funded by coal and oil interests, ranging from
U.S. coal mining firms to the government of
Kuwait. He lists grants provide by fossil-fuel interests to a few scientists who regularly issue
statements challenging the global warming hypothesis and creating confusion in the public
mind. This technique of using "hired guns" is
reminiscent of the tobacco industry's earlier use
of medical experts to deny the relationship between cigarette smoking and lung cancer, a
practice they have now abandoned.[56]

Mustering the needed political support is
hampered by the difficulty in understanding the
complex interactions among three distinct systems: the ecosystem, the economic system, and
the political system. Analyzing any one of these
is difficult enough, but understanding the ongoing interaction among the three is infinitely
more complex, thoroughly challenging our intellectual capacities. Although there are reasonably good computer models for the global
economy, there are none that simulate the behavior of the Earth's ecosystem or the global political system. For the ecosystem, modeling just
the climate segment taxes our abilities.

The challenge is how to cross political
thresholds—how to raise awareness and understanding to a level that will support the needed
change. We change our behavior as the result of
new information, new experiences, or some
combination of the two. If information does not
bring about change when it is needed, then suffering the consequences of failing to act may
bring change if it is not too late. After World War
I, for instance, many people were convinced of

the need for the League of Nations. U.S. President Woodrow Wilson was one of the most ardent supporters, but he could not convince the
U.S. Congress to support it. It took another war,
unprecedented human suffering, and the loss of
some 40 million lives to convince the world, including the U.S. Congress, that such an organization was indeed needed.

Public concern about environmental deterioration is reflected in the formation of thousands
of environmental groups, many of them small,
local, single-issue groups, such as those organized to oppose construction of a nuclear power
plant in Niigata Prefecture in Japan or the burning off of the Amazonian rainforest by cattle
ranchers. Others operate at the national level on
a broad range of environmental issues, such as
the Korean Federation for Environmental Movement, a group with a full-time membership of
36,000 and a staff of 60. And some go on to become prominent at the international level, such
as Greenpeace, the World Wide Fund for Nature,
and Friends of the Earth. Some of the larger U.S.
environmental membership groups, including
the National Wildlife Federation, have budgets
that rival that of the U.N. Environment Programme. Even much of the research that under-
pins environmental policymaking comes from
nongovernmental environmental research insti-
tutes. In few areas of public policy do non-
governmental organizations play such a prominent role.[57]

Many countries have crossed key sustainability thresholds on basic environmental issues
based on new information. One of the best
known is China's effort to stabilize the size of its
population before its growing demands overwhelmed the carrying capacity of its life-support
systems. When Chinese leaders undertook a series of population and resource projections during the early post-Mao era, they discovered that
even if they moved to a two-child family they
were faced with the addition to their already
huge population of as many people as then lived

in India. They realized there simply was not enough land and water to provide adequate diets for such an increase. And they decided to press for a one-child family, an action for which they have been widely criticized. Yet the criticism should not be for adopting this program, but for the delay in facing the population issue until there was no rational alternative but to press for a one-child family, and for the way the program was administered.[58]

Another example of how information can change behavior is found in the United States, where tens of millions of people have quit smoking over the last 35 years. This massive shift in social behavior was the result of a continuous flow of information that was launched in 1963 with the first Surgeon General's report on smoking and health. Every year since then, this report has been updated, triggering literally thousands of research projects on smoking and health, the findings of which are covered regularly by the news media. The result was a steady rise in public understanding of the effect of cigarette smoke, both direct and passive, on health—and a widespread decline in smoking.[59]

With the big steps that are still needed—stabilizing population and stabilizing climate—some countries have crossed the thresholds, others have not. Some have policies to stabilize their populations; others do not even recognize the need to do so. Some countries are pushing for heavy cuts in carbon emissions; others refuse even to consider doing so.

A reduction in carbon emissions is supported by some segments of the global community, but the support is not yet strong enough to bring about a major reorientation of energy policy. . . . Will we respond to the information on the threat posed by global warming, or will we delay until we are shocked into action by the result of failing to do so—possibly by crop-withering heat waves that abruptly reduce the world grain harvest, creating chaos in world grain markets? The mainstream scientific community, as represented by the 2,500 scientists on the Intergovernmental Panel for Climate Change, is quite clear on the need to reduce carbon emissions. The Alliance of Small Island States, a group of some 36 island countries that feel particularly vulnerable to rising sea levels and more powerful storms, is also actively pressing for a reduction in global carbon emissions.[60]

Another major challenge to the existing industrial development model is coming from the insurance industry. Shaken by an increase in weather-related insurance claims from $17 billion during the 1980s to $66 billion thus far during the 1990s, the insurance industry is urging a reduction in carbon emissions—in effect, a reduction in the use of fossil fuels. Some 60 of the world's leading insurance companies have signed a statement urging governments to move in this direction, marking perhaps the first time in history that one major industry has pressured governments to reduce the output of another major industry.[61]

Within the fossil fuel industry itself, as noted earlier, some companies such as Enron, British Petroleum, and Royal Dutch Shell are already looking to the future, and beginning to invest in alternative energy sources. Enron's chairman, Ken Lay, who publicly discusses the need to reduce carbon emissions and to stabilize climate, sees Enron at the heart of the transition from fossil fuels to renewable energy sources. The infrastructure it has built to store and distribute natural gas can one day be used for hydrogen as the solar/hydrogen economy unfolds.[62]

In an important speech at Stanford University in May 1997, British Petroleum's CEO, John Browne, said, "The time to consider the policy dimensions of climate change is not when the link between greenhouse gases and climate change is conclusively proven, but when the possibility cannot be discounted and is taken seriously by the society of which we are a part. We in BP have reached that point." This was a big jump for big oil.[63]

Realization that the existing fossil-fuel-based industrial development model that evolved in the West and Japan is not viable for the entire world is beginning to emerge in some unexpected quarters. For example, . . . a group of eminent scientists in China, many of them in the National Academy of Sciences, challenged the government's decision to develop an automobile-centered transportation system in a white paper, arguing that their country did not have enough land both to accommodate the automobile and to feed its people. Beyond that, they noted the problems of a growing dependence on imported oil, traffic congestion, and air pollution.[64]

A few other corporate leaders are also beginning to grasp this new reality. Among this new breed of corporate CEOs is Robert Shapiro of Monsanto, who puts it simply: "The whole system has to change." Hiroyuki Fujimura, the head of EBARA, a large Japanese corporation involved in water cleaning and purification, is equally blunt. He argues that the only acceptable way to keep water safe for human use is not to pollute it in the first place. Firms such as his that install end-of-the-pipe cleanup technologies are losing the battle to provide safe water as their efforts to purify water are overwhelmed by countless thousands of dangerous compounds being released into the environment. The only viable alternative, Fujimura says, is redesigning the economy.[65]

Shapiro has gone further than perhaps any other CEO in developing a strategic plan by asking, What will an environmentally sustainable economy look like and how can Monsanto use its resources to help get from here to there? In this vein, Monsanto has sold off its pesticides division, choosing to focus on the use of genetic engineering to breed pest-resistant crop varieties. Shapiro sees the encrypting of genetic information in crops to enable them to resist insects and diseases as being part of the information revolution. He believes this is less of a threat than that posed by pesticides as the world

tries to double world food output over the next several decades. Further, Shapiro believes that corporations that do not chart their course by the vision of an environmentally sustainable future will become obsolete and disappear.[66]

Among corporations, there will be winners and there will be losers. Farsighted, well-managed firms will anticipate the opportunities and exploit them. The same is true of countries. Some have crossed the political threshold and are working hard to create an environmentally sustainable economic system. Others actively oppose it. The two extremes can be seen in Denmark and Saudi Arabia. On the big issues of stabilizing population, stabilizing climate, and ensuring future food supplies, Denmark is well positioned. It has stabilized its population at just over 5 million and it has done so within the limits of its food-producing capacity. On the energy front, although it ranks high in carbon emissions per person, it has recently refused to license the construction of coal-fired power plants and is investing heavily in wind power, which now supplies 5 percent of its electricity.[67]

In contrast, Saudi Arabia still has not recognized the threat posed by its population growth of 3 percent a year, a rate that will ensure a 20-fold increase over the next century. Ideally positioned to benefit from the fossil fuel age, it refuses to recognize global warming as a threat, and at international gatherings the Saudis actively oppose meaningful efforts to reduce carbon emissions. Just as Denmark is well endowed with wind energy, so is Saudi Arabia richly endowed with solar energy, but it is doing little to exploit this environmentally benign energy source.[68]

If we care about the next generation, then we have little choice but to launch a full-court press to stabilize population as soon as possible everywhere. The difference between an all-out effort now and a continuation of business-as-usual could be the difference between a population that will stabilize around 8 billion and one that will approach 11 billion—the difference, in other words, between adding 2 billion and 5 billion more people. We need to do this not because it is easy or necessarily popular, but because future political stability and economic progress may depend on it.[69]

In a world where the pressures on deteriorating natural support systems continue to build, business-as-usual is not likely to continue much longer. Reversing the trends that are undermining our future depends on a massive mobilization of resources, one comparable to that associated with World War II. The educational effort needed to support change on this scale requires the dissemination of a vast amount of information, which can only be led by national governments.

During the Depression Decade of the 1930s, an earlier time of crisis, U.S. President Franklin Roosevelt launched the "Fireside Chats" over nationwide radio as he worked to restore confidence in the country's future. In September 1997, as the Clinton White House also recognized the need to better inform the American people on climate change and to counter industry's disinformation campaign, it began organizing special media events. One was a White House press conference featuring six of the country's leading scientists addressing the various dimensions of the climate change issue. And in another effort to reach the public, the Clinton White House organized a briefing on climate change for television weather forecasters. The goal was to help them better understand climate change so they could report daily weather events not as isolated matters but in a broader context. In this way, they can help the public better understand the reason for record-high temperatures, more destructive storms, or more intense droughts.[70]

All the major news organizations bear a responsibility for helping people understand that business-as-usual is no longer a viable strategy, that sustaining the technological and social progress that has been a hallmark of human civ-ilization now depends urgently on changes in policies and priorities. One defining characteristic of a civilized society is a sense of responsibility to the next generation. If we do not assume that responsibility, environmental deterioration leading to economic decline and social disintegration could threaten the survival of civilization as we know it.[71]

Although governments must lead this effort, only the global communications media—print and electronic—can disseminate the needed information in the time available. This puts a heavy burden on such electronic giants as the British Broadcasting Corporation, Voice of America, and Cable News Network (CNN) as well as on wire services, such as the Associated Press and Reuters, and the leading weekly news magazines, such as *Time, Newsweek,* and the *Economist.* While heads of the world's major news organizations may not have sought this responsibility, only they have the tools to disseminate the information needed to fuel change on the scale required and in the time available.

The need today is for leadership—and not just for marginal, incremental change, but for a boldness of leadership of the caliber demonstrated by Ted Turner, founder of the Turner Broadcasting System and CNN, when he announced in September 1997 that he would be giving $1 billion to the United Nations over the next 10 years to be spent on population, environment, and humanitarian relief programs. His gift reflected a deep concern with our failure to address the great challenges of our time effectively, the need for a global approach to the key issues facing humanity, and the futility of endlessly accumulating wealth to be passed on to the next generation while leaving them a planet so degraded that their world would be declining economically and disintegrating socially. One of Turner's goals is to encourage other billionaires not merely to be more charitable, but also to respond to the great issues of our day.[72]

If ever there was a need for leadership, it is now. It is time for corporate leaders to step forward, recognizing that they are responsible for more than just the short-term bottom line, that they can help keep the dream of a better life alive. While it is true that "the business of business is business," it is also true that corporations have a stake in building an economy in which economic progress can continue.

In a world of resource scarcity, political leadership is the scarcest of all. History judges political leaders by whether or not they respond to the great issues of their time. For Lincoln, the challenge was to free the slaves. For Churchill, it was to turn the tide of war in Europe. For Nelson Mandela, it was to end apartheid. For Bill Clinton, the challenge is to build a new economy.

Notes

1. Historic data from Herbert R. Block, *The Planetary Product in 1980: A Creative Pause?* (Washington, DC: U.S. Department of State, 1981); current data from International Monetary Fund (IMF), *World Economic Outlook, May 1997* (Washington, DC: 1997).

2. Current global output from IMF, op. cit. note 1.

3. Population increase from United Nations, *World Population Prospects: The 1996 Revision* (New York: forthcoming); information on idled cropland from K. F. Isherwood and K. G. Soh, "Short Term Prospects for World Agriculture and Fertilizer Use," presented at 21st Enlarged Council Meeting, International Fertilizer Industry Association, Paris, 15–17 November 1995, and U.S. Department of Agriculture (USDA), Foreign Agricultural Service (FAS), *World Agricultural Production* (Washington, DC: October 1995); grain stocks data from USDA, *Production, Supply, and Distribution* (PS&D), electronic database, Washington, DC, updated May 1997, and from USDA, FAS, *Grain: World Markets and Trade* (Washington, DC: September 1997).

4. Sandra Postel, *Last Oasis,* rev. ed. (New York: W. W. Norton & Company, 1997); grain import data from USDA, PS&D, op. cit. note 3.

5. Postel, op. cit. note 4; Thomas F. Homer-Dixon, Jeffrey H. Boutwell, and George W. Rathjens, "Environmental Change and Violent Conflict," *Scientific American,* February 1993.

6. IMF, *International Financial Statistics* (Washington, DC: 1996).

7. "Tension in Jordan After Bread Riots," Reuters, 17 August 1996; Jamal Halaby, "More Jordanians Riot In Bread Price Protest," *Washington Post,* 18 August 1996; Serge Schmemann, "In Jordan, Bread-Price Protests Signal Deep Anger," *New York Times,* 21 August 1996; Pakistan information from "Surge in Wheat Imports by Several Nations Offset China and Russia Declines," in USDA, FAS, *Grain: World Markets and Trade* (Washington, DC: August 1997).

8. Paul McKeague, "Nation's Environment Abuse Decried," *Southam Newspapers,* 1 April 1997.

9. Population from United Nations, op. cit. note 3; grain data and Figure 1 from USDA, PS&D, op. cit. note 3.

10. Example of "leapfrogging" to cellular phones in "Can China Reform?" *Business Week,* 29 September 1997.

11. Scrap recycling data for 1996 from William Heanan, Steel Recycling Institute, discussion with author (Mitchell), 12 August 1997; Steel Recycling Institute, "The Inherent Recycled Content of Today's Steel," fact sheet (Pittsburgh, PA: July 1997); energy savings from Nicholas Lenssen and David Malin Roodman, "Making Better Buildings," in Lester R. Brown et al., *State of the World 1995* (Washington, DC: W. W. Norton & Company, 1995).

12. Jerry Powell, "The Coming Crisis in Steel Recycling: The Rising Role of Scrap Substitutes," *Resource Recycling,* July 1997; Steel Recycling Institute, op. cit. note 11.

13. Maureen Smith, *The U.S. Paper Industry* (Cambridge, MA: The MIT Press, 1997).

14. Brenda Platt and David Morris, *The Economic Benefits of Recycling* (Washington, DC: Institute for Local Self-Reliance, January 1993).

15. Data on jobs from ibid.; German data from "Green Dot Recycling Program Reports Rise in Level of Packaging Waste Collected in 1996," *International Environment Reporter,* 14 May 1997, and from "Government to Try Again to Get Parliament to Approve Changes to Packaging Ordinance," *International Environment Reporter,* 11 June 1997.

16. "Industrial Ecology: Case Histories," Indigo Development, Competitive Industries in Sustainable Communities Through Industrial Ecology, CA, <http://www.indigodev. com/Cases.html>, viewed 31 July 1997; Nicholas Gertler, "Industrial Ecosystems: Developing Sustainable Industrial Structures," Master's Thesis, Massachusetts Institute of Technology, Cambridge, MA, 1995.

17. "Industrial Ecology: Case Histories," op. cit. note 16; Gunter Pauli, Executive Director, Zero Emissions Research Institute, discussion with author (Brown), Tokyo, Japan, 15 September 1997.

18.   Information on the Conservation Reserve Program from Isherwood and Soh, op. cit. note 3, and from USDA, Natural Resources Conservation Service, *America's Private Land: A Geography of Hope* (Washington, DC: December 1996).

19.   Information on Japan from Noel Grove, "Rice, The Essential Harvest," *National Geographic,* May 1994, and from USDA, PS&D, op. cit. note 3; "Chinese Reform Burial Customs," *Mazingira,* March 1984; information on Viet Nam from "South Korean Golf Course Exempted from Decree on Rice Fields," *New Frontiers,* June 1995.

20.   Gary Gardner, *Shrinking Fields: Cropland Loss in a World of Eight Billion,* Worldwatch Paper 131 (Washington, DC: Worldwatch Institute, July 1996); Lester Brown, "Higher Crop Yields?" *World Watch,* July/August 1997.

21.   Sandra Postel, *Dividing the Waters: Food Security, Ecosystem Health, and the New Politics of Scarcity,* Worldwatch Paper 132 (Washington, DC: Worldwatch Institute, September 1996).

22.   Ibid.; Postel, op. cit. note 4; shifting land from USDA, PS&D, op. cit. note 3.

23.   Grain-to-poultry ratio derived from Robert V. Bishop et al., *The World Poultry Market—Government Intervention and Multilateral Policy Reform* (Washington, DC: USDA, 1990); grain-to-beef conversion ratio based on Allen Baker, Feed Situation and Outlook Staff, Economic Research Service (ERS), USDA, Washington, DC, discussion with author (Brown), 27 April 1992; Figure 2 from USDA, PS&D, op. cit. note 3, and from USDA, FAS, *Livestock and Poultry: World Markets and Trade* (Washington, DC: March 1997).

24.   United Nations, op. cit. note 3; water needed based on Wulf Klohn and Hans Wolter, "Perspectives of Food Security and Water Development," unpublished paper, and on Postel, op. cit. note 4; grain needed based on USDA, PS&D, op. cit. note 3. Water calculation assumes that 40 percent of the water required to produce the additional grain comes from irrigation.

25.   United Nations, op. cit. note 3.

26.   U.S. Bureau of the Census, *International Data Base,* Suitland, MD, 10 October 1997; John Cleland and Louisiana Lush, "Population and Policies in Bangladesh, Pakistan," *Forum for Applied Research and Public Policy,* Summer 1997; Figure 3 from United Nations, op. cit. note 3.

27.   United Nations, op. cit. note. 3.

28.   John Bongaarts, "Population Policy Options in the Developing World," *Science,* 11 February 1994; Barbara Shane, *Family Planning Saves Lives* (Washington, DC: Population Reference Bureau, January 1997).

29.   Nada Chaya, "Contraceptive Choice: Worldwide Access to Family Planning," wall chart (Washington, DC: Population Action International, 1997); Macro International, *Contraceptive Knowledge, Use, and Sources: Comparative Studies Number 19* (Calverton, MD: 1996).

30.   "Pakistan: Family Planning with Male Involvement Project of Mardan," in *Family Planning Programs: Diverse Solutions For a Global Challenge,* package by Population Reference Bureau, Washington, DC, November 1993; information on spousal consent from John A. Ross, W. Parker Mauldin, and Vincent C. Miller, *Family Planning and Population: A Compendium of International Statistics* (New York: The Population Council, 1993), and from "Zambia: New Family Planning Policy Applauded," *Comtex Newswire,* 6 October 1997. In some countries, it may be beneficial for a woman to receive her husband's consent for sterilization so that her inability to reproduce is not used against her in the future.

31.   G. Tyler Miller, "Cops and Rubbers Day in Thailand," in *Living in the Environment,* 8th ed. (Belmont, CA: Wadsworth Publishing Company, 1994); growth rates from United Nations, op. cit. note 3.

32.   Bongaarts, op. cit. note 28.

33.   David Bornstein, "The Garmeen Bank—Trying to Put Poverty in Museums," *Why,* Summer 1997.

34.   Macro International, *Bangladesh Demographic and Health Survey, 1996–97,* Preliminary Report (Calverton, MD: June 1997).

35.   Shane, op. cit. note 28.

36.   Ann Austin, "State of Grace," *Earthwatch,* March/April 1993.

37.   Bongaarts, op. cit. note 28.

38.   Ibid.

39.   "Bangladesh: National Family Planning Program," in *Family Planning Programs: Diverse Solutions for a Global Challenge,* package by Population Reference Bureau, Washington, DC, February 1994.

40.   United Nations Population Fund (UNFPA), "Meeting the Goals of the ICPD: Consequences of Resource Shortfalls up to the Year 2000," paper presented to the Executive Board of the U.N. Development Programme and the UNFPA, New York, 12–23 May 1997.

41.   Ibid.; Michael Vlassoff, UNFPA, conversation with author (Mitchell), 28 October 1997.

42.   UNFPA, op. cit. note 40.

43.   Sharon L. Camp, "Population: The Critical Decade," *Foreign Policy,* Spring 1993.

44.   Global temperatures from James Hansen et al., Goddard Institute for Space Studies Surface Air Temperature

Analyses, "Table of Global Mean Monthly, Annual and Seasonal Land Ocean Temperature Index, 1950–Present," <http://www.giss.nasa.gov/Data/GISTEMP>, 19 January 1996; information on the insurance industry from Michael Tucker, "Climate Change and the Insurance Industry; The Cost of Increased Risk and the Impetus for Action," *Ecological Economics,* no. 22, 1997.

45.   World Resources Institute et al., *World Resources 1996–97* (New York: Oxford University Press, 1996).

46.   Bicycle data from United Nations, *Industrial Commodity Statistics Yearbook 1994* (New York: 1996); automobile statistics from American Automobile Manufacturers Association (AAMA), *World Motor Vehicle Data,* 1996 ed. (Detroit, MI: 1996), from AAMA, *Motor Vehicle Facts and Figures 1996* (Detroit, MI: 1996), and from DRI/McGraw-Hill, *World Car Industry Forecast Report* (London: November 1996).

47.   China bicycle data from "World Market Report," *1997 Interbike Directory* (Newport Beach, CA: Primedia, Inc. 1997); Figure 4 from United Nations, op. cit. note 46, from "World Market Report," op. cit. this note, from AAMA, *World Motor Vehicle Data,* op. cit. note 46, from AAMA, *Facts and Figures 1996,* op. cit. note 46, and from DRI/ McGraw-Hill, op cit. note 46; Amsterdam information from "Civilized Servants," *IBF News* (International Bicycle Fund, Seattle), no. 2, 1995; Lima information from Deike Peters, "Bikeways Come to Lima's Mean Streets," *Sustainable Transport,* Winter 1997; U.K. information from "Government Sets Target to Quadruple Bicycle Use," *ENDS Report 258,* July 1996.

48.   Toni Nelson, "Sales of Compact Fluorescents Soar," in Lester R. Brown, Christopher Flavin, and Hal Kane, *Vital Signs 1996* (New York: W. W. Norton & Company, 1996); David Malin Roodman, "Compact Fluorescents Remain Strong," in Lester R. Brown, Nicholas Lenssen, and Hal Kane, *Vital Signs 1995* (New York: W. W. Norton & Company, 1995). Figure 5 has 1988 data from Evan Mills, Lawrence Berkeley Laboratory, Berkeley, CA, per discussion with David Malin Roodman, Worldwatch Institute, 3 February 1993; 1989–92 data from Nils Borg, "Global CFL Sales," *International Association for Energy-Efficient Lighting (IAEEL) Newsletter,* Stockholm, Sweden, April 1994; and 1993–95 data from Nils Borg, IAEEL/National Board for Industrial and Technical Development, Stockholm, Sweden, discussion with Toni Nelson, Worldwatch Institute, 5 February 1996.

49.   Firewood data from U.N. Food and Agriculture Organization, *State of the World's Forests 1997* (Oxford, U.K.: 1997); hydropower data from Energy Information Administration, *International Energy Annual 1995* (Washington, DC: Department of Energy, December 1996); installed wind

generating capacity is a preliminary Worldwatch estimate based on Christopher Flavin, "Wind Power Growth Continues," in Lester R. Brown, Michael Renner, and Christopher Flavin, *Vital Signs 1997* (New York: W. W. Norton & Company, 1997), on *The Solar Letter,* various issues, and on *Windpower Monthly,* various issues; California wind farms from Mike Batham, California Energy Commission, Sacramento, CA, discussion with Christopher Flavin, Worldwatch Institute, 7 April 1994; Figure 6 from Birger Madsen, BTM Consult, "International Wind Energy Development" (Ringkobing, Denmark: 17 January 1997), from Paul Gipe and Associates, Tehachapi, CA, discussion with Christopher Flavin, Worldwatch Institute, 19 February 1996, and from Knud Rehfeldt, Deutsches Windenergie-Institut, letter to Christopher Flavin, Worldwatch Institute, 13 January 1997.

50.   D. L. Elliott, L. L. Windell, and G. L. Gower, *An Assessment of the Available Windy Land Area and Wind Energy Potential in the Contiguous United States* (Richland, WA: Pacific Northwest Laboratory, 1991); China data from Christopher Flavin, "Worldwide Growth of Wind Energy," *World Watch,* September/October 1996.

51.   Christopher Flavin, "Clean as a Breeze," *Time Special Issue,* November 1997.

52.   Neville Williams, Solar Electric Light Fund, Washington, DC, discussion with Christopher Flavin, Worldwatch Institute, 29 January 1997.

53.   Flavin, op. cit. note 51; information on Japan from "Japanese PVPS Would Go Further," *The Solar Letter,* 9 May 1997.

54.   Enron Corp, "Enron Forms Enron Renewable Energy Corp: Acquire Zond Corporation, Leading Developer of Wind Energy Power," press release (Houston, TX: 6 January 1997); Martha M. Hamilton, "Energizing Solar Power," *Washington Post,* 26 August 1997.

55.   Hamilton, op. cit. note 54; Robert Corzine, "Shell: £300m Spent on Renewable Energy," *Financial Times,* 17 October 1997; Flavin, op. cit. note 51.

56.   Ross Gelbspan, *The Heat Is On* (New York: Addison-Wesley Publishing Company, Inc., 1997).

57.   Teresa Watanbe, "In Historic Vote, Japanese Town Rejects Nuclear Plant," *Los Angeles Times,* 5 August 1997; Lester R. Brown, "We Are All Rubber Tappers," *World Watch,* March/April 1989; Yul Choi, Secretary General of the Korean Federation for Environmental Movement, discussion with authors, 6 October 1997; National Wildlife Federation, *1996 Annual Report* (Washington, DC: 1996); *United Nations Environment Programme (UNEP) Source of Funds, 1992–1996,* provided by Jim Sniffen, UNEP, New York, discussion with Hilary French, Worldwatch Institute, 19 February 1997.

58. Lester R. Brown, *Who Will Feed China?* (New York: W. W. Norton & Company, 1995).

59. "Surgeon General's Reports," Office of Smoking and Health, Centers for Disease Control and Prevention, http://www.cdc.gov/nccdphp/osh/sgrpage.htm, viewed 27 October 1997.

60. J. T. Houghton et al., eds. *Climate Change 1995: The Science of Climate Change,* Contribution of Working Group I to the Second Assessment Report of the International Panel on Climate Change (Cambridge, U.K.: Cambridge University Press, 1996); Colin D. Woodroffe, "Preliminary Assessment of the Vulnerability of Kiribati to Accelerated Sea Level Rise," in Joan O'Callahan, ed. *Global Climate Change and the Rising Challenge of the Sea,* Proceedings of the IPCC Workshop held at Margarita Island, Venezuela, March 9–13, 1992 (Silver Spring, MD: National Oceanic and Atmospheric Administration, 1992).

61. Gerhard A. Berz, Muchener Ruckversicherungs-Gesellschaff, press release (Munich, Germany: 23 December 1996); UNEP Insurance Initiative, *Position Paper on Climate Change* (Geneva: UNEP, 9 July 1996).

62. Ken Lay, Chairman and Chief Executive Officer, Enron, USA, "Too Hot For Business? The Implications of Global Warming?" lunch session at the World Economic Forum Annual Meeting, Davos, Switzerland, 1 February 1997.

63. John Browne, Group Chief Executive, British Petroleum (BP America), Climate Change Speech, Stanford University, 19 May 1997.

64. Patrick E. Tyler, "China's Transport Gridlock: Cars vs. Mass Transit," *New York Times,* 4 May 1996.

65. Shapiro quoted in Joan Magretta, "Growth Through Global Sustainability," *Harvard Business Review,* January–February 1997; EBARA information from Pauli, op. cit. note 17.

66. Monsanto in Magretta, op. cit. note 70.

67. United Nations, op. cit. note 3; USDA, PS&D, op. cit. note 3; information on Denmark's restriction of coal-fired power plants from Climate Network Europe and US Climate Action Network (US CAN), *Independent NGO Evaluations of National Plans for Climate Change Mitigation, Fifth Review* (Washington, DC: US CAN, November 1997); wind power data from Madsen, op. cit. note 49.

68. United Nations, op. cit. note 3; Saudi data from Seth S. Dunn, "The Geneva Conference: Implications for U.N. Framework Convention on Climate Change," *International Environment Reporter,* 2 October 1997.

69. United Nations, op. cit. note 3.

70. Stephen H. Schneider, "Global Warming Balance Sheet: What Do We Really Know," *Christian Science Monitor,* 8 August 1997; Howard Kurtz, "The White House Hopes to Warm up TV Weathercasters," *Washington Post,* 18 September 1997.

71. For more on this, see Peter M. Vitousek et al., "Human Domination of Earth's Ecosystems," *Science,* 25 July 1997.

72. David Rohde, "Ted Turner Plans a $1 Billion Gift for U.N. Agencies," *New York Times,* 19 September 1997; John Goshko, "For United Nations, $1 Billion Is a Good Round Figure," *Washington Post,* 20 September 1997.

Part 2

The Institutional Setting of Environmental Issues

THE SECOND PART of this book considers the ethical, regulatory, and economic settings in which environmental issues arise, are confronted, and are resolved. Partly intended to stimulate learning about the institutions involved and partly intended to provoke critical discussion about their roles in the recognition and resolution of environmental challenges, the readings provide a coherent sense of the interaction of the environment with the institutional realities created by humankind.

A reading from Aldo Leopold's classic, *A Sand County Almanac,* begins by sketching out a moral argument for environmental stewardship. Leopold, a University of Wisconsin naturalist, was passionate in his advocacy of the value of preserving wilderness. Leopold held that the abuse of land by humankind was a direct result of humans imposing the values of ownership on their surroundings. Viewed as a holistic community, of which humans are merely one constituent, the natural world takes on a completely different character and demands our respect and affection.

The next reading addresses what is perhaps the root cause of environmental degradation: overconsumption. In "Asking How Much Is Enough," Alan Durning, now of the Northwest Environment Watch, argues that the purchasing of ever more material goods within developed countries strains the earth's resources. This is a peculiar tendency, given that there is no direct correlation between material possessions and happiness, and that materialism is frowned on by all major religions. Thus, this article points to a basic ethical question confronting corporations—the extent to which they should promote consumption for its own sake.

Garrett Hardin's classic "The Tragedy of the Commons" forms a bridge between ethics and economics. Although a microbiologist and not an economist by training, Hardin does an excellent job of explaining how a common, free pool of exhaustible resources can lead to overconsumption and environmental degradation. The reading also illustrates the idea of economic externalities, which occur when one party produces ill outcomes for which it does not pay or positive outcomes for which it is not fully compensated. Hardin also purveys very provocative ideas for solving such problems.

Is the relationship outlined by Hardin inevitable? How might economics be reconstituted to enhance environmental quality? These are some of the questions that are addressed in the next several readings, which spotlight the role of regulation and of economic institutions in environmental challenges and their solutions.

Regulation of corporate behavior is the starting point for Paul R. Portney of Resources for the Future, in his "EPA and the Evolution of Federal Regulation." The reading begins by briefly reviewing the genesis of the main federal environmental regulatory body in the United States; the Environmental Protection Agency. Rather than explore the minutiae of detailed regulation, Portney provides a broader understanding of the fundamental choices that face policy makers as they approach the regulatory task. Thus he provides readers with a clean appreciation of the issues that Congress and other bodies face when they consider reform of environmental regulation in the United States, as well as an idea of how economists view these choices.

The increasing use of market-based instruments to promote environmental quality suggests a very important question: How can value be placed on goods that are not bought or sold? If market-based solutions are to be used, prices for such goods must be explicitly or implicitly determined. Frances Cairncross, former environmental editor of *The Economist,* addresses

this very question in the next reading, "Costs and Benefits." In this piece, excerpted from her book *Costing the Earth,* Cairncross renders this very complex subject down to its essential elements, providing the reader with an appreciation of the innovative ways in which the value of elements of the natural world can be established.

The University of Maryland's Timothy J. Brennan then contributes "Discounting the Future: Economics and Ethics," a discussion of one of the most basic elements in economic analysis: discounting. Discounting is the practice of lowering the value of benefits and costs that will occur in the future, compared to current costs and benefits. After explaining discounting and presenting several examples, Brennan provides an interesting discourse on the ethical pros and cons of discounting. It is a thought-provoking discussion that subjects a basic, widely accepted economic practice to an uncommon level of scrutiny.

The final three readings in this section take a step back and describe the global picture. In "Behind the Scenes," Harvard University's Raymond Vernon provides an in-depth view of how the major developed countries approach environmental regulation. Writing from the political science discipline, he compares and contrasts the approach to environmental policy employed by the United States, Japan, and Europe. With considerable differences apparent, he then highlights the role of nongovernmental organizations in bridging national differences, and producing consensus and improvements in environmental stewardship.

Our section on the institutional setting of environmental issues concludes with two readings that provide for a debate on trade and the environment, a subject that synthesizes ethical, political, and economic issues. Author and lecturer Edward Goldsmith, in "Global Trade and the Environment," attacks the idea of further liberalization of international trade. He argues that the expansion of economic growth has assaulted the environment, resulting in widespread de-spoilage and human loss. He questions the notion that expanded wealth created by trade will result in greater environmental awareness and enhancement. Daniel C. Esty of Yale University takes the opposite view in "Making Trade Work for the Environment." He provides documenta-tion supporting the notion that beyond a threshold level of gross domestic product, pollution declines. Thus, trade indeed will improve environmental quality. He then outlines a number of policy recommendations for aligning trade with the environment.

3

The Land Ethic
Aldo Leopold

When god-like Odysseus returned from the wars in Troy, he hanged all on one rope a dozen slave-girls of his household whom he suspected of misbehavior during his absence.

This hanging involved no question of propriety. The girls were property. The disposal of property was then, as now, a matter of expediency, not of right and wrong.

Concepts of right and wrong were not lacking from Odysseus' Greece: witness the fidelity of his wife through the long years before at last his black-prowed galleys clove the wine-dark seas for home. The ethical structure of that day covered wives, but had not yet been extended to human chattels. During the three thousand years which have since elapsed, ethical criteria have been extended to many fields of conduct, with corresponding shrinkages in those judged by expediency only.

THE ETHICAL SEQUENCE

This extension of ethics, so far studied only by philosophers, is actually a process in ecological evolution. Its sequences may be described in ecological as well as in philosophical terms. An ethic, ecologically, is a limitation on freedom of action in the struggle for existence. An ethic,

●

philosophically, is a differentiation of social from anti-social conduct. These are two definitions of one thing. The thing has its origin in the tendency of interdependent individuals or groups to evolve modes of co-operation. The ecologist calls these symbioses. Politics and economics are advanced symbioses in which the original free-for-all competition has been replaced, in part, by co-operative mechanisms with an ethical content.

The complexity of co-operative mechanisms has increased with population density, and with the efficiency of tools. It was simpler, for example, to define the anti-social uses of sticks and stones in the days of the mastodons than of bullets and billboards in the age of motors.

The first ethics dealt with the relation between individuals; the Mosaic Decalogue is an example. Later accretions dealt with the relation between the individual and society. The Golden Rule tries to integrate the individual to society; democracy to integrate social organization to the individual.

There is as yet no ethic dealing with man's relation to land and to the animals and plants which grow upon it. Land, like Odysseus' slave-girls, is still property. The land-relation is still strictly economic, entailing privileges but not obligations.

The extension of ethics to this third element in human environment is, if I read the evidence correctly, an evolutionary possibility and an ecological necessity. It is the third step in a sequence. The first two have already been taken. Individual thinkers since the days of Ezekiel and Isaiah have asserted that the despoliation of land is not only inexpedient but wrong. Society, however, has not yet affirmed their belief. I regard the present conservation movement as the embryo of such an affirmation.

An ethic may be regarded as a mode of guidance for meeting ecological situations so new or intricate, or involving such deferred reactions, that the path of social expediency is not discernible to the average individual. Animal instincts are modes of guidance for the individual in meeting such situations. Ethics are possibly a kind of community instinct in-the-making.

THE COMMUNITY CONCEPT

All ethics so far evolved rest upon a single premise: that the individual is a member of a community of interdependent parts. His instincts prompt him to compete for his place in that community, but his ethics prompt him also to co-operate (perhaps in order that there may be a place to compete for).

The land ethic simply enlarges the boundaries of the community to include soils, waters, plants, and animals, or collectively, the land.

This sounds simple: do we not already sing our love for and obligation to the land of the free and the home of the brave? Yes, but just what and whom do we love? Certainly not the soil, which we are sending helter-skelter downriver. Certainly not the waters, which we assume have no function except to turn turbines, float barges, and carry off sewage. Certainly not the plants, of which we exterminate whole communities without batting an eye. Certainly not the animals, of which we have already extirpated many of the largest and most beautiful species. A land ethic of course cannot prevent the alteration, management, and use of these "resources," but it does affirm their right to continued existence, and, at least in spots, their continued existence in a natural state.

In short, a land ethic changes the role of *Homo sapiens* from conqueror of the land-community to plain member and citizen of it. It implies respect for his fellow-members, and also respect for the community as such.

In human history, we have learned (I hope) that the conqueror role is eventually self-defeating. Why? Because it is implicit in such a role that the conqueror knows, *ex cathedra,* just what makes the community clock tick, and just what and who is valuable, and what and who is worthless, in community life. It always turns out that he knows neither, and this is why his conquests eventually defeat themselves.

In the biotic community, a parallel situation exists. Abraham knew exactly what the land was for: it was to drip milk and honey into Abraham's mouth. At the present moment, the assurance with which we regard this assumption is inverse to the degree of our education.

The ordinary citizen today assumes that science knows what makes the community clock tick; the scientist is equally sure that he does not. He knows that the biotic mechanism is so complex that its workings may never be fully understood.

That man is, in fact, only a member of a biotic team is shown by an ecological interpretation of history. Many historical events, hitherto explained solely in terms of human enterprise, were actually biotic interactions between people and land. The characteristics of the land determined the facts quite as potently as the characteristics of the men who lived on it.

Consider, for example, the settlement of the Mississippi valley. In the years following the Revolution, three groups were contending for its control: the native Indian, the French and English traders, and the American settlers. Historians wonder what would have happened if the English at Detroit had thrown a little more weight into the Indian side of those tipsy scales which decided the outcome of the colonial migration into the cane-lands of Kentucky. It is time now to ponder the fact that the cane-lands, when subjected to the particular mixture of forces represented by the cow, plow, fire, and axe of the pioneer, became bluegrass. What if the plant succession inherent in this dark and bloody ground had, under the impact of these forces, given us some worthless sedge, shrub, or weed? Would Boone and Kenton have held out? Would there have been any overflow into Ohio, Indiana, Illinois, and Missouri? Any Louisiana Purchase? Any transcontinental union of new states? Any Civil War?

Kentucky was one sentence in the drama of history. We are commonly told what the human actors in this drama tried to do, but we are seldom told that their success, or the lack of it, hung in large degree on the reaction of particular soils to the impact of the particular forces exerted by their occupancy. In the case of Kentucky, we do not even know where the bluegrass came from—whether it is a native species, or a stowaway from Europe.

Contrast the cane-lands with what hindsight tells us about the Southwest, where the pioneers were equally brave, resourceful, and persevering. The impact of occupancy here brought no bluegrass, or other plant fitted to withstand the bumps and buffetings of hard use. This region, when grazed by livestock, reverted through a series of more and more worthless grasses, shrubs, and weeds to a condition of unstable equilibrium. Each recession of plant types bred erosion; each increment to erosion bred a further recession of plants. The result today is a progressive and mutual deterioration, not only of plants and soils, but of the animal community subsisting thereon. The early settlers did not expect this: on the ciénegas of New Mexico some even cut the ditches to hasten it. So subtle has been its progress that few residents of the region are aware of it. It is quite invisible to the tourist who finds this wrecked landscape colorful and charming (as indeed it is, but it bears scant resemblance to what it was in 1848).

This same landscape was "developed" once before, but with quite different results. The Pueblo Indians settled the Southwest in pre-Columbian times, but they happened *not* to be equipped with range livestock. Their civilization expired, but not because their land expired.

In India, regions devoid of any sod-forming grass have been settled, apparently without wrecking the land, by the simple expedient of carrying the grass to the cow, rather than vice versa. (Was this the result of some deep wisdom, or was it just good luck? I do not know.)

In short, the plant succession steered the course of history; the pioneer simply demonstrated, for good or ill, what successions inhered in the land. Is history taught in this spirit? It will be, once the concept of land as a community really penetrates our intellectual life.

THE ECOLOGICAL CONSCIENCE

Conservation is a state of harmony between men and land. Despite nearly a century of propaganda, conservation still proceeds at a snail's pace; progress still consists largely of letterhead pieties and convention oratory. On the back forty we still slip two steps backward for each forward stride.

The usual answer to this dilemma is "more conservation education." No one will debate this, but is it certain that only the *volume* of education needs stepping up? Is something lacking in the *content* as well?

It is difficult to give a fair summary of its content in brief form, but, as I understand it, the content is substantially this: obey the law, vote right, join some organizations, and practice what conservation is profitable on your own land; the government will do the rest.

Is not this formula too easy to accomplish anything worthwhile? It defines no right or wrong, assigns no obligation, calls for no sacrifice, implies no change in the current philosophy of values. In respect to land-use, it urges only enlightened self-interest. Just how far will such education take us? An example will perhaps yield a partial answer.

By 1930 it had become clear to all except the ecologically blind that southwestern Wisconsin's topsoil was slipping seaward. In 1933 the farmers were told that if they would adopt certain remedial practices for five years, the public would donate CCC labor to install them, plus the necessary machinery and materials. The offer was widely accepted, but the practices were widely forgotten when the five-year contract period was up. The farmers continued only those practices that yielded an immediate and visible economic gain for themselves.

This led to the idea that maybe farmers would learn more quickly if they themselves wrote the rules. Accordingly the Wisconsin Legislature in 1937 passed the Soil Conservation District Law. This said to farmers, in effect: *We, the public, will furnish you free technical service and loan you specialized machinery, if you will write your own rules for land-use. Each county may write its own rules, and these will have the force of law.* Nearly all the counties promptly organized to accept the proffered help, but after a decade of operation, *no county has yet written a single rule.* There has been visible progress in such practices as strip-cropping, pasture renovation, and soil liming, but none in fencing woodlots against grazing, and none in excluding plow and cow from steep slopes. The farmers, in short, have selected those remedial practices which were profitable anyhow, and ignored those which were profitable to the community, but not clearly profitable to themselves.

When one asks why no rules have been written, one is told that the community is not yet ready to support them; education must precede rules. But the education actually in progress makes no mention of obligations to land over and above those dictated by self-interest. The net result is that we have more education but less soil, fewer healthy woods, and as many floods as in 1937.

The puzzling aspect of such situations is that the existence of obligations over and above self-interest is taken for granted in such rural community enterprises as the betterment of roads, schools, churches, and baseball teams. Their existence is not taken for granted, nor as yet seriously discussed, in bettering the behavior of the water that falls on the land, or in the preserving of the beauty or diversity of the farm landscape. Land-use ethics are still governed wholly by economic self-interest, just as social ethics were a century ago.

To sum up: we asked the farmer to do what he conveniently could to save his soil, and he has done just that, and only that. The farmer who clears the woods off a 75 per cent slope, turns his cows into the clearing, and dumps its rainfall, rocks, and soil into the community creek, is still (if otherwise decent) a respected member of society. If he puts lime on his fields and plants his crops on contour, he is still entitled to all the privileges and emoluments of his Soil Conservation District. The District is a beautiful piece of social machinery, but it is coughing along on two cylinders because we have been too timid, and too anxious for quick success, to tell the farmer the true magnitude of his obligations. Obligations have no meaning without conscience, and the problem we face is the extension of the social conscience from people to land.

No important change in ethics was ever accomplished without an internal change in our intellectual emphasis, loyalties, affections, and convictions. The proof that conservation has not yet touched these foundations of conduct lies in the fact that philosophy and religion have not yet heard of it. In our attempt to make conservation easy, we have made it trivial.

SUBSTITUTES FOR A LAND ETHIC

When the logic of history hungers for bread and we hand out a stone, we are at pains to explain how much the stone resembles bread. I now describe some of the stones which serve in lieu of a land ethic.

One basic weakness in a conservation system based wholly on economic motives is that most members of the land community have no economic value. Wildflowers and songbirds are examples. Of the 22,000 higher plants and animals native to Wisconsin, it is doubtful whether more than 5 per cent can be sold, fed, eaten, or otherwise put to economic use. Yet these creatures are members of the biotic community, and if (as I believe) its stability depends on its integrity, they are entitled to continuance.

When one of these non-economic categories is threatened, and if we happen to love it, we invent subterfuges to give it economic importance. At the beginning of the century songbirds were supposed to be disappearing. Ornithologists jumped to the rescue with some distinctly shaky evidence to the effect that insects would eat us up if birds failed to control them. The evidence had to be economic in order to be valid.

It is painful to read these circumlocutions today. We have no land ethic yet, but we have at least drawn nearer the point of admitting that birds should continue as a matter of biotic right, regardless of the presence or absence of economic advantage to us.

A parallel situation exists in respect of predatory mammals, raptorial birds, and fish-eating birds. Time was when biologists somewhat overworked the evidence that these creatures preserve the health of game by killing weaklings, or that they control rodents for the farmer, or that they prey only on "worthless" species. Here again, the evidence had to be economic in order to be valid. It is only in recent years that we hear the more honest argument that predators are members of the community, and that no special interest has the right to exterminate them for the sake of a benefit, real or fancied, to itself. Unfortunately this enlightened view is still in the talk stage. In the field the extermination of predators goes merrily on: witness the impending erasure of the timber wolf by fiat of Congress, the Conservation Bureaus, and many state legislatures.

Some species of trees have been "read out of the party" by economics-minded foresters because they grow too slowly, or have too low a sale value to pay as timber crops: white cedar, tamarack, cypress, beech, and hemlock are examples. In Europe, where forestry is ecologically more advanced, the non-commercial tree species are recognized as members of the native forest community, to be preserved as such, within reason. Moreover, some (like beech) have been found to have a valuable function in building up soil fertility. The interdependence of the forest and its constituent tree species, ground flora, and fauna is taken for granted.

Lack of economic value is sometimes a character not only of species or groups, but of entire biotic communities: marshes, bogs, dunes, and "deserts" are examples. Our formula in such cases is to relegate their conservation to government as refugees, monuments, or parks. The difficulty is that these communities are usually interspersed with more valuable private lands; the government cannot possibly own or control such scattered parcels. The net effect is that we have relegated some of them to ultimate extinction over large areas. If the private owner were ecologically minded, he would be proud to be the custodian of a reasonable proportion of such areas, which add diversity and beauty to his farm and to his community.

In some instances, the assumed lack of profit in these "waste" areas has proved to be wrong, but only after most of them had been done away with. The present scramble to reflood muskrat marshes is a case in point.

There is a clear tendency in American conservation to relegate to government all necessary jobs that private landowners fail to perform. Government ownership, operation, subsidy, or regulation is now widely prevalent in forestry, range management, soil and watershed management, park and wilderness conservation, fisheries management, and migratory bird management, with more to come. Most of this growth in governmental conservation is proper and logical, some of it is inevitable. That I imply no disapproval of it is implicit in the fact that I have spent most of my life working for it. Nevertheless the question arises: What is the ultimate magnitude of the enterprise? Will the tax base carry its eventual ramifications? At what point will governmental conservation, like the mastodon, become handicapped by its own dimensions? The answer, if there is any, seems to be in a land ethic, or some other force which assigns more obligation to the private landowner.

Industrial landowners and users, especially lumbermen and stockmen, are inclined to wail long and loudly about the extension of government ownership and regulation to land, but (with notable exceptions) they show little disposition to develop the only visible alternative: the voluntary practice of conservation on their own lands.

When the private landowner is asked to perform some unprofitable act for the good of the community, he today assents only with outstretched palm. If the act costs him cash this is fair and proper, but when it costs only forethought, open-mindedness, or time, the issue is at least debatable. The overwhelming growth of land-use subsidies in recent years must be ascribed, in large part, to the government's own agencies for conservation education: the land bureaus, the agricultural colleges, and the extension services. As far as I can detect, no ethical obligation toward land is taught in these institutions.

To sum up: a system of conservation based solely on economic self-interest is hopelessly lopsided. It tends to ignore, and thus eventually to eliminate, many elements in the land community that lack commercial value, but that are (as far as we know) essential to its healthy functioning. It assumes, falsely, I think, that the economic parts of the biotic clock will function without the uneconomic parts. It tends to relegate to government many functions eventually too large, too complex, or too widely dispersed to be performed by government.

An ethical obligation on the part of the private owner is the only visible remedy for these situations.

THE LAND PYRAMID

An ethic to supplement and guide the economic relation to land presupposes the existence of some mental image of land as a biotic mechanism. We can be ethical only in relation to something we can see, feel, understand, love, or otherwise have faith in.

The image commonly employed in conservation education is "the balance of nature." For reasons too lengthy to detail here, this figure of speech fails to describe accurately what little we know about the land mechanism. A much truer image is the one employed in ecology: the biotic pyramid. I shall first sketch the pyramid as a symbol of land, and later develop some of its implications in terms of land-use.

Plants absorb energy from the sun. This energy flows through a circuit called the biota, which may be represented by a pyramid consisting of layers. The bottom layer is the soil. A plant layer rests on the soil, an insect layer on the plants, a bird and rodent layer on the insects, and so on up through various animal groups to the apex layer, which consists of the larger carnivores.

The species of a layer are alike not in where they came from, or in what they look like, but rather in what they eat. Each successive layer depends on those below it for food and often for other services, and each in turn furnishes food and services to those above. Proceeding upward, each successive layer decreases in numerical abundance. Thus, for every carnivore there are hundreds of his prey, thousands of their prey, millions of insects, uncountable plants. The pyramidal form of the system reflects this numerical progression from apex to base. Man shares an intermediate layer with the bears, raccoons, and squirrels which eat both meat and vegetables.

The lines of dependency for food and other services are called food chains. Thus soil-oak-deer-Indian is a chain that has now been largely converted to soil-corn-cow-farmer. Each species, including ourselves, is a link in many chains. The deer eats a hundred plants other than oak, and the cow a hundred plants other than corn. Both, then, are links in a hundred chains. The pyramid is a tangle of chains so complex as to seem disorderly, yet the stability of the system proves it to be a highly organized structure. Its functioning depends on the co-operation and competition of its diverse parts.

In the beginning, the pyramid of life was low and squat, the food chains short and simple. Evolution has added layer after layer, link after link. Man is one of thousands of accretions to the height and complexity of the pyramid. Science has given us many doubts, but it has given us at least one certainty: the trend of evolution is to elaborate and diversify the biota.

Land, then, is not merely soil; it is a fountain of energy flowing through a circuit of soils, plants, and animals. Food chains are the living channels which conduct energy upward; death and decay return it to the soil. The circuit is not closed; some energy is dissipated in decay, some is added by absorption from the air, some is stored in soils, peats, and long-lived forests; but it is a sustained circuit, like a slowly augmented revolving fund of life. There is always a net loss by downhill wash, but this is normally small and offset by the decay of rocks. It is deposited in the ocean and, in the course of geological time, raised to form new lands and new pyramids.

The velocity and character of the upward flow of energy depend on the complex structure of the plant and animal community, much as the upward flow of sap in a tree depends on its complex cellular organization. Without this complexity, normal circulation would presumably not occur. Structure means the characteristic numbers, as well as the characteristic kinds and functions, of the component species. This interdependence between the complex structure of the land and its smooth functioning as an energy unit is one of its basic attributes.

When a change occurs in one part of the circuit, many other parts must adjust themselves to it. Change does not necessarily obstruct or divert the flow of energy; evolution is a long series of self-induced changes, the net result of which has been to elaborate the flow mechanism and to lengthen the circuit. Evolutionary changes, however, are usually slow and local. Man's invention of tools has enabled him to make changes of unprecedented violence, rapidity, and scope.

One change is in the composition of floras and faunas. The larger predators are lopped off the apex of the pyramid; food chains, for the first time in history, become shorter rather than longer. Domesticated species from other lands are substituted for wild ones, and wild ones are moved to new habitats. In this world-wide pooling of faunas and floras, some species get out of bounds as pests and diseases; others are extinguished. Such effects are seldom intended or foreseen; they represent unpredicted and often untraceable readjustments in the structure. Agricultural science is largely a race between the emergence of new pests and the emergence of new techniques for their control.

Another change touches the flow of energy through plants and animals and its return to the soil. Fertility is the ability of soil to receive, store, and release energy. Agriculture, by overdrafts on the soil, or by too radical a substitution of domestic for native species in the superstructure, may derange the channels of flow or deplete storage. Soils depleted of their storage, or of the organic matter which anchors it, wash away faster than they form. This is erosion.

Waters, like soil, are part of the energy circuit. Industry, by polluting waters or obstructing them with dams, may exclude the plants and animals necessary to keep energy in circulation.

Transportation brings about another basic change: the plants or animals grown in one region are now consumed and returned to the soil in another. Transportation taps the energy stored in rocks, and in the air, and uses it elsewhere; thus we fertilize the garden with nitrogen gleaned by the guano birds from the fishes of seas on the other side of the Equator. Thus the formerly localized and self-contained circuits are pooled on a world-wide scale.

The process of altering the pyramid for human occupation releases stored energy, and this often gives rise, during the pioneering period, to a deceptive exuberance of plant and animal life, both wild and tame. These releases of biotic capital tend to becloud or postpone the penalties of violence.

This thumbnail sketch of land as an energy circuit conveys three basic ideas:

(1) That land is not merely soil.

(2) That the native plants and animals kept the energy circuit open; others may or may not.

(3) That man-made changes are of a different order than evolutionary changes, and have effects more comprehensive than is intended or foreseen.

These ideas, collectively, raise two basic issues: Can the land adjust itself to the new order? Can the desired alterations be accomplished with less violence?

Biotas seem to differ in their capacity to sustain violent conversion. Western Europe, for example, carries a far different pyramid than Caesar found there. Some large animals are lost; swampy forests have become meadows or plowland; many new plants and animals are introduced, some of which escape as pests; the remaining natives are greatly changed in distribution and abundance. Yet the soil is still there and, with the help of imported nutrients, still fertile; the waters flow normally; the new structure seems to function and to persist. There is no visible stoppage or derangement of the circuit.

Western Europe, then, has a resistant biota. Its inner processes are tough, elastic, resistant to strain. No matter how violent the alterations, the pyramid, so far, has developed some new *modus vivendi* which preserves its habitability for man, and for most of the other natives.

Japan seems to present another instance of radical conversion without disorganization.

Most other civilized regions, and some as yet barely touched by civilization, display various stages of disorganization, varying from initial symptoms to advanced wastage. In Asia Minor and North Africa diagnosis is confused by climatic changes, which may have been either the cause or the effect of advanced wastage. In the United States the degree of disorganization varies locally; it is worst in the Southwest, the Ozarks, and parts of the South, and least in New England and the Northwest. Better land-uses may still arrest it in the less advanced regions. In parts of Mexico, South America, South Africa, and Australia a violent and accelerating wastage is in progress, but I cannot assess the prospects.

This almost world-wide display of disorganization in the land seems to be similar to disease in an animal, except that it never culminates in complete disorganization or death. The land recovers, but at some reduced level of complexity, and with a reduced carrying capacity for people, plants, and animals. Many biotas currently regarded as "lands of opportunity" are in fact already subsisting on exploitative agriculture, i.e. they have already exceeded their sustained carrying capacity. Most of South America is overpopulated in this sense.

In arid regions we attempt to offset the process of wastage by reclamation, but it is only too evident that the prospective longevity of reclamation projects is often short. In our own West, the best of them may not last a century.

The combined evidence of history and ecology seem to support one general deduction: the less violent the man-made changes, the greater the probability of successful readjustment in the pyramid. Violence, in turn, varies with human population density; a dense population requires a more violent conversion. In this respect, North America has a better chance for permanence than Europe, if she can contrive to limit her density.

This deduction runs counter to our current philosophy, which assumes that because a small increase in density enriched human life, an indefinite increase will enrich it indefinitely. Ecology knows of no density relationship that holds for indefinitely wide limits. All gains from density are subject to a law of diminishing returns.

Whatever may be the equation for men and land, it is improbable that we as yet know all its terms. Recent discoveries in mineral and vitamin nutrition reveal unsuspected dependencies in the up-circuit: incredibly minute quantities of certain substances determine the value of soils to plants, of plants to animals. What of the down-circuit? What of the vanishing species, the preservation of which we now regard as an esthetic luxury? They helped build the soil; in what unsuspected ways may they be essential to its maintenance? Professor Weaver proposes that we use prairie flowers to reflocculate the wasting soils of the dust bowl; who knows for what purpose cranes and condors, otters and grizzlies may some day be used?

LAND HEALTH AND THE A-B CLEAVAGE

A land ethic, then, reflects the existence of an ecological conscience, and this in turn reflects a conviction of individual responsibility for the health of the land. Health is the capacity of the land for self-renewal. Conservation is our effort to understand and preserve this capacity.

Conservationists are notorious for their dissensions. Superficially these seem to add up to mere confusion, but a more careful scrutiny reveals a single plane of cleavage common to many specialized fields. In each field one group (A) regards the land as soil, and its function as commodity-production; another group (B) regards the land as a biota, and its function as something broader. How much broader is admittedly in a state of doubt and confusion.

In my own field, forestry, group A is quite content to grow trees like cabbages, with cellulose as the basic forest commodity. It feels no inhibition against violence; its ideology is agronomic. Group B, on the other hand, sees forestry as fundamentally different from agronomy because it employs natural species, and manages a natural environment rather than creating an artificial one. Group B prefers natural reproduction on principle. It worries on biotic as well as economic grounds about the loss of species like chestnut, and the threatened loss of the white pines. It worries about a whole series of secondary forest functions: wildlife, recreation, watersheds, wilderness areas. To my mind, Group B feels the stirrings of an ecological conscience.

In the wildlife field, a parallel cleavage exists. For Group A the basic commodities are sport and meat; the yardsticks of production are ciphers of take in pheasants and trout. Artificial propagation is acceptable as a permanent as well as a temporary recourse—if its unit costs permit. Group B, on the other hand, worries about a whole series of biotic side-issues. What is the cost in predators of producing a game crop? Should we have further recourse to exotics? How can management restore the shrinking species, like prairie grouse, already hopeless as shootable game? How can management restore the threatened rarities, like trumpeter swan and whooping crane? Can management principles be extended to wildflowers? Here again it is clear to me that we have the same A-B cleavage as in forestry.

In the larger field of agriculture I am less competent to speak, but there seem to be somewhat parallel cleavages. Scientific agriculture was actively developing before ecology was born; hence a slower penetration of ecological concepts might be expected. Moreover the farmer, by the very nature of his techniques, must modify the biota more radically than the forester or the wildlife manager. Nevertheless, there are many discontents in agriculture which seem to add up to a new vision of "biotic farming."

Perhaps the most important of these is the new evidence that poundage or tonnage is no measure of the food-value of farm crops; the products of fertile soil may be qualitatively as well as quantitatively superior. We can bolster poundage from depleted soils by pouring on imported fertility, but we are not necessarily bolstering food-value. The possible ultimate ramifications of this idea are so immense that I must leave their exposition to abler pens.

The discontent that labels itself "organic farming," while bearing some of the earmarks of a cult, is nevertheless biotic in its direction, particularly in its insistence on the importance of soil flora and fauna.

The ecological fundamentals of agriculture are just as poorly known to the public as in other fields of land-use. For example, few educated people realize that the marvelous advances in technique made during recent decades are improvements in the pump, rather than the well. Acre for acre, they have barely sufficed to offset the sinking level of fertility.

In all of these cleavages, we see repeated the same basic paradoxes: man the conqueror *versus* man the biotic citizen; science the sharpener of his sword *versus* science the searchlight on his universe; land the slave and servant *versus* land the collective organism. Robinson's injunction to Tristram may well be applied, at this juncture, to *Homo sapiens* as a species in geological time:

Whether you will or not
You are a King, Tristram, for you are one

Of the time-tested few that leave the world,
When they are gone, not the same place it
    was.
Mark what you leave.

THE OUTLOOK

It is inconceivable to me that an ethical relation to land can exist without love, respect, and admiration for land, and a high regard for its value. By value, I of course mean something far broader than mere economic value; I mean value in the philosophical sense.

Perhaps the most serious obstacle impeding the evolution of a land ethic is the fact that our educational and economic system is headed away from, rather than toward, an intense consciousness of land. Your true modern is separated from the land by many middlemen, and by innumerable physical gadgets. He has no vital relation to it; to him it is the space between cities on which crops grow. Turn him loose for a day on the land, and if the spot does not happen to be a golf links or a "scenic" area, he is bored stiff. If crops could be raised by hydroponics instead of farming, it would suit him very well. Synthetic substitutes for wood, leather, wool, and other natural land products suit him better than the originals. In short, land is something he has "outgrown."

Almost equally serious as an obstacle to a land ethic is the attitude of the farmer for whom the land is still an adversary, or a taskmaster that keeps him in slavery. Theoretically, the mechanization of farming ought to cut the farmer's chains, but whether it really does is debatable.

One of the requisites for an ecological comprehension of land is an understanding of ecology, and this is by no means co-extensive with "education"; in fact, much higher education seems deliberately to avoid ecological concepts. An understanding of ecology does not necessarily originate in courses bearing ecological labels; it is quite as likely to be labeled geography, botany, agronomy, history, or economics. This is as it should be, but whatever the label, ecological training is scarce.

The case for a land ethic would appear hopeless but for the minority which is in obvious revolt against these "modern" trends.

The "key-log" which must be moved to release the evolutionary process for an ethic is simply this: quit thinking about decent land-use as solely an economic problem. Examine each question in terms of what is ethically and esthetically right, as well as what is economically expedient. A thing is right when it tends to preserve the integrity, stability, and beauty of the biotic community. It is wrong when it tends otherwise.

It of course goes without saying that economic feasibility limits the tether of what can or cannot be done for land. It always has and it always will. The fallacy the economic determinists have tied around our collective neck, and which we now need to cast off, is the belief that economics determines *all* land-use. This is simply not true. An innumerable host of actions and attitudes, comprising perhaps the bulk of all land relations, is determined by the land-users' tastes and predilections, rather than by his purse. The bulk of all land relations hinges on investments of time, forethought, skill, and faith rather than on investments of cash. As a land-user thinketh, so is he.

I have purposely presented the land ethic as a product of social evolution because nothing so important as an ethic is ever "written." Only the most superficial student of history supposes that Moses "wrote" the Decalogue; it evolved in the minds of a thinking community, and Moses wrote a tentative summary of it for a "seminar." I say tentative because evolution never stops.

The evolution of a land ethic is an intellectual as well as emotional process. Conservation is paved with good intentions which prove to be futile, or even dangerous, because they are devoid of critical understanding either of the land, or of economic land-use. I think it is a truism that as the ethical frontier advances from the individual to the community, its intellectual content increases.

The mechanism of operation is the same for any ethic: social approbation for right actions; social disapproval for wrong actions.

By and large, our present problem is one of attitudes and implements. We are remodeling the Alhambra with a steamshovel, and we are proud of our yardage. We shall hardly relinquish the shovel, which after all has many good points, but we are in need of a gentler and more objective criteria for its successful use.

4

Asking How Much Is Enough
Alan Durning

Early in the age of affluence that followed World War II, an American retailing analyst named Victor Lebow proclaimed, "Our enormously productive economy . . . demands that we make consumption our way of life, that we convert the buying and use of goods into rituals, that we seek our spiritual satisfaction, our ego satisfaction, in consumption . . . We need things consumed, burned up, worn out, replaced, and discarded at an ever increasing rate." Americans have responded to Mr. Lebow's call, and much of the world has followed.[1]

Consumption has become a central pillar of life in industrial lands, and is even embedded in social values. Opinion surveys in the world's two largest economies—Japan and the United States—show consumerist definitions of success becoming ever more prevalent. In Taiwan, a billboard demands "Why Aren't You a Millionaire Yet?" The Japanese speak of the "new three sacred treasures": color television, air conditioning, and the automobile.[2]

The affluent life-style born in the United States is emulated by those who can afford it around the world. And many can: the average person today is four-and-a-half times richer than were his or her great-grandparents at the turn of the century. Needless to say, that new global

wealth is not evenly spread among the earth's people. One billion live in unprecedented luxury; 1 billion live in destitution. Even American children have more pocket money—$230 a year—than the half-billion poorest people alive.[3]

Overconsumption by the world's fortunate is an environmental problem unmatched in severity by anything but perhaps population growth. Their surging exploitation of resources threatens to exhaust or unalterably disfigure forests, soils, water, air, and climate. Ironically, high consumption may be a mixed blessing in human terms too. The time-honored values of integrity of character, good work, friendship, family, and community have often been sacrificed in the rush to riches. Thus, many in the industrial lands have a sense that their world of plenty is somehow hollow—that, hoodwinked by a consumerist culture, they have been fruitlessly attempting to satisfy what are essentially social, psychological, and spiritual needs with material things.[4]

Of course, the opposite of overconsumption—poverty—is no solution to either environmental or human problems. It is infinitely worse for people and bad for the natural world too. Dispossessed peasants slash and burn their way into the rain forests of Latin America, and hungry nomads turn their herds out onto fragile African rangeland, reducing it to desert. If environmental destruction results when people have either too little or too much, we are left to wonder how much is enough. What level of consumption can the earth support? When does having more cease to add appreciably to human satisfaction?

Answering these questions definitively is impossible, but for each of us in the world's consuming class, asking is essential nonetheless. Unless we see that more is not always better, our efforts to forestall ecological decline will be overwhelmed by our appetites.

THE CONSUMING SOCIETY

Skyrocketing consumption is the hallmark of our era. The headlong advance of technology, rising earnings, and consequently cheaper material goods have lifted overall consumption to levels never dreamed of a century ago. The trend is visible in statistics for almost any per capita indicator. Worldwide, since mid-century the intake of copper, energy, meat, steel, and wood has approximately doubled; car ownership and cement consumption have quadrupled; plastic use has quintupled; aluminum consumption has grown sevenfold; and air travel has multiplied 32 times.[5]

Moneyed regions account for the largest waves of consumption since 1950. In the United States, the world's premier consuming society, on average people today own twice as many cars, drive two-and-a-half times as far, use 21 times as much plastic, and travel 25 times as far by air as did their parents in 1950. Air conditioning spread from 15 percent of households in 1960 to 64 percent in 1987, and color televisions from 1 to 93 percent. Microwave ovens and video cassette recorders found their way into almost two thirds of American homes during the eighties alone. (See Figure 1.)[6]

That decade was a period of marked extravagance in the United States; not since the roaring twenties had conspicuous consumption been so lauded. Between 1978 and 1987, sales of Jaguar automobiles increased eightfold, and the average age of first-time fur coat buyers fell from 50 to 26. The select club of American millionaires more than doubled its membership from 600,000 to 1.5 million over the decade, while

FIGURE 1. ● U.S. Household Ownership of Appliances, 1960–88.

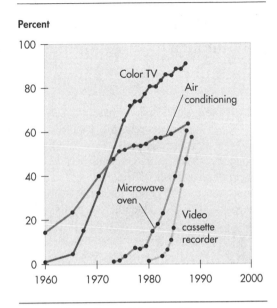

Sources: Census Bureau, U.S. Dept. of Energy

the number of American billionaires reached 58 by 1990.[7]

Japan and Western Europe have displayed parallel trends. Per person, the Japanese of today consume more than four times as much aluminum, almost five times as much energy, and 25 times as much steel as people in Japan did in 1950. They also own four times as many cars and eat nearly twice as much meat. In 1972, 1 million Japanese traveled abroad; in 1990, the number was expected to top 10 million. As in the United States, the eighties were a particularly consumerist decade in Japan, with sales of BMW automobiles rising tenfold over the decade. Ironically, in 1990 a *reja bumu* (leisure boom) combined with concern for nature to create two new status symbols: four-wheel drive Range Rovers from England and cabins made of imported American logs.[8]

Still, Japan has come to the high consumption ethos hesitantly. Many older Japanese still hold to their time-honored belief in frugality. Yorimoto Katsumi of Waseda University in Tokyo writes, "Members of the older generation . . . are careful to save every scrap of paper and bit of string for future use." A recent wave of stratospheric spending—cups of coffee that cost $350 and mink coats for dogs—has created a crisis of values in the society. Says one student, "Japanese people are materialistically well-off, but not inside. . . . We never have time to find ourselves, or what we should seek in life."[9]

Like the Japanese, West Europeans' consumption levels are only one notch below Americans'. Taken together, France, West Germany, and the United Kingdom almost doubled their per capita use of steel, more than doubled their intake of cement and aluminum, and tripled their paper consumption since mid-century. Just in the first half of the eighties, per capita consumption of frozen prepared meals—with their excessive packaging—rose more than 30 percent in every West European country except Finland; in Switzerland, the jump was 180 percent. As trade barriers come down in the move toward a single European market by 1992, prices will likely fall and product promotion grow more aggressive, boosting consumption higher.[10]

The collapse of socialist governments in Eastern Europe, meanwhile, unleashed a tidal wave of consumer demand that had gone unsatisfied in the region's ossified state-controlled economies. A young man in a Budapest bar captured his country's mood when he told a western reporter: "People in the West think that we in Hungary don't know how they live. Well, we do know how they live, and we want to live like that, too." Says German banker Ulrich Ramm, "The East Germans want cars, videos and Marlboros." Seventy percent of those living in the former East Germany hope to enter the world's automobile class soon; they bought 200,000 used western cars in the first half of 1990 alone.

Western carmakers' plans for Eastern Europe promise to give the region the largest number of new car factories in the world.[11]

The late eighties saw some poor societies begin the transition to consuming ways. In China, the sudden surge in spending on consumer durables shows up clearly in data from the State Statistical Bureau: between 1982 and 1987, color televisions spread from 1 percent to 35 percent of urban Chinese homes, the share with washing machines quadrupled from 16 to 67 percent, and refrigerators grew in prevalence from 1 percent to 20 percent of homes.[12]

Meanwhile, in India, the emergence of a middle class with perhaps 100 million members, along with liberalization of the consumer market and the introduction of buying on credit, has led to explosive growth in sales of everything from automobiles and motorbikes to televisions and frozen dinners. The *Wall Street Journal* gloats, "The traditional conservative Indian who believes in modesty and savings is gradually giving way to a new generation that thinks as freely as it spends."[13]

Few would begrudge anyone the simple advantages of cold food storage or mechanized clothes washing. The point, rather, is that even the non-western nations with the longest histories are increasingly emulating the high-consumption style of life. The lure of "modern" things is hard to resist: Coca-Cola soft drink is sold in more than 160 countries, and "Dallas," the television series that portrays the richest class of Americans, is avidly followed in many of the world's poorest nations.[14]

Long before all the world's people could achieve the American dream, however, the planet would be laid waste. The world's 1 billion meat eaters, car drivers, and throwaway consumers are responsible for the lion's share of the damage humans have caused to common global resources. For one thing, supporting the life-style of the affluent requires resources from far away. A Dutch person's consumption of food, wood, natural fibers, and other products of the soil involves exploitation of five times as much land outside the country as inside—much of it in the Third World. Industrial nations account for close to two thirds of global use of steel, more than two thirds of aluminum, copper, lead, nickel, tin, and zinc, and three fourths of energy.[15]

Those in the wealthiest fifth of humanity have built more than 99 percent of the world's nuclear warheads. Their appetite for wood is a driving force behind destruction of the tropical rain forests, and the resulting extinction of countless species.... Over the past century, their economies have pumped out two thirds of the greenhouse gases that threaten the earth's climate, and each year their energy use releases perhaps three fourths of the sulfur and nitrogen oxides that cause acid rain. Their industries generate most of the world's hazardous chemical wastes, and their air conditioners, aerosol sprays, and factories release almost 90 percent of the chlorofluorocarbons that destroy the earth's protective ozone layer. Clearly, even 1 billion profligate consumers is too much for the earth.[16]

Beyond the environmental costs of acquisitiveness, some perplexing findings of social scientists throw doubt on the wisdom of high consumption as a personal and national goal: rich societies have had little success in turning consumption into fulfillment. Regular surveys by the National Opinion Research Center of the University of Chicago reveal, for example, that no more Americans report they are "very happy" now than in 1957. The share has fluctuated around one third since then, despite a doubling of personal consumption expenditures per capita. Whatever Americans are buying, it does not seem to be enough.[17]

Likewise, a landmark study in 1974 revealed that Nigerians, Filipinos, Panamanians, Yugoslavians, Japanese, Israelis, and West Germans all ranked themselves near the middle of a happiness scale. Confounding any attempt to correlate affluence and happiness, poor Cubans and rich Americans were both found to be considerably happier than the norm, and citizens of India and the Dominican Republic, less so. As Oxford psychologist Michael Argyle writes, "there is very little difference in the levels of reported happiness found in rich and very poor countries."[18]

Measured in constant dollars, the world's people have consumed as many goods and services since 1950 as all previous generations put together.... Since 1940 Americans alone have used up as large a share of the earth's mineral resources as did everyone before them combined. If the effectiveness of that consumption in providing personal fulfillment is questionable, perhaps environmental concerns can help us redefine our goals.[19]

IN SEARCH OF SUFFICIENCY

In simplified terms, an economy's total burden on the ecological systems that undergird it is a function of three factors: the size of the population, average consumption, and the broad set of technologies—everything from mundane clotheslines to the most sophisticated satellite communications systems—the economy uses to provide goods and services.

Changing agricultural patterns, transportation systems, urban design, energy use, and the like could radically reduce the total environmental damage caused by the consuming societies, while allowing those at the bottom of the economic ladder to rise without producing such egregious effects. Japan, for example, uses a third as much energy as the Soviet Union to produce a dollar's worth of goods and services, and Norwegians use half as much paper and cardboard apiece as their neighbors in Sweden, though they are equals in literacy and richer in monetary terms.[20]

Eventually, though, technological change will need its complement in the reduction of material wants. José Goldemberg of the University of São Paulo and an international team of researchers conducted a careful study of the potential to cut fossil fuel consumption through greater efficiency and use of renewable energy. The entire world population, Goldemberg concludes, could live with the quality of energy services now enjoyed by West Europeans—things like modest but comfortable homes, refrigeration for food, and ready access to public transit, augmented by limited auto use.[21]

The study's implicit conclusion, however, is that the entire world decidedly could *not* live in the style of Americans, with their larger homes, more numerous electrical gadgets, and auto-centered transportation systems. Technological change and the political forces that must drive it hold extraordinary potential, but are ultimately limited by the compulsion to consume. If money saved through frugal use of materials and energy is simply spent buying private jets for weekend excursions to Antarctica, what hope is there for the biosphere? In the end, the ability of the earth to support billions of human beings depends on whether we continue to equate consumption with fulfillment.

Some guidance on what the earth can sustain emerges from an examination of current consumption patterns around the world. For three of the most ecologically important types of consumption—transportation, diet, and use of raw materials—the world's people are distributed unevenly over a vast range. Those at the bottom clearly fall below the "too little" line, while those at the top, in what could be called the cars-meat-and-disposables class, clearly consume too much.

About 1 billion people do most of their traveling, aside from the occasional donkey or bus ride, on foot, many of them never going more than 100 kilometers from their birthplaces. Unable to get to jobs easily, attend school, or bring their complaints before government offices, they are severely hindered by the lack of transportation options.[22]

The massive middle class of the world, numbering some 3 billion, travels by bus and bicycle. Kilometer for kilometer, bikes are cheaper than any other vehicles, costing less than $100 new in most of the Third World and requiring no fuel. The world's automobile class is relatively small: only 8 percent of humans, about 400 million people, own cars. Their vehicles are directly responsible for an estimated 13 percent of carbon dioxide emissions from fossil fuels worldwide, along with air pollution, acid rain, and a quarter-million traffic fatalities a year.[23]

Car owners bear indirect responsibility for the far-reaching impacts of their chosen vehicle. The automobile makes itself indispensable: cities sprawl, public transit atrophies, shopping centers multiply, workplaces scatter. . . . As suburbs spread, families start to need a car for each driver. One fifth of American households own three or more vehicles, more than half own at least two, and 65 percent of new American houses are built with two-car garages. Today, working Americans spend nine hours a week behind the wheel. To make these homes-away-from-home more comfortable, 90 percent of new cars have air-conditioning, doubling their contribution to climate change and adding emissions of ozone-depleting chlorofluorocarbons.[24]

Around the world, the great marketing achievement of the auto industry has been to turn its machines into cultural icons. As French philosopher Roland Barthes writes, "cars today are almost the exact equivalent of the great Gothic cathedrals . . . the supreme creation of an era, conceived with passion by unknown artists, and consumed in image if not in usage by a whole population which appropriates them as . . . purely magical object[s]."[25]

Some in the auto class are also members of a more select group: the global jet set. Although an estimated 1 billion people travel by air each year, the overwhelming majority of trips are taken by a small group. The 4 million Americans who account for 41 percent of domestic trips, for example, cover five times as many kilometers a year as average Americans. Furthermore, because each kilometer traveled by air uses more energy than one traveled by car, jet-setters consume six-and-a-half times as much energy for transportation as other car-class members.[26]

The global food consumption ladder has three rungs. At the bottom, the world's 630 million poorest people are unable to provide themselves with a healthy diet according to the latest World Bank estimates. On the next rung, the 3.4 billion grain eaters of the world's middle class get enough calories and plenty of plant-based protein, giving them the healthiest basic diet of the world's people. They typically receive less than 20 percent of their calories from fat, a level low enough to protect them from the consequences of excessive dietary fat.[27]

The top of the ladder is populated by the meat eaters, those who obtain close to 40 percent of their calories from fat. These 1.25 billion people eat three times as much fat per person as the remaining 4 billion, mostly because they eat so much red meat. (See Table 1.) The meat class pays the price of its diet in high death rates from the so-called diseases of affluence—heart disease, stroke, and certain types of cancer.[28]

In 1990, the U.S. government officially endorsed recommendations that have long come from the medical profession, urging Americans to limit their fat intake to no more than 30 percent of their calories. Meanwhile, early results of the largest-ever study of diet and health, which has been monitoring thousands of Chinese villagers, provides compelling evidence that the healthiest diet for humans is nearly vegetarian, containing 10–15 percent of calories from fat.[29]

TABLE 1. ● Consumption of Red Meat Per Capita, Selected Countries, 1989

Country	*Red Meat[1]* *(kilograms)*
East Germany	96
United States	76
Argentina	73
France	66
Soviet Union	57
Japan	27
Brazil	22
China	21
Egypt	12
India	1

[1]Beef, veal, pork, lamb, mutton, and goat, in carcass weight equivalents.
Source: Foreign Agricultural Service, U.S. Department of Agriculture, "World Livestock Situation," Washington, D.C., March 1990.

The earth also pays for the high-fat diet. Indirectly, the meat-eating quarter of humanity consumes nearly 40 percent of the world's grain—grain that fattens the livestock they eat. Meat production is behind a substantial share of the environmental strains induced by the present global agricultural system, from soil erosion to overpumping of underground water. In the extreme case of American beef, producing 1 kilogram of steak requires 5 kilograms of grain and the energy equivalent of 2 liters of gasoline, not to mention the associated soil erosion, water consumption, pesticide and fertilizer runoff, groundwater depletion, and emissions of the greenhouse gas methane.[30]

Beyond the effects of livestock production, the affluent diet rings up an ecological bill through its heavy dependence on long-distance transport. North Europeans eat lettuce trucked from Greece and decorate their tables with flowers flown in from Kenya. Japanese eat turkey from the United States and ostrich from Australia. One fourth of the grapes eaten in the United States are grown 11,000 kilometers away, in Chile, and the typical mouthful of American food travels 2,000 kilometers from farm field to dinner plate. This far-flung agribusiness food system is only partly a product of agronomic forces. It is also a result of farm policies and health standards that favor large producers, massive government subsidies for western irrigation water, and a national highway system that makes trucking economical by transferring the tax burden from truckers to other highway users.[31]

Processing and packaging add further resource costs to the way the affluent eat. Extensively packaged foods are energy gluttons, but even seemingly simple foods need a surprising amount of energy to prepare: gram for gram, getting canned corn to the consumer takes 10 times the energy of providing fresh corn in season. Frozen corn, if left in the freezer for much time, takes even more energy. To be sure, canned and frozen vegetables make a healthy diet easy even in the dead of winter; more of a concern are the new generation of microwave-ready instant meals. Loaded with disposable pans and multi-layer packaging, their resource inputs are orders of magnitude larger than preparing the same dishes at home from scratch.[32]

Global beverage consumption reveals a similar pattern. The 1.75 billion people at the bottom are clearly deprived: they have no option but to drink water that is often contaminated with human, animal, and chemical wastes. Those in the next group up, in this case nearly 2 billion people, take more than 80 percent of their liquid refreshment in the form of clean drinking water, with the remainder coming from commercial beverages such as tea, coffee, and, for children, milk. At the quantities consumed, these beverages pose few environmental problems; they are packaged minimally, and transport energy needs

are low because they are moved only short distances or in a dry form.[33]

In the top class once again are the billion people in industrial countries. At a growing rate, they imbibe soft drinks, bottled water, and other prepared commercial beverages packaged in single-use containers and transported over great distances—sometimes even across oceans. Ironically, where tap water is purest and most accessible, its use as a beverage is declining. It now typically accounts for only a quarter of drinks in industrial countries. In the extreme case of the United States, per capita consumption of soft drinks rose to 176 liters in 1989 (nearly seven times the global mean), compared with water intake of 141 liters. Americans now drink more soda pop than water from the kitchen sink.[34]

In raw material consumption, the same pattern emerges. About 1 billion rural people subsist on local biomass collected from the immediate environment. Most of what they use each day—about a half-kilogram of grain, 1 kilogram of fuelwood, and fodder for their animals—could be self-replenishing renewable resources. Unfortunately, because these people are often pushed by landlessness and population growth into fragile, unproductive ecosystems, their minimal needs are not always met.[35]

These materially destitute billion are part of a larger group that lacks many of the benefits provided by modest use of nonrenewable resources—particularly durable things like radios, refrigerators, water pipes, high-quality tools, and carts with lightweight wheels and ball bearings. More than 2 billion people live in countries where per capita consumption of steel, the most basic modern material, falls below 50 kilograms a year. In those same countries, per capita energy use—a fairly good indirect indicator of overall use of materials—is lower than 20 gigajoules per year. (See Table 2.)[36]

Roughly 1.5 billion live in the middle class of materials use. Providing each of them with durable goods every year uses between 50 and

TABLE 2. ● Steel and Energy Consumption Per Capita, Selected Countries, 1987

Country	Steel (kilograms)	Energy (gigajoules)
United States	417	280
Soviet Union	582	194
West Germany	457	165
Japan	582	110
Mexico	93	50
Turkey	149	29
Brazil	99	22
China	64	22
Indonesia	21	8
India	20	8
Nigeria	8	5
Bangladesh	5	2

Sources: U.S. Bureau of the Census, *Statistical Abstract of the United States: 1990* (Washington, D.C.: U.S. Government Printing Office, 1990); World Resources Institute, *World Resources 1990–91* (New York: Oxford University Press, 1990).

150 kilograms of steel and 20–50 gigajoules of energy. At the top of the heap is the throwaway class, which uses raw materials extravagantly. A typical resident of the industrialized fourth of the world uses 15 times as much paper, 10 times as much steel, and 12 times as much fuel as a Third World resident. The extreme case is again the United States, where the average person consumes most of his or her own weight in basic materials each day—18 kilograms of petroleum and coal, 13 kilograms of other minerals, 12 kilograms of agricultural products, and 9 kilograms of forest products.[37]

In the throwaway economy, packaging becomes an end in itself, disposables proliferate, and durability suffers. . . . Four percent of consumer expenditures on goods in the United States goes for packaging—$225 per person a year. Likewise, the Japanese use 30 million "disposable" single-roll cameras each year, and the British dump 2.5 billion diapers. Americans toss away 180 million razors annually, enough paper and plastic plates and cups to feed the world a picnic six times a year, and enough aluminum cans to make 6,000 DC-10 airplanes.[38]

Where disposability and planned obsolescence fail to accelerate the trip from cash register to junk heap, fashion sometimes succeeds. Most clothing goes out of style long before it is worn out; lately, the realm of fashion has even colonized sports footwear. Kevin Ventrudo, chief financial officer of California-based L.A. Gear, which saw sales multiply 50 times over in four years, told the *Washington Post,* "If you talk about shoe performance, you only need one or two pairs. If you're talking fashion, you're talking endless pairs of shoes."[39]

In transportation, diet, and use of raw materials, as consumption rises on the economic scale so does waste—both of resources and of health. Bicycles and public transit are cheaper, more efficient, and healthier transport options than cars. A diet founded on the basics of grains and water is gentle to the earth and the body. And a lifestyle that makes full use of raw materials for durable goods without succumbing to the throwaway mentality is ecologically sound while still affording many of the comforts of modernity. Yet despite these arguments in favor of modest consumption, few people who can afford high consumption levels opt to live simply. What prompts us, then, to consume so much?

THE CULTIVATION OF NEEDS

"The avarice of mankind is insatiable," wrote Aristotle 23 centuries ago, describing the way that as each of our desires is satisfied a new one seems to appear in its place. That observation, on which all of economic theory is based, provides the most obvious answer to the question of why people never seem satisfied with what they have. If our wants are insatiable, there is simply no such thing as enough.[40]

Much confirms this view of human nature. The Roman philosopher Lucretius wrote a century before Christ: "We have lost our taste for acorns. So [too] we have abandoned those couches littered with herbage and heaped with leaves. So the wearing of wild beasts' skins has gone out of fashion. . . . skins yesterday, purple and gold today—such are the baubles that embitter human life with resentment." Nearly 2,000 years later, Russian novelist Leo Tolstoy echoed Lucretius: "Seek among men, from beggar to millionaire, one who is contented with his lot, and you will not find one such in a thousand. . . . Today we must buy an overcoat and galoshes, tomorrow, a watch and a chain; the next day we must install ourselves in an apartment with a sofa and a bronze lamp; then we must have carpets and velvet gowns; then a house, horses and carriages, paintings and decorations."[41]

What distinguishes modern consuming habits from those of interest to Lucretius and Tolstoy, some would say, is simply that we are much richer than our ancestors, and consequently have more ruinous effects on nature. There is no doubt a great deal of truth in that view, but there is also reason to believe that certain forces in the modern world encourage people to act on their consumptive desires as rarely before. Five distinctly modern factors seem to play a role in cultivating particularly voracious appetites: the influence of social pressures in mass societies, advertising, the shopping culture, various government policies, and the expansion of the mass market into the traditional realm of household and local self-reliance.

In the anonymous mass societies of advanced industrial nations, daily interactions with the economy lack the face-to-face character that prevails in surviving local communities. Traditional virtues such as integrity, honesty, and skill are too hard to measure to serve as yardsticks of

social worth. By default, they are gradually supplanted by a simple, single indicator—money. As one Wall Street Banker put it bluntly to the *New York Times,* "Net worth equals self-worth." Under this definition, consumption becomes a treadmill, with everyone judging their status by who is ahead and who is behind.[42]

Psychological data from several nations confirm that the satisfaction derived from money does not come from simply having it. It comes from having more of it than others do, and from having more this year than last. Thus, the bulk of survey data reveals that the upper classes in any society are more satisfied with their lives than the lower classes are, but they are no more satisfied than the upper classes of much poorer countries—nor than the upper classes were in the less-affluent past.[43]

More striking, perhaps, most psychological data show that the main determinants of happiness in life are not related to consumption at all: prominent among them are satisfaction with family life, especially marriage, followed by satisfaction with work, leisure, and friendships. Indeed, in a comprehensive inquiry into the relationship between affluence and satisfaction, social commentator Jonathan Freedman notes, "Above the poverty level, the relationship between income and happiness is remarkably small."[44]

Yet when alternative measures of success are not available, the deep human need to be valued and respected by others is acted out through consumption. Buying things becomes both a proof of self-esteem ("I'm worth it," chants one advertising slogan) and a means to social acceptance—as token of what turn-of-the-century economist Thorstein Veblen termed "pecuniary decency."[45]

Beyond social pressures, the affluent live completely enveloped in proconsumption advertising messages. The sales pitch is everywhere. One analyst estimates that the typical American is exposed to 50–100 advertisements each morning before nine o'clock. Along with their weekly

22-hour diet of television, American teenagers are typically exposed to 3–4 hours of TV advertisements a week, adding up to at least 100,000 ads between birth and high school graduation.[46]

Marketers have found ever more ways to push their products. Advertisements are broadcast by over 10,000 television and radio stations in the United States, towed behind airplanes, plastered on billboards and in sports stadiums, bounced around the planet from satellites. They are posted on chair-lift poles on ski slopes, and played through closed circuit televisions at bus stops, in subway stations, and on wall-sized video screens at shopping malls.[47]

Ads are piped into classrooms and doctors' offices, woven into the plots of feature films, placed on board games, mounted in bathroom stalls, and played back between rings on public phones in the Kansas City airport. Even the food supply may soon go mass media: the Viskase company of Chicago now offers to print edible ad slogans on hot dogs, and Eggverts International is using a similar technique to advertise on thousands of eggs in Israel.[48]

Advertising has been one of the fastest growing industries during the past half-century. In the United States, ad expenditures rose from $198 per capita in 1950 to $498 in 1989. Total global advertising expenditures, meanwhile, rose from an estimated $39 billion in 1950 to $237 billion in 1988, growing far faster than economic output. Over the same period, per person advertising expenditures grew from $15 to $46. (See Figure 2.) In developing countries, the increases have been astonishing. Advertising billings in India jumped fivefold in the eighties, and South Korea's advertising industry has recently grown 35–40 percent annually.[49]

The proliferation of shopping centers has, in a roundabout way, also promoted the compulsion to consume. Mall design itself encourages acquisitive impulses, many critics believe. But perhaps more important, suburban malls and commercial strips suck commerce away from

FIGURE 2. ● World Advertising Expenditures Per Capita, 1970–88

1989 dollars

Sources: Internat. Advertising Assoc., Census Bureau, Pop. Reference Bureau

downtown and neighborhood merchants. Shopping by public transit or on foot becomes difficult, auto traffic increases, and sprawl accelerates. In the end, public places such as town squares and city streets are robbed of their vitality, leaving people fewer attractive places to go besides the malls that set the whole shopping process in motion. Perhaps by default, malls have even become popular spots to exercise. Avia, a leading sports footwear manufacturer, introduced a shoe designed for the rigors of mall walking.[50]

Particularly in the United States, shopping seems to have become a primary cultural activity. Americans spend 6 hours a week doing various types of shopping, and they go to shopping centers on an average once a week—more often than they go to church or synagogue. Some 93 percent of American teenage girls surveyed in 1987 deemed shopping their favorite pastime.

The 32,563 shopping centers in the country surpassed high schools in number in 1987. Just from 1986 to 1989, total retail space in these centers grew by 65 million square meters, or 20 percent. Shopping centers now garner 55 percent of retail sales in the United States, compared with 16 percent in France and 4 percent in Spain.[51]

Shopping centers are sprouting across the landscape in many industrial lands. Spain's 90-odd centers are expected to triple in number by 1992. Britain's bevy of one-stop superstores doubled to about 500 during the eighties. Italy, despite a strong tradition of community merchants, has recently relaxed controls on mall development, leading to predictions that its shopping centers will multiply from 35 to 100 in five years.[52]

Countless government policies also play a role both in promoting high consumption and in worsening its ecological impact. Urban and transport planning favor private vehicles—and motorized ones—to the exclusion of cleaner modes. The British tax code encourages businesses to buy thousands of large company cars for employee use. . . . Most governments in both North and South America subsidize beef production on a massive scale. Tax law in the United States allows virtually unlimited deductions for purchases of houses: the more homes a family buys, the more taxes they save. Partly as a consequence, 10 million Americans now have two or more homes, while at bare minimum 300,000 are homeless.[53]

Land use and materials policies in most of the world undervalue renewable resources, ignore natural services provided by ecosystems, and underprice raw materials extracted from the public domain. . . . More fundamentally, national economic goals are built squarely on the assumption that more is better. National statistics, for example, refer to people more frequently as consumers than as citizens. Economic policy, because it is based on modern economics' system of partial accounting, views as healthy growth what is often feverish and debilitating overconsumption. . . .

Finally, the sweeping advance of the commercial mass market into realms once dominated by family members and local enterprise has made consumption far more wasteful than in the past, as American history illustrates. The modern consumer economy was born in the United States in the twenties, when brand names became household words, packaged foods made their large-scale debut, and the automobile assumed its place at the center of American culture.

After World War II, the consuming society came of age. In 1946, *Fortune* magazine heralded the arrival of a "dream era . . . The Great American Boom is on." Government subsidies for housing loans and highway construction helped unleash the suburbanization of the country: the urban-to-suburban migration of the fifties involved five times as many people as the unprecedented influx of European immigrants in the century's first decade. Human settlements spread across the countryside, locking people into wasteful ways of using energy and materials. In turn, status competition got a boost from the atomization of cities into unattached suburban bungalows, each housing a single family.[54]

Over the past century, the mass market has taken over an increasing number of the productive tasks once provided within the household. More and more, flush with cash but pressed for time, households opt for the questionable "conveniences" of prepared, packaged foods, miracle cleaning products, and disposable everythings—from napkins to shower curtains. All these things, while saving the householders time, cost the earth dearly, and change households from the primary unit of the economy to passive, consuming entities. Shifting one economic activity after another out of the home does boost the gross national product (GNP)—but that is largely a fiction of bookkeeping, an economic sleight of hand.[55]

Like the household, the community economy has atrophied—or been dismembered—under the blind force of the money economy. Shopping malls, superhighways, and "strips" have replaced corner stores, local restaurants, and neighborhood theaters—the very things that help to create a sense of common identity and community in an area. Traditional vegetable stands and fish shops in Japan are giving way to supermarkets and convenience stores; along the way styrofoam and plastic film have replaced yesterday's newspaper as fish wrap. Even in France, where the passion for fresh foods is legend, the microwave and the *grande surface* (shopping mall) are edging out bakeries, dairies, and farmers' markets.[56]

The recycling ethos of the past was built upon a materials economy that valued things, and it embodied that value in institutions. Not long ago in western lands—and to this day in nonindustrial regions—rag pickers, junkyard dealers, scrap collectors, and dairy deliverers kept used materials and containers flowing back into the economy. In the United States, where the demise of local economies is furthest advanced, many neighborhoods are little more than a place to sleep. Americans move, on average, every five years, and develop little attachment to those who live near them.[57]

The search for social status in massive and anonymous societies, omnipresent advertising messages, a shopping culture that edges out nonconsuming alternatives, government biases favoring consumption, and the spread of the commercial market into most aspects of private life—all these things nurture the acquisitive desires that everyone has. Can we, as individuals and as citizens, act to confront these forces?

A CULTURE OF PERMANENCE

When Moses came down from Mount Sinai he could count the rules of ethical behavior on the fingers of his two hands. In the complex global economy of the late twentieth century, in which the simple act of turning on an air conditioner sends greenhouse gases up into the atmosphere, the rules for ecologically sustainable living run into the hundreds. The basic value of a sustainable society, though, the ecological equivalent of the Golden Rule, is simple: each generation should meet its needs without jeopardizing the prospects of future generations to meet their own needs. What is lacking is the thorough practical knowledge—at each level of society—of what living by that principle means.[58]

Ethics, after all, exist only in practice, in the fine grain of everyday decisions. As Aristotle argued, "In ethics, the decision lies with perception." When most people see a large automobile and think first of the air pollution it causes, rather than the social status it conveys, environmental ethics will have arrived. In a fragile biosphere, the ultimate fate of humanity may depend on whether we can cultivate deeper sources of fulfillment, founded on a widespread ethic of limiting consumption and finding nonmaterial enrichment. An ethic becomes widespread enough to restrain antisocial behavior effectively, moreover, only when it is encoded in culture, in society's collective memory, experience, and wisdom.[59]

For individuals, the decision to live a life of sufficiency—to find their own answer to the question "How much is enough?"—is to begin a highly personal process. The goal is to put consumption in its proper place among the many sources of personal fulfillment, and to find ways of living within the means of the earth. One great inspiration in this quest is the body of human wisdom passed down over the ages.

Materialism was denounced by all the sages, from Buddha to Muhammed. (See Table 3.) "These religious founders," observed historian Arnold Toynbee, "disagreed with each other in the pictures of what is the nature of the universe, the nature of the spiritual life, the nature of ultimate reality. But they all agreed in their

TABLE 3. ● Teachings of World Religions and Major Cultures on Consumption

Religion or Culture	Teaching and Source
American Indian	"Miserable as we seem in thy eyes, we consider ourselves . . . much happier than thou, in this that we are very content with the little that we have." (Micmac chief)
Buddhist	"Whoever in this world overcomes his selfish cravings, his sorrows fall away from him, like drops of water from a lotus flower." (*Dhammapada,* 336)
Christian	It is "easier for a camel to go through the eye of a needle than for a rich man to enter into the kingdom of God." (*Matt.* 19:23–24)
Confucian	"Excess and deficiency are equally at fault." (Confucius, XI.15)
Ancient Greek	"Nothing in Excess." (Inscribed at Oracle of Delphi)
Hindu	"That person who lives completely free from desires, without longing . . . attains peace." (*Bhagavad-Gita,* 11.71)
Islamic	"Poverty is my pride." (Muhammad)
Jewish	"Give me neither poverty nor riches." (*Proverbs* 30:8)
Taoist	"He who knows he has enough is rich." (*Tao Te Ching*)

Sources: Compiled by Worldwatch Institute.

ethical precepts. . . . They all said with one voice that if we made material wealth our paramount aim, this would lead to disaster." The Christian Bible echoes most of human wisdom when it asks "What shall it profit a man if he shall gain the whole world and lose his own soul?"[60]

The attempt to live by nonmaterialistic definitions of success is not new. Social researcher Duane Elgin estimated in 1981—perhaps optimistically—that 10 million adult Americans were experimenting "wholeheartedly" with voluntary simplicity. India, the Netherlands, Norway, the former West Germany, and the United Kingdom all have small segments of their populations who try to adhere to a nonconsuming philosophy. For these practitioners, motivated by the desire to live justly in an unjust world, to walk gently on the earth, and to avoid distraction, clutter, and pretense, the goal is not ascetic self-denial. What they are after is personal ful-

fillment; they just do not think consuming more is likely to provide it.[61]

Still, shifting emphasis from material to nonmaterial satisfaction is no mean feat: it means trying both to curb personal appetites and to resist the tide of external forces encouraging consumption. Mahatma Gandhi testified to the difficulty of living frugally: "I must confess to you that progress at first was slow. And now, as I recall those days of struggle, I remember that it was also painful in the beginning. . . . But as days went by, I saw that I had to throw overboard many other things which I used to consider as mine, and a time came when it became a matter of positive joy to give up those things."[62]

Many people find simpler living offers rewards all its own. They say life can become more deliberate as well as spontaneous, and even gain a sort of unadorned elegance. Vicki Robin, president of the Seattle-based New Road Map Foundation, which offers courses on getting off the more-is-better treadmill, notices that those who succeed in her program always have "a sense of purpose larger than their own needs, wants, and desires." Many find that sense of purpose in working to foster a more just, sustainable world. As French novelist Albert Camus wrote, "Without work, all life goes rotten, but when work is soulless, life stifles and dies."[63]

Others describe the way simpler technologies add unexpected qualities to life. Some come to feel, for example, that clotheslines, window shades, and bicycles have a utilitarian elegance that clothes dryers, air conditioners, and automobiles lack. These modest devices are silent, manually operated, fire-proof, ozone- and climate-friendly, easily repaired, and inexpensive. While certainly less "convenient," they require a degree of forethought and attention to the weather that grounds life in place and time.[64]

Realistically, voluntary simplicity is unlikely to gain ground rapidly against the onslaught of consumerist values. As historian David Shi of North Carolina's Davidson College chronicles, the call for a simpler life has been perennial through the history of North America, from the Puritans of Massachusetts Bay to the back-to-the-landers of the seventies. None of these movements ever gained more than a slim minority of adherents. Elsewhere, entire nations such as China and Vietnam have dedicated themselves to rebuilding human character— sometimes through brutal techniques—in a less self-centered mold, but nowhere have they succeeded with more than a token few of their citizens.[65]

It would be naive to believe that entire populations will suddenly experience a moral awakening, renouncing greed, envy, and avarice. What can be hoped for is a gradual weakening of the consumerist ethos of affluent societies. The challenge before humanity is to bring environmental matters under cultural controls, and the goal of creating a sustainable culture—a culture of permanence—is a task that will occupy several gen-

erations. Just as smoking has lost its social cachet in the United States in the space of a decade, conspicuous consumption of all types may be susceptible to social pressure over a longer period.

Ultimately, personal restraint will do little, though, if not wedded to bold political steps against the forces promoting consumption. In addition to the oft-repeated agenda of environmental and social reforms necessary to achieve sustainability, such as overhauling energy systems, stabilizing population, and ending poverty, action is needed to restrain the excesses of advertising, to curb the shopping culture, to abolish policies that push consumption, and to revitalize household and community economies as human-scale alternatives to the high-consumption life-style. Such changes promise to help both the environment, by reducing the burden of overconsumption, and our peace of mind, by taming the forces that keep us dissatisfied with our lot.

The advertising industry is a formidable foe and on the march around the world. But it is already vulnerable where it pushes products demonstrably dangerous to human health. Tobacco ads are or soon will be banished from television throughout the West, and alcohol advertising is under attack as never before. By limiting advertisers' access to the most vulnerable consumers, their influence can be further dulled. In late 1990, the U.S. Congress, for example, wisely hemmed in television commercials aimed at children, and the European Communities' standards on television for Europe after 1992 will put strict limits on some types of ads.[66]

At the grassroots level, the Vancouver-based Media Foundation has set out to build a movement boldly aimed at turning television to anti-consuming ends. The premiere spot in their High on the Hog campaign shows a gigantic animated pig frolicking on a map of North America while a narrator intones: "Five percent of the people in the world consume *one-third* of the planet's resources . . . those people are us." The pig belches.[67]

Irreverence aside, the Media Foundation is on target: commercial television will need fundamental reorientation in a culture of permanence. As religious historian Robert Bellah put it, "That happiness is to be attained through limitless material acquisition is denied by every religion and philosophy known to humankind, but is preached incessantly by every American television set."[68]

Some countries have resisted the advancing shopping culture, though only rarely is the motivation opposition to consumerism itself. England and Wales have restricted trading on Sundays for 400 years, and labor groups beat back the most recent proposal to lift those limits. Similarly, the protected green belts around British cities have slowed the pace of development of suburban malls there. As in much of Europe, German stores must close most evenings at 6:00 p.m. and have limited weekend hours as well. In Japan, most shopping continues to take place in neighborhood shopping lanes, which are closed to traffic during certain hours to become *hokoosha tengoku,* literally "pedestrian heavens."[69]

All these things help control the consumerist influence of marketing on the shape and spirit of public space. Shopping is less likely to become an end in itself if it takes place in stores thoroughly knit into the fabric of the community rather than in massive, insular agglomerations of retail outlets each planned in minute detail to stimulate spendthrift ways. The design of communities shapes human culture.

Direct incentives for overconsumption are also essential targets for reform. If goods' prices reflected something closer to the environmental cost of their production, through revised subsidies and tax systems, the market itself would guide consumers toward less damaging forms of consumption. Disposables and packaging would rise in price relative to durable, less-packaged goods; local unprocessed food would fall in price relative to prepared products trucked from far away.

The net effect might also be lower overall consumption as people's effective purchasing power declined. As currently constituted, unfortunately, economies penalize the poor when aggregate consumption contracts—unemployment skyrockets and inequalities grow. Thus arises one of the greatest challenges for sustainable economics in rich societies: finding ways to ensure basic employment opportunities for all without constantly having to stoke the fires of GNP growth.

Ultimately, efforts to revitalize household and community economies may prove the decisive element in the attempt to create a culture less prone to consumption. At a personal level, commitment to nonmaterial fulfillment is hard to sustain without reinforcement from family, friends, and neighbors. At a political level, vastly strengthened local institutions may be the only counterweight to the colossus of vested interests—ranging from gas stations to multinational marketing conglomerates—that currently benefit from profligate consumption.

Despite the ominous scale of the challenge, there could be many more people ready to begin saying "enough" than prevailing opinion suggests. After all, much of what we consume is wasted or unwanted in the first place. How much of the packaging that we put out with the household trash each year—78 kilograms apiece in the Netherlands—would we rather never see? How much of the rural land built up into housing developments, "industrial parks," and commercial strips—23 square kilometers a day in the United States—could be left alone if we insisted on well-planned land use inside city limits?[70]

How many of the unsolicited sales pitches each of us receives daily in the post—37 percent of all mail in the United States—are nothing but bothersome junk? How many of the 18 kilograms of nonrefillable beverage bottles each Japanese throws out each year could not just as easily be reused if the facilities existed? How much of the advertising in our morning newspapers—covering 65 percent of the newsprint in U.S. papers—would we not gladly see left out? How many of the kilometers we drive—6,160 a year apiece in the former West Germany— would we not gladly give up if livable neighborhoods were closer to work, a variety of local merchants closer to home, streets safe to walk and bike, and public transit easier and faster?[71]

In many ways, we might be happier with less. In the final analysis, accepting and living by sufficiency rather than excess offers a return to what is, culturally speaking, the human home: to the ancient order of family, community, good work, and good life; to a reverence for excellence of skilled handiwork; to a true materialism that does not just care *about* things but cares *for* them; to communities worth spending a lifetime in. Maybe Henry David Thoreau had it right when he scribbled in his notebook beside Walden Pond, "A man is rich in proportion to the things he can afford to let alone."[72]

For the luckiest among us, a human lifetime on earth encompasses perhaps a hundred trips around the sun. The sense of fulfillment received on that journey—regardless of a person's religious faith—has to do with the timeless virtues of discipline, hope, allegiance to principle, and character. Consumption itself has little part in the playful camaraderie that inspires the young, the bonds of love and friendship that nourish adults, the golden memories that sustain the elderly. The very things that make life worth living, that give depth and bounty to human existence, are infinitely sustainable.

Notes

1. Victor Lebow in *Journal of Retailing,* quoted in Vance Packard, *The Waste Makers* (New York: David McKay, 1960).

2. Sepp Linhart, "From Industrial to Postindustrial Society: Changes in Japanese Leisure-Related Values and Behavior," *Journal of Japanese Studies,* Summer 1988; Richard A. Easterlin and Eileen M. Crimmins, "Recent Social Trends: Changes in Personal Aspirations of American Youth," *Sociology and Social Research,* July 1988; Taiwan from "Asian Century," *Newsweek,* February 22, 1988.

3. Per capita income from Angus Maddison, *The World Economy in the 20th Century* (Paris: Organisation for Economic Co-operation and Development, 1989); income of American children, defined as 4- to 12-year-olds, from James McNeal, "Children as Customers," *American Demographics,* September 1990; poorest 500 million people based on Alan B. Durning, *Poverty and the Environment: Reversing the Downward Spiral,* Worldwatch Paper 92 (Washington, D.C.: Worldwatch Institute, November 1989), and on World Bank, *World Development Report 1990* (New York: Oxford University Press, 1990).

4. Paul Wachtel, *The Poverty of Affluence* (Philadelphia: New Society Publishers, 1989); Amy Saltzman, "The New Meaning of Success," *U.S. News & World Report,* September 17, 1990; Joseph T. Plummer, "Changing Values," *The Futurist,* January/February 1989; Ronald Henkoff, "Is Greed Dead?" *Fortune,* August 14, 1989.

5. Worldwatch Institute estimates, based on the following: copper and aluminum from United Nations (UN), *Statistical Yearbook, 1953* (New York: 1954), and from UN, *Statistical Yearbook, 1985/86* (New York: 1988); energy from UN, *World Energy Supplies 1950–1974* (New York: 1976), and from UN, *1987 Energy Statistics Yearbook* (New York: 1989); meat from UN, *Statistical Yearbook, 1953,* and from Linda M. Bailey, agricultural economist, U.S. Department of Agriculture (USDA), Washington, D.C., private communication, September 11, 1990; steel, wood, cement, and air travel from UN, *Statistical Yearbook, 1953,* and from U.S. Bureau of the Census, *Statistical Abstract of the United States: 1990* (Washington, D.C.: U.S. Government Printing Office, 1990); car ownership from UN, *Statistical Yearbook, 1953,* and from Motor Vehicle Manufacturers Association (MVMA), *Facts and Figures '90* (Detroit, Mich.: 1990); plastic from UN, *Statistical Yearbook, 1970* (New York: 1971), and from UN, *Statistical Yearbook, 1983/84* (New York: 1985). Throughout this chapter, population data used to calculate per capita consumption are from UN, *Statistical Yearbook, 1975* (New York: 1975), from UN, *Statistical Yearbook, 1983/84* (New York: 1985), and from UN, *Statistical Yearbook, 1985/86,* with two exceptions: most recent years from Population Reference Bureau, *1988 Population Data Sheet* and *1990 Population Data Sheet* (Washington, D.C.: 1988 and 1990), and data for United States from U.S. Bureau of the Census, *Statistical Abstract of the United States: 1979* (Washington, D.C.: U.S. Government Printing Office, 1979), and from Bureau of the Census, *Statistical Abstract of the United States: 1990.*

6. Cars from MVMA, *Facts and Figures '90,* and from MVMA, Detroit, Mich., private communication, July 10,

1990; car-miles from U.S. Department of Energy (DOE), Energy Information Administration (EIA), *Annual Energy Review 1988* (Washington, D.C.: 1989), and from Paul Svercl, Federal Highway Administration, Washington, D.C., private communication, August 21, 1990; plastics from Sara Spivey, Society for the Plastics Industry, Washington D.C., private communication, August 23, 1990; air travel from Mary C. Holcomb et al., *Transportation Energy Data Book: Edition 9* (Oak Ridge, Tenn.: Oak Ridge National Laboratory, 1987), and from Federal Aviation Administration, Washington, D.C., private communication, August 17, 1990; air conditioning, color TVs, and microwaves form Bureau of the Census, *Statistical Abstract of the United States: 1979,* and from DOE, EIA, *Annual Energy Review 1988;* VCRs from Bureau of the Census, *Statistical Abstract of the United States: 1990.*

7. Jaguars and fur coats from Myron Magnet, "The Money Society," *Fortune,* July 6, 1987; millionaires in 1980 and 1990 from Kevin P. Phillips, "Reagan's America: A Capital Offense," *New York Times Magazine,* June 18, 1990; billionaires from Andrew Erdman, "The Billionaires," *Fortune,* September 10, 1990.

8. Japanese travel in 1972 from Linhart, "From Industrial to Postindustrial Society"; 1990 travel from "Rich Girls with Wanderlust," *Japan Economic Journal,* March 3, 1990; consumer spending surge from "Japan's Baby Boomers Spending Lavishly in Singleminded Pursuit of the Good Life," *Japan Economic Journal,* April 11, 1990; "Retail Sales Up 7 Percent; Capital Outlays Raised," *Japan Economic Journal,* July 14, 1990; BMW sales from *Japan Economic Journal,* September 8, 1990; Range Rovers from T. R. Reid, "U.S. Automakers Grind Gears in Japan," *Washington Post,* September 23, 1990; "With Permit Rules Relaxed, Log Cabin Sales Are Soaring," *Japan Economic Journal,* August 4, 1990.

9. Yorimoto Katsumi, "Tokyo's Serious Waste Problem," *Japan Quarterly,* July/September 1990; spending and student quote from Fred Hiatt and Margaret Shapiro, "Sudden Riches Creating Conflict and Self-Doubt," *Washington Post,* February 11, 1990.

10. Steel, cement, aluminum, and paper from Eric Larsen, Center for Energy and Environmental Studies, Princeton University, Princeton, N.J., unpublished data, 1990; frozen meals from Euromonitor Publications Ltd., *Consumer Europe 1985* (London: 1985).

11. Budapest from Timothy Harper, "In Budapest, the Lines are at McDonald's," *Shopping Centers Today,* May 1989; Ramm quote, auto demand, and used car sales from Marc Fisher, "East Germany and the Wheels of Fortune," *Washington Post,* June 3, 1990; auto plant projection from "Motor Industry Banks on Eastern Promise," *Business Europe* (London), May 18, 1990.

12. State Statistical Bureau, cited in "TV Now in 50% of Homes," *China Daily,* February 15, 1988.

13. Prakash Chandra, "India: Middle-Class Spending," *Third World Week* (Institute for Current World Affairs, Hanover, N.H.), March 2, 1990; Anthony Spaeth, "A Thriving Middle Class Is Changing the Face of India," *Wall Street Journal,* May 19, 1988.

14. Coca-Cola from Matthew Cooper et al., "Global Goliath: Coke Conquers the World," *U.S. News and World Report,* August 13, 1990.

15. Netherlands study from the University of Amsterdam cited in Anil Agarwal, "The North-South Perspective: Alienation or Interdependence?" *Ambio,* April 1990; minerals consumption based on World Resources Institute (WRI), *World Resources 1990–91* (New York: Oxford University Press, 1990).

16. Nuclear warheads from Swedish International Peace Research Institute, *SIPRI Yearbook 1990: World Armaments and Disarmament* (Oxford: Oxford University Press, 1990); global warming, acid rain, hazardous chemicals, and chlorofluorocarbons are Worldwatch Institute estimates based on WRI, *World Resources 1990–91.*

17. Michael Worley, National Opinion Research Center, University of Chicago, Chicago, Ill., private communication, September 19, 1990; personal consumption expenditures from U.S. Bureau of the Census, *Statistical Abstract of the United States: 1989* (Washington, D.C.: U.S. Government Printing Office, 1989).

18. International comparison from R. A. Easterlin, "Does Economic Growth Improve the Human Lot? Some Empirical Evidence," cited in Michael Argyle, *The Psychology of Happiness* (London: Methuen, 1987); similar arguments are found in Angus Campbell, *The Sense of Well-being in America: Recent Patterns and Trends* (New York: McGraw-Hill, 1981), in Wachtel, *Poverty of Affluence,* and in F. E. Trainer, *Abandon Affluence* (Atlantic Highlands, N.J.: Zed Books, 1985).

19. Worldwatch Institute estimate of consumption since 1950 based on gross world product data from Maddison, *World Economy in the 20th Century.*

20. Japan and Soviet Union from Christopher Flavin and Alan B. Durning, *Building on Success: The Age of Energy Efficiency,* Worldwatch Paper 82 (Washington, D.C.: Worldwatch Institute, March 1988); Norway and Sweden paper use from Greenpeace, *The Greenpeace Guide to Paper* (Vancouver: 1990); literacy and income from World Bank, *World Development Report 1990.*

21. José Goldemberg et al., *Energy for a Sustainable World* (Washington, D.C.: WRI, 1987).

22. Marcia D. Lowe, *Alternatives to the Automobile: Transport for Livable Cities,* Worldwatch Paper 98 (Washington, D.C.: Worldwatch Institute, October 1990); Marcia D. Lowe, *The Bicycle: Vehicle for a Small Planet,* Worldwatch Paper 90 (Washington, D.C.: Worldwatch Institute, September 1989).

23. Auto fleet from MVMA, *Facts and Figures '90;* carbon emissions and traffic fatalities from Lowe, *Alternatives to the Automobile.*

24. Car ownership from Stacy C. Davis et al., *Transportation Energy Data Book: Edition 10* (Oak Ridge, Tenn.: Oak Ridge National Laboratory, 1989); two-car garages from "Motor Motels," *American Demographics,* April 1989; driving hours from John P. Robinson, "Americans on the Road," *American Demographics,* September 1989; air-conditioned cars from MVMA, Detroit, Mich., private communication, September 10, 1990; impact of CFCs on climate change from Mark A. DeLuchi, "Emissions of Greenhouse Gases from the Use of Gasoline, Methanol, and Other Alternative Transportation Fuels" (draft), Transportation Research Group, University of California, Davis, Calif., 1990.

25. Quoted in Wachtel, *Poverty of Affluence.*

26. One billion air travellers from "High Hopes and Expectations," *Europe,* September 1990; 4 million and 41 percent from Air Transport Association, Washington, D.C., private communication, September 12, 1990; jet set's extra distance and energy consumption are Worldwatch Institute estimates based on average trip lengths and energy use of air travel from Davis et al., *Transportation Energy Data Book, Edition 10.*

27. World Bank, *World Development Report 1990;* dietary fat is Worldwatch Institute estimate based on World Commission on Environment and Development (WCED), *Our Common Future* (Oxford: Oxford University Press, 1987).

28. Gina Kolata, "Report Urges Low-Fat Diet for Everyone," *New York Times,* February 28, 1990; WCED, *Our Common Future.*

29. Kolata, "Report Urges Low-Fat Diet for Everyone"; China from Jane E. Brody, "Huge Study of Diet Indicts Fat and Meat," *New York Times,* May 8, 1990.

30. Share of world grain from Peter Riley, grains analyst, Economic Research Service, USDA, Washington, D.C., private communication, September 13, 1990; grain input per beef produced is Worldwatch Institute estimate based on Economic Research Service, USDA, Washington, D.C., various private communications; energy based on David Pimentel et al., "The Potential for Grass-Fed Livestock: Resource Constraints," *Science,* February 22, 1980, and on David Pimentel, Professor, Cornell University, Ithaca, N.Y.,

private communication, August 29, 1990; other environmental effects from Molly O'Neill, "An Icon of the Good Life Ends Up On a Crowded Planet's Hit Lists," *New York Times,* May 6, 1990.

31. Chile grapes from Bradley Graham, "South American Grapes: Tale of Two Countries," *Washington Post,* February 2, 1988; travel of average mouthful of food from U.S. Department of Defense, *U.S. Agriculture: Potential Vulnerabilities,* cited in Cornucopia Project, *Empty Breadbasket?* (Emmaus, Pa.: Rodale Press, 1981); farm policies favor large producers from Marty Strange, *Family Farming: A New Economic Vision* (Lincoln, Neb.: University of Nebraska Press, 1989); health standards from Wendell Berry, "Sanitation and the Small Farm," in *The Gift of Good Land* (San Francisco: North Point Press, 1981); irrigation subsidies from E. Phillip LeVeen and Laura B. King, *Turning Off the Tap on Federal Water Subsidies, Vol. 1* (San Francisco: Natural Resources Defense Council and California Rural Legal Assistance Foundation, 1985); truck subsidies from Harriet Parcells, "Big Trucks Getting a Free Ride," National Association of Railroad Passengers, Washington, D.C., April 1990.

32. David Pimentel, "Energy Flow in the Food System," in David Pimentel and Carl W. Hall, eds., *Food and Energy Resources* (Orlando, Fla.: Academic Press, 1984).

33. Population without safe water from U.N. Development Program, *Human Development Report 1990* (New York: Oxford University Press, 1990); drinking classes from Frederick Clairmonte and John Cavanagh, *Merchants of Drink* (Penang, Malaysia: Third World Network, 1988).

34. Global mean soft drink consumption from Clairmonte and Cavanagh, *Merchants of Drink;* 1989 soft drinks and water consumption from *Beverage Industry,* Cleveland, Ohio, private communication, September 14, 1990.

35. Durning, *Poverty and the Environment.*

36. Worldwatch Institute estimates based on steel figures from Bureau of the Census, *Statistical Abstract of the United States: 1990,* and on energy consumption (excludes subsistence use of fuelwood) from WRI, *World Resources 1990–91.*

37. Comparisons of industrial and developing countries from WCED, *Our Common Future;* U.S. per capita consumption of materials is Worldwatch Institute estimate based on petroleum and coal from DOE, EIA, *Annual Energy Review 1988,* on other minerals and agricultural products from Bureau of the Census, *Statistical Abstract of the United States: 1990,* and on forest products from Alice Ulrich, *U.S. Timber Production, Trade, Consumption, and Price Statistics 1950–87* (Washington, D.C.: USDA Forest Service, 1989).

38. Expenditures for packaging from U.S. Congress, Office of Technology Assessment, *Facing America's Trash:*

What Next for Municipal Solid Waste? (Washington, D.C.: U.S. Government Printing Office, 1989); Steve Usdin, "Snap Happy: Throwaway Cameras Are an Instant Hit," *Intersect,* June 1990; diapers from Karen Christensen, independent researcher, Boulder, Colo., private communication, October 18, 1990; razors from Cheryl Russell, "Guilty as Charged," *American Demographics,* February 1989; plates, cups, and cans are Worldwatch Institute estimates based on Environmental Protection Agency, Office of Solid Waste and Emergency Response, "Characterization of Municipal Solid Waste in the United States: 1990 Update," Washington, D.C., June 1990; aluminum in DC-10 from Elaine Bendell, McDonnell Douglas, Long Beach, Calif., private communication, September 20, 1990.

39.   Spencer S. Hsu, "The Sneaker Steps Out," *Washington Post,* July 22, 1990.

40.   Aristotle, *Politics,* quoted in Goldian VandenBroeck, ed., *Less Is More: The Art of Voluntary Poverty* (New York: Harper & Row, 1978).

41.   Lucretius, *On the Nature of the Universe,* and Tolstoy, *My Religion,* both quoted in VandenBroeck, *Less Is More.*

42.   Brooke Kroeger, "Feeling Poor on $600,000 a Year," *New York Times,* April 26, 1987.

43.   Argyle, *Psychology of Happiness.*

44.   Determinants of happiness from ibid.; Freedman quoted in Wachtel, *Poverty of Affluence.*

45.   Veblen quoted in Lewis H. Lapham, *Money and Class in America* (New York: Weidenfeld & Nicolson, 1988).

46.   Ads in the morning from Andrew Sullivan, "Buying and Nothingness," *The New Republic,* May 8, 1989; teenagers, defined as aged 12 to 17, from John Schwartz, "Stalking the Youth Market," *Newsweek Special Issue,* June 1990; childhood total is Worldwatch Institute estimate based on Action for Children's Television, Boston, Mass., private communication, October 17, 1990.

47.   TV and radio stations from Bureau of the Census, *Statistical Abstract of the United States: 1990;* chair lifts, bus stops, and subway stations from Paula Span, "Ads: They're Everywhere!" *Washington Post,* April 28, 1990; Paula J. Silbey, "Merchants Star on Mall's Video Wall," *Shopping Centers Today,* August 1989.

48.   Classrooms and doctors' offices from Randall Rothenberg, "Two Views on Whittle's TV Reports," *New York Times,* June 1, 1990; feature films from Randall Rothenberg, "Messages From Sponsors Become Harder to Detect," *New York Times,* November 19, 1989; Randall Rothenberg, "$30,000 Lands Product on Game Board," *New York Times,* February 6, 1989; bathrooms from Robert Geiger and Larry Teitelbaum, "Restaurants, Airlines Privy to New Medium," *Adver-*

tising Age, October 24, 1988; phones from "Commercials Invade Ma Bell," *Family Circle,* April 24, 1990; hot dogs from Spain, "Ads: They're Everywhere!"; eggs from "Which Came First? Adman or Egg?" *Fortune,* April 9, 1990.

49.   Monetary figures are adjusted for inflation and expressed in 1989 dollars. U.S. per capita from U.S. Department of Commerce, *Historical Statistics of the United States, Colonial Times to 1970, Bicentennial Edition, Part 2* (Washington, D.C.: 1975), and from Bureau of the Census, *Statistical Abstract of the United States: 1990;* world per capita from Robert J. Coen, *International Herald Tribune,* October 10, 1984, and from Tracy Poltie, International Advertising Association, New York, private communication, August 29, 1990; advertising growth faster than economic output based on Maddison, *World Economy in the 20th Century;* India from Chandra, "India: Middle-Class Spending"; Korea from "Asia's Network Boom," *Asiaweek,* July 6, 1990.

50.   Roberta Brandes Gratz, "Malling the Northeast," *New York Times Magazine,* April 1, 1990; mall walkers from Mark J. Schoifet, "To AVIA, Mall Walking Is No Joke," *Shopping Centers Today,* January 1989; Bill Mintiens, Product Marketing Director for Walking, Avia, Portland, Oreg., private communication, July 3, 1990.

51.   Time spent shopping from John P. Robinson, "When the Going Gets Tough," *American Demographics,* February 1989; shopping and church from Robert Fishman, "Megalopolis Unbound," *Wilson Quarterly,* Winter 1990; teenage girls from Magnet, "Money Society"; number of malls from Bureau of the Census, *Statistical Abstract of the United States: 1990;* high schools from Herbert I. Schiller, *Culture, Inc.* (New York: Oxford University Press, 1989); retail space growth (figures exclude automotive outlets) from International Council of Shopping Centers, "The Scope of the Shopping Center Industry in the U.S.," New York, 1989; U.S. sales from Donald L. Pendley, Director of Public Relations, International Council of Shopping Centers, New York, in "Malls Still Dominant" (letter), *American Demographics,* September 1990; France and Spain from Paula J. Silbey, "Spain Leads European Growth," *Shopping Centers Today,* March 1989.

52.   Silbey, "Spain Leads European Growth"; Britain from Carl Gardner and Julie Sheppard, *Consuming Passion: The Rise of Retail Culture* (London: Unwin Hyman, 1990); Paula J. Silbey, "Italian Centers Expected to Triple in Number Soon," *Shopping Centers Today,* May 1989.

53.   Malcolm Fergusson, "Subsidized Pollution: Company Cars and the Greenhouse Effect," report prepared for Greenpeace U.K., London, January 1990; subsidized beef from Keith Schneider, "Come What May, Congress Stays True to the Critters," *New York Times,* May 6, 1990, and from George Ledec, "New Directions for Livestock Policy in

Latin America," Department of Forestry and Resource Management, University of California, Berkeley, October 1988; taxes on homes from Peter Dreier and John Atlas, "Deductio Ad Absurdam," *Washington Monthly,* February 1990, and from Peter Dreier, Director of Housing, Boston Redevelopment Authority, Boston, Mass., private communication, October 12, 1990; multiple home owners from American Housing Survey, U.S. Bureau of the Census, Suitland, Md., private communication, October 16, 1990; homelessness estimate from "Examining Homelessness," *Science,* March 23, 1990.

54.   *Fortune* quoted in David E. Shi, *Simple Life: Plain Living and High Thinking in American Culture* (New York: Oxford University Press, 1985); urban-to-suburban migrations from Stuart Ewen, *Captains of Consciousness* (New York: McGraw-Hill, 1976), and from Delores Hayden, *Redesigning the American Dream: The Future of Housing, Work, and Family Life* (New York: W. W. Norton & Co., 1984).

55.   Scott Burns, *Home, Inc.* (Garden City, N.Y.: Doubleday, 1975).

56.   Katsumi, "Tokyo's Serious Waste Problem"; "France: Aging but Dynamic," *Market: Europe* (Ithaca, N.Y.), September 1990.

57.   History from Susan Strasser, *Satisfaction Guaranteed: The Making of the American Mass Market* (New York: Pantheon Books, 1989); American neighborhoods from Robert Reich, "A Question of Geography," *New Republic,* May 9, 1988.

58.   Basic value of sustainable society from WCED, *Our Common Future.*

59.   Aristotle, *Nicomachean Ethics* 1109b23.

60.   Toynbee quoted in Wachtel, *Poverty of Affluence.*

61.   Duane Elgin, *Voluntary Simplicity* (New York: William Morrow and Company, 1981); India from Mark Shepard, *Gandhi Today: A Report on Mahatma Gandhi's Successors* (Arcata, Calif.: Simple Productions, 1987); Netherlands and Norway from Elgin, *Voluntary Simplicity;* United Kingdom and West Germany from Pierre Pradervand, independent researcher, Geneva, Switzerland, private communication, July 14, 1990, and from Groupe de Beaulieu, *Construire L'Esperance* (Lausanne: Editions de l'Aire, 1990).

62.   Quoted in VandenBroeck, *Less Is More.*

63.   Vicki Robin, "How Much Is Enough?" *In Context* (Bainbridge Island, Wash.), Summer 1990; Camus quoted

in E. F. Schumacher, *Good Work* (New York: Harper & Row, 1979).

64.   Berry, *The Gift of Good Land;* "What Is Enough?" *In Context* (Bainbridge Island, Wash.), Summer 1990; Katy Butler, "Paté Poverty: Downwardly Mobile Baby Boomers Lust After Luxury," *Utne Reader,* September/October 1989.

65.   Shi, *Simple Life.*

66.   Children's television restriction from Howard Kurtz, "Bush May Let Children's TV Measure Become Law," *Washington Post,* October 3, 1990, and from Action for Children's Television, private communication; Jeannine Johnson, "In Search of . . . the European T.V. Show," *Europe,* November 1989.

67.   "American Excess," *Adbusters* (Vancouver), Summer 1990.

68.   Robert Bellah, *The Broken Covenant* (New York: Seabury Press, 1975).

69.   Timothy Harper, "British Sunday Law Intact—for Now," *Shopping Centers Today,* May 1989; green belts from Timothy Harper, "Rulings Slow U.K. Mall Development," *Shopping Centers Today,* May 1989; Japan from Arthur Getz, "Small Town Economics, West and East," letter to Peter Martin, Institute of Current World Affairs, Hanover, N.H., December 26, 1989.

70.   Dutch household packaging waste is Worldwatch Institute estimate based on J. M. Joosten et al., *Informative Document: Packaging Waste* (Bilthoven, Netherlands: National Institute of Public Health and Environmental Protection, 1989); land developed from Jim Riggle, Director of Operations, American Farmland Trust, Washington, D.C., private communication, October 17, 1990.

71.   Mail from Blayne Cutler, "Meet Jane Doe," *American Demographics,* June 1989; Japanese bottles figure is Worldwatch Institute estimate based on Hidefumi Kurasaka, Chief of Planning Section, Environmental Agency, Government of Japan, private communication, August 7, 1990; newspaper advertising from Sullivan, "Buying and Nothingness"; car travel is 1988 vehicle-kilometers per capita based on International Roads Federation, *World Road Statistics 1984–88* (Washington, D.C.: 1989).

72.   Henry David Thoreau, *Walden* (1854; reprint, Boston: Houghton Mifflin, 1957).

5

The Tragedy of the Commons
Garrett Hardin

At the end of a thoughtful article on the future of nuclear war, Wiesner and York concluded that:

> Both sides in the arms race are . . . confronted by the dilemma of steadily increasing military power and steadily decreasing national security. It is *our considered professional judgment that this dilemma has no technical solution.* If the great powers continue to look for solutions in the area of science and technology only, the result will be to worsen the situation.[1]

I would like to focus your attention not on the subject of the article (national security in a nuclear world) but on the kind of conclusion they reached, namely that there is no technical solution to the problem. An implicit and almost universal assumption of discussions published in professional and semipopular scientific journals is that the problem under discussion has a technical solution. A technical solution may be defined as one that requires a change only in the techniques of the natural sciences, demanding little or nothing in the way of change in human values or ideas of morality.

In our day (though not in earlier times) technical solutions are always welcome. Because of previous failures in prophecy, it takes

courage to assert that a desired technical solution is not possible. Wiesner and York exhibited this courage; publishing in a science journal, they insisted that the solution to the problem was not to be found in the natural sciences. They cautiously qualified their statement with the phrase "It is our considered professional judgment." Whether they were right or not is not the concern of the present article. Rather, the concern here is with the important concept of a class of human problems which can be called "no technical solution problems," and, more specifically, with the identification and discussion of one of these.

It is easy to show that the class is not a null class. Recall the game of tick-tack-toe. Consider the problem "How can I win the game of tick-tack-toe?" It is well known that I cannot, if I assume (in keeping with the conventions of game theory) that my opponent understands the game perfectly. Put another way, there is no "technical solution" to the problem. I can win only by giving a radical meaning to the word "win." I can hit my opponent over the head; or I can drug him; or I can falsify the records. Every way in which I "win" involves, in some sense, an abandonment of the game, as we intuitively understand it. (I can also, of course, openly abandon the game—refuse to play it. This is what most adults do.)

The class of "no technical solution problems" has members. My thesis is that the "population problem," as conventionally conceived, is a member of this class. How it is conventionally conceived needs some comment. It is fair to say that most people who anguish over the population problem are trying to find a way to avoid the evils of overpopulation without relinquishing any of the privileges they now enjoy. They think that farming the seas or developing new strains of wheat will solve the problem—technologically. I try to show here that the solution they seek cannot be found. The population problem cannot be solved in a technical way, any more than can the problem of winning the game of tick-tack-toe.

WHAT SHALL WE MAXIMIZE?

Population, as Malthus said, naturally tends to grow "geometrically," or, as we would now say, exponentially. In a finite world this means that the per capita share of the world's goods must steadily decrease. Is ours a finite world?

A fair defense can be put forward for the view that the world is infinite; or that we do not know that it is not. But, in terms of the practical problems that we must face in the next few generations with the foreseeable technology, it is clear that we will greatly increase human misery if we do not, during the immediate future, assume that the world available to the terrestrial human population is finite. "Space" is no escape.[2]

A finite world can support only a finite population; therefore, population growth must eventually equal zero. (The case of perpetual wide fluctuations above and below zero is a trivial variant that need not be discussed.) When this condition is met, what will be the situation of mankind? Specifically, can Bentham's goal of "the greatest good for the greatest number" be realized?

No—for two reasons, each sufficient by itself. The first is a theoretical one. It is not mathematically possible to maximize for two (or more) variables at the same time. This was clearly stated by von Neumann and Morgenstern,[3] but the principle is implicit in the theory

of partial differential equations, dating back at least to D'Alembert (1717–1783).

The second reason springs directly from biological facts. To live, any organism must have a source of energy (for example, food). This energy is utilized for two purposes: mere maintenance and work. For man, maintenance of life requires about 1,600 kilocalories a day ("maintenance calories"). Anything that he does over and above merely staying alive will be defined as work, and is supported by "work calories" which he takes in. Work calories are used not only for what we call work in common speech; they are also required for all forms of enjoyment, from swimming and automobile racing to playing music and writing poetry. If our goal is to maximize population it is obvious what we must do: We must make the work calories per person approach as close to zero as possible. No gourmet meals, no vacations, no sports, no music, no literature, no art. . . . I think that everyone will grant, without argument or proof, that maximizing population does not maximize goods. Bentham's goal is impossible.

In reaching this conclusion I have made the usual assumption that it is the acquisition of energy that is the problem. The appearance of atomic energy has led some to question this assumption. However, given an infinite source of energy, population growth still produces an inescapable problem. The problem of the acquisition of energy is replaced by the problem of its dissipation, as J. H. Fremlin has so wittily shown.[4] The arithmetic signs in the analysis are, as it were, reversed; but Bentham's goal is still unobtainable.

The optimum population is, then, less than the maximum. The difficulty of defining the optimum is enormous; so far as I know, no one has seriously tackled this problem. Reaching an acceptable and stable solution will surely require more than one generation of hard analytical work—and much persuasion.

We want the maximum good per person; but what is good? To one person it is wilderness, to another it is ski lodges for thousands. To one it is estuaries to nourish ducks for hunters to shoot; to another it is factory land. Comparing one good with another is, we usually say, impossible because goods are incommensurable. Incommensurables cannot be compared.

Theoretically this may be true; but in real life incommensurables *are* commensurable. Only a criterion of judgment and a system of weighting are needed. In nature the criterion is survival. Is it better for a species to be small and hidable, or large and powerful? Natural selection commensurates the incommensurables. The compromise achieved depends on a natural weighting of the values of the variables.

Man must imitate this process. There is no doubt that in fact he already does, but unconsciously. It is when the hidden decisions are made explicit that the arguments begin. The problem for the years ahead is to work out an acceptable theory of weighting. Synergistic effects, nonlinear variation, and difficulties in discounting the future make the intellectual problem difficult, but not (in principle) insoluble.

Has any cultural group solved this practical problem at the present time, even on an intuitive level? One simple fact proves that none has: there is no prosperous population in the world today that has, and has had for some time, a growth rate of zero. Any people that has intuitively identified its optimum point will soon reach it, after which its growth rate becomes and remains zero.[5]

Of course, a positive growth rate might be taken as evidence that a population is below its optimum. However, by any reasonable standards, the most rapidly growing populations on earth today are (in general) the most miserable. This association (which need not be invariable) casts doubt on the optimistic assumption that the positive growth rate of a population is evidence that it has yet to reach its optimum.

We can make little progress in working toward optimum population size until we explicitly exorcize the spirit of Adam Smith in the field of practical demography. In economic affairs, *The Wealth of Nations* (1776) popularized the "invisible hand," the idea that an individual who "intends only his own gain" is, as it were, "led by an invisible hand to promote . . . the public interest."[6] Adam Smith did not assert that this was invariably true, and perhaps neither did any of his followers. But he contributed to a dominant tendency of thought that has ever since interfered with positive action based on rational analysis, namely, the tendency to assume that decisions reached individually will, in fact, be the best decisions for an entire society. If this assumption is correct it justifies the continuance of our present policy of laissez-faire in reproduction. If it is correct we can assume that men will control their individual fecundity so as to produce the optimum population. If the assumption is not correct, we need to reexamine our individual freedoms to see which ones are defensible.

THE TRAGEDY OF FREEDOM IN A COMMONS

The rebuttal to the invisible hand in population control is to be found in a scenario first sketched in a little-known pamphlet in 1833 by a mathematical amateur named William Forster Lloyd (1794–1852).[7] We may well call it "the tragedy of the commons," using the word "tragedy" as the philosopher Whitehead used it: "The essence of dramatic tragedy is not unhappiness. It resides in the solemnity of the remorseless working of things." He then goes on to say, "This inevitableness of destiny can only be illustrated in terms of human life by incidents which in fact involve unhappiness. For it is only by them that the futility of escape can be made evident in the drama."[8]

The tragedy of the commons develops in this way. Picture a pasture open to all. It is to be expected that each herdsman will try to keep as many cattle as possible on the commons. Such an arrangement may work reasonably satisfactorily for centuries because tribal wars, poaching, and disease keep the numbers of both man and beast well below the carrying capacity of the land. Finally, however, comes the day of reckoning, that is, the day when the long-desired goal of social stability becomes a reality. At this point, the inherent logic of the commons remorselessly generates tragedy.

As a rational being, each herdsman seeks to maximize his gain. Explicitly or implicitly, more or less consciously, he asks, "What is the utility to me of adding one more animal to my herd?" This utility has one negative and one positive component.

1. The positive component is a function of the increment of one animal. Since the herdsman receives all the proceeds from the sale of the additional animal, the positive utility is nearly +1.

2. The negative component is a function of the additional overgrazing created by one more animal. Since, however, the effects of overgrazing are shared by all the herdsmen, the negative utility for any particular decision-making herdsman is only a fraction of −1.

Adding together the component partial utilities, the rational herdsman concludes that the only sensible course for him to pursue is to add another animal to his herd. And another; and another. . . . But this is the conclusion reached by each and every rational herdsman sharing a commons. Therein is the tragedy. Each man is locked into a system that compels him to increase his herd without limit—in a world that is limited. Ruin is the destination toward which all men rush, each pursuing his own best interest in a society that believes in the freedom of the commons. Freedom in a commons brings ruin to all.

Some would say that this is a platitude. Would that it were! In a sense, it was learned thousands of years ago, but natural selection favors the forces of psychological denial.[9] The individual benefits as an individual from his ability to deny the truth even though society as a whole, of which he is a part, suffers. Education can counteract the natural tendency to do the wrong thing, but the inexorable succession of generations requires that the basis for this knowledge be constantly refreshed.

A simple incident that occurred a few years ago in Leominster, Massachusetts, shows how perishable the knowledge is. During the Christmas shopping season the parking meters downtown were covered with plastic bags that bore tags reading: "Do not open until after Christmas. Free parking courtesy of the mayor and city council." In other words, facing the prospect of an increased demand for already scarce space, the city fathers reinstituted the system of the commons. (Cynically, we suspect that they gained more votes than they lost by this retrogressive act.)

In an approximate way, the logic of the commons has been understood for a long time, perhaps since the discovery of agriculture or the invention of private property in real estate. But it is understood mostly only in special cases which are not sufficiently generalized. Even at this late date, cattlemen leasing national land on the western ranges demonstrate no more than an ambivalent understanding, in constantly pressuring federal authorities to increase the head count to the point where overgrazing produces erosion and weed dominance. Likewise, the oceans of the world continue to suffer from the survival of the philosophy of the commons. Maritime nations still respond automatically to the shibboleth of the "freedom of the seas." Professing to believe in the "inexhaustible resources of the oceans," they bring species after species of fish and whales closer to extinction.[10]

The national parks present another instance

of the working out of the tragedy of the commons. At present, they are open to all, without limit. The parks themselves are limited in extent—there is only one Yosemite Valley—whereas population seems to grow without limit. The values that visitors seek in the parks are steadily eroded. Plainly, we must soon cease to treat the parks as commons or they will be of no value to anyone.

What shall we do? We have several options. We might sell them off as private property. We might keep them as public property, but allocate the right to enter them. The allocation might be on the basis of wealth by the use of an auction system. It might be on the basis of merit, as defined by some agreed-upon standards. It might be by lottery. Or it might be on a first-come, first-served basis, administered to long queues. These, I think, are all the reasonable possibilities. They are all objectionable. But we must choose—or acquiesce in the destruction of the commons that we call our national parks.

POLLUTION

In a reverse way, the tragedy of the commons reappears in problems of pollution. Here it is not a question of taking something out of the commons, but of putting something in—sewage, or chemical, radioactive, and heat wastes into water; noxious and dangerous fumes into the air; and distracting and unpleasant advertising signs into the light of sight. The calculations of utility are much the same as before. The rational man finds that his share of the cost of the wastes he discharges into the commons is less than the cost of purifying his wastes before releasing them. Since this is true for everyone, we are locked into a system of "fouling our own nest," so long as we behave only as independent, rational, free enterprisers.

The tragedy of the commons as a food basket is averted by private property, or something formally like it. But the air and waters surrounding us cannot readily be fenced, and so the tragedy of the commons as a cesspool must be prevented by different means, by coercive laws or taxing devices that make it cheaper for the polluter to treat his pollutants than to discharge them untreated. We have not progressed as far with the solution of this problem as we have with the first. Indeed, our particular concept of private property, which deters us from exhausting the positive resources of the earth, favors pollution. The owner of a factory on the bank of a stream—whose property extends to the middle of the stream—often has difficulty seeing why it is not his natural right to muddy the waters flowing past his door. The law, always behind the times, requires elaborate stitching and fitting to adapt it to this newly perceived aspect of the commons.

The pollution problem is a consequence of population. It did not much matter how a lonely American frontiersman disposed of his waste. "Flowing water purifies itself every ten miles," my grandfather used to say, and the myth was near enough to the truth when he was a boy, for there were not too many people. But as population became denser, the natural chemical and biological recycling processes became overloaded, calling for a redefinition of property rights.

HOW TO LEGISLATE TEMPERANCE?

Analysis of the pollution problem as a function of population density uncovers a not generally recognized principle of morality, namely: *the morality of an act is a function of the state of the system at the time it is performed.*[11] Using the commons as a cesspool does not harm the general public under frontier conditions, because there is no public; the same behavior in a metropolis is unbearable. A hundred and fifty years ago a plainsman could kill an American bison, cut out only the tongue for his dinner, and discard the rest of the animal. He was not in any important sense being wasteful. Today, with only a few thousand bison left, we would be appalled at such behavior.

In passing, it is worth noting that the morality of an act cannot be determined from a photograph. One does not know whether a man killing an elephant or setting fire to the grassland is harming others until one knows the total system in which his act appears. "One picture is worth a thousand words," said an ancient Chinese; but it may take 10,000 words to validate it. It is as tempting to ecologists as it is to reformers in general to try to persuade others by way of the photographic shortcut. But the essence of an argument cannot be photographed: it must be presented rationally—in words.

That morality is system-sensitive escaped the attention of most codifiers of ethics in the past. "Thou shalt not . . ." is the form of traditional ethical directives which make no allowance for particular circumstances. The laws of our society follow the pattern of ancient ethics, and therefore are poorly suited to governing a complex, crowded, changeable world. Our epicyclic solution is to augment statutory law with administrative law. Since it is practically impossible to spell out all the conditions under which it is safe to burn trash in the back yard or to run an automobile without smog control, by law we delegate the details to bureaus. The result is administrative law, which is rightly feared for an ancient reason—*Quis custodiet ipsos custodes?*—"Who shall watch the watchers themselves?" John Adams said that we must have "a government of laws and not men." Bureau administrators, trying to evaluate the morality of acts in the total system, are singularly liable to corruption, producing a government by men, not laws.

Prohibition is easy to legislate (though not necessarily to enforce); but how do we legislate temperance? Experience indicates that it can be accomplished best through the mediation of administrative law. We limit possibilities unneces-

sarily if we suppose that the sentiment of *Quis custodiet* denies us the use of administrative law. We should rather retain the phrase as a perpetual reminder of fearful dangers we cannot avoid. The great challenge facing us now is to invent the corrective feedbacks that are needed to keep custodians honest. We must find ways to legitimate the needed authority of both the custodians and the corrective feedbacks.

FREEDOM TO BREED IS INTOLERABLE

The tragedy of the commons is involved in population problems in another way. In a world governed solely by the principle of "dog eat dog"—if indeed there ever was such a world—how many children a family had would not be a matter of public concern. Parents who bred too exuberantly would leave fewer descendants, not more, because they would be unable to care adequately for their children. David Lack and others have found that such a negative feedback demonstrably controls the fecundity of birds.[12] But men are not birds, and have not acted like them for millenniums, at least.

If each human family were dependent only on its own resources; *if* the children of improvident parents starved to death; *if,* thus, overbreeding brought its own "punishment" to the germ line—*then* there would be no public interest in controlling the breeding of families. But our society is deeply committed to the welfare state,[13] and hence is confronted with another aspect of the tragedy of the commons.

In a welfare state, how shall we deal with the family, the religion, the race, or the class (or indeed any distinguishable and cohesive group) that adopts overbreeding as a policy to secure its own aggrandizement?[14] To couple the concept of freedom to breed with the belief that everyone born has an equal right to the commons is to lock the world into a tragic course of action.

Unfortunately this is just the course of action that is being pursued by the United Nations.

In late 1967, some thirty nations agreed to the following:

> The Universal Declaration of Human Rights describes the family as the natural and fundamental unit of society. It follows that any choice and decision with regard to the size of the family must irrevocably rest with the family itself, and cannot be made by someone else.[15]

It is painful to have to deny categorically the validity of this right; denying it, one feels as uncomfortable as a resident of Salem, Massachusetts, who denied the reality of witches in the seventeenth century. At the present time, in liberal quarters, something like a taboo acts to inhibit criticism of the United Nations. There is a feeling that the United Nations is "our last and best hope," that we shouldn't find fault with it; we shouldn't play into the hands of the archconservatives. However, let us not forget what Robert Louis Stevenson said: "The truth that is suppressed by friends is the readiest weapon of the enemy." If we love the truth we must openly deny the validity of the Universal Declaration of Human Rights, even though it is promoted by the United Nations. We should also join with Kingsley Davis[16] in attempting to get Planned Parenthood–World Population to see the error of its ways in embracing the same tragic ideal.

CONSCIENCE IS SELF-ELIMINATING

It is a mistake to think that we can control the breeding of mankind in the long run by an appeal to conscience. Charles Galton Darwin made this point when he spoke on the centennial of the publication of his grandfather's great book. The argument is straightforward and Darwinian.

People vary. Confronted with appeals to limit breeding, some people will undoubtedly respond to the plea more than others. Those who have more children will produce a larger fraction of the next generation than those with more susceptible consciences. The difference will be accentuated, generation by generation.

In C. G. Darwin's words: "It may well be that it would take hundreds of generations for the progenitive instinct to develop in this way, but if it should do so, nature would have taken her revenge, and the variety *Homo contracipiens* would become extinct and would be replaced by the variety *Homo progenitivus*."[17]

The argument assumes that conscience or the desire for children (no matter which) is hereditary—but hereditary only in the most general formal sense. The result will be the same whether the attitude is transmitted through germ cells, or exosomatically, to use A. J. Lotka's term. (If one denies the latter possibility as well as the former, then what's the point of education?) The argument has here been stated in the context of the population problem, but it applies equally well to any instance in which society appeals to an individual exploiting a commons to restrain himself for the general good—by means of his conscience. To make such an appeal is to set up a selective system that works toward the elimination of conscience from the race.

PATHOGENIC EFFECTS OF CONSCIENCE

The long-term disadvantage of an appeal to conscience should be enough to condemn it; but it has serious short-term disadvantages as well. If we ask a man who is exploiting a commons to desist "in the name of conscience," what are we saying to him? What does he hear?—not only at the moment but also in the wee small hours of the night when, half asleep, he remembers not merely the words we used but also the nonverbal communication cues we gave him unawares? Sooner or later, consciously or subconsciously, he senses that he has received two communications, and that they are contradictory: (1, the intended communication) "If you don't do as we ask, we will openly condemn you for not acting like a responsible citizen"; (2, the unintended communication) "If you *do* behave as we ask, we will secretly condemn you for a simpleton who can be shamed into standing aside while the rest of us exploit the commons."

Everyman then is caught in what Bateson has called a "double bind." Bateson and his co-workers have made a plausible case for viewing the double bind as an important causative factor in the genesis of schizophrenia.[18] The double bind may not always be so damaging, but it always endangers the mental health of anyone to whom it is applied. "A bad conscience," said Nietzsche, "is a kind of illness."

To conjure up a conscience in others is tempting to anyone who wishes to extend his control beyond the legal limits. Leaders at the highest level succumb to this temptation. Has any President during the past generation failed to call on labor unions to moderate voluntarily their demands for higher wages, or to steel companies to honor voluntary guidelines on prices? I can recall none. The rhetoric used on such occasions is designed to produce feelings of guilt in noncooperators.

For centuries it was assumed without proof that guilt was a valuable, perhaps even an indispensable, ingredient of the civilized life. Now, in this post-Freudian world, we doubt it. Paul Goodman speaks from the modern point of view when he says: "No good has ever come from feeling guilty, neither intelligence, policy, nor compassion. The guilty do not pay attention to the object but only to themselves, and not even to their own interests, which might make sense, but to their anxieties."[19]

One does not have to be a professional psychiatrist to see the consequences of anxiety. We in the Western world are just emerging from a dreadful two-centuries-long Dark Ages of Eros that was sustained partly by prohibition laws, but perhaps more effectively by the anxiety-generating mechanisms of education. Alex

Comfort has told the story well in *The Anxiety Makers;*[20] it is not a pretty one.

Since proof is difficult, we may even concede that the results of anxiety may sometimes, from certain points of view, be desirable. The larger question we should ask is whether, as a matter of policy, we should ever encourage the use of a technique the tendency (if not the intention) of which is psychologically pathogenic. We hear much talk these days of responsible parenthood; the coupled words are incorporated into the titles of some organizations devoted to birth control. Some people have proposed massive propaganda campaigns to instill responsibility into the nation's (or the world's) breeders. But what is the meaning of the word responsibility in this context? Is it not merely a synonym for the word conscience? When we use the word responsibility in the absence of substantial sanctions we are not trying to browbeat a free man in a commons into acting against his own interest? Responsibility is a verbal counterfeit for a substantial *quid pro quo*. It is an attempt to get something for nothing.

If the word responsibility is to be used at all, I suggest that it be in the sense Charles Frankel uses it.[21] "Responsibility," says this philosopher, "is the product of definite social arrangements." Notice that Frankel calls for social arrangements—not propaganda.

MUTUAL COERCION MUTUALLY AGREED UPON

The social arrangements that produce responsibility are arrangements that create coercion, of some sort. Consider bank robbing. The man who takes money from a bank acts as if the bank were a commons. How do we prevent such action? Certainly not by trying to control his behavior solely by a verbal appeal to his sense of responsibility. Rather than rely on propaganda we follow Frankel's lead and insist that a bank is not a commons; we seek the definite social arrangements that will keep it from becoming a commons. That we thereby infringe on the freedom of would-be robbers we neither deny nor regret.

The morality of bank robbing is particularly easy to understand because we accept complete prohibition of this activity. We are willing to say "Thou shalt not rob banks," without providing for exceptions. But temperance also can be created by coercion. Taxing is a good coercive device. To keep downtown shoppers temperate in their use of parking space we introduce parking meters for short periods, and traffic fines for longer ones. We need not actually forbid a citizen to park as long as he wants to; we need merely make it increasingly expensive for him to do so. Not prohibition, but carefully biased options are what we offer him. A Madison Avenue man might call this persuasion; I prefer the greater candor of the word coercion.

Coercion is a dirty word to most liberals now, but it need not forever be so. As with the four-letter words, its dirtiness can be cleansed away by exposure to the light, by saying it over and over without apology or embarrassment. To many, the word coercion implies arbitrary decisions of distant and irresponsible bureaucrats; but this is not a necessary part of its meaning. The only kind of coercion I recommend is mutual coercion, mutually agreed upon by the majority of the people affected.

To say that we mutually agree to coercion is not to say that we are required to enjoy it, or even to pretend we enjoy it. Who enjoys taxes? We all grumble about them. But we accept compulsory taxes because we recognize that voluntary taxes would favor the conscienceless. We institute and (grumblingly) support taxes and other coercive devices to escape the horror of the commons.

An alternative to the commons need not be perfectly just to be preferable. With real estate and other material goods, the alternative we have chosen is the institution of private property coupled with legal inheritance. Is this system perfectly just? As a genetically trained biologist I deny that it is. It seems to me that, if there are

to be differences in individual inheritance, legal possession should be perfectly correlated with biological inheritance—that those who are biologically more fit to be the custodians of property and power should legally inherit more. But genetic recombination continually makes a mockery of the doctrine of "like father, like son" implicit in our laws of legal inheritance. An idiot can inherit millions, and a trust fund can keep his estate intact. We must admit that our legal system of private property plus inheritance is unjust—but we put up with it because we are not convinced, at the moment, that anyone has invented a better system. The alternative of the commons is too horrifying to contemplate. Injustice is preferable to total ruin.

It is one of the peculiarities of the warfare between reform and the status quo that it is thoughtlessly governed by a double standard. Whenever a reform measure is proposed it is often defeated when its opponents triumphantly discover a flaw in it. As Kingsley Davis has pointed out, worshippers of the status quo sometimes imply that no reform is possible without unanimous agreement, an implication contrary to historical fact.[22] As nearly as I can make out, automatic rejection of proposed reforms is based on one of two unconscious assumptions: (1) that the status quo is perfect; or (2) that the choice we face is between reform and no action; if the proposed reform is imperfect, we presumably should take no action at all, while we wait for a perfect proposal.

But we can never do nothing. That which we have done for thousands of years is also action. It also produces evils. Once we are aware that the status quo is action, we can then compare its discoverable advantages and disadvantages with the predicted advantages and disadvantages of the proposed reform, discounting as best we can for our lack of experience. On the basis of such a comparison, we can make a rational decision which will not involve the unworkable assumption that only perfect systems are tolerable.

RECOGNITION OF NECESSITY

Perhaps the simplest summary of this analysis of man's population problems is this: the commons, if justifiable at all, is justifiable only under conditions of low population density. As the human population has increased, the commons has had to be abandoned in one aspect after another.

First we abandoned the commons in food gathering, enclosing farm land and restricting pastures and hunting and fishing areas. These restrictions are still not complete throughout the world.

Somewhat later we saw that the commons as a place for waste disposal would also have to be abandoned. Restrictions on the disposal of domestic sewage are widely accepted in the Western world; we are still struggling to close the commons to pollution by automobiles, factories, insecticide sprayers, fertilizing operations, and atomic energy installations.

In a still more embryonic state is our recognition of the evils of the commons in matters of pleasure. There is almost no restriction on the propagation of sound waves in the public medium. The shopping public is assaulted with mindless music, without its consent. Our government is paying out billions of dollars to create supersonic transport which will disturb 50,000 people for every one person who is whisked from coast to coast three hours faster. Advertisers muddy the airwaves of radio and television and pollute the view of travelers. We are a long way from outlawing the commons in matters of pleasure. Is this because our Puritan inheritance makes us view pleasure as something of a sin, and pain (that is, the pollution of advertising) as the sign of virtue?

Every new enclosure of the commons involves the infringement of somebody's personal liberty. Infringements made in the distant past are accepted because no contemporary complains of a loss. It is the newly proposed infringements that we vigorously oppose; cries of "rights" and "freedom" fill the air. But what does "freedom" mean? When men mutually agreed to pass laws against robbing, mankind became more free, not less so. Individuals locked into the logic of the commons are free only to bring on universal ruin; once they see the necessity of mutual coercion, they become free to pursue other goals. I believe it was Hegel who said, "Freedom is the recognition of necessity."

The most important aspect of necessity that we must now recognize is the necessity of abandoning the commons in breeding. No technical solution can rescue us from the misery of overpopulation. Freedom to breed will bring ruin to all. At the moment, to avoid hard decisions many of us are tempted to propagandize for conscience and responsible parenthood. The temptation must be resisted, because an appeal to independently acting consciences selects for the disappearance of all conscience in the long run, and an increase in anxiety in the short.

The only way we can preserve and nurture other and more precious freedoms is by relinquishing the freedom to breed, and that very soon. "Freedom is the recognition of necessity"—and it is the role of education to reveal to all the necessity of abandoning the freedom to breed. Only so can we put an end to this aspect of the tragedy of the commons.

Notes

1. J. B. Wiesner and H. F. York, *Scientific American* 211, no. 4 (1964), 27. Offprint 319.

2. G. Hardin, *Journal of Heredity* 50 (1959), 68; S. von Hoernor, *Science* 137 (1962), 18.

3. J. von Neumann and O. Morgenstern, *Theory of Games and Economic Behavior* (Princeton, N.J.: Princeton University Press, 1947), p. 11.

4. J. H. Fremlin, *New Science,* no. 415 (1964), 285.

5. [Editors' note: Several European countries now have stable or declining populations.]

6. A. Smith, *The Wealth of Nations* (New York: Modern Library, 1937), p. 423.

7. W. F. Lloyd, *Two Lectures on the Checks to Population* (Oxford: Oxford University Press, 1833), reprinted (in part) in G. Hardin, ed., *Population, Evolution, and Birth Control,* 2d ed. (San Francisco: W. H. Freeman and Company, 1969), p. 28.

8. A. N. Whitehead, *Science and the Modern World* (New York: Mentor, 1948), p. 17.

9. Hardin, *Population, Evolution, and Birth Control,* p. 46.

10. S. McVay, *Scientific American* 216, no. 8 (1966), 13. Offprint 1046.

11. J. Fletcher, *Situation Ethics* (Philadelphia: Westminster, 1966).

12. D. Lack, *The Natural Regulation of Animal Numbers* (Oxford: Clarendon Press, 1954).

13. H. Girvetz, *From Wealth to Welfare* (Stanford, Calif.: Stanford University Press, 1950).

14. G. Hardin, *Perspectives in Biology and Medicine* 6 (1963), 366.

15. U Thant, *International Planned Parenthood News,* no. 168 (February 1968), 3.

16. K. Davis, *Science* 158 (1967), 730.

17. S. Tax, ed., *Evolution after Darwin* (Chicago: University of Chicago Press, 1960), 2:469.

18. G. Bateson, D. D. Jackson, J. Haley, J. Weakland, *Behavioral Science* 1 (1956), 251.

19. P. Goodman, *New York Review of Books* 10, no. 8 (23 May 1968), 22.

20. A. Comfort, *The Anxiety Makers* (London: Nelson, 1967).

21. C. Frankel, *The Case for Modern Man* (New York: Harper, 1955), p. 203.

22. J. D. Roslansky, *Genetics and the Future of Man* (New York: Appleton-Century-Crofts, 1966), p. 177.

6

EPA and the Evolution of Federal Regulation
Paul R. Portney

By comparison with many other federal regulatory agencies, the EPA and its siblings of the 1970s are relative newcomers. Indeed, it was more than a century ago, in 1887, that Congress created the Interstate Commerce Commission to regulate surface transportation industries, and it has been more than seventy years since the Federal Reserve Board and Federal Trade Commission were created to regulate commercial banks and deceptive trade practices, respectively. The first great burst of federal regulatory activity took place in the 1930s, during which Congress created the Federal Power Commission, the Food and Drug Administration, the Federal Home and Loan Bank Board, the Federal Deposit Insurance Corporation, the Securities and Exchange Commission, the Federal Communications Commission, the Federal Maritime Commission, and the Civil Aeronautics Board.

Between 1938 and 1970 little took place in the way of new federal regulatory activity.[1] Following this lull, however, came the second major burst of federal regulation. In quick order were created the EPA, the National Highway Traffic Safety Administration, the Consumer Product Safety Commission, the Occupational Safety and Health Administration, the Mining Safety and Health Administration, the Nuclear Regulatory Commission, the Commodity Futures Trading Commission, and the Office of Surface Mining Reclamation and Enforcement. Along with the Food and Drug Administration (FDA) (and omitting the Commodity Futures Trading Commission), these have come to be known as the "social" regulatory agencies. Generally speaking, they are those having to do with environmental protection and the safety and health of consumers and workers.

Aside from age, there are at least three important distinctions between the "old-line" agencies and the newer, social regulators like the EPA.[2] The first has to do with their reasons for being. In principle at least, all regulatory agencies have been created to remedy a perceived failure of the free market to allocate resources efficiently. Except for the FDA, the older agencies were meant either to control "natural monopolies" or to protect individuals from fraudulent advertising or unsound financial practices on the part of financial intermediaries or depository institutions.[3] (The latter justification was clearly a reaction to the calamitous Great Depression, during which many of these agencies were created.)

Federal intervention in the areas of environmental protection and the safety and health of workers and consumers has a very different rationale. Here, it is argued, the government must intervene because of externalities or imperfect information. The former arise when the production of a good or service results in some costs

Reprinted by permission from, "EPA and the Evolution of Federal Regulation," by Paul R. Portney, *Resources,* published by Resources for the Future, Washington, D.C.

(like pollution damage) which, in the absence of regulation, are unlikely to be borne by the producer. In such cases, the prices of products will not reflect what society must give up to have them, so that Adam Smith's "invisible hand" will steer us awry. In the case of imperfect information, workers or consumers may be only dimly aware of the health hazards associated with various occupations or consumer products or foodstuffs. If so, they will be unable to trade off higher risks for either higher wages or lower prices in an informed way, so that the unaided market would not necessarily result in either the right amount or the correct distribution of risk.

The newer regulatory agencies differ from their elders in another important way, having to do with the specificity of their focus. The older agencies can be thought of as dealing with a single industry—the Interstate Commerce Commission (ICC) with surface transportation, the Federal Communications Commission (FCC) with communications, the Civil Aeronautics Board (CAB) with airlines, and so on. This is not true of the newer social regulatory agencies. Thus, for instance, the Occupational Safety and Health Administration (OSHA) regulates workplace conditions in a wide variety of industries ranging from chemicals to agriculture. Similarly, the EPA regulates emissions of air and water pollution from the electric utility, steel, food-processing, petroleum-refining, and many other industries. The broader mandate of the social regulatory agencies may be a more difficult one to satisfy, since it requires each agency to become knowledgeable about and sensitive to the special problems and production technologies in many different industries.

A final distinction between the old-line agencies and their newer counterparts concerns recent developments in the scope of their activities. While it is always difficult to generalize over members of such a diverse group, the thrust of recent legislation and administrative actions at the older regulatory agencies has been in the direction of a sharp curtailment in the extent of their intervention in the markets they have regulated. This has been most pronounced in the case of the CAB, which was legislated out of existence in 1985 after it was recognized that the airline industry was ripe for competition. Similarly, the FCC has proposed significant reductions in the scope of its own activity, and both the trucking and railroad industries have been substantially deregulated through recent legislation and through administrative rulemakings at the ICC. The financial regulatory agencies and the Federal Energy Regulatory Commission (FERC, the successor to the Federal Power Commission) have also seen their powers eroded over time.

In general, this has not been the case at the newer, social regulatory agencies. While many have questioned the *way* these agencies have pursued their goals, relatively few have suggested that there is no need for them at all. It would be difficult to argue that unfettered competition among firms would lead to the right amount of pollution, product safety, or workplace risk so long as the problems of external effects or imperfect information characterize the conditions of production or consumption. Thus, while there is much agitation for regulatory reform—about which more is said below—there are very few calls for the abolition of the EPA, OSHA, FDA, or other social regulatory agencies. Indeed, in the case of the EPA at least, new responsibilities and regulatory programs have been added to the old almost continually since its creation. Trying to initiate new programs while struggling to master the existing ones is one of the problems with which the EPA has had to contend constantly.

THE CREATION AND GROWTH OF THE EPA

At the vanguard of the new social regulatory agencies, the Environmental Protection Agency got its start on July 9, 1970 when President Nixon submitted Reorganization Plan No. 3 of

1970 for congressional approval. That reorganization plan proposed to consolidate under one roof—the EPA's—various functions being performed at that time by the departments of Interior, Health, Education and Welfare, and Agriculture, as well as by the Atomic Energy Commission, the Federal Radiation Council, and the Council on Environmental Quality. By December 1970 the plan had been approved by Congress and the EPA was in action.

Because it was created out of existing programs, the EPA was never a very small agency. In 1971, its first full year of existence, it had about 7,000 employees and a budget of $3.3 billion, $512 million of which went to operate the agency, with the remainder being passed through the EPA in grants to state and local governments. By 1980, the agency had grown to more than 12,000 employees; its budget by that time was more than $5 billion, $1.5 billion of which went to the operation of the agency itself.

The budget of the Environmental Protection Agency, like that of most federal agencies, shrank during the Reagan years. In its final budget submission, just before George Bush was sworn in as president, the Reagan administration requested $4.8 billion for the EPA for fiscal year 1989—$1.6 billion for operations, $1.5 billion for sewage treatment grants, and $1.6 billion for the Superfund (in 1989 dollars). Ignoring the latter program, which did not exist in 1980, and adjusting for inflation, the operating budget of the EPA has fallen by about 15 percent in real terms since 1980.

One must be careful not to ascribe too much importance to the budget of the Environmental Protection Agency (or any other regulatory agency). While the budget may provide some guidance as to the agency's capabilities, its spending authority is less important than the costs incurred by those subject to the agency's various regulations. The latter, called compliance costs by economists, never show up in the agency's budget, yet they can dwarf its operating costs. For example, in 1981 the EPA spent $1.8 billion on outside research, salaries, rent, and other operating expenses (expressed in 1988 dollars). Yet in that same year, as indicated above, those subject to the EPA's air and water pollution control regulations were forced to spend some $52 billion to comply with EPA requirements. These expenditures—for pollution control equipment, cleaner fuels, sludge removal, additional manpower—give a much more accurate picture of the economic importance of the EPA than does its budget. (. . . Environmental regulations may of course result in substantial benefits as well. One must look at both costs and benefits before passing judgment on the overall worth of a particular regulatory program.)

The rapid growth of off-budget environmental compliance costs (they were estimated to be only $29 billion in 1973) has led to periodic concern about the possible effects of pollution control spending on the overall performance of the economy. While this is not the place to review in any detail the many studies on this subject, it may be useful to summarize them briefly.[4] With a fair degree of consistency, these studies have found that pollution control spending has had a relatively minor impact on macroeconomic performance. It has exacerbated inflation somewhat and slowed the rate of growth of productivity and of the GNP. On the other hand, studies have found that pollution control spending appears to have provided some very modest stimulus to employment, at least during the time when spending for sewage treatment plant construction was high. None of this should be too surprising. While annual expenditures of $52 billion or more are hardly trivial, they are small in comparison to a $5 trillion GNP like that of the United States. Thus it is unlikely that environmental or other regulatory programs on the present scale will ever be found to exert a significant impact on the measured performance of the economy.[5]

FUNDAMENTAL CHOICES IN ENVIRONMENTAL REGULATION

It may prove helpful . . . to review some of the basic choices that must be made in environmental regulation. The first question is one whose answer is often taken for granted—whether to regulate at all. While today we tend to take the need for regulation as a given, there are several possible alternatives to environmental regulation. These include the private use of our legal system as well as private negotiation or mediation.

Both alternatives depend upon a clear prior definition of property rights. Imagine that it was clearly understood that any citizen had an absolute right to be compensated fully for the damages from any kind of pollution. If the smoke from a neighbor's wood stove or a factory were ruining your laundry business, you could take the offending party to court. If your damages could be accurately assessed, and if the polluter were held liable for them, the legal approach would create the right incentives for polluters. They would undertake certain pollution control measures if the costs of these measures were less than the damages they would have to pay you. And they would continue to emit some pollution—and pay you for the damage it does—if it were more expensive to control than it was to reimburse you. Economists like such solutions because they minimize the total costs—control expenditures plus residual damages—associated with pollution control. Until the start of the twentieth century, all air pollution problems were handled under the nuisance and trespass provisions of common law.

Unfortunately, the real world is much more complicated than this simple example would suggest, and the added complexity makes a purely legal approach to environmental protection much less practical. First, it is not perfectly clear where property rights in clean air are, or even ought to be, vested in our society. This may

seem puzzling, since most people accept the right of the citizenry to be free from pollution. Yet even this apparently sensible proposition seems strained in, say, the case of a laundry that deliberately moves from a clean location to one directly adjacent to a factory and then demands compensation for smoke damage. In other words, it seems to make some difference who was there first. Furthermore, if property values and rents are lower in polluted areas than in clean ones (as they generally are), the launderer seems to be on shakier ground still, since he would have already reaped some savings in operating costs (lower rent) by virtue of his new location. In one sense, he would be getting double benefits if the factory were forced to curtail its operations. Not surprisingly, arguments like these are often advanced in defense of firms resisting pollution control. They are not wholly without merit.[6]

Even if property rights were clearly defined, environmental protection via the legal system or private negotiation would not be without difficulties. For instance, pollution rarely occurs on a one-to-one basis as in the simple example above. There are often many polluters, thus making it difficult or impossible to know which factory, car, or wood stove is responsible for which damages. Also, there are generally many "pollutees," no one of whom may be suffering sufficient damages to merit taking legal action or initiating mediation or negotiation alone. Legal transaction costs may be so high that they inhibit the filing of class action suits, even though aggregate damages across all pollutees may be significant. Finally, some of the damaging effects of pollution may be both more subtle yet more serious than mere dirty laundry. For example, pollution may be one of the causes of cancer and other serious illnesses. Yet the long latency period between exposure and manifestation, coupled with the possibility of other causes, will make it virtually impossible to assess liability satisfactorily in a courtroom or arbitration chamber. Add to this the difficulty of valuing the pain and suffering from such illnesses, and one can quickly understand the possible shortcomings of alternative approaches to government intervention.

Having said this much, it is time to make one more quite important point. Proponents of government action, regulatory or otherwise, are quick to point as justification to the imperfections inherent in free markets. Public goods, externalities, natural monopolies, and imperfect information—these are all problems economists recognize as standing in the way of efficient resource allocation. Yet regulation seldom goes exactly as planned when it is substituted for the forces of the market.[7] It is often poorly conceived, time-consuming, arbitrary, and manipulated for political purposes completely unrelated to its original intent. Thus the real comparison one must make in contemplating a regulatory intervention is that between an admittedly imperfect market and what will inevitably be imperfect regulation. Until it is recognized that this is the dilemma before us, we will be dissatisfied with either approach.[8]

If government intervention *is* deemed desirable, one must then ask, at what level should intervention take place? While environmental protection is very important, so too are public school quality, police and fire protection, income assistance, and criminal justice. Yet the latter are all functions which, in our federal system, are entrusted largely to local or state governments. Thus it is not obvious that all or even more environmental regulation should take place at the federal level. This is a key decision that must be made in designing interventions, and . . . one recent trend is in the direction of much more state and local regulatory activity.

Once the decision has been made to intervene at some level of government, the next choice to be made is, how should we decide how much protection to provide? There are a number of frameworks for deciding the answer, and Congress has directed different social regulatory agencies to use different frameworks in establishing levels of protection.[9] In fact, even within the EPA the approach differs depending on the regulatory program in question.

One way to select the degree of protection might be called the zero-risk or safe-levels approach. The administrator of the Environmental Protection Agency would be directed to set a particular environmental standard at a level that would ensure against any adverse health (or other kind of) effect. . . . This approach is not uncommon. And on its face, it certainly seems reasonable. After all, would we want a standard to be set at a level that poses some recognizable threat to health? Surprisingly, perhaps, the answer is maybe.

Science and economics contribute to this unexpected response. Accumulated research in physiology, toxicology, and other health sciences suggests that for a number of environmental pollutants, particularly carcinogens, there may be no threshold concentrations below which exposures are safe. This implies that standards for these pollutants must be set at zero concentrations if the populace really is to be protected against all risks. Here economics intrudes in a jarring way. Simply put, it is impossible to eliminate all traces of environmental pollution without at the same time shutting down all economic activity, an outcome which neither the Congress nor the public would abide. Yet this is where the zero-risk framework often appears to lead if interpreted literally.

Having raised this disquieting possibility, let us push it further to consider another interesting case. Suppose a particular pollutant was harmful at ambient (or outdoor) levels to one very large group of people—the one-third of U.S. adults who choose to smoke cigarettes— but only this group. If the costs of reducing ambient concentrations of the contaminant were very large, might society not decide to forgo this health protection? It might well, in view of the role that the sensitive population has played in predisposing itself to environmental illness.

Here too, then, the zero-risk approach would cause problems.

Perhaps more realistically, decisions to live with some risk might be reached even if the group at risk had done nothing to create its sensitive status. At some point, the costs of additional protection might be judged by society to be too great if the added health benefits are relatively small. Painful though such decisions may be, they are the rule rather than the exception in environmental and other policy areas. The problem with the zero-risk approach is that it prevents such tradeoffs from being made.

Another approach to the how-much-protection question is a variant of the above. It is often referred to as the technology-based approach. Under this framework, the only pollution permitted is that remaining after sources have installed "best available" or other state-of-the-art control technology. The underlying idea is simply that all technologically feasible pollution control measures will be required, and only after that will residual risks be accepted. This approach is somewhat weaker than a strict zero-risk approach since it admits the possibility of some risks. But in its strictest form, it is uncompromising with respect to trading off cost savings for less strict pollution control. For this reason, it appeals to many.

In its application, however, the technology-based approach faces several drawbacks. First, there is no unambiguously "best" technology—emissions can always be reduced further for additional control expenditures. In the limit, of course, sources could be closed down entirely—an ultimate, perhaps draconian, form of best technology. Moreover, implicit in the technology-based approach is the assumption that the control that results must be worth the cost. This might well depend upon the particulars. For instance, very strict control may be deemed essential for polluters in densely populated areas but much less important for those in remote, unpopulated regions. Yet the uniform technological approach has the liability of pre-

cluding the tradeoffs necessary to decide such questions. In addition, the technology-based approach suffers in a dynamic setting because it locks sources into specific means of control. It is unlikely that a firm required to meet this year's best technology will be told to scrap that equipment if next year's is even better. Thus this approach may deprive us of the opportunity to reduce the costs and increase the efficiency of pollution control over time.

The final framework for standard-setting discussed here formalizes the notion of balancing and incorporates it into environmental law. The relevant statutory language might direct the administrator of the EPA to set standards to protect health and other values while at the same time taking account of the costs and other adverse consequences of the regulations. The advantage of this approach is that it makes possible, indeed mandatory, the kinds of tradeoffs we have suggested might be desirable. On the other hand, it also forces the administrator to make very difficult decisions. Moreover, if all favorable and unfavorable effects are supposed to be expressed in dollars, so that precise benefit-cost ratios are required, this approach would impose a burden that economic analysis is not prepared to bear. In spite of the recent progress in valuing environmental benefits and costs,[10] the science is still far short of being able to make such comparisons in a precise way. For this reason, the balancing approach is best left in a qualitative or judgmental form.

At this point, some might reasonably chafe at the balancing framework. Why compromise citizens' health or welfare so that corporate or other polluters might remain economically healthy? This very natural question deserves a straightforward answer, one which proceeds along the following lines. While it would be nice if there were, there are no disembodied corporate entities into whose deep pockets we can reach for pollution control spending without at the same time imposing losses on ourselves or our fellow citizens. This is because corporations are merely legal creations, the financial returns to which all accrue to individuals in one capacity or another. Thus if corporations spend more for pollution control, these costs may be passed on to others in the form of higher product prices.[11] Alternatively, if costs cannot be shifted to consumers, then stockholders, laborers, or the management of the corporations will suffer reduced earnings.

Thus far the tradeoff may still seem appealing since it is expressed in terms of dollars versus health. However, the reduced incomes of consumers, stockholders, or employees will eventually mean less spending on goods and services they value. At this point, then, the tradeoff becomes more stark. Pollution control spending can sometimes protect health, but at an eventual cost to society of forgone health, education, shelter, or other valued things.[12] The real trick in environmental policy—or any other area of government intervention—is to ensure that the value of the resulting output is greater than that which must be sacrificed. And this sacrifice will take place regardless of the framework for standard-setting that is being employed. In the economists' view of things, the balancing approach is desirable not only because it is a natural way to make decisions, but also because it brings out in the open the terms of trade, so to speak. If we dislike the compromises being made by our regulatory officials, we can demand their removal.

Once environmental standards (or ambient standards, as they are sometimes called) have been selected, the next step is deciding on the means of attainment. In other words, how do we control the sources of pollution so that the environmental goals are met? While there are other possibilities, the two most common approaches are via direct, centralized regulation, or through an incentive-based, decentralized system.[13] Under the first, individual polluters are assigned specific emissions reductions; under the latter, they are given more latitude.

Under the centralized approach, the regulating authority has considerable discretion in apportioning the emission reductions required to meet the ambient standard. Only when there is but one source of pollution is it clear where emissions must be reduced.[14] More typically, there are multiple sources; in such cases the authority has to decide how much each source must curtail its offending activities. There are several ways this decision can be made.

If aggregate emissions must be reduced by 25 percent to meet the environmental standard, for example, each source could be required to cut back its own emissions by 25 percent. This equiproportional rule has the very attractive feature of *appearing* fair. Why only the appearance of fairness? Because of the very great diversity of sources for many environmental contaminants, ranging from neighborhood dry-cleaners or car-repair shops to complex steel mills or large chemical plants. The differing characteristics and technological circumstances of these sources mean that one source may be able to reduce its emissions by 25 percent quite inexpensively, perhaps by switching to a less polluting fuel or altering slightly its manufacturing technique. Yet another source might find that it can meet its 25 percent reduction only through the installation of expensive control technology. Thus a requirement for equal-percentage reductions may mean very unequal financial burdens.

Under another approach, emission reductions might be apportioned on the basis of affordability—that is, the largest cutbacks might be required of those in the best financial shape. This, too, has some obvious appeal. Indeed, under our present individual income tax system, we ask those in higher income brackets to pay a higher percentage of their income in taxes, and this would seem to extend that principle to pollution control.

On closer inspection, however, assigning

emission reductions on the basis of ability to pay also has serious drawbacks. First, it would penalize successful, well-managed firms and reward laggards that may well be largely responsible for their own poor financial state. In this sense, then, the approach gives exactly the wrong set of signals to firms and slows the replacement of failing enterprises with newer, more efficient ones. Second, there may be no relation whatsoever between a source's emissions and its financial condition. Thus a very profitable firm may have very low emissions (particularly if it has continually modernized) but under this approach would still be forced to spend heavily on further emission reductions; meanwhile, a smoke-belching firm in perilous financial condition would be let off lightly. For these reasons, an affordability criterion is less attractive than it may at first appear.

Finally, the regulatory authority could try to apportion emission reductions among sources in such a way that the required aggregate reduction was accomplished at the least total cost to society. In other words, the central regulator could look across all sources and ask where the first ton of emissions might be reduced most inexpensively, then require it to be removed there. The second ton of emissions reductions would then be assigned, again to the source that could accomplish it most cheaply. And so on until the aggregate emissions goal had been met.

This approach has the advantage of ensuring that society (through the affected sources) gives up as little as possible to get the emission reductions. But it raises the possibility of another sort of inequity. Suppose that one source, among a large number of polluters in a particular area, was always the lowest-cost abater? This is unlikely to be the case in reality, but it might hold true in certain circumstances. It would hardly seem fair to place the entire burden of emissions control on that source merely because it could reduce pollution more inexpensively

than the other sources. Thus, although the cost-minimization approach has some obvious appeal, it is not ideal.

Decentralized approaches, on the other hand, do address certain of these problems, although they present difficulties of their own. Perhaps the best-known of the decentralized approaches is the effluent charge or pollution tax.[15] Under this scheme, the regulatory authority imposes a tax or fee on each unit of the environmental contaminant discharged. In its purest form, the charge would be set to reflect the damage done by each unit of emissions. Rather than tell each firm how much to reduce emissions, the authority would leave it to the firm to respond to the charge however the firm best sees fit. Some sources would reduce their emissions immediately—those will be the ones that can do so at unit costs less than the amount of the charge. By doing so, they save the difference between their per-unit cost of control and the per-unit charge. Other sources will find it economical to continue discharging—they will be the ones finding it cheaper to pay the tax than to incur the required control costs.

Such an approach has several advantages. First, it ensures that the sources that do elect to take control measures are those with the lowest control costs. In other words, it mimics the least-cost approach under command-and-control, but does so without requiring the central authority to specify emission reductions for each and every source. Second, and perhaps more important, it provides a continuing incentive for firms to reduce their costs of pollution control. Since they must continue to pay the per-unit charge, it continues to be economical for them to find ways to reduce emissions for less than that charge. Third, this system requires something from all sources— either they must reduce pollution to escape the charge, or they must continue to pay the charge. No one gets off scot-free.

As might be expected, the effluent-charge

route has shortcomings, which at least some economists have been slow to recognize or acknowledge.[16] For one thing, it is no picnic to determine the damage done by each unit of pollution; in practice this could only be approximated at best. Some have suggested that the difficulty of apportioning damage is such a liability of the charge approach that a modified version of the approach should be used.[17] Under this variant, the central authority would first select the desired level of environmental quality and would then set the charge at a level sufficient to induce the emissions control that would achieve it. Yet even such a variant would require some trial and error, and the uncertainty this might create could make firms reluctant to come to their initial emissions control decisions. The effluent-charge route also presents one serious political problem. Under this approach, the emissions that sources are free to discharge under the current permit system would be subject to the charge. Thus many sources that presently complain about over-regulation would have a new complaint: a major effluent-tax liability.

A second variant of the incentive-based approach involves marketable pollution "rights" or permits. This approach could work in one of two basic ways. Under one version, the central authority would first decide how much total pollution was consistent with the predetermined environmental goal. It would then print up individual discharge permits, the total quantity of which added up to the maximum amount permitted. No one without a permit would be allowed to discharge the regulated pollutants. The permits could be allocated among sources in one of several ways. First, a sale might be held at which all of the permits were auctioned off to the highest bidders. Alternatively, the permits could be distributed free of charge on some predetermined (or even random) basis—perhaps on the basis of historical levels of pollution. Either

way, the permits would be marketable anytime after the initial distribution.

The incentive effect under a system of marketable permits is not unlike that of the effluent charge discussed above. Those sources that currently pollute but which could reduce pollution for less than the cost of a permit would take control measures. Those sources finding it very expensive to reduce pollution would buy discharge permits instead. Thus, as if guided by the same invisible hand, the emission reductions would take place at the low-cost sources, thereby minimizing the costs associated with a given reduction in emissions. Similarly, those firms buying permits would have a continuing incentive to reduce their costs of pollution control—as soon as they could do so, they could stop buying permits and save themselves money in the process.

The permit approach has one major advantage when compared to the effluent charge: the permit approach looks more like the existing system, which involves permits issued by the EPA or state environmental authorities, than does the latter. This may sound strange, but radical change is almost always more difficult to accommodate than gradual change. Since the marketable permit system is capable of accomplishing most of the same things as the effluent charge, why not advance it if it will be easier to put in place? This logic appears to have prevailed, and the inroads made by incentive-based approaches in environmental policy over the last ten years have featured permits.

Marketable permits are not without shortcomings, of course. One concern has to do with the possibility that certain sources might buy up all the permits as an anti-competitive tactic. While this ought to be rectifiable through governmental antitrust actions, in practice such actions might take time. Another question concerns the initial distribution of permits before the development of secondary markets. If all the permits are auctioned off, this approach would fall prey to the small political problems that arise under a charge approach—some sources would have to pay for emissions they are granted free under the existing system. Thus political problems could become formidable. If the initial permits are to be distributed free of charge, how should they be allocated? On the basis of previous emissions? To all citizens equally? To environmental and industry groups? This too is a potentially thorny problem, although not an insurmountable one.

A fifth and final question that arises in environmental policy is often overlooked: How do we monitor for compliance with the standards we set, and take enforcement actions against those in violation? . . . Suffice it to say now that the choice of both environmental and individual sources discharge standards ought to be (but often is not) influenced by the realities of monitoring and enforcement. Key issues involve the extent of reliance on financial penalties for noncompliance, the comparative strengths and weaknesses of civil as opposed to criminal penalties, and the choice of a monitoring strategy in a world of limited resources. All these issues and more must be addressed in designing sensible environmental policies.

U.S. ENVIRONMENTAL POLICY: A HYBRID APPROACH

As one might suspect, the fundamental questions raised above have been answered in an eclectic and hybrid way as environmental policy has evolved in the United States. With respect to the decision on intervention, federal, state, and local governments have all decided to intervene. Environmental statutes exist at all three levels—in fact, special districts have been formed in many areas around environmental problems. Thus long ago the decision was made not to entrust environmental problems and disputes solely to markets, to the courts, or to mediation services.

This observation also suggests the level at which intervention has taken place—at every level. Even federal environmental laws reserve important functions for state and local governments. For instance, under the Clean Air and Clean Water acts, the federal government (as embodied in the EPA) sets important ambient environmental and source discharge standards, yet the monitoring and enforcement of these standards is left largely to the states and localities. In fact, some ambient and source discharge standards are themselves reserved for lower levels of government in certain important cases. In other words, even federal laws are "federalist" in nature.

As to the choice of goals (How safe should we be?), U.S. environmental laws embody a range of approaches. A number of the most important environmental laws, or parts thereof, reflect the zero-risk (or threshold) philosophy. For instance, the Clean Air Act directs that ambient standards for common air pollutants be set at levels that provide an "adequate margin of safety" against adverse health effects, while standards for the so-called hazardous air pollutants are to provide an "ample margin of safety." Under the Clean Water Act, ambient water quality standards—which are left to the states rather than the federal government to establish—are also to include a margin of safety for the protection of aquatic life.

Other environmental standards are based on the technological approach to goal-setting. This is true of the Clean Air and Clean Water acts, the Resource Conservation and Recovery Act, and the Safe Drinking Water Act. . . . The notion of best-available technology—along with its cousins "best-conventional" and "reasonably available" technology and "lowest-achievable emissions," as well as others—plays a big role in U.S. environmental policy, even in those statutes which in other places embrace the zero-risk goal.

Even the balancing framework favored by economists is alive and well in environmental policy. For although balancing appears to be prohibited under certain sections of the Clean Air and Clean Water acts, it is *mandated* under the most important parts of the Toxic Substances Control Act and the basic pesticide law, the Federal Insecticide, Fungicide, and Rodenticide Act. One is tempted to throw up one's hands and say, You figure it out! . . .

In one important respect, the environmental laws have been rather uniform. When it comes to the means of pursuing environmental goals, the centralized or command-and-control approach has been given precedence over incentive-based approaches. Congress has rather consistently written regulations directing the EPA to establish emissions standards (with the help of states and localities) and to issue and enforce permits specifying those standards. However, it is certain that a variety of factors have influenced the emission reductions the Environmental Protection Agency has required. While the agency often claims to have pursued a least-cost strategy, the uniform rollback and ability-to-pay criteria have clearly dominated in apportioning emission cutbacks.

The effluent charge approach has never really gotten off the ground in U.S. environmental policy, although a tax on emissions of sulfur into the air was proposed by the Nixon administration in the EPA's first year and once again in 1988. Recently, however, the standards-and-permits approach to air pollution control has evolved in the direction of marketable permits, and there is talk of applying this approach more widely in air pollution control as well as in other regulatory programs. Needless to say, this is an important development. . . .

Before concluding this chapter, some mention should be made of several generic problems

that have arisen in the hybrid U.S. environmental policy since 1970. These problems have nothing to do with the well-known difficulties that arose at the Environmental Protection Agency between 1981 and early 1983;[18] rather, they have to do with the fundamental approach that Congress has taken in environmental regulation. . . .

These problems are of four sorts.[19] The first has to do with the tremendous complexity of our environmental laws and their penchant for promising a very great deal in a very short time. For instance, the clean air and clean water laws promise "safe" air and water quality, call for the establishment of literally tens of thousands of discharge standards, mandate the creation of comprehensive monitoring networks, and impose numerous other important tasks on the administrator of the EPA. Yet the laws allotted just 180 days for completion of many of these responsibilities. Today, more than seventeen years after passage of the laws, many of those assignments have yet to be carried out.

Similarly, the Toxic Substances Control Act calls for the promulgation of separate testing rules for each new chemical. Yet although such chemicals come on the market at the rate of 1,000 per year, the EPA has issued testing rules for only a few substances. Of the more than 50,000 existing chemicals in commerce, only a small fraction have been tested for carcinogenicity or other harmful effects. Each of the environmental laws provides examples like this where Congress either misunderstood the time required to issue careful regulations, or disregarded it in the rush to get legislation on the books. The EPA has tried to run faster and faster since its creation, but has fallen farther and farther behind because of its impossible burden and an occasional lack of will.

Problems of the second sort have to do with the spotty compliance with those standards that have been issued, and our poor ability to know which standards are being violated and which sources are responsible. The reason for these problems are two, it would appear. First, monitoring both ambient environmental quality and the emissions from individual sources is much more complicated and expensive than one would imagine. Monitoring is not a straightforward matter, as might be supposed from reading the laws. Second, monitoring and enforcement have always been poor stepsisters in the eyes of Congress. Apparently it is more fashionable to write new laws and call attention to problems with existing laws than it is to engage in the dirty work of fashioning an enforceable and scientifically meaningful set of standards. Thus enforcement programs have always suffered financially at the expense of new and emerging regulatory programs.

The third sort of generic problem concerns the frequent emphasis in environmental statutes on absolutist goals. Waters are to be "fishable and swimmable" as one step toward a world of "zero discharges" into rivers, lakes, and the oceans. Conventional and hazardous air pollutants are to be at "safe" levels, as are drinking water contaminants. Such an approach has obvious political appeal—it is comforting to tell voters that they will be safe from all environmental threats. But that will simply not be the case unless standards are to be set at zero, an impossibility for most pollutants. Thus, although it is surely done, the balancing of environmental versus other important goals, economic and otherwise, is done implicitly. This has resulted in setting some standards at levels that appear to be hard to justify on any rational basis.

Finally, and perhaps inevitably, environmental statutes have become contaminated by redistributive goals which often work against the environmental programs in which they are nested—the fourth sort of problem. For example, newly built electric power plants are forbidden to reduce sulfur dioxide emissions by switching from high-sulfur to low-sulfur coal in

order to protect the jobs of a small number of high-sulfur coal miners. This prohibition exists in spite of the tremendous cost savings that might be reaped if fuel-switching were permitted. Similarly, federal subsidies for the construction of sewage treatment plants have been continued even though the plants seem to have had a questionable impact on water quality in many areas, and although the federal subsidy has crowded out state and local spending for these same plants. Apparently, the pork-barrel aspects of the program have proved too attractive to eliminate. Water pollution from farms and other non-point sources has been overlooked altogether because of the political power of the parties that would be affected by tighter controls. Some evidence also suggests that environmental regulations have been structured to protect declining regions of the country from the effects of further economic growth in faster-growing sunbelt states. While all these contortions of environmental policy are understandable, they also stand in the way of an effective and less costly approach to environmental protection. As such, they deserve to be starkly highlighted.

Notes

1. Exceptions were the creation of the Federal Aviation Administration, the Federal Highway Administration, and the Federal Railroad Administration to oversee safety in the respective industries.

2. See George C. Eads and Michael Fix, *Relief or Reform? Reagan's Regulatory Dilemma* (Washington, D.C., Urban Institute Press, 1984) pp. 12–15.

3. A natural monopoly is said to exist when the per-unit cost of producing a good or service continues to fall with increases in output. In such a case, it is argued, consumers will enjoy the lowest prices if one firm serves the whole market rather than sharing it with two or more competitors, as long as the single provider is regulated so as not to abuse its monopoly position. Natural monopolies are thought to arise most often when the fixed costs of doing business are a large proportion of total costs. The traditional examples are local

telephone service, electricity distribution, and natural gas pipelines.

4. See Paul R. Portney, "The Macroeconomic Impacts of Federal Environmental Regulation," *Natural Resources Journal* vol. 21 (July 1981) pp. 459–488.

5. If regulation is the barrier to entry and discouragement to new growth that some maintain it is, and if these effects could be quantified, this conclusion could change.

6. In the real world, in fact, property rights appear to be shared. Even under existing regulation, firms are generally permitted to emit at least some pollution without being held responsible for the damage it may cause. In addition, tax breaks are provided for some investments in pollution control equipment. In effect, this shifts some of the costs of pollution control to the taxpayer, as would be the case if the property right were initially vested in the polluter.

7. See Charles Wolf, Jr., *Markets or Government* (Cambridge, Mass., MIT Press, 1988).

8. While it is probably inappropriate in the case of environmental problems, there is a third alternative to regulation in cases involving occupational hazards or dangerous consumer products. There the government could limit its role to the provision of information about the risks inherent in different jobs and/or products. Workers and consumers could then hold out for higher wages for risky jobs (as they do now) or pay low prices for risky products. Employers or producers would then have to decide whether it was in their interest to continue to pay higher wages or receive lower prices rather than reduce the hazards. In this way, too, market forces would work toward optimal riskiness. It should be noted, of course, that this model would be successful only if workers and consumers were fully informed about such risks and only if they had a range of jobs and products from which to choose.

9. See Lester B. Lave, *The Strategy of Social Regulation* (Washington, D.C., Brookings Institution, 1981).

10. See A. Myrick Freeman III, *The Benefits of Environmental Improvement: Theory and Practice* (Baltimore, The Johns Hopkins University Press for Resources for the Future, 1979); and Allen V. Kneese, *Measuring the Benefits of Clean Air and Water* (Washington, D.C., Resources for the Future, 1984).

11. This is the point of such regulations, in fact, since the higher prices discourage consumers from purchasing products whose production generates pollution.

12. Recently an effort was made to link spending like that necessitated by pollution controls to possible premature mortality via reductions in individuals' wealth. See Ralph L. Keeney, "Mortality Risks Induced by Economic Expenditures," working paper, University of Southern California, Systems Science Department (July 1988).

13. Other possibilities are moral suasion and direct government purchase of pollution control equipment. See William J. Baumol and Wallace E. Oates, *Economics, Environmental Policy, and the Quality of Life* (Englewood Cliffs, N.J., Prentice-Hall, 1979) pp. 217–224.

14. Even in this apparently simple case the matter is not so straightforward, because nature accounts for a share of many major pollutants. For instance, particulate matter can be blown from fields or roadways just as it can be generated by steel mills or cement plants. In such cases, the man-made share must first be assessed before required cutbacks can be determined.

15. For a comprehensive description and discussion, see Peter Bohm and Clifford S. Russell, "Comparative Analysis of Alternative Policy Instruments," in Allen V. Kneese and James L. Sweeney, eds., *Handbook of Natural Resource and Energy Economics,* vol. 1 (New York, North-Holland, 1985) pp. 395–460; see also Frederick R. Anderson, Allen V. Kneese, Phillip D. Reed, Serge Taylor, and Russell B. Stevenson, *Environmental Improvement Through Economic Incentives* (Washington, D.C., Resources for the Future, 1977).

16. For an interesting analysis of attitudes toward effluent charges, see Steven Kelman, *What Price Incentives?* (Boston, Auburn House, 1981).

17. William J. Baumol and Wallace E. Oates, "The Use of Standards and Prices for Protection of the Environment," *Swedish Journal of Economics* vol. 73 (March 1971) pp. 42–54.

18. These difficulties were quite serious, to be sure. Never before had the competence or commitment of the EPA's top management been questioned. Ultimately all but one of the agency's highest-ranking officials resigned or were fired. See Robert W. Crandall and Paul R. Portney, "Environmental Policy," in Paul R. Portney, ed., *Natural Resources and the Environment: The Reagan Approach* (Washington, D.C., Urban Institute, 1984) pp. 47–81.

19. Ibid., pp. 47–55.

7

Costs and Benefits
Frances Cairncross

Nothing so annoys environmentalists about economists as their attempt to put a price on nature's bounty. "What am I bid for one ozone layer in poor condition?" they tease. "How much is the spotted owl worth?" The idea seems ludicrous. Yet society puts prices on environmental assets all the time by deciding which policies to pursue. It is surely better to try to make sure that those prices reflect the value of the environment as accurately as possible than to pretend that they do not exist.

Most real-world decisions involve conflicts of interest. If a factory pollutes a beach, those who once swam there carry the cost. If a logging company chops down a forest, the creatures that lived in it suffer. If a view is blocked by a building, those who once enjoyed it lose, while those who rent out the building gain. In a world where money talks, the environment needs value to give it a voice.

Values are often placed on the environment almost by default. Governments implicitly judge the costs and benefits of environmental action, whether deciding to sign the Montreal Protocol on CFCs or passing laws about the permitted level of water pollution. They do implicit sums when deciding whether to run a road through a

●

Reprinted by permission of Harvard Business School Press, from *Costing the Earth: The Challenge for Governments, the Opportunities for Business* by Frances Cairncross. Boston, MA, 1992, pp. 43–62. Copyright © 1992 by the President and Fellows of Harvard College; all rights reserved.

beauty spot; so do companies when carrying out an assessment of environmental impact.

Of course, political pressures are often the way governments measure environmental benefit. Newspapers, whipped up by environmental lobbyists, clamor for action; governments publicly accept that a problem exists and announce that they will solve it, without first asking what the solution will cost, or what benefits it will bring. This may be a highly inefficient way to allocate scarce resources to protect the planet. Voters do not always get most excited about the things that do the most environmental damage.

Without putting a value on environmental gains, it is also impossible to know how far an environmental policy should go. Ought every scrap of pollution to be eliminated? Economists point out, incontrovertibly, that although the first steps in cleaning up are relatively cheap, each additional step produces smaller and smaller results. The costs of getting rid of a pollutant will rise steeply as it diminishes. Environmentalists, who tend to think in absolutes, often argue that no level of pollution is safe. Economists disagree. Some kinds of pollution, they admit, ought to be totally prevented: thus a nuclear power plant should never leave highly radioactive waste lying about, nor should factories dump cyanide in the local river. In general, though, economists think that it may be wiser to tolerate some pollution than to try to get rid of it all, whatever the cost.

MEASURING THE THREAT

Economists use two basic approaches to set values on environmental assets. One is direct; they ask people questions. The other approach is in-direct. Economists hunt for a real-world market in which to try to capture the value of environmental assets.

The questions asked in the direct approach are, at their simplest, along the lines of "What would you be willing to pay to stop the Grand Canyon from being shrouded in smog?" Some answers are shown in Table 1. Over time, such questions have become more and more refined in order, for instance, to try to stop people from naming huge sums on the sensible assumption that others will share the bill through higher taxes. Some surveys ask a set of questions once, then give interviewees a pep talk on the environmental issue at stake, and ask the questions again. Not surprisingly, such experiments prove

TABLE 1 ● A Value on Nature: Non-Use Values for Unique Natural Assets ($, mid-1980s)

Asset	Value per adult
ANIMAL SPECIES	
Whooping crane	1
Emerald shiner	4
Bottlenose dolphin	6
Bighorn sheep	7
California sea otter	7
Northern elephant seal	7
Blue whale	8
Bald eagle	11
Grizzly bear	15
NATURAL AMENITIES	
Water quality (S. Platte river basin)	4
Visibility (Grand Canyon)	22

Source: K. Samples, M. Gowen, and J. Dixon, "The Validity of the Contingent Valuation Method for Estimating Non-Use Components of Preservation Values for Unique Natural Resources," paper presented to the American Agricultural Economics Association, Reno, Nevada, July 1986.

the importance of environmental education in raising people's willingness to pay to prevent environmental damage. People name even larger values if they are given a day or two to reflect after the pep talk.

Surveys have some advantages over the second method of establishing environmental values. The use of indirect valuation captures only the market value of some environmental assets. That may not be the whole story. For example, what people spend to travel to a park gives a guide to the value they put on the experience. But travel costs say nothing about the values of those who might like to travel to a park the next year and would pay to keep that option open. Surveys capture more of the picture: what people say they would pay reflects, at least in theory, not only the market value of some environmental assets, for instance the higher price their house commands because it fronts onto an unpolluted river, but also the priceless enjoyment a person might get from fishing on that river, and the value that might be derived by another person, far away, from the comforting thought that the river was clean. Only surveys can hope to capture the most metaphysical of all the values that economists attach to the environment: those that reflect the benefit people draw from simply knowing that species or habitats continue to exist.

This kind of psychic value is important. One of the advantages of using surveys is that they are the only way to discover values put on some environmental assets by people who do not actually make use of them. People in industrial countries especially may put a value on a species or a habitat they may never see, even if they know they will never see it. They may be pleased to know that the oceans still contain whales and the Himalayas snow leopards. They may even attach value, however hazily, to the notion that these creatures will continue to exist long after they do. An indication of this is the size of voluntary contributions people are prepared to make to conservation bodies that hope to save wild species and places. The World Wildlife Fund (WWF), largest of all, receives nearly $100 million a year. Another is the effort that people in rich countries particularly will put into conservation campaigns.

Surveys have drawbacks, too. One is the large differences that regularly appear between the answer to the question "What would you be willing to pay for a 50% improvement in air quality?" and the apparently similar question "What would you accept as compensation for a 50% worsening in air quality?" When these questions were put to 2,000 people in Haifa, Israel, the answer to the first question was about $12 per household per year (1987 prices).[1] But the compensation the households wanted if air quality were to worsen was roughly four times as much. Sometimes surveys find that people simply say that nothing would be enough to compensate them for an environmental loss, implying that its value to them is infinite. Ask a "What would you pay" type question, and the numbers are always much more modest (see Table 2). One possible explanation is that people feel more strongly about losses imposed on them than about gains that they choose. The loss of something a person already "owns," like clean air, is valued more highly than the potential gain of something new, like even cleaner air. People feel that they are the owners of an endowment of environmental rights, which they are deeply unwilling to abandon.

This may be why companies trying to site a polluting plant seem to find it easier to give the local community a sense of control over the decision. But the differences between what economists dub "WTP" (willingness to pay) and "WTA" (willingness to accept) questions are interesting from another point of view. Normally, economists draw curves to show how people are willing to trade, say, apples for oranges, or money for matches. They assume that people are willing to move smoothly—"indifferently"— along these curves, trading gradually increasing

TABLE 2 ● Calculation Disparities of Models in Various Studies, Between WTP, "willingness to pay," and WTA, "willingness to accept" (year-of-study $)

Study	WTP	WTA
Hammack and Brown (1974)	247.00	1,044.00
Banford et al. (1977)	43.00	120.00
	22.00	93.00
Sinclair (1976)	35.00	100.00
Bishop and Heberlein (1979)	21.00	101.00
Brookshire et al. (1980)	43.64	68.52
	54.07	142.60
	32.00	207.07
Rowe et al. (1980)	4.75	24.47
	6.54	71.44
	3.53	46.63
	6.85	113.68
Hovis et al. (1983)	2.50	9.50
	2.75	4.50
Knetsch and Sinden (1983)	1.28	5.18

Source: Cummings et al. (1986), quoted in David Pearce and Kerry Turner, *Economics of Natural Resources and the Environment* (London: Harvester Wheatsheaf, 1990).

amounts of apples for rising numbers of oranges, or a few pennies less for a declining number of matchboxes. Some environmental economists argue that the answers to their valuation surveys suggest that this key assumption of conventional economics may be meaningless in the real world. Such curves may simply not exist. People's reactions may depend on whether they are paying to get more or being compensated to accept less.

USING THE MARKET

The indirect approach to discovering environmental values involves trying to find a real market that offers some guidance. In developing countries, where the environment is literally what most people live off, such markets are often easy to find. In richer countries, the link between environmental damage and a real market may be more tenuous. Take the property market. If two identical houses on neighboring streets sell for widely differing amounts, and the less expensive one is on the street with the noisiest traffic, it is reasonable to assume that the price difference may at least partly reflect the value people put on quiet streets. In fact, it may be hard to disentangle environmental nuisance from many other factors. A study by economists at Salford University of 3,500 houses in Stockport, England, found that those in the areas most affected by noise from Manchester Airport were on average 6% less expensive than others; but most of this price difference could be explained by other characteristics of the neighborhood and the houses.[2] Even if they had not been under the flight path, the houses would still have been less expensive.

Sometimes environmental damage has measurable costs. When air pollution corrodes stone, the cost of repairs can be reckoned. That is one way to get at the value of cleaner air. When polluted water makes people ill, economists may try to put a value on the loss of health.

In third world countries, it is often much easier to use these indirect measurement techniques. Natural resources have values that can be readily estimated. The products of wild nature are harvested commercially. Examples range from animal skins, ivory, fish, and timber to resins, rattans, mushrooms, and game. The cash value of wild products is often the only way in which biological resources appear in national income accounts. In some countries their impact on the economy may be considerable. This is especially true for countries with forests: timber from wild forests has been Indonesia's second largest source of foreign exchange, and teak is now providing Burma with hard currency. Other kinds of forest products may also be important exports: two-thirds of India's forestry exports in the early 1980s came from products other than timber. That might be true for other forested countries, if statistics were available, but figures on the value of forest products other than timber are rarely collated.

Local people may use wild nature as an important source of food that may well pass through no market and so not appear in national accounts.[3] Without wild protein, firewood, medicines, and building materials, though, people would be poorer; and it is possible to calculate with some precision just how much poorer they would be. For example, one study by the New York Botanical Gardens of the net present value of fruit, latex, and timber from a patch of Amazon rain forest looked at the price of these products in local markets.[4] Using those values, it reckoned that a hectare of forest was worth $9,000 (but only $3,000 if destroyed and used for cow pasture). The timber alone was worth only 10% of the total, and if cutting down a tree for timber killed latex or fruit trees, the gain from logging was wiped out.

Forests are a source of food, fuel, and furniture for the world's 500 million forest dwellers. In many African countries, wild food is an important part of diet, especially for the poor. In Ghana, for example, three-quarters of the population depends largely on wild foods such as fish, caterpillars, maggots, and snails. In Zaire, three-quarters of the animal protein that people eat comes from wild sources.

Amazonia is not the only place where the value of products harvested from the wild exceeds the value of the same land when used for unfamiliar domesticated animals. In developed countries the value of wild food may be tiny compared with the value of the industries that grow up around hunting and fishing. The market value of the hooked salmon or shot pheasant is a fraction of the amount human predators frequently pay to catch them. Robert Scott, a rancher from western Montana, dreams of turning the cattle off the Montana great plains, where they have grazed for not much more than a century, and replacing them with species that preceded them. He yearns to persuade the owners of 12 million acres, on which live 3,000 people and 350,000 cattle, to pool their land, which now brings in a net agricultural income of less than zero (offset by the government subsidies on which people live). Fences would fall, cattle would go, and in their place would be wandering bison, elk, antelope, bighorn sheep, and hunters. The revenue from hunting fees, guiding, accommodation, and butchering would bring in perhaps $60 million. Conservationists would have a wilderness, hunters a paradise, and landowners a genuine income.

Wildlife tourism is another way in which protected nature can earn a cash return. Tourism, mainly to see wild animals, is Kenya's biggest foreign-exchange earner. One estimate gives each lion in Amboseli National Park a value of $27,000 a year in visitor pulling-power. The park's net earnings, mainly from tourism, run at about $40 per hectare per year, a net profit 50 times as high as the most optimistic projection for agricultural use.

Some of the functions of wild nature have enormous value in making possible other kinds of economic activity, but are nonetheless hard to quantify. Wild trees may pollinate domestic ones; wild birds may keep down pests. If either go, the cost will be lost crops or money spent on developing man-made alternatives. One example is the brazil nut, which needs a particular species of bee to pollinate it, and a forest-dwelling rodent called the agouti to open its hard shell and allow the tree to seed itself. As the bee needs pollen from a forest orchid to mate, and the orchids need insects or hummingbirds to pollinate them in turn, the continued production of brazil nuts needs enough forest to accommodate bees, insects, hummingbirds, orchids, and agoutis. Other examples are marshes and wetlands, rich homes for wildlife, which often play an important role in purifying water supplies or preventing floods. One study estimated that retaining a swamp outside Boston, Massachusetts, saved $17 million in flood protection alone.[5] In other countries, coastal mangroves and coral reefs provide barriers against the fury of the sea and at the same time sustain valuable fisheries.

The functions performed by trees are even more profuse and valuable. Their roots stabilize soil and regulate the run-off of rainfall. Streams in forested areas continue to flow in dry weather and are less likely to flood when storms come. Their enormous value in preventing soil erosion has been recognized in Venezuela, where the government recently tripled the size of Canaima National Park, which safeguards a watershed that feeds some of the country's most important hydroelectric facilities. In Honduras the 7,500-hectare La Tigra National Park guards more than 40% of the water supply for Tegucigalpa, the country's capital. Rain forest has an even more important economic function, that of feeding rainfall as well as absorbing it. Cut down the trees and nearby regions suffer higher temperatures and more drought. The destruction of Africa's rain forests may well have caused the Sahara to advance, fatally impoverishing millions; destroy the Amazon, and large tracts of central and northern Brazil may suffer the same fate.

Most of the uses for wild nature accrue locally. A price can be put on them without too much ingenuity. But there are other, less quantifiable ways in which natural resources may have considerable value to the human race as a whole, but where it is difficult to turn that value into earnings for the country that has to preserve species.

Those would-be tourists who will never go to Amboseli reward television companies, not Kenyans, when they watch nature programs. Many medicines on the shelves of Western chemists have been developed from plants or (more rarely) animals and bugs. In the mid-1980s, the value of prescription and over-the-counter, plant-based drugs in OECD countries was put at about $43 billion. Tropical species are especially useful because they are often chock-a-block with poisons that scare off predators. Those poisons—like curare, used by Brazil's Yanomani Indians to tip their arrows, and by doctors as a muscle relaxant—may be the active ingredient in modern drugs. But drug companies have rarely put money into drug research in developing countries.

Wild species also play an essential role in restoring or replacing domesticated ones. The tiny group of domesticated species that account for most foods on supermarket shelves need to be able to draw on the gene pool of their wild relatives to maintain or increase yields. Ever since 1845, when potato blight wiped out the Irish potato crop, people have been aware that the genetic uniformity of cultivated plants makes them highly susceptible to disease and pests. Stripe rust in American wheat was defeated in the 1960s with germ plasma from a wild wheat found in Turkey.

Russ Mittermeier, a former official of the World Wildlife Fund in Washington, DC, used to thrill American audiences by pointing out that "Democracy in Latin America may depend on conservation in Madagascar. If rust hits the coffee crop, the continent could lose its main source of income. There are 50 species of wild coffee, many of them caffeine-free, in the rain forests of eastern Madagascar." His audiences particularly liked the bit about "caffeine-free." Some primitive farmers recognize the importance of genetic diversity for agriculture by planting several varieties of a crop in the same field. Modern farming uses plant breeding for the same effect. Most domesticated plants and animals come from countries other than those in which they are most used. In America, for example, at least nine out of ten commercially grown species are not native. They rely on wild relatives growing in other countries for periodic reinforcement. Only a small proportion of the wild relatives of many commercial crops have been collected and stored in seed banks (see Table 3).

Little-known plants, fish, and animals sometimes turn out to be valuable foods. In Panama and Costa Rica attempts are being made to domesticate the endangered but edible green iguana. Quinua, once a staple grain of the Incas, turns out to be one of the world's most productive sources of plant protein. Teosinte nearly became extinct. That is the name local people gave

TABLE 3 ● Wild Species in the Bank

Crop	Wild species held in all seed banks as % total holdings	Estimated % wild species still to be collected
CEREALS		
Rice	2	70
Wheat	10	20–25
Sorghum	0.5	9
Pearl millet	10	50
Barley	5	0–10
Corn (maize)	5	50
Minor millets	0.5	90
ROOT CROPS		
Potato	40	30
Cassava	2	80
Sweet potato	10	40
LEGUMES		
Beans	1.2	50
Chickpea	0.5	50
Cowpea	0.5	70
Groundnut	6.0	30
Pigeonpea	0.5	40

Source: International Board for Plant Genetic Resources, 1988 estimates.

to a species of maize found in 1979 on a small hillside in Mexico that was being cleared. Unlike other known species of maize, it was a perennial, and is now being used to develop a perennial hybrid for commercial cultivation.

But however valuable teosinte may turn out to be for commercial agriculture (and one study hazarded a figure of nearly $7 billion), not a penny is likely to go back to the owner of the Mexican hillside. A recurrent problem with all these returns on biological diversity is the virtual impossibility of turning them into cash for the people who might see it as an incentive to continue conserving. In the past the royalties on medicines made from useful medicinal plants have accrued to drug companies, not the Yanomani. Several Western schools of botany—including the New York Botanical Gardens and the Royal Botanic Gardens at Kew—now insist, before they will undertake a research contract on medical applications of tropical plants, that the commissioning companies agree to pay a share of any royalties to support research by local scientists. That is a big advance. But drug companies are not likely to use for long a plant that must be collected from the wild. Supplies are likely to be too erratic. Instead, they usually either cultivate the plant nearer home (which means in the developed world) or synthesize it. Either way, the plant's native country loses income.

Of all the ways in which nature makes possible those economic activities that are more readily measurable, none is more important than its role in regulating the planet's life support system. Plants and plankton help recycle oxygen, absorb carbon dioxide, and regulate rainfall. Individual countries may make this possible by the way they preserve their natural resources; all humanity gains.

However refined the methods by which economists value the environment, politicians and businesses may take more notice of cash payments than the value people say they derive from this or that aspect of environmentalism. One of the great dilemmas of the coming years will be to find ways of rewarding poor countries for their contribution to the public good. There may be no mechanism that enables those who want to protect a resource to compensate those who want to destroy it.

A PREMIUM FOR INSURANCE

One complication in setting environmental benefit against the costs of taking action is the difficulty of proving what will happen if nothing is done. Because environmental science is an uncertain art, most policy decisions involve a weighting for risk. If sulphur dioxide from coal-burning power stations were undoubtedly the cause of acid rain, then the decision to install scrubbers would be a (relatively) simple matter of balancing their cost against the value people place on forests. But there are probably several causes, including nitrogen oxides from car exhausts, and disentangling the main culprit will take time. In the meantime, governments have to decide whether to compel power stations to cut sulphur-dioxide output now or to wait for harder proof. If power stations are indeed the problem, then the sooner governments take action, the less it will cost; if they are not, then governments waste money by making electricity more expensive than gas.

The difficulty in making such decisions is compounded where the consequences of inactivity are likely to be irreversible. Clean the sewage out of a river and the fish will come back; stop homes from burning coal and air quality will improve. Many important environmental improvements of this very sort have occurred in the past few decades. But once the rhino is extinct, no earthly power can reinvent it; once the Amazon forest has gone, it probably can never be replanted; once the world has warmed up, we will have to wait for the next ice age to cool it again; and once genetically engineered organisms have escaped, they may never be recaptured. The problems that most preoccupy environmentalists are precisely the irreversible sort. The stakes are highest, and often the costs of correction are highest, too.

Politicians frequently turn to scientists to help them measure environmental damage. But scientists will not necessarily agree with one another—any more than economists. Establishing scientific proof of environmental damage is much harder than, say, finding a link between a falling apple and the force of gravity or even cigarette smoking and lung cancer. Environmental damage may occur far from the original cause. Acid rain in Norway may be caused by British coal-fired power stations or by German cars. It may take place long after the original event, too late for preventive action. Nitrates in the water supply may come from spreading nitrogen fertilizers today or from ploughing grassland 20 years ago. By the time we know for sure how the greenhouse effect will warm the earth, large amounts of warming gases will already have built up in the atmosphere. The only option for politicians who want to be environmentalists may be to pick their scientists and bet voters' money on the pet view.

To deal with the problems of risk and irreversibility, some governments have adopted the "precautionary principle," the precept that it may sometimes be wise to take action before scientific knowledge is sufficiently advanced to justify it. The British government tried to spell out what that meant in its environmental policy paper of September 1990. The paragraph proved the hardest one to draft in the entire lengthy document. In the end, it set out a concept against which the government had previously fought tooth and nail:

> Where the state of our planet is at stake, the risks can be so high, and the costs of corrective action so great, that prevention is better and cheaper than cure. Where

there are significant risks of damage to the environment, the government will be prepared to take precautionary action to limit the use of potentially dangerous pollutants, even where scientific knowledge is not conclusive, if the balance of likely costs and benefits justifies it.

GAUGING BENEFIT

One reason for trying to set environmental benefits against the costs of taking action is to make sure the public realizes the price it is paying for a particular gain. Governments may often be tempted—or lobbied—to pursue policies that will bring little environmental benefit, at huge expense. This is particularly true of policies whose immediate costs fall on companies in industrial countries. Companies, after all, may lobby, but they do not vote.

One of the oddities of human behavior that has played a large part in determining environmental policy is an apparently irrational attitude toward risk. Although people in rich countries live longer than ever, they are more fearful than their ancestors were about the world about them. One reason may be nervousness about new technology. Another is mistrust of scientists, who have too often claimed that a process or substance is safe and then changed their minds. Familiar risks are less frightening than the unfamiliar; visible risks less scary than the invisible sort. People clearly feel more frightened by the remote risk of a large catastrophe than by the greater risk of an equivalent number of deaths spread out over a long period. Hence the greater fear of nuclear power stations than coal-mining fatalities, and of aircraft crashes than road accidents. People feel more frightened by risks over which they feel they have no control than by those they inflict on themselves. Hence the greater desire for regulation of pesticide use than of alcohol consumption. One study found people willing to accept risks from voluntary activities (such as skiing) roughly 1,000 times as great as those they would tolerate from involuntary hazards, such as food preservatives, that brought much the same level of benefit—as far as such different commodities could be compared.[6] Better measurement techniques bring no reassurance: on the contrary, it seems that many people find the idea of one part per billion more frightening than one part per million, on the innumerate grounds that a billion is a larger number.

Such quirks may not matter when they influence the behavior of an individual. It is a different matter when the quirks become votes and the votes become government policy, as has happened in some countries with environmental policy. Much environmental regulation, especially in the United States, is dominated by a view common in the early 1970s that the "environment" is responsible for 80% to 90% of all cancers. Since then, epidemiologists have generally become convinced that only a few human cancers are caused by exposure to contaminated air, water, or soil. Cigarettes are responsible for 30% of all avoidable cancer deaths (plus many deaths from heart disease and other causes); polluted drinking water, in developed countries, for well under 1%. The best estimates suggest that 2% to 3% of all cancers are associated with environmental pollution, and 3% to 6% with radiation. Research by the Environmental Protection Agency (EPA) suggests that up to half of all cancer deaths from environmental risks each year may be caused by one factor: exposure to indoor radon, a radioactive gas that seeps into houses through the soil. Just under a quarter may be caused by exposure to ultraviolet light as a result of the depletion of stratospheric ozone.

Research by Michael Gough of Resources for the Future suggests that, at the outside, regulation by the EPA might be able to prevent about 6,400 American cancer deaths a year.[7] If cancer risks are estimated by means of a method employed not by the EPA but by the Food and Drug Administration, the numbers are tinier still. On

that basis, the entire expensive panoply of EPA regulations might prevent a mere 1,400 of America's 485,000 cancer deaths—or fewer than 1%.

Sometimes, environmental regulations expose people to greater, not lesser, risks. This view has been repeatedly set out by Bruce Ames, a leading American cancer specialist and director of the Environmental Health Sciences Center at Berkeley, California. Environmental regulation has been based heavily on tests carried out on rats and mice. But those tests may be misleading. Of 392 chemicals tested on both rats and mice, 226 were carcinogenic in at least one test, but 96 of them—almost half—were carcinogenic in mice but not in rats or vice versa. Common sense and Ames both suggest that if rats and mice, closely related species, react so differently to different substances, then the entirely different human species may react even more differently.

Ames also argues: "Our normal diet contains many rodent carcinogens, all perfectly natural or traditional (for example, from the cooking of food)."[8] Even if a food is natural, he points out, it may still be laced with naturally occurring chemicals that are toxic, as Table 4 shows. Most plants generate natural pesticides as part of their protective mechanism. Americans, he calculates, ingest at least 10,000 times more by weight of natural pesticides than of the man-made kind. Only a few of these chemicals have been tested on rodents, and many of those have turned out to be carcinogens.

Ames is concerned less with stopping people from sprinkling their food with black pepper or eating grilled chicken, both effective ways of eating large doses of rodent-killing chemicals, than with restoring a sense of proportion to environmental policy. "The total amount of browned and burnt material eaten in a typical day is at least several hundred times more than that inhaled from severe air pollution," he protests. Sometimes, banning a product may prevent some cancers but raise the risk of others.

TABLE 4 ● Natural Cancer-Causing Pesticides Found in Food

Food	Carcinogen[a]	Parts per m
Celery (stressed)	5-and 8-methoxypsoralen	25
Parsnip (cooked)	5-and 8-methoxypsoralen	32
Honey	benzyle acetate	15
Jasmine tea	benzyle acetate	230
Apple	caffeic acid	50–200
Carrot	caffeic acid	50–200
Coffee (roasted beans)	caffeic acid	1,800
Coffee (roasted beans)	catechol	100
Mushroom (commercial)	glutamyl-p-hydrazinobenzoate	42
Orange juice	limonene	31
Black pepper	limonene	8,000
Nutmeg	safrole	3,000
Mace	safrole	10,000
Cabbage	sinigrin (allyl isothiocyanate)	35–590
Brussels sprouts	sinigrin	110–1,560
Mustard (brown)	sinigrin	16,000–72,000

[a]Cancer-causing in rodents

Source: Bruce Ames, quoted in *Financial Times,* October 9, 1990.

He cites the EPA's decision to ban EDB, the active component in the most commonly used grain fumigant in America, after a risk assessment, which concluded that, at worst, residues in grain might cause 1% of all American cancers. Yet peanut butter is a much more potent source of rodent tumors and remains unbanned. And EDB was banned without any attempt to decide whether the alternatives, such as food irradiation or more mold, might be more hazardous to humans.

Because environmentalism is fashionable and scientific proof is hard to obtain, people may readily assume that pollution causes problems when the truth may be simpler but less welcome. A striking example of this is to be found in Eastern Europe, where many attempts have been made to link people's lower life expectancy with the high levels of pollution in those countries. Life expectancy is undoubtedly lower (67 years for a male Pole at birth, compared with 74 years for a man in nearby Sweden). It has been declining. Pollution is high and rising. Some links between pollution (especially air pollution) and health clearly exist. But consider the following: 81% of Polish men and 57% of Polish women in their early thirties smoke cigarettes; cigarette smoking did not decline between the mid-1970s and mid-1980s; Polish cigarettes are probably more harmful than those smoked in the West; and cigarette smoking almost certainly compounds the respiratory harm done by air pollution. If you combine all these factors, many Poles could clearly enjoy a cheap shortcut to better health by stopping smoking.

WHEN COSTS EXCEED BENEFITS

As industrial countries become cleaner, the benefit from additional pollution control will inevitably diminish. The amount of money that governments will need to spend to achieve further improvements will increase. A review of America's policies by the EPA estimated that the cost of complying with them was already higher as a proportion of GNP than in any other country (except, perhaps, West Germany), and would rise to at least 2.6% of GNP by the end of the century.[9] Already, such policies cost one-third of the nation's spending on medical care. The bigger the cost, the more it matters that it should not be wasted.

The Clean Air Act of 1990 will add about $4 billion to $5 billion annually to the costs of controlling emissions of sulphur dioxide from America's power stations. It is not clear that the environmental benefits from these measures will justify their cost. A ten-year study by the federal government, through the National Acid Precipitation Assessment Program, found that fewer lakes were acidified than had been feared; that acid rain had virtually no effect on agricultural output and that it damaged forests mainly on mountaintops in the northeastern United States; and that it was hard to calculate harm to buildings. All these findings reduce the benefits to be expected from curbing sulphur dioxide.

In a study of benefits and costs of the Clean Air Act, Paul Portney of Resources for the Future added in something for improved visibility and for a reduction in illnesses caused by air pollution.[10] Even then, he guesses at benefits total-ing between $2 billion and $8 billion—in other words, maybe half or maybe double the cost of the controls. Measures for improving air quality through cleaning up car exhausts are included in his figures. These might, he thinks, add $19 billion to $22 billion to the annual cost of compliance by the year 2005. The main results might be better health and gains in farm output. Added together, the figures indicate that the overall environmental benefits might be $4 billion to $12 billion a year. Controls for reducing toxic air pollutants from industrial plants will cost from $6 billion to $12 billion a year. At the outside, such controls might prevent 500 cases of cancer a year.

Trying to put a value on a human life is always difficult. But if each of those 500 cases were to result in death, the best techniques for valuing life would suggest the total cost might come to $1.5 billion. Adding all three measures together, Portney concludes that the United States may be committing itself to spending an extra $29 billion to $39 billion a year (or $300 to $400 for every household) to gain benefits worth, perhaps, about $14 billion. Why are people willing to accept that? One possibility is that they simply do not realize what the costs are. One of the beauties of regulation, from a politician's point of view, is that its true costs are largely buried; this is even more the case if the regulation falls on companies in the first instance rather than on individuals. Another possible explanation is that people are prepared to pay an extraordinarily high price for each cancer death avoided.

William Reilly, [former] EPA administrator, has called for more public debate on environmental priorities. These are mainly imposed on him by Congress, which expects the EPA to devote more than a third of its budget to cleaning up hazardous waste dumps. Yet two scientific reports have told the EPA that such sites should have lower priority than other environmental problems, including threats to wildlife habitats, which voters seem to care less about.[11]

How to change public perceptions of environmental risk? Better education is essential. People have to understand that some environmental goals must come before others. Public education may help; better mathematics teaching certainly would. In the meantime, companies find it impossible to talk sensibly to the public about the concept of "acceptable risk": any cancer risk is unacceptable.

The people with the greatest power to reassure or to disturb are environmental lobbyists. They should think carefully about environmental costs and benefits before demanding regulatory change. Irrational the public may be, but only up to a point. If people discover that enormous costs have been imposed on them to achieve environmental goals that have little value, they may revolt against the pursuit of goals that really are worthwhile. To win on toxic waste and lose on global warming would be a hollow victory for environmentalism.

Notes

1. Quoted in Per-Olav Johansson, "Valuing Environmental Damage," *Oxford Review of Economic Policy,* vol. 6, no. 1 (Spring 1990), p. 46.

2. G. Pennington, N. Topham, and R. Ward, "Aircraft Noise and Residential Property Values," *Journal of Transport Economics and Policy,* vol. xxiv, no. 1 (1990), pp. 49–60.

3. This chapter draws on Jeffrey A. McNeely, *Economists and Biological Diversity, Developing Incentives to Conserve Natural Resources* (Gland, Switzerland: International Union for the Conservation of Nature, 1988).

4. C. M. Peters, A. H. Gentry, and R. Mendelsohn, "Valuation of an Amazonian Rain Forest," *Nature,* vol. 339 (June 29, 1989).

5. David Pearce and Kerry Turner, *Economics of Natural Resources and the Environment* (London: Harvester Wheatsheaf, 1990).

6. C. Starr, *Science,* vol. 165, no. 1232 (1969), quoted by Paul Slovic, "Perceptions of Risk," *Science,* vol. 236 (April 17, 1987), pp. 280–285.

7. Michael Gough, "How Much Cancer Can EPA Regulate Anyway?" *Risk Analysis,* vol. 10, no. 1 (1990), pp. 1–6.

8. Bruce Ames, Renae Magaw, and Lois Swirsky Gold, "Ranking Possible Carcinogenic Hazards," *Science,* vol. 236 (April 17, 1987), pp. 271–280.

9. Environmental Protection Agency, "Environmental Investments: The Cost of a Clean Environment" (Washington, DC, December 1990).

10. P. R. Portney, "Economics and the Clean Air Act," *Journal of Environmental Protection,* vol. 4 (1990), pp. 173–178.

11. Environmental Protection Agency, "Unfinished Business: A Comparative Assessment of Environmental Problems" (Washington, DC: Office of Policy, Planning and Evaluation, February 1987); and Environmental Protection Agency, *Reducing Risk: Setting Priorities and Strategies for Environmental Protection* (Washington, DC: Science Advisory Board, SAB-EC-90-021, September 1990).

8

Discounting the Future: Economics and Ethics
Timothy J. Brennan

How much do we care about people whose lives won't begin until long after our own have ended? How much *should* we care about them? These questions come up when we contemplate environmental projects that benefit people who are separated by many years or even by generations from those who pay the costs. Whether the interests of future generations will be at all significant in determining how much we should limit carbon emissions, preserve the ozone layer, or protect endangered species depends on whether a dollar's worth of future benefits is worth less than a dollar's worth of present costs—what economists mean by *discounting*.

Much controversy surrounds the practice of discounting. Divisive caricatures of the discounting wars pit economists, who allegedly view the environment as just another capital asset, against ethicists, who look out for the interests of people born in the future, and environmentalists, who advocate the inherent, noneconomic values in sustaining nature. In reality, discounting battles rage even among economists. Two leading experts on the economics of public projects, William Nordhaus of Yale University and Joseph Stiglitz of the president's Council of Economic Advisers, disagree over the appropriate way to discount the future costs and benefits of climate change.

●

Reprinted with permission from *Resources,* Summer, 1995, published by Resources for the Future, Washington, D.C.

When an issue has defied resolution for so long, perhaps the difficulty is a misunderstanding of the fundamental questions. Indeed, the difficulty may be that *all* the seemingly contrary positions on discounting have some validity. One cannot hope to resolve discounting debates among economists or to allay the intensifying criticisms of discounting from those outside economics, but reflecting on the central arguments and illuminating the relationships between their economic and ethical sides may add a little light to the heat.

WHAT IS DISCOUNTING?

One way to understand how discounting works is to compare it with the compounding of interest on savings. Most people are familiar with the way compound interest increases the value of one's savings over time, in an accelerating way. For example, $100 invested today at 6 percent interest will be worth $106 in a year. Because the 6 percent interest will be earned on not just the initial $100 but the added $6 as well, the gains in the second year will be $6.36. Over time, these compounding gains become substantial. At 6 percent interest, the $100 investment will be worth about $200 in twelve years, $400 in twenty-four years, and $800 in thirty-six years. It will be worth around $3,300 in sixty years and almost $34,000 in a hundred years. A penny saved is more than a penny earned; after a century, the penny becomes $3.40. In 1626,

Dutch explorers bought Manhattan for a mere $24; if that sum had been invested at just over 6 percent per year, it would have yielded more than $40 billion in 1990—about the total income generated in Manhattan that year.

Discounting operates in the opposite way. While compounding measures how much present-day investments will be worth in the future, discounting measures how much future benefits are worth today. To figure out this discounted present value, we must first choose a discount rate to transform benefits a year from now into benefits today. If we choose the same discounting rate as the interest rate in the above example of compounding, $106 a year from now would be equal in value to $100 today. Discounting the benefits of a project that generates $200 in twelve years by a discount rate of 6 percent per year would tell us that those benefits are worth $100 today.

To economists, this is the same as saying that $100 invested at an interest rate of 6 percent will generate $200 in twelve years. For this reason, they often use the terms discount rate and interest rate interchangeably, although *discount rate* properly refers to how much we value future benefits today, while *interest rate* properly refers to how much present investments will produce over time.

The paramount consideration in assessing future environmental benefits is the size of the discount rate: The larger the discount rate, the less future benefits will count when compared with current costs. If the discount rate were 10 percent, $200 in twelve years would be worth only about $64 today; if the rate were 3 percent, the current value would be $140. At a zero discount rate, $1 of benefits in the future would be worth $1 in cost today. Differences in discount rates become crucial for benefits spanning very long periods.

THE OBVIOUS CASES FOR AND AGAINST DISCOUNTING

The close relationship between interest rates and discount rates is the basis for the obvious case in favor of discounting. Suppose that an environmental program costing $100 today would bring $150 in benefits twelve years from now. If other public or business projects yield 6 percent per year, however, those future benefits of $150 would be "worth" only about $75 today after discounting. By investing the $100 today in one of these alternative projects, we could produce $200 in benefits in twelve years, leaving $50 more for the future.

Whether we view the environmental investment in terms of the present value of benefits ($75 as compared with $100) or in terms of an alternative investment that produces benefits of greater value ($200 as compared with $150), it fails the test of the market. Using a bit of economic jargon, we can call this market test the *opportunity-cost rationale* for discounting. Here, opportunity cost refers to the most value we can get by investing $100 in something other than the environment. According to the opportunity-cost rationale, we should discount future benefits from a current project to see if these benefits are worth *at least* as much to people in the future as the benefits they would have if we invested current dollars in medical research, education, more productive technology, and so on.

In effect, the opportunity-cost rationale tells us that our discount rate should be the market interest rate. Consequently, looking at the four factors that produce the interest rates that we see in financial markets will help explain what lies behind discount rates. The first factor is the level of economic activity. If investors want a lot of money for a lot of projects, they will have to pay a higher interest rate for loans; during slow economic times, investors will require fewer loans, leading to a lower interest rate. The second factor is inflation. Future dollars will be discounted if one cannot buy as much with them in the future as one can today. The third factor is risk; a guaranteed bird in the present hand may be worth a chancy two in the future bush. The fourth factor, and the most controversial one in environmental assessments, is what economists call *pure time preference.* This preference refers to the apparent fact that people require more than $1 in promised future benefits in order to be willing to give up $1 in goods today.

Critics of the opportunity-cost rationale often find that discounting leads to a present-day valuation of future environmental benefits that they believe is too low. Threats to life and nature from environmental degradation are notoriously hard to measure and, in the views of many, impossible to compare with the "mere" economic benefits that accrue from investing in a business project. Moreover, the benefits from a business investment might accrue to the wealthy or be frittered away today, while the benefits from an

How much we value future dollars today: The effect of time and the discount rate

Discounting operates in the reverse direction of compounding. While compounding measures how much present-day investments will be worth in the future, discounting measures how much future benefits are worth today. The figure below shows how the discounted present value of future benefits can shrink to very small amounts as time goes on. Specifically, it shows how much $100 earned now and in 20, 40, 60, 80, and 100 years is worth today when a 3 percent discount rate is applied.

Along with the passage of time, increases in the discount rate also can dramatically shrink the discounted present value of future benefits. The figure below shows how much $100 in benefits 100 years from now would be worth today at discount rates ranging from 0 to 6 percent.

When we see how small variations in the timing or discounting of future benefits can make large differences in deciding how much the benefits are worth today, it's easy to understand why discounting can lead to such heated policy debates.

environmental project are likely to be distributed more widely across society and into the future.

Environmental benefits may or may not be overestimated in policy evaluations, and they may or may not be distributed more equitably than the returns from other investments. Those well-known criticisms, however, apply to cost-benefit tests in *any* context. The specific case against discounting fundamentally concerns pure time preference. A principle in most prominent ethical philosophies is that no individual's interests should count more than another's in deciding how social benefits should be distributed. If all men are created equal, as Thomas Jefferson wrote, there can be no justification for regarding the well-being of present generations as more important than that of future generations simply because of the difference in time. Given that principle, are we really justified in refusing to sacrifice $24 in 1995 if that $24 would bring "only" $4 billion—and not $40 billion—to people living in the year 2359? Substituting lives, or the capacity of wealth to save lives, for dollars makes this question even more vivid and pressing. How could a future life, no matter how distant, be worth less than a present one? Using the language of philosophers and lawyers, we might call the insistence that future lives be valued equally to present ones the *equal standing* argument against discounting future benefits.

MIGHT CASES FOR AND AGAINST DISCOUNTING BOTH BE VALID?

Suppose we ask whether present generations should sacrifice short-run economic growth to undertake a particular program to improve the environment and leave more resources for future generations. Proponents of opportunity cost, who would discount future benefits, might say no, but proponents of equal standing, who would not discount future benefits, might say yes.

When a question has two compelling yet contradictory answers, it may really combine two questions in one. A close look at the question "should we undertake this environmental policy now to benefit future generations?" reveals that it asks a question about obligation (what duty do we have to sacrifice today to benefit future generations?) *and* a question about description (if we should sacrifice, do we help future generations more by implementing the proposed environmental policy or by doing something else?).

The economist's opportunity-cost rationale speaks to the question about description. If the goal is to improve the welfare of future generations, we should choose a policy that achieves the largest improvement for a given present cost. Consequently, we should compare the returns to the proposed environmental policy with those to other investments in order to see which are largest. Consider, for example, other investments with the same present-day costs as the environmental policy. If the discounted future benefits from these alternative policies are larger than those from the environmental policy, we should consider implementing the alternative policies instead. We may be able to do more for future generations by subsidizing basic scientific and medical research or promoting education than by protecting the environment.

An obvious response would be to ask, "Why not invest in environmental protection *and* medical research?" This response brings us to the question about obligation—whether and how much to sacrifice. Unlike the question that asks us to describe and compare the benefits of one program to another, the obligation question asks us to contemplate our duties to future generations. As such, it fundamentally concerns ethical values rather than economic facts. Accordingly, equal standing is a more appropriate perspective from which to answer this question than is opportunity cost.

Proponents of the equal-standing principle have no problem with discounting for inflation or risk. But they find the pure-time-preference component of discounting to be morally controversial, even though the pure-time-preference discount rate is half the 6 percent discount rate drawn from today's markets. While a 19:1 ratio (present value to future value yielded by a 3 percent discount rate) is less philosophically forbidding than the 340:1 ratio (yielded by a 6 percent discount rate), it still is hard to reconcile with the equal-standing principle.

VIOLATING "HUME'S LAW"

Separating environmental policy questions into questions about description and about obligation uncovers the root of much of the discounting controversy within economic circles and across disciplinary boundaries. This controversy is a consequence of trying to use facts about how people *do* discount to tell us how policymakers *should* discount. This attempt violates a maxim derived from eighteenth-century British philosopher David Hume, who asserted that facts alone cannot tell us what we should do. Any recommendation for what you, I, or society ought to do embodies some ethical principles as well as factual judgments. For example, to recommend policies if and only if their economic benefits exceed their costs would imply the ethical principle that increasing net economic benefits is the only worthy goal for society.

The fact that we *do* have time preferences may not tell us much about how we ought to regard future generations. Imagine a world where generations do not overlap. In this world, people are like long-lived tulips; every eighty years, a new batch comes to life after the previous batch disappears. Suppose the people in one of those generations happen not to care about any subsequent generations. They would then choose to exhaust resources and degrade the environment without regard for how these actions might lower the quality of life of the people who succeed them. The *fact* of this disregard, however,

does not invalidate an ethical principle that people born far in the future deserve a good quality of life as much as people already living.

Using market discount rates to examine ethical questions has made the economics of discounting more complicated than it perhaps needs to be. For example, economists have long argued about whether to calculate pure-time-preference discount rates based on the returns that investors receive before they pay taxes or after they pay taxes and, if after, whether to include corporate income taxes or personal income taxes in the calculation. If pure time preference has only limited ethical relevance in determining how much we should discount, these issues become relatively unimportant.

Divergence between equal-standing and opportunity-cost discount rates would be less important if policies that always did the best from one perspective did the best from the other as well. Unfortunately, this does not always hold. A policy that generates benefits in the short run may have a higher discounted value in an opportunity-cost sense than a policy that produces benefits much later. If we use a lower discount rate—that is, one reflecting more equal standing—the policy with long-term benefits may come out on top. We might need to do more for future generations; moreover, we might be doing the wrong things now. At opportunity-cost discount rates, development of an urban park may be more beneficial than an equally costly plan to reduce greenhouse gas emissions by taxing gasoline. At low or zero discount rates, the gasoline tax may be the more beneficial policy.

Philosopher Mark Sagoff of the University of Maryland suggests that market discount rates may not be a good indicator of the ethical value that people, upon reflection, would place on protecting future generations. Accordingly, we might resolve the discounting issue by having the government set policy based on people's stated ethical views regarding how to weigh current lives and dollars against future lives and dollars. Through a telephone survey of 3,000 U.S. households, Maureen Cropper, Sema Aydede, and Paul R. Portney of RFF determined that the rate at which people apparently discount lives saved is comparable to after-tax returns in financial markets. For example, people discount lives a century from now at about 4 percent per year. Equal-standing advocates can draw scant comfort from such data, which might tell us how a democracy would react if it followed the public's pure time preferences but, according to Hume, don't tell us what the right time preferences are.

ETHICALLY JUSTIFIED DISCOUNTING

Reconciling discounting with ethics may seem impossible, but there is some hope. To say that present and future generations have equal standing in an ethical sense does not necessarily imply that they have the same claim on present resources, because the general level of wealth or well-being may be changing over time. If we follow the ideas of a recent Nobel Prize winner in economics, John Harsanyi of the University of California–Berkeley, we should sacrifice today for the benefit of future generations only if the average well-being of people in the future goes up by more than we lose on average today. If present trends continue, advances in technology and knowledge will make people better off in the future than we are today. In that case, more than a dollar of gains to them would be needed to make up for a dollar lost to us. Any future returns should then be discounted by this difference to ensure that future generations' gains in well-being exceed our losses. According to the view proposed by Harvard University philosopher John Rawls, we might not be justified in making *any* sacrifice for future genera-

tions if they would be better off than we are now. If we expect future generations to be worse off then we are, however, Rawls' framework suggests that we should make present-day sacrifices.

More promising justifications for discounting come from critiques of the equal-standing idea itself. Philosophers such as Susan Wolf of Johns Hopkins University and Martha Nussbaum of Brown University have pointed out that to say that everyone has equal standing is to say that no one has special standing—including our families, friends, and fellow citizens. Insistence on equal standing denies the value that special interpersonal relationships hold for us and without which we could not be fully human. This argument may provide some support for asserting that generations closer to us should mean more to us than generations far in the future. (Thomas Schelling of the University of Maryland points out the irony of worrying so much about the welfare of future generations while doing so little to improve the welfare of many of the most destitute among us today.)

As long as resource scarcity makes trade-offs between the present generation and future generations inevitable, no consideration of environmental policies to benefit future generations should ignore economic opportunity cost. Ultimately, decisions to implement or not to implement such proposed policies will be the result of political processes, with all their virtues and imperfections. Justifications for the policies, which are tied in large measure to the degree of discounting, unavoidably involve ethical reflection and judgment. An appreciation of the necessary roles of both economics and ethics should clarify the nature of discounting and promote better understanding of our obligations toward future generations and how to meet them.

9

Behind the Scenes: How Policymaking in the European Community, Japan, and the United States Affects Global Negotiations
Raymond Vernon

All signs indicate that the world is in the earliest stages of a prolonged era of intensive international negotiations over the environment.[1] Some of these negotiations may be inspired by the UN Environment Programme (UNEP); some may take place within existing international organizations, such as the World Health Organization and the Food and Agriculture Organization; some will be regional or bilateral, such as those conducted between the United States and Mexico.

Understandably, then, environmental, political science, and negotiations literature are rich with speculation and analysis aimed at helping to steer all parties toward agreements that will respond to their joint concerns.[2] Among many other issues, two basic questions have been the subject of extended discussions: Given the concerns of the parties, what can be negotiated? And what will prove effective if negotiated? Studies regarding these questions characteristically have analyzed the past performance of various types of international regimes and looked for some hint of the connection between their structure and their effectiveness.[3] In that context, the usual

questions have been asked: Should agreements be mandatory or hortatory? Should they be rules-based or results-based? Should they be global or regional? Should monitoring and enforcement be supported by a formal organization? If yes, what kind of organization?

Other, equally important questions, however, about the internal processes of the negotiating countries themselves have received less attention. The responses of countries participating in international negotiations are deeply influenced by their distinctive histories, values, and institutions. Thus, insights may be gained by looking at three key players in upcoming international environmental negotiations—the United States, Japan, and the European Union (EU)*—and exploring what connection may exist between their future roles in the negotiations and their respective national histories, values, and institutions. Studying the countries' internal processes could provide considerable help in explaining the behavior of these countries regarding environmental issues. At the same time, however, there appears to be something more to this causal mix: Grassroot responses that arise

●

*For most of its life, the European Union was known as the European Community. Its name was changed under the Maastricht treaty, which was executed in 1992.

outside of the established decisionmaking channels appear to play a larger role in this policy field than in other areas of policy.

An extensive literature already exists that aids in looking for generalizations regarding the behavior of the United States, Japan, and the EU when they formulate policies that affect the distribution of costs and benefits within their respective economies.[4] These studies demonstrate the power and persistence of national characteristics that are likely to distinguish the respective roles of these three actors in future environmental negotiations. Of course, other countries, such a Brazil, India, and China, are also likely to play major roles in shaping such negotiations. But for the present, the dominant role of the triad justifies some careful attention to the way that their internal processes are likely to shape their respective roles.

U.S. PATTERNS

Generalizations about national roles in international negotiations must be made with caution because there is always at least one memorable case that will not fit the posited pattern. There are strong grounds, however, for the generalization that U.S. representatives are more inclined than their counterparts in most other countries to take an activist role in the process; to place new propositions on the table; to organize blocking coalitions; and to modify or even reverse positions in the course of negotiations. It is doubtful that the propensity of U.S. representatives to take an activist line can be attributed to either greater wisdom or higher energy levels. Part of the reason probably lies in a persistent need of the country's negotiators to justify the United States' claimed position as the leader of a Western coalition. However, U.S. representatives could not respond with the seeming activism that often characterizes their international negotiating style if it were not for certain characteristics of the country's internal decision-making processes. In comparison with most countries, that process usually tolerates a relatively high degree of initiative and flexibility on the part of the U.S. representatives.

The Separation of Powers

It may seem paradoxical that representatives of a country whose government is built on an elaborate system of checks and balances should appear to have a relatively high degree of flexibility in international negotiations. However, the indispensable requirement for an effective system of checks and balances is the separation of powers of the various governmental entities involved. The separation of powers means that, within limits, each entity is free to act without securing the consent of the others in the system. Therefore, although the executive branch may consult congressional leaders about its positions in upcoming international negotiations, it will stop short of asking for advance congressional approval. Moreover, in the unlikely event that the executive branch asked for such approval, it would surely be rebuffed.

The flexibility of U.S. representatives in international negotiations is often enhanced by the fact that the principle of separation of powers creates walls not only among the three main branches of government but also among the departments and commissions that compose the executive branch. Agencies such as the Securities and Exchange Commission, the Federal Reserve Board, and the Environmental Protection Agency view their powers as being determined by statute, not by the White House; though ordinarily deferential to White House views, they are likely to defend their turf against any challengers. Tolerance by one agency for the views of other agencies in the executive branch affected by the exercise of its statutory powers, therefore, is often fairly limited.[5]

The Revolving Door

The probability that affected agencies will be slow to consult with one another over their common problems is due to other factors, as well. One important factor is the nature of the leadership of each administration. With each change in administration, a new group of about 3,000 officials is brought to Washington.[6] These officials are recruited from the four corners of the country, are trained in a variety of professions, share very little in background and values, and are exempted from civil service standards and appointment processes. All that the appointees can be expected to have in common is political credentials that have survived a screening conducted by the party occupying the White House. Individuals in the group characteristically have had only limited contact either with one another or with the agency to which they are assigned. Moreover, few of them have any expectation of building a career in the federal bureaucracy.[7]

These generalizations, of course, have been truer for some administrations and for some agencies than for others. They were more characteristic, for instance, of the Reagan era than of the Bush administration; and, with the turnover in top personnel attending the shift from a Republican to a Democratic president, these generalizations have gained in strength again. Also, although some of the political appointees involved in this revolving-door process may take their posts with deep personal commitments to some given line of policy, the prospect of a relatively short tenure places a high premium on making their mark early, with little regard for consistency or continuity.

For all these reasons, U.S. policymakers generally frame their objectives and shape their tactics for selling their proposed policies without much hope or expectation of developing a genuine consensus among the agencies that have a stake in the issue. Interagency committees may exist in profusion, but the persistent tendency of the policymaker will be to defend the power to operate autonomously and, if that option is not available, to look for a strategy—such as enlisting the president's personal support—that will allow the policymaker to finesse the process of consultation inside the executive branch.[8]

In a national decisionmaking structure in which consensus does not dominate, a major element of unpredictability is introduced into the positions that representatives are likely to take in international circles. The history and tradition of each agency prove to be uncertain predictors of its position on any new issue, and a great deal depends on the personal motivations and bureaucratic skill of the agency's top echelons. An agency head charged with a particular functional area such as the environment may not have the motivation or skill to overcome a blocking element in the White House staff. On the other hand, an agency head with an inside track to the White House will often be able to introduce proposals that represent abrupt departures from past policies.

The mercurial role of the U.S. executive branch in setting environmental policies has been strikingly apparent in the Carter, Reagan, and Bush administrations and promises to be characteristic of the Clinton administration, as well. Some of the sharp reversals in policy between the Carter and the Reagan administrations—such as the U.S. abandonment of its support for restrictions on the international movement of hazardous wastes—obviously reflected a difference in the values of the new White House occupant; it may even have mirrored a small shift in the national consensus on such matters. But the zig-zag course of the executive branch in the late 1980s and early 1990s seemed much more a product of tactical shifts in domestic politics, coupled with shifts in the preferences and objectives of a few key policy entrepreneurs in the Reagan and Bush administrations.[9]

The Role of Congress

Recognizing the principle of the separation of powers and the independence of the three federal branches of government, congressional leaders do not ordinarily question the right of the executive branch to launch any proposition for international discussion as long as Congress retains the opportunity eventually to rule on its merits. Sometimes, it is true, individual members of Congress may grouse at the executive's exercise of that discretion because they fear that the very introduction of a proposal in an international forum could tie the legislature's hands at a later stage. But at other times, members of Congress will heave a secret sigh of relief at not being required to take an early position on some contentious issue.

Moreover, the U.S. executive branch itself, when conducting an international negotiation over an economic policy, has been known to regard the independence of Congress as a negotiating advantage. At times, Congress' independence enables U.S. negotiators to threaten the representatives of other countries with the possibility of congressional displeasure and retribution if the other countries do not accept their proposals.[10]

But the congressional drive to retain power and independence means that the texts of laws and regulations take on special importance. They become centerpieces in struggles with the executive branch over national policies because, where the texts of laws and regulations are not explicit in prescribing the standards or procedures to be followed, the discretion of the executive branch grows at the expense of the legislature. This emphasis on standards and procedures elevates the role of adversarial proceedings and formal process, places the legal profession at the center of the controversy, and accordingly limits the powers of the bureaucracy to make complex judgments and to rely on inexplicit criteria.

Efforts to Cope

As numerous observers have pointed out, any international negotiation conducted among democratic governments is bound to proceed at two levels simultaneously. One level involves the interaction among governments, and the other involves the interaction of each government with its domestic interests. U.S. innovators commonly launch their proposals in international settings without first developing a broad national consensus. As a result, there is a high risk that the innovator may not be able to retain U.S. support for the position originally advanced. Some of the interests overlooked in the first phase of the negotiating process will be eager to make their position felt in subsequent rounds, and, in some instances, their late intervention may carry such weight as to require major changes in the U.S. position.[11]

The porousness of the U.S. decisionmaking structure represents an open invitation to any such neglected interest. If the opposition cannot capture a sympathetic ear in one agency, it may be able to do so in another.[12] And, if the executive branch is unmovable, Congress, the courts, or the media may offer an alternative channel. The system, therefore, places a premium on aggressive advocacy, a characteristic especially evident in the formulation of environmental policies. With such advocacy encouraged, the possibility of an interest group forcing a revision of a U.S. position in an international negotiation is relatively high. Therefore, the United States may abruptly shift course in the negotiation of an international agreement and may find itself obliged to breach agreements after they have been adopted.

At times in the past, the executive branch, in an effort to clear the path for an international negotiation, has tried to bypass Congress by claiming to have the power already to enter into agreements in the name of the United States. Experience suggests, however, that such an approach is highly vulnerable, especially when a policy area involves special interests and may require periodic changes in U.S. legislation. Executive agreements not expressly authorized or approved by Congress run the risk of being ostentatiously disregarded on Capitol Hill. For example, Congress has been cavalier about U.S. violations of its commitments under the General Agreement on Tariffs and Trade, sometimes ignoring the existence of the violations for long periods and sometimes grudgingly making an adjustment in response to international complaints.[13]

Moreover, there have been signs that the advantages that U.S. representatives derive from their autonomy in launching international negotiations are declining over time. Other countries have begun to realize that the proposals of U.S. representatives may not be backed by a broad U.S. consensus and that adversaries inside the United States may eventually force major alterations on a brave U.S. initiative. That, indeed, has been the history of international negotiations in matters of foreign trade. By the 1970s, the reluctance of other countries to negotiate with U.S. representatives on trade matters was so palpable that some remedy had to be found.

The remedy that was fashioned for the conduct of trade negotiations—the so-called fast-track provisions—provides a precedent that could conceivably be extended to other areas. Under the fast-track provisions, the executive branch agrees to conduct its negotiations in close consultation with private interest groups and with selected congressional representatives. In return, Congress agrees that it will vote for or against the negotiated agreement without delay and without qualification or amendment. In practice, other devices also sometimes allow the executive branch to engage in international negotiations with reasonable assurance that Congress will not block the resulting agreement. For

instance, agencies in the executive branch commonly negotiate memoranda of understanding with foreign countries under a congressional dispensation.

Even when the executive branch has acted well within its authority, however, Congress or the courts, responding to the initiatives of special interests, still can compel the U.S. government to act in disregard of existing international commitments. Asking the executive branch to meet this challenge may appear to be equivalent to asking the oceans to stand still. The challenge is not quite that great, however, because members of Congress often are looking for some insulation against the unremitting pressures of special interests. Some of their efforts in that direction, it is true, have had unfortunate consequences for the international negotiation process. In the area of trade, for example, in order for Congress to appear responsive to special interests without getting entangled in individual cases, it has commonly enacted provisions that increase the ability of special-interest groups to put pressure on the executive branch. These provisions typically open up new avenues of petition to executive agencies or the courts and lay down explicit standards that are supposed to guide the executive agencies and the courts toward a decision.[14]

Yet, on the whole, the executive branch and Congress often share a desire to limit their exposure to special-interest pressures in individual cases if they can find a way that is not too costly politically. This attitude opens up the possibility that international agreements that include compulsory arbitration clauses may sometimes be a welcome escape for both branches because such agreements offer a way to depoliticize the handling of individual cases.

The United States and Canada took a large step toward such depoliticization in the negotiation of the U.S.-Canadian free trade agreement by creating a binational court of appeals to deal with some contested issues and by providing for compulsory arbitration panels to deal with others. Such innovations could well point the way to the future structuring of other international agreements.

JAPANESE PATTERNS

By ordinary standards, Japan's economy would be described as market based and its political processes as democratic. But these standards allow plenty of room for variety, and Japan's approach to making and enforcing public programs, such as the protection of the environment, includes a number of very distinctive features. Although scholars do not agree on all the details of the critical factors that shape Japanese behavior, the various analyses of that behavior share much common ground.[15]

The Decisionmaking Structure

The "us versus them" syndrome, so pervasive in the formulation of most countries' foreign policies, has been especially strong during most of the history of modern Japan. This is hardly surprising given the fact that, for hundreds of years before the opening of Japan in 1868, the country was in danger of becoming a prize for the prowling navies of the Western powers.

During the century following the opening of Japan, numerous bitter struggles occurred among Japanese leaders over a variety of issues. Nevertheless, the leadership remained remarkably united in its view of the paramount domestic objectives. In 1868, it seemed obvious to the Japanese elite that their very existence as a nation depended on their ability to absorb the war-making technology of the West. Once that objective was within reach—by about the close of the First World War—the Japanese elite set about solving another threat to their national existence, their utter dependence on imports of raw materials. Repeated efforts by Japanese industry to gain direct access to sources of oil and minerals were

rebuffed by strong cartels composed of leading firms from Europe and North America.[16] Japan's invasion of China in the 1930s and its subsequent attack on Pearl Harbor were driven in considerable part by the desire of Japan's military to control sources of raw materials. During this phase, there were occasional signs that the unanimity among Japan's leaders that had apparently prevailed in earlier decades was not quite as complete. Deviants, however, were quickly brought into line by political assassinations and other forms of pressure.

With Japan's defeat in the Second World War, national priorities changed. Economic recovery became the consuming objective of the country, and, once again, it was difficult to find any part of the leadership prepared to subordinate that objective to some other purpose.

Not until the 1980s, therefore, could one see any significant modifications in the "us versus them" approach or any significant measure of recognition in Japan that it had a major stake in solving certain problems beyond its own borders. One indication of the extent of that change was Japan's willingness in 1987 to back the U.S.-inspired proposal for an international agreement to curb the use of chlorofluorocarbons (CFCs).[17]

Japan's tendency to present an unaccommodating, united front to the rest of the world, however, has been due to factors that cannot be expected to change very rapidly. Paradoxically, the strength, stability, and professionalism of the Japanese bureaucracy have tended to add to the appearance of a wooden, unaccommodating approach rather than to improve the country's image as an international negotiator. With lifetime commitments to their professions, bureaucrats engaged in policymaking usually have operated in a setting in which the identity of the principal players was highly predictable over extended periods of time. In such a setting, say game theorists, the players are encouraged to develop a reputation for team playing, albeit team playing

tempered by toughness. Some typical characteristics of U.S. bureaucratic behavior, therefore,
are frowned upon in Japan, including oppor-
tunistic innovation and tactics that take advantage of the absence or temporary weakness of
the opposition.

The stability of Japan's bureaucracy has
been matched by the stability of other elite sectors of Japan's decisionmaking structure. One
political party, the Liberal Democratic Party, has
dominated the government since the end of the
Second World War. Until the 1990s, the hold of
that party seemed unshakable. Although the
party was always strained by internal rivalries
among its so-called factions, each headed by a
prominent politician eager for the prime minister's office, that rivalry has not been strong
enough to threaten the party's control of the government.

In the business world, the stability of the
leadership during the postwar period also has
been remarkable in light of the degree of growth
and change in the economy. Scholars have attributed that stability to various factors, including the much-advertised lifetime career patterns
of Japanese business executives; the links
among large firms that are created by cross-
ownerships or by loyalty and that generate stable
business groups known as *keiretsu;* and the
dominant role of the Keidanren, a national association to which all major Japanese enterprises
belong, in coordinating business actions with
public policies. With so stable an elite in control,
the disposition of policymakers toward long-
term reputation building and team playing has
been high.

Such stability, of course, could not continue
indefinitely. In 1989, for instance, the Liberal
Democratic Party's perennial dominance over
Japanese politics was challenged for the first
time when the Socialist Party gained control of
the upper house of Japan's parliament. Similarly, the stability and predictability of the career
patterns of Japan's business executives are being

disturbed by a sharp increase in job-hopping and
an increase in demands for leisure time.[18] But
these countertrends are still too weak in the
1990s to portend any great change in Japan's
economic decisionmaking patterns.

Until the 1990s, the striking absence of
Japanese innovation or initiative was apparent in
practically all international issues, not just environmental ones. An explanation for this pervasive Japanese characteristic is the mirror image
of the preceding explanation for the opposite
propensities of U.S. representatives. Innovative
proposals usually entail a giant step into the unknown that involves latent risks and uncertain
benefits for some groups in the population. In a
move that is based partly on faith even when justified by reason, innovators typically are obliged
to ride roughshod over the doubts and misgivings of some groups at home likely to be affected by the proposed policy. In the U.S. system of decisionmaking, where consensus is
infeasible and artful dodging is a normal part of
the game, launching an innovative proposal that
embraces some general principle is sometimes
possible despite the existence of unassuaged
misgivings. In the Japanese system, where every
major interest is in a position to bring the negotiation to a standstill, the possibility of obtaining
agreement to take a leap into the dark by espousing a general principle is greatly reduced.

The same distinction helps to explain another characteristic of Japanese decisions: Foreign pressure, or *gaiatsu,* plays an important
role in determining Japanese moves, especially
when the breadth of the subject matter engages
the interests of several ministries. History suggests, however, that the use of foreign pressure
has its limits. If a significant part of the Japanese
establishment feels that such pressure is excessive and that a genuine internal consensus does
not exist, it may well take an independent course
in spite of the existence of a contrary international agreement. Foreign pressure, however,
provides Japanese negotiators with a way out of

their internal dilemma of trying to build a reputation as both a tough bargainer and a team player. To maintain such a position, the participants must ensure that the concessions made to achieve internal agreements are hard-won and small in scope. Foreign pressure, therefore, is critical because it gives a resisting group an excuse for yielding without losing its reputation as a tough bargainer.

One other characteristic of Japanese decisionmaking flows from this line of speculation. In contrast to the United States, the course of Japanese policies has some of the characteristics of a supertanker under way. The probability that some entity in the government structure will take an independent line and disregard or override an existing international agreement is low. Inertia and momentum play dominant roles. Any future change in direction, like the changes of the past, will only be effected slowly and with great effort.

Environmental Policies

Nevertheless, Japan's history in the adoption of national environmental policies has deviated sufficiently from its behavior in other policy fields to raise questions about Japan's likely future role at the international level. In a country that places great emphasis on avoiding confrontational tactics, the militant action of aberrant groups was largely responsible for placing the environmental issue on the national agenda. A few highlights of the Japanese record are helpful in exploring the extent to which the country's characteristic decisionmaking processes have been applied in the handling of environmental issues.[19]

Because of the high population densities on Japan's main islands and the spectacular growth of its industrial facilities in the 1950s and 1960s, Japan was one of the first industrialized market economies to react to some of the acute effects of modern industrial pollution. By the 1960s, the Japanese were discovering widespread instances of poisoning from toxic metals and chemicals—including the notorious minimata and itai-itai epidemics—as well as a mushrooming of bronchial asthma cases in some cities. But the policymaking machinery, resting securely in the hands of the bureaucracy, the Keidanren, and the dominant Liberal Democratic Party, seemed totally insulated from the local pressures of ordinary citizens. As long as these developments were confined to limited areas of the country and did not interfere with the achievement of the Japanese government's dominant objective of rapid, sustained economic growth, the affected groups seemed to have no choice but to endure.

Japanese environmental conditions as a whole were probably no worse than those of Western Europe or North America. Indeed, if life expectancy data are any guide, they may even have been better. But the consequences to the affected local areas in Japan were so shocking and the threat of further consequences so unremitting that local groups searched desperately for some remedy. One feature of the citizens' actions was thoroughly Japanese. They organized themselves into local cooperative groups that hammered away at local polluters and local government officials to develop an appropriate response. Another feature was remarkably aberrant and was presumably brought on by the gravity of the situation: Local citizens instituted civil suits in the courts to establish the responsibility of the polluters and obtain compensatory damages for those affected. The success of the plaintiffs in four celebrated cases created a landmark in Japanese environmental policy.[20]

By the 1970s, environmental issues in Japan were no longer the concern of local groups alone. Japan's mass media had used their influence in favor of environmental controls and had exposed the continuation of environmental degradation and the foot-dragging and indifference of Japan's leading polluters. For some years while public opinion was still being formed, the bureaucracy in Tokyo gave lip service to the environmental objectives. But, by the mid 1970s, key ministries in Tokyo, notably including the Ministry of Health and Welfare, had joined the media in an alliance against the industrial sources of pollution. With that shift, a new internal balance was achieved in Japan, and politicians and industry leaders, taking note of the shift, joined in framing a new set of environmental policies.[21]

Unlike similar public opinion changes in the United States, however, the transformation of Japanese public opinion from indifference to commitment was not accompanied by the development of strong national organizations or by the appearance of organized pressure groups in the capital. The struggle that eventually produced a shift in national policy was conducted through more ephemeral means—such as local movements and the media—that led eventually to a recognition among policymakers that the public had developed some new expectations of environmental policy. With that change in expectations recognized by the bureaucracy, the Liberal Democratic Party, and the Keidanren, the stage was set for concerted national action.

The programs of environmental control that emerged by the latter 1970s were exemplary in their stated goals and their initial achievements. The Ministry for International Trade and Industry's imposition of a ban on lead in gasoline in the 1970s, for example, stood in sharp contrast to the dreary trail of suits and countersuits over the same issue in the United States, where adversarial proceedings and statutory schedules were a normal part of the implementation process. In added contrast to U.S. practice, monetary support for those who were injured by the new restrictions played a major role in Japan's official programs.[22]

Also, in characteristic Japanese fashion, the paper trail created by Japanese programs contained few hard commitments or unambiguous standards; the effective guidelines, if they existed at all, were contained in the side-deals and confidential memoranda exchanged inside the bureaucracy.[23] Moreover, the affected industry groups were not regarded as adversaries in the process that shaped the relevant programs; on the contrary, their consultations with the bureaucracy were frequent and extensive. Finally, in exercising the broad discretion that typically resides in the Japanese bureaucracy, government officials proved themselves to be both flexible and supportive in their relations with the affected firms during the implementation phase by adjusting schedules and providing for special financing as required.

In the 1990s, however, the Japanese apparently have achieved enough progress in environmental issues on the home front that such issues have slipped off the front pages of Japanese newspapers. Substantial indications suggest that the policies adopted by the government are not being neglected by the bureaucracy and are being implemented with some care and efficiency. But unlike such efforts in the United States, the implementation of these programs has been shaped much more by expert opinion than by political pressure.[24] The forces that stimulate such experts to act in Japan are far less obvious, at least to the outside observer, than those which operate on policymakers in the United States. Despite Japan's domestic activism in environmental matters, there has been no accompanying development of national movements devoted to preserving the environment, such as the Greens in Europe or the Sierra Club and the Natural Resources Defense Council in the United States.[25] Nor have dedicated environmentalists often been included in the numerous advisory groups with which the Japanese bureaucracy consults. The crusading elements so evident in the European and U.S. environmental movements, therefore, are not to be seen in Japan's policymaking establishment. As best as one can tell, therefore, the stimulus for action seems to come from the periodic appraisals of the decisionmaking establishment that a national consensus has been forming to which it would be prudent to respond. The decisionmakers are helped in these appraisals by Japan's print media, which enjoy wide influence and circulation. But the more focused strategies of U.S. interest groups, such as rallying behind individual pieces of legislation and supporting key court cases, has no close Japanese equivalent.

EUROPEAN PATTERNS

European countries enter the present era of international activity in environmental controls with an extensive record of programs at the national level that have been in place for several decades.[26] Perhaps in part because of the novelty of certain environmental issues, these programs have reflected a great variety of approaches. Over time, however, national programs have become more similar in approach, pushed in common directions by the prodding of the European Union.[27] The polluter pays principle, for instance, has gradually begun to secure greater currency. But major national differences have persisted into the 1990s and reflect substantial variations in public opinion about the importance of environmental concerns and in legal traditions and regulatory practices.

Still, the European nations as a group can be distinguished from the United States in a number of explicit respects. The Europeans' overall approach to environmental controls is much more akin to that of the Japanese than to that of the Americans. Like the Japanese, Europeans are far less confrontational than are U.S. officials in how they formulate and enforce standards. Even Germany, which contains a highly vocal environmental lobby and is identified with strong environmental policies, nevertheless relies heavily on informal consultations and voluntary agreements.[28]

The contrast between European and U.S. practices is especially evident in how scientific opinion is amassed. In the United States, the government formally relies on the testimony of qualified experts that is accumulated largely through overt adversarial procedures—a process that usually generates a disparate set of conclusions, all purportedly supported by scientific authority and objectivity. In contrast, Europe's administrators garner their evidence, to the extent that it contributes to their decisions, from scientific sources largely of their own choosing.[29] Moreover, in both the formulation and enforcement of standards, the Europeans generally rely much more than the Americans on private consultations with the interests most affected. The responses of the Europeans to noncompliance, like the responses of the Japanese, tend to be far more flexible than the heavy-handed U.S. approach, which uses fines and court orders.[30]

Shared Responsibilities

Although the European Union's role in the environmental field has been somewhat influenced by the practices of its member countries, its unique treaty provisions and decisionmaking institutions have given its role a distinctive cast. To study the decisionmaking policies of the EU, however, is to close in on a rapidly moving target. The EU, barely three decades old, is still in the process of defining its goals, shaping its institutions, and settling on its patterns of governance.

The goals of the EU as originally defined in the Treaty of Rome that created it in 1958 made no mention of the environment. According to the treaty's text, its purpose was to lay the foundations of an ever-closer union among the European peoples by establishing a common market among its member countries. To create such a common market, the EU's member nations agreed eventually to surrender their powers over the transborder movement of goods, services, money, enterprises, and workers to the institutions of the EU. The countries also agreed that the lawmaking body of the EU, its Council of

Ministers, could enact the laws required to create the common market by a qualified majority vote rather than by the unanimous consent of its members.

During the first phase in the evolution of the EU, from 1958 to 1966, its member countries belatedly discovered just how narrowly the extraordinary commitments of the Rome treaty would limit their capacity for independent national action. For instance, France suddenly found itself unable to bar a foreign-owned enterprise, such as General Motors, from setting up a plant in its jurisdiction without considering the possibility that the plant might settle in Brussels and export its output to France. The dawning realization that the commitments of the Rome treaty created powerful restraints on the capacity of its member countries to act autonomously eventually produced a reaction from France's President Charles de Gaulle: Despite the treaty's provisions to the contrary, he exacted a commitment from member countries that issues that any member country defined as vital to its interests could only be settled by unanimous agreement.

That early decision seemed to throw a pall on the prospects of the EU being a significant actor in the economies of its member countries, much less a force in the environmental field. However, the vitality and persistence of the EU's other institutions, notably its Court of Justice, eventually opened up new possibilities. Despite the agreement that the Council of Ministers would rule by unanimity, the court still had to discharge its responsibilities as the ultimate interpreter of the meaning of the treaty and had to rule on complaints by individuals, national governments, and even the institutions of the EU itself regarding the legality of actions taken in light of the treaty's provisions. Such actions arose in a steady stream and covered a wide range of issues. The EU's executive arm, the European Commission, for instance, brought against national governments frequent actions that alleged that they were not living up to their treaty commitments. Individual enterprises commonly brought against the commission actions asserting that it had used its various executive powers in a manner inconsistent with treaty provisions.

This grist for the judicial mill produced a series of decisions from 1966 to 1985 that solidified and amplified the powers of the EU. During that period, the Court of Justice affirmed that the provisions of the Treaty of Rome and the regulations and directives enacted by its institutions to create the common market had "direct effect" upon the member countries—that is, they had the quality of national law and superseded existing national law wherever differences existed. The court also confirmed the principle that, in areas of policy in which the EU was exercising its powers under the treaty, the EU also had the sole responsibility for negotiations with outside countries.[31]

In one crucial area, however, the EU's powers were limited and would remain so for the indefinite future. Enforcement of the EU's decisions was left largely to the member countries. Over the years, the EU would develop various mechanisms to reduce the extent of noncompliance, including requirements for reports on the implementation of its directives and recommendations and appeals to the Court of Justice to find member countries in violation of their treaty obligations. Indeed, the Court of Justice would eventually rule that, in some circumstances, individuals could sue a member country for damages incurred by the country's failure to implement an EU directive. But the limitations on the EU's powers of enforcement still substantially affected its role.

Despite that caveat, the European Union's powers were vastly strengthened by court decisions in a process that, at the time, garnered little public attention. A small group of lawyers and scholars specializing in EU law followed these developments with avid interest. Until the 1980s, however, these critical developments went almost unnoticed by politicians, political scientists, and economists, not to mention the media and the public at large.

By the early 1970s, it began to be apparent that the EU could not forever remain aloof from the problems of environmental controls. Its mandate to create a common market eventually would require it to address any major obstacles that might stand in the market's way. On the other hand, the EU's authority to deal with such barriers as national environmental controls was not clear. In some circumstances, the programs of individual countries aimed at controlling their national environments—such as the efforts of some countries to curb the sale and use of motor vehicles that did not adhere to specified emission standards—could have the incidental effect of blocking international movements inside the common market. However, the treaty authorized member countries to limit exports and imports to protect the life and health of humans, animals, and plants, so long as they were not "a disguised restriction on trade."[32]

Despite the ambiguities surrounding the EU's powers in the environmental field, its member countries authorized the EU in 1972 to take a vigorous role in environmental controls. Much of the initiative for this development came from member countries with relatively high environmental standards—such as Germany and the Netherlands—who sought to spread those standards to other members of the EU.

Although the EU was obliged to act by unanimity, the new authorization nevertheless led to a series of EU sponsored environmental programs that were aimed mainly at controlling water pollution, air pollution, toxic substances, and waste disposal.[33] Three action plans that were adopted during the following 10 years gave rise to a stream of directives. The content of those programs showed that the EU shared the objective of controlling the degradation of the environment, although it strongly preferred measures that did not inhibit cross-border move-

ments within the common market. It was also apparent at times that the EU's involvement in environmental issues was raising the standards of some member countries that might otherwise have been slower to act. The study, for instance, attributes Britain's conversion in the late 1980s from laggard to leader on a wide range of environmental issues in part to the pressures to which Prime Minister Margaret Thatcher was exposed in EU discussions.[34]

In 1987, the Rome treaty was amended by the Single European Act, whose goal was to provide the EU with added authority to sweep away national regulations that inhibited the creation of a common market. For decisions aimed at achieving a common market by harmonizing national regulations, the principle of weighted majority voting was restored. Restrictions that inhibited the sale of services across national borders within the common market were identified as a major target for EU action. Technical barriers imposed in the name of public health and consumer safety provided another major target.

At the same time, the Single European Act recognized environmental policy as a common policy of the EU and one ostensibly equal in status to the creation of the common market. In the environmental field, however, the voting rules were complex and occasionally ambiguous: Those proposals that contributed to the common-market objective could be passed by a weighted majority, but those that could not be justified in such terms still required a unanimous vote.[35]

Apart from the ambiguities in the EU's voting rules for the exercise of its new environmental responsibilities, other provisions of the Single European Act created additional uncertainties regarding the EU's writ in environmental matters. According to one such provision, the new authority of the EU should be exercised with strict attention to the principle of subsidiarity—that is, the new authority was to be applied only when an EU program could perform better than programs pursued at the member-country level.[36] Moreover, national governments retained the right to enact environmental provisions that were more stringent than those enacted by the EU—provided, however, that the provisions were consistent with the treaty. Finally, member countries could enter into agreements with nonmember governments and international organizations in the areas in which they retained competence.

It was obvious from the first that the Court of Justice would eventually have to assist in untangling the legal snarl created by these provisions. At least one major case is now before it that might clarify the scope of the EU's competency.

The enactment of the Single European Act, however, was not the final episode in the evolution of the EU's powers over environmental regulations. In December 1991, representatives of the twelve member nations agreed that yet another round of treaty revisions—the so-called Maastricht treaty—would be submitted to their respective governments for ratification. To date, the ratification process has not yet been completed, having encountered a roadblock in Denmark and threats in a number of other countries. Nevertheless, one provision of the proposed amendments deserves special attention. According to that provision, in the future, the principle of subsidiarity is to be applied not only in the field of environmental controls but also in all fields in which the EU has competence.[37] Once adopted, that provision would presumably add weight and scope to the subsidiarity principle and place added limits on the EU's ability to speak for Europe.

A Closer View

To gain a sense of the decisionmaking process in the European Union, however, one cannot merely examine the interests and positions of the member countries and their collective decisions with regard to the EU. The institutions of the EU itself play a significant role that should be distinguished from the direct and indirect actions of the member countries.

This is not to belittle the power of the member countries in shaping the decisions of the European Union. As previously observed, member countries have used the EU as a medium for pushing their national objectives, such as persuading their fellow members to adopt new environmental measures. Moreover, representatives of the member countries permeate the decision-making processes of the EU. Without question, the hundreds of directives issued by the Council of Ministers under the powers bestowed by the Single European Act would not have survived without the support of the French prime minister and the German chancellor.

The measures taken to enforce EU directives also show the importance of the member countries' role. Although the EU may command, the member countries must carry out those commands. And in practice, national governments have commonly failed to meet their obligations and have generated long delays and lawsuits brought before the Court of Justice by the commission. Indeed, in 1990, the commission had nearly 400 cases outstanding that claimed noncompliance by member countries to the EU's many environmental regulations and directives.[38]

Nevertheless, the programs developed under the Single European Act owe much of their scope and power to the ingenuity and entrepreneurship of a few key officials in the commission, including its [former] chairman, Jacques Delors. And these initiatives could not have occurred without the groundbreaking decisions of the Court of Justice. Apart from the Court of Justice, other EU institutions involved in the shaping of EU policies have deviated at times from the wishes of the member countries. Even the EU's Council of Ministers—though ostensibly a body composed of national representatives—has produced results that were not just a simple reconciliation of national positions.

The Council of Ministers, the EU's lawmaking institution, is a body without precedent among international organizations. Although the council is composed of ministers representing each of the member countries, the identity of the ministers depends on the subject matter. Agricultural issues, for instance, are addressed by a council composed of agricultural ministers; environmental matters by environmental ministers; and trade matters by trade ministers. By one count, therefore, there are actually 23 separate Councils of Ministers, each drawn on functional lines.

One consequence of this odd structure has been the inhibition of the give and take across functional areas that ordinarily occurs in the policymaking bodies of democratic societies, such as national legislatures and national cabinets. And, while some member countries, such as France, have created elaborate national institutions for coordinating their instructions to their council representatives, such national structures still cannot control the ultimate decisions on any issue that take place inside the council. The fact that the deliberations of the Council of Ministers are held in secret has added to the sense that the laws it formulates are the products of a club of technocratic specialists. Some indications suggest that the secrecy surrounding the Council of Ministers' deliberations may be less pervasive in the future, but the extent of such a shift is not yet clear.[39]

Although the Council of Ministers is the ultimate lawgiver in the European Union, explicit proposals for the adoption of a directive must originate within the European Commission, which is composed of 17 members who are nominated for fixed terms by the member countries. The commissioners, who are assigned functional responsibilities inside the commission, are sworn neither to solicit nor to accept instructions from their governments; and, although some commissioners have been suspected of giving priority to national interests on certain issues, by and large,

the commissioners have played independent roles as good Europeans.

Surrounding the commission and operating between that body and the council is the Committee of Permanent Representatives to the Union (COREPER), whose members are quintessential agents of the member countries. Supported by a shifting network of subcommittees and working parties composed of national bureaucrats, COREPER performs both an initiating and a facilitating function by advising the commission on initiatives it thinks would be welcomed and on propositions it thinks would be tolerated by the committee members' respective governments; by explaining the commission's positions to the members' respective ministers; and by acting for the Council of Ministers on a wide range of routine issues.

Also on the list of the EU's key institutions is the European Parliament, an institution notable because it is the only body whose members are elected directly to the EU. The European Parliament is definitely not a parliament of national parliaments. Indeed, national parliaments are almost without power in the processes of the European Union, except in the case of Denmark, whose ministers are bound to follow the instructions of their national parliament when engaged in EU business.

The European Parliament is notable in another respect, as well: Despite its name, the parliament is little more than an advisory body, empowered to provide mainly advisory opinions on the commission's proposals and the council's prospective actions. True, the European Parliament is empowered to take some substantive actions, such as to reject *in toto* the EU's proposed budget and—in concert with the commission— to force the council to reconsider a decision. Moreover, the Maastricht agreement would slightly enlarge the parliament's powers by requiring the council to come to terms with the parliament if a council decision has not been made unanimously. But in the various tortuous sequences prescribed for the EU's decisionmaking, a unanimous decision of the council cannot be overridden by the parliament. Therefore, the one body in the EU that the various national electorates might conceivably identify as truly democratic is limited to an inconsequential role in the decisionmaking process.

The unprecedented nature of the decisionmaking structure of the European Union helps a little to explain its past role in matters of the environment. The European Parliament, free to play the role of keeper of the European conscience, has been aggressive in its support of advanced positions on environmental controls.[40] It is unlikely, however, that the parliament's aggressiveness would be quite so uninhibited if that body were to acquire substantial legislative powers. The EU's commission and its Council of Ministers have also been capable of substantial initiatives from time to time, as evidenced by the steady stream of environmental directives flowing from Brussels. The heavy tilt in the EU's decisionmaking structure toward the functional approach could have helped to give environmental ministers more freedom of action than they might have been able to exercise at home. But the many lapses of some members in responding to the EU's environmental directives and in enforcing those directives that have already been enshrined in national law are evidence of one of the structural limitations of the EU.

For the immediate future, then, two key factors must be taken into account in judging the likely scope of the European Union's authority to deal with environmental issues. One is that the EU's relative immunity from the checks and balances that are an integral part of any democratic system could be drawing to an end, which would reduce the EU's ability to reach strong decisions on environmental matters. A second factor, however, is the growing recognition of the EU's lack of control over the enforcement of its mandates, which could lead eventually to increases in the scope of the EU's authority.

ENVIRONMENTAL PROGRAMS

This cursory view of the decisionmaking processes of the governmental establishments in the United States, Japan, and Europe suggests that strong initiatives in support of international agreements on the environment may be forthcoming from time to time. In the U.S. case, as observed earlier, a necessary, though not a sufficient, condition for such an initiative might well be the decision of a high-level policy entrepreneur that the agreement is worth pursuing to make a mark. In the European case, such an initiative might depend on the conclusion that an international agreement that includes nonmember countries would ease the problems of the EU in making a single European market.[41]

Others who have studied the policymaking processes of the United States and other leading industrial countries see international initiatives on major environmental issues as being very slow in coming. For instance, Eugene Skolnikoff, who has devoted a professional lifetime to studying the formation of public policy in science, concludes that substantial international action on the global warming issue will not be forthcoming until the effects of the trend are far more palpable than they are today.[42]

Skolnikoff's plausible views can be buttressed by another line of argument. For more than a decade, scholars have observed a decline in the public's confidence in the efficiency of government in solving social and economic problems. That shift in public sentiment has arrested and even reversed the growth in the size and power of the public sector in the United States, Europe, and Japan, and it might reasonably have been expected to stop the environmental movement in its tracks.

Yet, when the domestic environmental programs of the United States, Japan, and the European Union are reviewed, they exhibit a vitality, a persistence, and a capacity for overcoming the resistance of groups with an adverse economic interest that could not easily have been anticipated 20 years ago. Popular activism appears with a frequency encountered in a very few other public issues, except perhaps that of abortion. A 1990 publication of the European Union reports that the commission "receives an increasing number of complaints about the actual situation in the Member States from non-government organizations, local authorities, Members of the European Parliament, local pressure groups and private individuals."[43] And in Europe, as well as in the United States and Japan, the political support that provides a basis for environmental programs has not often come through the traditional party structures; it has sprung up mainly through organizations that have cut across the parties. Indeed, in Germany, Belgium, France, Ireland, Sweden, the Netherlands, and the United Kingdom, the environmental issue has led to the creation of new green parties that concentrate entirely on environmental issues. Although, on the whole, green-party adherents have leaned toward the left, their willingness to sacrifice economic growth for environmental betterment has generated great antagonism from some of the traditional left-leaning European parties.[44]

Can it be, therefore, that the analysis of decisionmaking processes in the preceding pages will prove less important for environmental issues than for the usual business of governments? In the development of new initiatives to protect the environment, groups outside the usual decisionmaking structures in the United States, Europe, and Japan will probably play a considerable role in overcoming the resistance of those that see themselves bearing the costs.

Where new initiatives are concerned, the U.S. role, as usual, will be hard to predict. Observe, for instance, the refusal of the Bush administration to go along with definitive interna-

tional commitments aimed at slowing global warming at a time when public sentiment appeared to favor strongly such commitments; or the initiative of U.S. representatives in securing an international agreement to reduce the use of CFCs, despite strong misgivings among U.S. industrial leaders concerning the effects of such restrictions. Predicting the U.S. role is complicated further by the independence of Congress and the courts in deciding exactly how to treat the country's international commitments in the face of domestic pressures.

As for Japan, nothing in the record suggests that the usual decisionmakers will show much enthusiasm for international agreements on environmental measures; initiatives from that quarter are only likely to address issues that are immediately related to the problems of living on the crowded islands of Japan. Moreover, judging from history, the Japanese cannot be expected to embrace readily either specific standards or specific measures to achieve such standards, especially measures whose enforcement might involve adversarial proceedings and adjudication. Yet, one cannot be sure whether the new generation of cosmopolitan Japanese will follow in the steps of earlier generations.

In the end, therefore, international activism on environmental issues may depend on the out-of-channels pressures that have been indispensable in the past. The scholarly study of that phenomenon is already well under way, breeding such ponderous concepts as the "epistemic community," which is a group joined together across international borders by a common set of beliefs and values.[45]

In a world in which the costs of international communication are plummeting and the facilities for communication proliferating, the growing importance of transnational groups with common views regarding the environment seems inevitable. Their appearance was heralded a few decades ago by the proliferation of single-issue organizations in the political processes of various countries—such as the Sierra Club in the United States and the Greens in Germany—and followed up by the development of strong links among these national organizations. The trend has been accelerated by the growth of business organizations that straddle national boundaries, such as the multinational enterprises. Such transnational groups have figured prominently in the negotiations for the control of CFCs, as scientists and consumer groups exchanged information across borders and as Du Pont's recognition of the CFC problem spurred Great Britain's largest chemical company to shift its position.

That transnational communities may be critical in framing the content of international agreements, however, is an uncomfortable idea in a number of different respects. For one thing, it greatly complicates the structure of a well-known metaphor that political scientists apply in analyzing the international negotiating process—namely, the concept of the two-level chess game. With these transnational communities playing, the negotiations among national representatives begin to lose their adversarial character and take on some of the qualities of a joint conspiracy against the others in their respective national polities.

Communities that straddle national boundaries and that represent relatively specialized interests have, of course, been common in the conduct of international relations in the past. Long before the discovery of "epistemic communities," the monthly meetings of the world's chief central bankers in Basel, Switzerland, provided illustrations of the importance of such institutions. In this case, the monthly meetings evolved into an institution of some power and influence, which sometimes quietly engaged in an effort to bring free-spending national politicians to their senses. Also, for many decades, the world's principal airlines—speaking in the name of their respective governments—jointly determined the prices that international travelers would pay for their services and justified their

decisions by a shared belief in the efficacy of the system. The influence of such groups may have served good purposes or ill, but, quite obviously, their views did not always reflect the diverse interests and complex priorities of the countries they purportedly represented.

In any case, although transnational communities may play a critical role in the adoption of new international agreements, they probably would be much less effective in implementing such agreements. Although the adoption of new programs for the environment may be critical, making such a regime work is usually the ultimate test of its usefulness. In some environmental matters, for instance, the power to act or to avoid action is likely to revert to the day-to-day decisionmaking apparatus of the participating governments, including administrative agencies and the courts. In such cases, enforcement will probably depend on mundane processes and incremental measures that do not easily arouse the enthusiasm and commitment of ordinary citizens. It is at this stage that understanding the history, institutions, and values of national decisionmaking processes may prove especially critical.

Acknowledgments

The author has benefited enormously from the perceptive reactions to earlier drafts of this article by Nazli Choucri, Henry Lee, Marc Levy, Kalypso Nicolaidis, Susan J. Pharr, Louis T. Wells, Jr., and Philip Zelikow.

Notes

1. See N. Choucri, "Politics of Environmental Global Change: A Conceptual Framework" (Paper presented at the XV World Congress of the International Political Science Association, Buenos Aires, July 1991).

2. For an authoritative summary of such issues, see J. K. Sebenius, "Designing Negotiations Toward a New Regime," *International Security* 15, no. 4 (1991): 110–48. Also see R. E. Benedick, *Ozone Diplomacy: New Directions in Safeguarding the Planet* (Washington, D.C.: World Wildlife

Fund, 1990); J. T. Mathews, ed., *Preserving the Global Environment: The Challenge of Shared Leadership* (New York: W. W. Norton, 1990); and *Millennium* 19, no. 3 (Winter 1990), a special issue devoted to global environmental change and international relations.

3. See, for instance, G. Plant, "Institutional and Legal Responses to Global Climate Change," *Millennium,* note 2 above, pages 413–28.

4. Studies of U.S. policymaking are particularly rich. See, for instance, I. M. Destler, *American Trade Politics,* 2d ed. (Washington, D.C.: Institute for International Economics, 1992); and R. Vernon, D. L. Spar, and G. Tobin, *Iron Triangles and Revolving Doors: Case Studies in U.S. Foreign Economic Policymaking* (New York: Praeger, 1991).

5. J. W. Fesler, "Policymaking at the Top of Bureaucracy," in F. E. Rourke, ed., *Bureaucratic Power in National Policy Making* (Boston, Mass.: Little, Brown & Co., 1986), 317, 330; and R. B. Porter, *Presidential Decision Making: The Economic Policy Board* (Cambridge, England: Cambridge University Press, 1980), 5–21.

6. H. Heclo, *A Government of Strangers* (Washington, D.C.: Brookings Institution, 1977), 84–112.

7. R. B. Ripley and G. A. Franklin, *Congress, the Bureaucracy, and Public Policy* (Homewood, Ill.: Dorsey Press, 1980), 39, 45; and *Washington Post,* "Trading Places," 14 December 1990, A25.

8. S. D. Cohen, *The Making of United States International Economic Policy,* 3d ed. (New York: Praeger, 1988), 39–41; and Vernon, Spar, and Tobin, note 4 above, page 16.

9. The literature on this period is overwhelming in quantity and range. For a succinct summary of the international positions of the United States as they relate to domestic politics, see R. L. Paarlberg, "Ecodiplomacy: U.S. Environmental Policy Goes Abroad," in K. Oye, R. J. Lieber, and D. Rothschild, eds., *Eagle in a New World* (New York: Harper-Collins, 1992), 209–31. See, also, R. A. Harris and S. M. Milkis, *The Politics of Regulatory Change* (New York: Oxford University Press, 1989), 225–72.

10. See, for instance, T. C. Schelling, *The Strategy of Conflict* (Cambridge, Mass.: Harvard University Press, 1960), 27–28; R. Putnam, "The Logic of Two Level Games," *International Organization* 43 (1988):439–40; and H. R. Friman, "Rocks, Hard Places, and the New Protectionism: Textile Trade Policy Choices in the United States and Japan," *International Organization* 42 (August 1988):708–09.

11. See, for instance, J. K. Sebenius, *Negotiating the Law of the Sea* (Cambridge, Mass.: Harvard University Press, 1984), 71–109; and *The Economist,* "Faltering: GATT and Services," 14 July 1990, 70.

12. For a striking illustration, see Benedick, note 2 above, pages 58–67.

13. I. M. Destler, *American Trade Politics: System under Stress,* (Washington, D.C.: Institute for International Economics, 1986), 83–86.

14. See G. J. Ikenberry, "Manufacturing Consensus: The Institutionalization of American Private Interests in the Tokyo Trade Round," *Comparative Politics* 21, no. 3 (April 1989):295–301; and Destler, note 13 above, pages 19–22.

15. The literature on this topic is extensive. See, for instance, T. J. Pempel, "Japanese Foreign Economic Policy: The Domestic Bases for International Behavior," in P. J. Katzenstein, ed., *Between Power and Plenty: Foreign Economic Policies of Advanced Industrial States* (Madison, Wisc.: University of Wisconsin Press, 1978), 139–90; K. E. Calder, "Japanese Foreign Economic Policy Formation: Explaining the Reactive State," *World Politics* 40, no. 4 (July 1988):517–41; F. K. Upham, *Law and Social Change in Postwar Japan* (Cambridge, Mass.: Harvard University Press, 1987); D. I. Okimoto, "Political Inclusivity: The Domestic Structure of Trade," in T. Inoguchi and D. Okimoto, eds., *The Political Economy of Japan* vol. 2 (Stanford, Calif.: Stanford University Press, 1988), 345–78; and D. C. Hellman, "Japanese Politics and Foreign Policy," idem, 345–78.

16. See I. H. Anderson, "And Japan's Quest for Autonomy," in *The Standard-Vacuum Oil Company and the United States East Asian Policy, 1933–1941* (Princeton, N.J.: Princeton University Press, 1975), 71–103.

17. Benedick, note 2 above, page 75.

18. See, for instance, F. Koichi, "Wage Earners' Changing Attitudes," *Japan Echo* XV (1988):17–23; and *Financial Times,* "Japan's Employers Come to Terms with Young Job Hoppers," 24 September 1991, 10.

19. Detailed descriptions appear in S. Tsuru and H. Weidner, eds., *Environmental Policy in Japan* (Berlin: Ed Sigma Bohn, 1989); J. Gresser, K. Fujikura, and A. Morishima, *Environmental Law in Japan* (Cambridge, Mass.: MIT Press, 1981); and D. R. Kelley, K. R. Stunkel, and R. R. Wescott, *The Economic Superpowers and the Environment: The United States, the Soviet Union, and Japan* (San Francisco, Calif.: W. H. Freeman and Co., 1976). Especially useful is S. J. Pharr and J. L. Badaracco, Jr., "Coping with Crisis: Environmental Regulation," in T. K. McCraw, ed., *America Versus Japan* (Boston, Mass.: Harvard Business School Press, 1986), 229–60.

20. See M. A. McKean, *Environmental Protest and Citizen Politics in Japan* (Berkeley, Calif.: University of California Press, 1981); and N. Hudshle and M. Reich, *Island of*

Dreams: Environmental Crisis in Japan (Cambridge, Mass.: Schenkman Books, 1987), 14–23.

21. The interpretation draws heavily on Pharr and Badaracco, note 19 above.

22. For a detailed account of Japan's propensity to reduce conflict by payments to aggrieved parties, see K. E. Calder, *Crisis and Compensation: Public Policy and Political Stability in Japan, 1949–1986* (Princeton, N.J.: Princeton University Press, 1988).

23. See E. B. Keehn, "Managing Interests in the Japanese Bureaucracy: Informality and Discretion," *Asian Survey* XXX, no. II (November 1990):1021–37.

24. For the general tendency of Japan to maintain legal informality and to avoid hard-and-fast rules and standards, see, especially, Upham, note 15 above, pages 166–204. For these tendencies in the environmental field, see S. Nakamura and A. Toyonaga, "Making Environmental Policy in the United States and Japan: The Case of Global Warming," U.S.-Japan Program Occasional Paper 91–08 (Cambridge, Mass.: Harvard University, Program on U.S.-Japan Relations, 1991).

25. For a comparison of the U.S. and Japanese environmental movements, see McKean, note 20 above, pages 254–60.

26. Marc A. Levy of Princeton University in New Jersey generously gave the author access to some early drafts of his uncompleted doctoral thesis on environmental policies in Europe, which proved invaluable in bringing some critical details up to date. He bears no responsibility, however, for the author's interpretation of these facts.

27. See M. A. Levy, "The Greening of the United Kingdom: An Assessment of Competing Explanations" (Unpublished paper delivered at the annual meeting of the American Political Science Association, Washington, D.C., 29 August–1 September 1991).

28. C. Deck, "Negotiation and Compromise in German Environmental Politics: Government, Industry, and Public," in G. A. Mattox and A. B. Shingleton, *Germany at the Crossroads: Foreign and Domestic Policy Issues* (Boulder, Colo.: Westview Press, 1992), 149–61.

29. Compare with S. Jasanoff, "American Exceptionalism and the Political Acknowledgment of Risk," *Daedalus,* Fall 1990, 76.

30. See, for instance, A. J. Heidenheimer, H. Heclo, and C. Teich Adams, *Comparative Public Policy,* 3d ed. (New York: St. Martin's Press, 1990).

31. This tangled subject is well explored in N. Haigh, "The European Community and International Economic Policy," in A. Hurrell and B. Kingsbury, eds., *The International Politics of the Environment* (Oxford, England: Clarendon Press, 1992), 228–49; and A. Liberatore, "Problems of Transnational Policymaking: Environmental Policy in the European Community," *European Journal of Political Research* 19 (1991): 281–305.

32. Treaty of Rome, Article 36 (Brussels: European Documentation).

33. For a review, see J. Fairclough, "The Community's Environmental Policy," in R. Macrory, ed., *Britain, Europe and the Environment* (London: Imperial College, 1983), 19–34; D. P. Hackett and E. E. Lewis, "European Economic Community Environmental Requirements," in Practicing Law Institute, ed., *The European Economic Community's Product Liability Rules and Environmental Policy,* Course Handbook no. 388 (New York: Practicing Law Institute, 1990); and European Documentation, *Environmental Policy in the European Community,* 4th ed. (Brussels: European Documentation, 1990).

34. Levy, note 27 above, pages 20–28.

35. The revisions are found mainly in the provisions of the Treaty of Rome, note 32 above, Article 130.

36. Treaty of Rome, note 32 above, Article 130r.

37. Treaty on European Union (the Maastricht treaty) (Brussels: European Documentation), Article 3b.

38. *The Economist,* "The Dirty Dozen," 20 July 1991, 52.

39. In a meeting at Edinburgh in December 1992, the European Council, composed of the heads of member governments, agreed to various measures that would lift the curtain a little on the deliberations of the Council of Ministers.

40. See P. Ludlow, ed., *The Annual Review of European Community Affairs* (London: Brassey's, 1991), xxx–xxxiii.

41. The EC's proposal to adopt a carbon tax contingent on the United States and Japan following suit probably represents just such a case. See *Financial Times,* "Europeans Still Agonizing over Carbon Taxes," 19 February 1993, 3.

42. E. B. Skolnikoff, "The Policy Gridlock on Global Warming," *Foreign Policy* no. 79 (Summer 1990): 77–93.

43. *Environmental Policy in the European Community,* note 33 above, page 31.

44. A highly prescient article explores these trends in Europe; see S. Berger, "Politics and Antipolitics in Western Eu-

rope in the Seventies," *Daedalus* 108, no. 1 (Winter 1979): 27–50. In this article, Berger associates the trend with a general disillusionment with economic criteria as a basis for policy and thus offers an explanation of the survival and growth of environmental regulation.

45.   For reasons that escape the author, some scholars confine the concept of the epistemic community to organiza-tions that challenge the "habit-driven behavior" of the existing decisionmaking apparatus; see E. B. Haas, *When Knowledge Is Power* (Berkeley, Calif.: University of California Press, 1990), 40–49. But these transboundary communities may just as well be devoted to the preservation of existing habit-driven behavior and justify their position on the basis of their common beliefs.

10

Global Trade and the Environment
Edward Goldsmith

By now it should be clear that our environment is becoming ever less capable of sustaining the growing impact of our economic activities. Everywhere our forests are overlogged, our agricultural lands overcropped, our grasslands overgrazed, our wetlands overdrained, our groundwaters overtapped, our seas overfished, and nearly all our terrestrial and marine environment is overpolluted with chemical and radioactive poisons. Worse still, our atmospheric environment is becoming ever less capable of absorbing either the ozone-depleting gases or the greenhouse gases generated by these activities without creating new climatic conditions to which human beings cannot indefinitely adapt.

In such conditions, there can only be one way of maintaining the habitability of our planet, and that is to set out methodically to *reduce* the impact. Unfortunately, the overriding goal of just about every government in the world is to maximize this impact through economic globalization. Increased trade is seen to be the most effective way of increasing economic development, which we equate with progress and which is believed to provide a means of creating a material and technological paradise on Earth that will methodically eliminate all the problems that have confronted us thus far.

Unfortunately, economic development itself, by its very nature, *increases* the environ-

mental impact of our economic activities. This point is well illustrated by the terrible environmental destruction that has occurred in Taiwan and South Korea, the two principal newly industrialized countries that in the last decades, following the World Bank's dictates to permit heavy interventions by foreign transnational corporations, have achieved the most stunning rates of economic growth. The bank holds them up as models for all Third World countries to emulate.

THE CASE OF TAIWAN

In the case of Taiwan, as Walden Bello and Stephanie Rosenfeld have carefully documented in their book *Dragons in Distress* (1990), forests have been cleared to accommodate industrial and residential developments and to provide space on plantations for fast-growing conifers. The virgin broadleaf forests that once covered the entire eastern coast have now been almost completely destroyed. The vast network of roads built to open up the forests to logging, agriculture, and development have caused serious soil erosion, especially in the mountain areas, where whole slopes of bare soil have slid away.

Following "free trade" principles, efforts to maximize agricultural production for export-oriented plantations have led to the tripling of fertilizer use between 1952 and 1980, which has led to soil acidification, zinc losses, and decline in soil fertility, with water pollution and fertilizer runoff contaminating groundwater—the main source of drinking water for many Taiwanese. The use of pesticides has also increased massively, and it is a major source of contamination of Taiwan's surface waters and groundwaters. Because of deregulation, pesticide sale is subject to no effective government controls. The food produced is so contaminated with pesticides that, according to sociologist Michael Hsiao, "many farmers don't eat what they sell on the market. They grow another crop without using pesticides, and that is what they consume."

A substantial number of Taiwan's ninety thousand factories have been located in the countryside, on rice fields along waterways and near private residences. In order to maximize competitiveness, factory owners disregard whatever waste-disposal regulations exist and simply dump much of the waste into the nearest waterway. Not surprisingly, 20 percent of farmland, according to the government itself, is now polluted by industrial wastewater. Nor is it surprising that 30 percent of the rice grown in Taiwan is contaminated with heavy metals, including mercury, arsenic, and cadmium. Human waste, of which only about 1 percent receive even primary treatment, is flushed into rivers, providing nutrients for the unchecked growth of weeds, which use up the available oxygen and kill off the fish life. This also explains why Taiwan now has the world's highest incidence of hepatitis. Agricultural and industrial poisons and human waste have now severely polluted the lower reaches of nearly every one of Taiwan's major rivers, many of which are little more than flowing cesspools, devoid of fish. In Hou Jin, a small town near the city of Kaohsiung, forty years of pollution by the Taiwan Petroleum Company has not only made the water unfit to drink but actually combustible.

The shrimp-farming industry has achieved a fantastic growth rate, with prawn production increasing forty-five times in just ten years. Shrimp farmers, however, have themselves become deprived of the fresh water they need because of the buildup of toxic chemical wastes in rivers and wells from upstream industries. As a result, the mass deaths of prawns and fish have become a regular occurrence.

Air pollution has also increased massively, reaching levels that are double those judged harmful in the United States. The incidence of asthma has quadrupled since 1985, and cancer has now become the leading cause of death in Taiwan, its incidence having doubled since 1965. Even if the annual rate of economic growth in Taiwan were cut to 6.5 percent, stresses on Taiwan's already degraded environment would double in a decade—a horrifying thought.

Theoretically, once Taiwan has achieved a certain level of GNP, it might afford to install technological equipment to mitigate the destructiveness of the development process. However, with the advent of the global economy, competitiveness has become the order of the day. This has meant the elimination rather than the application of regulations, including environmental regulations, that increase costs to industry. In fact, not even the rich countries can now afford environmental controls, as the new GATT rules reflect.

THE CREATION OF CONSUMER CULTURES

Creating a global economy means seeking to *generalize* this destructive process, which means transforming the vast mass of still largely self-sufficient people living in the rural areas of the Third World into consumers of capital-intensive goods and services, mainly those provided by the transnational corporations (TNCs) (Menotti 1995).

For this to be possible, the cultural patterns that still imbue most Third World cultures and that commit them to their largely self-sufficient life-styles must be ruthlessly destroyed and supplanted by the culture and values of Western mass-consumer society. To this end, Western advertising firms, equipped with the latest global communication technologies, are already exporting the gospel of consumerism to the most distant areas of the Third World. Their purpose is to export the socially and environmentally devastating and utterly nonsustainable Western life-style to the five billion or so people who have not yet entirely adopted it. Of course, only the appetite for this life-style can be exported—the life-style itself only an insignificant minority will ever enjoy, and even then for but a brief period of time, for the whole enterprise is ecologically doomed.

The biosphere is incapable of sustaining all six billion of us at the consumption levels of the North. Indeed, the destruction that the global environment has suffered in the last fifty years, since global economic development has actually got under way, is certainly greater than all the destruction we have caused since the beginning of our tenancy on this planet. Our planet cannot possibly sustain a repetition of the last fifty years, let alone a similar period of still greater environmental destruction, without becoming incapable of sustaining complex forms of life.

To bring all Third World countries to the consumption level of the United States by the year 2060 would require 4 percent economic growth per year. The annual world output, however, and in effect the annual impact of our economic activities on the environment, would be 16 times what it is today—which is not even remotely conceivable. Nonetheless, America's Big Three automakers soon hope to finalize deals in China, with the hope of bringing automobiles to each person who now rides a bicycle or simply walks (Menotti 1995). The extra carbon dioxide emissions from several hundred million more automobiles would make nonsense of the tentative prognostics of the United Nations Intergovernmental Panel on Climate Change and lead to a massive escalation in global warming. If every Chinese were to have a refrigerator as well, which is an official goal of the Chinese government, emissions of CFCs, and HCFCs would make nonsense of the Montreal protocol to cut down on emissions of ozone-depleting substances.

THE EMPHASIS ON EXPORT

One of the principles of economic globalization and "free trade" is that countries should specialize in producing and exporting a few commodities that they produce particularly well and import almost everything else from other countries.

A very considerable portion of the world's most basic commodities is already produced for export—33 percent in the case of all plywood, 84 percent of coffee, 38 percent of fish, 47 percent of bauxite and alumina, 40 percent of iron ore, and 46 percent of crude oil (French 1993).

Since globalization has advanced, timber has also now become an export crop. In Malaysia, more than half the trees that are felled for timber are exported. This brings in one and a half billion dollars a year in foreign exchange but at a terrible environmental cost. Around 1945, Peninsula Malaysia was 70 to 80 percent forested. Today the trees are mostly gone. The result is escalating soil erosion, the fall of the water table in many areas, and a general increase in droughts and floods. The Malaysian states of Sarawak and Sabah are being stripped so rapidly by TNCs that in a few years all but the most inaccessible forests will be destroyed, and the culture and life-style of the local tribal people annihilated as well.

As country after country is logged out, the loggers simply move elsewhere. In Southeast Asia loggers move to New Guinea, Laos, Myanmar, and Cambodia, the last countries that are still forested—and, significantly, those that have remained outside the orbit of the world trading system. At the current rate of forest destruction, these countries will be deforested within the next decade. Already, Mitsubishi and Weyerhauser are moving into Siberia—the last major unlogged forest area on the planet.

Measures to control logging are unlikely. In most Southeast Asian countries, for instance, the politicians and their families own the concessions, and the transnational logging companies they deal with are too powerful to control (Marshall 1990). Only a collapse of the world economy is likely to save the remaining loggable forests.

Somalia has become increasingly dependent on exports of sheep, goats, and cattle, which have grown at least tenfold, and of camels, which have increased twentyfold since 1955. This has contributed to "a breakdown of the traditional, ecologically sensitive, nomadic system of livestock rearing—leading to overgrazing, soil erosion, and the degradation of range lands, all of which will diminish the ability of the land to provide sustenance for the Somali people" (French 1993). Internal warfare and gangsterism has been one result.

Tobacco is another crop grown for export worldwide, accounting for 1.5 percent of total agricultural export. In the case of Malawi it represents 55 percent of the country's foreign exchange earnings. Robert Goodland (1984) notes that "tobacco depletes soil nutrients at a much higher rate than most other crops, thus rapidly decreasing the life of the soil." But the heaviest environmental cost of tobacco production lies in the sheer volume of wood needed to fuel tobacco-curing barns. Every year, the world loses some 12,000 square kilometers of forest (some experts estimate 50,000 square kilometers), which are cut down, with 55 cubic meters of cut wood burnt for every ton of tobacco cured (Goldsmith and Hildyard 1990).

Coffee is also largely a high-export crop, and its production causes the most serious environmental degradation. As Georg Borgstrom (1967) writes: "The almost predatory exploitations by the coffee planters have ruined a considerable proportion of Brazil's soils."

The same can be said of peanut plantations in French West Africa. Indeed it has been estimated that "after only two successive years of peanut growing, there is a loss of thirty percent of the soil's organic matter and sixty percent of the colloidal humus. In two successive years of peanut planting, the second year's yield will be from twenty to forty percent lower than the first" (Franke and Chasin 1981).

What the export-oriented logging industry is doing to our forests and the livestock-rearing schemes and intensive plantations are doing to our land, the high-tech fishing industry, itself dependent on exports—with 38 percent of fish caught worldwide exported—is doing to the seas. Today, nine of the world's seventeen major fishing grounds are in decline, and four are already "fished out" commercially (Wilkes 1995). Total catches in the Northwest Atlantic have fallen by almost one-third during the last twenty years. In 1992, the great cod fisheries of the Grand Banks off Newfoundland in Canada were closed indefinitely, and in Europe mackerel stocks in the North Sea have decreased by fiftyfold since the 1960s.

As fish stocks are depleted in the North, the fleets are now congregating in the south, but the volume of fish exported from developing nations has increased by nearly four times since 1975, and southern fisheries are already under stress (French 1993). The predictable result is the depletion of Third World fisheries too, with the most drastic consequences for local fishing communities.

The expansion of many export-oriented industries gives rise to a whole range of adverse environmental consequences affecting most aspects of peoples' lives. An obvious case in point is the intensive prawn-farming industry that has been expanding rapidly not only in Taiwan but throughout Asia and some parts of the Americans and Africa.

To accommodate prawn farms, about half of the world's mangrove forests have already been cut down. In Ecuador 120,000 hectares of mangroves have been destroyed for this purpose. In Thailand the figure is 100,000 hectares. The consequences of mangrove destruction are catastrophic for local fishing communities, as many fish species necessarily spend the early part of their life cycle among the mangroves.

Another environmental consequence of prawn farms is a reduction in the availability of fresh water for irrigation in nearby rice paddies, the reason being that prawn farms require large amounts of a fresh water–sea water mix in order to produce the brackish water that the prawns require. In the Philippines the overextraction of groundwater for prawn farms in Negros Occidental "has caused shallow wells, orchards and ricelands to dry up, land to subside and salt water to intrude from the sea" (Wilkes 1995).

Because shrimps are carnivorous and feed on fishmeal, prawn farming has also further increased the pressure on world fish supplies. By 1991, 15 percent of world fishmeal supply was consumed by prawn farms. This has seriously reduced the supply of inexpensive locally available fish, such as sardines, for local consumption.

As more and more land is required for the cultivation of export crops, the food needs of rural peoples must be met by production from an evershrinking land base. Worse, it is always the good land that is devoted to export crops—land that lends itself to intensive, large-scale mass production. Production for export always has priority since it offers what governments are keenest to obtain: foreign exchange. The rural population is thus increasingly confined to often forested but nevertheless rocky and infertile lands, or steep slopes that are very vulnerable to erosion and totally unsuited to agriculture. These areas are rapidly stripped of their forest cover, ploughed up, and degraded. This has occurred, and continues to occur, just about everywhere in the Third World.

An example is provided by the rapid growth of the soya bean cultivation in Brazil—now the second largest soya bean exporter after the United States. One of the results of such growth has been the forced migration of vast numbers of peasants from their lands in the southern state of Rio Grande do Sul and into Amazonia, in particular to the states of Rondonia and Para, where they have cleared vast areas of forest to provide the land from which they must now derive their sustenance. The land, which is largely lateritic, is totally unsuitable to agriculture and after a few years becomes so degraded that it is no longer of any use. This forces the peasants to clear more forest, which provides them with land for another few years—a process that could theoretically continue until all available forest has been destroyed.

I recently toured the province of Kwa Zulu Natal, in the company of South Africa's leading conservationist, Ian Player, who for a long time was director of Natal's national parks. He showed me that most of the good agricultural land had been converted into plantations producing cash crops, in particular sugar cane and eucalyptus, largely for export. The "tribal lands" to which the bulk of the Zulu population has been consigned occupy rocky and infertile slopes that are eroding fast. The various tribal groups are desperately seeking more land. They know that they cannot obtain access to the plantations, because the lands provide foreign exchange, so they are lodging claims for much of the land that at present forms part of the national parks. In the meantime, because of the deforestation required to accommodate the plantations and the subsistence agriculture in the tribal lands—and also because sugar cane and eucalyptus are highly water-intensive crops (sugar cane being ten times more so than wheat for instance)—the local rivers have dried up and only flow during the rainy season. We flew over one dried-up river bed after another, where in Ian Player's youth there were magnificent rivers with clean water and abundant fish life.

INCREASED TRANSPORT

So far we have only considered the local effects of extractive export industries, such as logging, ranching, fishing, and prawn farming. But the produce of such industries and that of mining minerals, oil, coal, natural gas, and manufactured goods, must be transported to the countries that import them. With the development of the global economy the volume of such produce and the distances over which it must be transported increase significantly.

Already in 1991, four billion tons of freight were exported by ship worldwide, and this required 8.1 exajoules of energy, which is as much as was used by the entire economies of Brazil and Turkey combined. Seventy million tons of freight that year were sent by plane, and this used 0.6 exajoules, which is equal to the total annual energy use of the Philippines (French 1993).

A European Union task force calculated that the creation of the single market in Europe in 1993 would greatly increase cross-border traffic with a consequent increase in air pollution and noise by 30 to 50 percent. With the growth in trade between North America and Mexico, cross-border trucking has doubled since 1990, and this is even before trade barriers were reduced between the two countries. The U.S. government predicted that after the signature of the North American Free Trade Agreement (NAFTA), cross-border trucking would increase nearly sevenfold. The ratification of the GATT Uruguay Round can only increase the worldwide transport of goods even more dramatically—which means that a vast number of new highways, airports, harbors, and warehouses must be built, which in itself can only cause serious environmental destruction.

The trans-Amazonian highway, for instance, which is designed to supply Asian markets with more timber and minerals, is ripping through one of the most richly forested areas of the tropics. Like previous World Bank–funded highways carved through primary forests (such as the notorious Polonoereste Project, which catalyzed the deforestation of Rondonia and the annihilation of most of its tribal groups), the trans-Amazonian will fragment habitat and open up previously inaccessible lands to loggers, miners, ranchers, and settlers.

In its aim to expand and accelerate the transport of goods along the Río de la Plata, the Hidrovia project of the MercoSur countries will dry out Brazil's Pantanal (the world's largest wetland, which contains the highest diversity of mammals), while worsening flooding downstream. The building of more ports, essential for exporting and importing goods, destroys coastal habitats by demolishing wetlands and mangrove forests, increasing chemical spillage, and dredging the bottoms of bays and lagoons. The increased transport itself will give rise to even more environmental devastation, considering the pollution caused by the extra combustion of fossil fuels—particularly the effect of increased CO_2 emissions on global warming—and the accidents during transport that lead to oil and chemical spills. Indeed, if the environmental costs of increased transport were properly internalized, much of world trade would be revealed as uneconomic, and we would return to a more localized, less environmentally destructive trading system (Menotti 1995).

INCREASED COMPETITION

A European Community (EC) report has seriously questioned the effectiveness of current environmental regulations in protecting our environment as the impact on it continues to grow. The report points out that there has already been a 13 percent increase in the generation of municipal wastes between 1986 and 1991, a 35 percent increase in the EC's water withdrawal rate between 1970 and 1985, and a 63 percent increase in fertilizer use between 1986 and 1991. The report predicts that if current growth rates continue, carbon dioxide emissions will increase by 20 percent by the year 2010, rendering unapplicable the EU countries' commitment to stabilize them by the year 2000.

Clearly then, these regulations must be seriously strengthened. However, in the free-for-all of the global economy no country can strengthen environmental regulations that increase corporate costs without putting itself at a "comparative disadvantage" vis-à-vis its competitors—and running afoul of GATT.

The push for a global carbon tax illustrates the problem. The European Union (EU) and Japan both proposed adopting an international tax on fossil fuels as a first step in a campaign to reduce carbon dioxide emissions. In the United States, however, the Clinton administration decided that it could not get such a tax through Congress; it was called "electorally impossible." So the EU and Japan dropped the idea. Fossil fuel use and carbon dioxide emissions thereby remain almost entirely out of control (Menotti 1995).

In other words, responsible producers who seek to minimize environmental impacts must compete against those who do not and are therefore "more competitive." This, among other things, endangers—indeed condemns—the world's remaining ecologically sustainable economic activities.

An important example is the dilemma of Amazonia's rubber tappers, who extract latex from the rubber trees scattered throughout much of the Amazonian forests in a perfectly sustainable manner. They will encounter increasing difficulty in competing with rubber grown on Asian plantations that have been created by clearing entire tropical forests. They will especially feel pressure from transnational tire companies with plants in Brazil—such as Michelin and Goodyear—as tariffs on natural rubber imports are due to be eliminated in the next decade (Menotti 1995).

Also, in order to increase competitiveness, corporations are increasingly undertaking cost-cutting measures that include reducing, often drastically, the number of their employees. This can significantly increase environmental accidents. A case in point is the Exxon *Valdez* disaster, which would probably not have occurred if Exxon had not eliminated eighty thousand jobs, including reducing the crews of its supertankers by one-third (Hawken 1993). In addition, before the days of "competitiveness," the supertanker would normally have navigated in a safe but slow shipping lane. Instead, it moved to a much faster though more dangerous lane, passing through ice floes from the Columbia glacier. The Bhopal disaster also probably would not have occurred if Union Carbide had not indulged in cost-cutting measures at the risk of safety (Hultgren 1995).

DEREGULATION

Until recently, corporations were limited in their efforts to cut costs by a host of national regulations that protected the interests of labor, the unemployed, the poor, and, of course, the environment. To the hard-nosed businessman, these regulations were bureaucratic red tape, serving only to increase costs and reduce competitiveness and profit. Pressure has mounted everywhere to get rid of these regulations as quickly as possible. The term used to achieve this short-sighted goal is *deregulation,* and it has recently become the order of the day. When George Bush was vice president, he headed the Reagan administration's Task Force on Regulatory Relief, which, according to Public Citizen's Congress Watch, was involved in thwarting workers' safety regulations, obstructing consumer product safety controls, rolling back highway safety initiatives, and weakening environmental protection. In 1989, during the Bush administration, the work was taken over by Vice President Quayle's Council on Competitiveness. The council was active in opening up for development half of the United States' protected wetlands while tabling over a hundred amendments to the EPA's implementation proposals for the 1990s Clear Air Act.

Whatever deregulation could not be achieved within countries has now been neatly achieved by the new GATT and WTO agreements and through the creation of "free trade zones."

There are now some two hundred free trade zones in the Third World, usually situated near key communication centers. Foreign industries are enticed to establish themselves in these zones by being freed from any effective labor or environmental controls. In such areas, deregulation has been systematic and complete, and environmental devastation has occurred on a literally horrific scale. As Alexander Goldsmith argues in his chapter, the ratification of GATT effectively transforms the whole world into one vast free trade zone.

Further instances of the environmental consequences of increased competitiveness and deregulation are found in those Third World countries that in the last ten years have been subject to brutal International Monetary Fund (IMF) and World Bank structural adjustment programs.

For example, Costa Rica was subjected to nine IMF and World Bank structural adjustment programs between 1980 and 1989. The massive expansion of the banana industry and of heavily subsidized cattle ranching greatly facilitated the increase of exports. But the expansion took place at the cost of self-sufficient small-scale agriculture and of the country's forest cover, which dropped from 50 percent in 1970 to 37 percent in 1987 and still further since. Increasing banana production has also been directly destructive to the environment. Huge amounts of chemical fertilizers and pesticides have been used, which are washed into the rivers and end up in the sea, severely damaging coral reefs.

Ninety percent of such reefs have been annihilated in some areas.

By signing the GATT Uruguay Round Agreement, our politicians are effectively subjecting the entire world to one vast structural adjustment program, which ruthlessly subordinates all environmental, social, and indeed moral considerations to the overriding goal of maximizing trade. The environmental consequences can only be grave.

More effective than deregulation carried out by national governments within their own country is a process that we can call *cross deregulation*—deregulation that is conveniently imposed on countries by their own trading partners under the GATT Uruguay Round Agreement. For example, the EU's April 1994 *Report on U.S. Barriers to Trade and Investment* suggests that the commissioners should seek to overturn a large number of Californian and U.S. federal environmental laws that it felt can successfully be classified as GATT illegal trade barriers. These include California's Safe Drinking Water and Toxic Enforcement Act (Proposition 65), which requires warning labels on products containing known carcinogenic substances. Among the U.S. federal laws targeted by the EU are the "gas guzzler" law and other laws that aim to encourage the production of smaller, more fuel-efficient cars. [For a more extensive list of the laws threatened by GATT challenges, see chapter by Ralph Nader and Lori Wallach.]

It has been estimated by the U.S. chief negotiator at one of the preparatory meetings for the Rio environmental conference that 80 percent of America's environmental legislation could be challenged in this way, and most of it could be declared illegal before WTO panels.

Meanwhile, the United States and other countries can also obligingly challenge European Union environmental laws, resulting in a process whereby countries deregulate each other to the benefit of TNCs.

THE "STANDARDS" OF FREE TRADE

It is important to realize that the new free trade agreements were designed and promoted by associations of businesses for whom environmental regulations are no more than costs that interfere with profits and therefore must be minimized.

From the very start of the negotiations that led to the signing of these treaties, the environmental issue has been avoided altogether whenever possible. As Canadian Greenpeace activist Steven Shrybman reports (1990), the Canadian government actually sought to justify this omission in the case of the Canada-U.S. agreement on the grounds that "it is a commercial accord between the world's two largest trading partners. It is not an environmental agreement," and "the environment is not therefore a subject for negotiation; nor are environmental matters included in the text of the agreement." Shrybman goes on: "This is an astonishing statement, in view of the fact that the agreement explicitly deals with such issues as energy, agriculture, forest management, food safety and pesticide regulations, matters that could not bear more directly on the environment."

Nor is it surprising that the very word *environment* appears nowhere in the mandate of GATT. Neither is it mentioned in the constitution of the World Trade Organization, save in a cursory manner in the preamble.

Public pressure has, of course, forced the bureaucrats to take some notice of environmental issues, and there is even talk of "greening the GATT." But, whatever the rhetoric, environmental standards that will increase costs to industry are summarily rejected. Thus in 1971 the GATT secretariat stated that it was inadmissible to raise tariffs so as to take into account pollution abatement costs. In 1972 it refused to accept "the polluter pays principle," even though it had been adopted by the Organization for Economic Cooperation and Development (OECD) Council that same year.

It is thereby not surprising that the international standards for food safety set by the Codex Alimentarius (a little-known U.N. agency that now fixes international food safety standards) are not designed to influence countries to increase their pitifully lax environmental standards but, on the contrary, to reduce them. Thus 42 percent of the Codex standards for pesticides are lower than EPA and FDA standards. Fifty times more DDT, for instance, may be used on or left in residual amounts on peaches and bananas, and thirty three times more DDT may be applied on broccoli.

In the interests of the international harmonization of standards, the EPA and FDA standards will almost certainly be challenged. They are too high, but if they were lower, they would not be challenged, for, as Ralph Nader puts it, "the international standards provide a ceiling but not a floor" for environmental and health protection (testimony before the House Small Business Committee, April 26, 1994). Governments might theoretically set standards that are higher than the WTO standards, but only if the standards can avoid being classified as nontariff barriers to trade and hence as GATT-illegal. This is extremely difficult.

The global economy we are creating can therefore only massively increase environmental destruction—not only by increasing its impact on an environment that cannot sustain the present impact but also by eliminating regulations designed to contain this impact, and which necessarily increase corporate costs.

Clearly, there is no way of protecting our environment within the context of a global "free trade" economy committed to continued economic growth and hence to increasing the harmful impact of our activities on an already fragile environment.

We must reverse our course. As Tim Lang and Colin Hines recommend in their book, *The New Protectionism* (1993), we must seek to emphasize local production for local consumption, reduce global trade, and ensure strong environmental standards at all times. There is no evidence that trade or economic development are of any great value to humanity. World trade has increased by twelve times since 1950 and economic growth has increased fivefold, yet during this period there has been an unprecedented increase in poverty, unemployment, social disintegration, and environmental destruction. The environment, on the other hand, is our greatest wealth, and to kill it, as the TNCs are methodically doing, is an act of unparalleled criminality. What is more, it can only be in their own very short-term interests to do so, for, as their leaders should realize, there can be no trade and no economic development on a dead planet.

References

Bello, Walden, and Stephanie Rosenfeld, 1990. *Dragons in Distress: Asia's Miracle Economies in Crisis.* San Francisco: Institute for Food and Development Policy.

Borgstrom, Georg. 1967. *The Hungry Planet.* New York: Collier.

Franke, R., and B. Chasin. 1981. "Peasants, Peanuts, Profits and Pastoralists." *Ecologist* 11(4).

French, Hilary. 1993. "Costly Tradeoffs Reconciling Trade and the Environment." Washington, D.C.: WorldWatch Institute.

Goldsmith, Edward, and Nicholas Hildyard. 1990. "The Earth Report No. 2." London: Mitchell Beazley.

Goodland, Robert. 1984. "Environmental Management in Tropical Agriculture." Boulder, Colo.: Westview Press.

Hawken, Paul. 1993. *The Ecology of Commerce: A Declaration of Sustainability.* New York: HarperBusiness.

Hultgren, John. 1995. "International Political Economy and Sustainability." Oberlin College, Unpublished.

Lang, Tim, and Colin Hines. 1993. *The New Protectionism: Protecting the Future Against Free Trade.* New York: New Press.

Marshall, George. 1990. "The Political Economy of Logging: The Barnett Inquiry into Corruption in the Papua New Guinea Timber Industry." *Ecologist* 20(5).

Menotti, Victor. 1995. "Free Trade and the Environment." Unpublished.

Shrybman, Steven. 1990. "International Trade and the Environment: An Environmental Assessment of the General Agreement on Tariffs and Trade." *Ecologist* 20(1).

Wilkes, Alex. 1995. "Prawns, Profits and Protein: Aquaculture and Food Production." *Ecologist* 25(2–3).

11

Making Trade Work for the Environment
Daniel C. Esty

The proposition that trade harms the environment and that more trade harms it more (that is, trade liberalization is bad) has two separate environmental perspectives embedded within it. First, some environmentalists adhere to a "limits to growth" philosophy and are opposed to economic development and thus to almost all trade. Adherents to this no-growth world view have little interest in building environmental safeguards into the GATT. For them, no trade is good trade. Other environmentalists accept "sustainable development" as a goal and see economic growth as positive if it is achieved in ways that are sensitive to the environment. These "pragmatic" environmentalists seek to ensure that some of the gains from trade are in fact devoted to environmental purposes and that environmental safeguards put the economic activities promoted by trade on a sustainable course.

The elements of the environmental community that are convinced that trade and environmental protection are in inexorable conflict want to gut the GATT (Lang and Hines 1993). Adherents to a "small is beautiful" philosophy see trade liberalization resulting in unchecked development and economic growth resulting in more pollution, unsustainable resource use, and a buildup of waste in critical ecosystems. As Batra (1993, 245) bluntly declares: "Since trade

pollutes the earth, it is essential that it be kept to the minimum."

In fact, this line of criticism has nothing really to do with trade. It reflects the affinity of a vocal antigrowth minority in the environmental community for a nonmaterialistic world where individuals live simply with what they or others nearby can produce. From this point of view, international trade is not much worse than domestic exchange of goods. As one wag joked, adherents to this "deep ecology" philosophy support trade only to the extent possible by bicycle.

Although simplicity and less materialism may be virtues, this neo-Luddite vision of Nirvana holds little attraction for most people in the United States or around the world. Despite the underlying truth that unending population growth and the increased economic activity that accompanies it are not sustainable in the long run, the question is, when will the long run come and what will happen in the intervening time?

Herman Daly argues that the world is already 40 percent "full" (Goodland et al. 1992, 30) in the sense that nearly half of all arable land has been put into use for food production. He therefore concludes that the "limits to growth" are near. Others see population curves dipping down and foresee technological advances forestalling the Malthusian crisis[1]—making economic growth a positive force for centuries to come. Based on this latter view, the majority of environmentalists today have adopted a credo of sustainable development that supports economic growth so long as it builds in protection for public health and ecological resources.

But pro-growth environmentalists share

143

their no-growth colleagues' concern with the concept of pure free trade (Lallas, Esty, and Van Hoogstraten 1992). There is, they argue, no *a priori* reason in the absence of environmental safeguards to be confident that free trade will produce benefits that exceed its costs and therefore improve social welfare. A richer society is not necessarily a better society. If environmental problems are not properly accounted for, today's prosperity may be acquired under false pretenses that make society worse off over the long run. In pure economic terms, if the cost of addressing future environmental harms caused by today's economic activities is great enough, then the wealth acquired now and endowed to our progeny will not adequately compensate them for the environmental debts we also leave them.

Thus, sustainability cannot be assumed; it must be expressly provided for in trade agreements. Economists concede that to maximize social welfare, the benefits of trade must be weighed against the costs of ecological degradation from expanded economic activity (e.g., Anderson 1992). They recognize that, to be fully appropriate, this calculus must factor in all costs, including those that have traditionally not been part of the analysis because they were externalized and never translated into a price that someone paid. In fact, most economists would acknowledge that a number of assumptions about the functioning of the market must be fulfilled to be confident that market forces will produce an efficient social outcome.[2]

THE "TRADE IS PRO-ENVIRONMENT" CASE

GATT officials and others in the trade world do not perceive themselves or the international trade regime to be anti-environmental. Thus, the trade community was initially caught off guard by the force of the anti-trade green onslaught. As good economists, most free traders see both trade liberalization and environmental protection directed toward more efficient use of

resources and thus fundamentally compatible. Their confidence in this convergence of interests stems in particular from a conviction that trade generates wealth that can be used to address environmental problems and from a belief that market forces, if properly channeled, will protect the environment in the context of trade liberalization. Thus, free traders seemed taken aback at the outset of the trade and environment debate that their studious environmental agnosticism was viewed as heresy by environmental true believers.

Trade Generates Resources That Can Be Devoted to Environmental Protection

GATT experts are often puzzled by the failure of many environmentalists to see the links between trade, economic growth, and the availability of resources to invest in environmental protection. As Palmeter (1993, 69) suggests: "Any dispassionate study of the issue reveals . . . not only that the areas of potential conflict are limited and manageable, but also that expanded trade, by increasing overall world wealth, itself can contribute to the cause of a better environment." GATT officials frequently make the same point. In its sharply argued 1992 Trade and Environment Report (GATT 1992, 19), the GATT Secretariat observes that the international trade regime supports environmental protection by increasing the efficiency of resource use and raising incomes, making possible increased expenditures on the environment. Similarly, both the Bush and Clinton administrations argued that the North American Free Trade Agreement would advance the cause of environmental protection in Mexico by providing new funds through economic growth for much-needed environmental investments (USTR 1992 and 1993).

In building on this pro-growth, pro-environment proposition, the free traders are in good company. The widely heralded Brundtland Report, for example, argues that environmental protection supports long-term economic growth—that is, sustainable development—and that prosperity, promoted by trade liberalization, enhances the prospects for sustained support for environmental protection. In fact, the Brundtland Report can be read to make an even more fundamental point: poverty per se is a form of environmental degradation, and thus economic well-being is an environmental plus, regardless of its effects on pollution control or environmental protection efforts.

The correlation between prosperity and environmental protection seems logical (rich countries can afford higher environmental standards), appears consistent with observed data (despite higher levels of emissions, air and water quality is generally higher in OECD countries than in developing nations) and has some empirical support. Notably, Grossman and Krueger's (1993) study of pollution levels and national wealth concludes that although poor countries suffer increased pollution as they begin to industrialize, when they reach middle-income levels (about $5,000 GDP per capita), they invest more in pollution controls, and emission concentrations begin to fall (Figure 1).

In response, environmentalists observe that the correlation between economic conditions and pollution levels reflects only a theoretical relationship, not necessarily a causal connection (Lee 1992). Environmentalists remain suspicious that the invisible hand of market forces is

FIGURE 1 ● Income and Pollution

Concentrations of sulfur dioxide rise with income at low levels of per capita GDP, fall with income at middle levels of GDP, and eventually level off in the most advanced economies. The estimated turning point comes at a per capita income level of about $5,000 (1988 dollars).

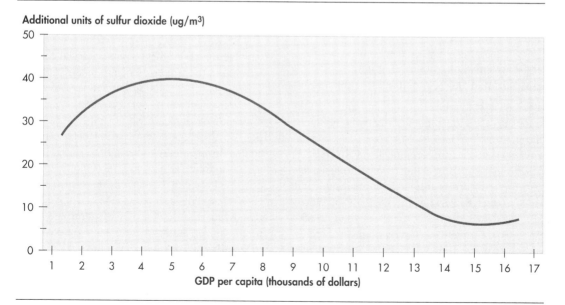

Source: Grossman and Krueger (1993), MIT Press. Reprinted by permission.

attached to an insufficiently environmentally conscious body. They argue that, in the trade liberalization context, the economic growth/environmental progress link should be made explicit, with environmental funding provisions accompanying all free trade agreements. Express environmental commitments are needed, they suggest, because political forces tend to neglect environmental considerations, and the time lags between economic growth and increases in environmental spending may be substantial. In addition, environmentalists point out that many studies, including Grossman and Krueger's, show increases in pollution in the short to medium run. Thus how growth takes place matters a good bit.

In light of this reality, trade liberalization efforts should be accompanied by environmental analyses designed to identify environmental harms that might be exacerbated by freer trade and to spot opportunities to advance environmental protection. These environmental impact assessments need not be exhaustive studies but should be designed to alert trade negotiators to the environmental variables they face and to alternative ways of dealing with them. . . .

The Economic Congruence of Trade Liberalization and Environmental Protection

The free traders' more dramatic argument is that trade liberalization ought to directly help protect the environment. At least in theory, the scope for environmental harm arising from liberalized trade can be greatly reduced or eliminated by ensuring that prices fully reflect environmental costs. In fact, Robert Repetto (1993a) and others (Richard Stewart 1992; Anderson and Blackhurst 1992) argue that there is no inherent trade and environment conflict since both trade liberalization and environmental regulation have similar aims—to make more efficient use of resources. Stephan Schmidheiny, chairman of the Business Council for Sustainable Development,

makes the same point in arguing for businesses to become "eco-efficient." Specifically, Schmidheiny (1992, xxiii) observes: "Conservation of the environment and successful business development should be opposite sides of the same coin—the coin being the measure of the progress of human civilization."

From this perspective, the key to reconciling trade and environmental policy goals is implementing the polluter pays principle and internalizing environmental harms. If environmental externalities are internalized,[3] free trade will increase welfare both nationally and globally.[4] Moreover, market forces, including free trade, result in more efficient resource use (reducing the stress on natural resources), encourage technological innovation, and lower the cost of environmental protection by improving productivity and permitting the same levels of output to be produced at lower costs both in monetary and environmental terms. As Young (1994) argues, if "social costs and nonmarket considerations could be factored into global markets, then the gains from trade liberalization would be unambiguously positive in a social and an economic sense."

The key issue, in laymen's language, is whether the prices that businesses and the public see reflect the full costs of producing and consuming goods, including burdens currently unaccounted for that are imposed on others through environmental spillovers such as pollution. In this regard, the tension between trade and environmental policies can be traced to pervasive market failures to which environmental policies have not adequately responded. Many environmentalists recognize the value of cost internalization both as a way of improving environmental protection per se and as a means of reconciling trade and environmental policies (Repetto et al. 1989; Meyer 1993). As Pearson (1994, 5) argues: "By allocating abatement costs to the private sector, market prices would more closely reflect the social cost of production. This would tend to encourage pollution abatement by reducing consumption of pollution-intensive products. . . . Thus the [polluter pays principle] supports improved efficiency in the allocation of natural and environmental resources (i.e., helps correct externality-distorted product prices). At the same time, it helps prevent a *trade* distortion."

But even economically minded environmentalists worry about the difficulties of putting this line of reasoning into practice. They note that the obverse of this argument is that market forces may not protect the environment if pollution effects and natural resources are inappropriately priced or given no value at all. They recognize that uncorrected market failures are the rule, not the exception, in the environmental realm (and other) areas and thus that trade liberalization does not now generally work to reduce environmental harms.[5] More specifically, because so many resources are improperly priced, market forces cannot today be relied upon to allocate scarce natural resources efficiently or to guarantee that polluters will face real incentives to minimize their emissions.[6]

Economists also recognize the difficulty of implementing the polluter pays principle. Pearson (1994, 3) notes: "Although durable and widely referenced, the [principle] is not without its ambiguities and idiosyncratic interpretations." He identifies a number of issues: who pays internalized costs, how much polluters should pay, which economic instruments are compatible with the principle, and how equity and fairness considerations are taken into account.

In addition to the ease with which pollution travels, another difficulty with getting environmental prices right is that natural resources tend to be communal property, or what economists call public goods—no one owns them exclusively. Air, for instance, is a public good; anyone can breath it or emit pollutants into it. Because of the difficulty of charging people for using or excluding people from taking advantage of these resources, they tend to be overused or exploited.

Economic theory offers two solutions to the public-goods problem. First, Pigou (1918) suggests that where free market competition systematically undervalues a resource, government intervention to correct this market failure through fees, taxes, or subsidies is required. Coase (1960) offers another approach based on the assignment of property rights in the overexploited resource. He argues that once resource ownership is established (no matter whether rights are assigned to the polluters or those affected by emissions) and assuming no transactions costs, the polluters and others who have an interest in the resource will negotiate a price and other terms for the use of the resource that will result in an optimal (sustainable) level of exploitation.

Society already relies on both of these mechanisms to regulate environmental amenities and natural resources. For example, escalating taxes have been placed on chlorofluorocarbons (CFCs) in the United States to protect the ozone layer—a public good. These fees have created an incentive not to use products that damage the ozone and have in fact resulted in a sharp drop in CFC consumption, ahead of the schedule mandated by the Montreal Protocol and its amendments. The assignment of property rights has also been used to improve environmental protection. For instance, the issuance of a limited number of permits to set lobster traps has stopped overharvesting and helped to stabilize the lobster population in Long Island Sound.

Most environmental regulation builds on both the assignment of property rights and efforts (albeit often crude) to adjust prices to reflect social costs. . . . One of the critical forces shaping the trade and environment conflict is the reassertion of public ownership over air and water, which had previously been viewed as a free good. With the property right established, the government can reduce exploitation by controlling access with permits or by charging emissions fees. Nevertheless, there are many resources over which property rights remain in doubt and an even greater number of cases in which pollution burdens or natural resources remain unpriced or underpriced.

Beyond the problem of externalities and the public-goods nature of environmental amenities, there is a third element of market failure that requires government intervention to ensure optimal attention to environmental protection: the intergenerational aspect of many environmental problems (Brown Weiss 1989). Specifically, because environmental problems often have long lead times and show threshold effects, it is possible for one generation to ignore issues at the expense of future generations, who will have to face the problems as they become visible and acute. In these circumstances, the market fails to produce an optimal outcome because future generations are not able to cast their market "votes" and bequest motives may not be strong enough to ensure optimal long-term outcomes (Diamond 1977; Brandts and de Bartolome 1988).

These market failures result in a sometimes significant divergence between private marginal costs and social marginal costs in the environmental realm—throwing off the price signals that would otherwise work to promote environmental efficiency (i.e., supporting long-term optimal consumption of natural resources and limiting use of the natural world as a waste dump). Cairncross (1992, 89) observes in *Costing the Earth:*

> . . . in environmental affairs, the invisible hand of the market fails to align the interests of the individual or the individual company with those of society at large. Individuals may drive their cars to work rather than take a bus; companies may use CFCs to insulate and cool refrigerators. In both cases, the costs to the environment

and thus to society at large exceed any private cost to individual or company. That is inefficient. Governments need to step in to align private costs with social costs.

Increasingly, economists and environmentalists agree that the way to respond to this failure is through full-cost pricing and adherence to the polluter pays principle. Moving in this policy direction would align economic forces and environmental protection needs. It would, more pointedly, help to ensure that the market incentives brought to bear by freer trade would also help to protect ecological values.

POLICY IMPLICATIONS

Several policy implications follow from the notion that the polluter pays principle and better cost internalization would not only correct the recognized market failures that plague environmental protection but also improve the environmental consequences of trade liberalization. First, efforts to convert environmental regulation from command-and-control requirements to market-based mechanisms ought to gain added impetus. If environmental regulations were market-based (not ad hoc emissions limits or technology requirements) and "monetized" (i.e., reduced to a price paid for the harm caused), then their scope for conflict with market access agreements and disciplines on standards would be much reduced. For example, if the United States sought to discourage gasoline consumption with a higher gas tax rather than the Corporate Average Fuel Efficiency (CAFE) fleetwide mileage requirements, Volvo, BMW, and Mercedes would have no basis for complaining about unfair treatment in the US market. Broad-based commitment to cost internalization would also reduce the need for using trade as leverage, except to ensure adherence to the polluter pays principle. Countries might still disagree over how much must be charged to internalize environmental costs, but such disputes would be a matter of degree.

Second, less-radical revision of the GATT would be required if progress were made in shifting from standards-based environmental regulation to cost internalization. In other words, GATT reform and environmental policy conversion are in some senses fungible. Even if one concludes (as this study does) that environmental cost internalization does not provide a "silver bullet" for integration of trade and environmental policymaking in the short term, it should remain a long-term priority.

A corollary of the "get prices right" proposition and the observation that trade restrictions are a poor substitute for proper environmental policies is the conclusion that the use of trade penalties to enforce environmental agreements or to promote environmental goals constitutes a second-best (or third- or fourth-best) policy mechanism. Environmental trade measures can easily become counterproductive from either an environmental or economic standpoint or both. Thus, in crafting such trade measures, policymakers should attend to the effectiveness of the programs they put in place and be aware of the danger that the measures may backfire.[7] When evidence of deleterious environmental results from environmental trade measures is found, officials should move quickly to reshape the policy in question.

ATTACKING THE MARKET FAILURE

The insight of economists—that important elements of the trade and environment conflict have arisen because the costs associated with environmental harms are not internalized—is significant. Unfortunately, having identified this market failure, trade analysts tend to believe the burden of resolving the conflict and implementing the polluter pays principle rests on the environmental community.

A spate of recent articles from trade experts

(e.g., Palmeter 1993; Jackson 1992; Bhagwati 1993) and even some environmental economists (Repetto 1993b) have therefore suggested that the dispute between trade and environmental interests is a "false conflict" and "much ado about little." In leaning too heavily on the conceptual opportunity presented by the polluter pays principle, economists and their trade colleagues tend to overstate the prospects for convergence. The real challenge lies in the practical obstacles to making trade and environmental policies mutually reinforcing. Disputes would still exist over what our environmental goals should be and how to value environmental amenities and harms. Valuation controversies are inevitable in the face of substantial scientific and risk uncertainties, variations in political priorities and judgments, and differences based on geography and level of development. . . . Market mechanisms are clearly not a panacea for all environmental problems, never mind all trade and environment issues.

Even where goals can be agreed upon, consensus on means is often elusive. Powerful political forces frequently intervene to prevent the internalization of costs in deference to industries or other policy actors with deeply entrenched interests in the status quo. The need to internationalize any commitment to the polluter pays principle adds further practical complexities. Moreover, society does not know how to get what it wants from environmental regulation. Science cannot say with certainty what is ecologically safe. Defining the dimensions and magnitude of environmental externalities—putting a price on pollution—therefore has an irreducible political element. Perhaps to a larger degree than in the trade realm, environmental regulation has a significant noneconomic dimension.[8]

In addition, in contrast with environmental regulation, trade liberalization is backed by a relatively coherent and well-accepted economic theory about what leads to greater social welfare. This theory has furthermore been translated into international rules.[9] Although there is a growing recognition of the conceptual power of cost internalization as the cornerstone for future programs to protect ecological resources and public health, environmental policymaking remains hobbled by the lack of a broadly accepted theoretical foundation. Thus, despite efforts to build in more analytic rigor through the use of better science, risk analysis, and economic tools, environmental regulation retains an important dimension that is art or philosophy. In this domain, political judgments are required, and experts disagree. It is in this zone of politics that the interests of free traders and environmentalists often clash.

We cannot hope to establish a common social welfare metric that will resolve all trade-environment strife unless we have answers to critical questions: How much is it worth to save a human life? What risk of cancer are we willing to accept? What is the value of a pretty view? Nonetheless, cost internalization, and particularly adoption of the polluter pays principle, offers a conceptual beacon on the horizon that should be followed for both the environmental and trade benefits it offers.

In the meantime, to the extent that environmental policies continue to obstruct the free flow of commerce, as they inevitably will, GATT reform is needed because the current system of trade rules and procedures lacks the balance necessary to adjudicate the relative merits of environmental and trade policies. How and when trade leverage should be employed to ensure compliance with a cost-internalization obligation or other principles will also continue to be controversial. Finally, the prospect of internalizing environmental harms does not fully address the offensive agenda of environmentalists who want to use trade measures to address competitiveness concerns.

Thus, even if one grants that full environmental cost internalization would significantly reduce the scope of trade and environment clashes, the suggestion that these disputes are "much ado about little" makes for an intellectual diet that is awfully rich on theory and rather thin on immediate policy application. In fact, this attitude belies the hard question that should be asked: why is it so difficult to get good environmental policies that internalize costs adopted?

Notes

1. Thomas Malthus first predicted the world's demographic demise based on a growing population and limited availability of food in his famous *Essay on the Principle of Population,* published in 1803 (available as *T.R. Malthus,* Donald Winch, ed., from Cambridge University Press, New York).

2. Environmental issues are, moreover, only the latest in a long list of "new" considerations such as the special needs of developing countries that have been folded in the trading system. Cooper (1972) reviews some of the earlier refinements.

3. Baumol and Oates (1975) provide the classic analysis of the problem of environmental externalities more broadly.

4. Of course, when professed free traders, particularly in the business community, are faced with the reality of cost internalization, they often demur, citing competitiveness concerns or other arguments why, in the case in question, internalizing costs will not work. The business community's broadly negative reaction to President Clinton's proposed energy tax offers a classic example of this behavior. This argues that resolution of the trade and environment conflict cannot rest on the polluter pays principle alone but must also build on an international regime that ensures worldwide adherence to cost internalization.

5. Some trade experts respond to this point by asking why, if these market failures are pervasive, the trade realm should be held responsible and singled out for special environmental rules. One answer to this question is that trade, by increasing the number of transactions at improper prices, may exacerbate pollution problems.

6. Kozloff and Dower (1993) provide an excellent discussion of how market prices fail to capture the environmental and other social costs of energy—and the market-distorting effect of this mispricing on society's mix of energy supplies. There is, of course, no agreed method for actually determining the correct value of environmental externalities (National Commission on the Environment 1993).

7. For instance, some observers have questioned the efficacy of the African ivory ban—arguing that limited sales of ivory on a sustainable basis would do more to protect elephants (Bonner 1993).

8. As pressures to consider issues such as human rights and labor standards gain currency as legitimate trade concerns, this noneconomic or "values" dimension of trade policymaking may expand.

9. Perhaps the contrast is between a single discipline field (economics) with a compelling theoretical foundation and a highly complex, multidisciplinary policy domain (biology, chemistry, economics, ecology, etc.) largely driven by observable natural reality.

References

Anderson, Kym. 1992. "Effects on the Environment and Welfare of Liberalizing World Trade: The Cases of Coal and Food." In Anderson and Blackhurst, *The Greening of World Trade Issues.* Ann Arbor: University of Michigan Press.

Anderson, Kym, and Richard Blackhurst. 1992. "Trade, the Environment and Public Policy." In Anderson and Blackhurst, *The Greening of World Trade.* Ann Arbor: University of Michigan Press.

Batra, Ravi. 1993. *The Myth of Free Trade.* New York: Macmillan.

Baumol, William, and Wallace Oates. 1975. *The Theory of Environmental Policy.* Englewood Cliffs, NJ: Prentice-Hall.

Bhagwati, Jagdish. 1993. "The Demands to Reduce Domestic Diversity among Trading Nations." Unpublished paper developed for Ford Foundation project. New York: Columbia University.

Bonner, Raymond. 1993. "Crying Wolf Over Elephants." *New York Times Magazine* (7 February): 17

Brandts, J., and C. de Bartolome. 1988. *Social Insurance and Population Uncertainty: Demographic Bias and Implications for Social Security.* C.V. Starr Center Economic Research Report #88–05 (February). New York: New York University.

Brown Weiss, Edith. 1989. *In Fairness to Future Generations: International Law, Common Patrimony, and Intergenerational Equity.* New York: Transnational Press.

Cairncross, Frances. 1992. *Costing the Earth.* London: Business Books Ltd.

Coase, Ronald. 1960. "The Problem of Social Cost." *Journal of Law and Economics* 3.

Diamond, Peter. 1977. "A Framework for Social Security Analysis." *Journal of Public Economics* (December).

General Agreement on Trade and Tariffs Secretariat. 1992. *Trade and Environment Report.* Geneva.

Goodland, Robert, Herman Daly, Salah El Serafy, and Bernd Von Droste. 1992. *Environmentally Sustainable. Development: Building on Brundtland.* Paris: United Nations Educational, Scientific and Cultural Organization.

Grossman, Gene M., and Alan B. Krueger. 1993. "Environmental Impacts of a North American Free Trade Agreement." In Peter M. Garber, *The Mexico-US Free Trade Agreement.* Cambridge, MA: MIT Press.

Jackson, John. 1992. "World Trade Rules and Environmental Policies: Congruence or Conflict?" *Washington and Lee Law Review* 49, no. 4 (Fall): 1227–78.

Kozloff, Keith Lee, and Roger C. Dower. 1993. *A New Power Base: Renewable Energy Policies for the Nineties and Beyond.* Washington: World Resources Institute.

Lallas, Peter L., Daniel C. Esty, and David J. Van Hoogstraten. 1992. "Environmental Protection and International Trade: Toward Mutually Supportive Rules and Policies." *The Harvard Environmental Law Review* 16, no. 2 (Fall).

Lang, Tim, and Colin Hines. 1993. *The New Protectionism.* New York: The New Press.

Lee, Thea. 1992. "NAFTA and the Environment: A Critique of Grossman and Krueger." Background Reading for Trade and Environment Workshop of the Center for International Environmental Law and The Pew Charitable Trusts, 30 October.

Meyer, Carrie A. 1993. *Environmental and Natural Resource Accounting: Where to Begin?* World Resources Institute Issues in Development Paper. Washington: WRI (November).

National Commission on the Environment. 1993. *Choosing a Sustainable Future* (The Train Commission Report). Washington: Island Press.

Palmeter, David. 1993. "Environment and Trade: Much Ado About Little." *Journal of World Trade* (June): 55–70.

Pearson, Charles. 1994. "Testing the System: GATT + PPP = ?" *Cornell International Law Journal* 27, no. 3 (Summer). Forthcoming.

Pigou, Arthur Cecil. 1918. *The Economics of Welfare.* London: Macmillan and Co.

Repetto, Robert. 1993a. "Trade and Environment Policies: Achieving Complimentarities and Avoiding Conflicts." *WRI Issues and Ideas* (July). Washington: World Resources Institute.

Repetto, Robert. 1993b. "A Note on Complimentarities Between Trade and Environmental Policies." In *The Greening of World Trade,* 78 (Pub. No. EPA 100-R-93-002). Washington: EPA.

Repetto, Robert, W. Magrath, M. Wells, C. Beer, and F. Rossini. 1989. *Wasting Assets: Natural Resources in the National Income Accounts.* Washington: World Resources Institute.

Schmidheiny, Stephan. 1992. *Changing Course: A Global Business Perspective on Development and the Environment.* Cambridge, MA.: MIT Press.

Stewart, Richard B. 1992. "International Trade and Environment: Lessons From the Federal Experience." *Washington and Lee Law Review* 49, no. 4 (Fall): 1329.

US Trade Representative. 1992. *Review of U.S.-Mexico Environmental Issues.* Washington: USTR (February).

US Trade Representative. 1993. *The NAFTA: Report on Environmental Issues.* Washington: USTR (November).

Young, M.D. 1994. "Ecologically-Accelerated Trade Liberalisation: A Set of Disciplines for Environment and Trade Agreements." *Ecological Economics* 9: 43–51.

Part

3

Managing to Be Environmentally Responsive

THIS SECTION OF readings examines linkages between the corporation and its most important human constituents. Balancing the demands of a broad set of stakeholders—from competitors to employees to environmental groups to customers—is critical to successful environmental management.

We begin with "Strategic Management for a Small Planet," by Ed and Jean Stead of East Tennessee State University. This reading deftly places environmental issues at the center of a discussion of competitive strategy. Beginning with a corporate philosophy that affirms the value of the natural environment, corporations can pursue ecologically sensitive policies which can lead to competitive advantages in the marketplace. This can also engender the type of supportive corporate culture that can create an enduring commitment to environmental stewardship.

Overcoming internal resistance to pollution prevention initiatives is the subject of "Corporate Obstacles to Pollution Prevention," by Peter Cebon of the University of Melbourne. Because preventing pollution at its source is inherently a cross-disciplinary endeavor, contextual information and technical information must be blended together. This can be a serious challenge, for a number of reasons that Cebon outlines. His purpose is to sensitize readers to the difficulty of overcoming these obstacles, by identifying such complicating factors as organizational tensions caused by cross-disciplinary team members' having multiple reporting responsibilities.

Another key constituency is formed by environmental groups. Frederick J. Long and Matthew B. Arnold of the Management Institute for Environment and Business, a nonprofit group dedicated to improving environmental literacy in business education, discuss "The Emergence of Environmental Partnerships." They see partnerships between corporations and environmental groups as having the potential to resolve problems more efficiently and less confrontationally than traditional regulatory methods. They survey several valuable partnerships and review what has been learned to date.

Perhaps the dominant connection between corporations and their constituents is through marketplace transactions. Private consultant Jacquelyn A. Ottman provides an in-depth view of how environmentalism manifests itself, in two chapters from the second edition of her book *Green Marketing*. In "Consumers with a Conscience," she discusses the long-term trends that underlie the rise of "green consumers." She also profiles green consumers, presenting the results of a study by the Roper organization, which breaks up the U.S. population according to extent of commitment to environmentally conscious purchasing habits. Finally, she provides a glimpse into the psychology of green purchasing. A followup reading by Ottman, "The Next Big Product Opportunity," then provides a guide to the development of more environmentally benign products. Here the emphasis is on designing pollution out of products, but also on adopting a broad view of the impacts of greening on the organization's processes. These more technical issues form the core of the remaining readings.

12

Strategic Management for a Small Planet
W. Edward Stead and Jean Garner Stead

... The Earth is a stakeholder with growing power and influence. Not only is it the ultimate source of natural capital and the ultimate receiver of wastes, it is represented in the immediate business environment by a growing cadre of green stakeholders. These stakeholders want less pollution and fewer wastes; they want more recycling; they want more renewable energy sources; they want products that are safer for the ecosystem, and so on. They are telling firms in a variety of ways that their ability to prosper in the future means finding economically feasible ways to operate within the biophysical limits of the planet.

Given this, strategic managers are faced with effectively implementing what we call *sustainable strategic management,* a broad term that encompasses all the processes necessary to integrate sustainability into the strategic core of organizations. Sustainable strategic management refers to internal cognitive, strategic, structural, and operational processes that are important for organizations wishing to function in sustainable ways. Further, as Throop, Starik, and Rands (1993) say, "Strategies promoting ecological sustainability . . . [must] recognize the interconnectedness of all firms and individuals in the global commons" (p. 75); therefore, sustainable strategic management also refers to myriad internal and external alliances, networks, and relationships that are important for organizations wishing to function in sustainable ways. Starik and Rands (1995) describe these alliances and networks as "a web of . . . sustainability relationships with individuals, other organizations, political-economic entities, and social-cultural entities" (p. 917).

Copious research in strategic management has pointed to the fact that successfully implementing long-term strategic efforts of any type requires that the core philosophies and value systems of the organization be consistent with the strategic initiative . . . and that the organization create the appropriate strategies, technologies, structures, and processes necessary to support the strategic effort over the long term (Banks & Wheelwright, 1979; Galbraith & Kazanjian, 1986; Hrebiniak & Joyce, 1984; Kerr, 1985; Kerr & Slocum, 1987; Noar, 1977; Salter, 1973; Stonich, 1981). Successfully implementing sustainable strategic management initiatives requires that organizations pay attention to these same factors. Further, because there are normally wide philosophical, ethical, operational, and structural differences between strategic initiatives based on hard growth and strategic initiatives that are based on sustainability, successfully instituting sustainable strategic management efforts in organizations often requires fundamental cultural change efforts (Post & Altman, 1992, 1994; Stead & Stead, 1994; Throop et al., 1993). Shrivastava (1992) refers to the wide variety of cultural and process changes necessary for effective sustainable strategic management as *corporate self-greenewal.*

In this [reading], we discuss several concepts that are important for focusing the attention and actions of strategic managers on the broad spectrum of processes related to integrating sustainability into their strategic decisions. When tied together, we believe that these concepts provide a sound framework for guiding strategic managers in their efforts to develop the philosophical and ethical underpinnings, strategies, production and operations systems, structures, and change processes necessary to support sustainable strategic management initiatives in organizations.

ECOCENTRIC MANAGEMENT: A PHILOSOPHY OF SUSTAINABILITY

In building a conceptual framework for successful sustainable strategic management, a very good place to begin is with Paul Shrivastava's (1995a) *ecocentric management paradigm.* Central to the ecocentric management paradigm is the assumption that the Earth is the ultimate stakeholder. In this regard, Shrivastava (1995a) says, "If organizations are to effectively address the ecological degradation inherent in risk societies, then they must use a new management orientation [that centers on] . . . the stakeholder that bears the most risks from industrial activities: Nature!" (p. 127).

The ecocentric management paradigm has embedded in it two fundamental concepts: industrial ecosystems, which are discussed at some length later in this chapter, and ecocentric management (Shrivastava, 1995a). Ecocentric management is essentially a philosophical ideal that Shrivastava (1995a) says is necessary for aligning the management processes of business organizations with the biophysical processes of the natural environment. According to Shrivastava (1995a), this means taking very different perspectives on at least seven organizational elements. He says that under the tenets of ecocentric management, compared with current or-

ganizational practices, the following should be true:

1. Organizational goals should emphasize "sustainability, quality of life, and stakeholder welfare" (p. 131).

2. Organizational values should reflect the importance of the central role of Nature as well as the importance of intuition and understanding.

3. Organizational products should be designed to be more ecologically sensitive.

4. Organizational production systems should use less energy and fewer resources and produce fewer wastes.

5. Organizational structures should be less hierarchical, more participative and decentralized, with lower income differentials between managers and the workforce.

6. Organizational environments should be interpreted to reflect the finite nature of the Earth's ability to provide energy and resources and to absorb wastes.

7. The basic organizational business functions of marketing, finance, accounting, and human resource management should reflect consumer education, long-term ecologically sustainable growth, accounting for full environmental costs, and a safe, healthful, and fulfilling work environment.

Shrivastava (1995a) says that the vision and mission of organizations applying ecocentric management should include commitments to "minimizing virgin-material and nonrenewable-energy use, eliminating emissions, effluents and accidents, and minimizing the life-cycle cost of products and services" (p. 131). He says that the input, throughput, and output processes of the firm should be designed to fulfill these commitments, with the ultimate goal of "closing the loop of output and input processes" (p. 133).

Many argue that the shift in the focus of management from anthropocentric to ecocentric would improperly emphasize Nature over humankind. At the root of such arguments is the Cartesian assumption that humankind is separate from and superior to Nature. However, as we demonstrated in earlier chapters, humankind is neither separate from nor superior to Nature. Instead, humankind and Nature are integrally intertwined, with the survival of each dependent on the other. Thus, ecocentric management is not designed to emphasize Nature over humankind. Rather, it is designed to emphasize Nature with humankind. As such, it provides an excellent philosophical view from which to set the processes of sustainable strategic management in motion. In this regard, Shrivastava (1995a) says,

> This [ecocentric] view of the firm suggests revising management's basic concepts of organizational objectives and strategy. . . . This new concept of strategy deals with the co-alignment of an organization with its environment. . . . This strategy must . . . address issues of impact of the firm's activities on the natural and social environments, and it must provide avenues for renewal of environmental resources that the organization uses. (p. 134)

ENTERPRISE STRATEGY: STANDING FOR SUSTAINABILITY

Enterprise strategy provides an excellent framework for developing organizational strategic processes that reflect the philosophies of ecocentric management. *Enterprise strategy* is an overarching level of strategy that allows firms to explicitly integrate ethical considerations into economic decisions. According to Ed Freeman (1984), enterprise strategy is designed to answer the question, "What do we stand for?" (p. 90). Thus, enterprise strategy reflects a firm's responsibili-

ties to the larger society in its strategic decision-making processes (Ansoff, 1979; Freeman, 1984; Schendel & Hofer, 1979).

The roots of enterprise strategy lie within the confines of stakeholder theory, which . . . has a strong ethical base. In this regard, Freeman (1984), Freeman and Gilbert (1988), and Hosmer (1994) all make cases that the true strength of enterprise strategy is that it provides a framework in which ethical concerns can be effectively incorporated into strategic management processes. They say that enterprise strategy specifically addresses the value systems of managers and stakeholders in concrete terms, focusing attention on what the firm *should* do.

At the heart of enterprise strategy formulation is *stakeholder analysis*. Stakeholder analysis identifies the firm's stakeholders along with the "stakes" that each has in the firm (economic, technological, social, etc.). This helps the firm to understand the roles that its various stakeholders play and to identify the interconnections between the stakeholders. Analyzing *stakeholder power,* that is, examining the scope and breadth of a stakeholder (discussed briefly in the previous chapter), is a critical component of stakeholder analysis. Such an analysis makes it possible to understand the "trump cards" held by each of the firm's stakeholders (Freeman & Gilbert, 1988). Also critical for stakeholder analysis is understanding the firm's *stakeholder management capability*—that is, its ability to meet the needs of stakeholders now and in the future (Freeman, 1984). Assessing stakeholder management capability involves comparing the firm's stakeholder maps with its standard operating procedures and the way it allocates resources and interacts with its stakeholders. Such an assessment provides an understanding of how well organizational processes fit with the external environment, and it provides a better understanding of how the firm's moral obligations to its stakeholders really come into play (Carroll, 1995).

According to Freeman (1984), analyzing a

firm's enterprise strategy requires integrating the results of stakeholder analysis with an analysis of the firm's values and an analysis of the societal issues it faces. *Values analysis* brings the ethical system of the firm to the surface, making it an explicit part of the strategy formulation process. Societal issues analysis allows the firm to incorporate the social context of the organization into strategy formulation. This stakeholders × values × issues analysis is very helpful in a firm's understanding of its enterprise strategy because it reveals "different moral views and different answers to the question, What do we stand for?" (Freeman, 1984, p. 101).

Thus, this analysis results in a clearer understanding of the type of enterprise strategy a firm is pursuing. Freeman (1984) and Freeman and Gilbert (1988) suggest several types of enterprise strategies, each based on different moral views and different assumptions about who the most important stakeholders are (the ones that hold the trump cards). For example, stockholder enterprise strategies reflect an overriding commitment to shareholders; managerial prerogative enterprise strategies reflect the dominant position of senior managers in the firm's hierarchy of stakeholders; and personal projects enterprise strategies reflect the firm's prevailing moral commitment to its employees as the most important stakeholders.

Once a firm includes the Earth as the ultimate stakeholder, stakeholders × values × issues analysis allows the firm to more thoroughly identify the scope, breadth, and power of the planet as a stakeholder in the organization, including the strength of its various green representatives in the immediate business arena. It also allows the firm to more clearly assess the degree to which sustainability has emerged as a core value in the firm, and it allows the firm to clarify the impacts of its operations on the Earth's resources, species, and systems. This analysis allows the firm to integrate the Earth as

a trump card into the organization's strategic thinking processes. Thus, from this process a new genre of enterprise strategy emerges in which the organization *stands for sustainability*.

SUSTAINABILITY STRATEGIES: FULFILLING GREEN VISIONS

Shrivastava (1996) says that a strategic vision "reflects a corporation's fundamental assumptions about itself, the very foundations on which it stands" (p. 174). In this regard, a firm's strategic vision is a reflection of its enterprise strategy. A strategic vision is an image that both guides and limits the firm's decision-making processes at all levels (Senge, 1990; Shrivastava, 1996). The vision serves as the foundation for developing the firm's mission, goals, objectives, and strategic actions. It also serves as a basis for determining what information the organization considers important and the ways the organization measures its success. Thus, a strategic vision provides the mold through which a firm's strategic actions can begin to take shape out of its enterprise strategy.

According to Hart (1995) and Shrivastava (1995a, 1996), instituting sustainable strategic management in organizations begins with a strategic vision based on sustainability. Such a vision provides the foundation for making decisions that support a new definition of long-term organizational prosperity, one that integrates the need to earn a profit with responsibility to protect the environment. Like a sailing craft in a race, the individual firm would see that the key to being competitive is the efficient and effective use of renewable resources and energy, the ability to be light and maneuverable, and the ability to leave no trace of operations in its wake.

As can be seen in Figure 1, such a vision demonstrates the interconnectedness between economic success and the health of the ecosystem; the organization would see itself as a part

Figure 1 ● Envisioning Sustainability Strategies

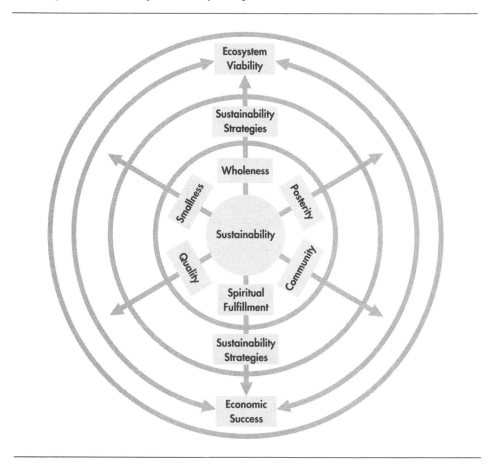

of a greater society and natural environment to which its survival is tied. Thus, this vision would serve as an excellent foundation for sustainable strategic management processes based on instrumental values such as wholeness, posterity, smallness, community, and spiritual fulfillment.

A vision based on sustainability "must be in place before complete corporate greening can be possible" (Shrivastava, 1996, p. 175). Once in place, operating within such a vision leads naturally to the development of competitive strate-

gies designed to simultaneously enhance the quality of the ecosystem and the long-term survivability of the firm (Hart, 1995; Keirnan, 1992; Shrivastava, 1995a, 1996). We refer to these strategies as *sustainability strategies*. Sustainability strategies are not compromise strategies; they are not designed merely to earn a profit while doing as little damage as possible to the ecosystem. Rather, they are integrative strategies; they provide competitive advantages to organizations by simultaneously enhancing the quality of the ecosystem and the long-term survivability of the firm. As Art Kleiner (1991) says, "In the long run, the principles of economic growth and environmental quality reinforce each other" (p. 38). Michael Porter (1991) reiterates this point, saying, "The conflict between environmental protection and economic competitiveness is a false dichotomy" (p. 168).

Sustainability strategies can be classified according to the nature of the competitive advantages they provide—that is, advantages based on lowering costs or providing opportunities for market differentiation (Hart, 1995; Porter, 1985; Shrivastava, 1996). *Process-driven sustainability strategies* are the first type. Economically, process-driven sustainability strategies are designed to provide firms with cost advantages through improved environmental efficiency (Hart, 1995; Shrivastava, 1995a, 1996; Stead & Stead, 1995). Ecologically, these strategies serve to reduce resource depletion, materials use, energy consumption, emissions, and effluents. Examples of activities often included in process-driven sustainability strategies include (a) redesigning pollution and waste control systems, (b) redesigning production processes to be more environmentally sensitive, (c) using recycled materials from production processes and/or outside sources, and (d) using renewable energy sources (Stead & Stead, 1995).

The second type are *market-driven sustainability strategies.* Economically, market-driven sustainability strategies are designed to provide firms with competitive advantages by allowing them to ecologically differentiate their products from their competitors in the marketplace. (Shrivastava, 1996; Stead & Stead, 1995). Ecologically, these strategies reflect *product stewardship* (Hart, 1995), the idea that environmental hazards and life-cycle costs should be minimized in products or services. Some of the activities that can make up market-driven sustainability strategies are (a) entering new environmental markets or market segments, (b)

introducing new environmentally oriented products, (c) redesigning products to be more environmentally sensitive, (d) advertising the environmental benefits of products, (e) redesigning product packaging, and (f) selling scrap once discarded as wastes (Stead & Stead, 1995).

Research reveals that sustainability strategy implementation has become pervasive in industry throughout the United States, Canada, and the European Community as firms seek to improve their environmental performance, enhance their competitiveness, and respond to pressures from green stakeholders such as regulators and consumers (Dillon & Fischer, 1992; Schot & Fisher, 1993; Stead & Stead, 1995; Throop et al., 1993; Williams, Medhurst, & Drew, 1993). Research also reveals that both market-driven and process-driven sustainability strategies can be economically feasible, even lucrative, for firms. Investments and payback periods are generally reasonable, and financial outcomes, including revenue enhancement, return on assets, return on investment, and return on equity, are often quite positive (Hart & Ahuja, 1994; Stead & Stead, 1995; Williams et al., 1993).

Stuart Hart (1995), in his natural-resource-based theory of the firm, greatly enriches the understanding of sustainability strategy formulation and implementation. He argues effectively that the natural environment offers firms some of the most important competitive advantages now and in the future. He develops a three-stage sustainability strategy progression: The first stage, which he refers to as *pollution prevention strategies,* essentially involves implementing process-driven strategies in order to simultaneously conserve resources and reduce costs. Because of the increasing demands for external scrutiny of environmental operations, Hart argues that pollution prevention strategies not only provide firms with competitive advantages, they also provide firms with opportunities to establish social legitimacy in the greater community.

In the next stage, which Hart (1995) calls

product stewardship, firms evolve from a pollution prevention focus to a focus on the complete life-cycle impacts of their products and processes. Product stewardship strategies are market driven in that they provide sustained opportunities for firms to differentiate themselves from their competitors, but they go well beyond this. Basing product stewardship strategies on life-cycle analysis means that this differentiation is achieved by attending to both process and market factors in strategy formulation and implementation. Further, total product stewardship is best achieved by involving all of the firm's external stakeholders—including suppliers, environmentalists, regulators, and the community—in its product development processes.

The third stage described by Hart (1995) is the development of *sustainable development strategies.* These are strategies that include the cost-saving, market differentiation, and social legitimacy dimensions of pollution prevention and product stewardship. however, they are a radical departure from these strategies because they shift the firm's focus from markets in developed nations of the world to markets in the developing world, primarily south of the equator (Hart, 1994, 1995). Hart says that the competitive advantages related to sustainable development strategies are garnered from the firm's keen sense of commitment to Nature and society. He says that a firm's long-term vision of sustainability must be the driving force behind sustainable development strategies. Formulating and implementing such strategies requires a willingness to make long-term commitments of organizational resources to the development of technologies that have low environmental impacts and serve the unique needs of customers in the developing nations of the world.

Hart (1995) points out that these three types of strategies are interconnected at a variety of levels. As implied in the discussion above, they are, to a large degree, cumulative and sequential. Pollution prevention strategies are both a benefi-

cial avenue to product stewardship strategies and an important part of product stewardship strategies. Product stewardship strategies are both helpful paths to and significant parts of sustainable development strategies. However, Hart points out that the interconnections between these three strategies flow in the other direction as well. He says that a strong vision of sustainable development is the most powerful foundation a firm can have for facilitating the formulation and implementation of pollution prevention and product stewardship strategies.

Hart's (1995) natural-resource-based theory of the firm is very valuable in explaining in some depth how sustainability strategies provide firms with sustained competitive advantages in developed markets across the globe. However, we believe that the theory's most important contribution may be that it opens an ecologically sensitive theoretical door through which firms can establish long-term niches in the rapidly growing markets of the developing world. Sustainable-development strategies as described by Hart are designed not only to bring economic success to organizations that are willing to make the long-term commitments necessary to compete in the developing world; these strategies also are designed to account for the unique social and environmental problems facing developing nations. Within this framework, Hart provides some economically feasible strategic pathways by which organizations can meaningfully contribute to the alleviation of the serious ecological and social problems plaguing the developing world—problems that must be faced if society is to truly achieve sustainability.

In essence, then, sustainability strategies are what organizations that *stand for sustainability* do: It is through sustainability strategies that the philosophies and ethics of sustainable strategic management become tangible. Sustainability strategies are thus excellent vehicles for operationally integrating the biophysical constraints of Nature into strategic decision-making processes. In short, sustainability strategies provide valuable avenues for bringing both the ecological and economic dimensions of an organization's green vision to life.

INDUSTRIAL ECOSYSTEMS: ALIGNING PRODUCTION WITH NATURE

We mentioned in the introduction of this chapter that sustainable strategic management requires that organizations operate within ecologically based networks with other firms and stakeholders. These networks are commonly referred to as *industrial ecosystems* because they model their production and market processes on the characteristics of mature natural systems (Richards, Allenby, & Frosch, 1994; Shrivastava, 1995a, 1995b). According to Shrivastava (1995a), "Conceptually, [an industrial ecosystem] consists of organizations that jointly seek to minimize environmental degradation by using each other's waste and by-products and by sharing and minimizing the use of natural resources" (p. 128). Richards et al. (1994) say, "In an industrial ecology, unit processes and industries are interacting systems rather than isolated components. . . . The focus changes from merely minimizing wastes from a particular process or facility, commonly known as pollution prevention, to minimizing waste produced by the larger system as a whole" (p. 3).

E. F. Schumacher's concept of "appropriate technology" (which he originally called "intermediate technology") is an important historical forerunner to the development of the concept of industrial ecosystems. In the mid-1950s, while working as an economic adviser to the British National Coal Board, Schumacher came to the conclusion that industrial technology was taking an irreparable toll on the natural environment because of its overuse of coal and other fossil fuels. In 1954, he warned that our current economic activities were creating dire problems because of technologies that relied on massive

amounts of nonrenewable energy and resources (Wood, 1984). Even though his warnings fell on deaf ears during the industrial expansion of the 1950s, this realization was a personal breakthrough for Schumacher. From that point on, it was abundantly clear to him that the technologies of the industrial age were built on dreams no more real than puffs of smoke (Wood, 1984). He saw these technologies as being inhuman, favoring the rich over the poor, and destroying the very Earth on which they existed. He realized that if society did not develop technologies more sensitive to human and environmental concerns, its days on this planet would be numbered (Schumacher, 1973).

From these concerns, Schumacher (1979) began to develop his ideas of appropriate technology. He describes appropriate technology using terminology very similar to that used later to define industrial ecosystems: He says that appropriate technology provides for "production which respects ecological principles and strives to work with Nature" (p. 57). He bases the development of appropriate technology on three assumptions: (a) It is possible to make things smaller; (b) it is possible to do things simpler; and (c) it is possible to do things cheaper. He says that production technologies based on these assumptions stress low-cost methods and equipment that are available to most people, can be used on a small scale, and are compatible with humankind's creative needs. By "low-cost technologies," Schumacher means total costs, measured not only in financial terms but also in terms of the depletion of the Earth's natural capital (Schumacher, 1973).

According to Richards et al. (1994), achieving an industrial ecosystem that is truly in concert with Nature's biophysical processes requires transcending three progressively difficult stages of industrial evolution. The first stage, the Type I industrial ecosystem, is the classical industrial model. In this stage, the global production and distribution systems operate on straight linear processes in which virgin raw materials and energy are converted into goods and services. The by-products of these processes are heat and material wastes that either dissipate into or must be disposed of in the natural environment. The second stage of industrial evolution, a Type II industrial ecosystem, involves some recycling of materials and energy in production processes but still requires the linear transformation of virgin inputs and energy into products and wastes that must be absorbed by Nature. The third stage of evolution is to a Type III industrial ecosystem in which the only inputs are renewable energy, and operations are totally closed-looped with virtually total materials reuse and recycling. Type III industrial ecosystems export only heat into the external environment. These Type III systems mimic mature natural ecosystems, which are generally quite stable, operating on minimal amounts of entropy.

From the above description, it is clear that humankind is still in the early stages of industrial ecosystem evolution. Currently, most efforts seem geared largely toward moving from Type I to Type II. The use of recycled materials and renewable energy are certainly on the rise in industry, and efforts such as pollution prevention and total quality environmental management (TQEM, discussed in the next chapter) have been particularly valuable in helping individual firms to improve their environmental management processes. However, at this point, Type III, closed-loop, interconnected networks of firms operating only on renewable energy and exporting only absorbable heat remain largely an ideal to be pursued. Nevertheless, simple Type III systems involving a few interacting firms are beginning to appear. Shrivastava (1995a) discusses such a system located in Kalundborg, Denmark, in which the management of raw materials, by-products, energy, water, and wastes is coordinated among six local organizations and several farms. The system has facilitated significant water savings, waste minimization, resource con-

servation, and energy conservation in Kalundborg. There are also ongoing efforts in the United States to promote the development of industrial ecosystems; an industrial-ecology park is being developed in upstate New York, and the city of Chattanooga, Tennessee, is attempting to develop industrial ecosystems as part of its efforts to become a "green city."

Though not yet a reality on a wide scale, Type III industrial ecosystems provide an excellent ideal upon which to design the production and operations management systems of firms seeking to implement sustainable strategic management processes. This ideal encourages firms to seek production methods that model Nature, using minimal resources and energy, generating minimal amounts of wastes, and developing ecologically symbiotic relationships with other organizations and stakeholders.

LEARNING ORGANIZATIONS: STRUCTURES FOR SUSTAINABILITY

It has long been recognized that increasing environmental turbulence and advancing technology dictate the need for more flexible, dynamic organizational structures that are flatter and that rely on more informal, knowledge-based decision-making processes (Burns & Stalker, 1961; Emery & Trist, 1965, 1973; Woodward, 1965). It has also long been recognized (although not always acknowledged) that interactions between business and the natural environment are significant features of this environmental turbulence (Emery & Trist, 1973; Schumacher, 1973, 1979).

Probably the first person to actually combine these two facts in a structural framework explicitly designed for organizations pursuing sustainable strategic management was (again) E. F. Schumacher (1973). He believed that large organizations inhibit freedom, creativity, and human dignity and that they damage the ecosystem. He believed that the only way to reverse the negative effects of vast organizations is to "achieve smallness within the large organization" (p. 242). It was on this premise that he based his theory of large-scale organization.

The theory consists of five principles. The first says that large organizations should be divided into *quasi firms,* which are small, autonomous teams designed to foster high levels of entrepreneurial spirit. The second principle says that accountability of the quasi firms to higher management should be based on a few items related to profitability. Decisions are made by the team members in ad hoc fashion without interference from upper management; upper management steps in only if the profitability goals are not being met. Third, the quasi firms should maintain their own economic identity; they should be allowed to have their own names and keep their own records. Their financial performance should not be merged with other units. Fourth, motivation for lower-level workers can be achieved only if the job is intellectually and spiritually fulfilling with ample opportunities to participate in decisions (that is, good work). Schumacher says that this can be achieved in two ways: One is to base the organization's structure on small, autonomous work teams; the other is to allow for more employee ownership and participation at the strategic level. The fifth principle of the theory of large-scale organization, the principle of the middle axiom, says that top management can transcend the divergent problem of balancing the need for employee freedom with the need for organizational control by setting broad, strategic directions and allowing the quasi firms to make their own decisions within these broad directions (Schumacher, 1973).

Schumacher (1979) says that firms organized around these principles would be structured "like Nature with little cells" (p. 83). He says that such organizations would resemble a helium balloon vendor at a carnival with a large number of balloons for sale. The vendor (who

represents top management) holds the balloons from below rather than lording over them from above. Each balloon represents an autonomous unit that shifts and sways on its own within the broad limits defined by the vendor.

As was the case with appropriate technology, many are now echoing Schumacher's sentiments. There is a growing consensus that achieving sustainable strategic management is most likely to occur in organizations that are driven by green visions and that have flat, informal, team-based, knowledge-based structures that allow for more control by employees (Halal, 1986; Hart, 1995; Post & Altman, 1992; Shrivastava, 1995a, 1996; Stead & Stead, 1994). Post and Altman (1992) have probably explored the structural dimensions of corporate greening in as much depth as anyone, and they believe that the most appropriate structural form for successful sustainable strategic management is the learning organization.

Learning organizations are holistic, interconnected structures that can successfully define their own futures through double-loop learning processes that allow them to question and change the foundation values, visions, and assumptions that underlie the way they think and behave. In the words of Beckhard and Pritchard (1992), learning organizations are structured to reach to "the very essence of organizations—their basic purposes, their identities, and their relationships" (p. 1). Learning organizations require vision-driven leadership that focuses on designing, teaching, and stewarding the organizational vision (Beckhard & Pritchard, 1992; Handy, 1989; Senge, 1990).

Peter Senge (1990) has probably contributed more than anyone to the development of learning organizations. He describes five interrelated *learning disciplines* that constitute the framework of learning organizations. The central discipline is systems thinking, which focuses on identifying points of leverage within circular, archetypical models that represent the long-term interrelationships between key variables. . . . The other four disciplines include personal mastery, or allowing for the pursuit of personal visions within the context of the organization; a shared organizational vision, which collectively and synergistically represents the employees' personal visions; a willingness to question mental models, that is, to examine basic values and assumptions that underlie organizational actions; and team learning processes, which emphasize double-loop learning and continuous, honest reflection and dialogue designed to bring the firm's underlying mental models to the surface as legitimate points of discussion and change.

Learning organizations provide a framework for a more intrinsic, spiritual view of the purpose of organizational life (Handy, 1989; Harman, 1988, 1991; Ray, 1991; Senge, 1990). Senge (1990) says that in learning organizations there is "a more sacred view of work" (p. 5) and that allowing employees the opportunity to be creative and self-directed in the pursuit of their personal visions is the "spiritual foundation" of learning organizations (p. 7). Ray (1991) says that adopting learning structures "is a move to the spirit, to inner qualities such as intuition, will, joy, strength, and compassion . . . , [and] to the power of inner wisdom and authority and the connection and wholeness in humanity" (p. 37).

Learning organizations are designed to continuously focus on and question the underlying values and assumptions that guide the firm. They bring a holistic, spiritual dimension into the psyche of organizations, and they are vision driven, team oriented, knowledge based, open, and free-flowing, allowing for increased employee participation in strategic decisions. In short, learning organizations are ideal structures for integrating sustainability into organizational values and visions, and they are ideal structures for facilitating the translation of these green values and visions into organizational strategic actions that

are in concert with both the economic success of the firm and the processes of Nature.

FUNDAMENTAL CHANGE: CREATING SUSTAINABILITY CULTURES

Thus, in sum, sustainable strategic management involves the following:

1. Adopting ecocentric management as the philosophical umbrella under which the firm's visions, missions, goals, inputs, throughputs, and outputs are developed

2. Integrating sustainability and related instrumental values into the core of the firm's enterprise strategy, creating an overarching organizational ethical system that encourages the firm to "stand for sustainability"

3. Translating this stance into a green vision and formulating and implementing sustainability strategies that provide the firm with competitive advantages in the pursuit of that vision.

4. Designing production and operations systems around the notion of Type III industrial ecosystems, which, like Nature, operate on a minimum of resource use, energy consumption, and waste generation

5. Creating and maintaining learning structures that provide the organizational frameworks necessary for tying together economic success, human spiritual fulfillment, and a vision of sustainability

If this summary clarifies anything, it is that most firms have an arduous journey ahead of them in their efforts to implement sustainable strategic management. If sustainable strategic management is to be successfully implemented in business organizations, it will likely require that organizations change their cultures in very fundamental ways (Post & Altman, 1992, 1994; Stead & Stead, 1994; Throop et al., 1993). Cultural change is a very difficult task that requires examining and redefining the core assumptions and values of the organization, the nature of the work, and the roles of the employees. Changing cultures generally involves developing new knowledge, skills, objectives, performance measures, reward systems, and training programs, as well as informal structures that support the new culture (Schein, 1985).

William Ruckelshaus (1991) uses an excellent analogy to explain the magnitude of the philosophical changes necessary for developing a culture to support sustainable strategic management. He points out that, whereas all organizations in capitalistic nations have a deep understanding and appreciation of the concept of profit, this concept had absolutely no meaning in old communist-bloc nations. He says that sustainability is as foreign a concept for strategic managers in capitalistic nations as profits used to be for communist managers. He says, "Sustainability has to be made the bones and belly of corporate life, to join the intrinsic concepts like profit and loss, debt and equity, capital and cost, that make our system work" (p. 7).

Jeffrey Heilpern and Terry Limpert (1991) of the Delta Consulting Group use the implementation of TQEM to illustrate the degree of change in organizational assumptions necessary to implement sustainable strategic management. They say that a basic problem with assisting firms in implementing basic total quality management (TQM) is that the firms usually are founded on "quality-hostile" assumptions, such as the idea that profits are all that really matter and that the organization is a lot smarter than its customers. Before TQM can be implemented, the firms must replace these with "quality-friendly" assumptions, such as the idea that quality is defined by the customer and that profits result from high quality. Adding the environmental (E) dimension to TQM presents an even more

difficult cultural dilemma. Firms must not only adopt quality-friendly assumptions, they also must adopt the environment-friendly assumptions that form the basis of sustainability.

The research of Post and Altman (1992) supports the contention of Ruckelshaus and the others that significant cultural change is generally necessary for implementing sustainable strategic management. Post and Altman (1992) conclude that successful adoption of sustainable strategic management generally requires organizations to achieve a *third-order* change, involving the development of new values, new objectives, new structures, new reward systems, and new norms. They say that "internal paradigm shifts and transformational change are necessary as companies attempt to adjust to the rapidly changing world of green politics and markets" (p. 13).

Third-order change is quite different from both first-order change (developing new ways to reinforce current objectives, values, norms, structures, etc.) and second-order change (purposefully modifying current objectives, values, norms, structures, etc.). Third-order change is discontinuous, requiring that organizations achieve and perpetuate an entirely different qualitative state (Bartunek & Moch, 1987). Organizations attempting third-order change cannot expect to be successful by taking the slow linear steps associated with lesser degrees of organizational change. Rather, third-order change requires fundamental efforts designed to completely shift the consciousness of the firm to a different level. Such efforts require the creation and stewardship of a new organizational vision until it is accepted as the very essence of the organization; this can be accomplished only by simultaneously changing all the systems and processes of the organization to support the new culture (Beckhard & Pritchard, 1992).

Research results are mixed regarding the adequacy of current organizational efforts to make the fundamental changes necessary to institute sustainable strategic management. Of the three firms Post and Altman (1992) studied, only one had made the cultural changes necessary to fully implement sustainable strategic management. Other research points to the fact that organizations are beginning to "talk the talk" of the environment very well, but their efforts to "walk the walk" are lagging behind their rhetoric. Firms are espousing Earth-friendly values and developing Earth-friendly policies, and they are appointing specialists, gathering information, and implementing programs related to these values and policies (Henriques & Sadorsky, 1995; Stead, Stead, Wilcox, & Zimmerer, 1994). However, their efforts to take the difficult steps necessary to actually fundamentally transform their organizational cultures so that sustainable strategic management will be perpetuated over the long run, such as redesigning structures and re-crafting performance, control, reward, and reporting systems, have been less than spectacular up to this point (Stead et al., 1994).

Although the third-order changes needed to achieve sustainable strategic management certainly pose some serious challenges for organizations, they can be overcome. Business organizations have proven time after time that they can successfully adapt their cultures to new environmental conditions when necessary. As ecological concerns continue to move into the forefront of the strategic issues facing business, organizations that adopt sustainability as the basis of their cultures will be prepared to develop the philosophies, strategies, technologies, structures, and management systems necessary to support the sustainable strategic management initiatives they will need to survive.

CONCLUSIONS

In a nutshell, sustainable strategic management is achievable when organizations can manage to institute the internal and external processes that will allow them to function as parts of larger net-works of ecologically interconnected firms and stakeholders, all of whom are stressing the processes of Nature, the common good of the human community, and the fulfillment of spiritual as well as economic needs as the proper paths to long-term economic success. This is no doubt an idealistic, utopian image—a dream, if you will. Yet it has been well documented that organizations that ascend to leadership positions often do so by committing themselves to the long-term pursuit of dreams that seem unattainable to others (Hamel & Prahalad, 1989; Hart, 1995). Yes, sustainable strategic management is indeed a dream, but it is a dream whose time has come. Firms who pursue it have the potential to succeed in the long term by integrating themselves with Nature.

References

Ansoff, I. (1979). The changing shape of the strategic problem. In D. Schendel & C. Hofer (Eds.), *Strategic management* (pp. 30–44). Boston, MA: Little, Brown.

Banks, R., & Wheelwright, S. (1979). Operations vs. strategy: Trading tomorrow for today. *Harvard Business Review, 57*(3), 112–120.

Bartunek, J. M., & Moch, M. K. (1987). First-order, second-order, and third-order change and organization development interventions: A cognitive approach. *Journal of Applied Behavioral Science, 23,* 483–500.

Beckhard, R., & Pritchard, W. (1992). *Changing the essence.* San Francisco: Jossey-Bass.

Burns, T., & Stalker, G. M. (1961). *The management of innovation.* London: Tavistock.

Carroll, A. B. (1995). Stakeholder thinking in three models of management morality: A perspective with strategic implications. In J. Nasi (Ed.), *Understanding stakeholder thinking* (pp. 47–74). Helsinki, Finland: LSR.

Dillon, P., & Fischer, K. (1992). *Environmental management in corporations: Methods and motivations.* Medford, MA: Tufts University, Center for Environmental Management.

Emery, F. E., & Trist, E. L. (1965). The causal texture of organizational environments. *Human Relations, 18,* 21–32.

Emery, F. E., & Trist, E. L. (1973). *Towards a social ecology: Contextual appreciations of the future in the present.* New York: Plenum.

Freeman, R. E. (1984). *Strategic management: A stakeholder approach.* Boston, MA: Pitman.

Freeman, R. E., & Gilbert, D. R., Jr. (1988). *Corporate strategy and the search for ethics.* Englewood Cliffs, NJ: Prentice Hall.

Galbraith, J., & Kazanjian, R. (1986). *Strategy implementation: Structure, systems, and process* (2nd ed.). St. Paul, MN: West.

Halal, W. E. (1986). *The new capitalism.* New York: John Wiley.

Hamel, G., & Prahalad, C. (1989, May/June). Strategic intent. *Harvard Business Review,* pp. 63–76.

Handy, C. (1989). *The age of unreason.* Boston, MA: Harvard Business School Press.

Harman, W. (1988). *Global mind change: The promises of the last years of the twentieth century.* Indianapolis, IN: Knowledge Systems.

Harman, W. (1991). 21st century business: A background for dialogue. In J. Renesch (Ed.), *New traditions in business* (pp. 19–30). San Francisco: Sterling & Stone.

Hart, S. (1995). A natural resource-based view of the firm. *Academy of Management Review, 20*(4), 966–1014.

Hart, S. L., & Ahuja, G. (1994, August). *Does it pay to be green? An empirical examination of the relationship between pollution prevention and firm performance.* Paper presented to the Academy of Management, Dallas, TX.

Heilpern, J. D., & Limpert, T. M. (1991). Building organizations for continuous improvement. In *Proceedings, Corporate Quality/Environmental Management: The First Conference* (pp. 11–15). Washington, DC: Global Environmental Management Initiative.

Henriques, I., & Sadorsky, P. (1995). The determinants of firms that formulate environmental plans. In D. Collins & M. Starik (Eds.), *Research in corporate social performance and policy, Supplement 1* (pp. 67–97). Greenwich, CT: JAI.

Hosmer, L. T. (1994). Strategic planning as if ethics mattered. *Strategic Management Journal, 15,* 17–34.

Hrebiniak, L., & Joyce, W. (1984). *Implementing strategy.* New York: Macmillan.

Kerr, J. (1985). Diversification strategies and managerial rewards: An empirical study. *Academy of Management Journal, 28*(1), 155–179.

Kerr, J., & Slocum, J. (1987). Managing corporate culture through reward systems. *Academy of Management Executive, 1*(2), 99–108.

Kiernan, M. J. (1992). The eco-industrial revolution: Reveille or requiem for international business. *Business and the Contemporary World, 4*(4), 133–143.

Kleiner, A. (1991, July/August). What does it mean to be green. *Harvard Business Review,* pp. 38–47.

Noar, J. (1997). How to motivate corporate executives to implement long-range plans. *MSU Business Topics, 25*(3), 41–42.

Porter, M. E. (1985). *Competitive advantage.* New York: Free Press.

Porter, M. E. (1991, April). America's green strategy. *Scientific American,* p. 168.

Post, J. E., & Altman, B. W. (1992). Models for corporate greening: How corporate social policy and organizational learning inform leading-edge environmental management. In J. Post (Ed.), *Research in corporate social policy and performance* (Vol. 13, pp. 3–29). Greenwich, CT: JAI.

Post, J. E., & Altman, B. W. (1994). Managing the environmental change process; Barriers and opportunities. *Journal of Organizational Change Management, 7*(4), 64–81.

Ray, M. L. (1991). The emerging new paradigm in business. In J. Renesch (Ed.), *New traditions in business* (pp. 33–45). San Francisco: Sterling & Stone.

Richards, D. J., Allenby, B. R., & Frosch, R. A. (1994). The greening of industrial ecosystems: Overview and perspective. In B. R. Allenby & D. J. Richards (Eds.), *The greening of industrial ecosystems* (pp. 1–19). Washington, DC: National Academy Press.

Ruckelshaus, W. D. (1991). Quality in the corporation: The key to sustainable development. In *Proceedings, Corporate Quality/Environmental Management: The First Conference* (pp. 5–9). Washington, DC: Global Environmental Management Initiative.

Salter, M. S. (1973). Tailor incentive compensation to strategy. *Harvard Business Review, 51*(2), 94–102.

Schein, E. H. (1985). *Organizational culture and leadership.* San Francisco: Jossey-Bass.

Schendel, D., & Hofer, C. (1979). Introduction. In D. Schendel & C. Hofer (Eds.), *Strategic management: A new view of business policy and planning* (pp. 1–22). Boston: Little, Brown.

Schumacher, E. F. (1973). *Small is beautiful: Economics as if people mattered.* New York: Harper & Row.

Schumacher, E. F. (1979). *Good work.* New York: Harper & Row.

Senge, P. M. (1990). *The fifth discipline: The art and practice of the learning organization.* Garden City, NY: Doubleday/Currency.

Shrivastava, P. (1992). Corporate self-greenewal: Strategic responses to environmentalism. *Business Strategy and the Environment, 1*(3), 9–21.

Shrivastava, P. (1995a). Ecocentric management in industrial ecosystems: Management paradigm for a risk society. *Academy of Management Review, 20*(1), 118–137.

Shrivastava, P. (1995b). The role of corporations in achieving ecological sustainability. *Academy of Management Review, 20*(4), 936–960.

Shrivastava, P. (1996). *Greening business.* Cincinnati, OH: Thompson Executive Press.

Starik, M., & Rands, G. (1995). Weaving an integrated web: Multilevel and multisystem perspectives of ecologically sustainable organizations. *Academy of Management Review, 20*(4), 908–935.

Stead, W. E., & Stead, J. G. (1994). Can humankind change the economic myth? Paradigm shifts necessary for eco-logically sustainable business. *Journal of Organizational Change Management, 7*(4), 15–31.

Stead, W. E., & Stead, J. G. (1995). An empirical investigation of sustainability strategy implementation in industrial organizations. In D. Collins & M. Starik (Eds.), *Research in corporate social performance and policy, Supplement 1* (pp. 43–66). Greenwich, CT: JAI.

Stead, W. E., Stead, J. G., Wilcox, A. S., & Zimmerer, T. W. (1994). An empirical investigation of industrial organizational efforts to institutionalize environmental performance. In *Proceedings, International Association of Business and Society.* Hilton Head, SC: International Association of Business and Society.

Stonich, P. J. (1981). Using rewards in implementing strategy. *Strategic Management Journal,* pp. 345–348.

Throop, G., Starik, M., & Rands, G. (1993). Sustainable strategy in a greening world: Integrating the natural environment into strategic management. *Advances in Strategic Management, 9,* 63–92.

Williams, H. E., Medhurst, J., & Drew, K. (1993). Corporate strategies for a sustainable future. In K. Fischer & J. Schot (Eds.), *Environmental strategies for industry* (pp. 117–146). Washington, DC: Island Press.

Wood, B. (1984). *E. F. Schumacher: His life and thought.* New York: Harper & Row.

13

Corporate Obstacles to Pollution Prevention
Peter Cebon

If pollution prevention is such a great thing, why doesn't it just happen? Plenty of case studies show it is a "win-win-win" alternative, benefitting the corporation, the community, and the countryside. Yet it took 10 years for government to take such an obvious idea seriously, and another five to create a semblance of regulatory interest. On the corporate side, very little happened before publication of the first Toxic Release Inventory in 1989 put public pressure on companies. Not all companies have found pollution prevention cheap or easy.

Pollution prevention is a complex subject ranging from small changes in operating technique to massive, research-driven endeavors to create new products and processes. To keep things manageable, let's focus here on one type of pollution prevention: incremental changes in existing technology. In this context, incremental change means the substitution of one or two steps in a production process; it may also mean changes in the relationships between production steps. Examples might include changes in a washing step, or redesigning the process to eliminate the need for washing altogether. Eliminating chlorofluorocarbons and saving energy by replacing a refrigeration process with a heat exchanger that can exploit waste cooling from an-

●

Reprinted from the July–September 1993 issue of *EPA Journal*, pp. 20–22.

other part of the process would likewise be incremental change.

For these incremental changes, three decision-making stages are critical: identifying a pollution prevention opportunity, finding a solution appropriate to that opportunity, and implementing that solution. It will be useful to examine how three important aspects of an organization—its culture, its ability to process information, and its politics—can affect these three stages. The discussion should demonstrate the importance of thinking of pollution prevention as a social, rather than simply a technical, activity.

What makes pollution prevention difficult in practice? The question can best be answered by first considering a second question, How is pollution prevention different from end-of-pipe emissions control? A key difference between the two is that pollution prevention opportunities are embedded deep within the plant and are tied to very specific physical locations. To determine whether a particular solution is feasible, people need a really intimate understanding of the way the plant works. This kind of understanding doesn't come from design drawings but from the uses and working idiosyncracies of the individual pieces of equipment.

Emissions control devices, on the other hand, are physically quite separate from the rest of the production process. All that's necessary to understand them is the composition of the material coming out the pipe. Because that tends to be the same from one plant to another, the solutions can be relatively independent of the process. One example: Despite different makes and ages of conventional boilers, different control systems, different histories, and different operating strategies, a scrubber is always a viable emissions control strategy for high-sulfur, coal-fired power stations.

A brief digression: In Monty Python's *Flying Circus,* an accountant tells us why his job is not boring. He recounts, in excruciating detail, the many "not at all boring" things that happen in his day. But why is this funny? Because it plays on a common stereotype that accountants are very boring people who find exciting exactly those routine details of daily life the rest of us dismiss as ordinary. For the stereotype to resemble reality, one of two things must be happening: Either people who choose to be accountants bore us, or the profession socializes new members to think and act in a way the rest of us find boring.

Organizational culture is the same. Organizations tend to recruit people who think in a way compatible with the organization's view of the world, or else socialize them to think that way. They train, reward, and punish employees to reinforce the organization's beliefs, and they allocate resources in accordance with those beliefs.

Now, suppose an organization makes a cultural assumption that technical expertise is the only really valid form of knowledge and, therefore, that knowledge built from hands-on experience has very little value outside of day-to-day operations. From what we said above, people in such a company are likely to make at least two kinds of errors. First, engineers who are reasonably—but not intimately—familiar with the process may conclude that there are no preventive opportunities because they can't see them. Second, the company may send in a "SWAT" team of technical experts to ferret out opportunities comparable to those described in many case studies. Not surprisingly, the team doesn't find many and concludes the opportunities don't exist.

Other important cultural beliefs also affect companies' prevention behavior regarding pollution prevention. Consider the way people conceptualize the production process. Do they think of it in terms of technology or people? How do they see their jobs and the jobs of others? Do they look for opportunities to improve things or wait for things to go wrong? Finally, do they see unusual events as problems to be solved or opportunities to get even deeper insights into the way things work?

Pollution prevention presents a difficult information processing problem because it requires people to understand more than the intimate details of the production process; they must also understand the technical possibilities. Such specialized information is generally carried into the organization by technical specialists or vendors. Such information is, for the most part, accessible only to people with the skills and communications links to get and understand it.

Pollution prevention solutions, then, require a nexus between two very dissimilar types of information: contextual and technical. The organizational problem lies in bringing the two together. This is notoriously difficult because they tend to be held by different actors in the organizational cast. We saw above that process engineers and "SWAT" teams are unlikely to find opportunities and solutions. Let's look at one last player, the environmental manager. Environmental managers, an obvious choice, are generally responsible for helping a firm comply with the law. While their work may expose them to many pollution prevention solutions, they often have trouble getting access to production areas. People in production often perceive them as "the compliance police." Also, most of their work—applying for permits, running treatment plants, reporting spills, and filling out waste manifests—doesn't require intimate process knowledge.

Instead of looking to individuals, we might think about combinations. The production operators—the people who turn the knobs and run the process—and production engineers—the people who help solve technical problems and design and implement changes in the production technology—could work together to find solutions. While the operators know exactly where the possibilities are, they rarely have the skills to realize them or knowledge of the smorgasbord of available solutions. Together with the production engineers, however, they have all the information. And, sometimes, the production engineers have both good enough relationships with the operators to find the problems *and* the skills and contacts to get the technical information to determine the solutions.

Suppose, then, that a pollution prevention manager wants to get engineers and operators working together. This can be intensely political because of competition from numerous other managers. Production engineers and operators generally report to production supervision, and most of their time is taken up with immediate production issues. The engineers must understand and remedy the day-to-day crises, ensure the product is up to standard, deal with the latest spill, make sure people work safely, and do myriad other jobs. Operators spend most of their time actually running the plant. The pollution prevention manager competes for their remaining time along with the safety, diversity, energy, quality, and training managers. All these managers have top management's endorsement, but that generally amounts to permission to compete, not to succeed.

That is not the end of the politics. The pollution prevention manager's solution requires the engineers and operators to work together. For that to happen, both groups must be amenable. In some chemical plants I've studied, the engineers have been young, they have lacked the interpersonal skills to solicit and obtain good help from the operators, and they have not fully

appreciated the operators' skills. The operators, on the other hand, have been older and not necessarily forthcoming with the latest know-it-all engineer breezing through the plant on a three-year rotation looking for career enhancing ideas.

Even when pollution prevention solutions are identified, resources such as capital and people are allocated by intensely political processes. Largely because pollution prevention projects are so often deeply embedded in the technology of a plant, assessing the return on a pollution prevention investment may be difficult. . . . This is important because in many companies discretionary capital is scarce and money for new projects is hard to come by. Unless the true costs and potential profitability of preventive options can be properly assessed, they are at a disadvantage in competition with other projects for discretionary company resources.

In sum, rather than being simple, as many case studies might have us believe, pollution prevention is often quite difficult to put into practice. As discussed, pollution prevention can be hampered by at least three realities of organizational life: The cultures of organizations can effectively limit their perspectives; in many organizations, it is very difficult to get the right information to the right people at the right time; and many aspects of organizational life are highly political. These realities, among others, inhibit organizations' abilities to carry out the three basic stages of decision making—identifying preventive opportunities, identifying specific solutions, and implementing those solutions.

But these barriers are not insurmountable. There are many encouraging case studies. A number of companies have managed to overcome existing barriers and find cost-effective preventive solutions to their environmental problems.

14

The Emergence of Environmental Partnerships

Frederick J. Long and
Matthew B. Arnold

EVIDENCE OF CHANGE

By the late 1980s, parties responsible for both pollution generation and regulation had begun to acknowledge their shortcomings and build the capacity to deal with changing expectations about environmental quality. Companies, mostly large, began to see the merits of managing environmental compliance. Once successful with compliance issues, many investigated what was previously considered unthinkable—beyond-compliance management.

Facing scientific evidence in the mid-1980s that chlorofluorocarbons (CFCs) contributed to stratospheric ozone depletion, Du Pont, the world's leading CFC producer, initially responded with stubborn denials. As international negotiators uncovered further evidence of the damage caused by CFCs, Du Pont began to see the debate in a different light. First, its international reputation could be damaged if consumers perceived it was dragging its feet on environmental issues. Second, if a multilateral accord was established to reduce CFC production, Du Pont could gain new market leadership through research on alternatives to CFCs. Du Pont decided to support the stringent CFC reductions that were

developed in 1987 through an international agreement called the Montreal Protocol.[1]

This is but one example of the new efforts being made by companies internationally. New associations have focused on development of best practices in environmental management and dissemination through business and environment publications. Statements of principles such as the International Chamber of Commerce's (ICC) Business Charter for Sustainable Development (see Exhibit 1) and Keidanren's Global Environment Charter evince growing corporate interest in beyond-compliance management. Still, the initiative for holistic environmentalism among companies remains with small, often private organizations such as the Body Shop, Patagonia, and AES Corporation.

The EPA has been building consensus and re-establishing priorities through public discussion, such as its landmark *Reducing Risk* report and through collaborative initiatives with industry and environmental groups to research the most efficient regulatory approach for particular industries.[2] Regulatory initiatives include:

- greater efforts to quantify the costs and benefits associated with regulation. (See Exhibit 2 for one attempt to compare environmental protection expenditures with environmental and health risks in the area of stratospheric ozone protection.)

- introduction of market mechanisms into regulations, providing incentives to pol-

Exhibit 1 ● The Business Charter for Sustainable Development

Principles for environmental management
Foreword

There is widespread recognition today that environmental protection must be among the highest priorities of every business.

In its milestone 1987 report "Our Common Future," the World Commission on Environment and Development (Brundtland Commission) emphasized the importance of environmental protection in the pursuit of sustainable development.

To help business around the world improve its environmental performance, the International Chamber of Commerce established a task force of business representatives to create this Business Charter for Sustainable Development. It comprises sixteen principles for environmental management which, for business, is a vitally important aspect of sustainable development.

This Charter will assist enterprises in fulfilling their commitment to environmental stewardship in a comprehensive fashion. It was formally launched in April 1991 at the Second World Industry Conference on Environmental Management.

Introduction

Sustainable development involves meeting the needs of the present without compromising the ability of future generations to meet their own needs.

Economic growth provides the conditions in which protection of the environment can best be achieved, and environmental protection, in balance with other human goals, is necessary to achieve growth that is sustainable.

In turn, versatile, dynamic, responsive and profitable businesses are required as the driving force for sustainable economic development and for providing managerial, technical and financial resources to contribute to the resolution of environmental challenges. Market economies, characterised by entrepreneurial initiatives, are essential to achieving this.

Business thus shares the view that there should be a common goal, not a conflict, between economic development and environmental protection, both now and for future generations.

Making market forces work in this way to protect and improve the quality of the environment—with the help of performance-based standards and judicious use of economic instruments in a harmonious regulatory framework—is one of the greatest challenges that the world faces in the next decade.

The 1987 report of the World Commission on Environment and Development, "Our Common Future," expresses the same challenge and calls on the cooperation of business in tackling it. To this end, business leaders have launched actions in their individual enterprises as well as through sectoral and crosssectoral associations.

In order that more businesses join this effort and that their environmental performance continues to improve, the International Chamber of Commerce hereby calls upon enterprises and their associations to use the following Principles as a basis for pursuing such improvement and to express publicly their support for them.

Individual programmes developed to implement these Principles will reflect the wide diversity among enterprises in size and function.

The objective is that the widest range of enterprises commit themselves to improving their environmental performance in accordance with these Principles, to having in place management practices to effect such improvement, to measuring their progress, and to reporting this progress as appropriate internally and externally.

Note: The term environment as used in this document also refers to environmentally related aspects of health, safety and product stewardship.

Exhibit 1 ● The Business Charter for Sustainable Development (*Continued*)

Principles

1. Corporate priority

To recognise environmental management as among the highest corporate priorities and as a key determinant to sustainable development; to establish policies, programmes and practices for conducting operations in an environmentally sound manner.

2. Integrated management

To integrate these policies, programmes and practices fully into each business as an essential element of management in all its functions.

3. Process of improvement

To continue to improve corporate policies, programmes and environmental performance, taking into account technical developments, scientific understanding, consumer needs and community expectations, with legal regulations as a starting point; and to apply the same environmental criteria internationally.

4. Employee education

To educate, train and motivate employees to conduct their activities in an environmentally responsible manner.

5. Prior assessment

To assess environmental impacts before starting a new activity or project and before decommissioning a facility or leaving a site.

6. Products and services

To develop and provide products or services that have no undue environmental impact and are safe in their intended use, that are efficient in their consumption of energy and natural resources, and that can be recycled, reused, or disposed of safely.

7. Customer advice

To advise, and where relevant educate, customers, distributors and the public in the safe use, transportation, storage and disposal of products provided; and to apply similar considerations to the provision of services.

8. Facilities and operations

To develop, design and operate facilities and conduct activities taking into consideration the efficient use of energy and materials, the sustainable use of renewable resources, the minimization of adverse environmental impact and waste generation, and the safe and responsible disposal of residual wastes.

9. Research

To conduct or support research on the environmental impacts of raw materials, products, processes, emissions and wastes associated with the enterprise and on the means of minimizing such adverse impacts.

10. Precautionary approach

To modify the manufacture, marketing or use of products or services or the conduct of activities, consistent with scientific and technical understanding, to prevent serious or irreversible environmental degradation.

11. Contractors and suppliers

To promote the adoption of these principles by contractors acting on behalf of the enterprise, encouraging and, where appropriate, requiring improvements in their practices to make them consistent with those of the enterprise; and to encourage the wider adoption of these principles by suppliers.

12. Emergency preparedness

To develop and maintain, where significant hazards exist, emergency preparedness plans in conjunction with the emergency services, relevant authorities and the local community, recognizing potential transboundary impacts.

Exhibit 1 ● The Business Charter for Sustainable Development (*Continued*)

---

13. Transfer of technology

To contribute to the transfer of environmentally sound technology and management methods throughout the industrial and public sectors.

14. Contributing to the common effort

To contribute to the development of public policy and to business, governmental and intergovernmental programmes and educational initiatives that will enhance environmental awareness and protection.

15. Openness to concerns

To foster openness and dialogue with employees, and the public, anticipating and responding to their concerns about the potential hazards and impact of operations, products, wastes or services, including those of transboundary or global significance.

16. Compliance and reporting

To measure environmental performance; to conduct regular environmental audits and assessment of compliance with company requirements, legal requirements and these principles; and periodically to provide appropriate information to the Board of Directors, shareholders, employees, the authorities and the public.

Source: International Chamber of Commerce, Paris.

luters to clean up. The Clean Air Act Amendments of 1990 created a trading market for sulphur dioxide emissions rights. The continuous financial incentive to reduce sulphur emissions below permitted levels may induce technology innovation beyond what command and control regulation would have mandated; and

- international accords such as the Montreal Protocol and industry-wide voluntary actions such as the 33/50 Toxics Reduction Program that allow for more creativity in achieving goals.[3]

Non-profits have also shown a new flexibility in their approaches to solving problems. Many have hired more scientists, policy experts, and resource specialists to complement the lawyers and activists who started the environmental movement. They have indicated willingness to work behind the scenes with legislators to draft more innovative components of environmental laws, and they have periodically worked together on conservation projects and regulatory

initiatives in order to harmonize their "voices" and increase the efficiency of their efforts.[4]

All these organizations, flexing their newfound capabilities to deal with changes in expectations and in science, have recognized the need for new paradigms of thought and action. As a first step toward resolving gridlock, societies need new ways of thinking about the economic impact of environmental protection. The World Commission on Environment and Development (also known as the Brundtland Commission) made significant strides when it popularized the phrase "sustainable development." The Commission stated:

> Humanity has the ability to make development sustainable—to ensure that it meets the needs of the present without compromising the ability of future generations to meet their own needs.[5]

For the first time, protection of the environment was not viewed independently from other societal goals. It had become an integral part of de-

Exhibit 2 ● Summary of US EPA's Benefit-cost Analysis of the Montreal Protocol

---

Benefits:
  Health benefits

Value of avoided premature deaths from skin cancer = $6,349 billion (EPA used a value of $3 million per life saved)

Value of avoided cases of skin cancer and cataracts = $65 billion (includes avoided medical and social costs)

Avoided damage from increased tropospheric ozone = $12.4 billion (increase tropospheric ozone predicted to increase deleterious effects)

  Other benefits

Avoided damage to crops from UV-B = $23.4 billion

Avoided damage to fish from UV-B = $5.5 billion

Avoided damage from sea level rise from global warming = $3.1 billion

Avoided damage to polymers from UV-B = $3.1 billion

Total benefits: $6,462.7 billion

(98% = Avoiding premature skin cancer deaths)

Total costs of regulation: $27 billion

Sources: US EPA. *Regulatory Impact Analysis: Protection of Stratospheric Ozone* (Washington, DC: December, 1987); Forest, Reinhardt, *"Du Pont Freon Products Division (A)"—Case Study* (Washington, DC: National Wildlife Federation), p. 24.

velopment strategies that could be sustained over long periods of time. In fact, it has taken nearly a decade for the principle of sustainable development to become an accepted term and for affected parties to consider what they must do in order to promote sustainability. Its major implications are that environmental protection and economic activity must be made part of the same strategy and that a more participatory process is required in order to accomplish this strategy.

Voluntary initiatives and the particular segment of these that we call "partnerships" represent a promising and imaginative approach to solving many of the priority setting, equity, and efficiency problems that society identifies when

it builds a strategy based upon sustainable development principles. Although regulation will undoubtedly remain the centerpiece of environmental protection, it is now recognized that setting goals must be a more participatory process, that implementation must become more flexible, and that planning should build on, rather than supersede, voluntary efforts that achieve desired goals.

"FIRST MOVERS" EXPERIMENT WITH PARTNERSHIPS

While the impetus for collaboration has become more compelling, organizations and the public at large still needed convincing that collaboration was not compromise or conspiracy. Through the mid-1980s, most existing models of environmental partnerships were based on traditional preservationist molds. When "gun and rod" enthusiasts worked voluntarily with other parties with similar purposes, this was not news the public seemed to notice. In the mid and late 1980s, however, a new wave of partnerships began to attract public attention:

Example: Starting in 1986, parties in Washington State that were frustrated with regulations governing timber harvesting practices sat down and began negotiating alternatives through a voluntary, mediated forum. Timber companies wanted a predictable basis on which to harvest their forest land assets, environmental groups wanted to preserve public resources that were damaged by private land-owner's harvesting methods, and American Indian tribal representatives wanted to ensure that their treaty rights to capture 50% of local fishing harvests would still provide them a modest living. In a process that became known as the Timber/Fish/Wildlife Agreement, changes in harvesting practices were agreed to in order to improve each party's position.[6]

Example: When the leaders of 1000 Friends of Oregon assessed progress towards their goal of reducing urban sprawl in the late 1980s, they were not satisfied. Too much was happening that they saw as outside their sphere of influence. When they looked for parties they could work with to achieve their goals, they found a surprising ally: the Homebuilders' Association of Metropolitan Portland. They jointly prepared recommendations on growth planning that would protect open space while increasing housing density in areas that had already been developed.[7]

Example: McDonald's Corporation and the Environmental Defense Fund worked together in 1990–1991 to analyze McDonald's solid waste problems. Based on joint research results,

McDonald's replaced styrofoam packaging with flexible paper packaging at all stores.[8] Both organizations have since participated in other partnerships, based in part on the success of this initial collaboration. The environmental partnership between McDonald's Corporation and the Environmental Defense Fund was clearly a landmark for environmental partnerships:

- It dealt with an environmental issue, solid waste, that was in the public's eye;
- it was a professional partnership that involved parties with only limited previous knowledge of each other;
- it involved respected organizations that seemed to come from "different worlds"; and
- for the first time, the public appeared to scrutinize both the goals and the process of collaboration employed by the participants.

All of these "first mover" partnerships were seen as innovative by researchers and observers, and received largely positive reviews from participants and affected stakeholders. When viewed as a group, these new partnerships reflect a significant break from the past:

They Deal Directly with Environmental Issues with Highly Uncertain Outcomes

Historically, environmental partnerships appear to have focused on implementing clearly defined solutions rather than seeking solutions in uncertain areas of environmental science. When great uncertainty existed, parties chose to go to court and take their chances with the judge's decision. New partnerships seem to reflect a higher risk profile, because the parties involved are willing to wade into uncertain environmental issue areas, working with partners that they may have known for only short periods of time.

They Involved Highly Respected Organizations Based in Significantly Different Industries

The cross-sectoral dimension of environmental partnerships appears to be broadening. While previous partnerships involved organizations in similar industries and with a high level of goal commonality, new activities seem to involve parties who work on the same "strategic" level.

They Were Proactive, Rather Than Reactive

Rather than waiting for conflict to occur, these stakeholders aggressively sought out and pursued solutions that could balance their interests with those of other parties. This new wave of partnerships is more clearly opportunity-based, with a "win-win" philosophy as its foundation. The parties to these partnerships may also see their collaborations as strategic efforts to become more competitive within their respective industries.

WHY PARTNERSHIPS MAKE SENSE

These early partnerships prompted a flurry of conjecture as to why the participants would choose such a strategy. Although answers differed, a series of common societal and organizational objectives is beginning to emerge. Societal benefits include:

Improved Effectiveness

When a company, agency, or non-profit seeks to protect a watershed or reduce polluting emissions, it faces many psychological and physical boundaries. Outsiders, for example, cannot force private landowners to change practices on their lands in order to improve wildlife habitat. If one of these parties chooses to work alone, it faces a strong possibility of failure. While the participation of a variety of organizations is time-consuming and difficult, a coordinated

plan may be critical to achieving the stated long-term environmental goal.

Increased Efficiency

An organization may have a variety of strategic options, each of which will produce a desired environmental goal. Faster implementation periods, lower execution costs, and lower expected resistance by affected parties are forms of efficiency that can be derived from partnerships. For example, if organizations are attempting to minimize negative impacts of mining, grazing, and timber harvesting on river water quality and fish populations, a voluntary collaboration that produces enforceable agreements will be more efficient, in terms of time and money, than a regulatory process or an extended period of litigation.

Enhanced Equity

Higher levels of participation through voluntary partnerships tend to improve the equity inherent in problem resolution and, just as important, enhance the perception of equity. Whether intentionally or unintentionally, environmental protection programs may allocate costs or benefits in ways that affected parties consider unfair. Alternatively, regulation may not yet have addressed a situation that is considered patently inequitable. Voluntary partnerships can accelerate both the debate over equity issues and the implementation of good solutions. For example, utilities that voluntarily cooperate with non-profit organizations and ratepayer groups become attuned to the fact that energy conservation programs tend to accrue to large industrial organizations that have the capital to invest in more efficient equipment. Special residential and low-income programs need to be developed as well. When companies in Mexico bring to the attention of local government the shortcomings of wastewater treatment capacity, they accelerate the development of infrastructure that serves both their needs and the needs of citizens whose health depends on clean water.[9]

A second set of reasons why partnerships are created concerns the benefits that participating organizations may gain. That the primary goal is protection of environmental quality should not distract us from decision-making reality. If there were no reason for participating in environmental partnerships other than "public spirit" or "social conscience," the driving force for effective partnerships would be lost. Corporations see voluntary partnerships as supportive of their mission, long-term health and profitability, and other measures by which their performance is calibrated. Non-profit organizations see partnerships as leverage for the often limited resources they possess. Governmental agencies view partnerships as a means of accelerating the fulfillment of agency goals and informing future regulatory development. Certain organizational benefits would apply to all participating organizations:

They Fulfill Their Missions More Effectively

In the non-profit sector, organizations often do not possess control of the resource they are attempting to protect. Thus, they must convince, cajole, and coerce others—whether companies, regulators, or individuals—to do what they believe is most appropriate. Likewise, agencies with a mandate to protect human health or natural resources cannot always use regulation to reach the parties most responsible for environmental degradation. Partnerships offer unique access to organizations over which a participant does not have control.

They Gain Access to Larger Resource Bases

Most non-profits, agencies, and corporations have been hit by flat or declining budgets since the late 1980s. Non-profit organizations that had experienced several years of growing budgets were shocked to find themselves competing directly with others for limited resources. Working through partnerships gives each organization expanded access to asset bases controlled by others. Furthermore, organizations that use partnerships as a strategy for accomplishing goals may receive expanded support from foundations and other funding sources that wish to avoid "making investments in futility" or "reinventing the wheel."

They Increase the Predictability of Operations and Financial Profit

Corporations are particularly sensitive to the potential of environmental issues to stop or delay core operations. Partnerships that help avoid litigation and work stoppages indirectly contribute to profitability. Agencies that establish regulations, only to find them disputed by regulated parties or litigious non-profits, can also increase operating predictability through partnerships that generate support for regulations before they are implemented.

They Improve Employee Morale and Public Relations

Employees work harder when they are happy in their jobs. Some companies in the chemicals sector have suggested that new graduates consider environmental track record and reputation as one factor in deciding which company to join.[10] How the public views companies' environmental record may also be a factor in purchase decisions and brand loyalty. These same factors are important at government agencies and non-profits that compete for workers and rely on public opinion. Voluntary environmental partnerships that involve employees and vest them with decision-making power enhance workers' skills and morale. When partnerships expand participation to include community-based organizations and non-profit groups, corporate and agency decisions that have environmental consequences tend to receive more public support.

Participants may also derive certain unique organizational benefits:

CORPORATIONS Companies have long-term growth and financial profitability as their primary organizational goals. Except for businesses that develop environmental technologies, they do not focus primarily on environmental protection. Still, they are regulated by law and must be constructive contributors to the communities in which they operate. Programs that go beyond what is required by law, such as community outreach and corporate philanthropy, may be justified as actions taken for the "public good." However, the justifications for environmental partnerships also transcend moral and ethical considerations. The Committee for Economic Development stated:

> Promoting the interest of the community is no longer seen as a peripheral exercise of good citizenship involving no more than annual philanthropic contributions or a matter of corporate social responsibility, a concept that implies a greater benefit to society than to the corporation. Rather, it is seen as a legitimate part of the corporation's long-run self-interest to which a variety of corporate activities and resources ought to be addressed.[11]

From a bottom line perspective, environmental partnerships may reduce long-term risk of environmental incidents, ensure predictability and sustainability of operations, create cost advantages, and empower employees. Because many of these benefits fit within a traditional analysis of "competitive advantage," we devote some time to this issue later in the chapter. In order for corporations to recognize these benefits in a material way, they must develop a system that con-

verts these obvious, but hard to quantify, benefits into hard numbers. This system can then be utilized to decide when participation in a partnership makes sense.

Non-profit Organizations Most non-profits that participate in environmental partnerships have environmental objectives as part of their fundamental mission statement. Thus, their decision to participate in a partnership must be essentially strategic: Is this better for achieving stated goals than other options such as litigation, lobbying, or independent research reports? From a strategic perspective, environmental partnerships may expand sources of funding and in-kind resources, broaden interest and participation in a challenge that has not previously received public attention, and enhance communication among non-profits and corporate and government entities. Non-profits face a unique challenge when they enter into partnerships. They risk losing ground in other areas when they gain ground through a partnership. Many environmental organizations were built on the principle of fighting the offenses of corporations and the intrusions of government. They receive financial support from thousands of individuals who value their "watchdog" role. When non-profits tap into the potential of partnerships, they must work hard to educate their membership and avoid compromising either their independence or their ability to maintain the public's trust.

Public Agencies Agencies have a wide range of roles and responsibilities, including protection and management of public resources, such as forests, land, and water supplies; protection of human health from pollution and toxic materials; and provision of services, such as education and economic development. This stewardship mission can probably best be realized by involving stakeholders in the development of programs.

Most regulatory programs provide for periods of public comment in which stakeholders state their views on a proposed regulation. However, this type of input differs from a true partnership in which stakeholders jointly define the agenda from the start of the process and agree to give up autonomy in exchange for the promise of better outcomes. From a strategic perspective, environmental partnerships may help agencies by improving the quality of regulation, by enhancing support for regulation, and by reducing the need for regulation. Agencies face internal and external challenges to participating in partnerships. Externally, they must reconcile their collaborative role with the regulatory mission that is provided to them by law. In some cases, agencies are prohibited from engaging in partnerships with regulated parties. Internally, agencies are concerned about giving power to companies they are supposed to regulate. Agency leaders must overcome the fear of loss of control and provide a supportive environment that allows policy makers to encourage partnerships and employees to drive partnerships without concern for loss of internal support.[12]

This analysis of benefits suggests that partnerships provide an opportunity to resolve difficult societal problems and to assist organizations in their pursuit of fundamental goals.

CATALYSTS FOR PARTNERSHIP FORMATION

The compelling theoretical benefits associated with partnerships—building an inclusionary process for environmental problem-solving and creating substantive strategies in pursuit of sustainable development—are not themselves sufficient to convert partnership opportunities into operating partnerships. Rather, they provide a context and they describe a trend towards increasing numbers of partnership opportunities.

As stated previously, partnerships are more about people than anything else. People feel frustration, opportunism, and vision, and they act upon these feelings to create partnerships from partnership opportunities. Nonetheless, a series of powerful catalysts can prod people into action: scientific uncertainty, the abundance of public interest in an environmental problem, the existence or threat of regulation, and the identification of a clear win-win opportunity.

Scientific Uncertainty

We still understand very little about the environmental challenges we are attempting to solve. Even when the public agrees that a resource must be protected, there is often uncertainty about how to protect the resource. When ecosystems reach thresholds where further degradation will create irreversible damage, partnerships can emerge. One example of such a situation is the Florida Everglades, where damming, irrigation, and enriched agricultural runoff are changing the characteristics of the ecosystem and threatening plant and animal life. Another estuary with systemic problems is the Chesapeake Bay, where oyster populations have been reduced to 1% of their early 1900s levels through combinations of pollution, degradation of habitat, and over-harvesting.[13] Uncertainties about the use of hundreds of toxic chemicals, about the risks of by-products such as dioxin, and about the relative benefits of various types of recycled paper are examples of long-standing debates among scientists and practitioners.

Broad Public Interest

In the past five years, coverage of environmental problems has expanded dramatically. When the public identifies an environmental problem, it can wield immense power in support of its concerns. Witness the public fights over chemical, power,

FACTORS CONTRIBUTING TO INTEREST IN PARTNERSHIPS

Factors contributing to the new activity in partnerships include the following:

Environmental protection is now a mainstream issue. Citizens value environmental quality highly. As much as 80% of U.S. citizens view themselves as environmentalists. Policy makers and corporate employees also view the environment as valuable. Thus, the idea that organizations would expend effort to protect the environment is no longer heretical.[*]

The complexity of environmental challenges is expanding. Damage such as stratospheric ozone depletion and erosion of wetlands quality often result from use of new technologies or the simple pressure created by more people consuming more resources. Our scientific ability to measure this damage is also improving. As behavioral changes are required of more and more parties in order to protect environmental quality, solutions also become more complex. We have solved many easy-to-solve problems. We are dealing with more complex or intractable ones, including many that go beyond our borders and are thus out of regulatory domain.

Governance of environmental issues is changing. As a result of substantial citizen interest in environmental protection, the non-profit environmental "industry" has grown in size and sophistication. The regulatory community has also improved its capacity to develop and enforce regulations. As scientists, lawyers, and management experts become more abundant, the public and non-profit sectors are more able to compete directly with larger corporations when conflicts arise. Furthermore, they possess enough expertise to be valuable to corporations as partners.

Organizations have tasted the success created by proactive, rather than reactive, environmental problem solving and want more powerful proactive tools. An appropriate analogy might be the use of a personal computer. When first using it, progress is slow. With experience, the user expects more—flexibility, power, capacity, and portability.

[*]*The Environment: Public Attitudes and Individual Behavior.* Prepared by the Roper Organization, Inc.

and waste facilities in recent years, which have usually been won by community groups, or the letter-writing campaigns that have brought companies to reconsider solid waste creation, materials use, and recycling strategies. When this public pressure is brought to bear on a single company or industry, the ground for partnerships is richer.

Existing or Threatened Regulation

Most activities that affect the environment or human health require some kind of regulatory or other governmental approval. Permits to operate, regulations to reduce or recycle, and requirements to train employees are examples of regulations that drive organizations to collaborate. When these types of approvals do not exist, but are threatened to be put in place, there is further stimulus for organizations to voluntarily collaborate to preclude the need for approvals or to inform the process by which the approval will be developed.[14]

Clearly Identifiable Opportunity

When parties identify an opportunity with a high probability of success and positive environmental impact, partnerships become a viable option for success. Major markets and businesses are created daily from the imagination of one person who sees things differently than others and is willing to try to make his or her vision real.

PARTNERSHIPS AS A SOURCE OF COMPETITIVE ADVANTAGE

As resource and environmental quality issues grow in importance, the rationale for partnering becomes more closely linked to organizational success. In a broader sense, individual organizations may develop some form of competitive advantage by seeking and executing successful environmental partnerships. By competitive advantage, we mean the achievement of one's goals—whether they are for market share, profitability, protection of wetlands, or regulatory development—better, sooner, and more cheaply than others that operate in the same activity area.

Michael Porter of the Harvard Business School hypothesized in a 1991 *Scientific American* article that environmental regulation, rather than serving as a deterrent to competitiveness, could be a boon by encouraging companies to develop innovations that would eventually be valuable as international markets adopted similar regulations.[15] Based on early results of a study by the Management Institute for Environment and Business (MEB), there is evidence to support this hypothesis.[16] This counter-intuitive

logic supports partnerships that involve investments beyond what is required by law.

McDonald's and the Environmental Defense Fund (EDF), two organizations that collaborated on solid waste reduction research that created new options for McDonald's operations, have benefited directly and indirectly from their interaction. McDonald's demonstrated its commitment to the public through a range of recycling programs, and has constructed new partnerships consistent with the organizational learning created by the solid waste project. McDonald's may well have avoided loss in market share—anticipated as a result of a negative letter-writing campaign—by responding quickly to demonstrate that it took the threat seriously, and effectively by choosing a high quality, reputable partner.

EDF is one of the fastest growing and most influential organizations in the environmental movement, with an annual budget of approximately $20 million in 1992. It attracts strong employees from scientific, legal, regulatory, and business backgrounds. While it is difficult to directly correlate their success with their willingness to engage in partnerships, most would agree that some portion of their success and public image is due to the fact that they work with corporations and government agencies rather than solely working against them.[17]

Other examples of competitiveness opportunities that arise from partnerships:

- Pacific Gas and Electric (PG&E), a participant with non-profit organizations and ratepayer groups in the development of conservation strategies, has profited from "megawatts," the reduction of energy use in an amount equivalent to a megawatt of electric power.

- The Wildlife Habitat Enhancement Council (WHEC), a non-profit organization that aims to protect habitat for wildlife, has leveraged its limited resources by getting corporations to commit to protect wildlife on their privately owned lands; and

- U.S. EPA has accelerated its mission to reduce toxic emissions by engaging in voluntary projects such as the 33/50 Program with industry leaders.

For some of the organizations participating in environmental partnerships, the experience has been so positive as to be almost transformational:

- Non-profit organizations participating in the North American Waterfowl Management Plan (NAWMP) revised their challenge to ecosystem protection rather than duck protection and have adjusted their staff capabilities accordingly;[18]
- Government agencies such as the EPA and the U.S. Department of Energy have increased their investments in voluntary programs in which their role is facilitative rather than regulatory; and
- Chemical companies such as Dow and Du Pont and other large multinationals like AT&T have dramatically reshaped business decision-making processes by involving outside organizations in the assessment of environmental issues.[19]

Many other examples like those highlighted in this book suggest that organizations may employ partnerships skills as a tool for getting ahead within industries or fields of activities. Roy Vagelos, Chairman and CEO of Merck & Co., stated, "The environment is, in these times, a competitive issue. If we can address it faster, more efficiently, we will have a competitive advantage."[20]

Notes

1. For information on the Du Pont-CFC story, see Forest Reinhardt, *Du Pont Freon Products Division (A)* (National Wildlife Federation, 1989). See also Richard Benedick, *Ozone Diplomacy* (Cambridge, MA: Harvard University Press, 1991).

2. U.S. Environmental Protection Agency. *Reducing Risk: Setting Priorities and Strategies for Environmental Protection* (September 1990).

3. The EPA's "33/50 Toxics Reduction Program" asked companies to reduce toxic emissions by 33% by 1992 and 50% by 1995.

4. During the negotiations over the 1990 Amendments to the Clean Air Act, the Environmental Defense Fund broke ranks with some environmentalists by contributing to the plans for the emissions trading scheme for sulphur dioxide emissions. During the 1993 negotiations over environmental side agreements for the North American Free Trade Agreement, seven environmental organizations worked as a team to expand their influence with policy makers.

5. World Commission on Environment and Development, *Our Common Future* (Oxford: Oxford University Press, 1987), p. 8.

6. The "Timber/Fish/Wildlife Agreement" is documented in Part IV.

7. "Growth Management Planning in Oregon" is documented in Part IV.

8. For the complete recommendations of the Task Force, see *McDonald's Corporation and Environmental Defense Fund Waste Reduction Task Force: Final Report,* April 1991.

9. Equity considerations were critical in both the cases cited—"California Demand Side Management Collaborative" and "Juarez Waste Water Treatment Plant Project"— that are presented in Part IV.

10. Monsanto has been cited as a company that is aware of the relationship between recruitment success and environmental performance.

11. Committee for Economic Development, *Public-Private Partnership: An Opportunity for Urban Communities,* (New York: Committee for Economic Development, 1982), p. 82.

12. Concerns about cooptation fall into the general category of "agency capture." For example, zoning boards in many communities are made up primarily of the developers who want to do business in the area.

13. Tom Horton, "Hanging in the Balance: Chesapeake Bay," *National Geographic,* Volume 183, No. 6, June 1993, p. 2.

14. EPA's Source Reduction Review Project, in which industries are targeted for multi-media regulation, is an example of an impending regulation that could motivate companies to move on a voluntary basis.

15.   Michael E. Porter, "America's Green Strategy," *Scientific American,* April 1991, p. 168. See also Porter's book, *The Competitive Advantage of Nations* (New York: Free Press, 1990).

16.   The Management Institute for Environment and Business, *The Competitive Implications of Environmental Regulations: Case Study Series* (Washington: MEB, 1994). Industries studied were paints and coatings, pulp and paper, electronics, printing inks, refrigerators, and batteries.

17.   EDF has been called the leader of the third wave of American environmentalism and one of America's leading environmental research and advocacy organizations. See, for instance, Forest Reinhardt, *Environmental Defense Fund,* Harvard Business School, November 1992, (Case NI-793-037).

18.   The "North American Waterfowl Management Plan" (NAWMP) is documented in Part IV.

19.   Du Pont, for example, has formed a Community Advisory Panel (CAP) at each of their facilities through which company representatives work directly with local leaders on key community challenges, including environmental quality.

20.   President's Commission on Environmental Quality, *Partnerships to Progress: The Report of the President's Commission on Environmental Quality,* (Washington: PCEQ, 1993), p. 12.

15

Consumers with a Conscience
Jacquelyn A. Ottman

The notion of a "typical green consumer" continues to be elusive. Unlike discrete target groups such as Hispanic women or college-age men, green consumers are hard to define demographically. Greenness extends throughout the population to varying degrees, and green consumers are extremely diverse, encompassing a wide range of issues from global climate change and gritty smokestacks, to graffiti and lawnmower noise on Sunday mornings.

However, research into recent buyers of green products and empirical evidence suggests that the consumers most receptive to environmentally oriented marketing appeals are educated women, 30–44, with $30,000-plus household incomes (see Exhibit 1). They are motivated by a desire to keep their loved ones free from harm and to make sure their children's future is secure. Influential in their community, they rally support for local environmental clubs and social causes. Their buying power and their potential to influence their peers make them a highly desirable marketing target.

That women are in the forefront of green purchasing cannot be underestimated. They do most of the shopping and although it sounds sexist, they may naturally exhibit a maternal consideration for the health and welfare of the next generation. Poll after poll shows that women

●

place a higher importance on environmental and social purchasing criteria than men. This may reflect differences in feelings of vulnerability and control between the sexes, leading men to feel relatively less threatened by environmental ills. However, not all green consumers are as "deep green" or as active as the women discussed here—there is a host of more passive green consumers as well.

MANY SHADES OF GREEN

In conventional marketing, demographics are often a key determinant of intent to buy specific products. But in green marketing, what seems to determine willingness to purchase environmentally conscious products—more than demographics or even levels of concern for a specific environmental issue—are the consumers' feelings of being able to act on these issues, or *empowerment.*[1]

After all, consumers may be concerned about a specific issue, such as fumes emanating from the local power plant or protecting a local wildlife sanctuary, and may have the time or money to act—but if they do not believe they can make a difference, they will likely not act.

Research has corroborated that the most accurate predictor of an individual's willingness to pay a premium for renewable energy is not education or income, but membership in—or prior contributions to—environmental groups. Supporters of such utility "green pricing" programs are "surprisingly diverse, including both urban professionals and rural families."[2]

Exhibit 1 ● Demographic Profile of Green Product Purchasers

Percent of People Who Ever Bought a Product Because the Advertising or the Label Said the Product Was Environmentally Safe or Biodegradable

	Yes, in Past 2 Months	Yes, But Not in Past 2 Months	No, Have Not Bought	Don't Know
SEX				
Total	26	19	49	6
M	22	18	53	7
F	29	20	46	5
AGE				
18–29	23	19	51	6
30–44	31	18	47	3
45–59	27	21	46	6
60+	18	18	55	8
HOUSEHOLD INCOME				
Under $15,000	19	13	61	7
$15,000–$30,000	21	17	55	6
$30,000–$50,000	28	22	45	5
$50,000+	35	22	40	4
$75,000+	34	25	38	3
EDUCATION				
Non–High School Grad	14	18	60	8
High School Grad	24	17	55	5
Some College	31	25	41	4
College Grad	33	18	42	8
OCCUPATION				
Exec./Professional	38	16	42	4
White Collar	28	23	43	6
Blue Collar	22	22	51	5
OTHER DEMO				
Parent of Kids 0–17	31	19	46	4
Household with Personal Computer	36	21	40	4

Source: Roper Starch Worldwide, Green Gauge, 1996. Used with permission

Levels of concern and feelings of empowerment, not surprisingly, vary among the population. A segmentation of consumers isolated by Roper ranges from a 15 percent core of educated, upscale individuals who say they are willing to pay a premium or forego certain conveniences to ensure a cleaner environment, to 37 percent of the public who are doggedly non-environmentalist, characterized more by indifference than by anti-environmentalist leanings. The in-betweeners are more or less pro-environmental—they label themselves "environmentalists" when pollsters ask, but for various reasons are not fully acting on their concerns (see Exhibit 2).

Roper has tracked these segments of consumers since 1990. As of 1996, the five segments, which have exhibited only modest movement overall since first identified, break out as in the following table:

	1990	1996	
True-Blue Greens	11%	10%	⎱ Active
Greenback Greens	11%	5%	⎰ environmentalists
Sprouts	26%	33%	Swing group
Grousers	24%	15%	⎱ Not active
Basic Browns	28%	37%	⎰ environmentalists

Source: Roper Starch Worldwide, Green Gauge, 1996. Used with permission

True-Blues

This 10 percent of the population hold strong environmental beliefs and live them. The most ardent of environmentalists, they believe they can personally make a difference in curing environmental ills. Politically and socially active, they dedicate time and energy to environmentally safe practices themselves and attempt to influence others to do the same. True-Blues are six times more apt to contribute money to environ-

mental groups and over four times more likely to shun products made by companies that are not environmentally responsible. Among the most educated of the five groups, these people are likely to be white females living in the Midwest or South. Almost one-third of them hold executive or professional jobs.

Greenbacks

Greenbacks, representing just 5 percent of the U.S. population, are so named because of their willingness to pay extra for environmentally preferable products. They make up that small group of consumers who say they will pay up to 22 percent more for green. They worry about the environment and support environmentalism, yet feel too busy to change their lifestyles. Although Greenbacks are generally not politically active, they are happy and eager to express their beliefs with their wallets; green purchasing within this group is very high.

Like the True-Blues, they are more likely than the average American to purchase any number of green products, such as environmentally preferable cleaning products, and products and packages made from recycled material or that can be refilled. Moreover, at 22 percent, they are twice as likely as the average American to avoid buying products from companies they perceive as environmentally irresponsible. Greenbacks are likely to be married white males living in the Midwest (35 percent) and West (24 percent). They are well educated, young (median age 37), and more likely than any of the other groups to hold white-collar jobs.

Sprouts

One-third of the U.S. population is classified as Sprouts. They are willing to engage in environmental activities from time to time but only when it requires little effort. Thus, recycling, which is curbside in many communities, is their

Exhibit 2 ● Demographic Composition of the Five Environmental Segments

	Total Public %	True-Blue Greens %	Greenback Greens %	Sprouts %	Grousers %	Basic Browns %
SEX						
Male	48	46	63	44	46	52
Female	52	57	37	56	54	48
MEDIAN AGE	42	42	37	43	42	42
MEDIAN INCOME	$28,000	$33,000	$33,000	$33,000	$28,000	$22,000
EDUCATION						
Less than HS	18	10	10	13	18	27
HS Grad	36	30	21	32	41	40
Some College	23	29	26	28	22	17
College Grad	22	29	44	26	19	15
OCCUPATION						
Exec./Professional	19	29	31	24	12	14
White Collar	18	20	25	18	21	16
Blue Collar	25	19	30	24	26	27
MARITAL STATUS						
Married	58	66	67	62	58	52
Single	42	34	33	37	42	48
POLITICAL/SOCIAL IDEOLOGY						
Conservative	39	31	24	39	42	40
Middle-of-the-Road	37	36	44	36	34	39
Liberal	20	29	28	20	21	16
REGION						
Northeast	20	22	19	21	23	18
Midwest	23	29	35	23	24	20
South	35	27	22	30	40	43
West	21	22	24	26	13	19
RACE						
White	84	91	92	90	78	79
Black	12	4	5	6	20	17
Asian	2	1	2	2	1	2
Other	2	2	1	3	1	2

Source: Roper Starch Worldwide, Green Gauge, 1996. Used with permission

main green activity. They read labels for greenness—although less often than the True-Blues and Greenbacks. Their greenness ends at the supermarket checkout: even though Sprouts and Greenbacks have similar median incomes, Sprouts generally won't choose a green product if it is more expensive than others on the shelf. When they do, they are only willing to pay up to 4 percent extra. More than half (56 percent) are female and at 43, they have the highest median age among the five groups. Sprouts are distributed evenly across the country. They are well educated, and just under two-thirds of them are married. They comprise the swing group that can go either way on any environmental issue. With more education, they are often the source for new Greenbacks and True-Blues.

Grousers

Fifteen percent of the U.S. population are Grousers. These people do not believe that individuals play any significant part in protecting the environment. Instead, they feel that the responsibility belongs to the government and large corporations. Often confused and uninformed about environmental problems, 45 percent of Grousers recycle bottles and cans regularly, but grudgingly; they do so to comply with local laws rather than to contribute to a better environment. They are far more likely than any other group, including Basic Browns, to use excuses to rationalize their lax environmental behavior. True to their name, Grousers complain that they are too busy, that it is hard to get involved, that green products cost too much and don't work as well, and, finally, that everything they do will be inconsequential in the whole scheme of things. Their overall attitude is that it is someone else's problem, so why bother. Demographically, Grousers are similar to the national average, although with a somewhat higher proportion of African-American members.

Basic Browns

Representing 37 percent of the population, Basic Browns are not tuned in or turned on to the environment. They are simply not convinced that environmental problems are all that serious. Basic Browns do not make excuses for their inactivity; they just don't care. The indifference of this group makes them less than half as likely as the average American to recycle and only 1 percent boycott products for environmental reasons as opposed to the 11 percent national average. Three percent buy recycled goods compared to 18 percent nationally. The largest of the five groups, Basic Browns have the lowest median income, the lowest level of education, and live disproportionately in the South. For the Basic Browns, there are just too many other things to worry about.

As noted in Exhibit 3, environmental behavior varies significantly across these segments, suggesting that not all categories of products or individual brands are affected equally by consumers' environmental concerns. A close look at the behavior of the most active segment, the True-Blues, demonstrates the relative depth of their commitment. Given their societal influence, this suggests the types of behavior that can be expected from a much bigger group of consumers in the future. More than half of the True-Blues return glass bottles, look for green messages on packages, recycle newspapers, and do the laundry with "biodegradable" detergents. As social and style leaders, their forceful presence can be expected to exert increasing pressure, particularly on the Greenbacks and the Sprouts—underscoring the opportunities of marketers who can win over these influential True-Blues.

Three Deep-Green Sub-Segments

Not all deep-green activists are alike. It is possible to further segment them into three groups mirroring the major types of environmental

Exhibit 3 ● Consumer Behavior to Protect the Environment, by Segment

Percent who do on a regular basis (1996)	*Total Public* %	*True-Blue Greens* %	*Greenback Greens* %	*Sprouts* %	*Grousers* %	*Basic Browns* %
RECYCLING						
Bottles, cans, glass	51	78	65	74	45	22
Newspapers	46	77	52	70	39	16
MARKET BEHAVIOR						
Use biodegradable soaps, detergents	22	60	27	36	13	2
Avoid buying aerosol products	20	50	30	31	15	1
Read labels to see if contents are environmentally safe	19	63	28	25	14	1
Buy products made or packaged in recycled materials	18	55	32	23	16	3
Buy products in packages that can be refilled	16	40	32	18	18	3
Avoid buying products from companies who aren't environmentally responsible	11	48	22	9	8	1
Avoid restaurants using styrofoam	8	44	15	4	4	1
OTHER BEHAVIOR						
Take hazardous waste to collection site	22	51	32	31	17	6
Compost yard waste	17	46	32	22	15	3
Take own bags to supermarket	10	36	9	11	11	1

Exhibit 3 ● Consumer Behavior to Protect the Environment, by Segment (*Continued*)

Cut down on car use	6	24	8	5	4	1
Contribute money to environmental causes	5	31	9	2	3	1
Volunteer for an environmental group	4	18	1	3	5	less than 1
Write to politicians	3	26	2	less than 1	less than 1	less than 1

Source: Roper Starch Worldwide, Green Gauge, 1996. Used with permission

issues and causes: Planet Passionates, Health Fanatics, and Animal Lovers (Exhibit 4).

With the goals of protecting wildlife and keeping the environment pristine for recreational purposes, Planet Passionates focus on issues relating to land, air, and water. They recycle bottles and cans, avoid overpackaged products, clean up bays and rivers, and boycott tropical hardwood.

As implied by their name, Health Fanatics focus on the health consequences of environmental problems. They worry about getting cancer from too much exposure to the sun, genetic

Exhibit 4 ● Segmentation by Consumer Motives

Planet Passionates	*Health Fanatics*	*Animal Lovers*
LIKELY TO BELONG TO:	*LIKELY TO BELONG TO:*	*LIKELY TO BELONG TO:*
Sierra Club	Americans for Safe Food	Greenpeace
Natural Resources Defense Council	Mothers and Others Against Pesticides	World Wildlife Fund National Audubon Society
American Rivers	National Coalition Against the	Humane Society
Rainforest Alliance	Misuse of Pesticides	PETA
Friends of the Earth		
LIKELY ENVIRONMENTAL BEHAVIOR:	*LIKELY ENVIRONMENTAL BEHAVIOR:*	*LIKELY ENVIRONMENTAL BEHAVIOR:*
Conserve energy, water	Buy organic foods and bottled water	Boycott tuna, ivory
Recycle bottles, cans	Use sunscreens	Buy "cruelty-free" cosmetics
Buy recycled paper	Buy unbleached coffee filters	Avoid fur
Avoid excessive packaging	Read *Organic Gardening,* *Prevention,* and *Delicious*	Boycott Exxon
Read *Sierra* Magazine and *Amicus Journal*		Read *Animal Agenda* and *Audubon*

Source: J. Ottman Consulting, Inc.

defects from radiation and toxic waste, and the long-term impact on their children's health of pesticides on fruit. Health Fanatics frequent natural-food stores, buy bottled water, and eat organic foods.

Animal Lovers, the third major group of deep greens, protect animal rights. They boycott tuna and fur, and their favorite causes include manatees and spotted owls. Animal Lovers check to see if products are "cruelty-free." They are likely to be vegetarians.

GREEN CONSUMER PSYCHOLOGY AND BUYING STRATEGIES

Although they express their environmental concerns in individual ways, green consumers are motivated by universal needs (see Exhibit 5). These needs translate into new purchasing strategies with implications for the way products are developed and marketed.

NEED FOR CONTROL

Green consumers put familiar products under a magnifying glass of environmental scrutiny, and their buzzwords signifying environmental compatibility abound. Starting in the late 1980s, such terms as "recyclable," "biodegradable," and "environmentally friendly" made cash registers ring throughout upper-middle-class neighborhoods from coast to coast. As we approach the millennium, "sustainable," "compostable," and "bio-based" are being added to the list.

As shown in Exhibit 6, the broad scope of these buzzwords suggests that green consumers scrutinize products at every phase of their life cycle, from raw material procurement, manufacturing, and production straight through to product reuse, repair, recycling, or eventual disposal. While in-use attributes continue to be of primary importance, environmental shopping agendas now increasingly encompass factors consumers can't feel or see. They want to know how far raw

Exhibit 5 ● Green Consumer Psychology and Buying Strategies

Needs	Strategies
Information	Read labels
Control	Take preventive measures
Make a difference/alleviate guilt	Switch brands
Maintain lifestyles	Buy interchangeable alternatives

Source: J. Ottman Consulting, Inc.

Exhibit 6 ● Green Purchasing Buzzwords

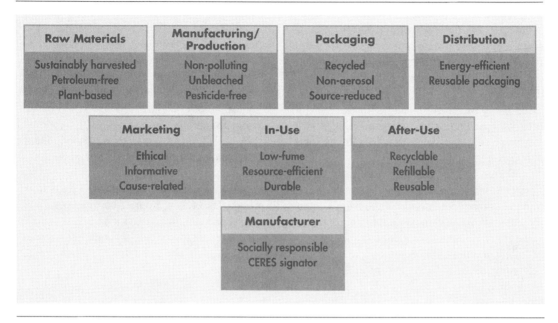

Source: J. Ottman Consulting, Inc.

materials are procured and where they come from, how food is grown, and what their potential impact is on the environment once they land in the trash bin.

As a second control strategy, green consumers patronize manufacturers and retailers they trust, and boycott the wares of suspected polluters. In the absence of complete knowledge about a product's environmental characteristics, purchasing from upright manufacturers and retailers provides an added layer of assurance that products are safe.

At 11 percent, a near-record number of consumers boycott brands of companies with poor environmental track records (see Exhibit 3). Apple growers well remember the boycott waged in 1989 by mothers who feared the long-term effects of the Alar pesticide on their children's

health. In 1995, to protest French nuclear tests in the Pacific, wine drinkers targeted the 25 million–30 million bottle harvest of Beaujolais. The market for Beaujolais "all but collapsed" in Japan, the Netherlands, and Scandinavia, and "disappeared" in Australia and New Zealand close to the testing.[3]

As a final control strategy, a small but growing number of consumers now search for simpler ways of living. In 1991, researchers of the *Yankelovich Monitor* reported on a long-term trend that showed new products, the lifeblood of marketers, were losing appeal. They attributed this to two factors—a growing dislike for shopping in general and the perception that "new" is risky.[4] For proof, consider what's happening to women's shopping habits.

The *New York Times* reports that women's

apparel sales are on a long-term slide (from a record $84 billion in 1989 to $73 billion in 1995), despite a 37 percent gain in overall personal spending during the same period. Apparently, women are deciding there are better ways to spend their money than shopping. Picking up the slack are "other passions, from one's children to investing, to a variety of goods and services being marketed as salves for a stressful life: backpacking trips and gardening tools, vanilla-scented candles, spiritual retreats, and manicures."[5]

Women are not the only ones tired of the "live-to-work, work-to-consume" rat race. A nationwide survey conducted for the Merck Family Fund shows that most Americans are concerned about materialistic values and the impact of indulgent consumption on our environment. According to the poll, 82 percent of Americans agree that "Most of us buy and consume far more than we need." Suggesting that consumers intuitively understand that today's lifestyles are unsustainable, 58 percent say it would make a "big difference" in helping the environment "if we taught our children to be less materialistic."[6] Attempting to reconcile values centered on family, responsibility, and community, more than a quarter said that "in the past five years, they had voluntarily made changes in their life which resulted in making less money in order to have a more balanced life." When asked what would make them happier, two-thirds said they wanted to spend more time with family and friends.

The mass consumer is still ambivalent about how to reconcile personal values with present consumption modes. However, a small but growing number of consumers address their needs to protect the environment, enhance spirituality, reduce stress, and build long-term financial security with strategies such as avoiding unnecessary purchases; buying high-quality, durable products; and using products that do several jobs. Representing a movement called Voluntary Simplicity, these lean consumers accounted for 4 percent of all Baby Boomers as of 1994, and are projected to represent 15 percent by the year 2000.[7]

Not to be confused with the back-to-basics crowd of the early 1970s, this small but growing contingent of upscale, educated adults do not reject consumption out of hand; some have secondhand BMWs in the driveway and designer clothes among their pared-down and largely monochromatic (black/white/gray) wardrobes. They happily trade in high-powered jobs and the hefty incomes they provide to spend additional time with loved ones, appreciate nature, and pursue creative activities. Expect their ways to depress sales of new homes, convenience foods, and second cars, while at the same time accelerating momentum in natural foods, easy-to-care-for clothes in classic styles, travel, and other leisure pursuits.

Case Study: Profile of a Simplifier

Kathy Bryant was living the American Dream. As an editor, writer, and photographer for Duke Power in Charlotte, North Carolina, her career was in the fast lane. But a key element was missing from her life.

In 1988 when her father died, Kathy realized she was too far from her home and family in College Park, Maryland—a town her great-grandfather had founded.

She called her uncle, a career utility executive, for advice. He urged her to "get off the phone and tell your boss you are quitting." She did.

A week before moving home she received an offer for freelance work. With her mother's support, Kathy restructured her life and work. As a freelancer, she controls when and for whom she works. She loves the variety of jobs she has done—including photographing Al Gore and Queen Elizabeth—opportunities she would never have had otherwise. And her mother benefits, too. Kathy provides companionship, helps care for the house, and encourages her mother to be active. Her mother is no longer lonely but thrives on the activity.

"I am really happy since I moved home. I cherish the time with my mother, the time in my garden. I can garden all day if I want," says Kathy. Managing her time required some discipline, she notes, as did learning to tailor her spending needs to her new income.

Kathy thinks in terms of life and happiness, not in terms of money and career. She has learned to live with less by eliminating small items like magazine subscriptions. When considering a purchase, she thinks about the articles she needs to write to pay for it. Being more deliberate about her purchases makes her spending "more real."

"Too much of our 'throw-away society' is based on creating and consuming," says Kathy. "Leading an alternative lifestyle demonstrates that you can consume less and have a very good life."

Kathy defines herself in terms of life choices, not career choices. She values the opportunity to create her own life. She looks for fun ways to make money, and volunteers with local organizations.

The quality of Kathy's life has increased dramatically, as has the quality of her work. "This is," admits Kathy, "the golden period of my life." She has found the vital ingredients previously absent—self-respect, self-definition, and satisfaction. That is Kathy Bryant's equation for fulfillment.[8]

A final control strategy relates to health and is best depicted in the revolution now underway called "clean food." Described as "a new standard for health and reliability," clean foods are "free of artificial preservatives, coloring, irradiation, synthetic pesticides, fungicides, rodenticides, ripening agents, fumigants, drug residues, and growth hormones," and exclude those foods that are "processed, packaged, transported, and stored to retain maximum nutritional value."

Motivated in part by lack of trust in government's ability to keep food pure, the appeal of clean foods has fueled escalating sales for organic produce, bottled water, health-food supermarkets, alternative medical treatments, and dietary supplements.[9]

Clean food and organic food provide irresistible aesthetic and spiritual benefits as well. According to Alice Waters, one of the first chefs to stress the importance of locally grown organic food for its taste and environmental preferability, "It's also a connection with the kind of food that is alive, fresh, seasonal, and a connection with the people who are growing it. A deep and lasting sensual connection is made, and once you eat food like that, you can't turn back."[10]

Keep an eye on this trend. Now representing a small (3 percent) portion of the population of those most concerned about food and its relation to health, it could engage up to 30 percent of the population in the next 20 years by one analyst's estimate.[11]

NEED TO MAKE A DIFFERENCE

Reflecting a deeply felt need of Baby Boomers to assume responsibility for their actions, green consumers want to feel that they can, at least in some small way, make a difference. It is no coincidence that they respond to such empowering promises as those represented by the bestseller, *50 Simple Things You Can Do to Save the Earth.* This need stems as much from a desire for control, as it does from the corresponding need to alleviate guilt.

Consumers feel especially guilty about environmental ills they can do something about, but do not. They readily acknowledge the role of their own consumption in despoiling the environment (see Exhibit 7), and while they feel they have improved slightly since the early 1990s, they rate themselves as just a little better than large businesses when asked, "Who's Dragging Their Feet on Environmental Protection?" (see Exhibit 8).

Exhibit 7 ● Root Causes of Environmental Problems

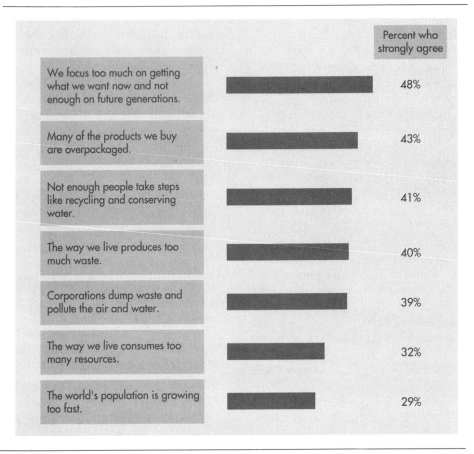

Source: "Yearning for Balance." A nationwide survey conducted by the Harwood Group from February 20 to March 1, 1995. Sponsored by the Merck Family Fund. Used with permission

They see themselves as being able to do little to fix serious problems like global climate change or ozone layer depletion. However, they do feel a responsibility to cut down on excess packaging and take steps like recycling and conserving water.

Everyday behavior, such as disposing of what is perceived as excessive packaging or keeping the water running while shaving, can serve as daily reminders of personal environmental transgressions. Use of products that are,

rightly or wrongly, associated with environmental blight—disposable diapers, plastic-foam cups, and aerosol spray cans—reinforces their guilt.

Consumers' desire to alleviate guilt manifests itself in indirect ways. New mothers may continue to use Pampers knowing they will wind up in a landfill. However, to compensate, they may go out of their way to recycle the family's bottles, cans, and newspapers to help offset the

Exhibit 8 ● "Who's Doing a Good Job on the Environment?"

	"Dragging Its Feet"	"Doing a Pretty Good Job"	% Change on "Doing a Pretty Good Job" Since 1993
The press	35%	37%	NC
Own state's Department of Environmental Quality	41%	34%	–1
Local government officials	47%	33%	–1
The American public	54%	33%	+3
Small businesses	43%	32%	–2
Large businesses	64%	20%	–1

Source: Roper Starch Worldwide, Green Gauge, 1996. Used with permission

space in the landfill taken up by the diaper. This compensatory behavior suggests that each consumer has a unique repertoire of activities and trade-offs he or she is willing to make to help out the planet. One's environmental repertoire likely reflects such factors as age, lifestyle, income, and particular environmental interests and concerns, as well as geographic location, including access to recycling and other after-use or disposal options. Consumers' feelings of guilt and eco-inadequacy have not been assuaged since the early 1990s; a lengthening of environmentally driven activities and purchasing continues to fill the gaps.

Green consumers are, by definition, very sincere in their intentions. As much as they are willing to do today, as their knowledge and commitment grows, they become more aware of what else they can do. The gap between what they feel they should be doing and what they are actually doing makes them feel guilty and sometimes defensive. Purchasing green products and taking measures around the house give environmentally concerned consumers a psychic lift by helping them align their beliefs with their actions.

For instance, anecdotal evidence suggests that consumers feel positively reinforced by recycling (typically one of their first steps down the path to green). Once engaged, they start asking, "What else can I do?" The significantly high levels of recycling that now occur may provide one explanation for the current rebound in green-product purchasing.

NEED FOR INFORMATION

Consumers heading off to supermarkets and health-food stores in search of greener goods need to know how to tell the "green" products from the "brown" ones, which stores or catalogs to find them in, and how to spot the products and packages that can be recycled in their community. Their task is tricky.

Such environmentally preferable products as mercury-free alkaline batteries or paper towels made from recycled content are often indistinguishable from "brown" ones. Some green products with as yet limited appeal like low-flow showerheads and citrus-based cleaning products are often tucked away in health-food shops and direct-mail catalogs beyond the reach of mainstream shoppers. Such alternative cleaning products as baking soda and white vinegar are easily found in supermarkets but are not necessarily labeled as "green."

Products representing new and unfamiliar technologies are constantly being launched onto supermarket shelves. Consumers' understanding of environmental issues is growing but continues to be low—only 8 percent of consumers claim to know a lot about environmental issues.[12] So even the most environmentally enthused consumers need to be educated on why some types of products represent less environmental harm than others. Providing such information and education still provides the biggest opportunity to expand the market to mainstream consumers.

Information aimed at filling in consumers' knowledge gaps is now in plentiful supply. Sources include manufacturers; packaging; advertising; consumer media, including several green shopping sites on the World Wide Web; and the specialty environmental press composed of consumer-oriented magazines, including *E, Mother Jones,* and *Utne Reader,* as well as such advocacy group publications as *Sierra, Audubon, World Watch,* and *Amicus Journal.* Although much of the information is more consistent and less confusing than its late 1980s counterparts, a profusion of labels, claims, eco-seals, and images on products and packaging, as well

as inconsistent media stories, often confuse and frustrate consumers who are just beginning to give green products another try.

Win consumers over by educating them with clear, consistent information about the environmental issues associated with your products.

NEED TO MAINTAIN LIFESTYLE

Although a small number of highly committed consumers will sacrifice in the name of altruism, the great majority of consumers, understandably, are still not prepared to give up such coveted product attributes as performance, quality, convenience, or price. Product efficacy continues to strongly influence consumer purchase decisions. As too many green marketers learned the hard way, environmentally preferable products must be priced competitively or project superior primary benefits in order to attract a wide market.

For the great many working women—and working mothers in particular—short-term, immediate concerns like getting through the day often preempt long-term and more remote environmental goals. Greened up versions of major products such as super-concentrated laundry detergents available at local supermarkets meet their needs and sell well as a result. Consumers want the products they buy to be delivered in a safe, sanitary, and attractive manner. Their desire to buy products with minimal packaging conflicts with their greater needs for safety (e.g., tamperproof lids) and convenience (e.g., microwavable food).

Historically, how food looks determined its appetite appeal and perceived purity. This is slowly changing, due largely to education efforts on the part of organic growers and more effective distribution methods. Fewer consumers now need to choose between organically grown apples with an inconsistent appearance and perfect-looking apples ripened with chemical agents.

Resistance to paying a premium will not go

away any time soon. Many consumers simply cannot afford to pay extra for any type of product, green or not; today's consumers are especially spoiled by everyday low-pricing strategies and mass-merchandiser discounting. Although wallets are gradually opening wider for green goods as a result of increased education, most consumers are still not willing to pay extra money upfront for products that promise a long-term payback, such as energy-efficient refrigerators or lightbulbs.

The inconsistent or even downright poor quality of green products offered in days gone by—low-flow showerheads that sputtered and green-hued florescent lighting that flickered, for example—seems to have given their modern-day successors a bad name. Happily, most of today's green products adeptly combine performance with environmental quality. Now that they can have their cake and eat it too, expect mainstream consumers to drop more green products into their shopping carts in the years ahead.

In the past, premium pricing and vaguely worded environmental claims made consumers suspect manufacturers of price gouging. If products are smaller, more compact, or simpler looking than their "brown" counterparts, consumers intuitively believe they should cost less, not more. But this is slowly changing. For example, a small but growing number of consumers seek out products and packaging that have been "source reduced." This is particularly true in the 1,800 or so U.S. municipalities that have volume-based, "pay as you throw" household waste-disposal fees, where consumers are typically charged for each bag of waste they drop at the curb.

Historical reluctance to pay a premium for green goods seems to be softening as consumers connect environmental responsibility with health or other direct benefits. Sales of organically grown "clean" foods, natural cosmetics, and cot-

tons grown without pesticides demonstrate that when it comes to green products, the greater the self-interest, the greater the perceived threat, the greater the willingness to pay. The small but growing Voluntary Simplifier movement suggests that some consumers will even go so far as to change jobs or rearrange their lifestyle altogether if the rewards of more time and a richer life are present. . . .

Notes

1. This is also referred to as "perceived consumer effectiveness" in "Green Consumers in the 1990s: Profile and Implications for Advertising," James A. Roberts, Baylor University, *Journal of Business Research,* Volume 36, p. 226.

2. Baugh, Keith, Brian Byrnes, Clive Jones, and Maribeth Rahimzadeh, "Green Pricing: Removing the Guesswork," *Public Utilities Fortnightly,* August 1995, p. 27.

3. Whitney, Craig R., "Nuclear Tests Cutting Sales of Beaujolais," *New York Times,* November 17, 1995, p. A10.

4. Hayward, Susan, of Yankelovich, Clancy, and Shulman, presentation to the American Marketing Association's "Environmental Conference: Green Marketing from a Marketer's Perspective," October 1991.

5. Steinhauer, Jennifer, and Constance C. R. White, "Women's New Relationship with Fashion," *New York Times,* August 5, 1996, p. D9.

6. "Yearning for Balance: Views of Americans on Consumption, Materialism, and the Environment," prepared for the Merck Family Fund by the Harwood Group, Bethesda, Maryland, July 1995.

7. Valdes, Alisa, "Living Simply. '90s Style Means Earning Less to Enjoy Life More," *Boston Globe,* September 1, 1994, p. A3.

8. Barry, Sam, "Kathy Bryant Profile," *Co-op America Quarterly,* Number 37, Summer 1995, p. 22.

9. Burros, Marian, "A New Goal Beyond Organic: Clean Food," *New York Times,* February 7, 1996, p. C1.

10. Ibid., p. C4.

11. Ibid., p. C4.

12. Roper Starch Worldwide, Green Gauge, 1995.

16

The Next Big Product Opportunity
Jacquelyn A. Ottman

Many green products on the market today represent small enhancement or "tweaks" to existing ones. Recycled content replaces virgin materials; packaging is lighter or designed to be refilled; washing machines save water and energy by tumbling clothes on a horizontal as opposed to a vertical axis. Although these are admirable and much-needed technical achievements, the reductions in environmental impact they represent may not be enough to meet future consumer needs in a sustainable fashion.

Finding solutions to environmental degradation involves much more than replacing one supermarket cartful of goods with another. That is because our present modes of production and consumption are simply not sustainable—"sustainability" is defined as meeting the needs of the present without compromising the ability of future generations to meet their own needs—in the face of a global population that is 5.8 billion today and expected to reach 10 billion by 2040.

Some experts go so far as to estimate that achieving sustainability over the next few decades requires a radical change in the entire production and consumption of industrial societies—a "system discontinuity," characterized by a 90 percent reduction in the consumption of environmental resources.[1] Societies that run at 90 percent "eco-efficiency" eat lower on the food chain (i.e., more plants and legumes as opposed to animal-based proteins); minimize the use of raw materials by recycling, reusing, and other means; and generate energy from renewable as opposed to fossil-fuel sources, which are not only quickly depleting but also contribute to global climate change and acid rain.

The issue of sustainability is especially critical for U.S. consumers. The United States represents 5 percent of the world's population but consumes 30 percent of the world's natural resources and creates 50 percent of global greenhouse gases. Since 1900, the U.S. population has tripled, while procurement of natural resources has multiplied 17 times.[2] Clearly, this is not sustainable. With developing countries looking to adopt Western lifestyles, pressures on global natural resources will intensify. Entire ecosystems such as the Florida Everglades are at risk of collapse.

Great strides are being made in the areas of information technology and "nano-technology," which uses resources superefficiently by building products one atom at a time. However, technological advances may not be enough. Major shifts in lifestyle will be necessary, as well as significant changes in how we meet basic human needs through the products and services we buy. We must leap rather then tweak.

Clearly, caring for the needs of a burgeoning population in a sustainable fashion presents opportunities for innovative companies. The purpose of this chapter is to provide a framework for thinking about solving environmentally related consumer issues creatively, and in doing so, offer some inspiration from history's preeminent problem-solver—Mother Nature.

WHAT IS GREEN?

Green products are typically durable, nontoxic, made from recycled materials, or minimally packaged. Of course, there are no completely green products, for they all use up energy and resources and create by-products and emissions during their manufacture, transport to warehouses and stores, usage, and eventual disposal. So green is relative, describing those products with less impact on the environment than their alternatives.

Ask the question "What is green?" If any certainty exists at all, too often the answer is "It depends." That's because the factors that make a product "green" often depend upon the specific product or product category, where it will be used, how often, by whom, and for what reason.

What Is the Product Category?

Biodegradability, for example, may be a highly desirable feature for laundry detergents whose suds can pollute local waterways, but it may not be relevant for paper cups or plastic trash bags destined for landfills where decomposition occurs slowly, if at all, and stability—if the landfill is to support a new airport, for instance—is preferred. Conventional alkaline batteries are considered green if they contain no added mercury, but they are highly toxic nevertheless, because of the other materials they contain.

Where Will the Product Be Used?

What might be green in my backyard may not be green in yours, because regional variations may exist in the amount or types of natural resources available, the local climatic and topographical conditions, and whether reduction, reuse, recycling, or composting are options. In a country as

diverse as the United States, such conditions can vary dramatically from state to state, even from town to town. So, broadly speaking, washable cloth diapers may be environmentally preferable in the Northeast where landfill space is at a premium and water is plentiful, but may be less desirable in the Southwest where water supplies are tight and there are still plenty of potential spots to bury trash. Because they take up less space, plastic supermarket bags may actually be environmentally preferable to paper bags where landfilling is the only option, but in areas where composting is a possibility, paper might be the optimal eco-choice.

How Will It Be Used?

Is a product likely to be used once and thrown away, or used over and over again? According to one chemist, if a ceramic mug will not be used at least 1,000 times, then the energy it takes to make it doesn't justify its presumed environmental preferability over polystyrene.[3] Compact fluorescent lightbulbs cost more than incandescents for a reason: all those weighty materials consume a lot of energy in their manufacture and transport. If they are used in lamps that are turned on and off frequently, the long-term energy savings likely won't be realized; incandescents may be preferable.

Are Alternative Technologies Available?

Environmental impact is literally designed into products up front. So existing products can only be tweaked so much before a jump to an entirely new or different technology capable of filling the same consumer need is necessary to make a significant improvement in environmental performance. For example, no amount of tinkering with incandescent lightbulbs (which throw off 90 percent of their energy in excess heat) will ever achieve the cooler-burning efficiency of compact fluorescents. Use recycled envelopes and stationery, fill the trucks with natural gas, but E-mail will always be environmentally preferable to even the greenest conceivable "snail mail."

Making "green" even tougher to pin down is the fact that no agreed-upon method exists to measure the precise relative environmental impact of one product against alternatives. In the debate over cloth versus disposable diapers, for example, value judgments come into play—plastic and paper production and solid waste, or cotton production and the water and energy to wash the diaper?

What Comes Next?

Environmental issues are constantly changing, reflecting new discoveries such as the hole in the ozone layer, shortages in natural resources, population shifts, and fewer places to bury everyone's trash. Technology is constantly advancing. Consumer tastes and attitudes evolve. Laws and marketing strategies are rewritten accordingly. Thus, no matter how well companies do their homework, what is accepted as "green" today may wind up being viewed as "brown" tomorrow. The aerosol industry and McDonald's learned this the hard way.

In the late 1970s, in response to reports linking chlorofluorocarbons to ozone layer depletion and subsequent consumer outcry, the aerosol-packaging industry quickly switched to hydrocarbon-based propellants. However, we now know that hydrocarbons create smog when mixed with sunlight; so the move is on to find a viable alternative, lest further sales be lost to pumps and other competitive technologies.

Since the 1970s, the packaging for McDonald's hamburgers has evolved from one technology to another in response to environmental as well as economic considerations. First, polystyrene foam replaced paper, but then was replaced altogether by quilt wraps. This much-heralded, source-reduced alternative may one

day be replaced itself by compostable packaging, now in test. Environmentally speaking, the folks at McDonald's can't rest. Because of escalating global food demands, coupled with the environmental degradation associated with cattle-raising, the very beef in McDonald's Big Macs may soon be under fire regardless of whether it is produced domestically or in the Amazon rain forest.

With green a moving target, planning gets tricky; industry can only respond as quickly as the market demands. This poses the risk of rushing greener products to market to serve the demands of influential consumers while mass consumers may be unaware of the need for a change. The green marketplace is rife with examples of less than perfect timing such as the following:

- When competitors were moving toward ½-cup laundry detergent concentrations, Church & Dwight answered with a ¼-cup formula for their own Arm & Hammer ultraliquid brand. But their sales suffered from confusion over the ½-cup "compacts" of other manufacturers. Acknowledging that consumers were prepared for only so much greenness at a time, the company reneged on the more concentrated alternative.[4]

- Introduced in response to a newly discovered need of chemophobics, Heinz's Cleaning Vinegar, a double-strength version of its normal product, flopped when introduced into supermarkets as an alternative cleaning aid. The mass consumer didn't seem to know what to make of it. While greater consumer marketing and educational efforts no doubt would have helped enhance its chance of success, the product opportunity may have been better served by a niche strategy, distributing the product in health-food stores and green-product catalogs until enough of the mass market was prepared to switch to the eco-logically conscious offering.

Lack of precise definitions for "green" coupled with the "moving target" syndrome tend to discourage industry from making the long-term investments needed to develop new technologies and market the greener products that result. Recent history is rife with examples of industry losing its sticking power in the face of market uncertainty for green technologies. Solar power is just one case in point.

After a rush of government funding in response to the oil crisis of the mid-1970s, U.S. industry geared up to develop photovoltaics (solar) technology. But when oil became cheap and plentiful again, and the Reagan Administration withdrew support for the fledgling technologies, industry sold outstanding key patents to Japan, a country deficient in natural-energy sources. The Japanese now hold the lead in this key future energy source. There is hope that American industry has learned that when it comes to the environment, it pays to think ahead.

NEED TO THINK IN NEW WAYS

Environmental concerns force today's consumers to question their assumptions about what types of products best meet their needs. Paper no longer has to be white. Recycled content, once deemed inferior—even unclean—is now preferable to virgin. Disposable products, once associated with feelings of satisfaction (we were so rich as a country we could afford to throw things away!), make us feel guilty.

Question your own assumptions. Reevaluate your business strategies. Think differently about what it takes to meet basic human needs in a sustainable fashion. In the not-too-distant future, advantage will accrue to corporations that can transcend existing paradigms and product categories, redefining existing notions of how best to meet consumer needs. The future belongs to companies that can invent new designs, mate-

rials, and technologies that meet consumer needs with minimal, if not zero, environmental impact. It belongs to companies who can reinvent how existing industries operate, or create entirely new industries if necessary.

Address consumers' concerns credibly and profitably by integrating environmental issues into new-product planning and overall corporate strategy, as follows.

Be Pro-Active

Because availabilities of natural resources are in constant flux, new materials and technologies are forever being developed. Learning is always taking place. So, be ever-vigilant and plan ahead.

Address Green Continuously

Because green is a "moving target," unexpected shifts in consumer sensibilities can occur with the potential to wipe out entire markets or tarnish corporate reputations. So address environmental issues on a continuous basis in order to better anticipate such consumer shifts, control your own destiny, and steal a march on competitors when the time to respond approaches.

Address Environmental Issues at the Design Stage

We cannot "tweak" our way to green. Design products and their packages *up front* to balance environmental challenges and consumers needs most satisfactorily. The introduction of the Woody Pen, marketed by the Goodkind Pen Company of Scarborough, Maine, demonstrates this strategy well.

Case Study: Woody Pens: Designed for the Environment

Rather than making its pens of plastic, Goodkind Pen Company uses birch scraps sourced from local furniture makers, and its pens are designed to be refillable. As an alternate to conventional "blister" packs, Goodkind Pen displays its pens in an innovative plastic clamshell that can be reused and recycled. Consumers simply unsnap the package components, remove the pen and its refill, and drop the package in a mailbox so that it can be returned to Goodkind.

By carefully designing its product up front for minimal environmental impact, Goodkind yields a product with a super-green profile and, in the process, enjoys a high level of satisfaction from both environmentally conscious consumers, as well as other consumers who enjoy the comfort and economic benefits of using a refillable wood-based pen.

Change the System, Not the Product

Environmental issues are holistic in nature. Often the most significant environmental impacts occur when the entire system of design, manufacturing, distribution, and reuse/disposal is overhauled, rather than just one or two features of a specific product or package. Knoll Furniture reduced packaging required for new office installations by 90 percent by lining the trucks and amending the loading docks rather than by "tweaking" the wrappings on individual pieces of furniture.

As a way to cut out milk-carton-type packaging altogether, Coca-Cola has explored siphoning syrup directly from trucks into holding bins at fountains and fast-food restaurants. In California, an entrepreneur sells carbonated-water taps along with syrup so consumers can make popular brands of soft drinks like Diet Coke and Sprite at home. His innovation represents a packaging and energy-saving alternative to pre-mixed bottles of pop that need to be transported to and from stores.

Changing the system by which products are designed and sold—or shall we say, changing the way benefits are delivered or consumer needs are met—suggests many opportunities for resource and energy-saving innovation, such as integrating products within the household infrastructure. Such staples as sugar, flour, salt, and pepper are sold in bulk, ready to be transferred within the home to permanent packages like sugar bowls, salt and pepper shakers, canisters, and the like. Similarly, household paper towels and toilet tissue are designed to fit neatly into permanent wall mounts. Why not consider selling permanent packages for your own products?

Some permanent packages are already finding their way onto supermarket shelves. Church & Dwight, for example, markets a refillable plastic shaker for its Arm & Hammer baking soda. Good Seasons salad dressing mix has long been accompanied by a free glass cruet. Liquid household and personal-care products, such as shampoos, liquid dishwashing detergents, and other cleaners, are starting to be sold in bulk for transferral to dispensers inside the home. Opportunities exist to market attractive dispensers. Given the flimsy nature of some spray bottles, an opportunity exists for manufacturers to sell permanent, dishwasher-safe packages designed for use with the collapsible-pouch packages now marketed as refills for popular household cleaning products.

One company that believes in the potential for permanent packaging is Rubbermaid, makers of Litterless Lunch Kits. Designed to replace brown bags, juice boxes, plastic baggies, and foil wraps, the kits are durable and reusable and come in an array of sizes and styles. For example, a whimsical Gilbert the Fish appeals to kids under five. Gilbert provides easy access to lunch through his oversized mouth, which unzips to fold down as a placemat. His tail fin hides a zippered compartment for milk money, keys, and other small items. Sold at Wal-Mart and grocery stores, the lunch kits retail from about $10.[5]

Consider refillables at retail. Where allowed by law, The Body Shop allows consumers to refill cosmetics jars from a special refill bar. In

Germany, consumers refill milk bottles from a steel cow. The potential for refilling suggests the prospect of in-store "real estate" for product manufacturers. Individual brands of cereal and coffee, for example, would be allotted permanent dispenser space on store shelves.

Be Flexible

Since environmental ills can vary by region as well as from season to season, opportunities exist for new market segmentations and line extensions akin to those used by sophisticated packaged-good marketers. Consider coffee.

Coffee drinkers have it made. At the supermarket shelf, they can pick among all-method grinds, drips as well as instant, freeze-dried, whole bean, and coffee-for-one "tea" bags. Coffee enthusiasts can shun the regular stuff for flavored coffees like French Vanilla and Swiss Mocha Almond, as well as espresso and the exotic blends like Arabian Mocha Sanai sold in specialty shops. Depending upon the distribution channel and the brand, packages can be steel cans, glass, aseptic packs, or kraft paper bags.

Marketers of green products can adopt similar flavor, formulation, and packaging variations. With the diversity of green issues around the country and around the world, a customized approach may represent the best chance for minimizing environmental impact.

Diversify Offerings

For example, allow consumers to choose packages made of materials that accommodate local capabilities for recycling, composting, or landfilling. Differentiate on the basis of product formulation. Melitta, for example, simultaneously markets both unbleached and bleached white coffee filters.

Although it sounds counterintuitive, offering a product with a "greener" profile right alongside one's historical "brown" product does not necessarily send a conflicting message about a company's green commitment. Empirical evidence suggests consumers are grateful for the choice. From a practical standpoint, the marketing of "greener" products alongside traditional offerings helps to serve the needs of that broad swath of consumers who may not yet be acting upon certain environmental issues, while having an alternative handy when they are ready to "trade up." Some marketers choose to avoid this dilemma in the first place through selective distribution strategies, alternative branding, or discontinuing the conventional product/technology at the "greener" one's introduction.

Take the High Road

Maximize the long-term payout of product development efforts by adopting the most environmentally sound technology, materials, or designs possible within the constraints of economics and consumer acceptance. This can also provide opportunities to preempt competition and avoid costly legislation. In the process, it can pay off in positive publicity and enhanced brand and corporate imagery often associated with leadership.

Case Study: The McDonough Collection: Textiles with Zero Impact

The William McDonough Collection of environmentally preferable fabrics manufactured by Design Tex Inc., of New York City, is just one example of a product line with the lofty goal of zero environmental impact. Created by the designer and architect for which it was named, the collection relies on a proprietary process that eliminates all toxic by-products at every step in the manufacturing process; the factory effluent actually leaves cleaner than it was when it came in! What's more, the fabric actually biodegrades safely into soil, leaving no carcinogens, persistent toxic chemicals, heavy metals, or other harmful substances. (Compare this to the estimated 127 heavy metals in the average silk tie!)

For the fabric, McDonough chose natural wool from New Zealand and ramie from the Philippines that is compostable and grown without pesticides or synthetic fertilizers. The fabrics are then dyed with a selection of only 16 pigments culled from a possible 4,500 commonly used in textiles that could be manufactured without releasing pollutants. By-products from the weaving process are shipped to strawberry farms near the manufacturing plant in Heerervegg, Switzerland, where the biodegradable scrap fabric is used in place of plastic as ground cover.

The fabrics have found a ready market among high-end furniture manufacturers, designers, and architects who appreciate its uncompromising attention to aesthetics as well as its environmental sensibilities.

Rethink the Value Your Products Provide

When it comes right down to it, consumers don't really *need* cellular telephones, designer clothing, or subcompact cars. They need to communicate, to stay warm, and to be transported from place to place. And if you really think about it, consumers don't need to *own* products per se; what they really need is the *utility* such products provide. Take a giant mental leap forward by rethinking your own products with these concepts in mind! You'll likely discover innumerable fresh new opportunities to increase profits and enhance customer loyalty. As long as you're thinking big, go so far as to consider selling *services* as replacements for, or adjuncts to, material products.

As identified by various, mostly European, experts working in what might just wind up to be the most exciting area of new product development in the future, four different groups of services are possible:

- Product-life extension services—services designed to extend the life of products,

e.g., technical assistance, repair, maintenance, and disposal service.

- Product-use services—the sharing of products as well as using products for some time without the need to buy, e.g., a "Greenwheels" car-sharing service now offered in the Netherlands.

- Intangible services—substituting products for labor-based services, e.g., automated bill-paying and in-home voice mail as a replacement for answering machines.

- Result services—services designed with the aim of reducing the need for material products, e.g., pedestrian access rather than cars, urban recreation facilities rather than forced tourism.[6]

Does your product pose a solid-waste challenge in terms of bulk and/or toxics? Consider leasing rather than selling it outright. Leasing provides an opportunity to maintain control over one's product throughout its entire life cycle. This translates to a cost-effective source of raw materials and it can help reduce liabilities stemming from irresponsible disposal by others. To reap these benefits, some chemical companies now lease their products, and some office equipment manufacturers now lease rather than sell copy machines. Although not marketed as such, manufacturers of toner cartridges who take their products back at the end of their useful lives (in this case, by providing for free pick-up at consumers' homes and offices) are in effect leasing the use of their products.

Many manufacturing companies can easily sell services as an adjunct or as a replacement to their own or another company's products. Appliance makers such as GE and Whirlpool already enjoy hefty revenues from service contracts. Electric-power utilities sell energy-conservation services in addition to power. Manufacturers of electric power mowers would do well to consider selling Xeriscaping services—using water-conserving native shrubs and grasses in water-short areas, for example—or potentially lose out to competitors outside their category. Ridding one's dress shirt of a greasy stain takes knowhow in addition to soap and elbow grease. Prediction: in addition to converting natural resources into Ajax and Biz, the big soap companies will convert *human resources* into paid-telephone-advice lines on spot removal.

Consider services, too, for their potential to lock in customers over time. It can be said that Ametek . . . is in the business of helping Ethan Allen protect furniture rather than manufacturing polypropylene. Instead of selling a product once, consider leasing, or even giving the product away and selling the refills. Think of the opportunities for manufacturers of coffeemakers, electric toothbrushes, and soap dispensers, all of whom have an incentive to make their initial products more durable, too.

GETTING STARTED: ASK "HOW WOULD MOTHER NATURE DO IT?"

The most fertile source of inspiration for companies in search of innovative methods to meet consumers' needs in environmentally sound ways is Mother Nature herself. For centuries, product and package designers have been inspired by her ingenious designs and technologies. Think about it. Cameras mimic the human eye. Helicopters hover and fly backward like hummingbirds. Velcro fasteners adopt the same entangled architecture as the prickly burrs attached to their Scottish inventor's boot.

By definition, green products are more nature-like: they are inherently efficient, easy to recycle, and often driven by solar power. Consider some of the greener products and technologies on the market today. Energy Star computers save on energy by hibernating when not in use. Solar cells on the roof of Mazda's 929 run a ventilating system when the car is parked in the sun.

Like peas in a pod, rolls of Kodak film stacked in one box instead of sold separately cut down on packaging waste.

The principles of nature have been incorporated into a creativity process invented by the author to generate concepts for new products and services that represent minimal environmental impact. Some of the strategies contained in this *Getting to Zero*[SM] process include the following:

Keep It Simple

A banana peel is a deceptively simple package. It protects its contents, it is easy to open, it eliminates the need for utensils, and it signals when its contents are ripe. How many human-designed packages can claim as much?

Trees are equally elegant in a multipurpose sort of way. When alive, they provide food, shelter, and shade, not to mention inspiration for poetry and a place of lofty refuge for kids. When naturally felled in the forest, they become food and home for a whole new host of organisms and wildlife. When felled by humans, they provide any number of useful products including paper, furniture, and wooden pencils.

In packaging a key to simplicity is source reduction—using designs that require less material in the first place. Since source reduction means the elimination of the very bells and whistles that make some types of packaging so convenient, this can be tricky. Colgate-Palmolive addressed this issue literally quite neatly in designing a new toothpaste tube that eliminated the need for an outer carton.

Colgate-Palmolive proved that one doesn't have to give up convenience in a source-reduced package when they introduced stand-up tubes in the fall of 1992. Prompted by retailers in Germany, where customers have the right to leave unwanted packaging behind, Colgate's innovation eliminates the traditional outer carton by allowing the tube to stand on its own via the use of a flat-top pad nozzle. Because it is powered by gravity, it solves the age-old problem of emptying the tube completely—a worthy environmental goal all by itself.

The revolutionary new tube design uses 20 percent less primary packaging material than a regular laminated tube and it has only four parts compared to as many as ten components in typical pumps. It also costs less than a pump. In the United States, it has attracted a loyal following of consumers who like its heightened convenience: the vertical storage feature keeps the toothpaste ready to dispense, and improves neatness and ease of use.

Grow Your Products Green

Nature's own economy is plant based and solar based. Biologically based products are starting to displace alternatives made from chemicals on supermarket shelves. Liquid Plumber, for example, markets a drain cleaner that uses the power of enzymes to literally eat through food and grease. Some consumers prefer cleaners that are made from d-limonene, nature's own solvent, extracted from orange peels in the orange-juice-making process.

Consider the stories of Fox Fibre and Citra-Solv, two innovative natural products on the market today.

Case Study: Fox Fibre: Dyed by Nature

Consumers know that a bright, white cotton T-shirt feels natural. What they don't know is that it takes tons of herbicides and pesticides and millions of gallons of water to grow the cotton plants, which are sprayed with a chemical defoliant to prevent leaf-staining. The resulting fiber is then saturated with bleach, or dyed with any number of potentially toxic chemicals.[7]

Sally Fox, founder of Natural Cotton Colours, Inc., of Wickenberg, Arizona, has a better idea: she grows cotton that is colored nat-

urally. Fox discovered that ancient peoples grew their cotton in bright colors. After ten years of experimentation, she produces cotton that yields beautifully colored fibers in hues of brown and green (she is currently working on blue). Her colored cotton is also naturally resistant to pests, so it requires fewer pesticides than conventional cotton. Also, because the resulting fabrics are naturally colorfast, there's no fading. In fact, the colors actually intensify with the first fifteen washings. The hues are naturally warm and elegant.

Starting with a mere six plants, Fox's business now grows enough product to supply cotton to yarn spinners in ten different countries. Companies such as Fieldcrest, IKEA, and Levi Strauss use this company's naturally colored fibers in their products. Timing has contributed to success—people concerned about the environment are drawn to Fox Fibre for its unique characteristics and are also willing to pay a slight premium. In 1993, when L. L. Bean first offered a Fox Fibre sweater for $39, it sold out in a week.[8]

Case Study: Citra-Solv: Nature's Own Cleaner

In a marketplace where all the leading products are made from a profusion of sometimes nasty-sounding synthetic chemicals, Shadow Lake's Citra-Solv® cleaner and degreaser stands apart. It is made almost entirely from d-limonene, nature's own degreaser, extracted from orange peels left over from the juice-making process.

Citra-Solv was originally created for the commercial and industrial markets. When OSHA regulations required that chemicals used in cleaning products be disclosed on product labels, Steven and Melissa Zeitler, founders of Shadow Lake, Inc., got the idea to take the product retail when employees, enamored with the product's fresh orange smell, asked to take some home.

Helping to debunk the myth that "green" products don't work as well as their "brown" counterparts, Citra-Solv quickly rubs out lipstick stains, chewing gum, adhesive goo, and easily tackles greasy barbecue grills and automobile wheel rims.

Distributed in over 90 percent of health-food stores and environmental-product catalogs, where it is typically a bestseller, and now a growing number of specialty-food stores, Citra-Solv represents a multimillion-dollar business. A recent partnership with the USDA's Alternative Agricultural Research and Commercialization Corporation providing marketing support promises to grow this product made from renewable resources even further.

Think in Circles

In nature there's no such thing as waste; everything is recycled. Soil, for example, represents decomposed plant and animal matter poised to support new life. Water is constantly being transformed in a neverending cycle consisting of evaporation, condensation, rainfall, and evaporation.

A growing brood of "industrial ecologists" now urges manufacturers to shift their thinking from a linear "cradle-to-grave" mode to a more circular "cradle-to-cradle" approach. Their recommended strategies—recycling, reuse, remanufacturing, and composting—all represent opportunities to create valuable new uses for products that would otherwise be dead-ended in landfills.

As Xerox has discovered, thinking in circles provides opportunities to save money and maximize return on assets through recycling and reuse of materials or components. New markets can be created for goods that are refurbished and resold. By thinking in circles, John Deere saves money and avoids landfill issues through an innovative reusable packaging system.

Case Study: Xerox: Where Thinking in Circles Pays Off

Xerox Corporation is a big believer in remanufacturing. No wonder. They have saved $200 million in materials and parts cost in less than five years by remanufacturing some of their copiers, using the same assembly line to produce newly manufactured as well as remanufactured machines.

In Europe, Rank Xerox markets the two types of machines as separate product lines. The lower-cost remanufactured line allows Xerox to competitively price against other manufacturers; in the United States, the machines are sold in the same product line. The remanufactured machines match Xerox's high expectations for new machines, and according to company surveys, consumer acceptance of the remanufactured machines, which come with a three-year performance guarantee, has increased in the past five years.[9]

Try recycling the wastes of another industry, or look for innovative ways for other manufacturers to turn your own waste into gold. The toy industry has created a huge market for the integrated circuit boards that are quickly made obsolete by rapid advances in computer chip technology. In a most symbiotic way, the used-chip market has flourished due to the growth in the number of toys utilizing computer technology, while the toy industry benefits from the availability of low-cost chips.[10]

Case Study: John Deere Saves Money Through Reuse

The John Deere Company of Horicon, Wisconsin, enjoys the opportunity it created to save money by pioneering the notion of reusable shipping crates. It chooses to go beyond compliance of state laws prohibiting the landfilling or burning of corrugated containers and opts for reusable/returnable plastic containers for the 5,000-plus components arriving at its farm-equipment factories. Deere, which owns the containers, provides them to its parts suppliers for shipping tractor components to assembly plants; the assembly plants return the empties in a continuous loop. Made of high-density polyethylene, the containers resist rust, mildew, and splintering and can be cleaned with soap and water.

By thinking in circles, Deere has eliminated 1,200 truckloads of non-recyclable corrugated cardboard going to landfills annually.[11] Disposal costs translated into bottom-line savings of approximately $1.5 million in 1995.[12]

Go with the Flow

Look for opportunities to harness nature's own technologies. This may include using gravity, as Colgate does, to "power" toothpaste tubes or lotions, or using green plants to filter indoor air pollutants. This may also include generating renewable sources of power, such as solar, wind, hydroelectric, or geothermal.

Solar power charges a host of devices ranging from $4 pocket calculators to $10,000 home-energy systems, now used in more than one million U.S. homes. The market for solar-powered appliances and photovoltaic home-energy systems is estimated at $1.5 billion in the United States and has grown 20 percent each year since 1992. Add in biomass, wind, geothermal, and other renewable energy technologies, and the market grows to $3.5 billion.[13] Many utilities, like Traverse City Light and Power, creators of an innovative "Green Rate" wind program, are beginning to notice the possibilities.

Case Study: The Coming Age of Renewable Power

"Green pricing" is catching on at electric power utilities across the nation. This refers to programs through which customers voluntarily pay a premium for electricity generated by renewable resources. Traverse City Light and Power, a municipal utility in Michigan, offers one of the most successful of such programs.

Under the plan, called "Green Rate," customers pay a 1.58¢-per-kilowatt-hour premium for wind power generated by a locally installed Vestas V-44 600-kW wind generator that towers over a local cornfield—the largest operating turbine in the United States.

Customers also agree to buy their electricity for a specific number of years—three years for residential, ten years for commercial customers. Customers are rewarded with locked-in rates—a benefit that can be offered since wind power is not subject to variable fuel costs. To date, 20 commercial customers and 245 residential customers (representing about 3 percent of the utility's patronage) have signed on despite the 17–23 percent premium, depending upon the rate class.[14]

To generate this kind of innovative thinking in your own company, start with some of the techniques used in the Getting to Zero[SM] process.[15] Distill the essence of your product's or package's function and ask: How would Mother Nature do it? Ask: How does nature protect things? Transport seeds? Get rid of waste? Communicate? Ask: What are some things in nature that are *like* our product or package? Search for some metaphors like banana peels and pea pods that can catalyze creativity. Ask: What would we do differently if, as in nature, landfills were not an option?

The next time you want to brainstorm, take your team to the woods instead of a sterile hotel room. Send your colleagues outdoors in search of innovative natural products and packages that are compatible with Earth. Take along some ecologists and biologists.

When taking these steps, keep in mind that using natural prototypes will not only accelerate your thinking, but it can shave light-years off your test market. After all, Mother Nature has been testing her concepts for over four billion years!

IDEAS FOR ACTION

Ask the following questions to uncover opportunities for innovative and pro-active product greening:

- What would it take for our product/industry to exist in a sustainable society? How could we deliver the same product benefits with zero environmental impact?

- Are there opportunities to offer variations in our product to cater to regional differences in climate, topography, and/or after-use/disposal options?

- Do consumers know how best to use our product so as to minimize environmental impact?

- How do consumers use our products? How can we alter our products to better match their needs and habits and still minimize environmental impact?

- Is the mass market ready for our eco-innovation? Should we pursue a niche distribution strategy?

- How do consumers view our products? Have their assumptions about what is environmentally correct for our product or category changed? What are their current expectations?

- What opportunities exist to impact the entire system of design, manufacturing, distribution, and reuse/disposal in which our product is made? Where are the opportunities to make the biggest environmentally oriented contribution?

- What would we have to do differently in order to achieve zero environmental impact?

- What are the opportunities to offer services as an adjunct or replacement to our products?

  —Can we extend the life of our own or another company's products through technical assistance, repair, maintenance, and/or disposal services?

  —Can we lease our products or make them available for paid sharing by a number of customers?

  —Can we offer the service replacement of our product, e.g., lawn-mowing service as opposed to selling lawn-mowers?

  —What are our opportunities to offer information or electronic-based substitutes for material products?

- How can we harness the power of nature as inspiration for green product and service development?

  —Are all of our employees trained in the basic principles of ecology?

  —Can we provide opportunities for our employees to interact with nature and professionals—such as ecologists and biologists—who can stimulate their thinking? . . .

Notes

1. "Sustainable Product-Services Development," introductory notes presented by Ezio Manzini at the Pioneer Industries on Sustainable Services workshop organized by the United Nations Environmental Programme—Working Group on Sustainable Product Development at the International Natural Engineers and Scientists Conference, "Challenges of Sustainable Development," Amsterdam, August 22–25, 1996.

2. Young, John, "The New Materialism: a Matter of Policy," *World Watch,* September/October 1994, p. 31.

3. Tierney, John, "Recycling Is Garbage," *New York Times Magazine,* June 30, 1996, p. 44.

4. Canning, Christine, "The Laundry Detergent Market," *Household and Personal Products Industry,* April 1996, p. 76.

5   "Juvenile Lunch Kits from Rubbermaid Bring Fun to Everyday Lunches," Rubbermaid press release, July 1996, p. 1.

6.   United Nations Environmental Program—Working Group on Sustainable Product Development, correspondence to members, January 23, 1997.

7.   Brookhart, Beth, "Cotton's Little Red Hen," *Farm Journal,* 1991, p. 8.

8.   "Organic Cotton Hits the Shelves," *In Business,* Volume 16, Number 3, May/June 1994, p. 21.

9.   Davis, John Bremer, "Product Stewardship and the Coming Age of Takeback: What Your Company Can Learn from the Electronics Industry's Experience," Cutter Information Corp., Arlington, Massachusetts, 1996, p. 38 and p. 108.

10.   Ibid., p. 39.

11.   *BioCycle,* December 1993, p. 26.

12.   John Deere Lawn and Grounds Care Division press release, 1996, p. 4.

13.   Personal communication with Scott Sklar, executive director, Solar Energy Industries Association, May 28, 1997.

14.   Telephone conversation with Steve Smiley, Bay Energy Services, February 18, 1997; and *Green Pricing Newsletter,* Ed Holt, ed., The Regulatory Assistance Project Number 3, April 1996.

15.   Getting to Zero is a service mark of J. Ottman Consulting, Inc.

Part 4

Principles of Corporate Ecology

THE FINAL SET of readings forms an agenda for corporations that are moving toward sustainable practices. In many respects, it is a tool kit, consisting of a set of skills that can be applied by various functional areas within a corporation, from product design to manufacturing to marketing. Yet, viewed holistically, these readings demonstrate the need for an integrative knowledge of environmental management which is informed by all functions in a balanced manner. The aim of these readings is to leave the student of corporate ecology with the background necessary to be conversant in topics of the corporate ecology field.

We begin with a discussion of life cycle costing. As discussed in the section on economics, one reason for the prevalence of pollution is that the prices of most, if not all, goods do not reflect their full environmental impact. One way this occurs is that the costs of a product over its entire life are not evaluated. So-called life cycle assessment is an attempt to analyze the environmental consequences of products, all the way from raw materials to their ultimate disposition. In "Note on Life Cycle Analysis," Susan Svoboda of Realia Group provides a broad overview of life cycle costing. Reducing a complex topic to its constituent elements, she explains the most useful segment of life cycle analysis for decision making: an inventory of all inputs and outputs that will occur throughout the life of a given product.

Developing information for decision making is the essence of accounting. The next reading, "An Introduction to Environmental Accounting as a Business Management Tool," orients students to the basic building blocks of environmental accounting. An Environmental Protection Agency publication, it explains how a great many pertinent costs and benefits elude traditional systems of accounting and how managers can begin to amend accounting conventions to incorporate them. Identification of costs is important, but in accounting, allocation of those costs to the proper products and processes is paramount.

A deeper consideration of the design elements of new products is the topic of the next reading, by AT&T's Braden R. Allenby. Entitled "Integrating Environment and Technology: Design for Environment," it is a concise introduction to the methodology of environmentally sensitive product design. Allenby stresses a systems approach, with a goal of achieving "environmentally-preferable manufacturing processes and products while maintaining desirable product price/performance characteristics." He introduces a simple matrix as a flexible approach to considering different alternatives. It looks at environmental impacts on various media as the product moves through its manufacturing, use, and reuse/recycling/disposal phases.

Our final reading is excerpted from *ISO 14000,* by Tom Tibor with Ira Feldman, who are private consultants in this area. It is an excellent overview of a new set of international standards that pertains to environmental management, spotlighting both products and processes for evaluation, but also the organization itself. Two elements are worth noting: the ISO standards are voluntary and not the product of government policy, and they do not delineate measurable pollution standards, only standards for an organization's environmental management system. Although there are considerable benefits and pitfalls of the ISO 14000 system, on balance Tibor and Feldman argue that adoption of the system will yield positive outcomes as it diffuses globally.

We conclude our readings with "The Natural Step to Sustainability," which appeared in the Johnson Foundation's *Wingspread Journal.* It was selected as the final reading because it takes the most farsighted perspective on sustainability, by linking human behaviors with the laws of the physical and life sciences. The centerpiece of the Natural Step program is the set of four "non-negotiable and absolute" conditions for sustainable life on the earth. Meticulously developed by a panel of 50 scientists, the conditions represent a clear set of guidelines not only for society but also for individual organizations.

17

Note on Life Cycle Analysis
Susan Svoboda

As corporations seek to improve their environmental performance, they require new methods and tools. Life cycle analysis (LCA) is one such tool that can help companies to understand the environmental impacts associated with their products, processes, and activities. LCA is controversial and still evolving as a methodology. However, the principles behind LCA thinking are being adopted rapidly by manufacturers and service organizations alike as a way of opening new perspectives and expanding the debate over environmentally sound products and processes. The goal of LCA is not to arrive at *the* answer but, rather, to provide important inputs to a broader strategic planning process.

THE ORIGIN OF LCA

LCA has its roots in the 1960s, when scientists concerned about the rapid depletion of fossil fuels developed it as an approach to understanding the impacts of energy consumption. A few years later, global-modeling studies predicted the effects of the world's changing population on the demand for finite raw materials and energy resource supplies.[1] The predictions of rapid depletion of fossil fuels and resulting climatological changes sparked interest in performing more detailed energy calculations on industrial pro-

cesses. In 1969, the Midwest Research Institute (and later, Franklin Associates) initiated a study of the Coca-Cola Company to determine which type of beverage container had the lowest releases to the environment and made the fewest demands for raw materials and energy.[2]

In the 1970s, the U.S. Environmental Protection Agency (EPA) refined this methodology, creating an approach known as Resource and Environmental Profile Analysis (REPA). Approximately 15 REPAs were performed between 1970 and 1975, driven by the oil crisis of 1973. Through this period a protocol, or standard methodology, for conducting these studies was developed.[3]

In the late 1970s and early 1980s, environmental concern shifted to issues of hazardous waste management. As a result, life cycle logic was incorporated into the emerging method of risk assessment, which was used with increasing frequency in the public policy community to develop environmental protection standards.[4] Risk assessments remain controversial procedures: the public is often disinclined to trust them, especially when conducted after-the-fact to justify an activity or when performed by an organization with a vested interest in their conclusions.[5]

When solid waste became a worldwide issue in the late 1980s, the life cycle analysis method developed in the REPA studies again became a tool for analyzing the problem. In 1990, for example, a life cycle assessment was completed for the Council for Solid Waste Solutions, which compared the energy and environmental impacts of paper to that of plastic grocery bags.[6]

A similar study comparing disposable diapers to washable cloth diapers was also conducted.

Environmental groups around the world have also adopted life cycle analysis; organizations such as Blue Angel, Green Cross, and Green Seal use and continue to improve LCA for the purpose of product labeling and evaluation. Thus, while initially limited to the public sector, LCA has been adopted by increasing numbers of corporations and nonprofit organizations as an aid to understanding the environmental impacts of their actions. And as demand for "green" products and pressures for environmental quality continue to mount, it is quite likely that industrial life cycle analysis will become in the 1990s what risk assessment was in the 1980s.

COMPONENTS OF LIFE CYCLE ANALYSIS

Life cycle analysis takes a systems approach to evaluating the environmental consequences of a particular product, process, or activity from "cradle to grave." By taking a "snapshot" of the entire life cycle of a product from extraction and processing of raw materials through final disposal, LCA is used to assess systematically the impact of each component process.

Ideally, a complete LCA would include three separate but interrelated components: an inventory analysis, an impact analysis, and an improvement analysis. The components are defined as follows:

- **Life Cycle Inventory.** An objective, data-based process of quantifying energy and raw materials requirements, air emissions, waterborne effluents, solid waste, and other environmental releases incurred throughout the life cycle of a product, process, or activity.
- **Life Cycle Impact Assessment.** An evaluative process of assessing the effects of the environmental findings identified in the inventory component. The impact assessment should address both ecological and

human health impacts, as well as social, cultural, and economic impacts.

- **Life Cycle Improvement Analysis.** An analysis of opportunities to reduce or mitigate the environmental impact throughout the whole life cycle of a product, process, or activity. This analysis may include both quantitative and qualitative measures of improvement, such as changes in product design, raw material usage, industrial processes, consumer use, and waste management.

To date, most LCAs have focused on the inventory component, as it is the most "objective" (and therefore, least controversial) analysis to perform. Franklin Associates, an industry leader in LCA, has been improving inventory-analysis methodology over the past 20 years.[7] However, it encourages clients to extend the inventory and add the impact and improvement assessments.

INVENTORY ANALYSIS

An inventory may be conducted to aid in decision-making by enabling companies or organizations to:

- Develop a baseline for a system's overall resource requirements for benchmarking efforts;
- Identify components of the process that are good targets for resource-reduction efforts;
- Aid in the development of new products or processes that will reduce resource requirements or emissions;
- Compare alternative materials, products, processes, or activities within the organization; or
- Compare internal inventory information to that of other manufacturers.

Managers using LCA to aid decision-making can improve the validity of the results and keep the analysis focused by precisely defining the scope of the "system" to be analyzed, considering practical constraints such as time and money. This step builds the foundation for the analysis that follows and should be understood and agreed upon by those responsible for commissioning the study. A system refers to a collection of operations that together perform some defined function. The system begins with all the raw materials taken from the environment and ends with the outputs released back to the environment (see Exhibit 1).

Within most systems, three main groups of operations may be defined: 1) operations of the production, use, transportation, and disposal of the product, 2) operations for the production of ancillary materials such as packaging, and 3) the energy production needed to power the system. A clearly defined scope will improve the results of subsequent steps when the total process is divided into subsystems. An example of typical subsystem categories is shown in Exhibit 2.

The linkages between subsystems make the process of collecting consistent measurements complex. For example, subsystems must be defined so that they are large enough to provide sufficient data for analysis but not so large that data is aggregated at a level that precludes detailed analysis. In addition, subsystems should be linked by a standard basis of comparison such as equivalent usage ratios. For example, two products or subsystems may use resources at different rates, have different densities, or have different performance levels. To resolve these issues, typical usage patterns for products need to be determined so that logical comparisons can be made. For many of the system inputs, equivalent weights or volumes may need to be calculated.

Managers using LCA to aid decision making must understand that the collection of data is a complex process and that many assumptions are made in the process. Absent or incomplete data,

Exhibit 1 ● Inputs and Outputs of a System

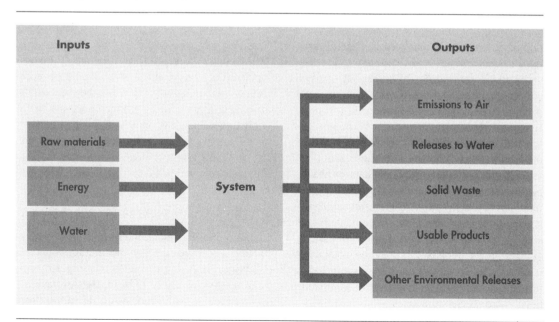

Exhibit 2 ● Defining System Boundaries

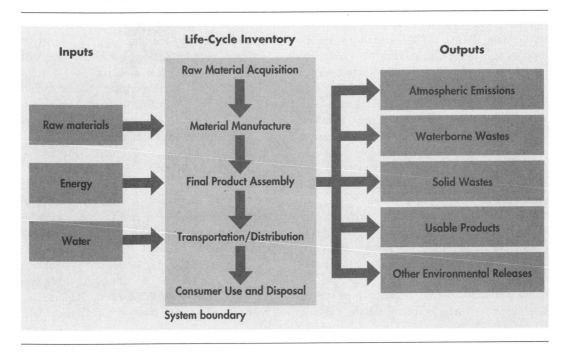

Source: Battelle & Franklin Associates, Ltd.

differences in the way data were collected, variations in technologies, and the number, diversity, and potential interactions of processing steps all contribute to the complexity. Either industry- or plant-level data may be used, depending on the scope and purpose of the study; government documents, federal regulations, technical literature, industry reports, published studies, and plant visits are all important sources of data. However, the selection of the source of data can substantially affect the inventory results, and any analysis should include complete documentation of sources, assumptions, limitations and omissions. For example, comparisons should be made using data from similar time periods, as manufacturing processes often change over time as companies adopt more efficient practices.

An important step in the inventory is the creation of a process-flow diagram that will serve as the "blueprint" for the data to be collected. Each step in the system should be represented in the diagram, including the steps for the production of ancillary products such as chemicals and packaging. This step is important because it clearly depicts the relative contribution of each subsystem to the entire production system and the final product.

OVERVIEW OF THE INVENTORY SUBSYSTEMS[8]

A thorough understanding of how an inventory analysis is conducted, and the limitations and assumptions inherent in the various stages is critical to effective use of LCA in decision making. The following is a synopsis of the various subsystems analyzed in an inventory analysis.

Raw Materials Acquisition

Data are collected for this subsystem on all activities required to obtain raw materials, including transportation of the materials to the point of manufacture (see Exhibit 3). Typically, raw materials are traced for the primary product and all primary, secondary and tertiary packaging. Managers should review the data to make sure equivalent comparisons are used. For example, a package containing recycled materials may need increased thickness to compensate for the decreased strength of recycled materials. In this case, managers must make a tradeoff between weight of materials that will someday become part of the waste stream and virgin material con-

tent. The inventory should also include all inputs of energy, materials, and equipment necessary for acquiring each raw material. Because this dramatically increases the complexity of the analysis, criteria must be determined to eliminate insignificant contributions. This may be done by establishing a threshold for inclusion. For example, any component contributing less than five percent of inputs might be ignored.

Ecosystems are impacted in many ways by the extraction or harvesting of raw materials, but only those effects that can be quantified, such as pesticide run-off from agriculture or soil loss from logging, should be included in the inventory. Effects that cannot be easily measured, such as loss of scenic or aesthetic value, may be

Exhibit 3 ● Raw Material Acquisition Subsystem

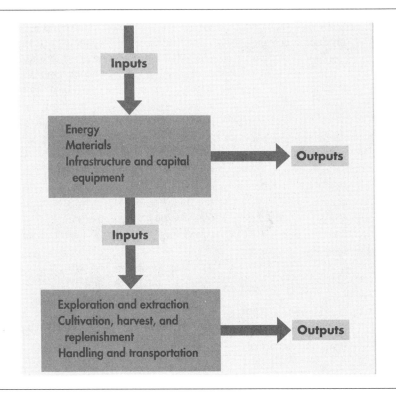

covered in the more subjective impact assessment. At this point, attempts to quantify renewable or nonrenewable resources for inventory calculations are subjective, as quantifiable data is not publicly available. However, maintaining separate lists of renewable and nonrenewable materials may be helpful if an impact assessment is later performed.

Energy acquisition is actually part of the materials-acquisition subsystem, but because of the complexity of the subject, it warrants its own analysis. Data collected should include all energy requirements and emissions attributed to the acquisition, transportation, and processing of fuels. This means that if gasoline is used as a transportation fuel, not only should emissions related to combustion be included, but also energy consumption and emissions due to extraction and refining. In the U.S., energy is derived from a number of sources including coal, natural gas, petroleum, hydropower, nuclear power, and wood. Utilities use many different types of energy sources to produce electricity, so the energy analysis must include a determination of the fuel mix used to generate the electricity. Generally, the national average fuel mix may be used, but industry-specific information is preferred.

Some materials are made from energy resources and are therefore assigned an energy value. For example, plastics, made from petroleum and natural gas, release energy when burned. This energy value is credited against the system requirements for the primary product, resulting in a new energy requirement that is less than the total energy requirements for the system.

Manufacture and Fabrication

Data collected for this subsystem includes all energy, material, or water inputs and environmental releases that occur during the manufacturing processes required to convert each raw material input into intermediate materials ready

for fabrication. This process may be repeated for several streams of resources as well as several intermediate cycles before final fabrication of the product (see Exhibit 4).

Often co-products—outputs that are neither products nor inputs elsewhere in the system— are generated in the manufacturing process. Co-products are included in LCA until they are separated from the primary product being analyzed. Raw materials, energy, and emissions should be allocated between the primary product and the co-products by their proportionate weight or volume. If scrap within one subsystem is used as an input within the same subsystem, the raw material or intermediate material required from the outside is reduced and should be factored into the analysis. If industrial scrap is used in another subsystem, it is considered to be a co-product and should be allocated to the same consumption and emission rates required to produce the primary material. Some scrap is simply discarded and should be counted as solid waste.

Differences in technology throughout the industry require certain assumptions to be made at this stage. Comparisons between different-size facilities, differing ages of equipment, different capacity-utilization rates, and differing energy consumption per unit of production must be made explicit.

The data collected for final product fabrication assesses the consumption of inputs and the emissions required to convert all materials into the final product ready for consumer purchase. Calculations follow the same procedure as in converting raw material to intermediate materials and include the same limitations.

Data collected for fabrication of the final product includes the inputs and releases associated with filling and packaging operations. As this is a necessary step for virtually any product, this step focuses on differences between processes or materials being compared. If the filling procedure is identical for the two products being compared, this step can be ignored. Both pri-

Exhibit 4 ● Manufacturing and Fabrication System

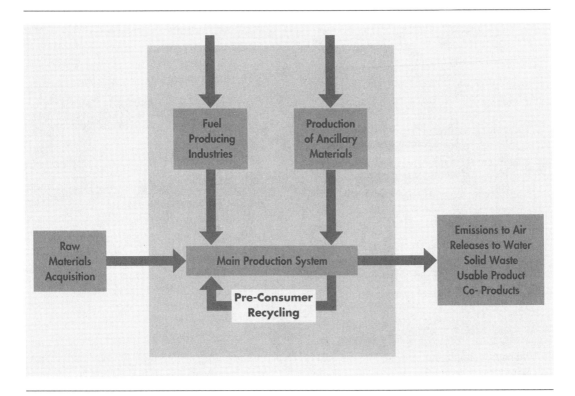

mary and secondary packaging must be included in the calculations, taking care to keep packaging per unit consistent between alternatives.

Transportation/Distribution

An inventory of the related transportation activities of the product to warehouses and end-users may be simplified by using standards for the average distance transported and the typical mode of transportation used (see Exhibit 5). Inventory of the distribution process includes warehousing, inventory control, and repackaging. Environmental controls such as refrigeration are components of both transportation and distribution. As in previous stages, clear boundaries must be established to define the extent to which

issues such as building and maintaining transportation and distribution equipment will be factored into the inventory results.

Consumer Use/Disposal

Data collected for this subsystem cover consumer activities including use (product consumption, storage, preparation, or operation), maintenance (repair), and reuse (see Exhibit 6). Issues to consider when defining the scope of the subsystem include:

- Time of product use before it is discarded
- Inputs used in the maintenance process
- The typical frequency of repair
- Potential product reuse options

Exhibit 5 ● Transportation/Distribution System

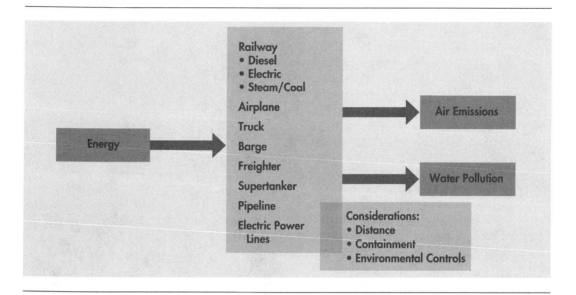

Managers should incorporate into the analysis any industry information on typical consumer usage patterns that may make the study's results more valid. For example, consumers may occasionally use two thinner paper cups to attain the strength of a single comparable polystyrene cup. Sources of data that may help this process include consumer surveys, published materials, and assumptions. Inventory reports must include documentation of assumptions including the timeliness of the data, potential biases, and other limitations.

Various disposal alternatives exist such as reuse, recycling, composting, incineration, and landfilling. Transportation and collection of post-consumer waste should also be included in the analysis. Inventories often use a national estimate of waste management methods, citing current averages for the percentage of waste disposed by landfilling, recycling, and incineration methods.

Recycling technology is expected to improve greatly in the future. Therefore, content levels and recycling rates should always be reported at current rates with documentation of study dates. Advances in technology will both increase rates and the number of products that are recyclable, altering both open- and closed-loop recycling options (see Exhibit 7).

Open-loop recycling means that a product is recycled into a different product that is disposed of after use. In these cases, the resource requirements and environmental emissions related to the recycling and final disposal of the recycled material is divided equally between the two products produced.

Closed-loop recycling refers to materials that can be recycled into the same product repeatedly. This means that the more times the product is recycled, the less virgin material is required and the greater the number of cycles over which the resources and emissions can be allo-

Exhibit 6 ● Consumer Use/Disposal System

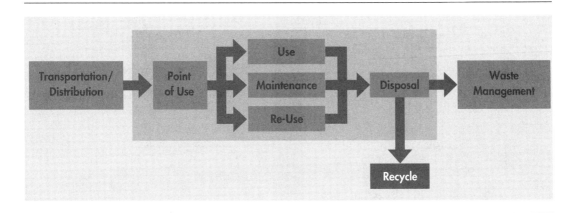

cated. The environmental effects of a closed-loop product will approach zero over the life of the product. For some products, a recycling infrastructure already exists, providing data on the collection, transportation, and processing of its materials. But for many products such information does not exist, leading to the use of data extrapolated from pilot programs or forecasts.

Wastes may be defined as materials that have no intrinsic or market value. Waste occurs in some form at every stage of the life cycle. Careful analysis of waste management issues is required as disposal options vary with the seasons, geography, and the technology used by a particular facility. Further complicating the inventory is the fact that many waste streams are combinations of materials derived from several subsystems, and that waste treatment facilities may produce a variety of releases including air, water, and solid wastes. For example, reported waterborne waste data should include an analysis of the water treatment system, the land associated with the treatment system, and atmospheric and solid wastes associated with the system. Information about emissions from solid waste is more difficult to find as there is no existing method to determine the emissions of a particular product once it has been mixed with municipal waste in a landfill or incinerator. If, however, a disposal process is being used for only one type of product (e.g., composting for yard waste or recycling for aluminum cans), accurate measures are available.

IMPACT ASSESSMENT AND IMPROVEMENT ANALYSIS

All life cycle analyses collect inventory data on raw material consumption, energy and water use, and waste production. However, a meaningful LCA should contain more than a mere inventory of inputs and outputs—it should also consider the overall contributions and risks to the environment and public health, as well as the social, cultural, and economic impacts of each option. In short, the products and processes being assessed should be seen in the context of the society they are intended to serve.

An impact assessment and improvement analysis thus *evaluates* the impacts caused by the proposed products, processes, or activities. The final result of an impact assessment is an en-

Exhibit 7 ● Recycling Subsystem

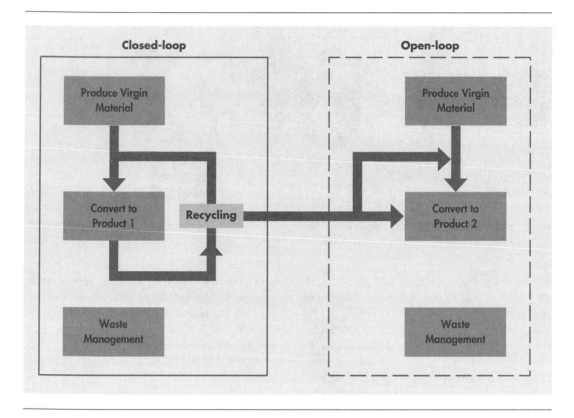

vironmental profile of the system. Impact assessment is one of the most challenging aspects of LCA since current methods for evaluating environmental impacts are incomplete at best.[9] Even when models exist, they can be based on many assumptions or require considerable data beyond that associated with the inventory.[10] Evaluating the importance and meaning of the data collected during the inventory requires judgement and interpretation. Thus, impact assessment inherits all the problems of inventory analysis while also introducing new methodological and measurement challenges.

Notes

1.   For example, D. Meadows, D. Meadows, and J. Randers. *Limits to Growth.* New York: Universe Books, 1972.

2.   Franklin, Associates. *Product Life-Cycle Assessment: Guidelines and Principles* (EPA Report #68-CO-0003). 1991.

3.   Hunt, R., J. Sellers, and W. Franklin. "Resource and Environmental Profile Analysis: A Life Cycle Environmental Assessment for Products and Procedures." *Environmental Impact Assessment Review,* Spring 1992.

4.   Stilwell, J., R. Canty, P. Kopf, and A. Montrone. *Packaging for the Environment.* New York: American Management Association, 1991.

5   See, for example, Lowrance, W. 1976. *Of Acceptable Risk*. Los Altos, CA: William Kaufmann, 1976.

6.   Council for Solid Waste Solutions. "Resource and Environmental Profile Analysis of Polyethylene and Unbleached Paper Grocery Sacks." CSWS (800-243-5790), Washington, DC, June 1990.

7.   Franklin Associates, Ibid.

8.   For details, see Franklin Associates, Ibid.

9.   U.S. EPA, Risk Reduction Engineering Lab. *Life Cycle Design Guidance Manual: Environmental Requirements and the Product System* (EPA #600/R-92/226). Prepared by Keoleian, Gregory A., and Dan Menerey. Cincinnati: EPA, 1993.

10.   For examples of the range of methods available, see Hart, S., G. Enk, and W. Hornick. *Improving Impact Assessment*. Boulder, CO: Westview Press, 1984.

An Introduction to Environmental Accounting as a Business Management Tool
United States Environmental Protection Agency

INTRODUCTION

The term *environmental accounting* has many meanings and uses. Environmental accounting can support national income accounting, financial accounting, or internal business managerial accounting. This primer focuses on the application of environmental accounting as a managerial accounting tool for internal business decisions. Moreover, the term *environmental cost* has at least two major dimensions: (1) it can refer solely to costs that directly impact a company's bottom line (here termed "private costs"), or (2) it also can encompass the costs to individuals, society, and the environment for which a company is not accountable (here termed "societal costs"). The discussion in this primer concentrates on private costs because that is where companies starting to implement environmental accounting typically begin. However, much of the material is applicable to societal costs as well.

WHY DO ENVIRONMENTAL ACCOUNTING?

Environmental costs are one of the many different types of costs businesses incur as they provide goods and services to their customers.

●

Reprinted from a publication of the United States Environmental Protection Agency, Office of Pollution Prevention and Toxics.

Environmental performance is one of the many important measures of business success. Environmental costs and performance deserve management attention for the following reasons:

1. Many environmental costs can be *significantly reduced or eliminated* as a result of business decisions, ranging from operational and housekeeping changes, to investment in "greener" process technology, to redesign of processes/ products. Many environmental costs (e.g., wasted raw materials) may provide no added value to a process, system, or product.

2. Environmental costs (and, thus, potential cost savings) *may be obscured in overhead accounts or otherwise overlooked.*

3. Many companies have discovered that *environmental costs can be offset by generating revenues* through sale of waste by-products or transferable pollution allowances, or licensing of clean technologies, for example.

4. Better management of environmental costs can result in *improved environmental performance and significant benefits to human health* as well as business success.

5. Understanding the environmental costs and performance of processes and products can promote *more accurate costing and pricing* of products and can aid companies in the *design of more environmentally preferable* processes, products, and services for the future.

6. *Competitive advantage* with customers can result from processes, products, and services that can be demonstrated to be environmentally preferable.

7. Accounting for environmental costs and performance can support a company's development and operation of an overall *environmental management system.* Such a system will soon be a necessity for companies engaged in international trade due to pending international consensus standard ISO 14001, developed by the International Organization for Standardization.[1]

EPA's work with key stakeholders leads it to believe that as businesses more fully account for environmental costs and benefits, they will clearly see the financial advantages of pollution prevention (P2) practices. Environmental costs often can be reduced or avoided through P2 practices such as product design changes, input materials substitution, process re-design, and improved operation and maintenance (O&M) practices. For example, increased environmental costs may result from use of chemical A (e.g., a chlorinated solvent), but not from chemical B (e.g., an aqueous-based solvent). This is true even though chemical A and chemical B can be substitutable. Another example: some environmental compliance costs are required only when use of a substance or generation of a waste exceeds a defined threshold. A company that can reduce chemical use below such thresholds or employ substitutes for regulated chemicals can realize substantial cost savings from design, engineering, and operational decisions.

In two of the most thorough reports on the subject of pollution prevention in the industrial community, the not-for-profit group INFORM[2] studied 29 companies in the organic chemical industry in 1985 and again in 1992. This research found that chemical "plants with some type of environmental cost accounting program" had "an average of three times as many" P2 projects "as plants with no cost accounting system."[3] The study also showed that the average annual savings per P2 project in production facilities, where data were available, were just over $351,000, which equalled an average savings of $3.49 for every dollar spent. Not only were sub-

stantial savings and returns on investment documented for P2 projects, but an average of 1.6 million pounds of waste were reduced for each project.

Results like these have highlighted the potential benefits of environmental accounting to the business community. For example, responses to a questionnaire administered by George Nagle of the Bristol-Myers Squibb Company at the Spring 1994 Global Environmental Management Initiative (GEMI) Conference showed that corporate professionals are placing a high priority on environmental accounting.[4] Of the 25 respondents to the informal survey, half stated that their company had some form of a tracking system for environmental costs. All but two reported that they believed environmental accounting issues would be more important to their companies in the near future. In addition, the Business Roundtable expects to turn its attention to environmental accounting issues in 1995, and companies of all sizes in the U.S. are beginning to consider implementing environmental accounting in their facilities.[5]

WHAT IS ENVIRONMENTAL ACCOUNTING?

Different uses of the umbrella term *environmental accounting* arise from three distinct contexts:

Type of Environmental Accounting	Focus	Audience
(1) national income accounting	nation	external
(2) financial accounting	firm	external
(3) managerial or management accounting	firm, division, facility, product line, or system	internal

National income accounting is a macroeconomic measure. Gross Domestic Product

(GDP) is an example. The GDP is a measure of the flow of goods and services through the economy. It is often cited as a key measure of our society's economic well-being. The term *environmental accounting* may refer to this national economic context. For example, environmental accounting can use physical or monetary units to refer to the consumption of the nation's natural resources, both renewable and nonrenewable. In this context, environmental accounting has been termed "natural resources accounting."

Financial accounting enables companies to prepare financial reports for use by investors, lenders, and others. Publicly held corporations report information on their financial condition and performance through quarterly and annual reports, governed by rules set by the U.S. Securities and Exchange Commission (SEC) with input from industry's self-regulatory body, the Financial Accounting Standards Board (FASB). Generally Accepted Accounting Principles (GAAP) are the basis for this reporting. Environmental accounting in this context refers to the estimation and public reporting of environmental liabilities and financially material environmental costs.

Management accounting is the process of identifying, collecting, and analyzing information principally for internal purposes.[6] Because a key purpose of management accounting is to support a business's forward-looking management decisions, it is the focus of the remainder of this primer. Management accounting can involve data on costs, production levels, inventory and backlog, and other vital aspects of a business. The information collected under a business's management accounting system is used to plan, evaluate, and control in a variety of ways:

1. planning and directing management attention,
2. informing decisions such as purchasing (e.g., make vs. buy), capital investments, product costing and pricing, risk management,

process/product design, and compliance strategies, and
3. controlling and motivating behavior to improve business results.

Unlike financial accounting, which is governed by Generally Accepted Accounting Principles (GAAP), management accounting practices and systems differ according to the needs of the businesses they serve. Some businesses have simple systems, others have elaborate ones. Just as management accounting refers to the use of a broad set of cost and performance data by a company's managers in making a myriad of business decisions, environmental accounting refers to the use of data about environmental costs and performance in business decisions and operations. Exhibit 1 lists many types of internal management decisions that can benefit from the consideration of environmental costs and benefits. This primer later summarizes how environmental accounting can be integrated into cost allocation, capital budgeting, and process/product design.

WHAT IS AN ENVIRONMENTAL COST?

Uncovering and recognizing *environmental costs* associated with a product, process, system,

Exhibit 1 ● Types of Management Decisions Benefitting from Environmental Cost Information

Product design	Capital investments
Process design	Cost control
Facility siting	Waste management
Purchasing	Cost allocation
Operational	Product retention and mix
Risk management	Product pricing
Environmental compliance strategies	Performance evaluations

or facility is important for good management decisions. Attaining such goals as reducing environmental expenses, increasing revenues, and improving environmental performance requires paying attention to current, future, and potential *environmental costs.* How a company defines an environmental cost depends on how it intends to use the information (e.g., cost allocation, capital budgeting, process/product design, other management decisions) and the scale and scope of the exercise. Moreover, it may not always be clear whether a cost is "environmental" or not; some costs fall into a gray zone or may be classified as partly environmental and partly not. Whether or not a cost is "environmental" is not critical; the goal is to ensure that relevant costs receive appropriate attention.

Identifying Environmental Costs

Environmental accounting terminology uses such words as *full, total, true,* and *life cycle* to emphasize that traditional approaches were incomplete in scope because they overlooked important environmental costs (and potential cost savings and revenues).[7] In looking for and uncovering relevant environmental costs, managers may want to use one or more organizing framework as tools. This section presents examples of environmental costs as well as a framework that has been used to identify and classify environmental costs.

There are many different ways to categorize costs. Accounting systems typically classify costs as:

1. direct materials and labor,

2. manufacturing or factory overhead (i.e., operating costs other than direct materials and labor),[8]

3. sales,

4. general and administrative (G&A) overhead,[9] and

5. research & development (R&D).

Environmental expenses may be classified in any or all of these categories in different companies. To better focus attention on environmental costs for management decisions, the *EPA Pollution Prevention Benefits Manual* and the Global Environmental Management Initiative (GEMI) environmental cost primer use similar organizing frameworks to distinguish costs that generally receive management attention, termed the "usual" costs or "direct" costs, from costs that may be obscured through treatment as overhead or R&D, distorted through improper allocation to cost centers, or simply overlooked, termed "hidden," "contingent," "liability" or "less tangible" costs.[10] Exhibit 2 lists examples of these costs under the labels "conventional," "potentially hidden," "contingent," and "image/relationship" costs.

Conventional Costs The costs of using raw materials, utilities, capital goods, and supplies are usually addressed in cost accounting and capital budgeting, but are not usually considered environmental costs. However, decreased use and less waste of raw materials, utilities, capital goods, and supplies are environmentally preferable, reducing both environmental degradation and consumption of nonrenewable resources. It is important to factor these costs into business decisions, whether or not they are viewed as "environmental" costs. The dashed line around these *conventional costs* in Exhibit 2 indicates that even these costs (and potential cost savings) may sometimes be overlooked in business decision-making.

Potentially Hidden Costs Exhibit 2 collects several types of environmental costs that may be potentially hidden from managers; first are *up-front environmental costs,* which are incurred *prior* to the operation of a process, system, or facility. These can include costs related to siting, design of environmentally preferable products or processes, qualifications of suppliers, evalua-

Exhibit 2 ● Examples of Environmental Costs Incurred by Firms

Potentially Hidden Costs

*Voluntary
(beyond compliance)*

Regulatory	*Upfront*	Community relations/outreach
Notification	Site studies	Monitoring/testing
Reporting	Site preparation	Training
Monitoring/testing	Permitting	Audits
Studies/modeling	R&D	Qualifying suppliers
Remediation	Engineering and procurement	Reports (e.g., annual
Recordkeeping	Installation	environmental reports)
Plans		Insurance
Training	*Conventional Costs*	Planning
Inspections	Capital equipment	Feasibility studies
Manifesting	Materials	Remediation
Labeling	Labor	Recycling
Preparedness	Supplies	Environmental studies
Protective equipment	Utilities	R & D
Medical surveillance	Structures	Habitat and wetland protection
Environmental insurance	Salvage value	Landscaping
Financial assurance		Other environmental projects
Pollution control	*Back-End*	Financial support to environmental
Spill response	Closure/decommissioning	groups and/or researchers
Stormwater management	Disposal of inventory	
Waste management	Post-closure care	
Taxes/fees	Site survey	

Contingent Costs

Future compliance costs	Remediation	Legal expenses
Penalties/fines	Property damage	Natural resource damages
Response to future releases	Personal injury damage	Economic loss damages

Image and relationship costs

Corporate image	Relationship with	Relationship with lenders
Relationship with customers	professional staff	Relationship with host
Relationships with investors	Relationship with workers	communities
Relationship with insurers	Relationship with suppliers	Relationship with regulators

tion of alternative pollution control equipment, and so on. Whether classified as overhead or R&D, these costs can easily be forgotten when managers and analysts focus on operating costs of processes, systems, and facilities. Second are *regulatory* and *voluntary environmental costs* incurred in *operating* a process, system, or facility; because many companies traditionally have treated these costs as overhead, they may not receive appropriate attention from managers and analysts responsible for day-to-day operations and business decisions. The magnitude of these costs also may be more difficult to determine as a result of their being pooled in overhead accounts. Third, while upfront and current operating costs may be obscured by management accounting practices, *back-end environmental costs* may not be entered into management accounting systems at all. These environmental costs of current operations are *prospective,* meaning they will occur at more or less well defined points in the future. Examples include the *future* cost of decommissioning a laboratory that uses licensed nuclear materials, closing a landfill cell, replacing a storage tank used to hold petroleum or hazardous substances, and complying with regulations that are not yet in effect but have been promulgated. Such back-end environmental costs may be overlooked if they are not well documented or accrued in accounting systems.

Exhibit 2 contains a lengthy list of *"potentially hidden" environmental costs,* including examples of the costs of upfront, operational, and back-end activities undertaken to (1) comply with environmental laws (i.e., regulatory costs) or (2) go beyond compliance (i.e., voluntary costs). In bringing these costs to light, it also may be useful to distinguish among costs incurred to respond to *past pollution* not related to *ongoing operations;* to control, clean up, or prevent pollution for *ongoing operations;* or to prevent or reduce pollution from *future operations.*

Contingent Costs   Costs that may or may not be incurred at some point in the future—here termed *"contingent costs"*—can best be described in probabilistic terms: their expected value, their range, or the probability of their exceeding some dollar amount. Examples include the costs of remedying and compensating for future accidental releases of contaminants into the environment (e.g., oil spills), fines and penalties for future regulatory infractions, and future costs due to unexpected consequences of permitted or intentional releases. These costs may also be termed "contingent liabilities" or "contingent liability costs." Because these costs may not currently need to be recognized for other purposes, they may not receive adequate attention in internal management accounting systems and forward-looking decisions.

Image and Relationship Costs   Some environmental costs are called "less tangible" or "intangible" because they are incurred to affect subjective (though measurable) perceptions of management, customers, employees, communities, and regulators. These costs have also been termed *"corporate image"* and *"relationship"* costs. This category can include the costs of annual environmental reports and community relations activities, costs incurred voluntarily for environmental activities (e.g., tree planting), and costs incurred for P2 award/recognition programs. The costs themselves are not "intangible," but the direct benefits that result from relationship/corporate image expenses often are.

Is It an "Environmental" Cost?

Costs incurred to comply with environmental laws are clearly environmental costs. Costs of environmental remediation, pollution control equipment, and noncompliance penalties are all unquestionably environmental costs. Other costs incurred for environmental protection are likewise clearly environmental costs, even if they are not explicitly required by regulations or go beyond regulatory compliance levels.

There are other costs, however, that may fall into a gray zone in terms of being considered environmental costs. For example, should the costs of production equipment be considered "environmental" if it is a "clean technology?" Is an energy-efficient turbine an "environmental" cost? Should efforts to monitor the shelf life of raw materials and supplies in inventory be considered "environmental" costs (if discarded, they become waste and result in environmental costs)? It may also be difficult to distinguish some environmental costs from health and safety costs or from risk management costs.

The success of environmental accounting does not depend on "correctly" classifying all the costs a firm incurs. Rather, its goal is to ensure that relevant information is made available to those who need or can use it. To handle costs in the gray zone, some firms use the following approaches:

- allowing a cost item to be treated as "environmental" for one purpose but not for another,
- treating part of the cost of an item or activity as "environmental," or
- treating costs as "environmental" for accounting purposes when a firm decides that a cost is more than 50% environmental.

There are many options. Companies can define what should constitute an "environmental cost" and how to classify it, based on their goals and intended uses for environmental accounting. For example, if a firm wants to encourage pollution prevention in capital budgeting, it might consider distinguishing (1) environmental costs that can be avoided by pollution prevention investments, from (2) environmental costs related to remedying contamination that has already occurred. But for product costing purposes, such a

distinction might not be necessary because both are costs of producing the good or service.

IS THERE A PROPER SCALE AND SCOPE FOR ENVIRONMENTAL ACCOUNTING?

Environmental accounting is a flexible tool that can be applied at different scales of use and different scopes of coverage. This section describes some of the options for applying environmental accounting.

Scale

Depending on corporate needs, interests, goals, and resources, environmental accounting can be applied at different scales, which include the following:

- individual *process* or group of processes (e.g., production line)
- *system* (e.g., lighting, wastewater treatment, packaging)
- *product* or product line
- *facility,* department, or all facilities at a single *location*
- *regional/geographical* groups of departments or facilities
- corporate division, affiliate, or the entire *company*

Specific environmental accounting issues or challenges may vary depending on the scale of its application.

Scope

Whatever the scale, there also is an issue of scope. An initial scope question is whether environmental accounting extends beyond conventional costs to include potentially hidden, future, contingent, and image/relationship costs. Another scope issue is whether companies intend to consider only those costs that directly affect their bottom line financial profit or loss (e.g., see examples of costs listed in Exhibit 2 above), or whether companies also want to recognize the environmental costs that result from their activities but for which they are not accountable, referred to as societal or external costs. These latter costs are described in Section F.

Thus, the *scope* of environmental accounting refers to the types of costs included. As the scope becomes more expansive, firms may find it more difficult to assess and measure certain environmental costs. This is illustrated by Exhibit 3.

WHAT IS THE DIFFERENCE BETWEEN PRIVATE COSTS AND SOCIETAL COSTS?

Understanding the distinction between private and societal costs is necessary when discussing environmental accounting, because common terms are often used inconsistently to refer to one or both of those cost categories. Exhibit 4 provides a graphical representation of the important difference between private and societal costs. It also shows that many private costs are

not currently considered in decision-making. This perspective can apply to a process, product, system, facility, or an entire company.

The innermost box labeled *"Conventional Company Costs"* includes the many costs businesses typically track well (e.g., capital costs, labor, material). Many of these costs may already be directly allocated to the responsible processes or products in cost accounting systems and be included in financial evaluations of capital expenditures. The larger unshaded box includes all of the potentially overlooked costs a business incurs. Examples of these costs are shown . . . at Exhibit 2. Together, the unshaded area represents *"private costs,"* which are the costs a business incurs or for which a business can be held accountable (i.e., legally responsible). These are the costs that can directly affect a firm's bottom line.

The outside shaded box labeled *"societal costs"* represents the costs of business' impacts on the environment and society for which business is not legally accountable. (These costs are also called "externalities" or "external costs.") Societal costs include both (1) environmental degradation for which firms are not legally liable and also (2) adverse impacts on human beings,

Exhibit 3 ● The Spectrum of Environmental Costs

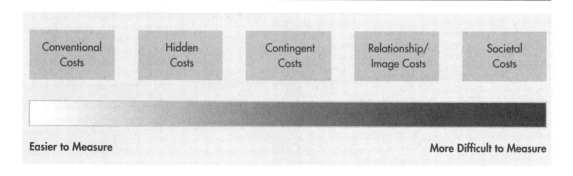

| Conventional Costs | Hidden Costs | Contingent Costs | Relationship/ Image Costs | Societal Costs |

Easier to Measure   **More Difficult to Measure**

Exhibit 4 ● Private and Societal Environmental Costs

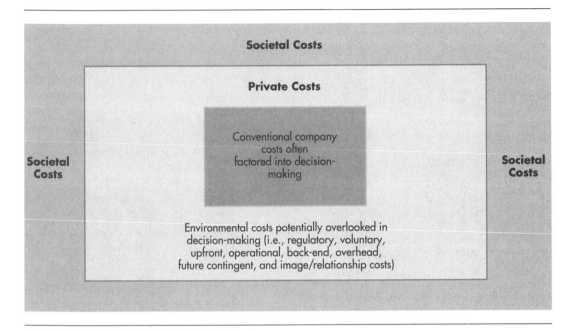

their property, and their welfare (e.g., employment impacts of spills) that cannot be compensated through the legal system. For example, damage caused to a river because of polluted wastewater discharges, or to ecosystems from solid waste disposal, or to asthmatics because of air pollutant emissions are all examples of societal costs for which a business often does not pay. Because laws can vary from state to state, the boundary between societal and private costs may differ as well. At present, valuing societal costs is both difficult and controversial; nevertheless, some businesses are attempting to address these costs and EPA supports their efforts. A major North American power utility, Ontario Hydro, has made a corporate commitment to determine external impacts and, to the extent possible, value societal costs in order to integrate them into its planning and decision-making.[12] EPA urges businesses to address all private envi-

ronmental costs shown on Exhibit 2, including hidden, future, contingent, and image/relationship costs, to the extent practical. Companies are also encouraged to move beyond consideration of private costs to incorporate societal costs, at least qualitatively, into their business decisions.

WHO CAN DO ENVIRONMENTAL ACCOUNTING?

Environmental accounting can be employed by firms large and small, in almost every industry in both the manufacturing and services sectors. It can be applied on a large scale or a small scale, systematically or on an as needed basis. The form it takes can reflect the goals and needs of the company using it. However, in any business, top management support and cross-functional teams are likely to be essential for the successful implementation of environmental accounting because:

LIFE CYCLE PERSPECTIVE CAN HELP TO IDENTIFY PRIVATE AND SOCIETAL COSTS

The life cycle of a product, process, system, or facility can refer to the suite of activities starting with acquisition (and upfront pre-acquisition activities) and concluding with back-end disposal/decommissioning that a specific firm performs or is responsible for. This life-cycle perspective can foster a thorough accounting of private costs (and potential cost savings) in addition to facilitating a more systematic and complete assessment of societal impacts and costs due to a firm's activities.

- Environmental accounting may entail a new way of looking at a company's environmental costs, performance, and decisions. Top management commitment can set a positive tone and articulate incentives for the organization to adopt environmental accounting.

- Companies will likely want to assemble cross-functional teams to implement environmental accounting, bringing together designers, chemists, engineers, production managers, operators, financial staff, environmental managers, purchasing personnel, and accountants who may not have worked together before. Because environmental accounting is not solely an accounting issue, and the information needed is split up among all of these groups, these people need to talk with each other to develop a common vision and language and make that vision a reality.

AT&T is one example of a company that has combined senior management support and use of a cross-functional team for its environmental accounting initiative.[13]

Companies with formal environmental management systems may want to institutional-ize environmental accounting because it is a logical decision support tool for these systems. Similarly, many companies have begun or are exploring new business approaches in which environmental accounting can play a part:

- Activity-Based Costing/Activity-Based Management
- Total Quality Management/Total Quality Environmental Management
- Business Process Re-Engineering/Cost Reduction
- Cost of Quality Model/Cost of Environmental Quality Model
- Design for Environment/Life-Cycle Design
- Life-Cycle Assessment/Life-Cycle Costing

All of these approaches are compatible with environmental accounting and can provide platforms for integrating environmental information into business decisions. Companies using or evaluating these approaches may want to consider explicitly adopting environmental accounting as part of these efforts.

Small businesses that may not have formal environmental management systems, or are not using any of the above approaches, have also successfully applied environmental accounting.

As with larger firms, management commitment and cross-functional involvement are necessary.

APPLYING ENVIRONMENTAL ACCOUNTING TO COST ALLOCATION

An important function of environmental accounting is to bring environmental costs to the attention of corporate stakeholders who may be able and motivated to identify ways of reducing or avoiding those costs while at the same time improving environmental quality. This can require, for example, pulling some environmental costs out of overhead and allocating those environmental costs to the appropriate accounts. By *allocating* environmental costs to the products or processes that generate them, a company can motivate affected managers and employees to find creative pollution prevention alternatives that lower those costs and enhance profitability. For example, Caterpillar's East Peoria, Illinois, plant no longer dumps waste disposal costs into an overhead account; rather, the costs of waste disposal are allocated to responsible commodity groups, triggering efforts to improve the bottom line through pollution prevention.[14]

Overhead is any cost that, in a given cost accounting system, is not wholly attributed to a single process, system, product, or facility. Examples can include supervisors' salaries, janito-

rial services, utilities, and waste disposal. Many environmental costs are often treated as overhead in corporate cost accounting systems. Traditionally, an overhead cost item has been handled in either one of two ways:

  1. it may be allocated on some basis to specific products, or

  2. it may be left in the pool of costs that are not attributed to any specific product.

If overhead is allocated incorrectly, one product may bear an overhead allocation greater than warranted, while another may bear an allocation smaller than its actual contribution. The result is poor product costing, which can affect pricing and profitability. Alternatively, some overhead costs may not be reflected at all in product cost and price. In both instances, managers cannot perceive the true cost of producing products and thus internal accounting reports provide inadequate incentives to find creative ways of reducing those costs.

Separating environmental costs from overhead accounts where they are often hidden and allocating them to the appropriate product, process, system, or facility directly responsible reveals these costs to managers, cost analysts, engineers, designers, and others. This is critical not only for a business to have accurate estimates of production costs for different product lines

---

STEPS IN ENVIRONMENTAL COST ALLOCATION

  1. Determine scale and scope
  2. Identify environmental costs
  3. Quantify those costs
  4. Allocate environmental costs to responsible process, product, system, or facility

and processes, but also to help managers target cost reduction activities that can also improve environmental quality. The axiom "one cannot manage what one cannot see" pertains here.

There are two general approaches to allocating environmental costs:

1. Build proper cost allocation directly into cost accounting systems, or

2. Handle cost allocation outside of automated accounting systems.

Companies may find that the latter approach can serve as an interim measure while the former option is being implemented.

A simple example illustrates the problem.[15]

Exhibit 5 depicts a traditional accounting system that assigns environmental and certain other costs to overhead. Such overhead costs generally are allocated to Widgets A and B in proportion to their consumption of labor and materials.

Exhibit 6 highlights the misallocation of environmental costs. Suppose Widget B is solely responsible for toxic waste management costs, and Widget A creates no toxic waste costs. The misallocation occurs because the toxic waste management cost is lumped together in an overhead cost pool that is misallocated to both Widgets A and B, even though none of the toxic waste management cost results from the production of Widget A. The effect is to distort the actual costs of producing Widget A and Widget B.

Exhibit 5 ● Traditional Cost Accounting System

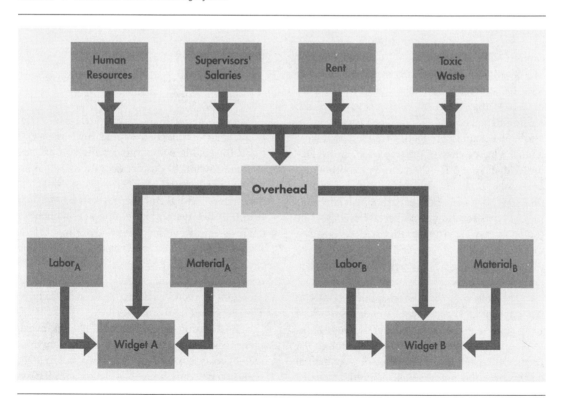

Exhibit 6 ● Misallocation of Environmental Costs Under Traditional Cost System

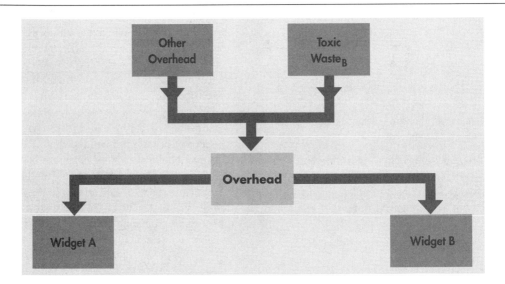

Exhibit 7 illustrates a cost accounting system that correctly attributes the environmental costs of Widget B only to Widget B. By breaking environmental costs out of overhead and directly attributing them to products, managers will have a much clearer view of the true costs of producing Widget A and B. Alternatively, environmental costs can be allocated to responsible processes, systems, or departments. Environmental costs resulting from several processes or products may need to be allocated based on a more complex analysis. And future costs (e.g., toxic waste disposal) may need to be amortized and allocated to proper cost centers.

The preceding discussion applies equally to the appropriate crediting of revenues derived from sale or use of by-products or recyclables (e.g., raw materials and supplies). Although the focus of cost allocation is on environmental costs, environmental revenues should be treated in a parallel fashion.

APPLYING ENVIRONMENTAL ACCOUNTING TO CAPITAL BUDGETING

Capital budgeting includes the process of developing a firm's planned capital investments. It typically entails comparing predicted cost and revenue streams of current operations and alternative investment projects against financial benchmarks in light of the costs of capital to a firm.[16] It has been quite common for financial analysis of investment alternatives to exclude many environmental costs, cost savings, and revenues. As a result, corporations may not have recognized financially attractive investments in pollution prevention and "clean technology." This is beginning to change.

When evaluating a potential capital investment it is important to fully consider environmental costs, cost savings, and revenues to place pollution prevention investments on a level playing field with other investment choices. To do

Exhibit 7 ● Revised Cost Accounting System

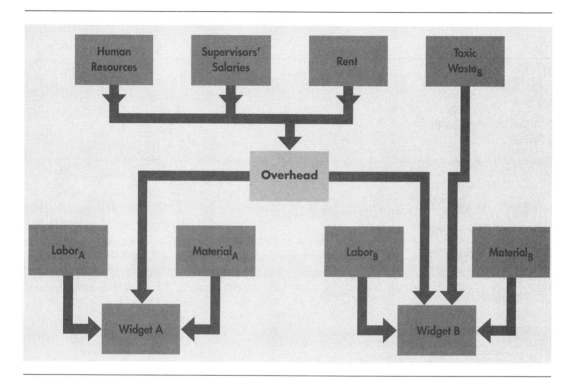

this, identify and include the *types* of costs (and revenues) (i.e., the "cost inventory") that will help to demonstrate the financial viability of a cleaner technology investment. Analyze qualitatively those data and issues that cannot be easily quantified, such as the potential less tangible benefits of pollution prevention investments. Exhibit 2 may help in identifying potentially relevant costs (and savings).

After collecting or developing environmental data (either from the accounting system or by manual means), allocate and project costs, cost savings, and potential revenues to the products, processes, systems, or facilities that are the focus of the capital budgeting decision. Begin with the easiest to estimate costs and revenues and work

toward the more difficult to estimate environmental costs and benefits such as contingencies and corporate image. The benefit of improved corporate image and relationships due to pollution prevention investments can impact costs and revenues in ways that may be challenging to project in dollars and cents. (See sidebar.) For example, a company selected as "Clean Air Partner of the Year" under a Colorado partnership program attracted several new clients from the positive publicity.[17] Information about past expenditures on corporate image also may be helpful in estimating future benefits (e.g., potential savings or reductions in those outlays resulting from the investment) for companies that want to go beyond the qualitative consideration of these benefits.

INTEGRATING ENVIRONMENTAL ACCOUNTING INTO CAPITAL BUDGETING

1. Inventory and quantify environmental costs
2. Allocate and project environmental costs and benefits
3. Use appropriate financial indicators
4. Set reasonable time horizon that captures environmental benefits

---

Be sure to use appropriate financial indicators that include the time value of money (i.e., a dollar today is worth more than a dollar next year). Sound financial indicators include net present value,[18] internal rate of return,[19] and other profitability indices. Payback,[20] although commonly used, does not recognize the time value of money. Further, payback may not recognize the long-term benefits of pollution prevention investments.

Consider cash flows and the profitability of a project over a sufficiently long time horizon (e.g., economic life of the capital investment) to capture the long-term benefits of pollution pre-

---

POTENTIAL LESS TANGIBLE BENEFITS OF POLLUTION PREVENTION INVESTMENTS

- Increased sales due to enhanced company or product image
- Better borrowing access and terms
- Equity more attractive to investors
- Health and safety cost savings
- Increased productivity and morale of employees, greater retention, reduced recruiting costs
- Faster, easier approvals of facility expansion plans or changes due to increased trust from host communities and regulators
- Enhanced image with stakeholders such as customers, employees, suppliers, lenders, stockholders, insurers, and host communities
- Improved relationships with regulators

INTEGRATING ENVIRONMENTAL ISSUES INTO DESIGN

1. Include environmental issues in needs analysis
   - consider environmental costs and performance in defining scope of design project
   - establish baseline environmental cost and performance
2. Add environmental requirements to design criteria
3. Evaluate alternate design solutions taking into account environmental cost, performance, cultural, and legal requirements.

---

vention investments. Finally, prepare the data and information in a format that managers and lenders can understand and find useful.

For more information on integrating environmental costs into capital budgeting, see EPA's *Total Cost Assessment: Accelerating Industrial Pollution Prevention through Innovative Project Financial Analysis* (EPA 741-R-92-002, May 1992).

APPLYING ENVIRONMENTAL ACCOUNTING TO PROCESS/PRODUCT DESIGN

The design of a process or product significantly affects environmental costs and performance. The design process involves balancing cost, performance, cultural, legal, and environmental criteria.[21]

Many companies are adopting "design for the environment" or "life cycle design" programs to take environmental considerations into account at an early stage. To do so, designers need information on the environmental costs and performance of alternative product/process designs, much like the information needed in making capital budgeting decisions. Thus, making environmental cost and performance information available to designers can facilitate the

design of environmentally preferable processes and products.

For example, the Rohm and Haas Company has developed a model to estimate in R&D the environmental cost of new processes. The model includes conventional, hidden, contingent, and relationship costs. In early phases of process development, the cost model prompts process researchers to select and justify process chemistries, operating conditions, and equipment that embody the principles of pollution prevention. As the project progresses, the model identifies environmental cost reduction opportunities. The model can provide financial analysts with an economic picture of the potential environmental risk of a new process prior to its commercialization.[22]

Notes

1. See ISO 14001: *Environmental Management System Specification* (Committee Draft, February 1995). ISO 14000 guidance document *General Guidelines on Principles and Supporting Techniques* (Committee Draft, February 1995) adds that tracking environmental benefits and costs can support the appropriate allocation of resources for achieving environmental objectives.

2. *Cutting Chemical Wastes* (1985), INFORM, New York, NY; *Environmental Dividends: Cutting More Chemical Wastes* (1992), INFORM, New York, NY.

3.   *Environmental Dividends,* at page 31.

4.   "Business Environmental Cost Accounting Survey," *Global Environmental Management Initiative '94 Conference Proceedings,* p. 243, March 16–17, 1994, Arlington, VA.

5.   See *Green Ledgers: Case Studies in Corporate Environmental Accounting,* edited by Daryl Ditz, Janet Ranganathan, and Darryl Banks (World Resources Institute, 1995) and *Environmental Accounting Case Studies,* EPA 742-R-95-00X (forthcoming).

6.   "Management accounting is the process of identification, measurement, accumulation, analysis, preparation, interpretation, and communication of financial information used by management to plan, evaluate, and control within an organization and to assure appropriate use of and accountability for its resources. . . ." Institute of Management Accountants Statement on Management Accounting, No. 1A.

7.   See, for example, Paul E. Bailey, "Full Cost Accounting for Life Cycle Costs—A Guide for Engineers and Financial Analysis," *Environmental Finance* (Spring 1991), pp. 13–29.

8.   Manufacturing or factory overhead typically includes indirect materials and labor, capital depreciation, rent, property taxes, insurance, supplies, utilities, repairs and maintenance, and other costs of operating a factory.

9.   General and administrative costs may be pooled with sales costs (i.e., SG&A) or as part of "technical, sales, and general administrative" costs (i.e., TSGA).

10.   The EPA's *Pollution Prevention Benefits Manual* (October 1989) introduced the terminology distinguishing among usual, hidden, liability, and less tangible costs. This framework was largely adopted in *Finding Cost-Effective Pollution Prevention Initiatives: Incorporating Environmental Costs into Business Decision Making* (1994, Global Environmental Management Initiative (GEMI), which uses the term direct, hidden, contingent liability, and less tangible costs.

11.   Adapted from Allen T. White, Monica Becker, and Deborah E. Savage, "Environmentally Smart Accounting: Using Total Cost Assessment to Advance Pollution Prevention," *Pollution Prevention Review* (Summer 1993), pp. 247–259.

12.   See *"Full Cost Accounting" at Ontario Hydro: A Case Study,* EPA 742-R-95-00X (forthcoming).

13.   See *Introducing "Green Accounting" at AT&T: A Case Study,* EPA 742-R-95-00X (forthcoming).

14.   Jean V. Owen (senior editor,) "Environmental Compliance: Managing the Mandates," *Manufacturing Engineering* (March 1995).

15.   This example and the diagrams are derived from Rebecca Todd, "Accounting for the Environment: Zero-Loss Environmental Accounting Systems," Presented at the National Academy of Engineering, Industrial Ecology/Design for Engineering Workshop, July 13–17, 1992.

16.   Allen White and Monica Becker, "Total Cost Assessment: Catalyzing Corporate Self Interest in Pollution Prevention," *New Solutions* (Winter, 1992), p. 34. See also, "Total Cost Assessment: Accelerating Industrial Pollution Prevention through Innovative Project Financial Analysis, With Applications to the Pulp and Paper Industry," U.S. Environmental Protection Agency (May, 1992) EPA-741-R-92-002.

17.   Reported by representative of Majestic Metals, March 22, 1995, at EPA Regional Office training program on pollution prevention.

18.   The present value of the future cash flows of an investment less the investment's current cost. It incorporates the time value of money.

19.   The discount rate at which the net present value of a project is equal to zero.

20.   The time period required for revenues or cost savings to equal costs; payback typically does not involve discounting.

21.   EPA *Life Cycle Design Guidance Manual: Environmental Requirements and the Product System,* EPA-600-R-92-226 (1993).

22.   Suzanne T. Thomas, Victoria Weber, Scott A. Berger, and I. Leo Klawiter, *Estimate the Environmental Cost of New Processes in R&D,* prepared for American Institute of Chemical Engineers (AIChE) Spring National Meeting (April, 1994).

19

Integrating Environment and Technology: Design for Environment
Braden R. Allenby

Twenty years ago environmental problems appeared simple and obvious: the Potomac and Hudson Rivers were so polluted that they could not be fished; the air in Los Angeles was foul; Love Canal and other sites were poisoned by toxic chemicals. Remedies were equally direct: the Clean Water Act, the Clean Air Act, Superfund, and the Resource Conservation and Recovery Act.

Now, with several decades of research and experience behind us, we have begun to recognize that we are treating the symptoms, not the disease. The problem is not individual rivers, airsheds, or hazardous waste sites, although they must be addressed. The problem is the relationship between human economic activity and the environment. It is a systems problem, arising from fundamental changes in the scale of human activity in relationship to supporting biological, physical, and chemical systems. Regional and global environmental perturbations cannot be adequately mitigated until this relationship is understood and regulatory and industrial practices are modified to reflect such an understanding.

A basis for developing a broad understanding of these issues, frequently termed "industrial ecology," is being established, albeit the effort is still in its infancy (Allenby, 1992a; Ayres, 1989; Frosch and Gallopoulos, 1989). Nonetheless, five fundamental principles upon which we may base development of improved methodologies for integrating technological and environmental systems can already be identified.

1. Methodologies should be comprehensive and systems-based.

2. Methodologies should be multidisciplinary, including technical, legal, economic, political, and cultural dimensions to the extent possible.

3. Mitigation of environmental perturbations can only be achieved by focusing on technology, and developing policies and practices that encourage the evolution of environmentally preferable process and product technologies.

4. Economic actors, including private firms, must internalize environmental considerations and constraints to the extent possible, given existing exogenous constraints on firm behavior (e.g., laws such as the antitrust statutes or the prices of inputs and competitive products).

5. Policies and regulations must reflect the need for experimentation and research as different paths and methodologies are tried (rigid micromanagement through command-and-control regulation will in many cases be incompatible with systems-based approaches embodied in methodolo-

gies such as Design for Environment (DFE), as the unfortunate negative impact of the Resource Conservation and Recovery Act on industrial recycling practices demonstrates (see, . . . more generally, Office of Technology Assessment [OTA], 1992).

Obviously, a great deal of work remains to be done before we begin to fully understand industrial ecology and apply it to current industrial ecosystems. . . . In the interim, however, there can be no excuse for evading the application of the approaches we do understand to ongoing regulatory and industrial behavior. Although just emerging and still generally untested at this point, DFE is one potential methodology for accomplishing this. Design for Environment should be regarded more as an approach, than as an existing, implemented system.

Before introducing DFE, it is important to recognize that our current unsophisticated approaches tend not to recognize important differences among classes of products and materials. Thus, for example, it is useful to differentiate between two classes of manufactured items: low-design/high-material items, such as packaging, consumer personal care items (e.g., soaps and shampoos), and bulk chemicals; and high-design/low-material products such as automobiles, electronic and communications equipment, and airplanes.

These product streams generally have different life cycles within the economy. For example, the former tend to be used up and dispersed into the environment rather than discarded (packaging being an obvious exception). Materials use in the two cases also implies different recycling and disposal requirements. Materials use in a low-design/high-material product stream tends to be relatively simple, and, in many cases, few materials are incorporated into individual items (this need not be the case, however; a snack chip bag only 0.002 inch thick con-

sists of nine separate layers of material [OTA, 1992]). Thus, recycling is fairly straightforward. On the other hand, the structure and materials use of a high-design/low-material product such as a printed writing board are highly complex, and many materials, including different plastics, ceramics, alloys, frits, and glasses, are often present in a single product. Recycling of materials for such a product is thus much more complicated and difficult.

Moreover, as implied by the designation, the design function is far less important for a low-design/high-material product than for a high-design/low-material product. This reflects a fundamental difference: the design of a complex high-design/low material product requires consideration of an additional, highly complex, system that low-design/high-material products do not—that is, the product itself. Associated upstream and downstream product and manufacturing process implications of changes to such a product or its associated manufacturing systems make the analysis far more complex than in the case of a low-design/high-material item. Moreover, the supplier/customer networks for high-design/low-material products tend to be far more complex than those for low-design/high-material products.

This has a number of policy implications, the primary one being that regulatory tools that may be effective in encouraging environmentally appropriate technology for high-design/low-material items may be dysfunctional or at least inefficient when applied to many low-design/high-material products. Thus, for example, post-consumer take-back requirements for high-design/low-material articles will drive firms (and thus designers) to produce products more easily disassembled and recycled. On the other hand, postconsumer take-back requirements imposed on low-design/high-material products such as consumer packaging, which generally require significant transportation of used product, may not be economically efficient.

DESIGN FOR ENVIRONMENT

As a practical matter, the only way the five principles enumerated above can be implemented by industry in practice, at least for high-design/low-material products and associated manufacturing processes, is by driving environmental considerations and constraints into the design process. Implementation of DFE practices is intended to accomplish this.

The idea behind DFE is to ensure that all relevant and ascertainable environmental considerations and constraints are integrated into a firm's product realization (design) process. The goal is to achieve environmentally preferable manufacturing processes and products while maintaining desirable product price/performance characteristics (Allenby, 1991).

DFE is intended as a module of an existing design system known as "Design for X," or DFX, where "X" is a desirable product characteristic such as testability, manufacturability, or safety (Gatenby and Foo, 1990). This has at least two critical advantages. For one, linking implementation of DFE to an existing process reduces the culture shock of integrating environmental considerations into product and process design and makes the entire package far more acceptable and easier to implement. For another, the need to create DFE to fit into an existing design procedure imposes a necessary discipline on DFE development that helps make DFE practical in a real operating environment.

Implementing DFE has a number of benefits for the firm. The major benefit is that it provides a mechanism for the firm to manage environmental issues as they evolve from simply overhead, "end-of-pipe," considerations to strategic and competitively critical. Thus, compliance with increasingly complex, sometimes contradictory, environmental regimes can be eased by designing to avoid emissions. Costs arising from taxes, fees, or burdensome regulations directed at inputs such as energy or virgin materials, or from wastes or carbon produced during manufacturing, can be identified and managed only through such a comprehensive approach.

Another important reason firms are adopting DFE is the need to meet increasing environmental concerns on the part of customers. There are two major components to this challenge for manufacturing firms.

The first is the much-discussed growing interest that consumers exhibit in "green" products. At this point, determining environmental preferability, or "greenness," over the life cycle of a product is frequently beyond the state of the art. Moreover, determining the depth and importance of environmental consumerism is somewhat problematic and depends to a great extent on the product and its market, as well as overall economic conditions. It is, however, clear that such preferences exist to some degree.

The second is more subtle and much harder to address ad hoc: the demands of sophisticated customers for products that reduce their potential environmental costs. Thus, for example, the U.S. Air Force may be concerned about a weapons system that requires chlorofluorocarbons (CFCs) for routine maintenance, or that produces significant used oil or chlorinated solvent waste streams. Sophisticated business customers may pressure component or subassembly suppliers to reduce their use of toxic substances such as lead solders or batteries containing cadmium, or to use environmentally preferable packaging. State and national laws require recycling of batteries and elimination of heavy metals in packaging or plastics. Such requirements frequently require design changes: they clearly cannot be addressed by traditional "end-of-pipe" means.

Comparing DFE with other environmental management and regulatory concepts helps demonstrate the comprehensive nature of the methodology. Perhaps the most familiar of these concepts is "pollution prevention" and such associated terms as "waste minimization" and "toxics use reduction." DFE incorporates these concepts, but as elements in a more complex multidimensional analysis. To a large extent, these concepts still reflect the "end-of-pipe" mind-set, in that they do not comprehend the need for a comprehensive, systems-based, technologically sophisticated approach to environmental management in a high-technology economy.

Other concepts involve aspects of the comprehensive DFE system as well. These include, for example, practices such as "Design for Disassembly," "Design for Refurbishment," "Design for Component Recyclability," and "Design for Materials Recyclability." Like pollution prevention, these are obviously necessary dimensions of a DFE system.

These single dimensions are important not just in themselves but because they offer firms a relatively easy path to begin implementing DFE. No firm has yet implemented a comprehensive DFE system, and, indeed, fully implementing DFE practices will in all likelihood require that most firms develop new competencies, organizations, and information systems. This will take time and, in many cases, changes in organizational cultures as well. Accordingly, the most practical path for firms to follow may be to concentrate on implementing a few of these concepts initially, such as pollution prevention and Design for Disassembly, and then move on to other aspects of DFE as experience is gained.

Life cycle analysis, or LCA, incorporates into DFE the concept that all environmental impacts of an item—from those attributable to inputs, to manufacture, to consumer use, to disposal—should be considered in evaluating the environmental preferability of the product (Society of Environmental Toxicology and Chemistry [SETAC], 1991). LCA is a means by which data on environmental impacts, an important component of a DFE approach, can be generated. LCA can thus be equated to the DFE Matrix System discussed below. While it is probable that both LCA and the DFE Matrix System will continue to evolve in similar directions, at present LCA appears to apply more to low-design/high-material products, in that proposed methodologies do not reflect the systems implications of manufacturing complex articles. Perhaps for similar reasons, LCA is also essentially an analytical method; it does not provide a mechanism by which identified environmental considerations and constraints can be introduced into product and process design, as DFE does.

A number of other generic terms, such as "green engineering" and "environmentally conscious manufacturing," are also in use. Although these efforts have generated useful ideas and specific technical practices, as currently defined they tend to follow a rather ad hoc approach to meeting environmental goals. The lack of a systems-based approach makes it difficult for firms, and designers, to implement these concepts in a comprehensive manner.

IMPLEMENTING DESIGN FOR ENVIRONMENT

The implementation of DFE practices involves two categories of activities: (a) global, comprehensive projects whose effect extends across all design functions; and (b) specific individual evaluations of products, processes, or inputs.

In the first category are projects that can be undertaken at any time and will help result in environmentally preferable products across the board. Such activities include review of all internal specification documents to determine whether unnecessary environmentally harmful processes (such as cleaning with chlorinated solvents) or components (lead solder where conductive epoxy systems might be used) are being required. Similarly, manufacturing firms should evaluate specifications and requests for proposals from their customers to determine whether unnecessary environmental impacts are being explicitly or implicitly required.

Using generic contract clauses to change

supplier behavior can also be effective. For example, several years ago AT&T began by contract to require that all suppliers use non-CFC packaging. Those who were unable to comply contacted AT&T, which then directed them to preferable alternatives. A general improvement of all packaging used by both AT&T and its suppliers was achieved.

Identifying unnecessary process steps can also be an effective way of reducing environmental impact across many operations. Thus, many electronics companies found they could reduce their use and emissions of CFCs and chlorinated solvents by eliminating some cleaning steps or by doubling-up cleaning operations. This activity can be driven back into the design process by identifying design decisions that require environmentally harmful processing activities, and selecting alternatives. Thus, for example, use of an open relay switch on a printed wiring board requires that the board be cleaned with a chlorinated solvent, since such relays "can't swim"; that is, they cannot be exposed to water. Substituting a sealed relay permits the use of environmentally preferable aqueous cleaning systems.

More specific DFE activities involve an analysis of options for specific design choices. Here, a particular product, process, or input would be evaluated using several basic steps.

1. *Scoping.* The target product, process, or input is chosen, and options are identified. This is a critical step, particularly because the process

FIGURE 1 ● Environmental primary matrix for bismuth.

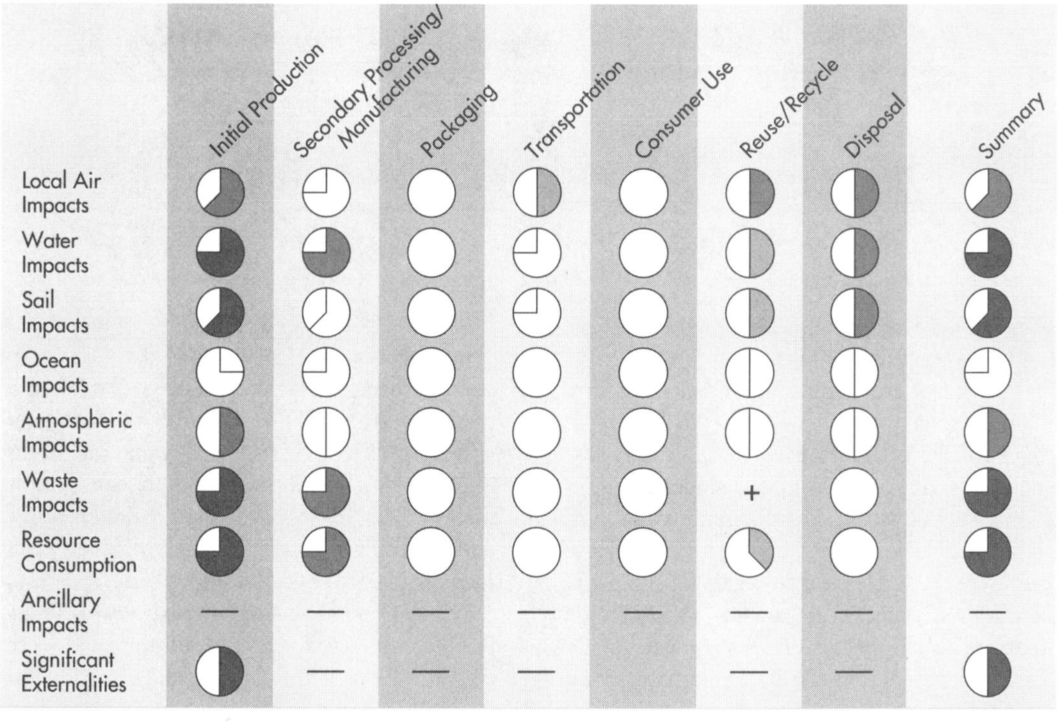

FIGURE 2 ● Manufacturing primary matrix for indium.

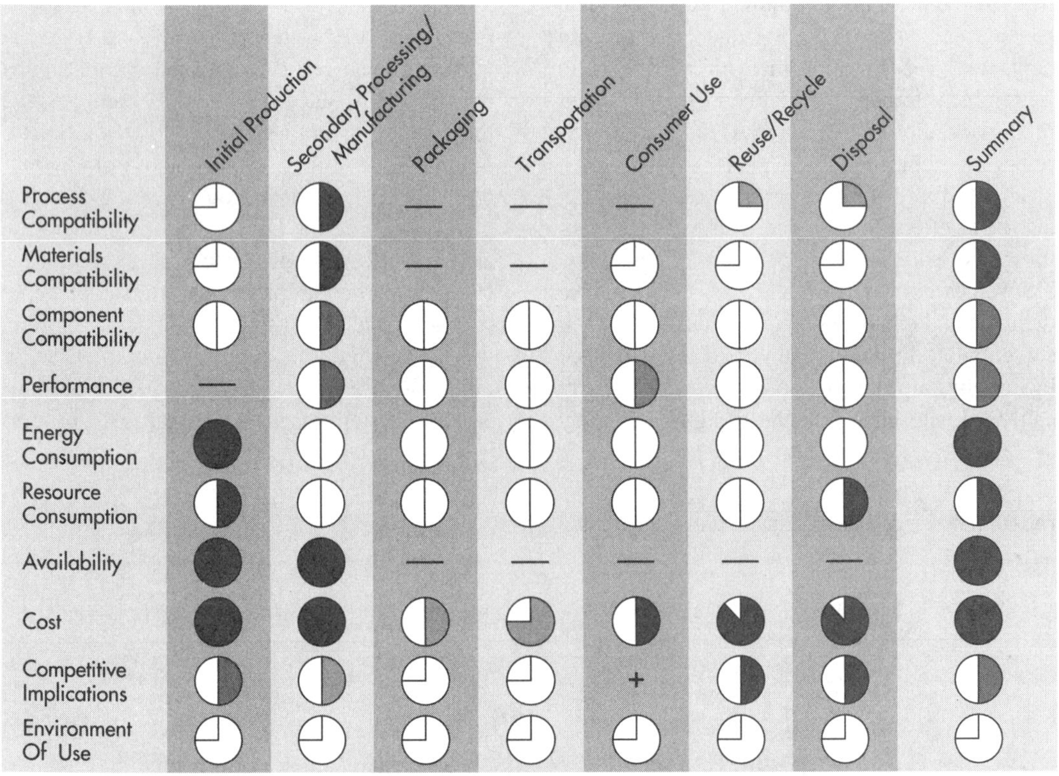

of identifying options also generates a set of potential competitive surprises.

A second important component of the scoping process is to determine the depth of analysis required. For a fundamental design decision—such as moving away from lead solder technologies in printed wiring board assembly—a fairly rigorous analysis would be appropriate. However, where incremental changes to an existing product or process are under consideration, there are relatively few options open to the designer, and a DFE analysis can be correspondingly limited.

2. *Data Gathering.* The next step is to gather and evaluate all relevant data. This may be done using LCA methodologies or, alternatively, by completing a data collection effort aimed specifically at DFE information needs. Such an effort revolves around collecting information in at least four areas, illustrated by the data collection matrices in Figures 1–5: environmental primary, manufacturing primary, social/political primary, and toxicity/exposure primary. A summary matrix then captures the most severe concern for each ranking. The data in the matrices shown in Figures 1–5 are drawn from an ex-

FIGURE 3 ● Social/political primary matrix for indium.

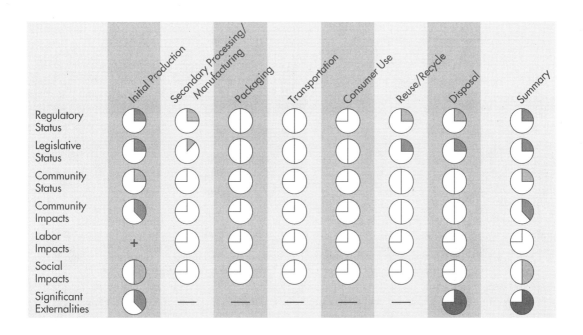

ample developed by the author and described later in this chapter.

There are three possible entries for each matrix cell (Figure 6). One or two pluses in a cell means the option has positive environmental effects for that category and indicates the relative degree of benefit. A straight line means the cell is inapplicable to the option. An oval indicates some degree of concern; an open, or blank, oval indicates minimal concern; dots indicate some concern; diagonal lines indicate moderate concern; and solid black indicates serious concern.

An important feature of this graphical approach is the ability to indicate relative degrees of uncertainty. Thus, the amount by which each oval is filled in (going clockwise from 12 o'clock, as illustrated in Figure 6) with the ap-

propriate pattern indicates the relative degree of uncertainty. For example, a solvent with potentially serious health effects, such as methylene chloride (a suspected carcinogen), would receive a solid black rating in the appropriate cell but, as those effects are quite uncertain, the oval might be only be half filled.

3. *Data Translation.* Once an analysis is completed, the information must be digested and turned into tools with which the design engineer or team can work. It is not very helpful, for example, to tell a designer that methylene chloride is a possible human carcinogen if the designer is unaware of alternatives. It is far more effective to create design tools, such as standardized components lists; design procedures, such as checklists that can be reviewed by environmental experts;

FIGURE 4 ● Toxicity/exposure primary matrix for lead.

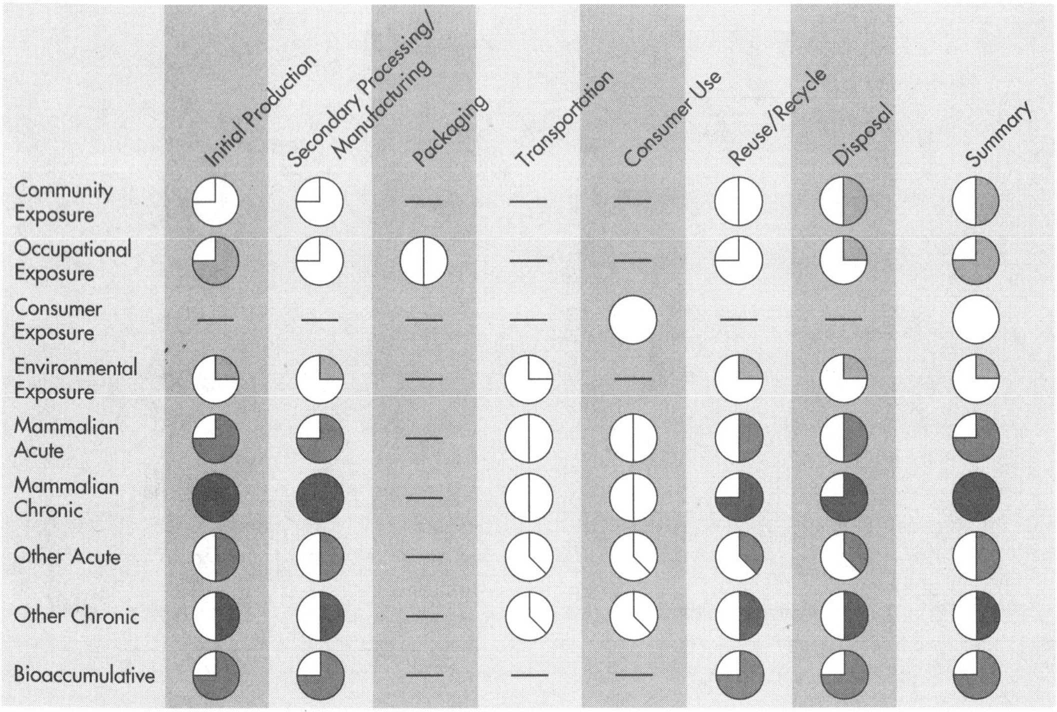

FIGURE 5 ● Summary matrix of the analysis.

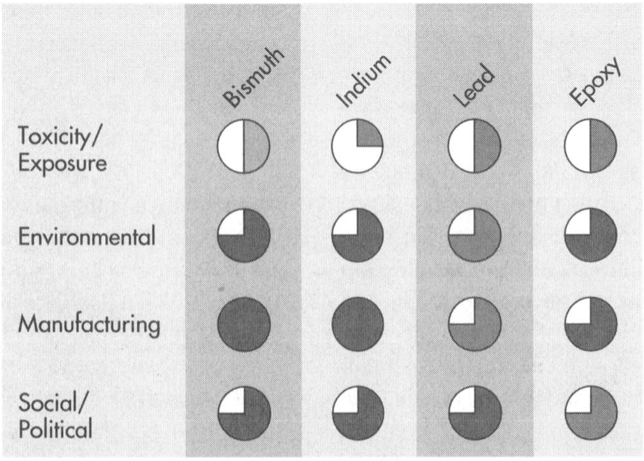

FIGURE 6 ● DFE Information System (DFEIS) symbols.

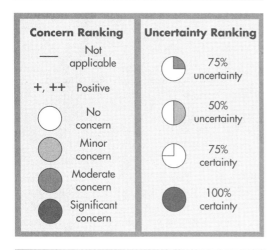

and software systems that incorporate these data into the design process without requiring further knowledge on the part of the designer.

These design tools can take many forms. For example, as AT&T phased out its use of CFCs in manufacturing, it created two useful tools. One, a handbook, listed all common solvents and, among other things, provided a color flag to indicate whether use of the material was acceptable from an environmental and regulatory perspective (for example, benzene would be red, or not acceptable, while water would be green, or acceptable under all circumstances). The other was a heuristic hierarchy of process choices (implementation of which frequently entailed changes in design process or product design). The preferable choice was to eliminate the cleaning step entirely; the second was to use an aqueous system; the third was to use a semiaqueous system (water/hydrocarbon); the fourth, temporary and least preferred, was to use a chlorinated solvent.

Another "design tool" is simply to require that all components be labeled to ease postcon-

sumer recycling. Thus, for example, plastic casings for computers or copiers increasingly have a label embossed on the inside giving the type of plastic, which facilitates material recycling. This need not concern the designer directly; it merely needs to be incorporated into the standard components list or required of the supplier through specifications.

DESIGN FOR ENVIRONMENT: TESTING THE SYSTEM

An experimental test of a formal DFE Information System (DFEIS) methodology was carried out by the author on a fairly controversial problem that AT&T confronted regarding the desirability of substituting indium alloys, bismuth alloys, or isotropic conductive epoxy technologies (using silver as the filler) for the lead solder currently used in assembly of printed wiring boards in electronics manufacturing (Allenby, 1992b). The results, presented in Figure 5, were counterintuitive, supporting a conclusion that significant substitution of indium, bismuth, or isotropic conductive epoxy technologies for lead solder would not be environmentally preferable.

None of the environmental effects that led to this conclusion occurred during the manufacturing or consumer use life cycle stages, the only ones that would have been considered in most standard industrial evaluations. Rather, they reflected basic characteristics of indium and bismuth ores (and, to a lesser degree, silver); namely, the low concentrations of indium and bismuth in virtually all ores, and the low world reserves of the metals taken as a whole. Under these circumstances, extraction would be very energy-intensive, and substantial environmental impacts, at least locally, could be anticipated (see Figure 1). Moreover, this raises obvious cost and availability concerns that should be addressed before relying on these options for a critical manufacturing function (see Figure 2).

Additionally, it was noteworthy that even this relatively limited, real world test of the DFEIS raised several unresolved ethical issues. For example, if indium or bismuth were to be substituted for lead solder, much of the environmental impact (and associated social and community impacts as well) would fall on localities where the mining and processing occurred, including some outside the United States. The potential environmental benefits, a reduction in the amount of lead solder from printed wiring boards in waste streams, would accrue primarily to localities near landfills or incinerators in the United States, where the electronic items would be disposed of. The asymmetrical geographic distribution of risk and benefit raises clear equity concerns, but I am aware of no generally accepted methods for resolving them.

A second issue, that of intergenerational resource allocation, is an extremely difficult equity problem. Since there is little indium in the world, is it appropriate to consume much of this limited stock in the manufacture of televisions and VCRs, where it will eventually end up in sinks from which it is virtually unrecoverable? Is this acceptable given that the risks posed by alternatives, such as lead solder, are probably minimal for this use? In essence, this amounts to buying little or no risk reduction for U.S. inhabitants today by loading potentially substantial costs on future generations. If other materials can substitute for indium completely, the answer might still be yes, but we have no way of knowing this: indium might have some unique value in the future. (This is the rationale behind the ranking of "serious concern" in the disposal life cycle stage/significant externalities category in Figure 3.)

At this point, at least, there are no generally accepted legal or economic answers to this conundrum. What is perhaps more interesting, however is that this very difficult issue arose in a relatively simple analysis of a serious existing design decision. Companies are deciding now whether to begin the difficult task of shifting to alternative joining technologies for printed wiring boards, so they will implicitly answer the ethical questions in any event. By failing to implement DFE practices, we are not avoiding problems; we are just ignoring them.

The toxicity/exposure primary matrix, containing the most familiar material, completes the matrix set, but even here there were important implications. Thus, as Figure 4 indicates, even for lead, a material whose toxic effects have been known since Roman times, considerable uncertainty over nonmammalian toxicity remains. Also it should be noted that data on exposure and on acute toxicity are integrated to provide the rankings captured in the summary matrix. This reflects the well-known toxicological principle that the hazard posed by any agent is a function of both the inherent toxicity of the agent and the concomitant exposure of the target population. Either exposure or toxicity alone does not generate hazard.

CONCLUSION

We are now at a stage where we are beginning to understand the multidisciplinary, systemic nature of the interrelationship between technology and environment. Current regulatory and industrial practices, however, are still predicated on an increasingly dysfunctional symptoms-oriented approach. Design for Environment practices provide a means by which industry—and regulators—can move beyond current single-dimensional, ad hoc approaches in the short term and evolve a system-based, comprehensive set of practices over the long term. Both the environment and industrial competitiveness will benefit as a result.

REFERENCES

Allenby, B. R. 1991. Design for environment: A tool whose time has come. SSA Journal September:5–9.

Allenby, B. R. 1992a. Industrial ecology: The materials scientist in an environmentally constrained world. MRS Bulletin 17(3):46–51.

Allenby, B. R. 1992b. Design for Environment: Implementing Industrial Ecology. Ph.D. dissertation, Rutgers University.

Ayres, R. U. 1989. Industrial metabolism. Pp. 23–49 in Technology and Environment, J. H. Ausubel and H. E. Sladovich, eds. Washington, D.C.: National Academy Press.

Frosch, R. A., and N. E. Gallopoulos. 1989. Strategies for manufacturing. Scientific American 261(3):144–152.

Gatenby, D. A., and G. Foo. 1990. Design for X: Key to competitive, profitable markets. AT&T Technical Journal 63(3):2–13.

Office of Technology Assessment. 1992. Green Products by Design: Choices for a Cleaner Environment. Washington, D.C.: U.S. Government Printing Office.

Society of Environmental Toxicology and Chemistry. 1991. A Technical Framework for Life-Cycle Assessment. Washington, D.C.: SETAC Foundation.

20

Introduction to ISO 14000
Tom Tibor with Ira Feldman

If you're an environmental manager, you're probably familiar with scenarios such as these:

- Management okays the new construction of a plant without fully considering the requirements of operating permits.

- The purchasing department shifts from a domestic to a foreign chemical supplier. However, the new chemical does not meet regulatory requirements.

- Downsizing at a plant proceeds, but no one is charged with reassessing key environmental responsibilities.

- A change in a materials specification requires a new Material Safety Data Sheet, which hasn't been developed by either the technical, marketing, or regulatory affairs departments.

- Management issues lofty policy statements lauding environmental improvement but does not accompany them with resources and personnel.

- The local community is concerned about the plant's discharges to a local stream but hasn't developed an effective communication program to ease the community's concerns.

- In general, the environmental staff is too busy putting out today's fires to find time to prevent those that may occur tomorrow.

What do these situations have in common? To a large extent, they are system failures. Either a good environmental management system doesn't exist, or if it does, it's not working as well as it should.

There's a set of standards . . . that may well change things. Known as the ISO 14000 series, it will affect every aspect of a company's management of its environmental responsibilities: how it performs environmental auditing; how it measures environmental performance; how it makes credible claims for its products; the way it analyzes the life cycle of its products and processes; and the way it reports environmental information to its employees and the public.

In short, the ISO 14000 standards will help any organization address environmental issues in a systematic way and thereby improve its environmental performance.

The ISO 14000 standards are being developed by Technical Committee 207 (TC 207) of the International Organization for Standardization (ISO) to provide organizations worldwide with a common approach to environmental management. Just as the ISO 9000 quality standards were developed to address quality management, the ISO 14000 standards are emerging to address a similar need in the environmental area.

WHAT IS AN ENVIRONMENTAL MANAGEMENT SYSTEM?

The ISO 14000 standards describe the basic elements of an effective environmental management

Reprinted with permission from *ISO 14000*.

system, routinely referred to by the acronym EMS. These elements include creating an environmental policy, setting objectives and targets, implementing a program to achieve those objectives, monitoring and measuring its effectiveness, correcting problems, and reviewing the system to improve it and overall environmental performance.

An effective environmental management system can help a company manage, measure, and improve the environmental aspects of its operations. It can lead to more efficient compliance with mandatory and voluntary environmental requirements. It can help companies effect a culture change as environmental management practices are incorporated into its overall business operations.

The ISO 14000 standards are based on a simple equation: better environmental management will lead to better environmental performance, increased efficiency, and a greater return on investment.

MANAGEMENT SYSTEMS AND TOOLS

The work of ISO's TC 207 encompasses standards in the following areas:

- Environmental management systems (EMS).
- Environmental auditing (EA).
- Environmental performance evaluation (EPE).
- Environmental labeling.
- Life cycle assessment (LCA).
- Environmental aspects in product standards (EAPS).
- Terms and definitions.

These areas fall into two general groups, as shown in Figure 1. The EMS, EA, and EPE standards are used to evaluate the organization. The EMS standards provide the basic framework for the management system. Environmental auditing and environmental performance evaluation are management tools that play a critical role in the successful implementation of the environmental management system.

The work in the areas of labeling, life cycle assessment, and environmental aspects in product standards will also play an important role in the environmental arena. The emphasis in these areas, however, is on the evaluation and analysis of product and process characteristics.

● ● ●

System, Not Performance

One key point that will facilitate an understanding of the standards is this: The ISO 14000 standards are *process*—not *performance*—standards. That is, ISO 14000 does not tell companies what environmental performance they must achieve. Instead, it offers companies the building blocks for a system that will help them achieve their own goals. The basic assumption is that better environmental management will lead indirectly to better environmental performance. The standards being developed by TC 207 do not, therefore, set performance levels or rates of improvement, nor do they prescribe specific goals, objectives, or policies.

One reason for this approach is that there are many different points of view on what constitutes good environmental management and performance. In part, this relates to diverse technologies to meet company objectives. That's why the goal of standards such as the ISO 14000 series is to lay a common foundation for more uniform, efficient, and effective environmental management worldwide. The result will be increased confidence among all stakeholders involved that the process put in place by a company will lead to better compliance with laws and other requirements and to high levels of environmental performance.

FIGURE 1 ● The ISO 14000 Series of Environmental Management Standards
Internal Organization for Standardization Technical Committee 207

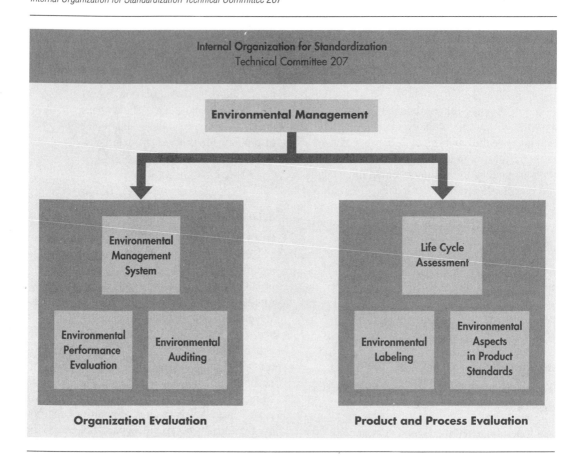

THE PACE OF DEVELOPMENT

Some of the standards in the ISO 14000 series are already in the form of Draft International Standards (DIS), one step away from published International Standards (IS). The EMS standards and the auditing standards could be published by mid-1996. Most standards developed at the international level take five years to reach publication. ISO 14000 has been in development less than two years. Why so fast?

Response to Proliferation

One reason is the growing proliferation of environmental management standards and voluntary initiatives. These are being developed by industry and government. At least a dozen countries have EMS standards, including the United Kingdom's BS 7750 and, in the United States, the NSF International's NSF 110 EMS standard.

Regional trading blocs such as the European Union have developed the Eco-Management and Audit Scheme regulation. Industry associations have developed codes of practice, such as the US Chemical Management Association's Responsible Care program; the Global Environmental Management Initiative's (GEMI) Environmental Self Assessment Program, and many others.

Without a common international standard, companies would be forced to deal with dozens of separate and potentially incompatible systems for every country in which they do business. This can increase the cost of doing business and pose trade barriers.

Environmental Stewardship and Accountability

The ISO 14000 standards setting activity is set against a broader tapestry. Generally speaking, the standards are developing quickly partly in response to the growing pressure on companies to demonstrate better environmental stewardship and accountability. Pressure is coming from the government, the public, stockholders, financial institutions, environmental groups, and others. With each passing month, anecdotal evidence of the trend accumulates.

Greener Products

As consumers, the public is also beginning to play a role. Consumer demand is increasing for green products, and companies are responding by taking a closer look at all environmental aspects of product design, production, packaging, distribution, and disposal. The investing public is taking a closer look at a company's environmental operations as a factor in its profitability.

For these reasons and others, ISO 14000 may well have an explosive impact on the global marketplace. Although designed as a voluntary standard, it could become a de facto market-driven requirement for companies both domestic and international. ISO 14000 may well become a company's global passport to doing business.

That's why proactive companies are already paying close attention to ISO 14000.

REASONS TO IMPLEMENT ISO 14000

First, there are strategic reasons to get involved. Increasingly, as we've discussed, there is a worldwide trend to focus on better environmental management. Environmental management has gone from an add-on function to an integral part of business operations. For many proactive companies, environmental management has become strategy-driven, not compliance-driven. ISO 14000 will provide a broad framework for implementing strategic environmental management.

Increasing Use of Voluntary Standards

There's also an emphasis on the use of voluntary international standards. The General Agreement on Tariffs and Trade (GATT) officially favors the use of international standards in its agreement on Technical Barriers to Trade (TBT).

This trend has been integrated into national policies. In the United States, for example, it's government policy to reference international standards whenever possible.[1]

The use of international standards can help level the international playing field. In countries with high compliance costs due to stringent regulations, companies can achieve more efficient compliance. In countries where compliance costs may be lower, due partly to a less stringent regulatory system, ISO 14000 may demand more of a commitment to effective environmental management.

Reduce Multiplicity/Duplication

The acceptance of a single international environmental standard can reduce the number of environmental audits conducted by customers, regulators, or registrars. By avoiding conflicting requirements, multinational corporations could reduce the cost of multiple inspections, certifications, and other conflicting requirements.

De Facto Requirement

Implementing an EMS that complies with ISO 14000 requirements and achieving third-party registration may well become a de facto requirement to do business. Foreign customers may require US suppliers to be ISO 14000 registered. This requirement could affect the ability of US companies to sell their products globally.

Even if ISO 14000 remains a purely voluntary standard, market pressure may drive registration. The pressure will not just be on large multinational companies but also on smaller companies that are part of the supplier chain. The trend is for companies to want to deal with environmentally responsible companies. ISO 14000 itself requires that organizations establish and maintain procedures related to the environmental aspects of goods and services that they use and communicate these procedures and requirements to suppliers and contractors. Since ISO 14000 registration is one way to demonstrate that a company has a system in place to achieve environmental performance objectives, companies may come to expect ISO 14000 registration of their suppliers and subcontractors.

Government Adoption

Another key player in the ISO 14000 movement could be government. Governments worldwide are looking at the role that ISO 14000 can play in their regulatory systems, their enforcement procedures, and their procurement policies. (See Box.)

In the European Union, ISO 14000 certification may satisfy the EMS requirements of the Eco-Management and Audit Scheme regulation. This is a voluntary scheme open to industrial sites in Europe that requires extensive EMA and auditing systems to be in place. . . .

Many other countries around the world are looking at ISO 14000, either to encourage their industries to get involved or to actually integrate the standard into their regulatory system in some fashion.

Governments in developed countries with strict environmental regulations are interested in ISO 14000 as a useful alternative to complex and expensive "command and control" regulations.

Other nations, especially in the developing countries, are looking at the use of ISO 14000 as a way to enhance regulatory systems that are either nonexistent or weak in their environmental performance requirements. In these countries, ISO 14000 registration may be an alternative method to achieve environmental goals.

In any case, even if the international standard isn't integrated into regulations, it may nevertheless influence national regulations by establishing a standard of care—a new level of expectations for EMS programs—that may guide the development of national regulations.

It may also affect enforcement policies. In the United States, the Environmental Protection Agency (EPA), the Department of Justice (DOJ), the Department of Energy (DOE), and the Department of Commerce (DOC) are among several agencies that are monitoring the ISO 14000 process and its role in regulation and enforcement.

Several countries are also considering giving preference in procurement contracts to companies that install an EMS that conforms to ISO 14000 requirements.[2]

Satisfy Stakeholder Interests

Companies are increasingly concerned with satisfying the expectations of a broad range of stakeholders, including investors, the public, and environmental groups. ISO 14000 registration can satisfy the public's need for corporate accountability. Companies with ISO 14000–registered EMS programs can provide confidence to the public that they are complying with regulations and continually improving their environmental management systems. ISO 14000 registration can demonstrate an organization's commitment and credibility regarding environmental issues. It demonstrates compliance not only with existing regulations but also with a publicly declared policy such as the ICC Charter.

Lower Insurance Rates and Better Access to Capital

Implementing an effective EMS can provide future savings in the form of lower insurance rates and better access to capital. Insurance companies will be more willing to issue coverage for pollution incidents if the company requesting coverage has a proven environmental management system in place. Some large institutional investors such as pension funds have begun to make investment decisions based on a corporation's environmental track record. This ties environmental management to future stock performance.

Internal Benefits

The discussion so far has focused on external pressures and benefits. What will ISO 14000 implementation do for an organization internally?

On a practical level, an ISO 14000 type of EMS program is likely to lead to cost savings through better management of the environmental aspects of an organization's operations.

To the extent that noncompliance with regulations is caused by systems deficiencies, implementing an EMS can reduce the number of noncompliances and increase overall operating efficiency. It can lead to waste reduction, pollution prevention, substitution of less toxic chemicals and other materials, less energy usage, cost

GOVERNMENT AND ISO 14000

Governments worldwide are closely monitoring the ISO 14000 process. The UK's Ministry of Defense may require potential vendors to achieve EMS registration, and it may offer favorable treatment regarding permit issuance to companies that comply with the UK's BS 7750 EMS standard. In the Netherlands, thousands of Dutch companies have agreed to implement EMS systems as part of government-industry covenants that supplement existing laws and regulations. The Dutch government may use EMS registration to issue permits and check compliance among regulated companies.

ISO 14000 registration can assist governments in using regulatory resources more efficiently. Germany, for example, is looking at the role ISO 14000 can play in deregulatory efforts and in simplification of its permitting procedures. Governments in South America—for example, those in Brazil, Argentina, and Chile—may apply pressure on companies in key sectors such as petroleum, mining, auto manufacturing, and the paper and pulp industries to implement ISO 14000. The same holds true for many Asian countries, many of whom have participated actively in the standards development process.

US GOVERNMENT AND ISO 14000

In the United States, many government agencies are monitoring the standards activities. The Department of Energy (DOE) may require major DOE contractors to put into place an environmental management system along the lines of ISO 14001 by 1997. The ISO 14000 standards may also play a role in the US government's procurement policies related to environmentally preferable products.[3]

The Environmental Protection Agency (EPA) has been participating actively in the standards drafting process. The EPA recognizes that ISO 14000 is a private-sector effort and thus, it is not at present considering the adoption of the ISO 14000 standards as a possible regulatory requirement. The EPA will likely find ISO 14000 to be a useful tool in its voluntary programs, as described below. In general, US industry would not welcome ISO 14000 implementation and/or third-party registration as a regulatory mandate.

As discussed in Appendix C, the EPA has developed policies that mitigate the enforcement response for companies performing environmental auditing and offer incentives for voluntary disclosure. In general, the EPA will follow the general US government trend to take into account a company's compliance assurance programs in its responses to violations. This is also true for the Department of Justice and the US Sentencing Commission.

As in other countries with complex regulatory schemes, the EPA is looking for ways to move away from its purely command and control posture and toward preventive approaches such as ISO 14000. The EPA anticipates more reliance by companies on independent auditing and self-certification as the primary way to prevent environmental problems and ensure regulatory compliance. One benefit to the EPA and to regulatory bodies in other countries that pursue the same strategy is greater regulatory efficiency; governments can ease oversight of environmental "good actors" and direct their attention to serious violators.

According to the EPA, possible uses of the ISO 14000 standard could include the following:

- Reduction of penalties and recognition of due diligence in complying with regulations.
- Special public recognition of some kind for ISO 14000–registered companies.
- A schedule of fewer routine inspections and regulatory audits in exchange for EMS implementation.
- Faster permitting procedures.
- Adoption by companies in place of compliance penalties in consent decree negotiations.
- Reduced or streamlined reporting and monitoring burdens and less paperwork.
- Some role in government supplier requirements, such as the environmentally preferable products orders.

(Continued)

ISO 14000 in voluntary programs. The ISO 14000 standards are likely to play a role in voluntary programs to encourage companies to comply with regulations and improve environmental performance.

   One such program is the EPA's Environmental Leadership Program (ELP), a one-year pilot project launched in March 1995 at 12 facilities. The basic concept of the program is to encourage companies to go beyond compliance by testing innovative management techniques such as environmental auditing, pollution prevention, and EMS programs. Another purpose of the program is to test criteria for auditing and for certification of voluntary compliance programs to standards such as ISO 14000.[4]

   The program will provide the EPA with more information about the elements of a state-of-the-art EMS program. If successful, the criteria developed through the pilot projects could lead to reduced inspections and public recognition for companies or agencies with successful compliance programs. Similar programs are being developed at the state level.

savings through recycling, and other such programs. It can facilitate obtaining operating permits and other authorizations.

   ISO 14000 can provide a mechanism for controlling existing management methods, integrating fragmented systems, or creating systems if none exist. It can help a company systematically monitor and measure its compliance status. It can help in training employees regarding their role in environmental protection and improvement. An effective EMS can integrate existing management systems to reduce costs and system duplication.

Pollution Prevention

ISO 14000 acceptance worldwide will provide more incentives to initiate pollution prevention activities. A company with an ISO 14000 system can gain some breathing room—instead of constantly putting out fires, it can prevent them from occurring in the first place. An effective EMS

program analyzes the cause of noncompliances and builds prevention into the company's overall operations.

   The key to prevention is successfully integrating environmental issues, business strategy, and operations. Prevention cuts costs by reducing the use of materials and energy, while end-of-pipe controls only save money from the avoidance of fines and penalties due to noncompliance.

Achieve Environmental Excellence

An effective EMS will help organizations implement their commitment to environmental excellence. The basic elements of ISO 14000 do not constitute an environmental excellence program in and of themselves; however, they are the foundation—the building blocks—for such a program. Stakeholder pressure, marketplace competition, and encouragement and recognition by government agencies are providing incentives for more companies to achieve environmental excellence.

On the broadest scale, better environmental management can protect human health and the environment from the impacts of industrial activity. An EMS can help an organization balance economic and environmental interests. It brings environmental issues into day-to-day decision-making processes. In short, ISO 14000 marries environmental management to business management.

CONCERNS AND CAVEATS

The benefits just discussed shouldn't disguise the concerns, caveats, and potential pitfalls in the ISO 14000 movement. In many cases, these are the flip side of the benefits.

Increased Costs

Implementing a comprehensive environmental management system can be expensive. Costs are especially critical for small and medium-size enterprises (SMEs), many of whom already have problems meeting environmental obligations. Depending on the definition of small business, anywhere from 75 to 90 percent of world industry is performed by SMEs. For small companies, the time and cost of ISO 14000 registration may be too high a price to play the game and thus the standard may pose a trade barrier for such companies.

The standards drafters claim that the ISO 14000 standards take into account the problems of industries in lesser developed countries and those of small companies. The ISO 14001 specification standard posits a gradual, baseline approach to managing environmental systems. Thus, a company need not start with the most sophisticated EMS. Implementing ISO 14000 effectively in SMEs, however, will remain an important challenge for the ISO 14000 movement.

Possible Nontariff Trade Barriers

International standards can facilitate a common industrial language, provide consumer confidence, and promote product safety. Standards can also encourage trade by making it more efficient and by simplifying testing and certification requirements for products and processes. Used improperly, however, standards can hinder worldwide trade by creating technical (nontariff) trade barriers.

A major goal of TC 207 is to facilitate trade and minimize trade barriers by leveling the playing field. But the standard could have the opposite effect and lead to imposing the requirements and management systems of advanced industrial nations on developing countries, requirements they lack the knowledge and resources to meet.

Voluntary or Mandated?

The basic purpose of a voluntary consensus standard is just that—to stay voluntary. Another trade barrier issue arises if the standard becomes a regulatory mandate. In this case, it could be used to prescribe requirements that are more stringent than existing regulations. This could pose a trade barrier to organizations located in countries where ISO 14000 is not required by law.

A related concern is that governments will use ISO 14000 to determine legal requirements and the government's enforcement responses and to calculate criminal penalties. A key principle of TC 207's work is that international standards should not be used to create or determine legal requirements.

Doesn't Actually Lead to Better Environmental Performance

Remember that the ISO 14000 standard is a process, not a performance standard. The expec-

ISO 14000 AND TRADE BARRIERS

The work of TC 207 does not exist in a vacuum but rather in a highly competitive international economy. This economy comprises nations at widely different levels of economic development, with varying degrees of environmental regulation. In this context, the aim of ISO 14000 is worldwide adoption by industry, improvements in environmental performance, and avoidance of trade barriers. ISO 14000 implementation, however, could actually create trade barriers. How could this happen?

Regulatory adoption by a country. ISO 14000 is a voluntary standard, and ISO 14001 registration is a voluntary scheme. Therefore, ISO 14000 does not create any official trade barrier as recognized by international agreements such as the General Agreement of Tariffs and Trade (GATT) in its agreement on Technical Barriers to Trade (TBT). If a country makes ISO 14000 registration a regulatory requirement for all companies doing business within its borders, however, this raises a potential barrier to foreign companies that find it difficult, for various reasons, to meet the requirements of the standard. This might apply especially if the foreign company facing the barrier is a subcontractor or vendor to a company located in the country with the requirement. Foreign suppliers who want to get contract awards but who cannot meet the "green" requirements of their customers, for whatever reason, may encounter market access barriers.

Barrier to developing countries. Requirements for ISO 14000 registration, whether government or marketplace mandated, can disadvantage developing nations. Even though ISO 14000 registration can be an opportunity for companies in developing nations to demonstrate effective environmental management, if ISO 14000 registration is expensive and the standards are too prescriptive to meet developing nations will be disadvantaged.

Another barrier faced by many countries is the lack of a registration and accreditation infrastructure. This may require companies in these countries to seek registrations from registrars in other nations, again potentially driving up costs and creating trade barriers.

tation, however, is that better management will lead to better performance. If companies achieve ISO 14000 certificates without demonstrating results, stakeholders who expect ISO registration to be a decisive indicator of environmental progress may lose confidence in the process.

Third-Party Registration Issues

Finally, there are concerns about the third-party registration process and the overall system for assessing conformity to the standards. Some of the key issues include:

- Consistent interpretation of the standards.
- The role of the self-declaration versus third-party registration for ISO 14000 implementation.
- Accreditation of the registrars (certification bodies).
- Competence of ISO 14000 auditors.
- Recognition of ISO 14000 registration certificates worldwide.

Notes

1. US regulations contain hundreds of standards from a variety of sources: local, national, regional, and global. Government policy favors the use of international standards to promote trade and ease technical trade barriers. In 1993, the Office of Management and Budget (OMB) issued a revised policy statement, OMB Circular A-119, "Federal Participation in the Development and Use of Voluntary Standards." A-119 provides federal agencies with guidance on the use of private standards and participation in voluntary standards bodies. Section 7a(2) of the circular states that "International standards should be considered in procurement and regulatory applications in the interests of pro-moting trade and implementing the provisions of the Agreement on Technical Barriers to Trade and the Agreement on Government Procurement."

2. Colombia, for example, plans to give preference in contracts to companies that comply with ISO 14000. (Reported in "Colombia, Chile, Argentina Prepare for ISO 14001," *International Environmental Systems Update,* July 1995, p. 1.)

3. Executive Order 12873—Federal Acquisition, Recycling and Waste Prevention, October 20, 1993. Published in the Federal Register, October 22, 1993.

4. If the EPA makes some use of ISO 14000, would registration be the only route companies could follow? On the one hand, independent third-party audits can provide the confidence that the marketplace and governments require. On the other hand, registration requires resources that many companies might not have. According to Mary McKiel, Director of the EPA's Standards Network, the EPA wants to have confidence that a company has properly implemented ISO 14000 but doesn't want to disadvantage those companies that, for whatever reason, prefer self-declaration as the means of demonstrating conformance. One possible approach for acceptance of self-declaration would be to set clear criteria and for the EPA to play an active role in developing certification/registration criteria for any proposed national accreditation system.

21

The Natural Step to Sustainability
Wingspread Journal

Up to now, much of the debate over the environment has had the character of monkey chatter amongst the withering leaves of a dying tree.

We are confronted with a series of seemingly unrelated questions: Is the greenhouse effect really a threat, or will it actually prevent another ice age? Is economic growth harmful, or does it provide resources for healing the environment? Will the costs of phasing out nonrenewable energy sources outweigh the benefits? Can communities, regions, or countries accomplish anything useful on their own, or must they wait for international agreements?

In the midst of all this chatter about the 'leaves' very few of us have been paying attention to the environment's trunk and branches. They are deteriorating as a result of processes about which there is little or no controversy; and the thousands of individual problems that are the subject of so much debate are, in fact, manifestations of systemic errors that are undermining the foundations of human society.

—Karl-Henrik Robèrt

The author of this passage is Karl-Henrik Robèrt, one of Sweden's leading cancer researchers. In 1989 he turned his attention from the chattering in the branches to see what could be done to address the rot in the trunk—systemic depletion of natural resources and increased proliferation of waste and toxic chemicals. The result of his efforts, a concept and an organization he calls The Natural Step, has been transforming the way individuals, communities, and business think about sustainability.

Robèrt began by trying to define the key environmental principles on which everyone could agree. He knew, for example, that while experts may disagree about acceptable levels of CFCs in the atmosphere, or at what pH value our environment is least productive, most could agree that ever increasing levels of CFCs and ever lowering values of pH are *not* acceptable. Robèrt sent the draft of his principles—21 times—to eminent Swedish scientists, inviting their comments, until he had their agreement on environmental principles consistent with science.

THE CYCLIC PRINCIPLE

What these scientific principles describe is actually a concept as simple as the circle. Our world, that is, the physical, natural, human, and atmospheric environment, is sustainable when what is taken out of the system for food or energy is restored to the system in waste that can be reused. The system works when waste—human, animal, and plant—does not systematically accumulate in nature and when the reconstitution of material quality is at least as large as its dissipation.

It makes intuitive sense, except that is not the way our current economy operates, nor the way most societies for the past hundred years have operated. Our linear economy converts resources to waste faster than nature can cope.

This linear system is transforming our resources into the useless waste we see in our garbage dumps and landfill sites, and also into the "molecular garbage" we don't see: the vast quantities of tiny particles daily dumped into our air, soil, and water.

In America, for example, each person uses, directly or indirectly, about 125 pounds of material every day, or about 23 tons per year. We use fuel, quarried materials like gravel, industrial minerals such as phosphate, industrial metals such as copper and aluminum, forestry products such as timber and pulpwood for paper, and agricultural products from milk and meat to grain and grapes. Every day, in order to feed us, U.S. farmers and ranchers draw out 20 billion more gallons of water from the ground than is replaced by rainfall.

Our waste is even more impressive. The total flow of our waste equals at least 250 trillion pounds, of which only about five percent is recycled. As author, environmentalist, and chairman of The Natural Step, U.S.A., Paul Hawken notes, "we are far better at making waste than at making products. For every 100 pounds of product we manufacture in the United States, we create at least 3,200 pounds of waste. In a decade, we transform 500 trillion pounds of molecules into nonproductive solids, liquids, and gases."

That "nonproductive garbage," produced by our linear way of living and working, never finds its way back into the cycles of society or of nature to be reused or absorbed. "As we busy ourselves with tearing down more than we rebuild," Robèrt notes, "we are racing toward world-wide poverty in a monstrous, poisonous garbage dump. The only thing that can save us from the consequences is the restoration of cyclical processes, where wastes become new resources for society or nature."

Creating a guide to thinking and acting in harmony with the earth's cyclical processes is what Robèrt has done with The Natural Step. As outlined in the table on the previous page, The Natural Step's Four System Conditions provide an easy-to-understand, pragmatic guide against which to measure our social, environmental, and economic actions. As Robèrt notes, people "at all levels—households, corporations, local authorities, nations—can systematically direct their activities to fit into this frame by requiring all secondary goals to function as steps toward achieving sustainability. In a program for development, small measures can be understood within the larger goal. . . . The Four System Conditions provide a model—a compass—pointing to sustainability." Like a compass, The Natural Step can point us in the direction we want to go and tell us when we are off track. Like a compass, it is based on laws of nature which are nonnegotiable. We can only change the way we respond to them.

TRANSLATING PRINCIPLES INTO ACTION

"What's unique about The Natural Step, is that it's the first time principles for sustainability have been defined in a concrete way that is operational and consistent with the laws that govern the functioning of the planet's ecosystem," says Molly Harriss Olson, former executive director of the President's Council on Sustainable Development and president of The Natural Step, U.S.A. "The Natural Step offers a science-based guide to sustainability."

What The Natural Step does *not* provide is a detailed program on how to get there. Instead, it trusts individuals to solve environmental problems in ways that fit their fields of expertise. Unlike many of the "Principles of Sustainability" that have been developed recently, The Natural Step is not prescriptive. And that may be its greatest strength.

"The principles are not judgmental," says Olson. "There are no values on what companies or individuals or groups can or can't do, as long as they work within the system conditions." This frees people, Olson says, to create solutions that

THE NATURAL STEP'S FOUR SYSTEM CONDITIONS

These conditions for sustainable life on earth are, in Robèrt's words, "non-negotiable and absolute." The beauty of this model, Robèrt adds, is that since it is absolute, you can audit yourself in that direction. That is the challenge of The Natural Step.

1. **Substances from the Earth's crust must not systematically increase in nature.**

Fossil fuels, metals, and other materials must not be extracted at a faster pace than their slow redeposit into the Earth's crust. Otherwise, quality will be lost due to the inevitable spread of wastes and their accumulation towards often unknown limits, beyond which irreversible changes occur. Today, in practical terms, this means radically decreased mining and use of fossil fuels.

2. **Substances produced by society must not systematically increase in nature.**

Substances must not be produced at a faster pace than they can be broken down and integrated into the cycles of nature or deposited into the Earth's crust. Otherwise, quality will be lost due to the inevitable spread of substances and their accumulation towards often unknown limits, beyond which irreversible changes occur. In practical terms, this means decreased production of natural substances that are accumulating, and a phase-out of all persistent and unnatural substances, such as plastic, freon, or PCBs.

3. **The physical basis for the productivity and diversity of nature must not be systematically diminished.**

The ecosystem must not be harvested or manipulated in such a way that productive capacity and diversity systematically diminish. Our health and prosperity depend on the capacity of nature to reconcentrate and restructure wastes into resources. Today, this means sweeping changes in our use of natural resources for agriculture, forestry, fishing, and planning of societies.

4. **Just and efficient use of energy and other resources.**

Basic human needs must be met with the most resource-efficient methods possible, including a just resource distribution. Humanity must prosper with a resource metabolism meeting the above three system conditions. This is necessary for social stability and cooperation in making future change. Today, in practical terms, this means an increased technical and organizational efficiency in the world, including a more resource-economical lifestyle in wealthier regions.

HITTING THE WALL

What happens if we don't begin to live more sustainably? According to Karl-Henrik Robèrt and The Natural Step, sooner or later our business, our community, or our planet will "hit the wall."

"Since we are now 5 billion people on earth, soon to become 10 billion, it is as if humanity were running into a funnel," says Robèrt. The walls of the funnel are the limits imposed by increasing population and consumption and decreasing resources. Violating the Four System Conditions by increasing the concentration of heavy metals brought up from below the earth's crust or large-scale dumping of man-made toxins into nature, for example, narrows our choices for living sustainably. The funnel walls become more and more narrow the faster the earth's resources are depleted or soiled.

If, however, we recognize the limits of the system, and target our activities *within* the parameters of the Four Conditions, we're living sustainably.

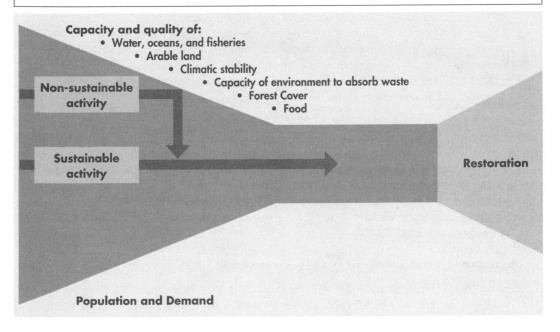

Capacity and quality of:
- Water, oceans, and fisheries
- Arable land
- Climatic stability
- Capacity of environment to absorb waste
- Forest Cover
- Food

Non-sustainable activity

Sustainable activity

Restoration

Population and Demand

© 1996 Paul Hawken, Karl-Henrik Robert, and The Natural Step.

not only produce sustainability, but also save money and create new opportunities.

Robèrt describes the process: "First we educate business leaders, politicians, and scientists in The Four System Conditions, and then we ask them for advice. Instead of telling them what to do, we say, 'How could this be applied in your world?' This sparks creativity and recruits enthusiasm into the process instead of defense mechanisms.

"Any expert in her field of expertise is much more clever than you or I," says Robèrt. "If you give her the overall principles, therefore, and then ask for advice, she finds much smarter solutions than Greenpeace or I or anybody else can. And we are very much in need of practical, creative solutions."

THE NATURAL STEP AND BUSINESS

The Natural Step approach is not just good for the environment, it is also good for business, as more than 60 major corporations around the world are discovering. Companies are recognizing that it just doesn't make good business sense to be dependent on resources that are getting more scarce, or to generate costly waste that could be re-used at a profit.

As Hawken writes, our economy will have a better chance to prosper if business fully values our natural resources. "The future belongs to those who understand that doing more with less is compassionate, prosperous, and enduring, and thus more intelligent, even competitive."

One company that has gotten the message is Interface, Inc., a $1 billion multinational carpet and flooring company. Carpeting usually lasts for about 12 years, after which Americans cosign it to landfills where it sits for another 20,000 years—at the rate of 3.5 billion pounds every year. Interface, as a result of its commitment to The Natural Step, has plans to lease its carpet service, replacing carpet tiles as they become worn, then recycling the old tiles into new ones for fresh carpeting.

Other innovative companies include Electrolux, which uses The Natural Step principles in creating more environmentally friendly products, IKEA furniture which has created a sofa that meets all four system conditions—and is one of its most popular products, and Monsanto, which has a team of more than 120 employees working on sustainability.

Today, just eight years after Robèrt began drafting his scientific principles, The Natural Step has national organizations in Sweden, Australia, the United States, Canada, France, the Netherlands, and the United Kingdom. Projects are also underway in New Zealand, Mexico, Brazil, and Japan.

Part 5

Environmental Management Cases

THE FOLLOWING SET of cases was designed not only to complement the readings but also to integrate the topics, so that the reader can appreciate "the big picture." Each case was chosen for specific value, but also to contribute to collective depth of knowledge, so that the knowledge gained from a group is maximized. Considerable diversity is displayed in the issues raised, the geographic settings in which they occur, and the tools that can be brought to bear on each situation.

Those familiar with case analysis will recognize that the usual frustrations apply here. First, in virtually all cases, complete information is not present. This makes drawing conclusions more difficult—one consequence of the real-world nature of cases. Lack of information also complicates the task of practicing managers as they face virtually any decision. Second, information may be inconsistent or, worse, contradictory. Here again, the condition is often mirrored in industry. As with managers, it is up to the reader to try to discern how a particular decision or issue is influenced by the weight of the evidence. Finally, class discussion is likely to result in the reader reappraising his or her assessments in light of other students' interpretations of the case. This is to be expected and is part of how case analysis promotes learning.

22

Bank of America and the Carlsbad Highlands Foreclosure (A)

Anne T. Lawrence

Jim Jackson opened the file lying on his desk marked "Carlsbad Highlands." Recently appointed to the position of Vice President, Corporate Real Estate, in Bank of America's Costa Mesa office in Orange County, California, Jackson had the job—as he somewhat delicately put it—of converting bad loans into assets. Bank of America (B of A) was in the business of loaning money, not in the business of marketing real estate. But, when a developer was unable, for whatever reason, to meet payments on a loan, the bank often acquired the property in foreclosure. It was Jackson's job to find the best price he could for these properties, if possible preventing the bank from taking a loss on the loan. His job was to sell real estate—much of it unimproved or partially improved land where a developer's project had somehow gone bad.

The Carlsbad Highlands property did not look promising. The upper left-hand corner was stamped "IN FORECLOSURE." He quickly skimmed the case file and appraiser's report forwarded to him by the bank's loan department.

●

The story was plain enough, if painful in its details. The 263-acre property in the foothills north of San Diego had been acquired by a developer in the mid-1980s with a five percent downpayment and a $6.8 million loan from B of A. At the time of acquisition, the property had been approved for 740 single-family homes. The developer had been preparing to begin construction when, in 1989, the bubble burst in the Southern California housing market, lowering the probable market value of the homes.

Compounding the developer's problems, the City of Carlsbad, where the parcel was located, had imposed a requirement that the developer construct a two-mile extension to an existing road, Cannon Road. The developer had planned to share the construction costs with neighboring developments, but these had not proceeded as anticipated, leaving the entire roadbuilding cost on his shoulders.

But the final blow to the project had been not the market downturn or infrastructure requirements, but an environmental problem. In March, 1993, the U.S. Fish and Wildlife Service (USFWS) listed the California gnatcatcher—a small, grayish bird with a call like a kitten's meow—as a "threatened" species under the Endangered Species Act of 1973. The gnatcatcher lived exclusively in the coastal sage scrub ecosystem—a mixture of sagebrush, cactus, and buckwheat that used to dominate much of coastal southern California. Under the pressure of relentless development, coastal sage scrub had dwindled to less than 400,000 fragmented acres between Los Angeles and the Mexican border. The USFWS, under law, had authority to block development that encroached on gnatcatcher habitat. Unhappily for its would-be developer, Carlsbad Highlands was about 40 percent coastal sage scrub—and, moreover, connected two other parcels of prime gnatcatcher habitat, thus forming an ecologically significant corridor. Since the development plan had been approved ten years earlier, it had not been designed to be sensitive to gnatcatcher habitat. Now, the U.S. Fish and Wildlife Service would surely not approve the necessary grading.

In July, 1993, just two months after the gnatcatcher listing, the beleaguered developer had finally thrown in the towel on the project and walked away from the loan, and the bank was left holding the property.

Now, just days later, Jackson's eye scanned down the appraiser's report to the bottom line: APPRAISED VALUE: $112,000. One hundred and twelve thousand dollars on a loan of almost seven million dollars! A native of San Diego, Jackson had had many years of experience as a land developer before coming to the bank, and he was all too familiar with the ups—and, more recently, downs—of the California land market. But the figures on Carlsbad Highlands were shocking even to his experienced eyes.

Within a few minutes, Jackson found himself in the car, driving south along the Pacific in Route 5, then turning up into the hills above the coastal city of Carlsbad. His route took him by several recent housing developments of the type planned for Carlsbad Highlands—compact communities of expensive, white stucco homes with red tile roofs, in the Mediterranean style favored by 1990s California homebuyers.

About five miles up, Jackson got out of his car and started hiking across the property. Much of the land was covered with unprepossessing, low-lying khaki-colored scrub—the kind preferred by the gnatcatcher, although Jackson could not see or hear any birds. Examining the

land carefully as he walked, Jackson could see the remnants of an old irrigation system, installed by an earlier owner who had used part of the property for farming tomatoes. Up ahead, the land had been torn up by dirt bikers, who had left broken vegetation and tire marks in their wake. To the east, the property line was marked by new subdivision housing, lying just over the border in the City of Oceanside. Their utilities could be extended, Jackson thought, if the cities would sign an agreement. To the west, the designated source of utilities, there was no development for a mile or more. Below and some five miles to the west, Pacific Ocean swells broke against the shore.

"If I had $112,000 in my pocket, I'd buy this property myself," Jackson mused to himself as he walked back to his car. "This property has got to be worth more than that, even if all you wanted to do with it was build a single ranch house and keep some horses up here. The view alone is worth that much."

BANK OF AMERICA'S ENVIRONMENTAL STRATEGY

Bank of America, the reluctant owner of the Carlsbad Highlands property, was unusual in the financial services industry in its commitment to corporate social responsibility as well as its sensitivity to environmental issues. Founded in 1904 in San Francisco by A. G. Giannini, the Bank of Italy—as B of A was then known—was committed to serving the unmet banking needs of California's immigrants and working classes. Throughout its history, the bank had tended to seek out unconventional opportunities for growth. Richard M. Rosenberg, who became chairman and CEO in 1989, characterized the bank's philosophy as the belief that "conventional wisdom is just that—predictable at best . . . not very interesting . . . and frequently wrong." The most effective strategy, he stated, was one that met "the rising expectations among our larger universe of stakeholders who believe that business should actively address the social challenges of our time."[1]

In March, 1990, Rosenberg formed an environmental task force, comprised of 30 top officers, charged with developing an environmental strategy. In part, this initiative reflected the new CEO's own values. A committed environmentalist, Rosenberg had met with representatives of the Environmental Defense Fund shortly before taking office to share ideas about the bank's environmental stewardship. In part, it reflected the bank's officers' perception of heightened stakeholder activism. The Exxon Valdez oil spill in 1989 had caused a public outcry, and shareholder activists had called on businesses to adopt a voluntary code of environmental responsibility, later known as the CERES (Coalition for Environmentally Responsible Economies) Principles. In late 1989, the Corporate Secretary had warned the CEO that the bank could become the target of a shareholder proxy election campaign, focused on environmental issues. Now, preparations for the 20th anniversary of Earth Day in April, 1990, had once more cast a spotlight on "green" concerns.

Bank executives clearly also saw environmentalism as an opportunity for competitive advantage. Since the mid-1980s, courts had held lending institutions liable for environmentally contaminated property, increasing credit risk. In the late 1980s, B of A had begun systematic environmental risk assessment before approving credit applications. The bank had established and staffed an Environmental Services Department, charged with assessing possible environmental liabilities of assets or real estate pledged as collateral against proposed loans. The active work of this group had succeeded in reducing the number of loans with environmental problems.

Rosenberg's environmental task force, working with a consultant—SRI International—produced a set of nine principles. These principles (Figure 1) were approved by the Board of Directors in December, 1990, making Bank of America the first major U.S. financial institution to adopt an explicit policy on environmental issues. To implement these principles, the bank established a full-time unit, the Department of Environmental Policies and Programs (DEPP), headed by senior vice president Richard Morrison, a well-

FIGURE 1 ● Bank of America's Environmental Principles

BankAmerica pledges to conduct business in a manner consistent with the following environmental principles:

1 BankAmerica will follow responsible environmental practices in all of its operations and places of business.

2 BankAmerica will make the environmental responsibilities displayed by customers and suppliers a factor in all relevant business decisions.

3 BankAmerica will solicit advice and technical expertise in the development and

management of its environmental programs and practices.

4 BankAmerica will make a special effort to identify businesses and organizations that are attempting to find solutions to environmental problems and provide appropriate support.

5 BankAmerica will provide employees and retirees with information regarding environmental issues in order to help them make informed decisions.

6 BankAmerica will expand its recycling, energy and waste management programs.

7 BankAmerica will recognize and reward employees for actions that support these principles.

8 BankAmerica will periodically assess its performance in identifying and addressing environmental issues.

9 BankAmerica is committed to improving the understanding of the full social impact of government and business actions that affect the environment and the economy.

Reprinted by permission.

respected officer with 25 years of line experience. To support the work of the unit, the bank created a 14-person environmental "team" consisting of top bank officials who remained in their functional and geographic organizations, where they were responsible for implementation. "Environmentalism at Bank of America is not a central staff function," Morrison commented. "It is the responsibility of the major line and staff departments."[2]

The Department immediately set about operationalizing the nine principles. Its first efforts, in Morrison's words, were "getting our own act together." The bank initiated internal programs to reduce consumption; recycle paper, plastic, and metals; and conserve water. Morrison's department staff worked with purchasing to buy recycled products where possible. They also worked with the Environmental Services Department to broaden pre-loan assessments to examine environmental benefits as well as costs. As Morrison put it, the objective was to "try harder to make an environmentally beneficial deal bankable [as well as] deny . . . credit to borrowers who show a blatant disregard for the environment."[3]

By its third year of operation—1993—Morrison's department had formulated four goals (Appendix A). On the first three—minimize environmental impact, enhance employee and public awareness, and clean air and water—the bank had already made significant progress. The fourth goal, however, represented a new challenge:

> Goal 4: Encourage activity that respects preservation of natural habitats and biological diversity

The bank had begun to address this goal in its loans to companies in the forest products industry of the Pacific Northwest, where it had worked with a consultant to evaluate whether or not a company's practices were consistent with sustainable harvesting. Beyond this, however, Morrison's department had made little progress in operationalizing the fourth goal.

By the time the Carlsbad Highlands foreclosure landed on Jim Jackson's desk, the Bank of America had clearly established itself as the leading environmental activist among U.S. banks and had established a goal, in principle, of promoting habitat protection and biodiversity. Few people in the bank, however, had given much thought to how this lofty aim would be implemented, or what it might mean to troops in the field like Jackson.

THE ENDANGERED SPECIES ACT AND PROPERTY RIGHTS

The Endangered Species Act (ESA)—under which the California gnatcatcher had been listed—was passed by Congress in 1973 to conserve species of fish and wildlife threatened with extinction and the habitats on which they depended. Under the law, the Department of the Interior (through its subdivision, the USFWS) was required to make a list of threatened and endangered species, to designate critical habitat, and to devise plans for the species' recovery. Under the law's "taking" provision, it was illegal to "harass, harm, pursue, hunt, shoot, wound, kill, trap, capture, or collect" a threatened or endangered species, or "to attempt to engage in any such conduct." The term "taking" was interpreted to include modifying habitat in a way that would injure or harm a protected species. Violations of the law were subject to both civil and criminal penalties.

Two provisions of the Act gave the Department of the Interior broad powers to conserve land. The first, the "jeopardy clause," stated that federal agencies could not authorize, fund, or carry out any actions that would jeopardize an endangered or threatened species or modify critical habitat. In effect, this clause gave Interior power not only to limit the uses of public lands such as national forests, but also to cut off federal funding for projects, such as roads, dams, or military contracts, that would modify habitat. In an important decision, the Supreme Court in 1978 blocked completion of the Tellico Dam (a Tennessee Valley Authority project) because it would flood a portion of the Little Tennessee River, the last remaining habitat of an endangered fish called the snail darter. The court ruled that the intent of the Endangered Species Act had been "to halt and reverse the trend toward species extinction, whatever the cost," and that the law did not include any mechanism for weighing the relative value of a particular species—in this case, the snail darter—against that of economic development—the dam. (Tellico was later completed, after Congress passed a special exemption for the project.)

But the law had important significance for private landowners, as well. The "taking" provision of the law was generally interpreted by Interior and by the courts as preventing private property owners from modifying their own land, if doing so would degrade habitat and disrupt important behavior patterns, such as nest-building. The law often had the effect, therefore, of reducing the market value of land that included endangered species' habitat. Property owners with a sensitive species on their land had a perverse incentive to destroy habitat—or even to kill the species—*before* it was listed, so that the owner's use of the property would not be impaired. In the words of David Howard, an officer of a property rights group known as the Alliance for America, many landowners had come to the conclusion that "the answer is often SSS—short for 'shoot, shovel, and shut up.'"[4]

During the 1970s and 1980s, various mechanisms had evolved in other environmental protection laws to accommodate private landowners with impacted property. Most common was the practice of case-by-case mitigation. For example, under the Clean Water Act, development of wetlands was strictly controlled. But landowners could apply for "dredge-and-fill" permits. These were often granted, subject to the landowner's agreement to mitigate the impact—for example, by leaving some of the wetlands undeveloped, buying and setting aside wetlands somewhere else, or paying a fee to support conservation efforts.

Not all affected stakeholders, however, were happy with this solution. Environmentalists were concerned that case-by-case mitigation tended to produce small, fragmented parcels of habitat, where species would be vulnerable to predators and isolated from others of their kind. They preferred larger, contiguous preserves, inhabited by larger populations, that could be actively managed. For their part, developers were aggravated by delays, uncertainty, and contradictory rulings by different regulatory authorities. In some cases, developers were actually required to purchase property for mitigation—land they otherwise had no interest in owning. The system also burdened regulators, who confronted a stream of discrete permit requests without an overall plan to guide individual decisions.

In 1982, Congress amended the Endangered Species Act to address the emerging conflict between habitat conservation and land development. Section 10 established a new mechanism, the habitat conservation plan, or HCP. An HCP was intended to be a comprehensive, regional plan to conserve habitat for one or more listed species, negotiated in a collaborative process by a range of affected stakeholders, including developers, environmentalists, and regulators. If the U.S. Fish and Wildlife Service approved an HCP, the agency could issue an "incidental taking permit," allowing some development to proceed in an endangered species' habitat if part of a pre-approved, area-wide conservation plan. HCPs were praised for "adding flexibility . . . and promoting compromise and negotiated settlements between the development and environmental communities."[5] HCPs were also superior to the case-by-case mitigation used in wetlands regulation because they allowed, in principle at least, for regional conservation planning.

Despite their apparent advantages, few HCPs were negotiated during the 1980s. One successful application of the HCP process occurred near San Francisco, where landowners seeking to build on San Bruno Mountain—home to the federally-listed mission blue butterfly— were able to negotiate with regulators a plan that allowed some development to proceed, while setting aside large sections of the property for butterfly habitat. Two other HCPs were approved in the 1980s, both also in California. Other habitat planning efforts were initiated, all in regions of the country that had both endangered species and strong real estate markets. In the "hill country" west of Austin, Texas; in the wetlands near Disney World in Orlando, Florida; and in the pine barrens of southeastern New Jersey, for example, stakeholders attempted to negotiate regional conservation plans. By 1992, however, none of these efforts had yet reached a successful conclusion. Some observers cited a lack of funding for habitat acquisition. Others pointed to a lack of support from the Reagan and Bush administrations, which some said "seemed to encourage conflicts as a means for building support from property owners, timber companies, and farmers to weaken the (endangered species) act."[6]

The Clinton administration, by contrast, moved aggressively to promote the habitat conservation plan model. In April, 1993, barely three months after taking office, President Clinton convened a well-publicized "forest conference" in Portland, Oregon, at which he attempted to bring together adversaries in the long-simmering controversy over the spotted owl to negotiate what was, in effect, a habitat conservation plan. Two weeks later, Clinton's Secretary of the Interior, Bruce Babbitt, seemed to signal the Administration's intentions when he announced that the government had negoti-

ated a plan with Georgia Pacific Corporation. The timber company had agreed to restrict logging on about 50,000 acres inhabited by the protected red-cockaded woodpecker; in exchange, the government had pledged not to use the ESA to curtail logging elsewhere on the company's timberlands in the southeastern states. This kind of negotiated settlement, Babbitt told the press, was the only way to avoid "the environmental and economic train wrecks we've seen in the past decade."[7]

DEVELOPMENT AND CONSERVATION PLANNING IN SAN DIEGO COUNTY

San Diego County, the site of Jim Jackson's problem, had all the ingredients of such a "train wreck." During the 1980s, the California population grew from 24 million to 30 million—a growth rate of 25 percent, among the highest in the industrial world. Half the state's people lived in the corridor from Los Angeles south to the Mexican border. San Diego County itself had grown by 35 percent during this decade, adding 647,300 residents. More people created tremendous pressure for the conversion of open land. During the 1980s, the amount of developed land (housing, commercial, and industrial) in the urbanized coastal cordon, where most people lived, increased by 24 percent.

The San Diego region was also unusually rich in natural biological diversity, with many species pushed to the brink by relentless development. Its wide variety of topography, climate, and soils had created many unique habitats, including beaches and dunes, coastal sage scrub, oak woodlands, montane coniferous forest, and desert. By the early 1990s, the USFWS had listed over 70 species in southern California (including 24 in the San Diego region) as threatened or endangered, and was considering adding over 300 more. In fact, a representative of the Nature Conservancy, writing in the early 1990s, called California the "epicenter of extinction in the continental United States."[8] Among the better known listed species in the San Diego area were the California gnatcatcher, the brown pelican, the golden eagle, and the mountain lion.

In 1991, California Governor Pete Wilson—a former mayor of San Diego who was familiar with the problems faced by developers there—and proposed a Natural Communities Conservation Program (NCCP) for the state. Intended as a kind of state version of the HCP, the NCCP aimed to develop habitat conservation plans that would simultaneously satisfy both the state's Department of Fish and Game (responsible for enforcing the state's own endangered species laws) and the USFWS. San Diego County's coastal scrub sage ecosystem was selected as the first pilot program.

Under the auspices of the NCCP, San Diego in 1991 initiated a multi-tiered regional planning process. The overall effort was directed by the San Diego Association of Governments (SANDAG), a regional agency. SANDAG began development of a comprehensive, regional multiple-species conservation plan and, subsumed under it, three sub-regional plans. One of these, the North County Multiple Habitat Conservation Program (MHCP), included the city of Carlsbad and the Carlsbad Highlands property. City of Carlsbad officials, like some other local jurisdictions, were also developing their own proposal, to be incorporated into the larger plans. The goal of this complex, multi-layered process was to develop a habitat conservation plan for the entire region that would successfully balance economic and environmental objectives. Proponents hoped, moreover, that the effort would facilitate development by removing regulatory uncertainty and minimizing the likelihood of future endangered species listings.

The San Diego effort, not surprisingly, attracted Secretary Babbitt's attention as a potential model for the rest of the nation. In an interview in *Rolling Stone* in July, 1993, Babbitt said of NCCP:

This experiment . . . is breathtaking in its magnitude. . . . The question is, can we invoke the land-use planning power of local communities, the enforcement power of the Endangered Species Act, and the framework of the state government to pull this off? . . . I think it's going to work.[9]

By the summer of 1993, however, this "breathtaking experiment" was still in its early stages. In the northern part of San Diego County, the working group was still busy trying to inventory biological resources and to draft a map of a workable system of preserves, consisting of parcels of high quality habitat and connecting corridors. There was still no good mechanism for paying for the preserves, and the plan was several years away from federal and state regulatory approval.

CONSIDERING THE OPTIONS

Over the next few days, Jackson began sketching out the bank's options for the Carlsbad Highlands property. The appraiser had been legally required to report a value on the land's "highest and best" use, which the appraiser judged to be speculation. Considering that the property's use for home development was compromised by the endangered species listing, the appraiser had assigned a rock-bottom estimate. The appraiser was probably right, Jackson thought, that the likelihood that the property would be approved for a big housing development any time soon was slim. However, a speculator might be willing to assume that risk or to buy at a low price and hold the land until it could be developed.

Considerable political uncertainty surrounded the Endangered Species Act and its enforcement. Clinton's Interior Secretary strongly supported the ESA and the concept of habitat conservation planning, and the federal courts had generally supported this position. However, some property rights groups had clamored for repeal or revision of the Act, and they had the ear of important Republicans in Congress. A political shift in Washington could change the risk equation significantly.

The land must have some conservation value, Jackson thought. But who would buy it? Was there a market for gnatcatcher habitat? Investigating further, Jackson learned that the 109 acres to the north of the property had been purchased within the past year by a developer as mitigation property. The buyer had paid a little over $1.4 million. However, this parcel had contained high quality coastal sage scrub and several documented pairs of nesting California gnatcatchers. A survey of the Carlsbad Highlands property had turned up only one pair of birds. Jackson's property probably was not worth as much, even if he could find a willing buyer.

Working the phones, Jackson learned that Caltrans, the California state transportation agency, was building a freeway in the City of Oceanside, a project that impacted coastal sage scrub. The USFWS had required that the agency buy 83 acres of coastal scrub elsewhere as mitigation, under the terms of a permit Caltrans had negotiated. Jackson soon had Caltrans on the phone. He described the property in detail. Were they interested? The Caltrans officer sounded discouraged. The agency was actively shopping for coastal sage scrub for mitigation, but the USFWS was very particular about what was acceptable and what was not. "Of course we're interested. But I doubt the feds would approve the Carlsbad Highlands property," the official responded glumly. "It doesn't have enough birds."

Agricultural development was a final possibility. The property had most recently been used for farming tomatoes, and Jackson had observed a rudimentary irrigation system in place that could be repaired and brought back into service. A farmer might be willing to pay up to $8,000 an acre, Jackson figured. His initial inquiries generated some promising leads. Within a few weeks, one farmer had made a formal offer of $1 million for the property, contingent on obtaining a permit to build a ranch house. The City of Carlsbad seemed favorable, since sale to a farmer would provide an intermediate use for the property until housing development would again become feasible. Without housing on the property, the City would never be able to afford improvements to Cannon Road. The farmer's offer was the best one on the table, Jackson thought. Perhaps the bank ought to accept it.

APPENDIX A: BANK OF AMERICA'S ENVIRONMENTAL GOALS

Goal 1: Help generate sustainable economic prosperity with minimum adverse impact on the environment.

Goal 2: Enhance awareness among employees, customers, and the public about environmental issues.

Goal 3: Encourage economic activity that upholds high standards for clean air and water.

Goal 4: Encourage economic activity that respects preservation of natural habitats and biological diversity.

Notes

1.   Rosenberg, Richard M., "Banking on the New America," speech delivered at the University of California, Berkeley, December 14, 1994, p. 2.

2.   Morrison, Richard, "Developing an Environmental Strategy in the Financial Services Industry," speech delivered at the University of California, Irvine, Graduate School of Management, November 1, 1991, p. 10.

3.   Ibid., p. 10.

4.   *Fortune,* "Environmentalists Are on the Run," September 19, 1994, p. 103.

5.   Timothy Beatley, "Preserving Biodiversity Through the Use of Habitat Conservation Plans," in Douglas R. Porter and David A. Salvesen, *Collaborative Planning for Wetlands and Wildlife,* Washington D.C.: Island Press, 1995, p. 57.

6.   "Accord Is Reached to Aid Forest Bird," *New York Times,* April 16, 1993.

7.   "Interior Secretary Is Pushing a New Way to Save Species," *New York Times,* February 17, 1993.

8.   Sally W. Smith, "Wildlife and Endangered Species: In Precipitous Decline," in Palmer, Tim, ed., *California's Threatened Environment: Restoring the Dream,* Washington D.C.: Island Press, 1993, p. 227.

9.   Interview with Bruce Babbitt, *Rolling Stone,* July, 1993.

23

Pacific Lumber Company[1]
Michael V. Russo and
Cindy Noblitt

TRADITIONS AND FORESTRY PRACTICES
AT PACIFIC LUMBER COMPANY

Pacific Lumber Company was the final destination of a circuitous journey that brought Simon Jones Murphy from Penobscot, Maine, to Scotia, California. As he moved west in search of new timber resources, Murphy's Irish roots seemed to bring him luck. While logging in Minnesota, he discovered iron ore beneath the trees; ranches he purchased in Arizona turned out to be sitting atop huge copper deposits.[2]

The redwoods of northwest California caught Murphy's eye next. At the time, redwood trees carpeted much of the coastal hills of northern California and southern Oregon. It was not unusual for the oldest redwoods to measure 15 feet across at their base and to have been seeded in the Middle Ages. Coast redwoods, the world's tallest living things, often soared to over 300 feet.[3] Coveted for their wood, which was rot-resistant, often knot-free, and strong enough for construction, they were felled with abandon during the late 1800s and early 1900s. The first to fall were stands within reach of San Francisco. Attention then turned to the dense forests of these giants that stood to the north, whose bounty fed sawmills as railroads gradually linked mills and forests. To gain a toehold, Murphy first purchased a number of small logging railroad lines near Eureka, California. By trading these lines to the Southern Pacific Railroad, he won his prize, a lumber mill and town surrounded by over 100,000 acres of virgin redwood trees.[4] In 1905, Pacific Lumber Company was founded and incorporated in Murphy's home state of Maine.

The company remained the province of the Murphy clan until late in its life, when Gene Elam's ascendancy as chief executive officer in 1982 marked the first hiring of a top manager without strong ties to the Murphys. Before that time, the company owed its sustenance to two key policies instituted by A. Stanwood (Stan) Murphy, who assumed the president's position in 1931 at the age of 39.[5] At the time, Pacific Lumber engaged in clearcutting, a practice wherein large sections of forest were completely cut and cleared. Murphy's first policy was to end clearcutting and instead to cut "selectively," harvesting no more than 70 percent of the mature trees in a stand. There were key environmental advantages to this practice, which allowed the remaining trees to stabilize the often-steep hillsides on which they remained and more rapidly regenerate the forest. Murphy was also cognizant of the westward movement of other lumber companies. Driven by their own rapid rate of cutting to seek new forests to exploit, they had sawed their way to the country's west coast. Murphy felt that these companies would never reduce their cut rate, even as their own resources were depleted. Murphy decided instead to cut only at the rate at which the forest could regenerate itself, in theory achieving a perpetual harvest called a "sustained yield." To the extent that other companies overharvested, such a strategy would only increase the value of his holdings over time.

Scotia, California, was Pacific Lumber's center of operations. The combination of sustained yield practices and the geographical isolation of Scotia created an insular world. The entire town was owned by Pacific Lumber, down to the rows of small bungalows that housed workers and their families. Lovingly portrayed in 1951 as "Paradise with a Waiting List," the town had two families waiting to live in company housing for every family then in town.[6] The polar opposite of prototypical mill towns that had suffered through cycles of boom and bust, Scotia had a steady population of roughly 1,000; a hotel; a theater; and a number of other businesses established to serve the residents. Within this setting, Stan Murphy had become a legendary figure, the patriarch of a company that wore its paternalism on its corporate sleeve. A well-respected leader, he never wavered in his commitment to Pacific Lumber or to Scotia. Pacific Lumber "lost money on the town," but considered the investment essential to a happy workforce.[7] In 1969, at a companywide party to celebrate Pacific Lumber's hundredth year, he promised that "we will never, ever, sell Pacific Lumber." Riotous applause erupted.[8]

Stability was a hallmark of the workforce, with multiple generations of the same family often working side by side. This constancy offered the luxury of a long-term perspective. In 1971, Corky Kemp, a 24-year-old timekeeper in the machine shop, said, "I got 41 years to go, and I can't see any reason I'd leave."[9] Workers were not unionized, but received raises matching those negotiated by unions representing mill workers at nearby operations.[10] A scholarship plan guaranteed each worker's child substantial support in meeting college tuition. Those who could handle the small-town atmosphere found Scotia a nearly ideal place to live and work. All this was aided by an absence of the trappings of hierarchy: almost no workers wore ties, and all employees at Scotia greeted each other by first name. Mutuality was also bolstered by actions taken during downturns. During a period of slack lumber demand in the 1970s, Pacific Lumber workers went to a four-day work week to avoid layoffs.[11]

In an industry marked by severe environmental impacts, dominated by firms that routinely battled environmentalists in court, Pacific Lumber stood out as an exception. In a 1982 documentary, *Mad River: Hard Times in Humboldt County,* the entire wood products industry was taken to task for poor business management, abuse of workers, and wholesale destruction of forest resources. Yet Pacific Lumber was held up as "proof that good business and good citizenship could, with wise management, go hand in hand."[12] Indeed, by the 1980s, Pacific Lumber controlled most of the nation's remaining privately owned virgin redwood stands. Its sustainability would be enhanced when its new on-site power plant, designed to burn wood chips to produce electricity, went on line.

THE ECOLOGY OF OLD-GROWTH FORESTS[13]

Old-growth forests represent unique ecosystems which have evolved over millions of years into specialized habitats for numerous plant and animal species. In the tropics and in temperate areas, forests perform valuable ecological functions that maintain the planet's life-support systems. In temperate areas of the Northwest, remaining old-growth stands protect and regulate water supplies, support healthy fish populations, anchor unstable steep slopes, and provide a home for many old growth–dependent species, such as the spotted owl and the marbled murrelet. Now an endangered species, the marbled murrelet makes a hollow in moss and other debris accumulated on high branches of old-growth trees instead of building a nest.[14]

An old-growth forest is characterized by a multistory canopy of various species of trees at different stages of growth. Once an established forest of dominant Douglas fir or coast redwood grows large enough to shade out other vegetation, shade-tolerant species such as the western hemlock or cedar thrive. It may take 350 years for an old-growth forest to reach its prime of growth and diversity. The temperate old-growth forests of the Pacific Northwest are unusually rich in wildlife for their latitude. They are able to hold vast amounts of moisture so that flooding is moderated and the forests are not devastated by fire.

Along the edges of forests, such as where forest meets river, abundant wildlife can be found. These areas receive more sunlight and support plants that many of the animals use for food, such as berries eaten by black bears or willow leaves coveted by blacktail deer. These animals rely on the cover and shelter that the forest furnishes. Predators like the gray fox and bobcat prey on small mammals such as brush rabbits and deer mice. Amphibians, such as the Pacific tree frog or the yellow-legged frog, are able to live in the pure streams flowing through the forests.[15] Biodiversity thrives.

In life and in death, every piece of organic matter contributes to the complex web of interrelationships that bind plants and wildlife together in mutually supportive and cooperative roles. The old-growth forests of the Northwest contain the highest accumulations of dead standing and fallen trees.[16] When a tree finally succumbs to age or a windstorm and falls to the ground, it begins a new life as a log. The downed log serves as homes for many animals. Many plants will take root and grow on these logs, which become spongy and thick with water as they gradually decompose. As a log rots, it releases nutrients to the soil and to other plants. Decomposers, such as banana slugs, redwood snails, and numerous kinds of fungi, begin to break down the leaves into nutrients which will be leached back into the soil by the rain. These nutrients can then be used by other trees and plants.[17]

Small mammals, such as red tree voles,

bats, flying squirrels, chipmunks, and squirrels, find shelter in the trees. The standing dead trees, or snags, serve as places for birds to nest. Ospreys along the river build their nests on the tops of these spiketop trees, where they will have a view of the river. Spotted owls use snags as nest sites as well.[18]

THE UNIQUE REDWOOD FOREST ECOSYSTEM

Coastal redwoods (*Sequoia sempervirens*) were a dominant tree of the Western Hemisphere in the days of the dinosaur. Now their range is restricted to a narrow coastal redwood belt, extending 500 miles up the coast from central California to southern Oregon and almost never more than 30 miles wide.[19] Redwoods thrive in the fog belt along the Pacific Coast, from Monterey County in mid-California to the southernmost area of southwest Oregon, in a range that varies in width from 10 to 40 miles, although its north-south continuity is broken in several places.[20] With less than 4 percent of the original 2 million acres of redwood forest that covered the West Coast when Europeans arrived still standing, the remaining redwood ecosystem is severely fragmented.

Redwoods (and sequoias) have evolved a number of unique characteristics. They are one of the plant world's most efficient practitioners of photosynthesis and can grow in spots where only 1 percent of the incoming sunlight ever makes it down to the leaves. Because most of their bulk is contained in their trunk and because they grow arrow-straight, the trees can get very tall yet still remain stable. Aiding balance is a network of roots on all sides. Measuring 50 feet in each direction, it anchors trees firmly into the ground. These roots are intertwined with the roots of other trees and plants within the area to further stabilize the trees.[21]

Redwoods require vast amounts of water daily—at least 300 gallons in a 24-hour period. An extraordinary network of vertical capillaries moves this water, 2,500 pounds worth, from the roots to the leaves. Hundreds of these tiny passageways fill every square inch of the wapwood, each only a few cells wide but hundreds of feet long.[22] The region receives large amounts of rainfall during parts of the year, but during dry spells or droughts, redwoods quench their thirst on the fog that moves inland from the coast. Through a phenomenon known as "fog drip," sea fog condenses on the trees' foliage and is steadily absorbed through the needles or falls to the ground as raindrops. In especially wet periods, a single tree can also release up to 500 gallons of moisture into the air per day.[23]

Through these processes, a coastal redwood forest creates its own localized climate, on which the other plant and animal life associated with a redwood forest depends. The redwoods influence the climate of the river canyons by transpiring moisture, which keeps the humidity high.[24] Temperature extremes are moderated. The forests stay cool in the summer and warmer in the winter than surrounding open areas. Pure stands of redwood exist naturally, but more commonly redwood forests contain numerous other species like Douglas fir, Sitka spruce, Port-Orford cedar, grand fir, western hemlock, western red cedar, California laurel, tanoak, red alder, bigleaf maple, and torreya.[25] The red tree vole and the northern flying squirrel live in the forest canopy. Under the canopy, animals such as bats and birds find shelter in the bark of the trees. In the water, river otters hunt for fish. Steelhead (sea-run rainbow trout), salmon (Coho and Chinook), California roach, and the nonnative Sacramento squawfish eat the many insects in the water.[26] Redwood forests are complex ecosystems of which the giant trees are just one component.

Redwoods may be killed by windthrow, floods, or fire. But when these trees are alive and healthy, they are remarkably resistant to the natural forces that tend to kill other trees. Many insects and fungi are repelled by the high level of bitter tannic acid in the bark of live trees. The bark can be up to a foot thick, which provides the tree with excellent insulation from fires. Floods, which deposit soil around the base of the trees, do not smother the roots of redwoods as they can those of other trees. Instead, redwoods can grow new roots up into the newly deposited soil.[27]

Fire plays an important role in the ecology of a redwood forest and has historically been a natural part of the cycle of life. Every quarter-century or so, a big fire burns some sections of the forest, with subsequent beneficial consequences for the redwoods, for other plants and animals, and for the Native Americans who once lived in the region.[28]

Low-intensity fires clear away undergrowth and material that has accumulated on the ground, opening clear areas on the forest floor and allowing seeds to germinate on clear soil. The ash from the burned material provides nutrients for the soil. Periodic fires burn off downed limbs and small trees. If these are not burned off, the material will accumulate to a dangerous level and create a fuel ladder which may allow a fire to spread to the crowns of the trees.[29] The increased sunlight on the forest floor creates an opportunity for other plants to grow—plants that provide food and shelter for wildlife. This cleared ground also gives redwood seeds a place to grow. Because approximately 90 percent of all redwood seeds are killed by fungus before they ever sprout, having a cleared place to grow increases their chances of survival.[30] Sprouting, in which new shoots come up from trees damaged or killed by logging or fire, is also an important method of reproduction for redwoods. The redwood is the only western conifer that will stump-sprout, making this an important method of natural regeneration.[31] Although redwoods produce copious amounts of cones, each containing 90 to 150 seeds, many seeds are empty, and normal redwood germination rates are as low as 3 to 10 percent. Additionally, few seedlings survive beyond the first three years, and natural regeneration of redwoods is a slow process.[32]

Fire also hollows out the inside of many trees, leaving behind cavernous holes. This does not kill the tree, as the major part burned is the heartwood, the dead wood inside a tree. The only living part of the wood is the cambium, a thin layer between the bark and the heartwood where all growth takes place. This is why trees have growth rings. Each year, a new layer of cells grows and produces a growth ring. Trees damaged by intense or repeated fires are able to sprout new trunks from tissue in their root collars called burl. Burl is bud tissue that remains dormant until some kind of damage occurs to the trunk of the parent tree. When the parent tree is damaged, the burl tissue begins to grow. A tree that has lost its top due to wind can grow a new top in this way. Redwoods also sprout from the base, in much the same way as rose bushes grow suckers. When the trunk is cut off, such as when a tree is logged or burned by fire, the tree will often develop a ring of sprouts around the stump. In areas that were logged many years ago, you can find these rings of trees, called "fairy rings" or "fire rings."

CHARLES HURWITZ, UNWELCOME SUITOR

It was 5:30 A.M. on September 30, 1985, when the phone rang, jolting Gene Elam, Pacific Lumber's CEO, out of a sound sleep. On the other end of the line, a fellow by the name of Charles Hurwitz introduced himself. He was a Texan, in the oil and gas business, and he said his call was a courtesy to Elam. In just a few minutes, he would announce a tender offer to purchase all outstanding shares of Pacific Lumber, and he wanted to fly out to San Francisco immediately to finalize negotiations on a friendly basis. After some apprehension, Elam agreed to meet late

that afternoon. Hurwitz closed the conversation by noting that Elam probably wouldn't need a shower to wake up that morning.[33]

Just who was Charles Hurwitz? In 1985, by the age of 45, he was a man with a personal history dense with financial success—and controversy. The son of a prosperous Kilgore, Texas, businessman, Hurwitz attended the University of Oklahoma and at first worked as a stockbroker. From the start, his sales skills were superlative, and other salesmen would "crowd around his desk, just to hear him work the phones, his drawl softening all the rough edges," until the sale was closed.[34] Yet, despite the professional success he was to enjoy in later life, from the beginning he placed a premium on his personal life and made time for his wife and sons. And he was not ostentatious; while others in the field enjoyed first-class air travel and other perks, he eschewed them.[35]

But Hurwitz was a magnet for litigation, which appeared to mount almost as quickly as his personal fortune. His first brush with the law came in 1971, when the Securities and Exchange Commission (SEC) charged Hurwitz and 40 others with conspiring to inflate the price of a stock.[36] A consent decree resulted. In 1978, Hurwitz was charged with fraud by New York regulators after an insurance company he controlled folded; those charges were later dropped. In the years leading up to the Pacific Lumber buyout, he had grown wealthy by buying undervalued, often poorly managed companies, stripping assets, and improving the bottom line of the remaining divisions.

He began with McCullough Oil in 1978. After taking a substantial position with the company, he was named CEO and returned the energy and real estate concern to profitability—taking control of the corporation as he did so. Hurwitz used McCullough Oil, renamed MCO Holdings, to purchase control of Simplicity Pattern Company in 1982. Hurwitz took control of the second-largest savings and loan company in

Texas, United Financial Group, in 1983, and turned it into an aggressive force in the Texas real estate market. Later that year, however, his umbrella company for these investments, Federated Development, was accused of using arcane methods to "freeze people out" and take Federated private for a fraction of its value.[37] United eventually failed, leaving the federal government with $1.6 billion in uncollectable debts. In 1984, after a run at Castle and Cooke, he was sued for acquiring his stake illegally, but the suit was dropped after Hurwitz accepted a premium for stock he had accumulated. Hurwitz also found himself in court in the early 1980s when he sued the resort city of Rancho Mirage, California, as well as its city council members individually, for trying to stop his plan to build a hotel, housing, and a golf course on a bluff above the town. The city's master plan had precluded building on the skyline, and Hurwitz's tract also invaded areas populated by the rare and protected Santa Rosa peninsular bighorn sheep.[38] Eventually the project moved ahead.

But regardless of his means, under his new umbrella company, Maxxam, Inc., Hurwitz had consolidated a major portfolio of assets by 1985. He bristled at the idea that he was a prototypical corporate raider who was interested in short-term gains. In a 1984 interview, Hurwitz said, "I invest in companies with intrinsic value and, often, where we can offer help. I buy to build, not to sell."[39] Still, questions about his character and litigious background haunted him. *Barron's* said about Hurwitz, "everything he touches seems to turn to litigation."[40] Another source in the investment business later said that Hurwitz's penchant for favoring himself over stockholders had led to Maxxam's stock price reflecting a "Hurwitz discount," due to the risk of Hurwitz's agenda diverging from his shareholders.[41] But both critics and admirers agreed that, in Hurwitz, Pacific Lumber Company had drawn an astute, well-seasoned, and extremely tenacious adversary.

PACIFIC LUMBER COMPANY AS A TARGET

Why did Charles Hurwitz find Pacific Lumber attractive? As with many companies that are viewed as takeover candidates, an argument could be made that the company was undervalued. Perhaps the most obvious indication was that the company really had only a vague idea of how much redwood it actually owned. The last aerial cruise to establish its reserves was undertaken in 1956. The estimate of marketable wood from the 1956 cruise was subsequently adjusted for growth and removal of trees annually, and in 1985 the company estimated that it owned 5.2 billion board-feet of timber.[42] Hurwitz, however, had secretly performed his own cruise, which suggested that the company owned 30 percent more timber and 45 percent more old-growth timber than it thought it had.[43]

A second reason why Pacific Lumber was attractive came from a look at its financial condition. While not wildly profitable, its allure lay in other areas. It had very little long-term debt and was so cash-rich that it was able to repurchase a large number of outstanding shares in 1984. One other aspect caught Hurwitz's eye: its pension fund was grossly overfunded. In fact, cash on hand exceeded expected payouts by at least $50 million.[44] Although Pacific Lumber had seen this as a way of ensuring pensions for its workers regardless of future conditions, a less conservative approach would free up the excess cash to help finance the takeover. A final reason to pursue Pacific Lumber was that several of its business units could be disposed of to help pay for the acquisition. Pacific Lumber had diversified since the late 1960s, in order to "provide a means of achieving real growth in excess of the long-term average growth expected from the company's forest products operations."[45] And though these operations were profitable, they were peripheral to its core business and could easily be spun off.

Still, for Hurwitz to finance the proposed acquisition, no small measure of daring would be necessary.

THE TAKEOVER BATTLE

Although Pacific Lumber's stock had been trading in the $25-per-share range during early 1985, a slow but perceptible rise began early in the summer. This movement had not escaped the scrutiny of Pacific Lumber's executives, whose perfunctory search for the source of the inflation turned up empty.[46] But it was then that Hurwitz began to accumulate shares in Pacific Lumber, using the services and advice of Drexel Burnham Lambert. At the time, Drexel was highly controversial for its role in popularizing the use of high-risk, high-yield bonds, widely referred to as "junk bonds."

Through the summer, Drexel accumulated for Hurwitz purchases in small blocks leading to a roughly $15 million stake in Pacific Lumber. Because going beyond this level of ownership would force Hurwitz to file public documents and expose his intentions, he chose to have further stock purchased for him by Boyd Jeffries, a Wall Street broker. The nature of this provocative agreement was never clarified and became the subject of hearings before Congress on the legality of Hurwitz's role in the takeover.[47] Specifically, accusations that Jeffries had "parked" the stock for Hurwitz under an informal agreement could never be proven. When the stock price had risen into the $33- to $34-per-share range by late summer, this block of stock was for no apparent reason sold to Hurwitz for $19.20 per share.[48]

By late summer, Hurwitz was ready to announce a bid for Pacific Lumber. Just prior to the takeover, however, a significant threat emerged. In the week before Hurwitz was to formally announce his tender offer, the price of Pacific Lumber stock suddenly gyrated higher. On Thursday, September 26, in the last two hours of the session, the stock, which had opened at $29 per share, shot up and closed at $33. Hurwitz, suspecting loose talk, angrily telephoned Drexel but was told that there was no such leak.[49] Yet speculators were onto the deal and were buying the stock in anticipation of a tender offer. They were led by Ivan Boesky, who had made a fortune by purchasing shares of companies just prior to takeover announcements. It would later be revealed that Boesky's timing indeed was too good to be true and that he was trading with inside information. In this case, and in others, suspicions arose that the information was funneled to him directly by Drexel's staff.[50] The spike in the stock price struck fear in Hurwitz, who was preparing a $36-per-share offer for Pacific Lumber. That price now represented a dwindling premium over the market's price. The whole deal could collapse if he was forced to increase his bid substantially to attract shares he did not already control. He dreaded what would happen to the stock price on Friday, certain that Thursday's jump would release a blood scent to Wall Street sharks.

Then fate intervened. Hurricane Gloria, which was to hit New York with gale force winds and rain, forced the closing of the stock market on Friday. Given this reprieve, after phoning Elam, Hurwitz hurriedly finalized and announced his $36 bid on Monday, September 30, increasing it to $38.50 per share later in the week after the stock continued to rise. But would Pacific Lumber's corporate board agree to negotiate with him on a friendly basis?

PACIFIC LUMBER'S RESPONSE

This was a critical question, for Pacific Lumber had defenses against undesired aggression. In 1981, its board had enacted several charter provisions that protected it from unwanted suitors, including one requiring that 80 percent of shareholders approve a hostile takeover.[51] Although such provisions could be attacked legally, and Hurwitz had moved to do so, negotiating his way to a friendly takeover would smooth the process considerably. Pacific Lumber had retained Salomon Brothers, a New York investment house, to represent it in its attempt to remain independent. In the event that the takeover took place anyway, Salomon would continue to represent Pacific Lumber. Under the terms of its agreement, however, Salomon, hired to defend Pacific Lumber, would actually earn substantially higher fees if the takeover proceeded, when it would earn a prespecified percentage of the deal's value.[52]

Ultimately, after several meetings, the board capitulated, accepting a slightly sweetened bid of $40 per share, despite a Salomon Brothers' valuation that set the company's worth "in excess of $60 per share."[53] One reason for this acquiescence was rooted in the arcane legal doctrine surrounding takeovers, the fiduciary responsibilities of board members, and the culpability of board members as individuals. Because they had no idea of the true worth of the company, publicizing the Salomon Brothers estimate of timber holdings would have been "equivalent to pleading guilty to incompetence," "invoking the wrath—and lawsuits—of shareholders."[54] But there was a way for the board members to protect themselves personally: by requiring Hurwitz to indemnify them for subsequent lawsuits. This turned out be prescient, for in the end, the actions of the board did elicit several suits, including one from dissident members of the Murphy family. Eventually, these actions resulted in a $52 million settlement, in which Maxxam agreed to compensate former Pacific Lumber stockholders for the fraud, deception, and breach of fiduciary duties by the Pacific Lumber board during the takeover.[55]

There were other reasons for the board's decision to agree to a friendly acquisition. One was the lack of clear alternatives. Despite its pleas of distress, only one "white knight" emerged, offering only a weakly competitive counteroffer to Hurwitz's.[56] Another reason was the potential value that some board members saw in Hurwitz as an agent for change. For some time, it was hinted that philosophical differences had split the board between allies of the Murphy family, including his widow, and a cadre of newer members, led by Elam, who wanted to revitalize a company that they felt had fallen behind the times.[57] The takeover offered such an opportunity.

The total price tag for Pacific Lumber was $868 million dollars. The transaction was financed almost exclusively with debt. A bridge loan of up to $300 million dollars was arranged with Irving Trust, to cover expenses until some assets could be sold, and roughly $450 of high-yield, or junk, bonds were offered by Drexel Burnham Lambert.[58] The remaining costs would be funded with Maxxam equity and a plan to pull out roughly $50 million from Pacific Lumber's overfunded pension plan. With this plan, a company whose balance sheet showed very little debt was metamorphosed into a risky, highly leveraged enterprise. A pivotal question remained: with interest costs running in the neighborhood of $70 to $90 million annually, and Pacific Lumber's net income running in the $30 to $50 million range historically, how would the debt be serviced? Contemplated sales of assets, including the cutting tools division of Pacific Lumber (eventually sold for $320 million), as well as the sale of its San Francisco office building for $30 million, reduced the debt substantially.[59] But questions still remained.

EMPLOYEE REACTIONS TO THE TAKEOVER

The initial reaction throughout Scotia to Hurwitz's move was surprise, for most workers simply did not understand how someone could buy a company that was not for sale. When the details of the plan came to light, the mood became feisty. Who was this guy from Houston? How could Elam have let Hurwitz pull this stunt? Why, if Stan Murphy was alive when Hurwitz came along, "he would have kicked his ass all the way back to Texas, end of story."[60] Workers signed a petition protesting the takeover and hung Gene Elam in effigy for bowing to Hurwitz.[61] But the deal was consummated, and workers crowded into the Winema Theater in Scotia in late October for the opportunity to see their nemesis, Charles Hurwitz, who had flown in to address them.

After assuring them of his long-term commitment to the company, Hurwitz took questions from the workers filling the redwood-paneled theater. The general thrust of his responses was that little would change, except perhaps a small increase in the rate of cutting. Combining humor with evasion of the more pointed questions, he offered a glimpse of his philosophy by offering his version of the Golden Rule: "Those who have the gold rule." That line drew a roar of laughter from the attendees.[62] Hurwitz's performance, often recounted in the press, marked a turning point in his relationship with the workers. His rehabilitation in their eyes was aided by his commitment to guarantee their wages and benefits for three years. While many of the workers continued to fear the long-term consequences of his actions and profoundly distrusted him, others approved of the prospects for overtime wages and the sustenance of their cherished fringe benefits.

In retrospect, it was easy to understand Hurwitz's guarantees to workers—he needed them. In early 1986, Pacific Lumber moved to increase cash flow from timber operations. The company announced that it would double the redwood harvest on Pacific Lumber lands.[63] The idea was that clearcutting of remaining old-growth redwoods could take place for 20 years, and that rotation of cutting thereafter could be sustained indefinitely. To put this plan into action, Pacific Lumber purchased a nearby sawmill in Carlotta,

California, and invested millions in productivity improvements. But all did not go as planned, for in staffing up to increase the cut, it hired inexperienced loggers who sometimes ruined redwoods through poor cutting and felling techniques.[64]

THE CONTROVERSY OVER CLEARCUTTING

In contemporary times, the most common practice of harvesting conifers such as redwoods has been clearcutting—the total removal of all trees. But this practice can be particularly damaging to a redwood forest, as the sudden exposure causes rapid deterioration of the special forest environment on which redwoods depend. Even residual isolated, mature trees die within 10 to 15 years once this environment is destroyed, weakened through gradual deterioration to the point at which wind can easily blow them down. Formerly, the more common selective harvesting allowed for abundant resprouting from cut redwood stumps and to some extent maintained the essential elements of the protective forest environment.[65]

Mudslides occur more frequently and are much more severe on heavily logged slopes and areas associated with road building. In addition to the economic and sometimes personal losses that flooding and slides incur, critical wildlife habitat is also damaged. The precipitous decline of Coho salmon is due in large part to clearcutting within their habitat. Northern California runs of Coho salmon were recently put on the endangered species list.[66]

The support provided by the root systems of large trees, which hold soil in place, especially on steep mountain slopes, cannot be overstated. The volume of water that the ground can absorb when it is covered with vegetation is also much greater than in a clearcut. Ground cover slows the flow of water, root systems carry it up, and trees transpire moisture into the air. The volume of soil gripped by a coastal redwood's roots is capable of holding more than 130,000 gallons of water.[67] After logging, the roots of the stumps that once were trees gradually decompose over a period of years (around 10 in a Douglas fir forest, closer to 20 for a redwood forest) and lose their ability to hold soil in place. The soil is more quickly saturated, and water not absorbed runs off downhill, causing damaging erosion and the runoff of topsoil. Often the silt and debris run into streams and rivers, damaging critical fish habitat and spawning grounds. The redwood's ability to sprout from stumps has led foresters to believe that slope failure is less likely after a redwood forest is logged than a Douglas fir–dominant forest, but conditions that promote the unique forest environment in which redwoods thrive do not exist after an area is clearcut.

Although slides occur in uncut old-growth as well as on slopes that have been cut over, strong evidence suggests that the risk is dramatically greater for slides emanating from clearcuts or associated with roadbuilding, and that such slides are larger and more severe. The assertion that clearcutting is ecologically comparable to natural disasters such as firestorms has also been made. But expert foresters argue that fires are less frequent, do not damage soils, and do not kill all trees in a stand.[68]

A survey of scientific studies performed to date documents evidence that clearcuts and forest roads are associated with dramatic increases in both the number and the volume of slides relative to natural forest conditions.[69] It shows that landslide rates in clearcut areas average 13 times higher than the background landslide rate observed in forested areas. The volume of soil displaced is also markedly higher.[70]

ENVIRONMENTALIST REACTIONS TO PACIFIC LUMBER'S NEW AGENDA

Pacific Lumber's accelerated harvest deepened suspicions among environmentalists about Hur-

witz's motives. To them, Pacific Lumber, formerly a model wood products company, had metamorphosed into a corporate criminal, responsible for vast destruction of forest ecosystems. A small group of activists associated with the group Earth First! were the first to mobilize.

Earth First! was founded in 1980 by Dave Foreman, a former marine and self-described Barry Goldwater Republican. His establishment of the group, which had no official membership, no dues, and no bylaws (but did circulate its own newsletter), was a response to what he perceived as the enfeeblement of mainstream environmental groups. To him, their keen sense of purpose had been blunted by too many years of compromise with the Washington establishment. Instead, what was needed was a "militant, uncompromising group unafraid to say what was needed to be said or to back it up with stronger actions that the established organizations were unwilling to take."[71] The Earth First! view was that "human life was but one life form on the planet and has no right to take exclusive possession."[72] Said Greg King, one of the leaders of the Earth First! activities against Pacific Lumber: "I don't see much difference between bombing a city and clearcutting an old-growth forest."[73]

Earth First! was willing to take strong, often illegal actions in its campaigns. In fact, Foreman had authored a book, *Ecodefense: A Field Guide to Monkey Wrenching,* which described methods for sabotaging activities of organizations that it considered antienvironment. The most controversial of the tactics ascribed to Earth First! was the practice of tree-spiking, in which long steel spikes were driven into loggable trees. If such spikes, which were not often visible afterward, were encountered during the cutting of the tree, they would destroy the chain saw being used to fell the tree, but more importantly, cause life-threatening danger to the logger when the chain broke loose at high speed. If the spike survived the cut, it would be encountered at the saw mill, where it could maim not only a large saw blade, but possibly nearby mill workers as well. Earth First! claimed that, after spiking trees, it would notify the owners of those forests, to prevent logging. But the practice itself was loathed by loggers.

Its willingness to take such strong, and often illegal, actions made Earth First! extremely controversial. Many of the mainstream environmental groups that it reviled felt that Earth First! tactics went far over the line. Jay Hair, president of the National Wildlife Federation, said, "They are terrorists and they have no right being considered environmentalists."[74] An attorney who argued a case for an Idaho company whose machinery was sabotaged in an Earth First! protest called their activists "modern day gangsters and thugs," after a jury awarded his client $1 million in mostly punitive damages.[75] Nonetheless, the media had taken an interest in Earth First! which broadened the outcry over northwest forests. Later, a number of prodevelopment groups, such as the Yellow Ribbon Coalition, were formed as a way to engage in nonviolent activism and to publicize their side of the story.[76]

In the Pacific Lumber case, the initial Earth First! actions were waged before regulators and in the courts. The first stop in attacking Pacific Lumber plans was to challenge timber harvest plans (THPs) submitted to the California Department of Forestry (DOF) for review. Among other responsibilities, the DOF is charged with assessing the environmental impact of a proposed harvest and the system of roads required to service the cut. Under the structure of California law, if the DOF does not raise an issue with the plan, it is automatically approved. In order to challenge plans in court, anyone wanting to stop a THP must first participate in the hearings held prior to its approval.

When the THP that would cut a key tract of virgin forest, a 4,500-acre grove that came to be known as the Headwaters Forest, was brought up for approval, Earth First! activists decided to bring matters to a head.[77] At the public meetings

they encountered behavior that illustrated how the approval process had become a procedural formality. Exposed to questioning, many experts' cursory review of the plans became clear. In one instance, an expert from the California Department of Fish and Game disagreed with DOF conclusions, arguing that its conclusions about the biological impacts of logging the tract were far too optimistic. Nonetheless, the DOF approved the harvest plan, and although Pacific Lumber decided voluntarily not to log the tracts, a lawsuit to be filed by the environmentalists would challenge the approval.[78]

In early fall of 1987, the case of *EPIC* v. *Maxxam* went to trial. EPIC was the Environmental Protection Information Center, the local organization established by the Earth First! activists. In the trial, a DOF forester stated that he had not conducted a vigorous search for endangered species, but had not seen any in the proposed cut area. Although he claimed to be familiar with those species because he had seen photographs of them, on cross-examination he revealed that he had first seen pictures of several species in the office of the Pacific Lumber attorney, just one week previously.[79] The judge in the case ruled that the THP was illegal, because it violated the California Environmental Quality Act, so that a new plan would have to be filed by Pacific Lumber. However, a side approval to build roads in the area had been approved, and the company later began building preparatory roads in the Headwaters Forest. In 1989, it resubmitted a THP for the area but later voluntarily removed the plans from consideration.

TAKING THE CASE TO CALIFORNIA'S VOTERS

Denied much enduring satisfaction in the regulatory system and the courts, and tired of fighting Pacific Lumber THP by THP, environmentalists decided to take their case for reform directly to the people. A loose affiliation of activists and established environmental groups banded together to collect the 600,000 signatures necessary to place an initiative on the November 1990 California statewide ballot. Officially named the Forest and Wildlife Protection Bond Act of 1990, but popularly known as the Forests Forever initiative, it would have mandated broad and fundamental changes in forest management in the state.

Clearcutting in an area beyond 2.5 acres would have been banned. Under the initiative, all timber harvest plans would have had to include a detailed wildlife survey. The measure would have reformulated the policy-making body of the Department of Forestry, the Board of Forestry, reallocating slots reserved for industry representatives to environmental groups. Companies would have been restricted to cutting no more than 60 percent of the total timber in a stand. Logging roads would have had to have been removed after being taken out of service. Finally, a $750 million bond issue would have funded purchase of forest tracts that enjoyed significant biodiversity.[80]

In the meantime, a small group of Earth First! activists, led by Judi Bari, Darryl Cherney, and Greg King, announced in February 1990 that the coming summer would be "Redwood Summer," a season-long protest over the logging practices of Pacific Lumber. Their aspiration was to draw thousands of protesters to Northwest California, to publicize their struggle with Pacific Lumber and to gain sympathy for their cause. Tensions between environmentalists and loggers heightened, with environmentalists receiving death threats more or less continually. In Oakland, California, in May 1990, a bomb under the driver's seat of a Subaru carrying Darryl Cherney and Judi Bari exploded. Both were severely injured, and Bari nearly died. Although initially prime suspects in the case, the two were exonerated later. The perpetrators have yet to be found, and activities associated with

Cherney and Bari's lawsuit against the FBI continue.[81]

Protests in Northern California turned ugly. Pacific Lumber employees and others began to object much more vociferously about the threat to their livelihood that they felt the environmentalists posed. To them, reduced costs meant fewer hours and losses in personal welfare. They also objected to environmentalists, most of whom they saw as outsiders to the area, trying to impose their values on Pacific Lumber. Antagonism was reaching a fever pitch. Environmentalists distributed posters portraying a small army of stiff-legged ghouls, each resembling Charles Hurwitz, in an effort to dramatize their belief that he would eventually leave Scotia a ghost town. Pacific Lumber responses included distribution by the public relations firm Hill and Knowlton of a flyer that portrayed Earth First! activists advocating tree-spiking as a means to fight for the redwoods. Pacific Lumber's executives were aware, even as the leaflet was being distributed, that it was most likely a fake.[82] The summer culminated in a Labor Day march into a town near Scotia, Fortuna, by 500 environmental activists. When they reached the town's borders, they met a hostile crowd, some armed with baseball bats, some with eggs, paintballs, and rocks.[83] Yet no major violence occurred in Humboldt County, and Redwood Summer concluded quietly.

Meanwhile, the fight to pass the Forest Forever initiative was considerably complicated by the addition of no less than three environmentally oriented initiatives on the California ballot, one of which competed directly with it. The "Global Warming and Clearcutting Reduction, Wildlife Protection, and Reforestation Act of 1990" was an initiative sponsored by the timber industry, written to override the Forests Forever initiative should both be passed by voters. In many respects, the initiative appeared to represent a move toward greater stewardship by companies, but media reports identified numerous loopholes that would significantly weaken its restrictions on clearcutting and wildlife endangerment. An industry attorney disclosed that the initiative's language contained "ambiguities" and "drafting errors"; detractors claimed that it actually could accelerate clearcutting and remove oversight from forestry.[84]

The campaign over the initiatives was riddled with charges of deceptive advertising and sensational estimates about the impacts of the two initiatives. Most of the criticism was targeted at the timber-financed initiative, which received the lion's share of campaign funds divided between the two initiatives. Its media campaign, which the Sierra Club called "a monumental attempt to deceive the voters,"[85] featured widespread messages in which the timber company–sponsored proposition was portrayed as the best way "to protect our ancient redwoods and dwindling forests," and in which the titles of the two initiatives were deliberately transposed.[86] So questionable were the tactics of the consultants hired to support passage of the timber company–sponsored initiatives that, six years later, the *San Francisco Examiner* used the campaign to illustrate the pitfalls of an initiative process that it argued was irreparably flawed.[87]

In November 1990, The Forests Forever initiative lost 52 percent to 48 percent; the timber company–sponsored initiative lost 71 to 29 percent.

THE BATTLE OVER THE HEADWATERS FOREST

Following the 1990 electoral campaign, efforts began to concentrate on saving the Headwaters Forest. After the campaign, the focus shifted to state oversight of forestry. In January 1991, California's Board of Forestry (the parent organization of the DOF) voted 5 to 3 against Pacific Lumber plans to harvest 564 acres deep within the Headwaters Forest, on the grounds that it would negatively impact the marbled murrelet, a rare bird found only in a few coastal forests.[88] Of the roughly 2,000 remaining murrelets, 300 to 500 were estimated to dwell on Pacific Lumber property.[89] But board Chairman Carlton Yee refused to foreclose the possibility of a later harvest plan's being approved, saying that the decision should not "be interpreted by the people here today as the denial of the legal right of Pacific Lumber to harvest timber in that area."[90]

Later in 1991, word began to emerge of a scheme to save the Headwaters Forest through what was essentially a "debt-for-nature" swap. Such deals had begun with developing countries, where debt accrued in financing infrastructure was waived by the major financial institutions in return for the preservation of sensitive environmental lands within those countries. But within America? Although Pacific Lumber claimed to be receptive to such an arrangement, federal officials backed away, for unclear reasons. Perhaps out of exasperation, Maxxam weighed selling Pacific Lumber in late 1994, but could find no buyers among the timber companies to whom the deal was brought. One problem was the price, reportedly $1.0 to 1.2 billion, for all of Pacific Lumber's assets except the Headwaters Forest, which was to be retained for unspecified purposes.[91] Another issue was apprehension about the possibility that environmentalist and government actions would preclude major tracts of Pacific Lumber lands ever being harvested.[92]

For the next several years, ideas came and went, but no definitive plan to preserve the Headwaters Forest emerged. By mid-1995, Pacific Lumber told state forestry officials that it would halt its self-imposed five-year moratorium on approaching the Department of Forestry and Fire Protection, and again asked the Board of Forestry to approve harvest of Headwaters trees. But it also served notice that, in accordance with the California Forest Practices Act, which permitted removal of 10 percent of dead and dying trees, it wished to begin logging operations.[93] This time, logging was stopped when the Clinton administration stepped forward with a more aggressive plan to purchase the forest. This was seen by observers as one way for the president to make environmental amends for signing a law that contained the so-called salvage rider. This law, which allowed limited logging in virtually all national forests—including previously untouchable tracts—was assailed by environmental groups.[94]

A new variant of the debt-for-nature deal was advanced. As noted above, Hurwitz had played a controlling role at the United Financial Group, a failed Texas thrift that had saddled the federal government with $1.6 billion in bad debt. Federal regulators were suing Hurwitz to recoup some of this shortfall and thought that perhaps some forgiveness of debt could be traded for transmittal to public ownership of the Headwaters Forest. Environmentalists saw the deal as a windfall for Hurwitz, who hoped to capture as much as $600 million for the acreage. Critics of the deal pointed out that Clinton and Hurwitz had been photographed together at a Houston fundraiser, and wondered why the federal government hadn't been a tougher negotiator.[95] But this deal, too, fizzled.

LOSING PATIENCE

At this point, Pacific Lumber made public statements that distressed environmentalists greatly. President John Campbell's weariness over the fight to save the Headwaters Forest was clear:

> We've indicated that if people want to buy the Headwaters Forest, we are a willing seller. We've had it set aside for over six years. No one has stepped up to do this, and quite frankly, our patience is a little thin. And it is a very valuable asset of the company, and quite frankly, if they don't do something soon, we are going to move ahead to harvest it for what it's zoned for by the state of California—for timber production.[96]

Was time running out?

Notes

1. This case is intended to be used as a basis for class discussion rather than as an illustration of either effective or ineffective handling of the situation. This case was prepared by Michael V. Russo and Cindy Noblitt. Copyright © 1998 by Michael V. Russo. Reprinted with permission.

2. Frank J. Taylor, "Paradise with a waiting list," *Saturday Evening Post,* 24 February 1951, 36–38, 103–108.

3. Doug Stewart, "Green Giants," *Discover,* April 1990, 61–64.

4. Taylor, "Paradise."

5. David Harris, *The Last Stand* (New York: Times Books, 1995), 18–19.

6. Taylor, "Paradise," 103.

7. Hugh Wilkerson and John Van der Zee, *Life in the Peace Zone* (New York: Collier Books, 1971), 150.

8. Alston Chase, *In a Dark Wood* (Boston: Houghton Mifflin, 1995), 67.

9. Wilkerson and Van der Zee, *Peace Zone,* 49.

10. J. A. Savage, "The Last of the One-Company Towns," *Business and Society Review,* Fall 1984, 27.

11. Ellen Schultz, "A Raider's Ruckus in the Redwoods," *Fortune,* 24 April 1989, 176.

12. Cited in Lisa H. Newton, "Chainsaws of Greed: The Case of Pacific Lumber," in *The Corporation, Ethics, and the Environment,* ed. W. Michael Hoffman, Robert Frederick, and Edward S. Petry, Jr., (New York: Quorum Books, 1990), 91.

13. This section and the sections entitled "The Unique Redwood Forest Ecosystem" and "The Controversy over Clearcutting" were written by Cindy Noblitt.

14. "Redwood Forest Ecology," from the Humboldt State Park web page, http://www.northcoast.com/~hrsp/ecology.html

15. "The World Famous Rockefeller Forest," from the Humboldt State Park web page, http://www.northcoast.com/_hrsp/rockfrst.html

16.   G. Tyler Miller, Jr., *Living in the Environment,* 7th ed., (Belmont, CA: Wadsworth, 1992), p. 282.

17.   "Redwood Forest Ecology."

18.   "Redwood Forest Ecology."

19.   Rudolf U. Becking, *Pocket Flora of the Redwood Forest* (Washington, D.C.: Island Press, 1982) and Stewart, "Green Giants," 64.

20.   Warren R. Randall, Robert F. Keniston, Dale N. Bever, and Edward C. Jensen, *Manual of Oregon Trees and Shrubs,* 6th ed. (Corvallis, OR, OSU Book Stores, 1990), 87.

21.   Stewart, "Green Giants," 62.

22.   Ibid.

23.   "Redwood Forest Ecology."

24.   Ibid.

25.   Randall et al., *Manual,* 87.

26.   "The World Famous Rockefeller Forest."

27.   "Redwood Forest Ecology."

28.   "Burls, Goosepens, Fairy Rings and Fire: The Wonders of the Coast Redwood Forest," March 1997, found at http://www.northcoast.com/~hrsp/burls.html

29.   "Redwood Forest Ecology."

30.   "Burls, Goosepens, Fairy Rings and Fire."

31.   Randall et al., *Manual,* 87.

32.   Becking, *Pocket Flora,* 4.

33.   Harris, *The Last Stand,* 62–63.

34.   Harris, *The Last Stand,* 25.

35.   Harris, *The Last Stand,* 22–25.

36.   This financial history appears in Mark Ivey, "Charles Hurwitz Doesn't Bark, He Just Bites," *Business Week,* 10 December 1984, 73–74.

37.   Pamela Sherrid, "A split too far?" *Fortune,* 14 February 1983, 55–56.

38.   Michael Parrish, "Western Environmentalists' Enemy Number 1," *Los Angeles Times,* 19 August 1990.

39.   Ivey, "Charles Hurwitz Doesn't Bark," 73.

40.   Diana Henriques, "The Redwood Raider," *Barron's,* 28 September 1987, 14.

41.   Debra Sparks, "Rogue Elephant," *Financial World,* 12 September 1995, 36.

42.   A board-foot, the standard measure in the industry, was a block measuring 12 inches by 1 inch by 1 inch.

43.   Parrish, "Enemy Number 1."

44.   Schultz, "Raider's Ruckus," 180.

45.   Annual Report to Stockholders, 1984, page 7.

46.   Harris, *The Last Stand,* 36.

47.   Hearings before the Subcommittee on Oversight and Investigations of the Committee on Energy and Commerce of the House of Representatives, October 5, 1987, Serial Number 100–116.

48.   Ralph S. Janvey, "Parking of Stock," *Securities Regulation Law Journal,* 1988, 164–178.

49.   Harris, *The Last Stand,* 58.

50.   James B. Stewart and Daniel Hertz, "Deal in Boesky Probes Shows Increasing Links With Drexel Burnham," *Wall Street Journal,* 5 December 1986, A1.

51.   Schultz, "Raider's Ruckus," 180.

52.   Mike Geniella, "Pacific Lumber stung with second suit," *Santa Rosa Press Democrat,* 11 February 1989, E-1.

53.   Ibid.

54.   Chase, *In a Dark Wood,* 211.

55.   Michael Parrish, "Settlement Reached in Pacific Lumber Suits," *Los Angeles Times,* 18 May 1994, D2.

56.   "Pacific Lumber Rejects Higher Bid for Maxxam Offer," *Wall Street Journal,* 28 October 1985, 12.

57.   Schultz, "Raider's Ruckus," 180.

58.   "Pacific Lumber to be Acquired for $868 Million," *Wall Street Journal,* 24 October 1985, A8.

59.   "Maxxam to Sell Most of PALCO for 320 Million," *Wall Street Journal,* 18 August 1987, A14.

60.   Harris, *The Last Stand,* 72.

61.   Ilana DeBare, "A Tale of Two Owners," *Los Angeles Times,* 29 April 1987, 1.

62.   Harris, *The Last Stand,* 111.

63.   James P. Miller, "Maxxam Group Plans to Double Redwood Harvest," *Wall Street Journal,* 3 July 1986, 27.

64.   Schultz, "Raider's Ruckus," 181.

65.   Becking, *Pocket Flora,* 4–5.

66.   Greenpeace, "Cutting the Heart out of the Ancient Redwoods," *Greenpeace Quarterly,* Spring 1997, 4–5.

67.   Stewart, "Green Giants," 62.

68.   J. F. Franklin, "Characteristics of Old-Growth Douglas Fir Forests," Proceedings of the 1983 Society of American Foresters Convention (Bethesda, MD: Society of American Foresters, 1983).

69.   Doug Heiken, "Landslides and Clearcuts: What Does Science Really Say," Oregon Natural Resources Council, 1997. Found on IGC EcoNet conference: wall.events.

70.   Ibid.

71.   Dave Foreman, "Earth First!" *The Progressive,* October 1981, 39–42.

72.   Ibid.

73.   Mark A. Stein, "From Rhetoric to 'Ecotage,'" *Los Angeles Times,* 29 November 1987, 1.

74.   Jamie Malanowski, "Monkey-Wrenching Around," *The Nation,* 2 May 1987, 569.

75.   Michael Ybarra, "She May Be Broken, But She Remains Unbowed," *Los Angeles Times,* 24 January 1997, E1.

76.   Chase, *In a Dark Wood,* 272.

77.   Acreage ascribed to the Headwaters Forest varies Environmentalists used "Headwaters Complex" to refer to a contiguous area of roughly 60,000 acres that they wanted Pacific Lumber to preserve as wilderness.

78.   Harris, *The Last Stand,* 184–186.

79.   Harris, *The Last Stand,* 198–199.

80.   Harris, *The Last Stand,* 285, and Richard C. Paddock, "California Elections," *Los Angeles Times,* 18 October 1990, A3.

81.   Ybarra, *She May Be Broken.*

82.   David Helvarg, "The Big Green Spin Machine," *Amicus Journal,* Summer 1996, 13–21.

83.   Harris, *The Last Stand,* 338–339.

84.   Paddock, "California Elections," 18 October 1990.

85.   Richard C. Paddock, "Logging Firms Portray Themselves as Environmentalists," *Los Angeles Times,* 3 November 1990, A26.

86.   Ibid.

87.   "Reform the Reforms," *San Francisco Examiner,* 28 October 1996, A-16.

88.   Richard C. Paddock, "Logging in the Headwaters Forest Rejected," *Los Angeles Times,* 10 January 1991, A3.

89.   Ibid.

90.   Ibid.

91.   Charles McCoy, "Charles Hurwitz Seeking to Sell Pacific Lumber," *Wall Street Journal,* 8 November 1994, A3, and "Maxxam Confirms It Studies Options for Lumber Unit," *Wall Street Journal,* 9 November 1994, A8.

92.   Ibid.

93.   Michael Parrish, "Pacific Lumber to End Moratorium on Old Redwoods," *Los Angeles Times,* 4 March 1995.

94.   See, for example, "Does He Deserve Your Vote? Bill Clinton's Environmental Record," *Sierra,* September 1996, 38.

95.   Alexander Cockburn, "The Feds Blinked on Redwood Swap," *Los Angeles Times,* 2 August 1996, B9.

96.   Interview on Morning Edition, National Public Radio, 2 July 1996.

24

The International Climate Change Partnership: An Industry Association Faces the Climate Change Issue

David L. Levy

The ozone treaty is widely cited as the most successful example of international environmental cooperation to date and the best model for progress on such issues as climate change. Some argue, though, that ozone was an easy issue—that strong scientific evidence, the lack of coherent industry opposition, and the availability of alternatives meant that CFCs would have been eliminated with or without effective international institutions.[1]

In January 1996, Kevin Fay, director of the International Climate Change Partnership (ICCP), was reassessing the options facing the industry association he led. His immediate task was to formulate a response to a major scientific report recently released by the respected United Nations Intergovernmental Panel on Climate Change (IPCC), which confirmed that emissions of greenhouse gases were warming the earth (see Exhibit 1 for a timeline of key events). The media were giving increasing coverage to the issue. The *New York Times* had just reported that 1995 was the warmest year on record,[2] and *Newsweek* ran a cover story that blamed global warming for the blizzard that shut down much of the east coast of the United States in January 1996.[3] In the next few months, Fay would also need to reexamine his association's strategy for participating in the international negotiations on a treaty to limit emissions of greenhouse gases.

Many of the ICCP's member companies had also been active in another industry association, the Alliance for Responsible CFC Policy, which played a major role in shaping the 1987 Montreal Protocol on Substances that Deplete the Ozone Layer. This international treaty, which took seven years to negotiate under the auspices of the United Nations Environment Programme (UNEP), phased out worldwide production and use of most ozone depleting substances. The treaty culminated 13 years of intense research and debate, sparked by the publication of a paper by two American scientists in 1974 that hypothesized a link between CFC gases and ozone destruction—work which was to earn the scientists the Nobel Prize for Chemistry in 1995.[4]

Political momentum was now building for a

Reprinted by permission of The Management Institute for Environment and Business, a program of the World Resources Institute.

The author would like to thank the World Resources Institute BELL Program and the University of Massachusetts, Boston, for funding the development of this case.

EXHIBIT 1 ● Timeline of Key Events on Climate Change

1977	National Academy of Sciences report discusses CO_2 and the "climate problem."
1979	WMO and UNEP sponsor the first World Climate Conference.
1988	Toronto conference calls for a 20 percent cut in emissions by 2005.
	United States EPA issues a report identifying the need for a broad range of regulatory and fiscal measures to stabilize/reduce emissions.
1990	Second World Climate Conference.
	IPCC releases first scientific assessment report.
1991	Negotiations begin on a climate convention.
1992	June—Framework Convention on Climate Change signed at Earth Summit in Rio. No mandatory limits on emissions, but parties agree to negotiate a protocol.
1995	Feb.—First Conference of the Parties (COP 1) held in Berlin.
	Dec.—IPCC releases second assessment report, which concludes that some global warming is already under way.
1996	Jan.—*New York Times* reports that 1995 was warmest year on record. *Newsweek* runs cover story linking east coast blizzard to global warming.
	July—Second Conference of the Parties held in Geneva. Parties call for legally-binding emissions reductions.
1997	Target for Third Conference of the Parties and adoption of a protocol with "targets and timetables" for emissions reductions.

similar protocol to limit emissions of carbon dioxide and other greenhouse gases; negotiators were hoping to conclude a treaty by the end of 1997. Fay knew, however, that climate change was a much more complex issue than ozone depletion. As he put it, "A handful of companies manufactured ozone-depleting chemicals, and there were a limited number of uses for them. Controlling carbon dioxide emissions would affect every aspect of life on earth." Any treaty to limit emissions would certainly have a major impact on the ICCP's member companies, which included Dupont, British Petroleum, AT&T, Enron, 3M, Allied Signal, American Standard, and Carrier Corporation. Fay was considering how best to promote his members' interests, but he recognized that these companies represented a very diverse range of products and services; a mandatory reduction in emissions of

greenhouse gases would present opportunities as well as threats.

BACKGROUND

Climate change is caused by the buildup of greenhouse gases, particularly carbon dioxide (CO_2), in the earth's atmosphere. The scientific evidence for greenhouse warming was strong but not totally conclusive. It was an example of "global commons" issues: gases emitted into the atmosphere from any one country affect the whole world. Most countries in the world produced and emitted these gases in amounts that, individually, would not have much impact on the global environment (Exhibit 2). Few countries would be willing to bear the costs of controlling emissions if others did not commit to doing likewise. Nevertheless, the sum total of global emis-

EXHIBIT 2 ● Carbon Emissions from Fossil Fuel Burning, Selected Countries, 1994

Country	Total Emissions (million tons)	Emissions per person (tons)	Emissions per $ GNP (tons/m.$)	Emissions Growth 1990–94 (percent)
United States	1,371	5.26	210	4.4
China	835	0.71	330	13.0
Russia	455	3.08	590	−24.1
Japan	299	2.39	110	0.1
Germany	234	2.89	140	−9.9
India	222	0.24	160	23.5
U.K.	153	2.62	150	−0.3
France	90	1.56	80	−3.2
Poland	89	2.31	460	−4.5
S. Korea	88	1.98	200	43.7
Mexico	88	0.96	140	7.1
S. Africa	85	2.07	680	9.1

Source: Adapted from Lester Brown et al. (1996), *State of the World 1996,* p. 30 (Norton/Worldwatch Institute).

sions could have potentially disastrous effects on the ecosystem.

Negotiating an agreement on climate change was a high-stakes game with uncertain odds. Many businesses that produced or relied on fossil-fuel energy expressed concern that premature action to curb emissions could impose huge economic costs. The costs of inaction, however, could also be massive. Global warming could lead to rising ocean levels, droughts and hurricanes, endangering coastal cities and disrupting the global food supply. Some environmentalists warned that waiting for more definitive proof of global warming could be disastrous, due to time lags in the climate system—as one Greenpeace member put it, we "should step on the brakes before we see the edge of the cliff."

A series of unusual events in 1994 and 1995 led some to claim that global warming was already under way. In a series of articles in the British medical journal *The Lancet,* it was reported that disease-spreading mosquitoes were expanding their habitats to areas previously considered too cold for them. A new orbiting radar gun detected a rise in sea level of three millimeters a year. Siberia was warmer than at any time since the Middle Ages, and the permafrost was retreating in the Canadian Arctic. And in early 1995, a Rhode Island–sized chunk of the Larsen Ice Shelf in the Antarctic broke off into the South Atlantic, exposing rocks that had been buried for 20,000 years.[5]

THE SCIENTIFIC BASIS FOR INTERNATIONAL ACTION

Scientists had known for decades that CO_2, methane, and other "greenhouse" gases warm the earth by allowing in and trapping the sun's heat. The first World Climate Conference in 1979 concluded that "there is serious concern that the continued expansion of man's activities may cause significant extended regional and even global changes of climate." Nevertheless, there was considerable debate about the extent to which human activity might change the climate. Fossil fuel combustion released about 22 billion metric tons of CO_2 a year worldwide, and deforestation added another three to six billion tons a year. Concentrations of methane—with 20 times the heat trapping potential of CO_2—had nearly doubled in the past 100 years, from sources such as livestock and rice-growing (Exhibit 3).

The level of carbon dioxide in the atmosphere had risen from about 285 parts per million (ppm) 100 years ago to 350 ppm in 1995, and the rate of increase continued to grow. During this period, global mean temperatures had increased by 0.3° to 0.6° Celsius.[6] The oceans

were warming, polar ice caps were shrinking, and sea levels had risen about four to six inches in 100 years. The Intergovernmental Panel on Climate Change (IPCC), a group of scientists convened by the UN and the World Meteorological Organization, projected that if greenhouse gases continued to grow unchecked, mean global temperatures would increase by 0.8° to 3.5°C by the year 2100, and sea levels would rise a further 4 to 30 inches (Exhibit 4).

While these numbers may sound quite modest, they "indicate changes more rapid than any experienced in the last 10,000 years."[7] The IPCC report predicted that some ecosystems would not be able to cope with this rate of change, leading to loss of species. The changes would be more pronounced outside the tropics, and more extreme local weather patterns, such as floods, droughts and hurricanes, were predicted. The projected temperature changes could be put into perspective by comparing them to the ice-ages, when av-

EXHIBIT 3 ● Sources of Greenhouse Warming, by Gas and Economic Activity

Relative global warming potential reflects both the amount of each gas emitted and its heat-trapping potential. For example, CFCs have a relatively large contribution to global warming despite low emission levels because they trap thousands of times more heat than CO_2 and remain in the atmosphere much longer.

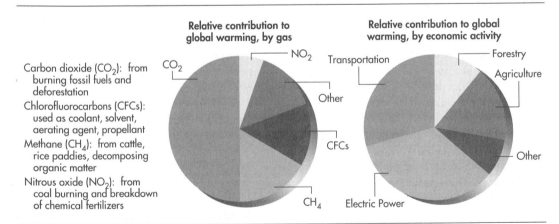

Source: Adapted from World Resources 1994–95 and other sources.

EXHIBIT 4 ● Global Average Temperature and Carbon Dioxide Concentration 158,000 B.C.–1994 A.D.

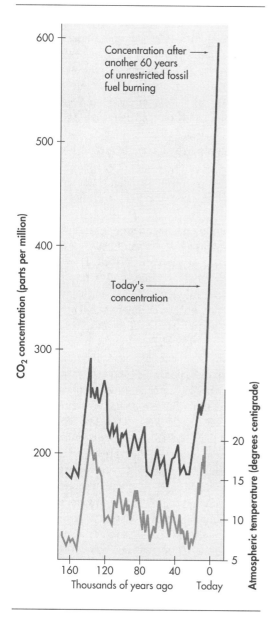

Source: Christopher Flavin, "Storm Warnings," *World Watch,* Nov/Dec. 1994. Reprinted by permission.

erage global temperatures were about three to four degrees Celsius cooler, and ice-sheets covered much of North America and Europe.

The wide range of forecasts of temperature changes was due to the complexity of the global climate system, and the natural variability in weather patterns. Scientists attempted to simulate the climate using "general circulation models" that divided the earth's atmosphere and oceans into three-dimensional grids and solved hundreds of equations for each cell in the grid. These highly complex computer models were still only coarse approximations and did not account well for changing cloud cover and ocean currents. Until the early 1990s, most general circulation models predicted temperature increases nearly twice as great as those observed. Only recently had these models included the effect of aerosols—small particles emitted from burning fossil fuels—that act to cool the earth by reflecting some sunlight back out to space. Current models predicted very well the amount of cooling that resulted from the eruption of the Mount Pinatubo volcano in 1991. James Hansen, Director of NASA's Goddard Institute for Space Studies, argued that "these models can now reproduce quite accurately climate changes of the distant past as well as the global warming of this century."[8]

There was considerable debate about the direction and size of climatic feedback mechanisms; for example, increased CO_2 and higher temperatures could lead to faster rates of forest growth, which would absorb more of the carbon being put into the air. Cloud cover could increase due to greater evaporation of water at higher temperatures, blocking more of the sun's solar energy. On the other hand, some thought that higher temperatures could accelerate the emission of CO_2 and methane from decomposing organic matter, and that the retreat of polar ice caps would lead to more absorption of solar energy.

The level of complexity and uncertainty of

climate change led some to characterize it as a "chaotic" system, meaning a complex, dynamic, non-linear system in which small changes could cause large, sudden, and potentially irreversible consequences.[9] Researchers from the Woods Hole Oceanographic Institute, who studied ocean sediments and ice core samples, reported that the earth's climate appears to snap suddenly into and out of ice ages in a matter of decades. According to researcher Scott Lehman, "Our results suggest that the present climate system is very delicately poised. Shifts could happen very rapidly if conditions are right, and we cannot predict when that will occur."[10] One scenario was that Arctic snowmelts could dilute the salinity of the Atlantic Ocean, causing the Gulf Stream to flow in a more southerly direction, giving England a Siberian climate.

Due to the buffering effect of the oceans and other time lags, the full effect of changes in CO_2 levels would not be felt for decades; just to stabilize the level of greenhouse gases in the atmosphere, emissions would have to be reduced by about 50 percent from 1990 levels. As in the case of ozone depletion, however, global warming also had its skeptics. Astrophysicist Sallie Baliunas, at the Harvard-Smithsonian center for Astrophysics, claimed that "There is no observed change in global . . . mean temperature that is outside the bounds of natural variability. . . . There is no scientific basis for a catastrophic global warming produced by the buildup of greenhouse gases from fossil-fuel burning."[11] Although this view was shared by only a few reputable scientists, they tended to be vociferous in their views and received considerable attention in the media and in Congress. Some pointed out that these enviro-skeptics received significant sums from the coal and oil industries; for example, Fred Singer, who had moved on from ozone to the climate change issue, received consulting fees from Exxon, Shell, Unocal, ARCO, and Sun Oil.[12]

COUNTRY POSITIONS IN INTERNATIONAL NEGOTIATIONS

In their efforts to reach international agreements that would address global environmental problems, different countries brought a wide range of interests and concerns to the negotiating table, depending on their economic structure, sensitivity to public opinion, and geography. The richer, industrialized countries tended to see ozone depletion, climate change, marine pollution, and biodiversity as the most critical issues facing the earth, while developing countries were more interested in clean water, desertification, and securing resources to ensure economic growth.

International negotiations to limit emissions of greenhouse gases began in earnest at the first Conference of the Parties (COP I) in Berlin in February 1995. A Framework Convention had already been signed by 153 countries at the U.N. Conference on Environment and Development "Earth Summit" in Rio de Janeiro in June 1992. Despite the 1990 IPCC report indicating that emissions of greenhouse gases might have to be cut by up to 60 percent to prevent further climate change, the Rio agreement was little more than an expression of intent to stabilize emissions at 1990 levels by the year 2000. The UN forecast in 1995 that 9 of 18 major industrialized countries would miss even this target. The US, which had instituted a number of voluntary programs to encourage firms to cut emissions, blamed strong economic growth and low energy prices for its failure to meet the target.

A number of countries represented in Berlin supported a 20 percent cut below 1990 emissions levels by the year 2005. The US, however, reversing its strong support for controls in the ozone case, played a key role in blocking any move toward a binding agreement. Environmental groups blamed the US stance on industry pressure, and pointed out that the US was the largest emitter of CO_2 in the world and had substantial reserves of oil and coal (Exhibit 5). The U.S. delegation argued that, instead of rushing to adopt costly and arbitrary reductions goals, further economic and technical analysis was needed to understand what steps were feasible. One American delegate remarked privately that "other countries are willing to make bold commitments without any idea of how to achieve them. Some of them are simply using the US for cover—they don't want mandated reductions any more than we do."

Canada, a major exporter of energy, joined the US in opposing specific emissions limits. Japan also joined in blocking a 20 percent reduction, though it was prepared to support a freeze at 1990 levels. Japan was planning to increase its use of nuclear power from 27 percent of generating capacity in 1990 to more than 40 percent by 2010. Members of OPEC, led by Saudi Arabia and Kuwait, were among the most vociferous opponents of any restriction.

European governments were unable to present a united front. France and Germany both supported the 20 percent reduction, but for different reasons. France already obtained more than 60 percent of its electricity from nuclear plants, and was perhaps hoping that controls on fossil fuels might spur exports of its nuclear technology. Germany had a strong environmental lobby, and was also expecting substantial cuts in emissions from the closure of outdated and inefficient power plants and factories in the former East Germany. The U.K., which had led an attack on a proposed European carbon tax, had supported the U.S. position since 1992. During 1995, the U.K. government changed course and endorsed some controls—this change occurred the same year that the government announced its intention to shut down much of the British coal industry, which was inefficient and heavily subsidized. Four poorer members of the European Union, Spain, Portugal,

Greece and Ireland, opposed specific restrictions on emissions and expressed fears that emissions controls would stifle economic growth.

Much of the developing world, which already accounted for an estimated 45 percent of total greenhouse gas emissions, was firmly opposed to any agreement. China, with one-third of the world's proven reserves of coal, relied on coal for around 80 percent of its energy needs, and was already the third largest emitter of CO_2. China planned to expand its coal production five-fold to three billion tons a year by 2020, which would increase global CO_2 emissions nearly 50 percent.[13] Brazil, Indonesia, and Malaysia were home to much of the world's tropical rain forest, whose destruction contributed a significant amount to CO_2 releases.

The strongest support for firm action came from a group of 32 countries known as the Association of Small Island States (AOSIS), which also included countries like Bangladesh with large populations in low-lying coastal areas. Despite their relatively weak bargaining position, these countries were able to exert some moral suasion over the negotiations, due to the threat to their very existence.

INDUSTRIES AFFECTED AND BUSINESS RESPONSE

Companies that extracted and processed fossil fuels such as coal and oil would obviously suffer from any effort to limit their use. The largest emitters of CO_2 were the electric utilities and the transportation sector (Exhibit 6). A much broader range of industries relied on energy inputs, and the more energy-intensive ones, such as steel, aluminum, cement, and chemicals, would be particularly hard hit by higher energy prices. Yet another group of industries could be affected by changes in climate; agriculture and forestry are sensitive to temperature and rainfall, and some in the insurance industry were beginning to express concern at the potentially enormous losses from flooding, drought, and hurricanes. Frank Nutter, the president of the Reinsurance Association of America, was quoted as saying that climate change "could bankrupt the industry."[14]

Energy Sources

U.S. power plants accounted for about 36 percent of U.S. emissions of CO_2, and the demand for this energy was split roughly equally among residential, commercial, and industrial uses (Exhibit 5). Each kilowatt-hour (kWh) of coal-derived electricity put more than two pounds of CO_2 into the air; the corresponding figure for oil was 1.7 pounds, and 1.3 pounds for natural gas (Exhibit 6).[15] U.S. demand for electricity was forecast to nearly double by 2025, and demand

EXHIBIT 5 ● Demand for Electricity by End Use

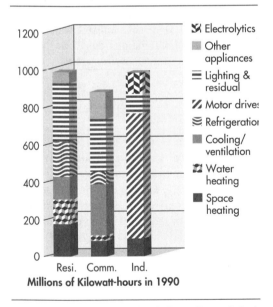

Millions of Kilowatt-hours in 1990

Source: Copyright © 1991. Electric Power Research Institute. EPRI CU-7440. *Saving Energy and Reducing CO$_2$ with Electricity.* Reprinted with permission.

in less developed countries was expected to increase even faster; the average American consumed about 11,000 kWh, compared to 700 kWh in Asia and 400 kWh in China.

Given this rapid growth in demand for energy, the U.N. goal of stabilizing CO_2 emissions at 1990 levels appeared to be a daunting task. It would entail a substantial switch to gas, nuclear, or renewable sources of power such as solar or wind, as well as increased efficiency in energy use. Most of the world's fossil fuel reserves, however, were in the form of coal, and this was still the cheapest form of power. Nuclear power had become a very expensive alternative due to safety requirements, decommissioning costs, and the time required to license and construct a plant.

Renewable energy sources supplied about 20 percent of the world's electricity, mostly from hydropower. There was limited scope for expanding hydropower, partly due to environmental concerns about the impact of large dams. Wind power had become competitive in certain locations, at around six cents per kWh, but photovoltaic cells, which convert the sun's energy directly into electricity, were still very expensive at about 30 cents per kWh—in full sunlight. Photovoltaics were finding applications in rural areas in developing countries, as they had low distribution costs and required relatively little maintenance. Solar thermal energy, which focuses the sun's energy to boil a liquid and drive a turbine, was more competitive at around 10 cents per kWh, and several small plants had been installed in California. In recent years, utilities had found that conservation—termed "demand management" by the industry—was the cheapest and cleanest way to free capacity to meet demand; investing in insulation and energy efficient lighting, for example, saved electricity at an estimated cost of three cents per kWh.

With a few exceptions, the large coal, oil, and utility companies that dominated the energy

EXHIBIT 6 ● U.S. Electricity Fuel Mix and Related CO_2 Emissions

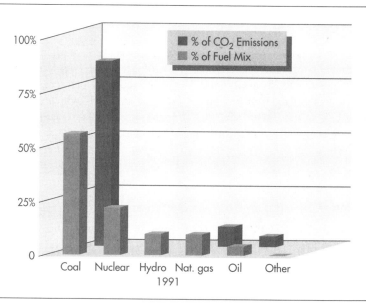

Source: U.S. Department of Energy and Investor Responsibility Research Center.

industry had not invested very much in renewable energy sources. Companies developing wind and solar power technologies tended to be small and undercapitalized. Luz International, the only commercial company supplying solar thermal plants, filed for bankruptcy in 1991. The U.S. government encouraged renewable energy with tax credits during the Carter administration, but under presidents Reagan and Bush the Department of Energy gave very low priority to renewables: the lion's share of federal resources had gone to fusion research, even though commercial application was not expected for 40 years or more.

Economic Impacts

There had been various proposals for a tax on fossil fuels to promote energy efficiency and a switch to renewable sources. Some economists argued that a carbon tax based on the CO_2 emitted per unit of energy would provide the lowest cost route to cutting emissions; the tax revenues could be used to fund research into alternative energy sources and to reduce income taxes. Estimates of the cost to the economy of curbing greenhouse gas emissions varied widely. According to *The Economist,* "One of the few certainties about global warming is that the costs of severely curbing emissions of greenhouse gases now would be huge."[16] By contrast, the U.S. Office of Technology Assessment estimated that taxes and controls on greenhouse gases could yield a reduction of more than 20 percent in emissions by 2015, and that savings from conservation and new technologies would more than offset the costs.[17]

One economic study indicated that a carbon

tax of $120 per ton would stabilize CO_2 emissions at 1990 levels, at a cost to the U.S. economy of $150 billion a year.[18] This cost represented about two percent of the U.S. GNP—but would not necessarily slow the economy's *rate* of growth. Other economists pointed out that energy was already taxed in arbitrary ways; the implicit tax on oil ranged from $65 per ton of carbon in the U.S. to more than $300 in France and Italy, while coal was actually subsidized to the tune of $40 a ton of carbon in Germany and the UK.[19]

Other Industry Groups

With the experience of the ban on CFCs fresh in their minds, a number of industry groups began to organize to protect their members' interests. A proposal in 1991 for a combination energy/carbon tax in the European Union, which would have increased electricity prices by about 20 percent, was defeated after strong lobbying by European industry associations representing utilities, oil companies, chemicals, and industrial energy users.[20] A modest fuel tax proposed by the Clinton administration in 1992 was quickly dropped in the face of pressure from the automobile and oil industries. The American Petroleum Institute paid $1.8 million in 1993 alone to the public relations firm of Burso-Marsteller, partly to help defeat the Clinton fuel tax. An association of U.S. utilities ran a series of advertisements in 1992 debunking global warming theory, but touting its benefits if it did occur: "Winter nights are warming and summer days appear to be cooling, promoting greater crop yields and more robust forests. CO_2 fertilization of the atmosphere helps produce more food for people and wildlife. Wildlife can flourish in more abundant habitat."

The Global Climate Coalition, which represented more than 50 companies and trade associations in the oil and coal, utility, chemicals, and auto industries, was the largest industry group working on this issue and was active at the international treaty negotiations in Berlin in February 1995. It spent nearly $1 million a year to convince policy makers that proposals to limit CO_2 emissions "are premature and are not justified by the state of scientific knowledge or the economic risks they create."[21] Don Pearlman's Climate Council, which worked closely with oil exporting countries such as Kuwait and Saudi Arabia as well as with some oil and coal companies, was also active in trying to forestall any international treaty with mandatory reductions in CO_2 emissions.

The Business Council for a Sustainable Energy Future represented businesses active in natural gas, energy efficiency, and renewable energy—sectors that stood to benefit from controls on carbon emissions. Although the BCSEF was much smaller than the CCG, it claimed success in demonstrating at Berlin that business was not united against an emissions treaty. The BCSEF supported proposals to curb CO_2 emissions, especially measures that would offer financial incentives for low-carbon alternatives and for the transfer of new technologies to LDCs. Trade associations representing U.S. gas, solar, and energy services industries estimated that more than 200,000 jobs could be created if energy taxes and subsidies were used to promote growth in these sectors.[22]

Other industries potentially affected by climate change had adopted a wait-and-see attitude. The insurance industry, concerned at payouts for natural disasters that jumped from an average of $3 billion a year in the 1980s to $10 billion a year in the 1990s, had begun to monitor the issue closely, but had not yet been active in international negotiations.[23] Agriculture and forestry in some areas could be hurt by changing temperature and rainfall—some models predicted that the U.S. Great Plains could be hit by severe droughts. Higher CO_2 levels and greater rainfall in other regions could enhance crop and tree growth. Companies in these industries had been studying the drought tolerance of various seeds, but had not yet entered the policy debates. Cynthia Rosenzweig, a Columbia University agronomist and co-author of a major study, concluded that "the overall outlook for climate change is not catastrophic."[24] Consumer prices for food would rise somewhat, and income in the agricultural sector in the U.S. could actually rise one to two percent due to higher prices and inelastic demand. The outlook for the rest of the world, where people spent more of their incomes on food and were more dependent on local crops, was less optimistic.

The ICCP

The ICCP was formed by a group of industrial companies which had been involved in the CFC issue, and were now concerned that HFCs, some of which were potent greenhouse gases, would also be regulated in a climate change treaty. These companies soon discovered, however, that they had a broad range of interests that could potentially be affected by efforts to limit greenhouse gas emissions. Some companies manufactured insulation and could benefit from increased incentives for energy efficiency. AT&T was promoting "tele-commuting" as an approach to reducing emissions from transportation. Enron had substantial interests in conventional power generation, but had recently invested in a joint venture with Amoco to produce photovoltaic panels. General Electric's gas turbine business could benefit from a switch away from coal, but its appliance and aircraft divisions could be hurt by emissions controls.

The ICCP stressed the need for more voluntary programs that would encourage companies to identify profitable opportunities to reduce emissions. If voluntary measures proved inadequate, the ICCP expressed a preference for market-based measures rather than command and control mandates. The ICCP wanted to ensure that any treaty to reduce emissions would be based on a detailed analysis of technological and economic feasibility, and would have a long timetable; this would give industry the time to design new products and processes, and prevent premature obsolescence of capital.

THE ROLE OF ENVIRONMENTAL GROUPS

By the early 1980s, it was estimated that about 13,000 environmental non-governmental organizations (NGOs) existed in industrialized countries, and another 2,000 or so in LDCs. Most were only national in scope with a narrow focus, but a growing number were taking an interest in international issues. Among them were activist organizations such as Greenpeace, and others that focused more on research, such as the Worldwatch Institute. The World Wildlife Fund had 23 national organizations with 3 million members in 1990, while Greenpeace, a loose global confederation, had more than 3 million members in 20 countries. The European Environmental Bureau was a confederation of 120 national environmental organizations with a combined membership of 20 million. Despite these impressive membership numbers, environmental groups did not appear to have much political influence. Only in Germany were environmentalists formally organized into political parties with significant strength. The green vote, comprising between 8 and 14 percent of the electorate, sometimes played a crucial swing role in the country's regional politics.

In the U.S., environmental NGOs had been especially successful at increasing consumer awareness of the dangers of CFCs. The British group, Friends of the Earth, also undertook a large public relations campaign against aerosols. It was largely pressure from consumers and environmental groups that led Johnson Wax and other companies to phase out their CFC use in aerosol sprays and foam packaging.

To work on the climate change issue, environmental NGOs from 22 countries formed a coalition called the Climate Action Network (CAN). This umbrella organization had a strong presence at the Berlin conference, holding press conferences and publishing a daily newsletter. CAN was quite well organized despite a relative lack of resources, and engendered respect among the UNEP staff for its independence. As Chris Flavin of the Worldwatch Institute put it, "the NGOs ran circles around the Global Climate Coalition." Influencing the national delegations was another matter, however. Environmental groups had not been very successful at galvanizing public opinion around this issue, and in the U.S. people seemed to be more focused on domestic issues such as the federal budget deficit. One environmentalist at Berlin complained that "the U.S. delegation is free to stall these negotiations without any worry about domestic repercussions."

AFTER BERLIN

The Berlin talks concluded with an agreement to negotiate a climate change protocol by 1997, though there was still great uncertainty concerning targets and timetables, and it was not clear how binding any protocol might be. The final deal in Berlin was "just enough to keep the climate treaty process from collapsing," according to the Climate Action Network.[25] Chris Flavin of the Worldwatch Institute, on a more optimistic note, thought that the agreement to negotiate a protocol by 1997 was "about the best that could be realistically expected at this time."

Despite the lack of agreement on specifics, a number of options had been explored in Berlin that could prove useful in moving the negotiations forward. One approach would involve granting CO_2 emission permits to each country, which in turn would assign permits to major CO_2 emitters such as coal-powered power plants. These permits would then be tradeable, encouraging companies to seek efficient ways to cut back on emissions.[26] Another idea that aroused considerable interest in Berlin was termed "joint implementation." This scheme would allow companies (and countries) to count activities performed in other countries toward their goal of emissions reductions: for example, an American utility would be able to claim credit for an overseas reforestation project, or for selling technology for more efficient electricity generation to a developing country.

Now, with the 1997 negotiation deadline looming, Fay needed to formulate a response to the IPCC scientific report that had just been released. In the past, business groups had tended to downplay any evidence of global warming and had emphasized the need for more research before any action was taken. Fay, along with most other business groups, still thought that the 1997 target for a treaty would not allow sufficient time for conducting detailed technical and economic assessments on a sector by sector basis. He feared that the imposition of severe curbs on emissions without having alternatives in place could lead to market chaos and significant disruption to the ICCP members' businesses.

Fay also knew that if business continued to drag its feet, it risked being sidelined in the treaty process. He wondered whether it might be time to change course; acknowledging that climate change was indeed a potential problem might give his group more credibility and influence in the negotiating process. The next round of talks was to be held in Geneva in the summer of 1996, and he knew that political momentum for a treaty was mounting. It would not be easy, however, to find common ground among the ICCP's diverse member companies. It would be even harder to present a united front with the other industry groups, such as the GCC and the BCSEF. While these divisions might weaken the influence of business at the negotiations, Fay thought it important that policy makers understand the broad range of business concerns. He hoped that the negotiators would see his group as the moderate voice of industry, with the resources and expertise to help find solutions to the greenhouse problem. He needed to make sure that the ICCP had a "seat at the table" in the process.

Notes

1. Edward A. Parson, "Protecting the Ozone Layer," in P. M. Haas, R. O. Keohane, and M. A. Levy, *Institutions for the Earth: Sources of Effective Environmental Protection* (Cambridge, Mass.: MIT Press, 1993), p. 27.

2. William K. Stevens, "'95 is Hottest Year on Record as the Global Trend Resumes," *New York Times,* Jan. 4, 1996, p. 1.

3. Daniel Gleck and Adam Rogers, "Going to Extremes," *Newsweek,* Jan. 22, 1996, p. 26.

4. Mario J. Molina and F. Sherwood Rowland, "Stratospheric Sink for Chlorofluorocarbons: Chlorine Atomic Catalyzed Destruction of Ozone," *Nature,* Vol. 249, No. 5460, 1994, pp. 810–812.

5. Ross Gelbspan, "The Heat is On," *Harper's Magazine,* December 1995, pp. 32–33; Chris Flavin, "Facing Up to the Risks of Climate Change," in Lester Brown et al. (eds.), *State of the World 1996* (New York: W.W. Norton; Washington, DC: Worldwatch Institute, 1996), p. 23.

6. IPCC, *The IPCC Second Assessment Synthesis Report: Draft Summary for Policy Makers* (Geneva: United Nations, 1995). A change of 1 degree Celsius equals a change of 1.8 degrees Fahrenheit.

7. Ibid., IPCC (1995).

8. Bette Hileman, "Climate Models Substantiate Global Warming Models," *Chemical and Engineering News,* Nov. 27, 1995, pp. 18–23.

9. Douglas Cogan, *The Greenhouse Gambit* (Washington, DC: Investor Responsibility Research Center, 1992).

10. Gelbspan, p. 33.

11. Paul Craig Roberts, "Quietly, Now, Let's Rethink the Ozone Apocalypse," *Business Week,* June 19, 1995, p. 26.

12. Gelbspan, p. 35.

13. Michael Grubb, "The Greenhouse Effect: Negotiating Targets," *International Affairs,* Vol. 66, No. 1, 1990, pp. 67–89.

14. Gelbspan, p. 35.

15. Cogan (1992), p. 350.

16. "Stay Cool," *The Economist,* April 1995, p. 11.

17. U.S. Office of Technology Assessment, *Changing by Degrees: Steps to Reduce Greenhouse Gases* OTA-0-482 (Washington, DC: U.S. Government Printing Office, 1991).

18. Neil A. Leary and Joel D. Scheraga, "The Costs of Different Energy Taxes for Stabilizing U.S. Carbon Dioxide Emissions: An Application of the Gemini Model," *World Resource Review,* Vol. 5, No. 3, 1995, pp. 372–386.

19. Peter Hoeller and Markku Wallin, "Energy prices, taxes and carbon dioxide emissions," *OECD Economic Studies,* Vol. 17 (Fall, 1991), pp. 91–104.

20. Tony Ikwue and Jim Skea, "Business and the genesis of the European carbon tax proposal," Working Paper, Programme on Environmental Policy and Regulation, Science Policy Research Unit, University of Sussex, 1994.

21. Global Climate Coalition press release, Feb. 9, 1995.

22. Cogan (1992), p. xviii.

23. Gelbspan, p. 35.

24. Cogan (1992), p. 74.

25. ECO Newsletter, April 7, 1995 (London: Climate Action Network).

26. Richard Lapper and Laurie Morse, "Market Makers in CO_2 Permits," *Financial Times,* March 1, 1995, p. 10.

25

Acid Rain: The Southern Company
Forest Reinhardt

Early in 1992, managers at the Southern Company were reexamining their strategy for complying with the acid rain provisions of the 1990 amendments to the Clean Air Act. The Southern Company was a holding company; its operating units were electric utilities in Georgia, Alabama, Mississippi, and Florida. The largest Southern subsidiaries, Georgia Power and Alabama Power, provided most of the electricity in their respective states.

Dozens of Southern Company executives had worked on compliance strategies since the Clean Air Act's passage in November 1990, but the time for analysis was just about over. Because of long lead times in installing pollution-control equipment, the final decisions on compliance strategy would have to be made in 1992 in order to meet the Act's 1995 effective date.

The choices that the company faced at Georgia Power's Bowen coal-fired plant were representative of the dilemmas the Clean Air Act posed for the Southern Company as a whole. The Bowen plant sat on the banks of the Etowah River near Taylorsville, Georgia, northwest of the city of Atlanta. Completed in 1975, it was capable, when all four of its generators were

running at capacity, of producing enough power to serve the residential, commercial, and industrial demands of 1 million people.

The Bowen plant was an unusually large, but otherwise fairly typical, coal-fired steam electric plant. Coal was burned in massive vessels. Steam, traveling through pipes that ran through these vessels, was heated by the energy from the burning coal. Adjacent turbines converted the energy in the steam to mechanical energy, which was then converted to electrical energy in the plant's generators. Large coal-fired plants like Bowen had high-fixed costs but relatively low variable costs and were designed to operate continuously. Utilities used them for baseload generation, supplementing the energy from the coal plants with power from oil- or gas-fired plants to meet peak demands.

Running the Bowen plant was an operation of vast scale. Hundreds of railroad cars, carrying coal from southeastern Kentucky, arrived at the plant each day, contributing to a pile of inventory that weighed over 1 million tons. During 1990, Bowen's generators consumed 8.338 million tons of coal (952 tons of coal every hour) and generated 21,551 million kilowatt-hours of electricity. The value of this electricity varied substantially across markets, but in 1990 the Southern Company realized an average of 5.6 cents per kilowatt-hour in revenues.

Also during 1990, over 30 tons of sulfur dioxide left the stacks of the Bowen plant each hour. This pollutant was an important precursor of acid deposition, or acid rain, which had been implicated in damage to lakes, forest ecosystems, and manmade materials like metals and paints. New legislation aimed at controlling acid rain, passed by Congress and signed by President Bush in November 1990, would regulate these emissions starting in 1995.

Most previous regulations for air pollution control had specified a particular quantity of pollution that a facility could emit. A firm faced fines or other sanctions if its emissions exceeded the permitted level, but it had no incentive to reduce its emissions below the level specified in the permit. The new acid rain law, by contrast, allowed firms to choose their own emissions levels. They would be granted allowances to emit a certain amount of sulfur dioxide, based on the amount of electricity they had generated in the past. Starting in 1995 (in "Phase One" of the law), each of about 100 large coal-fired utility plants across the country, including Bowen, would receive allowances to emit 2.5 pounds of sulfur dioxide per million British thermal units (MMBtu) of coal consumed. In the year 2000 ("Phase Two"), all coal-fired utility plants, including those regulated in Phase One, would get allowances worth 1.2 pounds per MMBtu of coal.

If they wished, utilities could reduce their emissions below the amount for which they had been given allowances and sell the extra allowances to other utilities. Alternatively, they could purchase additional allowances from other firms, which would permit them to release larger quantities of sulfur dioxide.

Compared to other plants that would be regulated in Phase One, Bowen was fairly clean; many other utility plants, including some in the Southern Company system, were emitting sulfur dioxide in quantities up to two times higher than Phase One levels. Nevertheless, Bowen would have to reduce its emissions by 1995, or purchase allowances, in order to comply with the law. Further reductions or increased purchases of allowances would be necessary beginning in the year 2000.

The Clean Air Act amendments specified the quantity of allowances Bowen would receive. The plant would receive allowances for 254,580 tons of sulfur dioxide in each of the five years beginning in 1995. Starting in the year 2000, it would receive allowances worth 122, 198 tons per year.

There were several options for complying with the new law. First, the company could continue to operate Bowen as it had in the past, burning high-sulfur Kentucky coal without scrubbing the exhaust gases. If it did, its emissions would exceed the amounts for which it would receive allowances. Each year beginning in 1995, Bowen would purchase allowances from other Southern Company plants or on the open market to make up the difference.

Second, the company could install scrubbers at the Bowen plant that would remove sulfur dioxide from the exhaust gases of the generators. The scrubbers could be installed from 1992 to 1994 so they would be on line during Phase One; in that case, Bowen would generate excess allowances that could be sold to other utilities or to other Southern Company plants. Alternatively, the company could delay the installation of the scrubbers until 1997 to 1999, in which case they would begin working in the year 2000; in that case, Bowen would generate excess allowances starting in 2000, but during 1995 through 1999 it would need to buy allowances from other plants.

The company's last option was to switch the Bowen plant to low-sulfur coal from Kentucky or West Virginia. This strategy would bring Bowen's emissions below the amount of its Phase One permits. In Phase Two, the Bowen plant would need to buy allowances. (Nothing prevented the Southern Company from switching fuels and also installing scrubbers, but this option made little sense economically. If a plant burned low-sulfur coal, the gases leaving its boilers would be sufficiently low in sulfur that scrubbers could not remove enough additional sulfur to pay for themselves.)

Under any of the options, the Bowen plant would continue to generate electricity at its 1990 levels through the year 2016. In 2016, Bowen was likely to be retired as new, more efficient plants came on stream, and its salvage value would be negligible.

Company planners expected the price of electricity to remain constant during the period Bowen was in operation. They also figured that operating costs exclusive of fuel and pollution-control expenditures, which had averaged 0.00281 dollars per kilowatt-hour in recent years, would stay about the same until the plant was retired.

The prices the Southern Company could charge for its electricity in Georgia were determined by the Public Service Commission, a body of five officials elected statewide. The utility customarily applied for rate increases to recover the costs of new construction or to pass on increases in operating costs. The Southern Company's government relations personnel were uncertain whether the commission would approve rate increases to cover the total costs of compliance with the Clean Air Act. The commission might force the company's shareholders to bear some of the costs of compliance rather than passing them on to its ratepayers. A second possibility was that the company might be allowed to recover its costs only if it could show that it had complied in the least-cost manner. In either case, the company executives felt that they ought to search for the cost-minimizing method of complying with the Act.

Numerous government agencies and private firms had developed predictions of the prices of allowances in Phase One and Phase Two. As a working estimate, company planners felt that the price of allowances would probably be $250 per ton of sulfur dioxide in 1995, the first year of Phase One, and that the price would rise at 10% per year through the year 2010. Thereafter, the allowances were expected to stay at their 2010

price. Allowances could be bought or sold on the open market, and a multiplant firm like the Southern Company could also move allowances from one of its plants to another in an internal transaction. From an economic standpoint, it was irrelevant whether allowances were traded within the firm or externally, since the value of an allowance—and hence the appropriate internal transfer price—would be determined in the external market (Exhibit 1).

In Georgia, the Southern Company paid federal and state income taxes at a combined effective rate of 37.7%. The company customarily used an after-tax discount rate of 10% in evaluating investment opportunities.

OPTION 1: BURN HIGH-SULFUR COAL WITHOUT SCRUBBERS; PURCHASE ALLOWANCES

Aside from capital costs, costs of fuel were the largest single expense at Bowen (Exhibit 2). Coals varied widely both in delivered price per ton and in heat content per pound, so prices were usually expressed in dollars per ton and in dollars per MMBtu.

The high-sulfur Kentucky coal burned at Bowen cost, on average, $41.46 per ton delivered to the plant. Starting in 1996, the price was expected to fall to $29.82 per ton, delivered. Bowen's generators required coal with a total heat content of 202.3 million MMBtu; the heat content of the coal was 24.262 MMBtu per ton, so that Bowen needed 202,300,000/24.262 or 8.338 million tons of that sort of coal per year.

The coal currently burned at Bowen contained an average of 1.6% sulfur by weight. Burning 8.338 million tons of this coal without installing additional pollution-control equipment would generate 266,550 tons of sulfur dioxide emissions.

EXHIBIT 1 ● Projected Operating Data for the Bowen Plant: Assumptions Common to All Options

OUTPUT	21,551 million kilowatt-hours	
REVENUE	$0.056 per kilowatt-hour	
INPUT REQUIRED	202.3 million MMBtu (Coal tonnage depends on heat content of coal.)	
SULFUR DIOXIDE ALLOWANCES	1995–1999	254,580 tons
	2000–2016	122,198
OPERATING COST (excluding fuel and pollution allowances)	$0.00281 per kilowatt-hour	
TAX RATE	37.7%	
DISCOUNT RATE (after tax)	10%	

OPTION 2: BURN HIGH-SULFUR COAL WITH SCRUBBERS; SELL ALLOWANCES

In order to reduce emissions of sulfur dioxide at Bowen, the Southern Company could install wet-limestone flue gas desulfurization (FGD) equipment, commonly known as scrubbers. The gases from the generator already went through one pollution-control device called an electrostatic precipitator before release to the atmosphere; the precipitator eliminated most of the ash and particles from the gas. If scrubbers were installed, the gases, after leaving the precipitator, would enter another large chamber where they would be mixed with a slurry of water and limestone. The limestone would react with the sulfur dioxide, forming a sludge that could be landfilled. The gases, with 90% of the sulfur dioxide removed, would then be vented to the air.

Scrubbers were enormous, as large as the generators themselves; they were also expensive. To install them at Bowen in time to reduce emissions in 1995 would require outlays of $143.85 million in 1992, $503.61 million in 1993, and $71.97 million in 1994. Once installed, the scrubbers would add 0.13 cents per kilowatt-hour to the operating costs of the Bowen plant, primarily for the purchase of limestone and the disposal of the sludge. They would also consume 2% of the

EXHIBIT 2 ● Projected Operating Data for the Bowen Plant: High-Sulfur Coal Without Scrubbers

FUEL		
Cost of coal per ton	1992–1995	$41.46
	1996–2016	29.82
Tons of coal to meet input requirements (per year)	8.338 million	
POLLUTION		
Sulfur dioxide emitted per year	266,550 tons	
ADDITIONAL COSTS	0	

EXHIBIT 3 ● Projected Operating Data for the Bowen Plant: High-Sulfur Coal with Scrubbers

FUEL		
Cost of coal per ton	1992–1995	$41.46
	1996–2016	29.82
Tons of coal to meet input requirements (per year)	8.338 million	
POLLUTION		
Sulfur dioxide emitted per year	before scrubbers are installed	266,550 tons
	once scrubbers are operational	26,655
ADDITIONAL COSTS		
Investment in Year 0	$143.85 million	
in Year 1	503.61 million	
in Year 2	71.97 million	
Additional operating costs ($/kwh)	$0.0013	
Energy consumption (% of revenue)	2%	

total amount of electricity generated at the plant once they were turned on. This would, in effect, reduce revenues by 2% (Exhibit 3).

The capital costs of the scrubbers could be depreciated over 20 years beginning in the first year of operation (i.e., beginning in 1995 if the scrubbers were installed to meet Phase One deadlines). In each of the first 5 years of the depreciation schedule, 14% of the capital costs could be depreciated; for the next 15 years, the company could depreciate 2% of the capital costs. These capital costs would include the capitalized interest (at 10% per year) on the scrubbers during the period when the devices were being installed. The scrubbers were not expected to have an appreciable salvage value.

The Southern Company could also wait to begin installing the scrubbers until 1997, bringing them on line in time for the more stringent Phase Two requirements. This strategy would delay the capital outlays of installing the scrubbers by five years, but in Phase One Bowen would have to buy allowances or burn lower-sulfur coal.

OPTION 3: BURN LOW-SULFUR COAL

Instead of installing the FGD equipment, the Southern Company could switch to low-sulfur coal from Kentucky or West Virginia. If Bowen chose to switch to this type of coal, it would wait until the beginning of 1996 to do so, since the utility's take-or-pay contract with its current supplier would expire at the end of 1995. The low-sulfur coal contained 1% sulfur by weight. It cost less than the company was currently paying for the coal burned at Bowen, but its cost was greater than the expected 1996 cost of high-sulfur coal. Its use, without scrubbers, would generate extra allowances under Phase One of the Clean Air Act. During Phase Two, Bowen would have to purchase some allowances.

Most coal was purchased and transported under contracts lasting from 5 to 20 years; the Southern Company could write contracts with mining companies and the railroads that would move the coal to Georgia, for any length of time it chose.

Low-sulfur coal with a heat content of

24.110 MMBtu per ton could be delivered to Bowen starting in 1996 for $30.37 per ton. Starting in 2000, however, its price was expected to rise to $34.92 per ton as the tighter controls in Phase Two drove up demand. It would take 8.391 million tons of this low-sulfur coal per year to generate electricity at Bowen at historic levels, and this coal would generate 167,650 tons of sulfur dioxide per year if burned without scrubbers.

Switching to low-sulfur coal would require changes in the electrostatic precipitators used to control airborne particulate matter (fly ash) at Bowen, since the equipment currently in place was designed to operate with high-sulfur coal. These investments would cost $22.1 million and would be depreciated like the investments in scrubbers (Exhibit 4).

OTHER CONSIDERATIONS

If the Southern Company installed scrubbers at Bowen, it would have to make modest investments in working capital, primarily to maintain an inventory of limestone. If it switched to low-sulfur coal for Phase One, it would burn its two-month inventory of high-sulfur coal at the beginning of 1996, so that 1996 emissions would be somewhat higher than emissions in 1997 and subsequent years. The effects of such changes were small, however, and did not materially alter the company's appraisal of its options.

EXHIBIT 4 ● Projected Operating Data for the Bowen Plant: Low-Sulfur Coal Without Scrubbers

FUEL		
Cost of coal per ton	1992–1995 (high-sulfur)	$41.46
	1996–1999	30.37
	2000–2016	34.92
Tons of coal to meet input requirements	high sulfur	8.338 million
	low sulfur	8.391 million
POLLUTION		
Sulfur dioxide emitted per year:	before switching	266,550 tons
	after switching	167,650
ADDITIONAL COSTS		
Investment in year switch occurs	$22.1 million	

26

SELF (A)
Scott B. Soneshein,
Michael Gorman,
and Patricia Werhane

The biggest threat to global warming and to greenhouse gases in the future is the unbridled development of the Third World.

—Neville Williams

Such a statement is quite bold coming from a man who strives to provide electricity to individuals living in developing nations. However, as bold as his statement is, Neville Williams has never backed down from a challenge. Williams, an ambitious scientist and scholar whose previous job experiences have included the promotion of renewable energy technologies for the Carter administration, has traveled to over 50 developing countries, including China. On such trips, Williams noticed how introducing electricity to developing nations drastically changed lives. At the same time, he was cognizant of how previous conventional electrification efforts have done irreversible environmental damage. For example, in 1990, carbon emission from fossil-fuel burning in China was 661 mil-

lion tons, or more than eleven percent of the world's total. From 1950 to 1990, world aggregate nitrogen emissions from fossil-fuel burning have increased from 6.8 to 26.5 million tons, and sulfur emissions from 30.1 to 68.7 million tons.

From his travels, Williams concluded that individuals living in developing nations "don't care about the environment," and only "care about getting electricity any way they can."[1] This presented him with a challenge: could he provide developing countries with environmentally friendly power? To this end, in 1990 he founded the Solar Electric Light Fund (SELF), a nonprofit, Washington, D.C.–based company that acts as a facilitator in providing persons in developing countries with an environmentally friendly power source. Williams formed his company with the underlying philosophy that all individuals are entitled to electricity, but at the same time, the entire planet is entitled to a safe environment. SELF's mission statement states that we must "address the issue of how 70 percent of the people in the Third World are going to get electricity without doing additional damage to the planet. Two billion people attempting to emerge from centuries of darkness into an electrically lighted future will be one of the critical issues of the 21st century."

Williams' first goal was to provide environmentally safe electricity to China, a country where some 20 million persons had no reliable source of power. His potential clients were some of the poorest individuals in the world. Cognizant of the relatively high energy costs in China, Williams knew that he needed to uncover some method of aiding the rural residents in obtaining power. However, restraining Williams' efforts was his strong interest in environmental preservation, a factor that he would not sacrifice.

Since everyone relies on scarce natural resources, China's environmental problems inevitably affect the entire world. Williams declares that "if the Third World develops in the way we did the world would be a wreck . . . because 70 to 80 percent of the people in developing countries don't even have electricity."[2] While past environmental damage cannot be reversed, future development can avoid the global environmental problems of previous electrification efforts. Conventional grid extensions of fossil-fuel power to the approximately two hundred million nonelectrified individuals in China would only add to the growing number of environmental problems and health risks. The obvious question arises: *How do individuals in China without access to electricity get a reliable power source without doing additional damage to the planet?*

ENERGY IN CHINA

Despite economic growth in China during the 1980s of approximately 10 to 14 percent annually, energy growth was significantly lower, at 4 to 6 percent. The gap between energy supply and energy demand has been widening at an astronomical pace, and by the year 2000 sources predict that there could be an energy shortage as high as 700 megatons (coal equivalent).[3]

One source attributed the growing gap between China's energy supply and energy demand to four key factors:[4]

1. Despite China's large population and energy production, China had a very low per-capita energy use, only 40 percent of the world average. Augmented economic growth would lead to an increase in income, of both urban and rural citizens. More income would increase power demand and therefore place additional strains on current energy sources.

2. China's energy consumption rate per US$ of GNP was four times that of Japan and five times that of France. In other words, it cost China four times the amount of money for electricity than it did Japan, and five times that of France. (See Exhibit 1.)

3. Investors infrequently funded the construction of power plants, opting for alternative projects which had shorter returns on investment.

4. Fossil-fuel reserves were not evenly distributed. This poor distribution of resources caused coal prices in Western Tibet to be 10 times higher than normal. Such high costs inevitably retarded economic growth.

Despite relatively high energy costs, China still relied heavily on traditional fossil fuels. A report on China's coal use concluded:

> [W]ith the rapid exploitation and high dependency of coal productivity, China is damaging not only the physical environment, but China is also creating health problems for Chinese people, and people in surrounding countries.[5]

Since approximately 70 percent of China's energy consumption comes from the burning of coal, it is not surprising that China's energy use has posed large-scale environmental problems to the entire world and severe health risks to Chinese citizens. Increased emissions of sulfur

Exhibit 1 ● SELF (A)

Energy Consumption for 1 US $ GNP (1989)

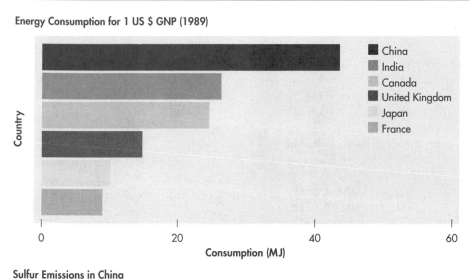

Sulfur Emissions in China

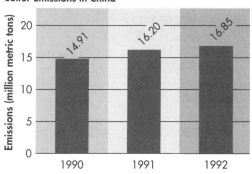

Source: China Economy Daily as cited in Yingjing Nan and Anhua Wang, *Alternative Energy Options with Reference,* and Trade and Environment Database, 1996

dioxide (SO_2) from the burning of fossil fuel have resulted in large amounts of air pollution. (See Exhibit 1.) This pollution has been far from negligible. In 1988, chronic obstructive pulmonary disease, an ailment caused primarily by SO_2 (and cigarette smoking) accounted for 26 percent of all deaths in China. Additionally, lung cancer deaths have drastically increased.

Coal burning has also heightened carbon dioxide (CO_2) emissions, which has subsequently exacerbated global warming. Besides global warming, acid rain has been linked to fossil fuel burning in China, the effects of which are easily noticed in China's urban areas:

When rain falls in metropolis cities in China, the pollution is clearly visible. Soot coats the pavement turning it into slippery muck, and turns the leaves a black-brown color . . . [Coal burning] has led to a rise in cancer and lung disease.[6]

Even with such obvious health and environmental risks, little has been done to improve China's energy problems. Plans for the construction of a new 2,640 megawatt coal-burning plant are underway. One report concluded: "Despite proof of toxic air pollutants and acid rain, China is making minimal efforts in converting coal-burning plants to more environmentally safe methods."[7]

Another report was slightly more optimistic:

China's energy-related pollution problems cannot be easily overlooked. They are likely to plague China for years because of the country's great potential for growth in energy use. However, China's success in de-coupling energy consumption and economic growth in the 1980s is cause for hope. Continued efforts to improve energy efficiency, use more renewable energy, and incorporate environmental factors into energy planning can help put China on a more sustainable energy path.[8]

THE MAGIACHA PROJECT IN GANSU, CHINA

Magiacha, a small village of about 200 families located in Tongwei County in Gansu, China, is situated about 1,200 miles west of Beijing. In 1992, none of the 850 villagers had access to electric power. Magiacha represented a specific target in China where Williams could attempt his mission—the village wanted some form of electricity and grid extension was not economically feasible. The villagers were not satisfied with their current power source. One villager observed:

We only had kerosene lamps, which gave us little light, like the stars do. It's so diffi-

cult for us to do any work in the evening time. The most dangerous thing was when we got up in the morning, our noses and mouths were filled with black ashes . . . [Kerosene makes us feel] dizzy in the head and dim of sight.[9]

Opportunity knocked for Williams; he had a village that he could electrify if he could find and demonstrate the affordability of a "new" technology. There were three such choices to consider: hydropower, photovoltaics, and clean coals.

HYDROPOWER

In 1990, China supplied almost five percent of the world's total hydroelectric generating capacity.[10] Touted as what would be the largest hydropower station and dam in the world, the Three Gorges Dam Project located in central China would provide 17 million kilowatts capacity of power and generate over 84 billion kilowatt-hours per year. The dam would operate by harnessing river currents, providing electricity without emitting pollution. The 1.2 mile dam would greatly contribute to China's increasing electricity needs. By the year 2015, China's power capacity would need to grow to 580 million kilowatts per year.

By supporting this project, Williams could help check China's coal consumption while providing energy for more individuals. However, various social and environmental costs would be incurred. Over 1.1 million individuals, many of whom were farmers, would have to be relocated. Cultural roots and river wildlife may be threatened and the risk of earthquakes and landslides would increase. Several endangered species including the Giant Panda, the Chinese Tiger and the Siberian Crane would be adversely impacted by the dam. Moreover, the cost of the dam would exceed any other single construction project in history.[11]

PHOTOVOLTAICS

Photovoltaic-generated power uses the sun's light to create energy. The National Renewable Energy Lab considers PV environmentally "benign." The systems rely exclusively on sun generated power and do not need fuel or cooling systems. PV panels, however, have a negative visual impact.

Williams' company found that for each PV user, over one quarter of a ton of carbon dioxide gas would have been produced by kerosene lamps supplying the same amount of light. In addition to the reduction of carbon dioxide emissions, finding an alternative to kerosene lamps will eliminate toxic, and potentially fatal fumes. In fact, 780 million women and children who are exposed to kerosene fumes inhale the equivalent of two packs of cigarettes a day.

Costs for photovoltaics in 1990 were relatively expensive, approximately $5.67 per watt.

CLEAN COAL

Approximately 70 percent of China's energy production comes from burning coal. Despite the fact that coal has been mined in China since 476 BC, it is estimated that the nation still has 4,490 billion tons of unmined coal. While most of China's coal consumption poses severe environmental damage, Williams could support technologies to minimize those threats. Cleaner-coal technology removes some of coal's toxic pollutants by using such methods as flue-gas desulphurization. The United States Department of Energy (DOE) considers the technology to be "an

investment in a cleaner [and] more secure energy future."[12] The department estimates that worldwide clean coal markets will be between $270 billion and $750 billion for the next 20 years. Besides the worldwide surge in clean coal demand, China has also recognized its benefits. China's vice minister of Power Industry has given top priority to developing clean coal technology.[13]

Notes

1. Neville Williams quoted in "Interview: 'SELF'—Working to Electrify the Third World," *Greenwire* 4 (Feb. 1992).

2. Ibid.

3. Yingjing Nan and Anhua Wang, *Alternative Energy Options with Reference to China* (Gansu National Energy Research Institute, 1992): 2.

4. Ibid.

5. Trade and Environment Database, "China Coal and Pollution, http://gurukul.ucc.american.edu/ted/CHINCOAL.HTML." (1996)

6. Ibid.

7. Ibid.

8. Congressional Testimony, *Views of Senator Arlen Spector,* 1994.

9. Ibid.

10. World Watch Data Disk, 1994.

11. Trade and Environment Database, "Three Gorges Dam," http://gurukul.ucc.american.edu/ted/THREEDAM.HTML

12. DOE Press Release, October 28, 1996.

13. *China Economic Daily News,* October 10, 1996.

SELF (B)
Scott B. Soneshein,
Michael Gorman,
and Patricia Werhane

Neville Williams's goal to achieve rural electrification of the Magiacha village in Gansu, China, with an environmentally friendly energy source led him to photovoltaics (PV). Williams hoped that this technology would provide a solution for China's energy crisis and mitigate environmental damage throughout the world.

He needed to act quickly. The task at hand for him was to be the first person to reach the nonelectrified individuals in China because, as he noted, "the first person to show up with electricity wins!"[1] Williams thought that if he did not electrify these people first with an environmentally safe power supply, another group would reach them using conventional fossil-fuel power, thereby augmenting a rapidly growing environmental disaster. While Williams might be the first person to introduce electricity, his problem was more complex: his clients were dirt poor. He notes: "You've got to give these people a way to afford 20 years of technology, which is

what a PV panel gives them. . . . But the cost . . . is generally what these people make in a year."[2]

PV technology is quite simple. Units harness the sun's rays and convert them to energy. For the most part, the energy is environmentally friendly. However, since the unit requires storage for energy when the sun is down, disposal of a battery will cause a relatively small environmental threat.

Williams chose individual PV house units with a 20-watt capacity. The $300 price was reasonable, yet still relatively expensive for the villagers. The capacity would be sufficient to satisfy most of their needs. Generating energy on the household level also seemed like a good match—expensive wiring and complex metering would not be needed.

The PV systems would drastically change the lives of the villagers. Their days would no longer end at sundown. This would allow children to have more time to read and become better educated. The units would provide energy for radios, a means of accessing information about the world.

Williams's nonprofit corporation, the Solar Electric Light Fund (SELF), makes it clear that it is not a charitable organization. SELF provides power only to individuals who have the financial means to purchase it. Such corporate ideology is grounded both pragmatically and philosophically. First, Williams notes that "there isn't enough money in the world to give this stuff (photovoltaics) away." Secondly, and more importantly, doling out electricity is inconsistent with SELF's corporate ideology of individual responsibility. Such a philosophy, SELF maintains, encourages villagers to both conserve energy and take care of their individual units. Additionally, ownership of property helps individuals in the developing world obtain a sense of pride.

Since SELF had both limited financial resources and a corporate philosophy that centered on individual responsibility, SELF would not provide free electricity to the villagers. While the PV units that Williams chose would provide only a modest supply of power, their cost would nevertheless place severe economic burdens on the villagers, as the cost of such units was equivalent to the villagers' annual incomes (see Exhibit 1).

A research report concluded:

> No market structure yet exists to handle the required capital flows [for solar technology]. The emerging [solar] industry . . . has been plagued by poor access to capital. Only about 5 percent of rural households in developing countries have the ability to purchase a system outright with cash.[3]

Magiacha was only a beginning for Williams; eventually, he hoped, no outside assistance would be needed to electrify the remaining areas of China. Such an ambitious project required that SELF "sow solar seeds" or facilitate initial purchases of PV units to begin the process of forming an independent solar market.

One possibility would be to secure funding from the Chinese government, which could be used to partially subsidize the PV units. Since the Chinese government was already subsidizing current grid extensions, it could easily direct some financial resources to purchasing PV units. Thus, instead of the Chinese government funding electrification projects that produce environmental problems, it could finance environmentally safe projects that would produce equivalent electrification results at the same time. In fact, since SELF asserted that any extension of existing electric-grid structures would require copper wiring at the cost of approximately $10,000/mile,[4] subsidizing PV technology would also be cheaper. While an extension of the electric-power grid would provide a greater power source, SELF argued that PV units would adequately meet the power demands of the villagers—individuals never before exposed to electric power. This solution would also allow the Chinese government to take responsibility for its own environmental problems by redirecting financial resources from environmentally devastating projects to environmentally friendly ones.

"SELF"

Use	Meaning
SELF-help	Demonstrate benefits of clean, decentralized, renewable energy
SELF-reliance	Families purchase their own solar-power systems.
SELF-determination	Ability to allow children to read after sundown and have access to electronic information
SELF-interest	Individual households are responsible for their own units, and ensure their efficient use
SELF-sufficiency	Become less dependent on oil; rural people become less dependent on urban grids
SELF-sustaining	Economic development as solar enterprises; employment and service businesses grow
SELF-improvement	People in agricultural areas raise their living standards in current rural locations

Exhibit 1 ● SELF (B): Cost of Photovoltaic

Average Costs for PV Units

Power (W)	Unit Cost ($)	Light Hours/Day	Capability
60	600.00	15	About six lights, some TV and radio most of the night
20	300.00	6	About two lights and a radio

Source: "Interview: 'SELF'—Working to Electrify the Third World," *Greenwire* (1992 Feb. 4).

Approximate Cost and Capacity of PV Cells

	1981	1992
Cost (Per peak watt of pv cells)	*$14.00*	*$6.00*
Capacity (MW)	5	55

Source: "Rural Development," *Energy Economist* (1993 Apr.)

As PV units spread throughout the country, SELF would eventually leave and private firms would enter the PV market, realizing a viable business endeavor and thus helping to facilitate electrification.

Williams might also look to organizations throughout the world who spend millions of dollars to preserve the environment and promote humanity. SELF could first argue that all individuals are entitled to a decent standard of living, and that such a standard requires electric power. Thus, it would only be fair that Magiacha receive electricity. In fact, China had already electrified 85 percent of its citizens, mostly through electric-grid extensions, and out of fair-

ness, some method of electrifying the rest of the country should be found. While most of China's electricity comes from fossil-fuel burning, however, SELF could push for private-sector charitable funding of PV technology, as an alternative to preserve the environment. This would enable the village to be electrified in an environmentally safe manner and would take advantage of the millions of dollars donated to environmental and humanitarian organizations. SELF would simply act as a catalyst in securing funds to individuals willing to purchase PV units. The funding would cover only down payments, ensuring that the villagers would pay for their electricity on a monthly basis and subsequently allowing the villagers to take individual responsibility for their own electricity. SELF would provide zero-interest loans for the difference between the subsidy and the unit cost.

As more individuals purchased solar units, for-profit corporations would also enter the solar market and electrification would proceed with two unique routes at twice the speed: subsidized

Financing Option A

Unit Cost	Chinese Govt. Subsidy	Balance upon Receipt
$300	$100	$200

Financing Option B

Unit Cost	Subsidy for Down Payment	Villager's Balance	Amount Per Month of Loan	Length of Loan
$300	$90	$210	$5.83-1.75	3–10 years

purchases via SELF organized funding and privatized market purchases.

Williams also considered securing working capital from environmental groups and governments to establish a "revolving credit fund" that provides zero-interest loans to villagers who purchase individual PV units. SELF would use the initial capital to purchase units. SELF would then turn over the units to the villagers. SELF would collect a down payment on the units from the villagers, followed by monthly installments, thereby having the villagers pay for the entire cost of the unit. Payments would be used to finance additional loans to other individuals wishing to acquire PV units. However, the villagers would need to pay back their loans in order for their neighbors to receive electricity and maintain the solvency of the revolving credit fund. In addition to providing more funding for other loans, the revolving credit fund would also promote borrowers to make timely—and some-

times early—payments to allow others access to loans. The fund would grow as more people made their payments and private solar markets would eventually develop. As a market began to form, SELF would exit China, thereby allowing the forces of the market to electrify China.

Williams pondered these three choices. In order to carry out this project he had to choose one.

Notes

1. Neville Williams quoted in "Interview: 'SELF'— Working to Electrify the Third World," *Greenwire,* Feb. 4. (1992).

2. Ibid.

3. Rockefeller Brothers, "Pocantico Paper Number Two" (1996).

4. "Solar Electric Light Fund Photovoltaic Rural Electrification," Official World Wide Web Site—Solar Electric Light Fund, Http://www.crest.org/renewables/self/newbroch.html.

Financing Option C

Unit Cost	Down Payment	Amount of Loan	Amount Per Month of Loan	Length of Loan
$300	$55	$245	$6.80-2.04	3–10 years

28

Deja Shoe (A): Creating the Environmental Footwear Company
Paul Hardy

Julie Lewis' interest in recycling began in the early 1960's when recycling wasn't fashionable. Recycling in her home was done out of necessity. She helped her mother crush aluminum cans and return them to the local recycling center. She became concerned with environmental issues as a high school student when national attention was focused on the first Earth Day and water restrictions made news in her native California. With the encouragement of her teacher, Lewis made a video on the "State of the Environment" for a class project. Combining her environmental awareness with her instilled habit of recycling, she endeavored to launch a program whereby students would sift through landfills to extract reyclables. However her effort was discouraged by landfill owners concerned about potential liabilities.

When she became active in environmental issues again years later, Lewis took note of existing recycling programs. Although her Oregon community had one of the most ambitious curbside collection programs in the state, little of the material collected was actually recycled. Most consumer products still used virgin materials in production processes, as potential uses for recyclables were largely misunderstood or unexplored. The faults in the recycling programs spurred her to act:

> The problem with the mandatory programs was that they didn't have any markets for the stuff, so a lot of it was put in warehouses and ended up in landfills anyway. Nobody wanted to pay to warehouse it and wait for markets to develop. I thought, "This is so stupid!" They should have thought of markets before they had this mandate. And so that became part of my mission—to create markets for recycled materials. I thought somebody has *got* to do this. I thought of shoes because, going back to my childhood again where I wore sandals from Mexico that had tire rubber soles, I thought we ought to be recycling tires again and putting them into shoe soles.

Lewis began calling mills in the southern United States to inquire about the possibilities of making a shoe fabric out of recyclables. After the mills did not respond to her inquiries, she contacted Bill Bowerman, founder of Nike and fellow Oregon resident, in order to discuss the viability of producing a recycled shoe. Bowerman recognized that the footwear industry engaged in wasteful practices and was intrigued by Lewis' idea to produce shoes from recycled materials. Bowerman recruited Nike executives to facilitate Lewis' interactions with manufacturers and with product designers. In the meantime, Lewis secured a $110,000 grant from a local agency that funded projects that attempted to broaden the market for recycled materials.

With seed funding and technical assistance secured, Lewis began to develop the strategy for launching the "environmental footwear company." Recycling underpinned the strategy. Lewis pointed to recycling as a way to minimize human impact on the environment and reduce the amount of material flowing into landfills. Raw materials for early "Deja shoes" included polystyrene cups, file folders, rejected coffee filters, baby diapers, plastic milk and soda bottles, paper bags and corrugated cardboard. Besides saving landfill space, she believed that recycling saved energy and helped minimize the air and water pollution emitted during the processing of virgin materials. She pointed out that recycling also protects landscapes and animal habitats, as mining, logging, oil production, and other extractive industries are curtailed. Finally, when consumers wore the shoes out, they could send them back to Deja to be recycled again.

Lewis also began initiating contacts with major international conservation organizations. She committed donating 5% of her company's pre-tax profits to the Species Survival Commission of the World Conservation Union in Switzerland. She endeavored to source raw materials that were sustainably harvested in developing countries, which in some cases would provide an alternative to slash and burn agriculture or clearcutting native forests.

Lewis articulated the company's vision of "sustainable development":

> We believe that economic growth for individuals, businesses, and societies should occur within ecological bounds and limitations set by nature. To be sustainable, development must meet present human needs without impacting future generations' ability to meet theirs.

Bowerman and other Nike executives were instrumental in helping her operationalize this vision. With technical assistance from the Amoco Corporation, Lewis had developed a prototype polypropylene fabric made from pre-consumer disposable diaper waste. On recommendation from her supporters at Nike, an Arkansas mill agreed to produce a run of five thousand pairs of shoes made from the recycled polypropylene. But as she boxed the shoes in her basement, Lewis noticed quality problems. Many pairs did not have the proper fit or had components that were not properly stitched and sealed. As a result, Lewis determined only a few thousand pairs could be salvaged from the production run.

THE MANAGEMENT TEAM

The experiment left Lewis over budget by $20,000 and with the realization she needed an experienced management team from the footwear industry to bring the product concept to the next stage. Lewis learned that Dean Croft, the former President of Avia, lived in her neighborhood. She visited her neighbor Croft at his home, who was impressed with what she was able to accomplish as an industry outsider. Croft referred her to Scott Taylor, Avia's former Chief Financial Officer. Taylor drew in Bruce MacGregor, another recently-departed Avia executive.

During his tenure with Avia, MacGregor had vice-presidential responsibilities for design, production, marketing, product development, and advertising and promotions at different times. MacGregor had just left Avia when he was contacted by Taylor. MacGregor recounts his initial conversations with Taylor about coming to work at the environmental footwear company:

> I had said that I'm going on sabbatical for a while and I don't want to talk business. He kept after me when I got back from Europe and I said fine. It was really more of a favor just to sit down with him and see what was up. So I ended up meeting Julie.

The idea intrigued me. I guess what intrigued me is that I saw a shoe that looked brand new. And that startled me.

The design, the fit, the comfort—all the aspects of the footwear itself were absolutely terrible. Nevertheless, the shoe looked brand new. That was really the first time I understood what she was trying to do here. I don't know what I was expecting, I guess maybe soiled shoes or worn shoes!

In 1991, the three partners divided responsibilities for managing the company. MacGregor became President of Deja, Inc. and Taylor became CFO. Lewis took on responsibility for new product development and materials sourcing as Vice-President for Research. The former Avia executives funded the next six months of operations out of their own pockets, moved the operation out of Lewis' basement and into a Portland area office and began drafting a business plan and raising capital.

MacGregor's and Taylor's experience in the footwear industry and familiarity with financial markets and Lewis' articulation of the sustainable product concept was received favorably by venture capitalists. In March 1992, Deja received its first round of equity funding. U.S. Venture Partners, Allstate Venture Capital, and BancBoston invested a total of $2.5 million. Some of the same venture capital firms had invested in Avia when Deja's new management team held leadership positions. During Taylor and MacGregor's tenure at Avia, the company's sales grew from $5 million a year to $200 million. Ann Doherty of Allstate Venture Capital in Chicago remarked:

> It was Julie's vision, zeal, and innovative approach to recycling technology that attracted the attention and backing of some key business people who have proven track records in the industry. Allstate reviews more than 600 potential investments every year in a wide variety of industries and

funds only about eight or ten. Deja had the right mix of timing, trends, and most importantly, a management team capable of pulling it off.

THE FOOTWEAR MARKET

The market for footwear in the U.S. is approximately 1 billion pairs of shoes per year. The market is divided into three primary segments: athletic, casual, and an "other" category that includes formal footwear and specialty footwear.

Athletic footwear constitutes nearly 35% of the total footwear market and is an extremely competitive segment. The athletic segment is dominated by industry giants Nike and Reebok, which together account for over 50% of the $8.7 billion athletic footwear market. Nike's and Reebok's athletic footwear are manufactured in Asia. For both companies, Indonesia and China were the number one and number two manufacturing locations. Thailand, Taiwan and South Korea are among the other nations which produce at least 10% of the footwear products for the companies. The low wage rates in Asia contributed to the companies' 40% gross margin on their footwear products.

Among the functions at Nike's and Reebok's U.S. headquarters are product design and marketing. Marketing was an area of particularly intense competition. Market trends showed that performance was an attribute of athletic footwear that influenced consumer's purchasing patterns. As a result, Nike and Reebok lured high profile athletic celebrities to endorse and promote their products. Income statements for Nike and Reebok can be found in Exhibit 1.

Smaller companies vie for share in specialty athletic markets by developing performance products for specific athletic activities. In the 1980's, Avia Group International, Inc. exploited such a niche by focusing on performance footwear for aerobics, cross-training, and tennis. This strategy led the company to the company's

Exhibit 1 ● Consolidated Statement of Income for Nike and Reebok

Nike: Consolidated Statement of Income	1993	1992
Revenues	$3,930,984	$3,405,211
Costs and expenses:		
Cost of sales	2,386,993	2,089,089
Selling and administrative expenses	922,261	761,498
Other expenses	27,214	32,806
Total expenses	$3,336,468	$2,883,393
Income before taxes	594,516	521,818
Income taxes	229,500	192,600
Net income	$ 365,016	$ 329,218
Net income per common share	$ 4.74	$ 4.30
Average number of common and common equivalent shares	77,063	76,602

Notes: Figures are for fiscal year ending May 31. All figures are in thousands, except per share data.

Reebok: Consolidated Statement of Income	1993	1992
Revenues	$2,893,933	$3,062,346
Costs and expenses:		
Cost of sales	1,719,869	1,809,304
Selling and administrative expenses	769,744	807,078
Other expenses	41,073	188,000
Total expenses	$2,530,686	$2,804,382
Income before taxes	363,247	257,964
Income taxes	139,832	143,146
Net income	$ 223,415	$ 114,818
Net income per common share	$ 2.53	$ 1.24
Average number of common and common equivalent shares	88,348	92,697

Notes: Figures are for fiscal year ending December 31. All figures are in thousands, except per share data.

explosive growth before being acquired by Reebok.

The casual footwear market accounts for approximately 30% of all footwear sales, generating between $3.5 billion and $4 billion in revenue. In contrast to the athletic footwear market, no major brand dominates the casual segment.

Companies competing in the premium casual segment include Rockport (a Reebok subsidiary), Dexter, Florsheim, Nine West (a Nike subsidiary), Teva, Doc Marten, and Birkenstock. Wholesale price for premium casual footwear is $20 or higher. Yet the largest segment of casual footwear has a wholesale price under $20. Value is the dominant purchasing criteria in this segment, which constitutes approximately 70% of casual footwear market.

Timberland is the largest company in the casual footwear market; the company's $418 million in sales in 1993 accounted for between 10%–12% of all casual footwear sold. Product design, marketing, and investor relations are handled from Timberland's corporate headquarters in New Hampshire. Timberland products are marketed to consumers in the outdoor casual segment that pay a premium for stylish leather designs and durability. Many Timberland walking shoes and workboots are waterproof and quadruple stitched.

Timberland products are manufactured primarily in the Dominican Republic, with some production occurring in Taiwan, Thailand, and other East Asian nations. Until early 1995, Timberland contracted with mills in North Carolina and Tennessee, but withdrew from U.S. production when quality standards could be achieved by off-shore manufacturers at a lower price. The company's costs for materials and production amount to between $18 and $20 per pair. Timberland's products retail for $80 on average. The Timberland Company's income statement can be found in Exhibit 2.

MANUFACTURING & MATERIALS

Deja shoes were manufactured in Asia. Manufacturing the shoes in Asia appeared to be a necessity. To manufacture in the United States would have meant incorporating the higher wages of U.S. workers into the price of the shoes. Yet because of the relatively small production orders, the costs associated with developing new materials, and no economies of scale over which to disperse these costs, the costs advantage of manufacturing in Asia was not as great as it was for the large companies in the athletic wear segment.

MacGregor, concerned that the start-up operation needed the lowest labor costs and the greatest manufacturing flexibility that it could

Exhibit 2 ● Consolidated Statement of Income for The Timberland Company

Timberland: Consolidated Statement of Income	1993	1992
Revenues	$418,918	$291,368
Costs and expenses:		
Cost of sales	266,211	183,510
Selling and administrative expenses	111,541	81,339
Other expenses	7,043	7,520
Total expenses	$384,795	$272,369
Income before taxes	34,123	18,999
Income taxes	11,602	6,080
Net income	$ 22,521	$ 12,919
Net income per common share	$ 2.01	$ 1.18
Average number of common and common equivalent shares	11,206	10,922

Notes: Figures are for fiscal year ending December 31. All figures are in thousands, except per share data.

find, made use of the Asian contacts developed while at Avia. However, manufacturing a Deja shoe imposed different requirements on factories than manufacturing footwear for traditional footwear companies. MacGregor explains that despite their extensive footwear manufacturing experience, Asian firms still faced a learning curve when it came to manufacturing Deja shoes:

> There's a lot of components that go into a shoe. If you're a traditional footwear company sourcing in Asia, you just give your specs to the factory and the manufacturers procure the materials. Or if you're sourcing in this country, you just give the specs to your manufacturing folks here and they source the materials. We gave our specs to the factories in Asia and they went, "Wait a minute!" Obviously they didn't know where to begin. "Excuse me, what's this? Ex-baby diapers and milk jugs?"

Deja's management recognized that the traditional industry relationship with Asian manufacturers would not serve the company's needs. The manufacturers' inexperience with recycled materials and an underdeveloped recycling infrastructure in Asia meant that the responsibility for material procurement would fall not to the manufacturers, but to Deja Inc. Sources for raw materials (i.e. baby diapers, milk jugs, etc.) were identified in the United States, the U.K., Canada, and Japan, purchased by Deja and then sent to a facility that could reprocess the materials into a fabric, sole, or other shoe component.

After the raw materials were recycled, Deja would ship the finished components to Asia for assembly into a Deja shoe. Deja's management considered producing shoes closer to the sources of recycled materials. However, the high wage rates in North America, Europe and Japan precluded this option.

At Deja, the company's deepening involvement in the sourcing and manufacturing processes

was viewed as a necessity, as the incorporation of recycled materials into footwear was the essence of their product's differentiation from other brands of footwear. "We basically had to become the material sourcing wing, which complicates things compared to traditional footwear start-up. But we had to do that," asserted MacGregor. As a result, Deja's cost for producing a shoe was around $22. MacGregor estimated that the environmental design and materials in Deja shoes resulted in at least a 20% premium over the cost of footwear produced by traditional footwear companies.

During his initial discussions with Lewis, MacGregor believed that Lewis had finalized the development of a high-strength polypropylene fabric made from recycled material. However, the polypropylene fabric was not perfected. Recycled polypropylene had more impurities than polypropylene made from virgin materials. In the production process, the recycled version had a higher melting point that resulted in damage to the extruders and other manufacturing equipment belonging to the Arkansas firm that produced the trial run of 5,000 pairs. The management team had to seek out a substitute material for the recycled polypropylene half-way through the development of the first product (to be released as the spring '93 line). MacGregor recounted the frustration of having to find an alternative for polypropylene mid-way through the design phase:

> We switched gears and found a canvass from Eco-Fibre in Canada. But it just wasn't the technical story that polypropylene told. It wasn't the environmental story or the technical story. There was a great environmental story to pre-consumer waste from the manufacturing of baby diapers. There's a great technical story because polypropylene is incredibly strong and wicks moisture. So we lost a lot of elements when we had to go to canvass.

Besides believing that Eco-Fibre's recycled canvass would not make the same deep impression among consumers that would be made by a material produced from recycled diapers, MacGregor had other reservations about the switch from polypropylene to canvass. Although some footwear products used canvass, MacGregor knew that 80%–90% of the footwear sold in the U.S. was leather. Furthermore, because the switch occurred late in the design phase, there was not adequate time to test how Eco-Fibre's canvass would perform. Although he considered delaying bringing the shoes to market until the spring '94 season, Deja's financial agreement with the venture capitalists was based on sales beginning in 1993.

THE MARKET FOR DEJA SHOES

Market research began in-house. Because Lewis seemed like a typical consumer, MacGregor asked her a series of questions. "What do you watch on TV and what do you like to eat? What do your friends eat? What do you wear?" were included among the questions that he fired at her. Lewis spent time in the library researching consumer preferences. This research, in combination with polling data concerning people's attitudes towards the environment, indicated that consumers would welcome green products. Deja's management reviewed the results of a New York Times/CBS News poll taken in April 1990. The poll revealed that 60% of the population believed that those involved in environmental groups are "reasonable" and only 27% believed they were "extremists." Furthermore, 71% of the respondents said that the environment should be protected even if it means increased spending and higher taxes. When viewed historically against previous polls, the percentages indicated that more of the public was identifying with environmentalists.

The polls also helped them estimate that up to 60% of the population views *itself* as core en-

vironmentalists but, as company documents illustrate, "these more 'conveniently green' consumers usually select the environmental product over others if they do not have to sacrifice function, value, or fashion." Management estimated that 5%–10% of the U.S. population consisted of consumers who would put environmental standards above other concerns when making purchasing decisions.

Successful businesses such as The Body Shop, Ben & Jerry's, and Patagonia further confirmed that a large market existed for products brought to market by socially-responsible businesses. Lewis and MacGregor sketched a profile of Deja's core consumer. The profile can be found in Exhibit 3. MacGregor summarized the results of the team's research efforts:

> . . . We had a lot of surveys on who considered themselves environmentalists, environmentally sensitive, etc. And this just wasn't from one survey. We took a combination of a Roper poll and a USA Today poll. Generally, about fifty percent of the population, it turned out through these polls, was our target audience. Particularly, women were more sensitive than men, which isn't surprising because women are generally more socially responsible and probably more moderate politically than men, as we now see in elections. So we went off these polls.

As a result, the 30–45 year old casual segment was targeted because market research suggested that women in this age group were the most environmentally-conscious consumers. Deja Inc. was entering the casual footwear market while this segment was undergoing rapid growth. Changes in lifestyles towards recreation and casual dress, and changes in footwear fashion from athletic styles to casual styles, are accredited with the increased demand for casual shoes. Another consideration for entering the casual

Exhibit 3 ● Consumer Profiles

Deja's management sketched the following consumer profiles based upon information from a Roper Poll and a USA Today poll.

Core Environmental Consumer 22%–29% of the U.S. Population	*Environmentally Sensitive Consumer 26%–31% of the U.S. Population*
At least half this group are baby boomers. (30–45 years old)	The majority of this group are Generation X. (18–29 years old)
Predominantly female.	Gender balanced.
Middle to upper income.	Generally middle income.
Most have college degrees.	Educated or still in school.
Think globally, act locally.	Think locally, act locally.
Pro-active on environmental issues, either with their time or money.	Act only on environmental issues that affect them.
Skeptical of commercial claims.	Skeptical of commercial claims.
Most will not pay much or any premium for environmentally correct product.	Will definitely not pay a premium for environmentally correct product.
Environmentalism is a lifestyle issue.	Environmentalism, when convenient.
Active in the outdoors.	Somewhat active in the outdoors.
See themselves as non-conforming.	More non-conforming.

---

footwear market was that the segment is highly fragmented, signifying the company would not have to displace dominant competitors to compete effectively. Based on sketches drawn by a friend of Lewis', the company introduced the Envirolite for women in the 30–45 year old group.

Deja's management also identified the 18–29 year old market segment—Generation X—as crucial to the company's success, due to the role this group has as a leader of fashion trends. Doc Marten, Teva, and Birkenstock were popular with Generation X. With the younger segment in mind, designers produced specs for the Eco-sneak.

Keeping with the firm's vision of sustainable development were provisions to take back Deja shoes after consumers had worn them out. Consumers were encouraged to send their used shoes back to the company's Oregon headquarters. The used shoes would then be recycled, thereby serving as raw material for the next gen-

eration of product. To facilitate the take-back, the Deja shoe box was designed to be easily turned inside out. The interior of the box was pre-printed with space for a mailing label, as well as with artwork depicting various endangered species.

MARKETING AND PROMOTION

Management also concluded that the majority of potential consumers reside in regions where the environment holds a prominent place on the civic agenda. These regions include the Pacific Coast and the Northeast, and to a lesser extent, the states located in the Upper Midwest and Rocky Mountains. Needing assistance in reaching retailers, the management team hired sales representatives which divided responsibility for covering the country on a geographic basis.

Retailers across the United States enthusiastically received Deja shoes, remarking on the innovation and timeliness of the product concept. A global conference held in Rio de Janeiro in 1992 had focused media attention on rainforest destruction, loss of biological diversity and other environmental issues. As the management team and sales staff introduced the shoes, major retailers signed on with very little hesitation, believing that the recycled footwear concept behind Deja's products would quickly translate into sales to an increasing environmentally-aware consumer base.

Within a few months, many retailers which catered to outdoor enthusiasts and green consumers, as well as major department stores, were promising to showcase Deja products in catalogs and in-store displays. MacGregor recalled the retailers' reactions:

> Once we got the spring '93 line together and started showing retailers . . . the reaction was amazing. L.L. Bean, who's very conservative, wanted to put us in their catalog the first time, which they did. Recreation Equipment Inc. (REI) was super excited and (also very conservative) gave us more space in the spring catalog than they gave either Rockport or Timberland. Then Nordstrom in Northern California put us on the cover of their spring men's catalog. So out of the box, never having shipped a shoe, retailers are raving about this.

Throughout the year, many other retailers, including Bloomingdales, also decided to carry Deja products. A partial list of Deja retailers is located in Exhibit 4. Although Deja finished 1993 with nearly 400 retail accounts across the United States served by 25 representatives, it was difficult for MacGregor to pinpoint why Deja shoes had made such an impression with the retailers.

> You're never quite sure breaking it down. It's just like if it doesn't work, it's more

than one factor and if it does work, it's more than one factor. But they loved the concept. They thought the public was ripe.

Green stores were more enthusiastic about Deja's products than mainstream retail outlets. Larger green businesses, such as Seventh Generation's catalog business, as well as smaller green outlets, welcomed the introduction of the recycled shoes. Such businesses tend not to specialize in any one product area, but rather act as one-stop shopping outlets for consumers whose purchasing choices are based on environmental concerns. A consumer could expect to find organically grown foods, clothing made from hemp, and chlorine-free recycled paper in a green retail outlet. Although they had no direct experience in the footwear industry or selling shoes, the green stores provided Deja's sales representatives with extensive orders. Moreover, because green businesses were a small, but rapidly growing retail sector, Deja's management had high expectations for future sales through this channel. Data that management used to understand the growth of the green product market can be found in Exhibit 5.

Deja's recycled footwear concept generated substantial attention from the mainstream press. Lewis' early efforts were highlighted in Portland's major newspapers. Lewis also was interviewed by a major wire service, which distributed the Deja story to media outlets across the nation. Each news story brought a flurry of inquiries from other news media as well as from prospective customers, retailers and other business partners. Lewis recalled that after Deja shoes were featured on the front page of the *Wall Street Journal's* Marketplace section, her phone would not stop ringing. She noted, "Every time that I returned to the house after being gone for a few hours, my answering machine would be full of messages!"

The company also received several high profile awards. Deja shoes won the National Recycling Coalition's Best Product Innovation

Exhibit 4 ● Partial List of Deja, Inc. Accounts

ATHLETIC FOOTWEAR STORES
- Athletic Attic
- Just for Feet
- Lady Footlocker
- Gart Bros.

DEPARTMENT STORES
- Parisian
- Nordstrom
- Bloomingdales
- Jacobson's
- Strawbridge & Clothier
- Barney's

SHOE STORES
- Chemins
- C & J Clark

SPECIALTY WALKING/COMFORT STORES
- Overland Trading Company
- The Walking Co.

SPECIALTY OUTDOOR RETAILERS
- Paragon
- Whole Earth Provisions
- The Great Outdoor Provision Company
- Recreational Equipment, Inc.
- L.L. Bean
- Eastern Mountain Sports

GREEN STORES
- What a World
- Earthsake
- Eco Habit
- The Nature Company

SPECIALTY APPAREL BOUTIQUES
- Passport
- Fast Forward
- Eileen Fisher Boutique

MAIL ORDER CATALOGS
- Eastbay
- Plow & Hearth
- Hanna Anderson

GREEN CATALOGS
- Real Goods Catalog
- Seventh Generation
- Eco Design

Award at the group's 1993 annual conference in Nashville, Tennessee. During the 75th commencement exercise at Connecticut College, the college's president bestowed Lewis with an honorable mention award in the college's first Inherit the Earth Award program.

The importance of the press attention was not lost on MacGregor. In contrast to the huge advertising budgets of dominant footwear industry players, marketing expenses accounted for only 6% to 7% of the start-up company's expenses. MacGregor estimated that the concept behind the recycled footwear generated $5 million a year in free advertising.

PRICING

The company's market research indicated that the 5%–10% of the population that were truly core environmentalists would pay a premium for

Exhibit 5 ● Data on Green Markets

New green product introductions have increased from 2.8% of all new product introductions in 1988 to 12.8% in 1993.
Source: Marketing Intelligence Ltd.

Sales of green household products are expected to increase from $2.1 billion in 1991 to $7.7 billion in 1996.
Source: Green Market Alert, March/April '92.

Sales of all green products are projected to increase from $26.1 billion in 1991 to $96.5 billion in 1996.
Source: Green Market Alert, March/April '92.

Deja shoes, but the roughly 50%–60% that was environmentally-aware was unlikely to do so. However, Deja's mainstream accounts insisted that their shoppers would pay a premium for a recycled product. They believed that Deja's radical innovations would be refreshing to a footwear market that had been used to only moderate innovations from incremental changes in style.

In 1993, Deja's canvass casual, the Envirolite, had a wholesale price of $30 and a retail price of $60, although most other canvass casuals retailed for between $20 and $30. Deja's Envirolite had an inner sole which provided more arch support than traditional canvass footwear. Management thought that the value-added pro-

vided by the sole would possibly justify the higher price. Yet the enthusiasm expressed by Nordstrom and other mainstream retailers was the factor which overcame skepticism about the "conveniently green" segment. MacGregor recalled rationalizing the adoption of the premium pricing strategy:

> For a canvass product, yes it was a premium. But despite all and any concerns, when you get that kind of reaction from three of the leading retailers in the country that have a lot of experience and a lot of savvy, you tend to say, "Well, if they think it's right, it's right. So let's go."

29

Procter & Gamble Inc.: Downy Enviro-Pak
Janet Lahey,
Chris Lane,
and Adrian B. Ryans

In February, 1989, Grad Schnurr, the brand manager for Downy fabric softener at Procter & Gamble Inc., needed to work fast to develop plans to launch a refill pouch called an Enviro-Pak for the Downy product line. The introduction of such packaging would result in a reduction in the solid waste created by the Downy fabric softener. Several key decisions had to be made regarding pricing and promotion. Senior management had a keen interest in this project, especially after seeing the success of Loblaws' Green Product line. The environment was now a significant concern to consumers, and P&G Inc. wanted to be the first major consumer goods company in the market with their response.

COMPANY HISTORY

Procter & Gamble (P&G) was founded in Cincinnati, Ohio in 1837 when William Procter, a candlemaker, and James Gamble, a soap maker,

●

formed a partnership that grew to become a leading international company. By 1988 P&G was selling more than 160 brands in 140 countries and was a global leader in household cleaning, health care, personal care, and food product markets. Total sales exceeded $20 billion in 1988. P&G's leading brands include Tide laundry detergent, Pampers diapers, Ivory soap, Downy fabric softener, Crest toothpaste, Crisco oil, Duncan Hines baking mixes, and Vicks cold care products.

PROCTER & GAMBLE INC.

Procter & Gamble Inc. (P&G Inc.) opened its first Canadian plant in 1915 in Hamilton, Ontario. It subsequently added three manufacturing sites in Belleville and Brockville, Ontario, and Pointe Claire, Quebec. P&G Inc. experienced substantial growth during the 1980s, with net sales doubling between 1978 and 1988. 1988 sales exceeded $1.2 billion, with net income of $78.9 million.

P&G Inc. was organized into four divisions: Laundry and Cleaning Products, Health and Beauty Care, Food, and Paper Products. In an effort to push down decision-making and increase responsiveness to the market, the company was organized on a category basis within each division (i.e., Fabric Softeners within the

Laundry and Cleaning Products division). Each category had managers from Marketing, Finance, Sales, Product Supply, and Marketing Research assigned to it.

Marketing was organized on a brand management basis, with a brand manager and one or two assistant managers concentrated on the business of one product/brand, such as Tide detergent or Downy fabric softener. Promotions and projects within a brand were executed by business teams which involved the other functional managers responsible for the category. During significant new product launches or promotions, these teams would meet every three or four weeks to review their progress.

Downy

Downy is a popular liquid fabric softener used in the washing machine to soften clothes, remove static from clothes and leave them with a fresh scent. In early 1989, regular Downy was being sold in 1L, 1.5L, and 3L plastic jugs, and concentrated Downy was being sold in 500 mL, 1L and 2L sizes. Overall, Downy was the number two brand in Canada in the liquid fabric softener category with a 12% share of the market. Its major competition consisted of a similar product called "Fleecy," manufactured by Colgate-Palmolive, as well as fabric softener dryer sheets which Procter & Gamble produced. There was little growth in this market segment, and competition usually took place on a price or incremental improvement (scent, efficacy) basis.

Pricing   The 3 litre bottle of Downy generated a contribution margin of 23%, and was sold to the trade at $5.99. The average shelf price of $7.30 reflected typical trade margin levels of 18% (calculated on retail price). When Downy was on deal, the shelf price would fall to about $5.99. Downy appeared to be priced at a pre-

mium versus competition, but on a price per use basis was on par with the major competitor.

Promotion   The 1989 Downy marketing plan included several promotions and incentives at both the consumer and trade levels. Events were scheduled to take place approximately every two months and would generally last four weeks. Approximately 70% of Downy was sold to the trade on deal.

ENVIRONMENTAL CONCERN

In 1989 the environment had become a significant issue to Canadian consumers. David Nichols of Loblaws gained celebrity status when he launched an innovative line of "Green Products" which claimed to be "environmentally friendly." In Ontario alone, Loblaws sold more than $5 million of Green products. It was clear that these products had a wide appeal. Business magazines were running articles concerning environmental management on a regular basis. One environmental concern, which was the primary focus of several lobby groups and which could be most readily addressed by consumers, was solid waste.

Landfill sites in urban communities like Toronto were projected to be full by the mid-90s. This posed a serious problem for government officials in determining locations for new sites, since "NIMBY" (not in my back yard) protests by the residents close to proposed landfill locations were increasingly effective. People were becoming aware of how much solid waste was being buried in the ground. As a result, some communities had started up "Blue Box" curbside recycling programs which were run by the government and partially funded by industry. Household residents stored particular types of waste, such as newspapers, soft drink bottles, and tin cans in a blue plastic box which were collected and sorted by municipal operators. The overwhelming success of these programs, with participation rates over 80%, indicated citizens were highly concerned about protecting their environment and were willing to make an effort to reduce the amount of solid waste being sent to landfill sites.

Government Action

The Ontario Government had legislated new regulations for the soft drink industry, under the Environmental Protection Act, requiring specific percentages of recyclable bottles. It had also stated a goal of a 25% reduction in the use of landfill sites by 1992. Other industries were speculating that the provincial government would soon require funding from them for recycling programs and were aware that legislation similar to the soft drink industry might also follow. Ontario was seen to be the leading province in dealing with environmental issues. Other provinces were expected to introduce similar programs after they had been proven in Ontario.

Procter & Gamble's Environmental Policy

P&G Inc. considered itself to be a community leader in terms of being a responsible business organization that contributed to the well-being of the environment. By 1989 it had already undertaken a number of environmental initiatives including:

1. Using recycled materials for P&G product cartons and shipping containers. Laundry detergent cartons were made of 100% recycled paper.

2. Introducing a paper recycling program in the corporate head office.

3. Eliminating heavy metals from printing inks to facilitate safer incineration.

P&G Inc.'s efforts in the solid waste area were a major responsibility of a division General Manager and the Director of Product Development. The corporate policy followed the generally accepted ranking of waste management priorities: source reduction, re-use, and re-cycling.

EUROPEAN ENVIRO-PAKS

In early 1989 Procter & Gamble Inc. was receiving consumer complaints regarding solid waste at an increasing rate. Disposable diapers were a particular area of concern. Calls about the environment had doubled in frequency over the past few months. P&G subsidiaries in Germany, Switzerland, and France had recently introduced "stand-up" pouches as refills for previously purchased bottles of Downy. These pouches (a type of Enviro-Pak) significantly reduced the solid waste generated by the Downy product. Grad Schnurr decided to review the results of the European launches to help him develop a strategy for a Canadian introduction (see Exhibit 1).

Product

A number of market research studies conducted in Europe indicated that the success of the pouch could be attributed primarily to its convenience and cost relative to the bottled Downy. Packages that reduced the amount of solid waste could generate further savings to German consumers, who were faced with financial penalties for excess garbage disposal.

Promotion

In Germany, the Downy pouch had been launched with substantial consumer and trade promotions including in-store refill demonstrations and give-aways, trade samples followed by telephone calls for orders, shopping bag advertising, trade incentives for display and direct delivery of display pallets.

Exhibit 1 ● European Enviro-Pak Results

	Downy Enviro-Pak Market Share	Enviro-Pak Share of Downy Business
Germany	11.2%	26%
France	2.3	14
Switzerland	4.1	19
Austria	3.1	31
Spain	0.7	12
Italy	0.7	8

Source: Company records

Pricing

The most popular package size for Downy in Europe was a 4 litre bottle. The European pouch had been originally priced at a 5% discount to this bottled version with very disappointing re-purchase results. The problem stemmed from the promotional price of the 4 litre bottle, which often made the consumer price of the pouch more expensive. The trade was not reducing the pouch prices because they wished to retain the good margins they provided. P&G conducted a test market in one city with the pouch priced at a 15% discount to the bottle on a per usage basis. This resulted in a significant volume improvement, with the pouch reaching a market share of 17% versus its previous share of 10%.

Share Results and Cannibalization

The pouch had been introduced in Germany and had achieved an 11% market share (see Exhibit 1). Although this was accompanied by a drop in the partner 4 litre size, the overall market share for Downy grew, taking Downy's share from 20% to 25% after the pouch was launched. Grad Schnurr wondered whether the same effect would occur in Canada, and what implications this had for the pricing of the pouch.

THE DOWNY ENVIRO-PAK

The Downy pouch or Enviro-Pak provided a significant reduction in solid waste after use, containing 85% less plastic than the 3 litre bottle it would refill. The pouch was similar to a plastic milk bag, but had a gusseted bottom so it could stand upright on the shelf. A consumer would cut the corner of the pouch off and then pour the product through a funnel into an empty 3 litre bottle. He or she would then add two litres of water, shake the bottle, and have three litres of fabric softener ready for use.

Grad Schnurr thought the Downy Enviro-Pak offered benefits for both consumers and the trade. Consumers would be attracted to the product for two reasons. First, by using the Enviro-Pak, they would be reducing the amount of household solid waste they generated. Second, the price could be lower than that of the regular bottle. Grad Schnurr recognized that the pouch represented a small inconvenience to consumers, as they had to do some preparation before they could use the product. Some consumers would

Exhibit 2 ● Downy Sales to the Trade in Canada

	Shipments (000 cases)*	Market Share
1988		
July	79	
August	72	13.8%
September	91	
October	78	12.6%
November	95	
December	69	12.5%
1989		
January	139	
February	96	12.6%
March**	89	
April**	70	14.2%
May**	73	
June	100	11.8%

*3 litre Downy was packed 6 bottles to a case

**Forecast

Source: Company records

also be concerned about spillage when they were refilling the bottle. These factors would need to be addressed through the Enviro-Pak's price and promotion plan.

The trade would also benefit in two ways. The pouches would attract environmentally conscious shoppers to their stores, away from competitors who did not carry such products. Also, the unique design of the Enviro-Pak provided more efficient use of space versus the bottled Downy. This second feature would provide decreased retailer handling and inventory costs.

Competitive Activity

Downy's three major competitors had also launched refill versions in Europe. No such activity had taken place in North America, but Canada would be a logical target for the next expansion, given the growing concern about the environment. However, Mr. Schnurr was unsure as to how applicable the German market results would be in predicting the response to the new package in Canada.

The logistics of the product launch also remained to be worked out. Given the likelihood of competitive activity in developing a more environmentally friendly package for Downy fabric softener, Grad Schnurr wasn't sure whether he should conduct a test market first or launch the Enviro-Pak in parts of Canada immediately. This decision was further complicated with trade rumours that Colgate-Palmolive was about to launch an environmental package. It would be much tougher trying to get retailers to list the Enviro-Paks if they already carried competitive versions. The brand that was able to introduce its environmental package first would gain an enviable reputation as a leading force in fighting the war on solid waste.

Manufacturing Issues

The manufacturing business team members estimated that their production schedule could support an August launch in Ontario and Quebec. These provinces were chosen for a number of reasons, including rising environmental awareness, potential volume, distribution time from plant, and competitive activity. The Hamilton plant estimated that it would take them an additional four months to get enough volume to fill the distribution pipeline and support ongoing shipments for the rest of the country. The cost of a packing line capable of producing 300,000 cases[1] annually of Enviro-Paks was estimated at $600,000.

Given the unique nature of this product, there was a high degree of uncertainty about the shipment forecasts. The last thing Grad Schnurr wanted was to have an overwhelming response to the Enviro-Pak with orders which P&G could not fill due to lack of supply.

Pricing

Grad Schnurr knew it would be vital to maintain the pouch price point below the comparable price of the 1.5 litre and 3 litre bottles. The pouch design provided a significant savings in the cost of goods sold. Its total delivered cost was 10% less than the 3 litre bottle. Grad Schnurr had to consider the total contribution of the brand and how much of this saving should be passed on to the trade and consumer. He was considering two options:

1. *An everyday low retail price ($6.29).* This option would give the Enviro-Pak a discount versus the regular price of the 3 litre size ($7.30) using a cost per use comparison. The price to retailers would be either $5.16 or $4.74, depending on whether they were offered an 18% or 25% margin. The higher margin would help assure fast acceptance, as retailers traditionally received 18% margins on the Downy bottle. To gain additional retailer support during the introductory period, retailers would be given a Purchase Allowance of $1.00 off each case. This amounted to an eleven cent saving per bottle.

   In this scenario, there would be no special promotion or discount periods when the regular Downy product was on deal. One concern Grad Schnurr had with this option was that the Enviro-Pak would be priced above the 3 litre bottles when the bottles were featured on promotion at $5.99.

2. *A moderately lower retail price ($7.00), with featuring.* Under this scenario, the trade would be offered discount pricing for the Enviro-Pak coinciding with the regular Downy promotion schedule. The regular trade price would be $5.74, while the promotional offers would provide for a 20% discount, or a price of $4.59 for the trade and $5.60 for consumers.

Promotion

Grad Schnurr had put together a preliminary promotion plan, including trade discounts, television, radio and print advertising. He was also considering using displayable shipping containers. These containers enabled retailers to build a display out of the Downy shipping containers by cutting off the top portion of each container and stacking them at aisle ends. The incremental cost of this style of container would be $0.95 per case.

Given the unique environmental properties of the Downy Enviro-Pak, the launch would need some extra consideration to ensure the product was accepted by environmental groups, as well as the trade and consumers. This was evident in the problems Loblaws had faced when some of its "green" products were disputed by environmental groups such as Pollution Probe and Friends of the Earth. Grad Schnurr wanted to make sure that consumers accepted the Enviro-Pak as a valid environmental package without giving the impression that P&G was exploiting this concern for the sake of profits. He wondered how to go about this tactical issue. Should some of the environmental lobby groups be consulted before the launch? What if they did not support the idea? Would early consultation risk the security of the launch plans? Grad Schnurr needed to consult with Barry Smith, P&G Inc.'s public relations manager to start planning their approach.

Note

1. Each case would contain 12 Enviro-Paks.

30

McDonald's Environmental Strategy
Susan Svoboda and
Stuart L. Hart

INTRODUCTION

Rooted in Ray Kroc's founding principles of Quality, Service, Cleanliness & Value (Q.S.C.&V.), McDonald's management has always believed in being a leader in issues that affect their customers. This philosophy is evident in McDonald's involvement in various community projects regarding education, health care, medical research, and rehabilitation facilities. These activities help the corporation to extend their image beyond fun and entertainment into social responsibility.

However, in the late 1980s, McDonald's began to face criticism for its environmental policies, especially those surrounding polystyrene clamshell containers. In 1987, McDonald's replaced CFCs, the blowing agent used in clamshell production, with weaker HCFC-22's after facing public criticism that CFC usage was contributing to ozone depletion. But this change was not enough for many grass-roots environmental groups that, led by the Citizens Clearinghouse for Hazardous Waste (CCHW), united in establishing a "Ronald McToxic Campaign" con-

●

This case was prepared by Susan Svoboda, then manager of the University of Michigan Corporate Environmental Management Program (CEMP) under the guidance of Stuart Hart, the director of CEMP. This case is intended to be used as a basis for class discussion rather than as an illustration of either effective or ineffective handling of the situation. ©1995 by the Regents of the University of Michigan. Reprinted with permission.

sisting of restaurant picketers and an organized effort to mail clamshells back to Oak Brook headquarters. When McDonald's later tested trash-to-energy on-site incinerators, CCHW quickly named the project "McPuff." By 1989, school children, the backbone of McDonald's customer base, founded a group called "Kids Against Polystyrene." Although they were not the only fast-food restaurant facing criticism for disposable packaging, McDonald's could not afford to let this situation escalate. One of their primary competitors, Burger King, was winning praise for its paperboard containers, which were claimed by some to be biodegradable.

COMPANY BACKGROUND

McDonald's Corporation grew from a single drive-in restaurant in San Bernardino, California, in 1948, to the largest food-service organization in the world. In 1991, McDonald's owned $13 billion of the $93 billion fast-food industry, operating 12,400 restaurants in 59 countries including company-owned restaurants, franchisees, and joint ventures. In the U.S. alone, more than 18 million people visit a McDonald's daily.[1] Exhibit 1 contains an 11-year financial summary for the company. McDonald's management intends to continue growing by: 1) maximizing sales and profits in existing restaurants, 2) adding new restaurants, and 3) improving international profitability.

Ray Kroc based his empire on the fundamental principles of Quality, Service, Cleanliness, and Value (Q.S.C.&V.) and developed tangible goals and specific operating practices to carry out his vision. An extensive team of field auditors monitor these practices, which are communicated to employees through continuing education that includes videotaped messages from Kroc himself. These values were integrated into McDonald's three strategic priorities for 1991, stated in the Annual Report as follows:

- to enhance the message that McDonald's is value-driven on behalf of its customers by emphasizing their profitable value-meal combinations;
- to provide exceptional customer care by exceeding customer expectations, including finding ways to add personal touches that go beyond convenient locations, quick service, clean restaurants, and quality products;
- to remain an efficient producer while maintaining quality by looking to innovations in food processing, construction, and design operations that will increase global profits.

Approximately 80 percent of McDonald's restaurants are franchises, paying a percentage of their monthly revenue for centralized marketing research and R&D. Franchise fees cover roughly the costs of corporate services; thus, if the franchises are not making money, neither is the corporation. This mutual dependence is considered by management to be a corporate strength. McDonald's Corporation revenues are derived from franchise fees plus company restaurant sales. The Corporation operates approximately 16 percent of U.S. McDonald's restaurants, and a higher percentage of international restaurants since they usually enter new countries with company restaurants and then franchise them after they are well established. McDonald's typically receives over 20,000 franchise inquiries per year. Twenty-year franchises are awarded to applicants after extensive screening, and additional restaurants are allocated to franchises with proven records of success.

McDonald's management style may be described as "tight-loose"—the corporation sets overall quality standards, but the franchisees are given the freedom to make localized decisions. Many new product innovations, such as the Filet O' Fish and the Egg McMuffin, originated with franchises. Recently, McDonald's has increased its new product development efforts, responding to customer's concern for nutrition. However, Tom Glasglow, Vice President and Chief Financial Officer, is concerned with maintaining the focus that has made McDonald's successful: in the 1991 Annual Report he stated, "We're in the business of serving a small number of products that have mass appeal. That's our niche."

McDonald's is the second-best-known global brand and intends to maintain this level of consumer awareness with a $1 billion marketing budget.[2] McDonald's launched a major new ad campaign in 1991, "Great Food at a Great Value," which was successful in promoting profitable value-meal combinations. High brand recognition is particularly important as many customers are impulse purchasers, often selecting McDonald's over competitors by the convenience of the location. Glasglow, discussing how McDonald's customers distinguish it from the competition, stated, "We are the easiest. The place that satisfies customers best, and gives them the best value." The emphasis McDonald's places on customer convenience is manifested in McDonald's self-description as a leader in the quick-service industry, rather than the fast-food industry.

A typical McDonald's may serve as many as 2,000 people per day, 60–70 percent of whom take their food outside the restaurant. McDonald's depends on the ability of their crew to be able to prepare hot, fresh food and to serve it to their customers within two minutes of the time they enter the restaurant. To do this, McDonald's engineering department has carefully designed the layout and equipment for its restaurants. Ex-

Exhibit 1 ● 11-Year Summary (dollars rounded to millions, except per common share data and average restaurant sales)

	1991	1990	1989	1988
System-wide sales	$19,928	$18,759	$17,333	$16,064
U.S.	12,519	12,252	12,012	11,380
Outside U.S.	7,409	6,507	5,321	4,684
System-wide sales by type				
Operated by franchisees	12,959	12,017	11,219	10,424
Operated by the company	4,908	5,019	4,601	4,196
Operated by affiliates	2,061	1,723	1,513	1,444
Average sales, restaurants				
open at least 1 yr. (in 1,000s)	1,658	1,649	1,621	1,596
Revenues, frnchsd. rstrnts.	1,787	1,621	1,465	1,325
Total revenues	6,695	6,640	6,066	5,521
Operating income	1,679	1,596	1,438	1,288
Inc. before prov. for inc. taxes	1,299	1,246	1,157	1,046
Net income	860	802	727	646
Cash provided by operations	1,423	1,301	1,246	1,177
Financial position at year-end				
Net property and equipment	9,559	9,047	7,758	6,800
Total assets	11,349	10,668	9,175	8,159
Long-term debt	4,267	4,429	3,902	3,111
Total shareholder equity	4,835	4,182	3,550	3,413
Per common share				
Net income	$2.35	$2.20	$1.95	$1.71
Dividends declared	.36	.33	.30	.27
Year-end shareholder equity	13.48	11.65	9.81	9.09
Market price at year-end	38	29 1/8	34 1/2	24 1/8
System-wide restaurants at year-end	$12,418	$11,803	$11,162	$10,513
Operated by franchisees	8,735	8,131	7,573	7,110
Operated by the company	2,547	2,643	2,691	2,600
Operated by affiliates	1,136	1,029	898	803
Systemwide restaurants at year-end:				
U.S.	8,764	8,576	8,270	7,907
Outside U.S.	3,654	3,227	2,892	2,606
Number of countries at year-end	59	53	51	50

*Before the cumulative prior years' benefit from the change in accounting for income taxes.

1987	1986	1985	1984	1983	1982	1981
$14,330	$12,432	$11,001	$10,007	$8,687	$7,809	$7,129
10,576	9,534	8,843	8,071	7,069	6,362	5,770
3,754	2,898	2,158	1,936	1,618	1,447	1,359
9,452	8,422	7,612	6,914	5,929	5,239	4,788
3,667	3,106	2,770	2,538	2,297	2,095	1,916
1,211	904	619	555	461	475	425
1,502	1,369	1,296	1,264	1,169	1,132	1,113
1,186	1,037	924	828	704	620	561
4,853	4,143	3,694	3,366	3,001	2,715	2,477
1,160	983	905	812	713	613	552
959	848	782	707	628	546	482
549*	480	433	389	343	301	265
1,051	852	813	701	618	505	434
5,820	4,878	4,164	3,521	3,183	2,765	2,497
6,982	5,969	5,043	4,230	3,727	3,263	2,899
2,685	2,131	1,638	1,268	1,171	1,056	926
2,917	2,506	2,245	2,009	1,755	1,529	1,371
$1.45*	$1.24	$1.11	$ .97	$ .85	$ .74	$ .65
.24	.21	.20	.17	.14	.12	.09
7.72	6.45	5.67	4.94	4.38	3.78	3.37
22	20 1/4	18	11 1/2	10 1/2	9	6 1/2
$9,911	$9,410	$8,901	$8,304	$7,778	$7,259	$6,739
6,760	6,406	6,150	5,724	5,371	4,911	4,580
2,399	2,301	2,165	2,053	1,949	1,846	1,746
752	703	586	527	458	502	413
7,567	7,272	6,972	6,595	6,251	5,918	5,554
2,344	2,138	1,929	1,709	1,527	1,341	1,185
47	46	42	36	32	31	30

Exhibit 2 ● Schematic of McDonald's Existing Food Delivery System

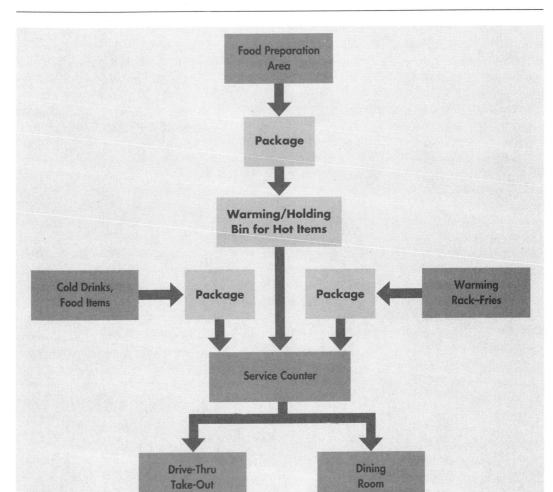

hibit 2 shows how all food flows from the back of the kitchen to the front as it is prepared, and is placed in a heated food "bin" awaiting customer delivery. Servers at the counter or drive-through window collect items from the bin and drink stations for customers. An important component of McDonald's operational strategy is to anticipate customer traffic patterns and food selection based on a detailed analysis of sales history and trends and to use this information to prepare various menu items in the right quantities and at the right times in order to have the food ready for their customers when they arrive. Food may be stored in the bin for up to ten minutes before it is discarded.

1991 marked the introduction of "Series

2000" design restaurants. These buildings are approximately half the size of traditional restaurants, designed to accommodate nearly the same level of sales but requiring a lower real estate investment. Series 2000 restaurants are targeted toward both small towns and major metropolitan areas.

All of McDonald's 600-plus suppliers are independent companies with whom long-term relationships have been developed. This strategy is intended to improve McDonald's ability to focus its efforts on its core business—restaurant operations. Most suppliers operate on a cost-plus basis. McDonald's often holds seminars and conferences for suppliers to discuss their needs.

Joint Task Force

Recognizing McDonald's potential to influence public opinion through its 18 million daily customers, the Environmental Defense Fund (EDF) approached McDonald's in 1989 to discuss environmental issues related to solid waste. At that time McDonald's was facing environmental protests in the form of demonstrations, letters, and customers mailing their polystyrene clamshells back to the company. Realizing that young people, traditionally loyal McDonald's customers, were demanding "greener" practices, McDonald's stepped up its recycling efforts. However, several U.S. cities were proposing a ban on polystyrene packaging altogether. Caught between seemingly conflicting environmental goals, McDonald's welcomed EDF's help.

EDF is a national nonprofit organization that links science, economics, and law to create innovative, economically sustainable solutions to environmental problems. It was founded in 1967 by scientists on Long Island, New York, to fight the spraying of the pesticide DDT. Today, EDF has a professional staff of more than 110

people located in six offices, and has support from over 200,000 members and 100 private foundations.

McDonald's and EDF created a joint task force to work together to understand the role of materials and packaging used at McDonald's (see Exhibit 3 for a list of task force participants). Each member spent one day working in a restaurant, and the task force held meetings with McDonald's food and packaging suppliers, toured McDonald's largest distribution center, and plastics and composting facilities.

MCDONALD'S ENVIRONMENTAL STRATEGY

One of the first results of the task force was the development of a strong company-wide environmental policy declaring that McDonald's is committed to protecting the environment for future generations, and that it believes that business leaders must also be environmental leaders. The policy takes a total lifecycle approach to reducing and managing solid waste: a sizable challenge, considering that each of McDonald's 8,600 U.S. restaurants[3] creates 238 pounds of waste per day and each of its 34 U.S. regional distribution centers disposes of another 900 pounds of waste per day.[4]

McDonald's has also been active in educating its customers about the company's environmental activities and positions. Brochures are available in restaurants informing customers about McDonald's position on such topics as ozone depletion, the rain forest, and packaging.

McDonald's is working to translate this environmental commitment into specific actions. In order to live up to its environmental policy, McDonald's Environmental Affairs Officer has been given the authority to enforce adherence to standards, and reports directly to the Board of Directors on a regular basis. McDonald's also plans to continue to seek counsel with environmental experts to take advantage of opportuni-

EXHIBIT 3: BIOGRAPHIES OF TASK FORCE MEMBERS

Terri K. Capatosto, Director of Communications, McDonald's Corporation. Ms. Capatosto joined the Corporation in 1984 and is responsible for managing McDonald's interaction with local and national news media as well as providing communications counsel, support, and training to the company's corporate and regional management and local owner-operators. Since 1988, she has also held specific responsibility for environmental issues, working with Operations, Purchasing, Environmental Affairs, and other key departments within McDonald's on the company's environmental initiatives. Ms. Capatosto has received numerous awards for leadership and outstanding performance, including McDonald's President's Award in 1987. Before joining McDonald's, Ms. Capatosto was a Captain in the U.S. Marine Corps. She holds B.A. degrees in Psychology and Music from the University of Utah.

Richard A. Denison, Senior Scientist, EDF. Mr. Denison, who holds a Ph.D. in Molecular Biophysics and Biochemistry from Yale, specializes in hazardous and solid waste management issues ranging from waste reduction and recycling to the health effects and regulatory requirements of landfilling and incineration. Prior to joining EDF in 1987, Mr. Denison was an Environmental Analyst at the U.S. Congress' Office of Technology Assessment and also conducted cancer research in a postdoctoral position at the University of California, San Francisco. He has authored numerous papers and reports on solid and hazardous waste management, and a recent book, *Recycling and Incineration: Evaluating the Choices.*

Robert L. Langert, Director of Environmental Affairs, The Perseco Company. Bob Langert is responsible for managing projects related to source reduction, recycling and other waste management alternatives for the Perseco Company, the exclusive packaging purchaser for McDonald's. His responsibilities include assisting in the coordination of McDonald's recycling initiatives across the country, and working with an extensive group of packaging suppliers on waste reduction initiatives. Prior to joining the McDonald's family, Mr. Langert was an operations manager for a McDonald's distributor, Perlman-Rocque, and served as Midwest logistics manager for the American Hospital Supply Corporation. He holds an M.B.A. degree from Northwestern University.

Keith Magnuson, Director, Operations Development Department, McDonald's. Mr. Magnuson works on developing new operating systems and improving store operations for the company's restaurants worldwide. Most recently, he has been involved in the development of McDonald's in-store recycling programs, packaging source reduction, and other environmental initiatives. Over the past 17 years, his positions have included store manager, area supervisor, field consultant, and operations development manager. He attended the University of Maryland.

(Continued)

S. Jackie Prince, Staff Scientist, EDF. Ms. Prince conducts research on a variety of solid waste issues, including recycling technologies and the use of product life cycle assessments in evaluating consumer products. Ms. Prince holds Master's degrees in Public and Private Management and Environmental Studies, and received her B.S. in chemical engineering, all from Yale. She is a former Project Manager/Engineer for the Waste Management Division of the U.S. Environmental Protection Agency, Region I, where she received the 1986 EPA Award For Excellence. She is the author of *Wetlands Assessments at Hazardous Waste Sites* and *Assessment of PCB Contamination in New Bedford Harbor.*

John F. Ruston, Economic Analyst, EDF. With a Master of City Planning degree from MIT, Mr. Ruston works on issues that link economic development and environmental quality. He is co-author of *Coming Full Circle: Successful Recycling Today; Recycling and Incineration: Evaluating the Choices;* and *The Economic Case for Recycling: Evidence from the Brooklyn Navy Yard Hearings.* Mr. Ruston received his B.S. from the University of California at Davis, where he also completed graduate work in economics and computer modeling.

Dan Sprehe, Environmental Affairs Consultant, Government Relations Department, McDonald's. Mr. Sprehe's duties include internal research on recycling and source reduction issues as well as serving as a McDonald's corporate spokesperson to environmental and government groups. He was previously a legislative analyst for the Illinois General Assembly's Senate Energy and Environmental Committee, where he helped draft legislation on numerous environmental issues, including the Illinois Solid Waste Management Act. Mr. Sprehe holds a B.S. in Political Science from Eastern Illinois University.

---

ties to improve its environmental performance on an ongoing basis. As part of its waste reduction action plan, McDonald's has committed to reviewing annually all food-service products and packaging items to identify opportunities for source reduction. McDonald's realizes that in order to achieve its waste reduction goals, it must collaborate with its suppliers. To promote collaboration, it has developed an annual environmental conference intended to train suppliers and has included environmental issues in its annual supplier reviews and evaluations.

The following initiatives were proposed by the task force.

SOURCE REDUCTION

McDonald's had already initiated several waste reduction efforts when EDF contacted it, but the ensuing discussions led to a proposal calling for a joint task force to create "a framework, a systematic approach and a strong scientific basis for McDonald's solid waste decisions."[5] The EPA's waste management hierarchy became the foundation for task force efforts.[6]

In the joint task force report, "waste reduction" was defined as any action that reduces the amount or toxicity of municipal solid waste, prior to incineration or landfill. "Source reduction" takes an even stronger environmental position than recycling by reducing the weight, volume, or toxicity of products or packaging prior to their use. Because source reduction decreases or eliminates waste at its point of generation, thus creating less to be reused, recycled, incinerated, or landfilled, the EPA gave it the highest priority on the waste management hierarchy. The task force identified the source reduction projects shown in Exhibit 4, which are being implemented as a result of revised supplier specifications. Annual waste characterization studies will be conducted to determine a baseline against which to measure future goals.

Consistent with McDonald's management style, the task force reasoned that its waste management strategy would have to be implemented in a tight-loose fashion, as centralized plans alone could not take into account all the differing local and regional waste disposal practices, infrastructures, and costs. They also realized that in many cases there was not one obvious solution to a problem. In fact, trade-offs involving environmental impacts, costs, and performance require complicated decision-making. For example, increasing the content of recycled paper in packaging may diminish the strength of the paper, requiring increased packaging thickness to compensate for decreased performance. In addition, when a packaging alternative significantly reduces the weight of material to be disposed, the material still might not have an existing recycling infrastructure.

McDonald's has made substantial progress in its source reduction efforts over the past 20 years. For example, McDonald's "average meal" in the 1970s—a Big Mac, fries and a shake—required 46 grams of packaging. Today, it requires 25 grams, a 46 percent reduction.[7] McDonald's has also reduced the weight of packaging in its sandwich wraps, hot cups, and napkins, removed corrugated dividers in some shipping cases, and switched to bulk containers

wherever possible. A summary of source reduction accomplishments is provided in Exhibit 5, which lists packaging changes approved for implementation in 1990.

As an example, orange juice had been shipped, stored, and served in individual containers. These have been replaced by concentrate mixed at the restaurant, resulting in a packaging reduction of two million pounds per year. In addition, a new Coke delivery system that pumps syrup directly from delivery trucks to storage tanks eliminates the need for intermediate containers, saving an additional two million pounds of packaging annually. Weight reductions, reductions in secondary packaging, and increased use of bulk packaging has reduced packaging by 24 million pounds annually.[8]

Further, McDonald's purchases materials from suppliers that use more benign manufacturing processes, such as non-chlorine-bleached paper bags, and has switched to french fry cartons made from mechanically pulped rather than chemically pulped paper.

When new opportunities for source reduction have been identified, operating practices are engineered and researched using one to five restaurants as test sites. During this process, customer perceptions are carefully monitored; past reductions have been imperceptible to most customers.

REUSE

Identifying immediately feasible opportunities for the reuse of materials was a difficult assignment for the task force as the time required to handle, collect, and clean materials would impact McDonald's ability to provide high-volume fast food. In addition, the committee's investigation showed that opportunities varied greatly according to behind-the-counter and over-the-counter operations.

Over-the-counter operations are currently

Exhibit 4 ● Current Source Reduction Projects

Project/Idea/Concept	*Potential % Reduction*
1. Cold Cups:	
A. Use unbleached/non-chlorine bleached paper.	TBD*
B. Eliminate lids on in-store purchases.	TBD
C. Drink-thru lid.	TBD
2. Sandwich Wraps:	
A. Explore different compostable barriers/coatings.	TBD
B. Use unbleached/non-chlorine bleached paper.	—
3. Cartons:	
A. Replace medium and large fry cartons with bags.	75%
B. New glue seam on cartons.	TBD
C. Replace hash brown carton with bag.	75%
D. Reduce amount of paperboard used in Happy Meal boxes.	20%
4. Straws:	
A. Reduce gauge.	6%
B. Convert to unwrapped bulk.	20%
5. Cutlery:	
A. Evaluate polypropylene.	TBD
B. Test and evaluate starch-based materials.	TBD
6. Foam Cups & Breakfast Entrees:	
A. Look for environmentally preferred alternatives to polystyrene foam.	TBD
7. Corrugated Shipping Containers:	
A. Continue examining ways to reduce amount of corrugated used in boxes.	TBD
B. Test reusable plastic containers (distribution center to restaurant and raw material supplier to distribution center).	TBD
C. Test recyclable coating for meat boxes.	TBD
8. Inner Pack PE Film Wrap:	
A. Color-tint only those which are not recyclable.	—
B. Convert all possible wraps to LDPE to enhance recyclability.	—
9. Condiment Packaging:	
A. Convert to 17 g. ketchup packet from current 11 g. packet.	—
10. Other Unbleached Products:	
A. Coffee Filters	TBD
B. Prep Pan Liners	—

*TBD = To be determined

Source: Task Force Report

Exhibit 5 ● 1990 Source Reduction Accomplishments

Accomplishments	% Weight Reduction
Redesign 16-oz. cold cup (one supplier).	10.2%
Reduce large cold cup.	6.0%
Reduce density of breakfast lids.	14.5%
Reduce density of slant McChicken package.	6.6%
Reduce density of small clamshell.	8.5%
Smaller napkin.	21.0%
Oriented unwrapped bulk cutlery.	11.0%
Convert to jumbo roll toilet tissue.	23.0%
Reduce gauge of sundae cup.	9.0%
Replace breakfast sandwich foam with sandwich wrap.	59.0%
Increase corrugated usage for 10:1 meat boxes.	15.0%
Replace sandwich foam with wraps:	
Weight	1.0%
Volume	90.0%
Down-sized McD.L.T. package	32.0%

*Note: Each change is based on its annual impact for that particular product line.

Source: Task Force Report

limited as McDonald's customers expect fast service even at peak times of the day. McDonald's operations are designed to anticipate the content of customer orders and to prepare food just before the customers arrive. However, McDonald's does not feel it can anticipate *where* its customers will choose to eat, and most reuse options require different packaging for dine-in or take-out customers. Repackaging food after the customer arrives or delaying its preparation until the order is taken would lengthen service time. Further, sanitation issues were also a concern of the task force, as single-serve, disposable packaging had basically eliminated the potential of packaging-related contamination. Dishware storage, both in the restaurant and behind-the-counter, and the placement of dishwashing equipment are potentially difficult in McDonald's already tightly designed kitchens. Consideration was also given to the environmental trade-offs of the dishwashing process, as it would require energy, water, and detergents.

Behind-the-counter opportunities appeared more promising: an on-premise study indicated that that is where 80 percent of restaurant waste was generated. Exhibit 6 shows the breakdown of over-the-counter and behind-the-counter waste based on a two-restaurant, one-week audit. Several easily implemented reuse options existed for behind-the-counter waste including the reuse of plastic (rather than cardboard) disposables, shipping trays for bakery items, and plastic shipping pallets that last at least three times longer than wooden pallets.

RECYCLING

Recycling efforts take two forms: use of products made from recycled materials, and the recycling of post-consumer/post-industrial waste.

Exhibit 6 ● McDonald's On-Premise Waste Study

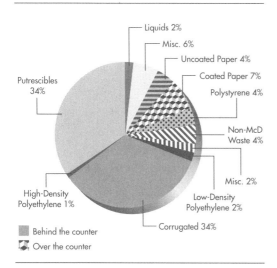

Liquids 2%
Misc. 6%
Uncoated Paper 4%
Coated Paper 7%
Polystyrene 4%
Non-McD Waste 4%
Misc. 2%
Putrescibles 34%
High-Density Polyethylene 1%
Low-Density Polyethylene 2%
Corrugated 34%

■ Behind the counter
▨ Over the counter

Source: McDonald's/EDF Task Force Report

Many of the technical aspects of post-production recycling of both plastic and paper have already been exploited by suppliers' internal reuse operations for scrap. However, little recycling has been done of post-consumer plastic and paper materials due to contamination problems. Unlike glass and metal, where food residue and bacteria contamination can be burned off, foam and paperboard are not easily cleaned.

McDonald's tries to use recycled materials whenever possible. For example, it is one of the largest users of recycled paper in the U.S. However, packaging that has direct contact with food, which constitutes approximately 42 percent of McDonald's packaging, is strictly regulated by the FDA not to contain post-consumer recycled materials. Therefore, McDonald's strives to increase the recycled content for nonfood packaging, such as corrugated boxes, which must be made of 35% recycled material according to a 1990 mandate. In addition, it uses recycled pa-

per for nonfood items such as Happy Meal boxes, carry-out drink trays, and paper towels.

In April 1990, McDonald's announced the McRecycle Program, a commitment to spend $100 million annually on the use of recycled materials, especially in the building and renovation of its restaurants. In 1991, it surpassed its goal, purchasing more than $200 million of recycled materials. It also created a clearinghouse of "environmental" product suppliers, which has received over 8,000 calls since the 800 number was published.

The focus of McDonald's recycling efforts on post-consumer, in-store waste has been polystyrene recycling. In 1989, McDonald's launched a polystyrene recycling effort followed by a 1990 packaging brochure stating, "Polystyrene foam is easily recycled." Ken Harman, chair of the National Polystyrene Recycling Center (NPRC), said,

> 1990 is going to be a pivotal year for polystyrene recycling. It will be the year that polystyrene recycling gains momentum due, in part, to the efforts of recycling facilities like our Plastics Again Center . . . and the commitment of institutional cafeterias, schools, and private companies.

However, implementation of McDonald's recycling program highlighted an inherent limitation of any recycling option—that is, benefits are only realized for the packaging that is actually collected and recycled.

McDonald's experimented with three different point-of-discard methods to educate and assist customers in separating their trash, but customers were generally either confused or overwhelmed by the instructions. In communities that did not have an existing curbside recycling program, participation was much lower than in communities where customers were already accustomed to sorting their trash.

Internal logistical problems increased recycling costs. A typical McDonald's restaurant produced five to ten bags of incorrectly separated materials, creating disposal problems. And the bulkiness of the clamshells made three pickup times a week a necessity, incurring expensive hauling costs as 90% of plastic is comprised of air. Further, the NPRC required incoming materials to be free of paper and food contamination, a standard that was not then being realized. To respond to this problem, McDonald's experimented with material recovery facilities to sort, clean, and consolidate materials, but the cost proved to be prohibitive.

Throughout this time, McDonald's continued to work with suppliers to develop packaging that was consistent with curbside recycling programs, to support the recycling of material that leaves the restaurant via takeout orders.

COMPOSTING

Composting is still in the formative stage. Therefore, much of the task force's work centered on gaining a better understanding of McDonald's composting options. Composting is an attractive disposal alternative as it diverts organic waste from landfills and incinerators and it improves soil quality.

Almost 50 percent of McDonald's waste stream consists of paper packaging and food organics that could be composted. McDonald's is reviewing the compostability of its packaging and studying materials such as the coatings used on its paper-based packaging to determine if they impair compostability. Where possible, it will replace materials that are not compostable with materials designed for compostability.

To make composting a viable option, McDonald's is investigating how to: 1) collect and separate materials, 2) balance the cost and environmental trade-offs of composting methods, and 3) identify markets for composted products.

McDonald's began testing the compostability of nine packaging items in January 1991. Several months later, nine McDonald's restaurants in Maine began sending their waste to Resource Conservation Services, a nearby composting company. Data from these tests will be used to determine the proper conditions for composting McDonald's waste and to determine the quality of the final compost product.

THE FUTURE

Environmental groups play an increasingly important role in influencing policy (See Exhibit 7 for an overview of leading environmental groups). Furthermore, during the past decade, membership in many of the leading environmental groups doubled in size. This growth may be attributed to both the public's concern that industry and government are not adequately addressing environmental issues and to public confidence in environmental groups. In fact, a recent study conducted by Golin/Harris Communication, Inc. found that 80 percent of those studied believe "some" of what environmental groups report while less than 40 percent believe "some" of what businesses report.[9]

The joint task force was one of the first collaborative efforts involving a leading environmental organization and a major corporation aimed at improving corporate solid waste practices. It posed opportunities and challenges for both sides. EDF wanted to create a model approach that could be used by other companies, yet it risked criticism from other environmentalists. McDonald's needed a way to respond to public criticism of their environmental practices, but knew that potential task force disagreements could be embarrassing.

An early outcome of the task force was McDonald's adoption of the waste management hierarchy. The hierarchy served as a means to guide early decision making, but the long-term

Exhibit 7 ● Descriptions of Some Environmental Groups

Citizen's Clearinghouse for Hazardous Waste
(1981) Mission: To assist grassroots leaders in creating and maintaining local community organizations that fight toxic polluters and environmental hazards.

Budget: $689,908 (1990)

Membership: Not available

Conservation International Foundation (1987)

Mission: To help develop the capacity to sustain biological diversity, ecosystems, and ecological processes that support life on Earth.

Budget: $8.9 million (1991)

Membership: 55,000 individuals

Earth First! (1980)

Mission: The preservation of natural diversity.

Budget: None

Membership: Not available

Environmental Defense Fund (1967)

Mission: Committed to a multidisciplinary approach to environmental problems, combining the efforts of scientists, economists, and attorneys to devise practical, environmentally sustainable solutions to these problems.

Budget: $15.1 million (1990)

Membership: 150,000 individuals

Friends of the Earth (1990)

Mission: To work at the local, national, and international levels to protect the planet; preserve biological, cultural, and ethnic diversity; and empower citizens to have a voice in decisions affecting their environments and lives.

Budget: $3 million (1990)

Membership: 50,000 individuals

Greenpeace USA (1971)

Mission: To preserve the environment through international campaigns in the areas of toxic waste, disarmament, ocean ecology, energy and atmospheric preservation, and rainforest preservation.

Budget: $34 million (1990)

Membership: 2.1 million individuals

Izaak Walton League of America (1922)

Mission: To defend America's soil, air, woods, waters, and wildlife through its local chapters, state divisions, and a national headquarters in the U.S. capital.

Budget: $1.8 million (1990)

Membership: 52,700 individuals

National Audubon Society (1905)

Mission: Long-term protection and the wise use of wildlife, land, water, and other natural resources; the promotion of rational strategies for energy development and use; the protection of life from pollution, radiation, and toxic substances; and solving global problems caused by overpopulation and the depletion of natural resources.

Budget: $35.8 million (1990)

Membership: Not available

Natural Resources Defense Council (1970)

Mission: Dedicated to conserving natural resources and improving the quality of the human environment.

Budget: $16 million (1990)

Membership: 170,240 individuals

The Nature Conservancy (1951)

Mission: To preserve plants, animals, and natural communities that represent the diversity of life on Earth by protecting the land and waters they need to survive.

Budget: $68 million (1990)

Membership: 580,000 individuals; 405 corporations

Sea Shepard Conservation Society (1977)

Mission: To protect and preserve marine wildlife and habitats for future and present generations.

Budget: $600,000 (1990)

Membership: 17,000 individuals

Sierra Club (1892)

Mission: To explore, enjoy, and protect the wild places of the earth; to practice and promote the responsible use of the earth's ecosystems and resources; to educate and enlist humanity to protect and restore the quality of the natural and human environment; and to use all lawful means to carry out these objectives.

Budget: $35 million (1990)

Membership: 650,000 individuals

Wilderness Society (1935)

Mission: Devoted primarily to the preservation of wilderness and the proper management of our country's public lands and natural resources.

Budget: $17.9 million (1990)

Membership: 383,000 individuals

World Wildlife Fund

Mission: To conserve nature by using the best available scientific knowledge and advancing that knowledge to preserve the diversity and abundance of life on earth and the health of ecological systems by protecting nat-ural areas and wild populations of plants and animals, including endangered species; to promote sustainable approaches to the use of renewable natural resources; and to promote more efficient use of resources and energy and the maximum reduction of pollution.

Budget: $54 million (1991)

---

success of the program will depend on both parties' ability to manage the partnership.

EDF's President Fred Krupp said, "Environmentalists and industry alike will be waiting to see what McDonald's does with the task force options and recommendations. That will be the ultimate test of this effort's success."

Notes

1.   Environmental Defense Fund and McDonald's Corporation. *Waste Reduction Task Force Final Report.* Oak Brook, IL: McDonald's, 1991. p. 22.

2.   McDonald's Corporation. *McDonald's 1991 Annual Report.* Oak Brook, IL: McDonald's. p. S4.

3.   The Task Force Study collected data for McDonald's 8,600 domestic restaurants only.

4.   Environmental Defense Fund. *Task Force Report.* pp. 31–34.

5.   Ibid., p. 3.

6.   The waste management hierarchy developed by the EPA—reduce, reuse, recycle, and incinerate/dispose—prioritizes solid waste practices and is widely accepted.

7.   Environmental Defense Fund. *Task Force Report.* p. 42.

8.   McDonald's Corporation. *McDonald's Packaging—The Facts.* Oak Brook, IL: McDonald's, 1990. p. 7.

9.   Foundation for Public Affairs. *Public Interest Group Profiles, 1992–93.* Washington: Congressional Quarterly, 1992.

31

The Clamshell Controversy
Susan Svoboda

INTRODUCTION

The Joint Task Force of McDonald's Corporation and the Environmental Defense Fund (EDF) was in its third month of collaboration when a decision needed to be made about the expansion of McDonald's polystyrene recycling program. The task force, formed through a mutual agreement between the parties, had been charged with finding ways to reduce McDonald's solid waste through source reduction, reuse, recycling, and composting. However, one aspect of McDonald's operations seemed to attract the public's attention—the polystyrene "clamshell" sandwich containers. Although these packages represented only a minute fraction of total municipal solid waste,[1] to the public they symbolized the "throw-away" society.

Debate over McDonald's packaging materials started in the 1970s when the public became concerned that too many trees were being cut down to make packaging. In response to this interest, Ray Kroc, McDonald's founder, commissioned the Stanford Research Institute (SRI) to conduct an environmental impact study comparing the paperboard packaging McDonald's was then using to polystyrene packaging. By analyz-

ing all aspects of the two alternatives from manufacturing through disposal, SRI concluded that plastic was preferred. They reasoned that the coating on the paperboard made it nearly impossible to recycle, while polystyrene was recyclable and used less energy in production.

As a result, McDonald's switched to polystyrene for their cups and sandwich containers, and launched an environmental education program to communicate to the public their rationale for the switch from paperboard to plastic. In 1989, McDonald's piloted a recycling program in 450 of their New England restaurants by asking in-store customers to sort their trash into designated trash bins. The polystyrene was then shipped to one of eight plastic recycling plants formed in a joint venture of eight plastics companies. The program gained enough success that soon it was expanded to California and Oregon at the request of state officials, and involved a total of 1,000 stores. McDonald's began planning a national expansion of the program. However, EDF Director Fred Krupp told Ed Rensi, Chief Operating Officer and President of McDonald's USA, that he would publicly refuse to endorse the recycling program, because he did not regard it as the best environmental solution.

PACKAGING IN THE WASTE STREAM

Packaging is essential to a product's performance. It protects the product throughout production, distribution and storage, provides consumers with product and usage information, and differentiates the product. Food manufacturers and distributors also expect packaging to extend

This case was prepared by Susan Svoboda, then manager of the University of Michigan Corporate Environmental Management Program (CEMP) under the guidance of Stuart Hart, the director of CEMP. This case is intended to be used as a basis for class discussion rather than as an illustration of either effective or ineffective handling of the situation. ©1995 by the Regents of the University of Michigan. Reprinted with permission.

the product's shelf life and to preserve the appearance, freshness, flavor, and moisture content of food. Effective packaging reduces food spoilage-rates and diverts more than its own weight from disposal.

The composition of solid waste has changed significantly over the past three decades. Paper and plastics have grown to a combined total of 50 percent, while metal, food and yard waste, and glass have decreased. See Exhibit 1 for a breakdown of municipal solid waste (MSW). Further, the total weight of packaging in MSW doubled between 1960 and 1990. However, as shown in Exhibit 2, the EPA estimates source reduction efforts will reduce the packaging content of MSW to 30 percent by the year 2000 (from a high of 36 percent in 1970).

The growing trends of single-parent families and dual-career couples have popularized single-use and microwave containers for which no recycling infrastructure currently exists. These packages offer convenience but often replace more durable or reusable options. If the present rate of growth continues, the proportion

Exhibit 2 ● Packaging in the Waste Stream

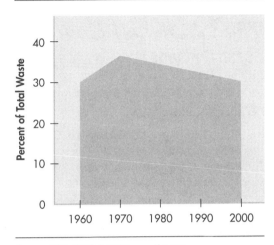

Source: EPA. 1990 & 2000 are estimates

Exhibit 1 ● Materials in Municipal Solid Waste (in 1986, by weight)

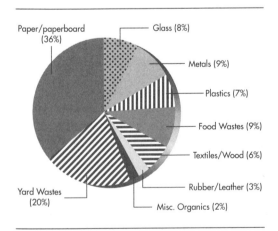

Source: Office of Technology Assessment

of plastics in packaging is expected to be 15 percent by the year 2000 (see Exhibit 3). Both manufacturers and consumers value the flexible, durable, and insulating properties of plastics. However, plastics have become a topic of debate as citizens try to reconcile the desire for convenience with "greening" attitudes.

Recent *Greenwatch* studies by J. Walter Thompson indicate that 78 percent of those surveyed say that they are willing to pay extra for products with recyclable or biodegradable components, and 77 percent report that their purchase decisions are influenced by a company's reputation on environmental issues. Although actual consumer behavior may not necessarily match intended behavior, this growing sentiment is prompting manufacturers to search for new technologies to make their packages thinner or lighter in order to "green" their packaging. In addition, many companies are looking to find ways to overcome the diminished performance characteristics of recycled materials so that they can replace virgin materials with recycled ones.

Exhibit 3 ● Plastics in Packaging

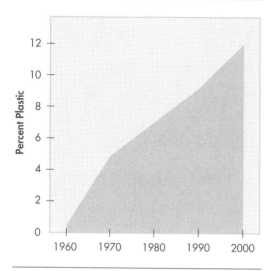

Source: EPA. 1990 & 2000 are estimates.

venient way to take food out while keeping it fresh, hot, and moist, since a typical McDonald's restaurant serves 2,000 people per day, 60–70 percent of whom take their food outside the restaurant.

As the task force began reviewing sandwich packaging options, they basically had two alternatives: paperboard containers costing approximately 2.5–3 cents per sandwich and polystyrene clamshells at approximately 2–2.5 cents per sandwich.[2] To help the joint task force understand how packaging was used in McDonald's operations, Perseco was requested to perform an audit of all packaging—primary, secondary, and tertiary—used in a restaurant. Secondary packaging, used to contain and ship supplies, includes corrugated cardboard, inner wraps, packs, and dividers. Tertiary packaging includes customer-related packaging such as utensils, napkins, carry-out bags, etc. The results, shown in Exhibit 4, indicated that paper

CLAMSHELLS, PAPERBOARD, AND QUILT-WRAP

McDonald's selects packaging based on long-standing criteria derived from its founding principles of Quality, Service, Cleanliness, and Value (Q.S.C.&V.) considering: packaging availability, its ability to keep food insulated and control its moisture level, its ease of handling, its customer appeal, and its cost. McDonald's packaging philosophy is to "evolve as new applications and materials that meet our customers' needs become available. If there is a better package . . . we'll use it!"

Perseco, an independent and privately owned company that purchases from over 100 suppliers, handles the procurement of all McDonald's paper and plastic food-service packaging, including direct food packaging as well as utensils, cups, bags, and napkins. McDonald's packaging must provide customers with a con-

Exhibit 4 ● McDonald's Packaging Materials (in 1989, by weight)

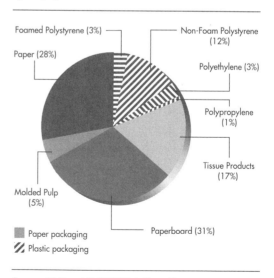

Source: McDonald's/EDF Task Force Report

products constitute 81 percent of McDonald's primary packaging.

As the task force members contemplated the complexity of the environmental issues before them, they knew that they must develop a comprehensive framework that would enable them to assess the advantages and disadvantages of various options. For example, some options aimed at improving one particular aspect of a package may have other detrimental environmental impacts. Foremost, the clamshell issue needed to be resolved. Although current public opinion opposed the clamshells, McDonald's had selected polystyrene clamshells over 20 years before because they were shown to be more environmentally "friendly" than coated paperboard, which could not be recycled. In the meantime, McDonald's had made a strong commitment to recycling polystyrene in both its relationship with the National Polystyrene Recycling Center and in its efforts to educate the public. Also, plain paper wraps had been eliminated as a viable alternative since they did not satisfactorily insulate the sandwiches.

The task force decided to let the waste management hierarchy and the life cycle assessment methodology guide their analysis. Life cycle assessment gives consideration to all impacts that occur during each stage of the product's or packaging material's life cycle, from extraction of the raw materials through manufacturing, transportation, use, and disposal. In addition, the team found that time spent learning about McDonald's operations, suppliers, and customers was invaluable to their decision-making when factoring in qualitative measures of public perception of the magnitude of an option's impact on the environment; the health or safety risk to McDonald's employees, customers, or the communities they serve; and how an option could be integrated into both pilot tests and full-scale operations. Finally, they considered the feasibility of the option being replicated in the many local conditions of the McDonald's restaurants and supporting communities.

TASK FORCE ADOPTS LIFE CYCLE METHODOLOGY

Understanding the important linkages between different stages of a package's or product's "life" is a dynamic process where, for example, a change in an input to the manufacturing process would result in corresponding changes in disposal figures. The analysis is further complicated by the fact that many inputs or releases have not been measured and tracked over time, and some are not even quantifiable. The task force turned to Franklin Associates Ltd., specialists in life cycle analysis, for a complete review of the relative merit of packaging materials.

Franklin Associates Ltd. gathered data from a number of sources including: material manufacturers, product manufacturers, published literature, government sources, and Franklin's existing materials and manufacturing database. Data from a 1990 Franklin Associates study, prepared for the Council of Solid Waste Solutions, compared polystyrene clamshell to bleached paperboard containers at various recycling rates . . . A second study compared clamshells to a new "quilt-wrap" packaging developed by the James River Corporation. Quilt-wrap is a layered paper package that was introduced while the task force was in progress. The inner tissue-paper layer protects the sandwich from absorbing grease. The middle layer is a thin polyethylene film that acts as a barrier to moisture and insulates the food. The outer layer of plastic gives the paper strength. This wrap is not recyclable and is estimated to cost 1.5–2 cents per sandwich.[3]

As both the public and government agencies have become more environmentally concerned over the past 20 years, several studies have been conducted to evaluate the impact of containers. However, confusion remains over how to measure and compare all the environmental risks associated with them. In many cases, impacts such as pollution emissions have not been measured, and in other cases the long-term risks have not been determined. Assumptions and limitations of the life cycle assessment methodology have spurred debate over the value of such assessments. Franklin Associates provides only life cycle inventories—listings of quantifiable environmental inputs and releases. Such inventories usually lead clients to develop improvement assessments—studies that use inventory results to pinpoint opportunities for improvement.

Other groups such as Green Cross and Green Seal have used life cycle data to attempt to estimate a product's environmental impact. However, consumer labeling efforts often attempt to make product comparisons of products for which comprehensive data have yet to be collected. Currently, no general formula is available to make this comparison, and comparison of entire categories such as plastics versus paper is virtually meaningless. The validity of environmental labelling without a scientific basis or widely accepted standard continues to be debated by environmental, business, and consumer groups.

LIFE CYCLE INVENTORY DATA— THE CLAMSHELL DECISION

The life cycle inventories prepared by Franklin Associates to aid task force decision-making provided information on the systems that produce the products, in this case sandwich packaging. Here a system is defined as "the collection of operations that together perform some defined function." Each individual stage or process can be viewed as a subsystem of the total system. . . . The following is a description of the systems used to produce polystyrene clamshell containers and paper-based sandwich wraps. Variations in the production of either paperboard or quilt-wrap are noted.

POLYSTYRENE PRODUCTION

Polystyrene containers result from a multistage process with several production and manufac-

turing subsystems (see Exhibit 5). A description of the various processes follows.

Raw Materials Acquisition

Crude Oil Production Oil is produced by drilling into porous rock formations several thousand feet under the earth's surface that contain oil. Pumps are used to extract the oil and the accompanying "brine" water. The brine is separated from the oil at the surface. Approximately 90 percent of water with minimal oil residue is sent to separate wells that are specifically designed for its storage, and the remaining 10 percent is discharged into surface water. Hydrocarbons may also be emitted to the air in this process as many oil fields also contain natural gas. Crude oil passes through a distillation and desalting process in order to remove salt, sediment, and water.

Natural Gas Production Although natural gas flows quite freely to the earth's surface, it requires energy to pump it to the surface. Hydrocarbons are released during the process. Since approximately 25 percent of natural gas is produced in combination with oil, brine water is produced at the same time as natural gas. Hydrocarbons are also produced with natural gas and are released into the air during venting at the well-site.

Transportation Oil and natural gas may be shipped in truck or railroad tanks, by ocean tanker, or by pipelines. Oil leaks and spills are potential risks. Transportation of highly explosive natural gas necessitates special equipment and safety precautions.

Material Manufacture

Natural Gas Processing Processing plants use compression, refrigeration, and oil absorption to extract light hydrocarbons. When components

Exhibit 5 ● Polystyrene Production

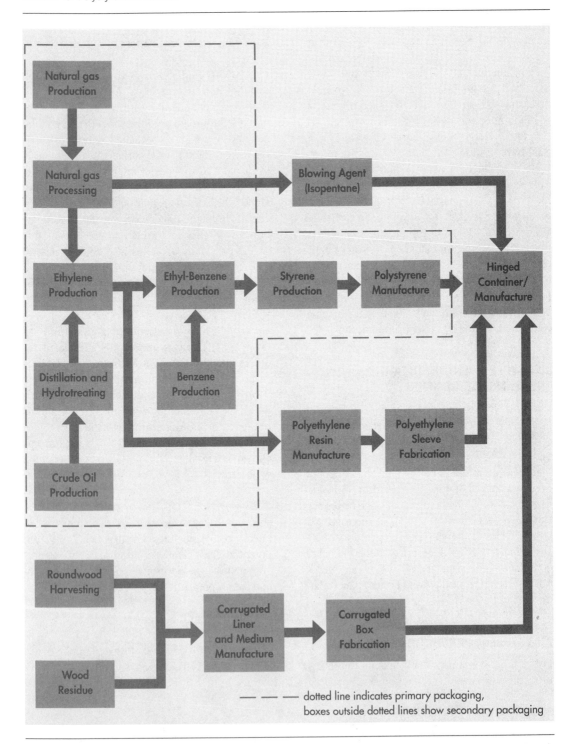

dotted line indicates primary packaging,
boxes outside dotted lines show secondary packaging

of the gas are removed they are stored in controlled conditions until being transported away. The primary pollutants in this process are hydrocarbons. In some cases, natural gas must undergo a "sweetening" process in which sulfur dioxide is emitted.

Ethylene Production   Ethylene is produced by a process called thermal cracking—hydrocarbons and steam are fed into the cracking furnace, where they are heated, compressed, and distilled. Typical feedstocks used in U.S. in this process are approximately 75 percent ethane/propane and 25 percent naphtha.

Benzene Production   Benzene is naturally produced from crude oil as it is distilled in the refining process. It can also be produced using a reforming operation that uses decontaminated naphtha from ethylene production. Benzene has been found to cause blood disorders and leukemia in workers exposed to high concentrations for a long period of time. It is regulated by the Comprehensive Environmental Response, Compensation and Liability Act (CERCLA/Superfund), the Resource Conservation and Recovery Act (RCRA), and the Occupational Safety and Health Administration (OSHA).

Styrene Production   Styrene is produced by combining benzene and ethylene using a catalyst and then dehydrogenating the resulting ethylbenzene. Ethylbenzene is listed as a volatile contaminant by the Environmental Protection Agency (EPA) and is a standard priority pollutant for monitoring of water discharges. Styrene is a clear, colorless liquid which is flammable and toxic and requires special precautions. Exposure to high levels may result in irritation to eyes, skin, and the respiratory tract. The Health Hazard Assessment Group and the EPA's Office of Drinking Water classifies styrene as a probable carcinogen; however, the Science Advisory Board refutes this claim. Styrene is regulated under Superfund and by OSHA and the Food and Drug Administration (FDA).

Polystyrene Resin   Styrene is converted to polystyrene by holding styrene in a chamber under controlled temperatures to remove solvents, unreacted materials, and other volatiles from the end product. It is then fed through a die where strands and pellets are formed.

Blowing Agent Production   Isopentane, n-pentane, isobutane, n-butane, CFCs, and HCFCs are all blowing agents for foam plastic. CFCs are commonly used in the production of polymer foams, but used only 2.3 percent of the time in the production of polystyrene. Of that 2.3 percent, most is used to produce insulation board. Common blowing agents for polystyrene include pentane and HCFCs. Pentane does not affect the ozone layer, but may contribute to low-level smog if not recovered. The EPA has endorsed HCFC-22 as an "excellent alternative" to CFCs as it reduces ozone depletion by 95 percent over CFCs. However, federal law requires a phase-out of all ozone-depleting chemicals, and by 1993 HCFC-22 will be prohibited by federal law from use in the production of foam packaging.[4]

Final Product Fabrication   Crystal polymers are combined with blowing agents under pressure in an extruder. The pressure drops as they exit the extruder, which causes the polystyrene to bubble and foam. Sheets are produced and thermoformed into desired shapes. Most of the solid waste generated during this stage is recycled.

Packaging and Transportation   Polystyrene products are typically wrapped in polyethylene sleeves and packaged in corrugated boxes and shipped by truck or rail.

Disposal

Landfilling   Plastics are an inert material that add stability to a landfill, first by acting as a liner that reduces leaching of toxins in landfills and second by not producing methane gas. Landfill characteristics do not foster the biodegradability of plastics. Plastics may take as long as 20 years to break down and even then will only break into smaller pieces, retaining the same volume. However, pressure within a landfill is estimated at 50 pounds per square inch, enough to compress all the air out of plastics, thereby reducing their volume.

Incineration   Plastics burn easily because the fuel value remaining in the plastic is released during incineration. The heat generated from combustion of polystyrene is much higher than that released by average MSW, and over twice that of paperboard containers.[5]

Recycling   After polystyrene is transported to the recycling facility, it is washed and food contaminants are removed as sludge. The polystyrene is ground, dried, re-extruded, and pelletized. Energy needed to melt plastics for recycling is 2–8 percent of the energy needed to make virgin plastics.[6] Recycling efforts are hampered by economic and operational factors. First, the sale of polystyrene waste to recyclers generates little revenue relative to hauling costs because recycled materials are generally purchased by weight and polystyrene is very light. Second, residual food contamination can hurt the quality of the recycled material making it potentially unsalable.

Operationally, cleaning is labor-intensive and requires large amounts of water. Recycled plastics are usually weaker or less durable than non-recycled plastics of the same weight, so they are often combined with additives or formed in multiple layers to increase strength. Biodegradable plastics complicate recycling efforts. Manufacturers are working to improve the degradability of plastics intended for landfill. However, biodegradable plastics, if recycled, may deteriorate while still in use. Finally, recycling post-

pones disposal, but it does not eliminate eventual disposal.

Paper Production

Paper, paperboard, and quilt-wrap packaging result from multistage processes with several production and manufacturing subsystems (see Exhibit 6). The various processes are essentially the same for each of the packaging materials unless otherwise noted.

Raw Material Acquisition

Logging Operations   Logging operations can be divided into the following four stages:

Harvest Planning. Decreasing timber supplies relative to expected demand has made the planning stage increasingly important to improve wood utilization and to reduce environmental impacts. Planning decisions include logging techniques, the volume and species to be harvested, and road layout.

Cutting Practices.   Trees are cut down as low to the ground as possible using power saws. Machines known as "feller-bunchers" cut the timber into smaller segments and gather them for transportation. The logs are then roughly scaled, classified for best usage, and graded and measured for length and diameter.

Yarding Practices.   Logs are moved from the forest to a centralized loading area using either tractors to pull the logs or cable lines to transport logs above the forest.

Loading and Hauling.   Logs are transported from the loading area to the manufacturing plant using truck, rail, or water.

Harvesting can lead to soil erosion, which causes the pesticides and fertilizer applied be-

Exhibit 6 ● Paper Production

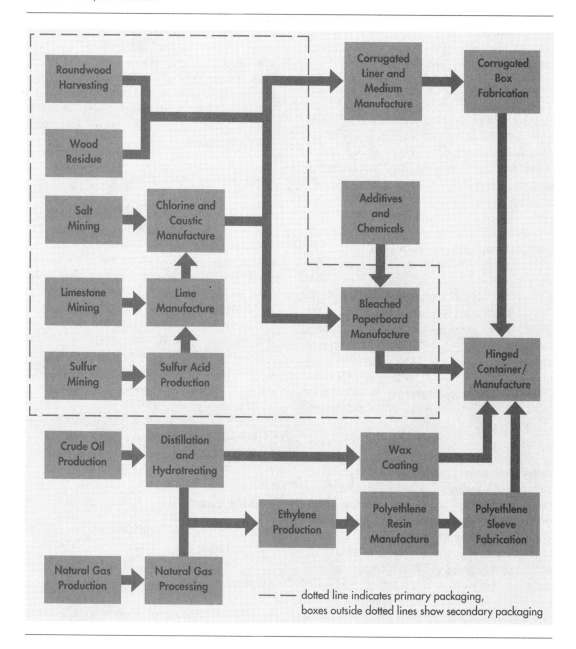

fore harvesting to be washed into the water as well as the soil. Ongoing erosion may change the run-off patterns of a watershed. And the power tools, tractors, and trucks used all consume energy and release emissions.

Materials Manufacture

Pulping   Pulping is a process whereby cellulose fiber, the material used to make paper, is separated from the other components found in wood. Wood is comprised of 50 percent cellulose fiber, 30 percent lignin, and 20 percent oils and carbohydrates.

   Mechanical Process.   Logs that do not meet lumber-quality standards are debarked by a rotating drum that wears away the bark. Logs are chopped into blocks which are combined with wood chips in a continuous grinding machine. A stream of water flows through the grinder and washes the pulp away. The sludge pulp is pumped over several screens to remove coarse material and water, and is stored in tanks until needed. Mechanical pulping tears the cellulose into shorter fibers and allows more lignin to be included in the pulp, which creates weaker paper that yellows easily.

   Chemical Process.   Debarked logs are chipped and placed in large steel tanks called digesters where they are "cooked" with a combination of soda, sulfite, and sulfate at high temperatures. This pulpy substance is blown into cyclones to remove steam and gas and then sent to large tanks where the cooking chemicals are separated from the pulp. The pulp is pumped over screens to remove the water, which is usually 100 to 500 tons of water per ton of pulp. The pulp is thickened and rolled through presses to make sheets of pulp, or moved directly into papermaking operations.

   Pulp and paper mills use an average of 50,000 gallons of water per ton of paper output.

The industry reuses water to conserve usage. In fact, total water use is usually three times higher than actual intake. In addition, mills employ internal recovery systems that recover the liquors used in pulpmaking. Emissions into the air include particulates of sulphur dioxide and organic sulfur compounds. Scrubbers that "wash" the air to collect fly ash, and boilers and furnaces equipped with air pollution controls are used to reduce emissions.

Final Product Fabrication

Bleaching   If bleached paper is desired, the pulp is either treated with an oxidizing agent such as chlorine or a reducing agent such as sulfate dioxide. Salt, limestone, and sulfur mining processes extract the raw materials used in the bleaching process. In the bleaching process, approximately 10 percent of the chlorine used combines with organic molecules in the wood and produces toxic chlorine compounds called organochlorines. One organochlorine that has received particular attention is dioxin. Bleaching is done in several stages with continuous agitation and washing to achieve the desired brightness. The bleaching process can be skipped if natural brown paper is acceptable to the customer, or accomplished with non-chlorine processes such as oxygen bleaching.

Packaging and Transportation

Paper wraps are packaged in corrugated boxes and shipped by truck or rail.

Disposal

Landfilling   Biodegradability is not a factor in modern landfills since the sunlight and air required for quick decomposition does not exist. In fact, the "Garbage Project" at the University of Arizona has been investigating and exhuming landfills since the 1970s and has determined that

40–50 percent of garbage is paper which has not decomposed.

Composting   Paper is organic so it is compostable so long as it is not wax coated or laminated.

Recycling   Waste paper is pulped using the same processes as virgin paper and is passed through a filter to remove any foreign materials. If de-inking is required, the pulp is aerated so that the ink rises to the surface as foam and is removed by a vacuum. In some processes, heat and chemicals aid the de-inking process. The rest of the process is the same as for virgin papermaking.

Recycling waste paper consumes less energy than is consumed during the harvesting, production, and transporting of lumber required for virgin paper. However, this is somewhat offset by the energy used to collect and transport waste paper to the recycling center. Neither paperboard nor quilt-wrap packaging is currently recyclable due to wax and polyethylene content, and possible food contamination.

THE DECISION

As the task force members considered their decision of whether or not to endorse McDonald's recycling program for clamshells, they reviewed the data found in the Franklin studies. They knew that they were going to have to make some assumptions about future disposal methods, unmeasured impacts and consumer response.

Clamshells had become a high-profile decision. Not only would this decision affect McDonald's environmental image but it may also be used to judge the effectiveness of this type of joint task force. Should McDonald's continue clamshell recycling efforts, or drop clamshells altogether?

Notes

1. Municipal Solid Waste (MSW) is solid waste generated by residences, commercial establishments, and institutions.

2. "The Greening of the Golden Arches," *Rolling Stone,* August 22, 1991, p. 36; personal communication with Jackie Prince, EDF, March 29, 1993.

3. Stillwell, J., Contz, C., Kopf, P., and Montrome, M., *Packaging for the Environment,* New York: American Management Association, 1991.

4. Environmental Defense Fund and McDonald's Corporation. "Waste Reduction Task Force Final Report," Oak Brook, IL: McDonald's, 1991. p. 22.

5. Personal Communication with Robert Langert, March 29, 1993.

6. Ibid.

The Procter & Gamble Company: Disposable and Reusable Diapers— A Life-Cycle Analysis
Management Institute for Environment and Business

When the Procter & Gamble (P&G) Company unveiled Pampers disposable diapers in the 1960s, consumer products manufacturers and parents considered it the product breakthrough of the decade. By the early 1990s, P&G's invention contributed over 18% to the company's annual revenues of $24 billion. The product has also presented consumers with a decision that has generated significant attention in recent years: which type of diapers to use—disposable or reusable? Used by environmental and consumer advocate groups as a symbol of the "throw away" mentality, disposable diapers account for 1–3% of America's yearly trash output, or 3.6 million tons. In an effort to deflect criticism, P&G decided to take matters into its own hands. In 1990, the company commissioned Arthur D. Little, Inc., an international management and technology consulting firm specializing in environmental issues, to analyze the full range of environmental impacts, or to conduct a "life-cycle analysis," of both types of diaper to settle the debate.

●

Reprinted by permission of The Management Institute for Environment and Business, a program of the World Resources Institute.

LIFE-CYCLE ANALYSIS

Life-cycle analysis (LCA) is a tool to measure and inventory the full range of environmental impacts associated with the inputs and outputs of raw materials, energy and waste during the life of a product—from the acquisition of raw materials, material manufacture, final product fabrication, packaging and distribution, to consumer use and disposal. LCA is a total process and product mapping methodology.

LCA is often used to compare two similar products in order to assess which is environmentally favorable. However, such a comparison presents three major difficulties. First, LCA analyses rarely determine that one product is evironmentally favorable in every category of environmental impact. Second, LCA studies typically measure different sorts of things, producing results which are largely inconclusive. And third, processing the information obtained from an LCA requires managers to weigh qualitative and quantitative data. Evaluations range from determining the health and environmental risks associated with a particular waste stream to choosing whether reducing air pollution is more important than water pollution.

Many environmentalists argue that LCA misses the point altogether. Such is the belief of Barry Commoner of New York University, who criticizes LCA and similar tools because they put "a badge of legitimacy on existing levels of pollution," rather than questioning whether that pollution is justifiable from society's perspective.

THE DIAPER LIFE-CYCLE ANALYSIS

Researchers at Arthur D. Little began their task by determining a prototypical weight and size of both a disposable and reusable diaper and gauging the weekly usage rates of each. They also mapped the life-cycle of each, as illustrated in Figures 1 and 2.

In constructing the life-cycle diagrams, Arthur D. Little staff made a number of simplifying assumptions concerning the ways in which diapers are used and disposed:

1. The number of daily diaper changes is the same for both disposables and resusables: The researchers assumed the same frequency rate of changes for both types of diapers, although disposables, due to their greater absorbency, generally require fewer changes.

FIGURE 1 ● Reusable Diaper Life-Cycle Analysis

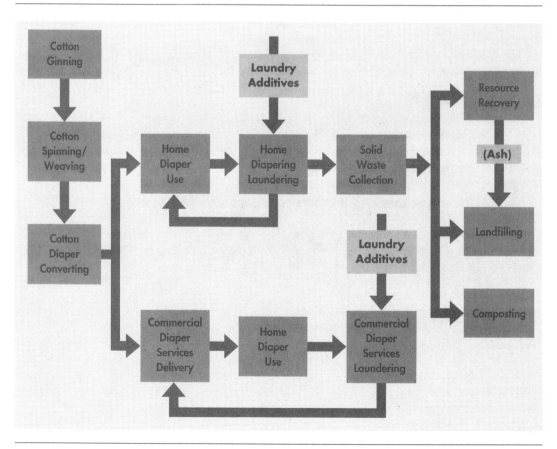

Source: Arthur D. Little, Inc.

FIGURE 2 ● Disposable Diaper Life-Cycle Analysis

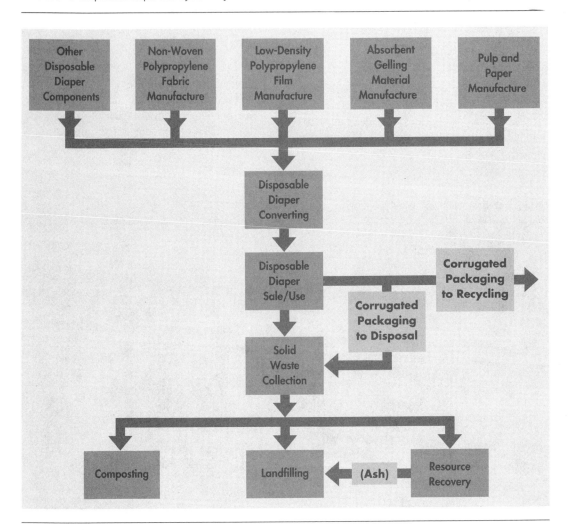

Source: Arthur D. Little, Inc.

2. 90% of all reusables are laundered at home: The researchers assumed that only 10% of consumers using reusable diapers subscribe to a diaper service. However, other estimates have placed this figure at a higher percentage.

Arthur D. Little emerged with the following results:

Life-Cycle Analysis of Disposable and Reusable Diapers (based on weekly diaper needs)

Category	Disposable	Reusable
Raw Materials Consumption (lbs)	25.30	3.60
Energy Consumption (Btu)	23,290.00	78,890.00
Water Consumption (gal)	23.60	144.00
Atmospheric Emissions (lbs)	0.09	0.86
Waste Water Effluents (lbs)	0.01	0.12
Process Solid Waste (lbs)	2.02	3.13
Post-Consumer Waste	22.18	0.24
Total Costs ($/week)	10.31	7.47–16.92

References

Arthur D. Little, Inc., *Disposable versus Reusable Diapers: Health, Environmental, and Economic Comparisons,* report to Procter & Gamble, March 16, 1990.

Society of Environmental Toxicology and Chemistry and SETAC Foundation for Environmental Education, *A Technical Framework for Life-Cycle Assessment,* Workshop Report, January 1991, p. xvii.

David Stipp, "Life-Cycle Analysis Measures Greenness, But Results May Not Be Black and White," *Wall Street Journal,* February 28, 1991.

33

DesignTex, Incorporated (A)

Matthew M. Mehalik
Michael E. Gorman
Andrea Larson
Patricia H. Werhane

The contract textile business is about offering choice, not volume.

—Susan Lyons

Susan Lyons, vice president of Design at DesignTex, a firm specializing in the design and manufacture of textiles for commercial interiors, knew the importance of looking ahead to the next design breakthrough. In February 1991, she had helped launch a new line of fabrics called the Portfolio Collection™, a design that evolved out of collaboration with very famous architects, Aldo Rossi, Robert Venturi, Denise Scott Brown, and Richard Meier. This collection was provocative in its aesthetic sense, and it also demonstrated that well-designed fabrics could be marketed at reasonable prices.

Although Lyons was proud of the latest collection, she wanted the next design to focus on an issue, not be just a change in aesthetics. The issue of environmental responsibility seemed

perfect. "Green" was popular in the trade literature and in the general media, and she had been receiving inquiries from DesignTex's customers about how environmentally responsible DesignTex's products were. Her desire to pursue an environmental agenda was not, however, simply the result of customer demand. It sprang from deep personal beliefs about environmentalism that reflected her mother's influence. Lyons' mother had been "way ahead of her time": she had been recycling trash and other items and had been conservation minded back in the 1960s when Lyons was growing up. These childhood experiences had made Lyons sensitive to environmental concerns, and she had a strong impulse to act upon them.

Such a breakthrough, thought Lyons, would maintain DesignTex's leadership in the commercial-fabrics design market. DesignTex was vying to be the largest member of the Association of Contract Textiles (ACT), the industry trade organization. Located in New York, DesignTex worked with over 40 mills around the world, many of which manufactured the designs created by DesignTex.

DesignTex was also a member of the Steelcase Design Partnership, a collection of design industries purchased in 1989 by Steelcase, a giant corporation located in Grand Rapids, Michigan, that manufactured office furniture and supplies. Steelcase formed this partnership to capture a market that otherwise eluded the firm. Although the company was able to turn out huge amounts of products very profitably, it was not responsive to customers such as architects, who demanded specialty or custom designs. Small, nimble, and entrepreneurial companies were able to meet the demands of this growing market better than Steelcase, and DesignTex was such a company.

In order to maintain DesignTex's ability to respond to the rapidly changing, custom-design market, Steelcase permitted DesignTex's management to operate autonomously. In fact, as a fabric supplier, DesignTex sometimes competed against Steelcase for contracts. Steelcase typically brought in DesignTex as a consultant, however, in matters involving specialty-fabrics design. Susan Lyons summarized the relationship, "DesignTex is very profitable, and Steelcase receives a large amount of money from DesignTex's operation with no oversight, so Steelcase is happy to let DesignTex do its own thing. However, this situation could change if DesignTex's profitability began to decline." By taking the lead in the still volatile environmental market, Lyons hoped DesignTex would maintain its autonomy.

To launch her project, she began surveying the trade literature, contacted yarn spinners who claimed to be environmentally "correct," and paid attention to competitors who were also attempting to enter this market. The work was difficult because (1) she was also looking at approximately 40 other new designs and design improvements, (2) she wanted the design to look like others in the DesignTex line and (3) she wanted the design to be durable as well as environmentally viable.

Lyons continued her "research" for about two years, from 1991 through 1993. What she found was a jumble of information. As she pointed out, there were "conflicting claims about environmentally safe materials." Cottons were often heavily bleached, and most manufacturers were reluctant to talk about what was in their dyes. She considered using foxfiber with

vegetable dyes, but the combination was available in only two colors. She considered using a yarn that was made from PET-recycled soda bottles. In fact, this appeared to be the most promising option, but the vendors were unreliable. These problems seemed difficult to reconcile with her belief that the "contract-textile business is about offering choice, not volume."[1]

THE CLIMATEX OPTION[2]

Because DesignTex also worked with over 40 contract mills around the world, Lyons contacted some of them to investigate their environmental efforts. In December 1992 she became interested in a sample of a fabric product line called Climatex. Albin Kaelin, managing director of Rohner Textil, a mill located in Switzerland, sent Lyons a sample. He and Rohner Textil had been pursuing an environmental agenda of their own, and he was willing to team up with Lyons and DesignTex in developing a new product based on Climatex.

The fabric, a patented combination of wool, ramie, and polyester, was unique because it wicked away moisture from a person who was in contact with the material over long periods. It was intended to improve comfort in wheelchairs and trucks, since those applications involved extended periods of contact between people and fabrics. Exhibit 1 contains additional information on Climatex.

Lyons also inquired about the possibility of recycling Climatex. Kaelin informed her that recycling fabrics was possible only if the material was pure (e.g., 100 percent wool or cotton), but not if it was a combination of materials. Because Climatex was a blend of wool, ramie, and polyester, no recycling was possible. In addition, Kaelin mentioned that recycling any commercial fabrics was questionable, because they were typically glued as upholstery, and the glue itself made recycling difficult. Nevertheless, he went on to add, "there is a far more important argu-

Exhibit 1 ● Information on Climatex[R]

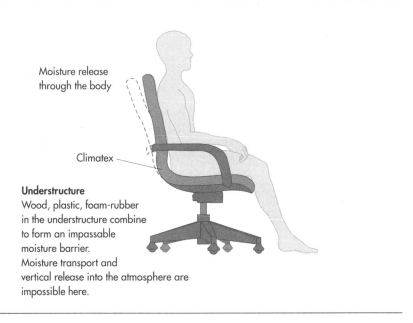

Moisture release
through the body

Climatex

Understructure
Wood, plastic, foam-rubber
in the understructure combine
to form an impassable
moisture barrier.
Moisture transport and
vertical release into the atmosphere are
impossible here.

ment on the aspect of ecology to Climatex." Since the fabric was created without any chemical treatments, "the yarn in the fabric can be burnt [sic] without any damaging chemical reaction and are consisting [sic] of a good heating factor." By "good heating factor," Kaelin meant that the fabric released a large amount of energy when burned, and he proposed using this energy in the operation of the mill. He also mentioned that Climatex was being tested in Germany by an independent institute, the International Association for Research and Testing in the Field of Textile Ecology (OEKO-Tex).[3]

Both Kaelin and Lyons were pleased when Climatex passed the OEKO-Tex inspections in May 1993. The institute, concerned with human-ecology issues, tested for pH value, content of free and partially releasable formaldehyde, residues of heavy metals, residues of pesticides, pentachorophenole content, carcinogenic compounds, and color fastness. Having passed these tests, Climatex could bear the OEKO-Tex trademark and was certified to be allergy-free. . . .

By the middle of 1993, Lyons had several options to consider for an environmental design. The most promising one seemed to be the Climatex fabric from Rohner, which was certified to be manufactured within the OEKO-Tex specifications. But she was worried that because the fabric was not recyclable, and because it was difficult to make a grand environmental statement using the OEKO-Tex label, that option might not be as good as it seemed. In addition, the product was not cheap. It was priced competitively within the worsted-wool market niche, but that particular niche was on the expensive end of the overall market. She considered using yarn made from PET-recycled soda bottles, but she was not confident that the vendors could deliver reliably. Her research uncovered promising options, but each had difficulties and risks.

In July 1993, DesignTex owner Ralph Saltzman, President Tom Hamilton, Consultant Steve Kroeter, and Lyons met to consider what the next generation of the Portfolio™ Collection would be. Launched in 1991, Portfolio™ had been a highly successful major product line. By mid-1993, however, the product's demand had peaked. At this meeting, the team agreed that the next Portfolio™ collection would have a major impact on the market if its design focused on the green issue.

During the meeting, Lyons brought up another factor that could not be neglected: aesthetics. In addition to being environmentally friendly the next Portfolio collection had to be as beautiful as the last. Lyons hoped to collaborate with a prestigious designer in producing beautiful fabrics for the new line, just as she had for the original Portfolio Collection™. At the meeting, Kroeter suggested that they contact Suzy Tompkins of the Esprit Clothing Company, which had just released a unique line of clothing based on organic cotton. Lyons suggested an architect who was well known for his environmental philosophy and his architectural-design accomplishments, William McDonough. The group agreed that they would contact both designers and invite them to participate in the next generation of Portfolio™. Tompkins declined to participate because as a clothing manufacturer, she rarely worked with commercial-fabric designers. Lyons did, however, receive a more enthusiastic response when she contacted McDonough.

WILLIAM MCDONOUGH

During her environmental-literature search, Lyons had come across the name of William McDonough in two places. She had read the March 1993 issue of *Interiors* magazine, which was dedicated entirely to McDonough and his projects. She had also seen an article about him in the *Wall Street Journal*.[4] McDonough had just accepted a job as the dean of Architecture at the University of Virginia. After reading about him, Lyons viewed him as the most high-profile person working with environmental concerns in the design industry.

McDonough had no immediate plans to develop sustainable fabrics, but he responded quite enthusiastically when she made the suggestion to him. He was looking for opportunities to apply his design philosophy. The fabric-design project fit into his plans perfectly.

McDonough came to visit DesignTex in early October 1993. During their meeting, Lyons described the options she had turned up in her literature and marketplace searches and suggested the idea of the PET soda bottle fabric to him. In turn, McDonough presented his design philosophy. . . .

"Two key principles hit home really hard," Lyons said, "the idea that waste equals food and the idea of a cradle-to-cradle design, not a cradle-to-grave design." McDonough stated that in order to meet the waste-equals-food and cradle-to-cradle design criteria, the product had to be able either (1) to compost completely with no negative environmental impact, thereby becoming food for other organisms (organic nutrients) or (2) to become raw material for another industrial product (technical nutrients). Furthermore, one should not mix the organic and the technical, or one would end up with a product that could be used neither as food for organisms nor as raw materials for technology. "The product should be manufactured without the release of carcinogens, bioaccumulatives, persistent toxic chemicals, mutagens, heavy metals, or endocrine disruptors." McDonough discouraged the use of the term "environmentally friendly" and instead proposed "environmentally intelligent" to describe this method of design, because it involved having the foresight to know that poisoning the earth is not merely unfriendly, but unintelligent.[5]

"The key to the project," McDonough stated, would be "getting the fabric mills to open up their manufacturing processes to inspection to see where problems arise." In addition, the mills would have to examine the processes of the mill partners—the farmers, yarn spinners, twisters, dyers, and finishers—so that they could also meet the design protocol. McDonough suggested that his close colleague, Dr. Michael Braungart of the Environmental Protection Encouragement Agency (EPEA) in Germany, could help with this project. Braungart's profession was chemistry and he had led the chemistry department of Greenpeace. He had collaborated before with McDonough in implementing McDonough's design protocols.

In addition to the environmental criteria, McDonough's proposal addressed the aesthetic component of the fabrics. "The fabrics needed to be incredibly beautiful as well." He suggested that they use the mathematics of fractals to generate the patterns. Fractals were appealing to McDonough because "they are like natural systems . . . the smallest component is the same as the whole." He was interested in harmonic proportions throughout nature, and he felt that the new designs should reflect natural harmonies in the protocols and in the esthetics.[6]

FORMING THE NETWORK

The day following the McDonough meeting, Lyons contacted Rohner Textil to see if Kaelin would be willing to participate in this project. He was encouraged by Lyons's report and looked forward to meeting McDonough, who traveled to Rohner a fortnight later. McDonough was encouraged by the Climatex project. Nevertheless the Climatex fabric was far from compostable, because the OEKO-Tex standards did not exclude all harmful chemicals that would be released during composting. In addition, Mc-

Donough was concerned about the use of polyester because it came from a fossil fuel. He explained to Kaelin his design protocols, which, according to Lyons, was like asking Kaelin to "reinvent his mill." Kaelin responded enthusiastically to McDonough's ideas and eagerly awaited Braungart, who would help begin the assessment of the manufacturing processes.

Braungart traveled to the mill in December 1993. He examined it closely to determine the changes needed to meet McDonough's design protocol. Braungart was "pleasantly surprised" by Climatex and its OEKO-Tex approval. He was also impressed with the mill, which, he thought, had dealt with ecology issues in a manner far ahead of everything he had seen up to that point. Braungart's early suggestions were, as expected, in agreement with McDonough's: produce the Climatex product without using polyester so that all-natural materials would be used, which would make the fabric compostable. The problem with Climatex, from McDonough's perspective, was that it mixed organic and technical nutrients, so the fabric could not be composted, yet the technical nutrients could not be recovered.

Braungart's evaluation required him to examine all stages of the fabric-construction process. Because the mill was involved with the fabric weaving, he also inspected the mill's suppliers: farmers, yarn spinners, yarn twisters, dyers, and finishers. Yarn spinners created a cord of yarn/thread from the pieces of individual material fibers, such as wool. Yarn twisters took two or more cords of thread/yarn and twisted them together, producing a much thicker, stronger piece of yarn. Dyers added the colors to the yarn. Finishers added chemicals to the finished weave to make it more durable, flame resistant, static resistant, and stain resistant, if these qualities were required.

Lyons was the main project coordinator and was responsible for creating the "construction," or generalized set of weaving patterns and color palette based on McDonough's designs. "Everyone on the project," she said, "knew that getting the mill contractors to open their books for Braungart's inspection would be difficult, and keeping track of the fabric's production would involve complex management well beyond the normal levels of supervision." Consequently, the team had concluded that the more they could do themselves, the easier it would be to produce the new fabrics. Acting on this philosophy, they intended to have the mill perform the role of dyer as well as of weaver. Kaelin agreed: "We need as few members in the pool as possible."[7]

THE PROJECT UNDERWAY?

By the end of January 1994, Kaelin had eliminated polyester from Climatex, producing a new blend of ramie and wool that preserved the fabric's moisture-wicking properties. He called this new fabric Climatex Lifecycle™. Using this fabric seemed easier than using material that reclaimed and reused polyester and other technical nutrients.

By the end of January, Kaelin had sent Braungart all of the security data sheets and production details pertaining to the chemicals and dye substances used in the manufacturing of Climatex Lifecycle™. The team hoped that this information would be enough for Braungart to make recommendations on how to proceed by the end of February 1994. They wanted Braungart's examination to be totally complete by the end of March 1994.

At the beginning of March 1994, Braungart had some bad news. The chemicals used in the dye materials did not meet the design protocol. Furthermore, questions about the manufacture of the dye chemicals could not be answered by examining the security data sheets, even though they had passed the OEKO-Tex standards.

DesignTex's next Portfolio Collection, McDonough's fractal patterns and design protocols, and Rohner's next generation of Climatex, depended on Braungart's ability to gain access to the manufacturing processes of the dye suppliers, which meant the dye suppliers had to open their books to Braungart. Kaelin contacted Rohner's dye suppliers and asked them to cooperate with Braungart's inspection and answer his questions. By the end of March, however, it was clear that cooperation was not forthcoming. Braungart had contacted over 60 chemical companies worldwide, none of which had agreed to open their books for his inspection.

Another concern was the project's cost. Someone needed to pay Braungart and the EPEA as he studied the manufacturing processes. Kaelin agreed to hire Braungart and the EPEA, because Rohner expected to acquire the patent rights for the next generation of Climatex. By the end of April, however, Braungart had already spent the funds Rohner had provided and needed an extension. Rohner was willing to consider an additional payment, but only after the product had been introduced into the marketplace. None of the team were sure how much more money Braungart would require.

Lyons reflected on the situation. DesignTex had made a large commitment to this project, hoping it would propel the firm into the lead of the commercial-fabric market. It had already been three years since DesignTex had launched the first Portfolio Collection™, and she was aware of the pressure to get a product out the door. Waiting for Braungart to gain access to the dye process risked the whole project and would dramatically increase its cost, even if he succeeded. On the one hand, perhaps it would be better to relax McDonough's and Braungart's standards a little and test the results of the manufacturing process without inspecting the dye suppliers' dye-production processes. After all, Climatex Lifecycle was already a major improvement over currently available environmental designs. On the other hand, the whole project was about making a breakthrough in environmental design, and it was not clear that anything short of the McDonough/Braungart approach would represent a sufficient leap forward.

Notes

1. The information in this section was obtained during an interview with Susan Lyons on 31 July 1995.

2. Climatex is a registered trademark of Rohner Textil, AG.

3. Kaelin quotes from correspondence from Kaelin to Lyons, 3 December 1992, supplemented by the Lyons interview of 31 July 1995.

4. *Wall Street Journal,* October 23, 1989.

5. The concepts "cradle-to-cradle," "waste equals food," "current solar income," "environmentally intelligent," and the design protocol discussed above are proprietary to William McDonough and are included in this document with his permission.

6. The material in this section was developed from interviews conducted with William McDonough on 29 June 1995, 16 August 1995, and 21 September 1995, and with Susan Lyons on 31 July 1995.

7. Interviews with Lyons on 21 July 1995.

34

Bayerische Motoren Werke AG
Christopher A. Cummings
Frank den Hond

In the late summer of 1990, the German government invited industry commentary on a proposed policy to make automobile manufacturers responsible for the final disassembly and disposal of their products, as well as for ensuring that most of each vehicle is recycled. Commonly known as product "take-back" requirements, such legislation is potentially revolutionary for manufacturers. The obligation to assume stewardship for a product long after it has been sold necessitates changes in product design, materials use and disassembly techniques that would have been unthinkable even ten years ago. Moreover, establishment of a reverse distribution network to collect discarded products requires a significant investment in apparently non-productive assets.

At BMW AG, it was the task of the recycling group (T-RC) to determine the company's response to the draft legislation, which was called "Draft: The Federal Government's Policy on the Reduction, Minimization, or Utilization of Scrapped Vehicle Wastes." Dr.-Ing. Horst-Henning Wolf and Dr.-Ing. Harald A. Franze would assume primary responsibility for developing BMW's proposals to the German Environment Ministry (BMU, Bundesministerium für Umwelt, Naturschutz und Reaktorsicherheit).

●

Reprinted by permission of The Management Institute for Environment and Business, a program of the World Resources Institute.

The contents of the draft legislation came as no surprise to BMW. Years earlier, Klaus Töpfer, head of the BMU and the federal government's champion of the legislation, visited BMW's corporate headquarters in Munich. Chairman Eberhard von Kuenheim, Wolf, Director of T-RC, and Franze, head of T-RC Development, briefed him on BMW's environmental program and the current vehicle recycling situation: due to a mushrooming diversity of materials used in vehicle manufacture, vehicle recyclability was declining. This trend increases the costs of dismantling and disposing of vehicles. The viability of the vehicle recycling industry, composed of dismantlers who separate and sell vehicle components, and shredders who process and reclaim component and body materials, was becoming increasingly tenuous.

Wolf and Franze had followed both the legislative and recycling industry developments carefully. As Wolf headed off to the Research and Engineering Centre and Franze back to his office, each wondered about the implications for BMW, the economics of recycling and how, if at all, the company should alter its operations and political strategies.

THE VEHICLE RECYCLING INDUSTRY

Approximately 4,000 dismantlers and 44 shredders recycle almost 95% of Germany's scrapped vehicles. In 1989, the network processed 2.1 million vehicles. The dismantling operation is a time consuming and very manual process of unscrewing things and requires relatively unskilled labor. Dismantling requires little capital investment other than property and manually operated tools. Companies serving this market are widely dispersed throughout Germany and tend to be fairly small and undermanaged. In contrast to dismantling, the shredding operation requires large machines to rip apart metal, a significant capital investment which limits the number of participants in the market. Both shredding and dismantling companies have relationships with remanufacturing and metals companies in order to ensure markets for their outputs. (See Exhibit 1 for a complete illustration of the parts and materials flow of spent vehicles through the recycling network.)

In a typical auto disposal situation, the final owner transports the old jalopy to a dismantler and negotiates a price for disposal. The make and condition of the model determine the residual value of the vehicle's parts and materials. The better the make and condition, the greater the residual value and the lower the cost. Depending on the value of the vehicle and its condition, the owner may pay the dismantler, the dismantler may pay the owner, or there may be no exchange of money. Dismantlers are under no legal obligation to accept used vehicles. BMWs typically fetch DM 200-300 from dismantlers, as high-value components and metal can be sold to reprocessing and scrap metals companies.

Dismantlers pull apart spent vehicles and separate and sell used, valuable components. Components are frequently remanufactured and reconditioned. The reconditioning is done by some dismantling companies, a number of dedicated remanufacturing companies and most vehicle manufacturers. These used parts—e.g. catalytic converters, batteries and gearings—are sold at a fraction of the cost of new parts. Dismantlers also sell used polymer components to polymer suppliers which grind them up and sell the recycled polymers. Finally, they typically

drain operating fluids, compact the vehicle and transport the remaining hulk to vehicle shredders.

Shredder companies, most of which are owned by major steel companies, use large shredding machines to process the remaining car hulks. They purchase the hulks from the dismantler, rip the vehicle hulk into fist-sized pieces and then use a variety of magnetic, air and aqueous separating machines to sort ferrous and non-ferrous metals that have resale value in metal markets. The ferrous scrap is sold to steel mills; the non-ferrous to specialized metal companies. Automotive Shredder Residue (ASR, known throughout the industry as "fluff") is a by-product of this separation process. Comprised of plastic, foam, rubber, glass and dirt, ASR cannot be recycled in mixed form and hence has no economic value for shredder operators. In order to complete the material disposal cycle, shredders must pay for the transport and disposal of ASR, either by landfill or incineration.

In total, dismantlers and shredders recoup nearly 75% of the material from a used or wrecked vehicle; ASR, the remaining 25%, presents the waste management challenge. (See Exhibit 2.) ASR accounts for 400,000 tonnes of solid waste—75% of total shredder waste and .65% of Germany's industrial annual solid waste stream. Exhibit 3 indicates the magnitudes of ASR and total shredder waste streams in EC countries. However, a number of current trends within the industry indicate that the challenges to the existing recycling network may be growing.

Improvements in materials technology, particularly in polymer technology, are enabling vehicle manufacturers to optimize the performance of individual components and simultaneously reduce the weight of the vehicle. (See Exhibits 7 and 8 for an indication of the increase in plastics use.) Weight reduction improves fuel efficiency and handling. However, the proliferation of these materials makes disassembly a more complicated and costly process. The end

Exhibit 1 ● Flow Chart for the German Recycling Network

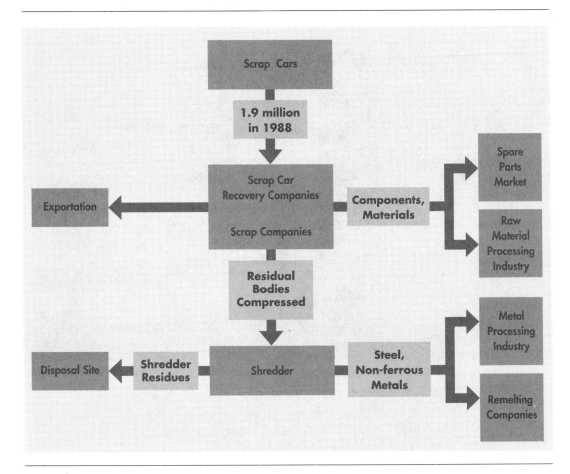

Source: Company information

result is an increase in the ASR percentage of vehicles, which reduces the residual value of the car, and increases the amount of material to be disposed in landfills or incinerators.

As the costs to the network of disassembling and disposing of vehicles increase, it must pass on the costs to the final owner. At some point, the owner will refuse to pay the fee, and may seek to illegally or improperly discard the vehicle, at no cost to him/herself. Hence, the decrease in vehicle recyclability not only weakens the dismantling industry, but may exacerbate Germany's solid waste problem. More ASR could find its way into environmentally sensitive areas; more vehicles into the Black Forest.

Exhibit 2 ● Material Flow in Scrap Vehicle Disposal

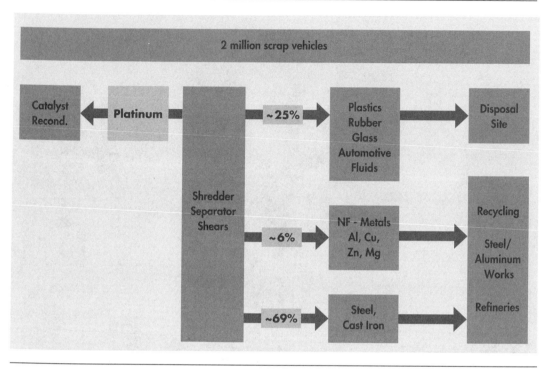

Source: Company information

A second disconcerting aspect of the recycling industry is that only 10% of the dismantlers currently operating in Germany have been certified for operation by the BMU. Most of these operations do not have leachate systems required for operations dealing with hazardous waste (i.e., waste oils and operating fluids), while others require significant remediation efforts in order to obtain certification. If requirements were enforced, most dismantlers would have to make significant outlays of capital to comply or close down.

THE GERMAN SOLID WASTE SITUATION

Like many other countries, Germany is afflicted with the dual pressures of increasing per capita waste generation, and a populace that is increasingly intolerant of traditional methods of waste disposal. So while the amount of garbage is on the rise, economically viable disposal options are on the wane. The pinch is particularly acute for large generators of industrial waste, such as the shredders that produce ASR. Germany's two most popular disposal methods—landfill and in-

Exhibit 3 ● Shredder Waste in Selected European Countries

Country	Vehicles Processed (000s)	ASR (000s tonnes)	Total Shredder Waste (000s tonnes)	ASR as % of Shredder Waste	Total Industrial Waste (000s tonnes)	ASR as % of Industrial Waste
Germany	2,100	400	530	75.5	61,400	0.65
UK	2,000	465	720	64.6	50,000	0.93
France	2,000	398	475	83.8	50,000	0.80
Italy	1,500	300	N/A	N/A	43,700	0.69
Netherlands	450	115	140	82.1	17,300	0.66
Denmark	75–90	10	40	25.0	1,600	0.63

Note: Differences in amounts of ASR reflect differences in approaches to waste management.
Source: Den Hond, CEST, VDA, Author Estimates, OECD reports.

cineration—are getting prohibitively expensive for such generators, who are then forced to develop more creative solutions.

Current Practices

Germany utilizes three disposal methods to process its annual municipal and industrial waste stream of 90 million tonnes.[1] Landfill operations handle approximately 50%, resource recovery (waste-to-energy) incinerators 35%, and recycling just 15%. See Exhibit 4 for a comparison of waste disposal practices in the United States, Japan and Germany.

Until recently, Germany was among the world's largest waste exporters. East Germany and the North Sea were the main disposal grounds for German waste. For instance, in 1988, West Germany exported 2.1 million tons of garbage to East Germany. However, BMU and the Bundestag, the German Parliament, recently enacted legislation banning exportation of waste and entered an agreement with the EC to eliminate ocean disposal as a management

option.[2] Germany will now be independently responsible for its own waste.

Landfill Disposal

Land disposal is the oldest and best-known method of solid waste management. In recent decades, the "not-in-my-backyard" (NIMBY) movement, a collective reference to grassroots, local initiatives that oppose new landfill development, has made new facility sitings extremely difficult for waste management companies and local municipalities. Nevertheless, many experts still believe that it is the appropriate approach. If population density is low, space is available, no groundwater or surface water sources will be threatened, and waste content is largely biodegradable, landfill disposal may be the safest and most efficient waste management approach.[3]

Landfill siting, design and technology have progressed significantly during the past two decades. In the past, siting decisions had more to do with convenience than the hydrologic setting and potential environmental impacts. Typical disposal areas were wetlands, marshes and spent

Exhibit 4 ● Waste Disposal Practices in Selected Countries, Late 1980s

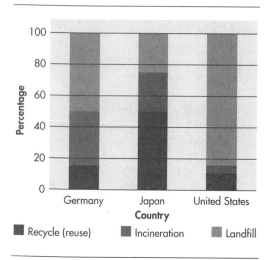

Recycle (reuse)   Incineration   Landfill

Source: Corson, p. 270.

mines, all of which are environmentally sensitive areas, and design and technology were afterthoughts. As a consequence, many landfill sites have been closed by regulatory authorities due to the adverse effects that operations have had on water and soil quality.

Environmental Impacts   Past problems, such as litter, odor, and rodent population, have given way to the more serious problems of leachate and methane generation.[4] Leachate is produced when water from rain or waste permeates the landfill, becomes acidic through various interactions with garbage content and dissolves elements and compounds from other wastes. Once a landfill's capacity to contain water is exhausted, leachate can escape into nearby surface waters and underground aquifers, contaminating ecosystems and drinking water. Leachate can contain toxic metals, such as cadmium, and polychlorinated biphenols, both of which pose

threats to public health.[5] Once contamination has occurred, affected areas, especially aquifers, are very difficult to remediate.

Methane production has also emerged as an environmental concern. A colorless, combustible and potentially explosive gas, methane is produced naturally during the microbiotic, anaerobic decomposition of waste.[6] It has been known to kill vegetation adjacent to landfills by depleting soil of oxygen and nutrients. Recently, landfill methane generation has been implicated in the global warming debate.[7]

Current Landfill Operations   State-of-the-art landfills are far more sophisticated than their predecessors:

● The geotechnical and hydrologic characteristics of newer landfill sites are carefully assessed prior to choosing the site, so as to minimize potential contamination from leachate.

● Plastic and clay liners are used to retain seepage and recovery systems are used to capture and process leachate prior to emission into surrounding ecosystems.

● Landfill gas systems (LGS) are used to harness landfill methane for productive purposes. Methane is captured, cleaned and sold to nearby gas and power companies, defraying and in some cases covering landfill operating costs.[8] Recovered methane has the same energy capacity as natural gas—1,000 btus per cubic foot. Although only a limited number of LGS systems have been incorporated into landfill systems around the world, experience indicates that they supply a steady and reliable source of energy and will be widely adopted in the future.

Status in Germany   Similar to the situation in the United States, the landfill population in Germany has decreased rapidly over the past two decades. In Bavaria, landfill facilities have decreased by 99%–from 4,000 to 40—and there are plans to close the remainder within 5 to 10 years.[9] Some sources indicate that Germany will run out of landfill disposal capacity within the next 5 years.

The vast majority of German landfills are not "state-of-the-art," and the public and public officials have become increasingly concerned over their environmental impact. A recent BMU regulatory campaign has led to stricter content and emissions standards for a number of pollutants, most notably PCBs. Under the requirements, PCB concentration levels for wastes entering landfills will fall from 50 ppm (parts per million) to 10 ppm over a two year period. At that time, if PCB levels are above 10 ppm in waste shipments, the waste load will not be accepted and will be reclassified as hazardous waste. Hazardous waste disposal is on the order of three or four times as expensive as solid waste landfill disposal in Germany. ASR will likely be among the kinds of waste that will be turned away from landfills. See Exhibit 5 for the current and projected costs of landfill disposal.

Incineration

Problems with landfill disposal have led to a search for new solid waste management options. Burning garbage, often to generate power, has been a prevalent secondary option in many industrialized countries, including Germany. As of 1987, more than 350 waste-to-energy facilities were operating in over 15 countries, more than half of which were in Western Europe.[10] Incinerators burn garbage at high temperatures and reduce waste volumes by nearly 90% (weight by 70%). However, concerns over negative environmental impacts, high costs of construction and maintenance, and potential obstruction of recycling programs have limited widespread reliance on incineration as a primary waste management option.

Exhibit 5 ● Landfill Disposal Prices—Current and Projected

Year	Costs (DM/Tonne)
1987	30
1988	40
1989	60
1990	120
1991*	200
1992–1993*	400–600
1994–1995*	500–1800

*Projected

Source: Company information, author estimates

Environmental Impacts　Air emissions from the incineration process are the fundamental environmental concern. Burning chlorinated material, metal and plastic potentially emits dioxins and furans, metals and PCBs, all of which are toxic and pose significant human health threats.[11] Although most incinerator facilities have taken steps to control emissions, potential negative effects on human health are a constant concern for incinerator operators and local communities.

Disposal of the residual ash also poses problems. Although there are uses for ash as feedstock for cement and gypsum, or road bed, unused ash is often landfilled. However, unburned metals in the ash make it quite toxic, and have prompted a movement in the US and Germany to disallow landfill disposal of ash. German officials are considering reclassifying ash as hazardous waste.

Incinerator Operations　Depending on the BTU value of the refuse, garbage can be an excellent source of energy for electricity. Incinerators burn waste at temperatures of 700 to 1200

degrees centigrade and recoup energy in the form of steam, which is used either by power companies or nearby manufacturing facilities. Current designs are equipped with multiple pollution control systems to reduce harmful emissions. In conjunction with BMU, all German incinerators report emissions each day and plants are shut down when incinerators are out of compliance with standards for one hour.

Status in Germany   Incineration has emerged as a critical component of German waste management strategy. The German incinerator population has grown from 7 in 1965 to 47 as of 1988. All but one are resource recovery incinerators and collectively they handle 35% of Germany's solid waste stream.[12] German officials expect 20 more plants to come on line by 1995 (as many as 35 by 2000) and the percentage of solid waste that they process to rise to 50%.[13] However, the cost of bringing a new incinerator on-line ranges from DM 240–320 million. Current incinerations prices are, on average, twice the price of landfill disposal.

The Green Party, a political unit with a primary aim of advancing environmental quality, is strongly opposed to these plans and has vowed to work with local environmental groups to oppose new facility sitings. Unfortunately for the automobile industry, incineration may no longer be a viable disposal option for ASR. The BMU is concerned about the environmental risk of plastic incineration, and does not want to reduce incentives to recycle.

MATERIALS TRENDS AND CHOICES IN THE AUTOMOTIVE INDUSTRY

A Polymer Primer

Polymers are composed of long repeating chains of monomers—small molecular units consisting of carbon atoms linked to hydrogen, nitrogen, oxygen, fluorine, sulphur, bromine, or chlorine atoms—that are chemically modified to create plastics. For example, ethylene monomers are reacted to create the polymer polyethylene.

Polymers were first used by the automotive industry in the late 1950s. Early polymers such as polypropylene (PP) and polyvinyl chloride (PVC) were relatively inexpensive and unsophisticated, and were used for a limited number of applications such as interior trim. Plastics technology rapidly evolved toward higher value added "engineering" and "specialty" polymers. These materials are formulated to exhibit properties specifically tailored for individual application needs, such as strength or heat resistance.

Polymers are generally separated into two classes:

- Thermoplastics consist of polymers that resemble intertwined bundles of spaghetti without direct connection between each polymer chain. Weak electrostatic forces hold the chains together. These forces can be strengthened by cooling or weakened by heating, making the polymer pliable under certain conditions. As a result, thermoplastics can be recycled under proper conditions. However, they experience some degradation in properties as a result of progressive reduction in molecular weight (chain length). Thermoplastics account for 85% by weight of all polymers produced.

- Thermosets, unlike thermoplastics, are linked together by chemical bonds. Due to their cross-linked structures, they are resistant to heat and many have great dimensional stability. Thermosets are not easily recycled, although numerous research efforts are underway.

Chemical suppliers alter the performance and quality of original polymer resins in order to customize polymers for specific functions in several ways:[14]

- Suppliers manipulate chain length and the degree of crystallization of the feedstock mix in order to adjust the properties of the final polymer or polymer blend.
- Processors use various additives, such as plasticizers for flexibility, lubricants for greater moldability, antioxidants for greater temperature stability and ultraviolet stabilizers for resistance to sunlight, and flame retardants.
- Fillers and reinforcements, such as fibers and hollow glass spheres, are added to increase strength and stiffness; chalk is added as a general filler to reduce cost.
- Certain polymers are mixed to create polymer blends or alloys, enabling the processor to achieve a wide range of physical and performance characteristics.

Advantages and Disadvantages of Plastics

Applications Qualities   Exhibit 7 documents the increase in polymer use in the automotive industry. While they continue to be used primarily for interiors, such as dashboards and seats, plastics are increasingly used in critical components, such as fuel tanks and body paneling. Metals still comprise the bulk of the car (i.e., the chassis and engine block), but plastic content continues to grow. In addition to weight advantages over metal, proponents point to several additional advantages:[15]

- High corrosion and chemical resistance
- Greater ease and efficiency in manufacturing through reduced steps in production
- Reduced number of parts needed for a single component, as plastics can be fashioned in complex shapes
- Greater versatility and adaptability to production changes and specific requirements

- Reduced energy consumption in manufacturing[16]
- Reduced expense on a volume basis

Critics charge that a number of plastics characteristics continue to make them unsuitable for many automotive applications:

- Low temperature stability
- Degradation under ultraviolet light
- Lengthy production time
- Lack of experience with polymers in critical applications
- Difficulty of achieving first class surface finish
- Current low level of recyclability

The drive toward acceptance in the automotive world has helped spur a corresponding effort by polymer manufacturers to engineer polymers for specific components and applications. According to Richard Dolinski, Vice President of Dow Chemical's Automotive Development Group, "one size does not fit all in the world of automotive materials, and that's as true of metal as it is of plastics. Both thermoplastics and thermosets serve us well. (We) use them when they are right for the application."[17] As a result, the number of polymers used in one vehicle has grown significantly; a typical vehicle contains more than 20 different polymers and alloys.

Recoverability.   The downfall of increased plastics use is the resulting reduction in the recyclable content of today's vehicles. Metals experience little degeneration from use, have value in secondary metal markets and an established set of buyers. As a result, reprocessed metals can be used for critical applications. While metal recycling is efficient and profitable, it is often not a "closed loop" recycling system; metals recaptured from spent vehicles are not frequently reused in production of new parts.

The plastic recycling technology and end-markets are markedly different. Recycling of thermoplastics is easier, cheaper and more effective than recycling thermosets. Some industries currently recycle thermoplastics, including the automotive industry, in which recent studies have shown that old plastic parts can be recycled even after ten years of use.[18] However, there are several complications that have precluded recycling activities in the past:

- Polymers can be recycled only with homogeneous polymers. Plastics must be separated into like waste streams before any recycling efforts can be undertaken. The greater the number of polymers used in a vehicle, the greater the complexity and effort required to separate them. Although Hoechst Celanese, Eastman Chemical, Dupont and others have developed ways to separate polymers, alloys, composites and additives into monomer feedstocks for some polymers, the technology is not yet effective for many.
- Insufficient labelling of plastic parts has hindered efforts to separate and recycle parts.
- Polymers can be contaminated by commonly used substances, such as paint, glue and other connecting materials, and additives and fillers. While certain additional substances, such as ultraviolet stabilizers that help preserve quality, can improve the recyclability of polymer parts, others can degrade and hence limit the value of the recycled resin.
- Polymers degrade during the regranulation and remelting process, reducing their quality and checking the development of markets for recycled plastics (see Exhibit 6).

Recycled Plastics   According to polymer experts, there is not a clear distinction between virgin and recycled polymers in automotive applications. Despite the degradation that occurs in the regranulation and remelting process, recycled polymers are frequently mixed with virgin polymers for specific applications. In such mixes, recycled polymers are unlikely to be more than 10% of the mix. The lack of a supply of recycled polymers has limited their use. When they have been used in automotive applications, recycled polymers traditionally have been relegated to non-critical applications, such as noise dampening pads, which are hidden from view, or luggage compartment linings.

Industry Materials Trends

Environmental considerations in vehicle design and performance emerged as focal points for German vehicle manufacturers in the mid-1970s. Energy efficiency and emission levels

Exhibit 6 ● Cascade Effect of Plastics Recycling

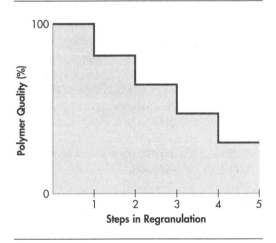

Source: Company information

came under regulation or voluntary agreement between BMU and vehicle manufacturers. What ensued was an industry-wide shift away from heavier metals toward lighter, high performance materials in an effort to meet fuel efficiency and emissions standards.

Over the past thirty years, net metal content of vehicles has dropped by 9.5% while plastic content has grown by 11% (see Exhibit 7). Iron, steel and other metals have been reduced in favor of aluminum and plastics. Although current prices may check aluminum growth rates, plastics content is expected to rise to 15% of vehicles in the coming years. In Germany, the automobile industry accounts for 7% of total plastic consumption.

BMW Materials Selection . . . Plastics comprise 10–11% of BMW's current product line; glass, rubber, fabric and other non-recyclable materials 12.5–15% (see Exhibit 8 for the weight and plastic content of each of BMW's models). . . . Franze predicts the plastic content of the company's product line will continue to experience growth through the 1990s.

THE BMU AND VEHICLE RECYCLING

Industry in the Federal Republic of Germany has taken on the commitment to employ its creativity, its expertise and technical know-how to continually develop environmentally favourable technologies. It recognises the need to incorporate environmental interests—right down to the question of managing the waste accruing from the products it manufactures—in its decision-making and planning activities. It regards environment policy as an indispensable component of an overall, future-orientated policy.[19]

—BMU, *Environmental Protection in Germany*

Environmental policy is beginning to reflect a new approach to waste generation and management in manufacturing industries. Increasingly, industries must examine the full range of environmental impacts associated with manufactured products, known as "life-cycle analysis." . . .

BMU's approach to this type of regulation is based on the idea of voluntary, industry-driven regulation rather than the strict command and control approach practiced in the United States. Under the approach, BMU sets goals for pollu-

Exhibit 7 ● Materials Choice in Automobiles, 1965–1995

Material	1965	1985	1995*
Steel, Iron	76.0%	68.0%	63.0%
Lead, Zinc, Copper	4.0%	4.0%	3.0%
Plastics	2.0%	9.0%	13.0%
Aluminum	2.0%	4.5%	6.5%
Other Non-Recyclables (fabric, rubber, glass)	16.0%	14.5%	14.5%
Total	100.0%	100.0%	100.0%

*Projected

Source: Weber, p. 144.

Exhibit 8 ● BMW's Product Line—Weight and Plastic Content

Model	Weight (kg)	Plastic Content (kg)	Plastic Content/Weight (%)
3 Series	1,050–1,250	130	11.3
5 series	1,350–1,475	150	10.6
6 series	1,450–1,650	170	10.9
7 series	1,550–1,750	160	10.3
8 series	1,750	170	9.7
Average	1,350–1,500	155	10.5

Source: Company information, author estimates

tion levels and industrial performance, and, in conjunction with regulators, industries create their own systems and implementation guidelines to achieve them. Although agreements between BMU and industry are voluntary, the agency can formally create and enforce regulations to achieve the desired outcome if "voluntarily-regulated" industries do not meet their objectives, such as:

New Waste Avoidance and Waste Management Act   In June 1988, the Bundestag passed *Actungesellschaft,* the "New Waste Avoidance and Waste Management Act."[20] The relevant provisions of *Actungesellschaft* are as follows:

- Industry has the responsibility to minimize waste generation through waste avoidance and waste utilization.
- Waste utilization techniques should take priority over traditional waste disposal.
- The federal government has the authority to issue general administrative regulations on future requirements for waste management.
- BMU has the authority to issue statutory regulations regarding the avoidance or re-

duction of noxious substances in waste or to ensure the environmentally-compatible management of such waste or to promote the reuse or recycling of such waste. BMU can issue a *verordnung,* or voluntary agreement, between government and industry to engage a particular environmental problem.

Verpackungsverordnung   In conjunction with the BMU, the Bundestag passed a sweeping piece of legislation in 1991 targeting the role of packaging waste in the German solid waste stream. The decree gives consumers the right to return all packaging materials directly to the point of sale, with deposits possible on some items, and the assurance that the returned packaging will be materially recycled unless it is technically infeasible.

Vehicle Recycling Legislation   In August 1990, Töpfer and BMU issued "Draft: The Federal Government's Policy on the Reduction, Minimization, or Utilization of Scrapped Vehicle Wastes," a voluntary agreement with vehicle manufacturers to address growing concerns over waste from used vehicles. The provisions of the draft are as follows:

- Vehicle manufacturers or their agents must accept used vehicles from the final vehicle owner.

- This transaction must be free of charge to the final vehicle owner.

- In vehicle disposal, reuse and recycling of parts and materials should take precedence over other disposal methods (i.e., landfilling or incineration) whenever technologically feasible, economically reasonable and markets exist for parts and materials.

- In order to achieve the goal of recycling, manufacturers must provide facilities where dismantling can occur, and must develop the supporting technology to effectively separate reusable products from toxic waste streams and other unusable matter.

- New vehicle designs should reflect the goal of increased reuse and recycling of components and materials once the vehicles' useful lives are terminated.

The ultimate goal of the draft legislation is the implementation of a nationwide take-back system by the end of 1993 and a reduction in automotive shredder waste by 60% of current levels to just over 200,000 tonnes per year. Manufacturers have the option to work with the existing recycling network or develop their own system, so long as the goal is achieved. In order to ensure a market for recycled polymers, BMU also is considering the creation of a recycled polymer content requirement. For example, recycled polymers may be required to comprise 25% of a manufacturer's total plastic consumption.

BAYERISCHE MOTOREN WERKE AG

We know it is important to react to developments with speed and agility. Equally, it is vital at an early stage to allow in our planning for possible future developments. After all, we are working today on cars that will not be on the roads for ten or even twenty years. Thus, we help to shape the future. A form of mobility not new to us is to imagine what is currently unimaginable.[21]
—Dr.-Ing. E.h. Eberhard von Kuenheim Chairman, Board of Management

Headquartered in Munich, Germany, Bayerische Motoren Werke AG was founded in 1916 as a high-performance engine manufacturer. After initial success in the aircraft engine business, the company branched out into development of motorcycles and automobiles. It quickly developed a reputation within the automobile and motorcycle racing circuits as a top-notch manufacturer, prompting the company to concentrate more heavily on the private automobile market. Today, automobile related revenues account for over 90% of company sales.

The company is controlled by heirs of Herbert Quandt, who provided $1 million to BMW in 1959 to help the company through a difficult period. The 65% share controlled by the Quandts is now worth nearly $3 billion. Dr.-Ing E.h. Eberhard von Kuenheim, BMW's Chairman, has held the position for two decades.

Business Strategy and Performance

Until the mid 1980's, when it entered the performance car market, BMW had a reputation for producing quality, functional automobiles. In 1980, the company sold 339,232 vehicles and 29,263 motorcycles, generating DM 6.89 billion in revenues and after tax profits of DM 160 million; domestic market share was 5.6%. Engineering improvements, new product introductions, a conscious shift into the upper bracket of the market boosted sales, and a 3 million vehicle domestic market boosted revenues and profits throughout the 1980's. Despite a tight worldwide market in 1989, BMW generated sales of 511,476 units, revenues of DM 20.9 billion, and annual growth of over 13% for the 10 year period; the company's share in the domestic market rose to 6.7%, accounting for 42% of revenues.

Product Line   BMW had always been known for its craftsmanship and engineering, but its target market did not fully exhaust its abilities. From the 1950s through the early 1980s, BMW's product line was targeted at the small, functional car market. BMW's 2 and 3 Series models—small, two-door vehicles that sold very well—were the collective cornerstone of the company.

The European penchant for small cars, however, led most of the other German companies to focus on the same market. Volkswagen AG, Ford-Werke AG and Adam Opel AG—significantly larger multinational corporations with more diversified product lines—provided BMW's main competition down-scale. Mercedes-Benz, the flagship German manufacturer, competed in the upscale performance market.

In 1986, BMW invaded the upper-intermediate performance luxury car segment (a market dominated by Mercedes-Benz) with the introduction of its new 7 Series luxury sedan, which became Europe's top-seller in the over $50,000 category. "We had to get away from the boxy look of our cars and create a model that people would want to look at and caress," explains chief designer Claus Luthe, who oversaw the design of several more expensive, adventurously-designed vehicles.[22] The company found success beyond its expectations in the intermediate luxury segment of the market with its 5 Series, introduced in 1988. BMW believes that its new 1990 3 Series will solidify BMW's position in the performance luxury market. According to von Kuenheim, "for almost 30 years, Mercedes-Benz had the monopoly in luxury vehicles. To their surprise, we've now ended that monopoly."[23]

The 3, 5 and 7 Series vehicles remain BMW's main products, together accounting for over 90% of all vehicles produced by the company. In the future, BMW intends to introduce new models or engines annually and make substantial engineering improvements throughout its operations.

Research and Development   BMW's design and engineering focus manifests itself in the company's commitment to extensive research and development and is reflected in continuous improvement in its product line. For example, according to BMW personnel, the new 325i model is larger, 13% more powerful, and 11% more fuel efficient than its predecessor, yet at $29,900, costs only 4% more than its predecessor in the 3 series line.

Over the course of the next five years, the company intends to spend DM 6.4 billion (approximately 3% of anticipated revenues over the same period) on research, development, engineering improvements and automation. Work was recently completed on a DM 960 million Research and Engineering facility in Munich-Milbertshofen which will serve as BMW's design and engineering headquarters and house 4,500 employees. The facility consolidates design, engineering development and manufacturing planning into a single site.

The company has also announced its intention to spend about DM 800 million annually to acquire companies (especially in the electronics industry) that have technological capabilities directly related to the automobile industry. The company, for example, recently gained controlling interest in DesignWorks USA, a California-based engineering design firm that BMW has used in the past to "audit" its internally-developed designs.[24]

Market Position   In the past decade, BMW's responsiveness to new market opportunities and demands has paid off—sales have grown at better than 10% annually since 1986, well above the industry growth rates. Most of its success is due to its expansion into the performance luxury car segment. It has also gained some advantage through its ability to produce semi-customized vehicles in an efficient manner, holding marginal costs down.[25] The company's European market share is 2.8% and world market share is 1.7% (see Exhibit 10).

Forbes notes the unique position BMW has garnered among vehicle purchasers— "BMW flourishes by selling to people who feel they are flaunting their affluence less ostentatiously and more intelligently than if they were driving similarly priced cars of other makers."[26] The typical BMW buyer wants performance and luxury, and is willing to pay for it. The company has been able to fill this need by tapping its engineering strengths to achieve attractive styling without sacrificing handling and agility.

Despite its past success, BMW, along with Mercedes and other European performance luxury car producers, faces a significant challenge from lower-priced Japanese competition. A majority of Japanese manufacturers have created subsidiaries in order to penetrate the European market. Honda's Acura, Toyota's Lexus, Nissan's Infiniti and Mitsubishi's Diamante units and new models from Mazda, each with high customer satisfaction ratings and on average lower prices, have found good success in the North American and Japanese markets, and are set to challenge in the European market. Von Kuenheim is skeptical of their ability to do so: "building luxury cars and a luxury image requires more than scissors and glue. Just because Toyota and Nissan are introducing cars that look like BMW and Mercedes doesn't mean they will succeed as we have."[27] Regardless, the market segment that was once controlled almost exclusively by Mercedes-Benz has become one of the most competitive within the automotive market.

BMW executives are concerned about the company's ability to sustain its competitive position. "Our real problem," asserts von Kuenheim, "is not whether we can sell $60,000 cars or $90,000 cars. It is whether we can be competitive with workers who have the highest wages, the shortest working time, the most benefits, and the longest holidays."[28]

BMW and Environment Stewardship

In 1972, a series of houses were built adjacent to BMW's Munich plant, which employs over 14,000 people, in order to address housing needs of the athletes and spectators of the 1972 Summer Olympic Games in Munich. When the Olympic Flame was extinguished, the houses were offered for sale, and many BMW plant workers took up residence. Residents in the housing complex became concerned about noise and emissions from the plant. In response, BMW appointed an *Umweltreferent* (environmental specialist) to analyze current operations and reduce local impacts.

BMW's environmental program has since expanded, and BMW views both its engineering and environmental initiatives as being compatible. As one trade publication described it, "BMW's reputation still hinges on great handling, but its research efforts indicate that the company is also well aware of its responsibilities to provide environmentally sound, economical, and safe automobiles."[29]

Components Remanufacturing Program   In the mid-1960s, BMW initiated a program to recondition and remanufacture high-value, used components for resale as used parts. The company found that used engines could be remanufactured and sold to buyers at 50 to 80% of the cost of new engines, with an acceptable profit above the costs of disassembly, logistics and labor. BMW expanded this program to an additional 1,700 individual parts, including starters, alternators, transmissions, waterpumps, final drive

Exhibit 9 ● BMW AG Financial and Production Data, Selected Years

		1989	1988
Net Sales	DM Million	20,957.8	19,883.7
% Change	%	5.4	12.6
Export Share	%	58.5	59.8
Production—Automobiles	Units	511,476.0	484,121.0
Production—Motorcycles	Units	25,761.0	23,817.0
Sales—Automobiles	Units	510,968.0	486,592.0
Sales—Motorcycles	Units	25,549.0	24,205.0
Investment	DM Million	1,508.7	1,309.1
In tangible/fixed assets	DM Million	1,416.7	1,254.9
In subdiaries	DM Million	92.0	54.2
Depreciation	DM Million	1,233.3	1,231.0
Fixed Assets	DM Million	4,272.3	4,019.1
Current Assets	DM Million	5,860.5	5,344.8
Subscribed Capital	DM Million	790.6	750.0
Reserves	DM Million	2,868.0	2,516.0
Shareholder Equity	DM Million	3,851.6	3,453.5
Long-Term Liabilities	DM Million	1,312.5	1,195.7
Long-Term Capital	DM Million	5,164.1	4,649.2
Balance Sheet Total	DM Million	10,132.8	9,363.9
Expenditure on Materials	DM Million	12,727.6	11,880.9
% of Production Value	%	60.5	59.4
Expenditure on Personnel	DM Million	4,126.6	4,000.2
% of Production Value	%	19.6	20.0
Taxes	DM Million	587.5	615.5
Net Income	DM Million	386.0	375.0
% Change	%	2.9	0.0
Workforce at Year End		57,087	56,981
Wage Earners		35,212	35,524
Salaried Employees		18,457	18,157

Source: BMW AG, Annual Reports

gearings and various electronic components. According to BMW spokespeople:

It is no coincidence that this high-value recycling is referred to as High-Tech

recycling: Using the most advanced technologies such as ultrasound cleaning or numerically-controlled grinding systems, each original BMW exchange part and component is carefully overhauled, recon-

1987	1986	1985	1984
17,656.7	14,994.3	14,246.4	12,931.6
17.8	5.2	10.2	12.6
65.9	65.7	65.0	61.1
461,340.0	446,438.0	445,233.0	431,995.0
27,508.0	32,054.0	37,104.0	34,001.0
459,502.0	446,109.0	440,732.0	4,342,665.0
27,811.0	31,731.0	36,320.0	33,912.0
1,643.4	1,821.8	941.5	669.2
1,541.2	1,735.0	906.5	663.8
102.2	86.8	35.0	5.4
1,145.6	948.9	751.6	707.9
39,964.2	3,486.9	2,592.0	2,410.6
4,661.5	4,564.3	3,980.6	3,496.0
750.0	750.0	600.0	600.0
2,328.5	2,141.0	1,320.3	1,160.1
3,266.0	3,059.8	2,070.3	1,910.1
1,161.1	1,125.9	1,268.4	1,183.0
4,427.1	4,185.7	3,338.7	3,093.1
8,625.7	8,051.2	6,572.9	5,906.6
10,260.3	8,606.6	7,890.8	6,915.0
57.8	57.1	55.1	53.6
3,586.4	3,173.7	2,918.5	2,792.5
20.2	21.1	20.4	21.7
551.0	706.8	731.5	692.7
375.0	337.5	300.0	329.6
11.1	12.5	−9	14.4
54,861	50,719	46,804	44,692
34,185	31,883	30,170	29,524
17,522	15,822	13,918	12,677

ditioned and tested according to strict quality standards.[30]

The company offers the same warranty condition on its remanufactured parts as it does on new parts. There is currently a substantial waiting list for these parts. In 1989, the company reprocessed 18,000 engines, 280,000 waterpumps, 20,000 transmissions and 9,500 electrical systems.

Exhibit 10 ● BMW AG Market Share Data, Selected Years

		1989	
Market	Total Market Units	BMW Sales Units	BMW Market Share %
Austria	276,100	9,600	3.48
Belgium	439,800	11,900	2.71
France	2,274,300	30,600	1.35
Germany	2,831,700	191,000	6.75
Great Britain	2,300,900	48,900	2.13
Italy	2,362,100	27,700	1.17
Netherlands	495,700	10,400	2.10
Spain	1,072,000	11,000	1.03
Switzerland	320,200	13,100	4.09
MAJOR EUROPEAN	12,372,800	354,200	2.86
Canada	987,600	4,300	0.44
United States	9,867,400	64,900	0.66
NORTH AMERICA	10,855,000	69,200	0.64
Australia	444,000	4,800	1.08
New Zealand	83,900	700	0.83
South Africa	221,300	18,700	8.45
Japan	4,403,800	33,100	0.75
WORLD	28,380,800	480,700	1.69

Source: BMW AG, Annual Reports

The ecological benefits of the program were largely an afterthought. The program prevents a significant portion of material from entering the waste stream. Engines, for example, may provide the best example: of a single engine that enters the reconditioning process, 94% of the engine is reconditioned, 5.5% is remelted for reuse, and the final 0.5% is landfilled.

BMW and Recycling

Recycling and Pollution Prevention in Production   Throughout the 1970s and 1980s, the company developed pollution prevention strategies for its production processes and implemented a number of programs:

- Production waste (used oils, gases, glass, plastics, etc.) is separated and reused as

	1988		1989 vs. 1988
Total Market Units	BMW Sales Units	BMW Market Share %	Change in Market Share %
253,300	8,700	3.43	+0.04
427,000	11,300	2.65	+0.06
2,208,100	31,600	1.43	−0.09
2,803,700	180,200	6.43	+0.32
2,233,900	42,900	1.92	+0.09
2,187,100	23,700	1.08	+0.09
481,300	11,600	2.41	−0.31
992,600	9,200	0.93	+0.09
320,200	14,100	4.40	−0.31
11,907,200	333,300	2.80	+0.06
1,050,700	5,000	0.48	−0.04
10,610,100	73,800	0.70	−0.04
11,660,800	78,800	0.68	−0.04
403,600	2,700	0.67	+0.41
71,100	600	0.84	−0.01
230,500	17,500	7.59	+0.86
3,732,000	26,900	0.72	+0.03
28,005,200	459,800	1.64	+0.05

an integral part of production activities. Used oils are reformulated and reused in new products, gases are collected and fed into manufacturing and paint units, and glass and plastic scraps are returned to suppliers.

- BMW requires its suppliers to take back homogenous plastic waste from all produc-

tion facilities. BMW collects plastics scrap, and suppliers pack, transport and reuse it.

- Water, primarily used in cleaning operations, is used and reused six times before it is disposed as effluent.

Dr.-Ing. Manfred Heller, who heads the Konzern Umweltschutz (TSU, environmental protection staff), claims that efforts like these allow the company to re-use 80% of its waste. The remaining 20% is landfilled, incinerated or treated as special waste. While these efforts have cost BMW DM 10 million in new equipment, he estimates that the company has saved over DM 70 million through reductions in materials procurement and disposal costs.

Post-Consumer Component Recycling   In collaboration with its component manufacturers and dealer network, BMW initiated a recycling program for catalytic converters in April 1987 in order to reuse the precious metals content. Six ounces of platinum and one ounce of rhodium are used in each catalytic converter to reduce vehicle emissions, but, at the end of the converter's life, the metals can be reused. The dealer network recoups catalytic converters from customers and ships them to BMW's production facilities, where the components are ground up and the metals recovered. Customers receive credits to their accounts to be used in the purchase of spare parts.

Post-Consumer Vehicle Recycling   In June 1990, the company's Board of Management added BMW's recycling group T-RC as a formal department housed within the TSU. The T-RC informally began in 1985 when various employees initiated meetings to discuss vehicle and polymer recycling out of personal concern and interest. T-RC is comprised of 10 people, representing materials, development, planning, production, logistics and finance disciplines. Dr.-Ing. Horst-Henning Wolf, the group's director, reports directly to Bernd Pischetsrieder, head of Technik (Production Division) and a member of the board.

In that same month, the company established a pilot disassembly site within its Landshut facility, the company's remanufacturing plant. The goals for the program are to study dis-

mantling and shredder techniques and economics for BMW vehicles.

THE COMPETITION

Other German manufacturers have undertaken initiatives to study the ASR problem, and some have taken differing approaches to solving it.[31]

Adam Opel AG   1989 was a very successful year for General Motor's German affiliate. The company generated DM 20.8 billion in revenues as production rose 11% to nearly 1.25 million vehicles and net profits rose 10% to DM 1.1 billion. (See Exhibit 11 for complete financial, production, and market share data for the German market.) Opel's share of the German market was 16.1%. The company has undertaken some preliminary investigation into vehicle dismantling and reuse of plastic components. Opel has been using plastic components since 1979 and has conducted preliminary research into plastics reuse. It currently uses a small percentage of recycled polymers in its bumpers, and sees new applications in air-cleaner housings, floor mats and sound-proofing materials.[32]

Ford-Werke AG   Ford maintained its German market share of 10.1 % and earned profits of DM 362 million. Ford is concentrating on developing new plastics recycling and automated sorting technologies, and labelling plastic components.

Mercedes-Benz AG   Mercedes produced almost 260,000 units and earned DM 1.4 billion in profits on sales of DM 56.3 billion. Mercedes-Benz is interested in testing vehicles for disassembly, but does not advocate recycling and reuse of polymer components. Mercedes-Benz feels the best use of waste plastic is a modified form of waste-to-energy incineration called metallurgical recycling. Using newly designed melt reactor technology, the manufacturer intends to strip high-value parts, drain operating fluids, compress the hulk and feed it into a melt reactor, which can reach temperatures of 2000 degrees Celsius. Steel is melted, heavy metals and plastics are gassified, and useful energy is created. Throughout the process, emissions are collected and fed into an optimized gas purification system in order to further combust or eliminate the environmentally undesirable content. Mercedes' first metallurgical recycling facility is scheduled to open in 1992, and subsequent additions to its network will be based on the results of that operation.[33]

Volkswagen AG VW produced and sold nearly 3 million vehicles, generating revenues of DM 65.3 billion and profits of DM 1 billion. Like BMW, Volkswagen has been actively involved in examining and addressing environmental issues. Internally, it is considering using partial recycled content for its parts and is experimenting with recycling bumper materials to be used in new components, but is still in the test phase. VW also labels all its thermoplastic components. Externally, VW prefers the idea of a number of regional dismantling and recovery centers, licensed by the company and the government, to handle the dismantling of all its spent vehicles.

Cooperation

In 1974, the Verband der Automobilindustrie e.V. (VDA, the German automobile association) established the Forschungsvereinigung Automobiltechnik e.V. (FAT) to study automobile recycling. The group initially focused on metals and plastics recycling techniques and works with the plastics, glass, rubber and other industries to develop techniques and technologies for recycling. In 1989, each of the five major German automobile companies—Adam Opel AG, BMW AG, Ford-Werke AG, Mercedes-Benz AG and Volkswagen AG—joined the effort, renaming the con-

sortium PRAVDA. PRAVDA presents the views of the automobile industry on vehicle recycling to regulators and the public.

BMW'S OPTIONS

Wolf and Franze sat down later that afternoon to analyze the relevant options available for its take-back and recycling strategy. While they believed that BMW had the ability to reuse certain recycled polymers, they questioned whether recycled polymers would uphold BMW's stringent performance standards. If recycled materials were to reduce quality or throughput, Pischetsrieder, von Kuenheim and the remainder of the Board of Management would not likely support their plan. Wolf concentrated on the take-back infrastructure, while Franze examined what role, if any, use of secondary materials should play in manufacturing operations.

Wolf, after consultation with Franze, outlined the following options available regarding the take-back infrastructure:

Option 1: Fight the Regulation BMW could argue that the proposed regulation would severely hamper the industry's costs of operations and, since PRAVDA was already attempting to address the same issue, the regulation was both burdensome and unnecessary.

Option 2: Create an Independent National Take-Back Infrastructure The company could create its own take-back infrastructure in order to handle disposal of all BMW vehicles. In such a network, all BMW vehicles would be transported to the company's pilot dismantling and reconditioning site at Landshut. BMW dismantlers would remove and pelletize polymer components, and dispose of the remaining ASR through landfill, incineration or an external plastics supplier. This would not only ensure the recovery and return of "remanufacturable" parts to BMW reconditioning operations, but through

Exhibit 11 ● Financial, Production and Market Share Data for Selected German Firms, 1989

		Audi AG	*Adam Opel AG*
FINANCIAL DATA			
Sales	*DM Million*	12,215.1	20,805.8
Profit	*DM Million*	114.0	1,123.8
Book Value of Assets	*DM Million*	4,855.6	9,038.6
Book Value of Equity	*DM Million*	1,143.7	2,664.0
Profit/Sales	*%*	0.01	0.05
Sales/Assets		2.52	2.30
Profit/Assets	*%*	0.02	0.12
Assets/Book Equity		4.25	3.39
Return on Book Equity	*%*	0.10	0.42
PRODUCTION DATA			
Production	*Units*	421,243	989,385
% Change from 1988	*%*	−1.22	+10.48
SALES/MARKET SHARE DATA			
Domestic Market Sales	*Units*	158,100	455,700
Domestic Market Share	*%*	5.6	16.1
% Change from 1988	*%*	−1.1	+0.8
European Market Sales	*Units*	380,000	1,454,400
European Market Share	*%*	2.8	10.8
% Change from 1988	*%*	−0.1	+0.4
North American Market Sales	*Units*	23,200	N/A
North American Market Share	*%*	0.5	N/A
% Change from 1988	*%*	0.0	N/A

Source: Moody's International Manual, vol. 1, 1991 (NY: Dun & Bradstreet Corp., 1991); Ward's Automotive Yearbook, 52nd Edition, 1990 (Detroit, MI: Ward's Communications, 1990).

the development of model-specific dismantling techniques, the company could cut dismantling times by 35% and reduce processing costs.

Option 3: Modify the Existing National Take-Back Infrastructure   BMW could work with the existing scrap vehicle processing infrastructure in order to ensure its continued viability. The company could develop model-specific re-

cycling techniques and disseminate them to existing dismantlers.

That afternoon session produced the following options for BMW's secondary materials strategy:

Option 1: Take-Back Processed Vehicles and Landfill ASR   BMW could opt to ensure the

BMW AG	Ford-Werke AG	Mercedes-Benz AG	Volkswagen AG
26,515.4	19,806.2	56,367.0	65,362.2
558.0	362.2	1,492.0	1,038.1
20,688.7	7,824.5	27,118.0	56,871.4
5,370.6	1,440.7	4,052.0	11,505.8
0.02	0.02	0.03	0.02
1.28	2.53	2.08	1.15
0.03	0.05	0.06	0.02
3.85	5.43	6.69	4.94
0.10	0.25	0.37	0.09
511,476	633,340	536,993	1,463,991
+5.65	+4.02	−3.02	+6.7
191,100	284,800	259,600	619,100
6.7	10.1	9.2	21.9
+0.3	+0.1	−0.8	−0.3
381,700	1,559,500	433,300	1,335,200
2.8	11.6	3.2	9.9
+0.1	+0.4	−0.2	0.0
69,200	N/A	79,800	155,100
1.6	N/A	1.8	3.6
−0.1	N/A	0.0	+0.1

take-back and proper disposal of its spent vehicles by funding landfill disposal of the remaining ASR. In this case, dismantlers and shredders would make no change to operations, but BMW intervention would ensure their economic viability. BMW would continue to use virgin polymers in new vehicle production.

Option 2: Take-Back Processed Vehicles and Incinerate ASR Akin to Mercedes-Benz, BMW could argue that the most efficient use of recycled plastics is waste-to-energy incineration. Vehicle hulks would continue to be processed for used metals, but polymers and other materials, such as foam, carpet and glass, would be gassified in melt reactors to recoup energy.

Option 3: Recycle Plastics for Use in Other Industries BMW could recover plastics from its vehicles to become feedstock for other industries. If BMW were to establish markets for its used plastics, dismantlers would have an economic incentive to undertake plastic component dismantling. Recovery of plastics would lower disposal costs, thereby reducing the economic burden on the shredder industry.

Option 4: Use Recycled Polymers in BMW Vehicles BMW could use recycled polymers for certain of its plastic components in order to help create a market for recycled plastics. While it might not be practical to implement a "closed-loop" recycling system at the present time, they could use recycled polymers for specific applications.[34] In order to evaluate this option, they would need to develop an approach to evaluate when the substitution of recycled polymers for virgin materials made economic sense. At Franze's suggestion, they chose a number of components to examine, including the bumpers on the new 3 series, in order to determine material flows and costs, recycling costs, and recycling logistics.

Option 5: Incorporate Design for Environment (DFE) Methodology In order to meet the current demands of the draft legislation, BMW could alter product and process designs to reduce, reuse and recycle waste. For example, they could incorporate greater amounts of additives and stabilizers in the polymer mix, label plastic components, design for use of recycled instead of virgin polymers, minimize component size and simplify disassembly. DFE could enhance the vehicle's recyclability and minimize negative environmental impacts of future disposal.

Wolf and Franze were supposed to meet with Pischetsrieder later that week. He would want an analysis of the problem, including the volumes of waste and disposal costs facing the recycling industry and BMW independently, and what factors BMW must consider when using secondary materials. Ultimately, he would also want to know what strategy BMW should pursue in response to the draft legislation and what system, if any, the company should advocate. With options before them, they thought carefully about BMW's future actions.

Notes

1. Organisation for Economic Co-operation and Development, *The State of the Environment* (Paris, France: OECD Publications, 1991), p. 149.

2. Newsday, *Rush to Burn: Solving America's Garbage Crisis?* (Washington, DC: Island Press, 1989), p. 87.

3. H. A. Neal and J. R. Schubel, *Solid Waste Management and the Environment: The Mounting Garbage and Trash Crisis* (Englewood Cliffs, NJ: Prentice-Hall, Inc., 1987), p. 37.

4. P. R. O'Leary, P. W. Walsh, and R. K. Ham, "Managing Solid Waste," *Scientific American,* Vol. 259, No. 6, December 1988, p. 40; C. Pollock, *Mining Urban Wastes: The Potential for Recycling,* Worldwatch Paper No. 76 (Washington, DC Worldwatch Institute, April 1987), pp. 14–15.

5. PCBs are industrial toxins typically found in electronics equipment and hydraulic fluids. They are known to cause cancer, birth defects, skin disease and gastro-intestinal damage in humans. In the United States, they are listed as a "medium" cancer risk and subject to numerous layers of regulation and reporting requirements.

6. The Global Tomorrow Coalition, *The Global Ecology Handbook,* ed. by Walter H. Corson (Boston: Beacon Press, 1990), p. 277.

7. J. Raloff, "Are landfills a major threat to climate?" *Science News,* Vol. 131, March 7, 1987, p. 150.

8. I. P. Wallace, "Landfill Gas-Fired Power Plant Pays Cost of Operating Landfill," *Power Engineering,* Vol. 59, No. 1, January 1991, p. 27.

9. Newsday, op. cit., p. 86.

10. Neal and Schubel, op. cit., p. 81.

11. Certain dioxins, such as tetrachlorodibenzo-p-dioxin (known as "Agent Orange"), are among the most toxic mol-

ecules in existence, and have been proven to break down immune systems and cause birth defects.

12.   L. Barniske, "Waste Incineration in the Federal Republic of Germany—State-of-the-Art Technology and Operating Experience as to Corrosion Problems," in *Incinerating Municipal and Industrial Waste: Fireside Problems and Prospects for Improvement,* ed. by R. W. Bryers (New York: Hemisphere Publishing, 1991), p. 9.

13.   Newsday, op. cit., p. 86.

14.   James F. Carley, "A Plastics Primer," *Modern Plastics Mid-October Encyclopedia Issue,* p. 4.

15.   F. den Hond and P. Groenwegen, "Innovation in the Context of Plastic Waste Management—The Automotive Industry," Report of the Commission of the European Communities, DG XII—Moniter-SAST Unit, Free University-CAV, Amsterdam, Netherlands, March, 1992.

16.   For example, in a comparison of energy requirements for fuel tank production, plastics need only 47% and aluminum 80% of the energy needed to create one steel fuel tank. L. Matysiak, "Design for Environment; An Analysis of German Recycling Legislation and Its Implications for Materials Trends and Corporate Strategies in the Automobile Industry," unpublished thesis (Cambridge, Mass: MIT, May, 1992), pp. 36, 42.

17.   A. Stuart Wood, "What To Do With Plastics, Cars When They're Junk?" *Modern Plastics,* June 1988, p. 62.

18.   Den Hond and Groenwegen, "Co-operation between Firms in the Automotive Branch and Strategies to Solve the Shredder Waste Problem," unpublished research paper presented at "The Greening of Industry: Research Needs and Policy Implications for a Sustainable Future" Conference, November 1991, Noordwijk, Netherlands, p. 5.

19.   Bundesministerium für Umwelt, Naturschutz und Reaktorsicherheit (BMU), *Environmental Protection in Germany.* Bonn, Germany: BMU Public Relations Division, 1992.

20.   Bundestag, Waste Avoidance and Waste Management Act, August 27th, 1986, *Article 14,* Bonn, Germany.

21.   BMW, *1990 Annual Report,* Munich, Germany, p. 6.

22.   P. Fuhrman, "The Company Behind the Image," *Forbes,* November 27th, 1989, p. 89.

23.   Fuhrman, op. cit., p. 89.

24.   These figures based on an exchange rate of DM 1.6/US $1.

25.   The production line at the Regensburg plant is responsible for the 3 basic models of the 3-Series (sedan, convertible and station wagon), each with some 40 types of stylistic choices, each with different component options, and each customized for over 10 different countries. BMW estimates that completely identical vehicles are produced, on average, four months apart.

26.   Fuhrman, op. cit., p. 89.

27.   Fuhrman, op. cit., p. 89.

28.   A. Taylor, "BMW and Mercedes," *Fortune,* August 12th, 1991, p. 62. According to von Kuenheim, autoworkers in Germany earn $8.37 to $11.16 (as compared to $16.58 to $19.42 in the US), but the level of benefits (unlimited medical care, free education for workers' children, and bonuses) they receive more than doubles their wages. They work 37.5 hour work weeks (as compared to 40 hour work weeks in the US) and have 6 weeks vacation (as compared to 4).

29.   Bill Siuru, "Fast Lane," *Mechanical Engineering,* October 1989, p. 66.

30.   Company Information.

31.   All production data from *Ward's Automotive Yearbook* (Detroit, MI: Ward's Communications, 1990); all financial data from Moody's Investors Service, *Moody's International Manual 1991. Volume 1* (New York: Moody's Investors Service, Inc., 1991).

32.   "Leading-edge Engineers Design for Recycling," *Machine Design,* January 24th, 1991, p. 13.

33.   Den Hond and Groenwegen, op. cit., p. 21.

34.   In a "closed-loop" system, end-waste materials are recovered and fully utilized in new products.

35

Industrial Products Inc. (A): Measuring Environmental Performance
Richard Wells

In September 1992 the environmental coordinators of Industrial Products Inc.'s (IPI) 12 divisions met in Knoxville, TN, for a three-day environmental retreat. The subject was improving the company's environmental performance. The topic of environmental improvement performance was becoming increasingly important at IPI. Several divisions' customers had inquired about the company's environmental policies; other customers were beginning to ask about the early life cycle stages of products they bought from IPI as part of larger life cycle analyses.

Most importantly, in IPI's case, the family owners (fourth generation descendants of the company's founder) were strongly committed to environmental performance. Industrial Products' Board of Directors, which was made up largely of family members, had recently informed Steve Barnes, the CEO, that they expected an increase of return on equity (from 3 to 9 percent), and they wanted to ensure that IPI's operations were conducted in a manner that had "no net impact on the environment."

Industrial Products Inc. is a highly diversified producer of products for a wide range of industrial customers. Its twelve divisions operate businesses in oil and gas exploration and pro-

duction, minerals mining, forest products, chemical manufacturing and electronic assembly. In these businesses IPI was a commodity supplier with little pricing flexibility; it competed instead on product and service quality. In 1992 its annual sales were just over $1 billion, making it a Fortune 350 company. Because it operated primarily in mature markets with little growth potential, IPI's return on equity was a low 3 percent. Moving into high growth markets and enhancing shareholder value were strategic priorities for IPI.

Industrial Products had a strong commitment to quality, and to the financial and human health of its employees. The commitment to product and service quality was pervasive throughout the company. Numerous plants, particularly in the Chemicals Division, had attained ISO 9000 certification and its managers "spoke SPCC."[1] The result of the company's quality focus was evident in its high customer retention and customer satisfaction. Because of this, IPI could compete and survive in low-margin industries. On the other hand, it had established a priority of shifting to higher-margin industries, where its quality commitment would contribute to higher shareholder value.

The company also had a protective stance toward its employees. Profit sharing and retirement plans were generous. In fact, one manager said that every employee who retired after a career at IPI retired a millionaire. Although this was, perhaps, an exaggeration, it was clear that IPI cared for its people. The manifestation of this care in the health and safety area was a highly successful "drive to zero" program whose objective was to eliminate work-related injuries. Several IPI divisions boasted of records of well over three years without a lost-time accident.

When IPI environmental coordinators met in Knoxville, they found a more mixed record in the environmental area. In general, their compliance record was enviable—few notices of violation (NOVs) every year. IPI was fortunate also in having few environmental liabilities. It was potentially a defendant in a citizens' suit brought in the Houston area, but this suit had little relation to IPI's operations. The environmental coordinators, however, realized that compliance and the absence of major liabilities were only part of the picture. They recognized that many of their facilities were having substantial impacts on the environment despite the fact that they complied with regulatory and permit requirements, and they recognized that they could improve their performance.

On the third day of the conference, IPI's environmental coordinators were joined by senior managers: Steve Barnes, the CEO, two group vice presidents, each in charge of six divisions, all twelve division presidents, and several corporate vice presidents including the director of strategic planning, the chief financial officer, and the director of human resources. The issue of the day was how IPI could improve its environmental performance.

John Rushmore, a consultant who had been studying corporate environmental activities, gave a talk, "From Compliance to Strategy," that suggested that environmental issues were increasingly becoming a strategic concern for corporate management. Ultimately, simple regulatory compliance would not be sufficient. Public information sources such as EPA's Toxics Release Inventory (TRI) meant that facility neighbors were much better informed.[2] Rushmore surprised the division presidents by giving four years of TRI data for IPI's divisions showing lit-

tle improvement of performance and in some cases a worsening of performance. In addition, he suggested that on the corporate side, recent activities of the Industrial Chamber of Commerce (ICC) and in the United States the Global Environmental Management Initiative (GEMI) indicated that leading companies were rethinking their environmental policies. In particular, Rushmore cited the ICC Business Charter for Sustainable Development and the proposal of an international corporate environmental management standard proposed by the International Standards Organization (ISO) at the recent Rio de Janeiro Summit Conference on Environment and Development.

Steve Barnes concluded the day by pointing out that the family owners of IPI wanted the company to reduce the impact of its operation on the environment. Since its founding, IPI had been concerned about stewardship of the environment from which it drew its resources. This philosophy had been developed when IPI was primarily a mining company. Priority needed to be given to this philosophy and it needed to be extended to all the environmental aspects of IPI's operations. To accomplish its goal, Steve committed the company to a 20 percent reduction of the impact of its operations on the environment per year. He assigned this task to Jim Weaver, one of the company's two group vice presidents.

During the discussion on the afternoon of the third day, several points were raised by the division presidents and environmental coordinators:

- No one had a clear picture of what the environmental aspects of IPI's operations were. The company had a good compliance record, but it was generally recognized that compliance alone was not an adequate measure of environmental performance.
- Steve Barnes had committed IPI to a 20 percent annual reduction of its impact on the environment, but no one had a measure

of "environmental impact." Certainly, compliance with regulations was an insufficient measure. In fact, most IPI managers believed regulatory requirements had little to do with true environmental performance. Rushmore's TRI data were little better—everyone recognized that many materials used by IPI were not on the TRI list and, in any case, many IPI operations such as oil and gas production, mining, and forest products were not covered by TRI.

- There would clearly have to be a balancing of business and environmental interests. Whatever IPI's environmental impact, reducing it by 20 percent per year would appear to add to IPI's costs. This commitment would be difficult to reconcile with IPI's other key commitment—to increase return on equity from 3 to 9 percent.

Several weeks after the Knoxville meeting, Jim Weaver called John Rushmore to meet at his office at IPI's headquarters. He had decided to accept Steve Barnes's challenge of reducing IPI's impact on the environment by 20 percent a year. He believed it could be done, based on his experience turning around IPI's safety performance, and he was personally committed to the owners' values. Jim pointed out that since leaving college, he had spent his entire career with IPI, rising from plant engineer to plant manager, division president, and ultimately to group vice president. Jim said that he had decided he would:

- Model the IPI's environmental program on the extremely successful "drive to zero" safety program, which he had championed;

- Base IPI's environmental program on measurement. He was convinced that "you manage what you measure." The key to improving performance was developing a continuous measure of performance that senior management, from the Chairman of the Board to the plant managers, could understand and would be responsible for;

- Utilize IPI's quality culture to implement environmental improvement. Like Rushmore, Weaver believed total quality management could be applied effectively to environmental management.

As they discussed IPI's commitment to environmental quality improvement, it became obvious to Jim and John that the central problem was how to measure environmental performance. The key difference between the safety program and the environmental program was that in safety there was a readily communicated way to measure success—the number and severity of work-related injuries. In environment, there was no comparable measure. Without a readily-communicated measure of success, it would be difficult to utilize IPI's quality programs to improve performance.

As they discussed the problem further, several other points became evident:

- Environmental performance had numerous, unrelated, aspects. The neighbors of a facility might be concerned about toxic chemical releases, but other concerns included the efficiency with which IPI used resources, and its releases of greenhouse gases and chlorofluorocarbons (CFCs), which were a potential concern to a broader, global community. There was no way to compare an impact at a local level to an impact at a global level because the types of impacts and stakeholders were different. In defining performance it would be important to "compare apples to apples."

- Even within one aspect of performance, such as local impacts, comparisons of effects were subject to very substantial scientific uncertainty. For the vast majority of the 70,000 chemicals in commerce maintained on EPA's "TSCA Inventory," there existed very little environmental effects data.[3] The information that existed was often imprecise.

- A major problem would be how to define a fair basis to compare among plants and divisions. Jim's goal was to create a measurable basis to reward (or penalize) division presidents or plant managers for their environmental performance. As a former plant manager and division president himself, he was sympathetic to their need to have a fair and objective basis to measure performance. It was clear to him, though, that he would have to apply a different yardstick to IPI oil and gas production operations than to its electronic equipment manufacturing operations.

- Performance had to be related to production levels. IPI's plants were both growing and declining. Jim did not want to confuse changes in levels of production with changes in environmental performance. It was difficult, however, to define a common physical unit of production between oil and gas production facilities and electronic equipment manufacturers. Financial measures such as revenues were also unsatisfactory because the value of inputs varied across divisions from 30 percent to over 90 percent of revenues.

- Efficiency of data collection was important. Jim did not want a system that would divert IPI's environmental coordinators' energies from their primary job of improving the company's environmental performance. For this reason, Jim specified that the performance system should require no more than four hours per plant or division to operate per month.

After several weeks of work, John proposed a system that would, he hoped, meet IPI's requirements—the Industrial Products Environmental Performance Index (IPEPI). It was a novel system based on John's previous work, but not one that had been implemented on a large scale before. The following were the key components of the system:

- Performance would be measured in four dimensions:

— *Local community welfare,* consisting of those aspects of IPI's operations that affected its neighbors. These aspects included both actual chemical releases and potential releases based on chemical use and storage, recognizing that chemical use and storage posed some risk of release to neighboring communities.

— *Global/regional welfare*—some aspects of IPI's activities could affect the global or regional environment. Some plants burned oil or natural gas releasing CO_2, a greenhouse gas, and sulfur and nitrogen dioxides considered acid rain precursors; the oil and gas operations released methane, a greenhouse gas, and some electronic equipment plants still used solvents containing CFCs; finally, all the facilities used electricity and Jim wanted to account for the environmental impacts of IPI's use of electricity.

— *Resource efficiency*—as a heavily resource-based company, IPI felt a strong commitment to using resources efficiently. Jim wanted to incorporate this commitment by tracking efficiency in the use of materials, water and energy.

— *Management systems development*—some activities undertaken by IPI plants were designed to anticipate problems by improving management systems, providing training to workers, performing audits or self assessments, and conducting outreach to facility neighbors. Jim did not want to ignore these activities in the measurement systems because he considered management systems development a "leading indicator" of environmental performance. He was concerned that by focusing too narrowly on physical measures of performance, IPI would neglect management systems improvement, which he was convinced was the long-term road to improvement.

- Each plant, division, and the corporate function would be assigned a baseline value of 1000 points reflecting its 1994 production-weighted performance. Each dimension would initially have a value of 250 points. The dimensions would be further divided into sub-dimensions of performance as necessary (Table 1).

- Improvements would be measured as continuous improvement against the baseline. Direct plant-to-plant comparisons in absolute performance would be avoided because neither Jim nor John felt that the data were reliable enough to permit such comparisons; in any case, Jim felt that it was unfair to penalize a plant or division because its processes were inherently dirtier than those of another plant in another industry. Rather, plants would be judged based on their performance compared to *their own* baseline performance. Nineteen-ninety-three would be established as a baseline year, each plant receiving 1000 points based on its 1993 performance. Success would be gauged as improvements over 1993 performance that reduced the 1000-point baseline value.

- Performance would be "rolled-up" from the plant to the division and corporate levels (see Exhibit 1). The performance index would be recalculated at the division and

TABLE 1 ● Allocation of Index Value Points Among IPEPI Dimensions

Dimension/Subdimension	Points	
COMMUNITY WELFARE	250	
Potential Releases		50
Actual Releases		200
GLOBAL/REGIONAL WELFARE	250	
Ozone Depletors*		10
Greenhouse Gases		120
Regional Pollutants (e.g., SO_x, NO_x)		120
RESOURCE EFFICIENCY	250	
Materials		100
Energy		100
Water		50
MANAGEMENT SYSTEMS DEVELOPMENT	250	
Preventive/Anticipatory		100
Compliance		100
Community Outreach		50
TOTAL	1000	

*Note: Few IPI facilities used ozone depletors.

Exhibit 1 ● Environmental Performance Index Structure

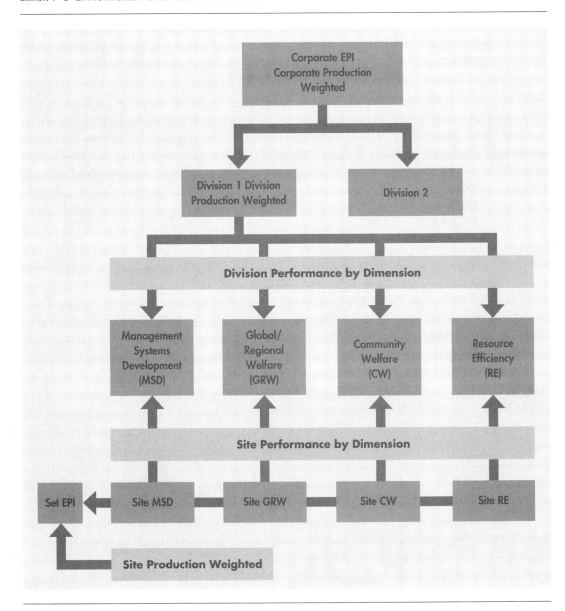

corporate levels using division and corporate production levels.

A key concept in the IPEPI was materials accounting, a less rigorous form of mass balance. Materials accounting is based on the proposition that any material input not converted into a product or saleable byproduct is a waste (Exhibit 2). Other concepts in the IPEPI included toxicity weighting and disposal practices weighting. IPI used a wide range of materials. By and large, these materials were large volume, low toxicity industrial materials. A few, however, were highly toxic. Toxicity weighting in the IPEPI provided a means to prioritize among materials by assigning them a toxicity-based weight of 1 to 1000. In addition, Jim Weaver wanted IPI to follow a waste management hier-

archy that established on-site reuse or recycling as the most preferable alternative and direct release to the environment as least preferable. To accomplish this, the IPEPI multiplied the waste quantity by a management practices factor (Table 2).

Thus, any material used was converted into Impact Units by multiplying its Waste Quantity by a Toxicity Weighting Factor and then by a Management Practices Factor. The sum of the weighted Impact Units for all materials used at the plant was divided by production quantity. This number was then multiplied by a baseline normalization factor (n) to convert it to the baseline Index Value (Exhibit 3).[4] Improvements in performance could be obtained by reducing waste byproducts, shifting to less toxic materials, or shifting to more preferred management

Exhibit 2 ● Resource Efficiency Dimension: Materials Accounting

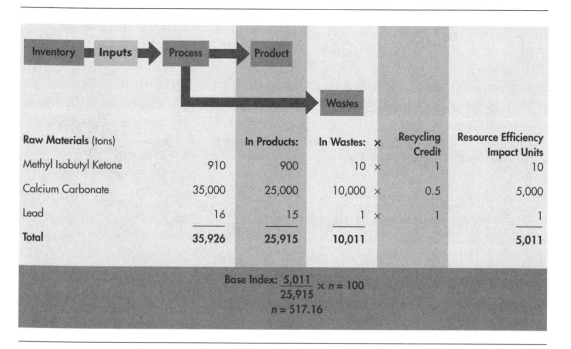

Raw Materials (tons)		In Products:	In Wastes: ×	Recycling Credit	Resource Efficiency Impact Units
Methyl Isobutyl Ketone	910	900	10 ×	1	10
Calcium Carbonate	35,000	25,000	10,000 ×	0.5	5,000
Lead	16	15	1 ×	1	1
Total	35,926	25,915	10,011		5,011

$$\text{Base Index: } \frac{5,011}{25,915} \times n = 100$$
$$n = 517.16$$

TABLE 2 ● IPEPI Toxicity Weighting and Management Practices Factors (Toxicity weighting factor in order of increasing toxicity: 1, 10, 100, 1000)

Management Practices Factors

Factor	Management Practice Factor
0	On-site recycling/reuse
1	Off-site recycling
2	On-site treatment
3	Off-site treatment/disposal
4	Direct release to the environment

practices (Exhibit 4). A similar procedure was followed for the global/regional dimension, except that in the case of combustion sources emissions were calculated using stack monitoring results (where available), engineering calculations, or emission factors, because materials accounting does not apply to combustion where all the fuel is converted into waste or energy.

In many respects, designing the system was the easy part; the major challenges were in implementation. Jim decided that above all, the system had to be accurate, fair, and practical. Moreover, he would have to gain the support of the plant managers and division presidents whose performance would be measured by the system.

Exhibit 3 ● Community Welfare Dimensions (Actual Releases): Prioritizing Environmental Loads

	Inventory → Inputs → Process → Product			
	Wastes:			
	Tons of Waste × Material	Toxicity Weighing × Factor (TWF)	Management Practices = Factor (MPF)	Impact Units (IU)
Methyl Isobutyl Ketone	10	100	4	4,000
Calcium Carbonate	10,000	1	1	10,000
Lead	1	1,000	3	3,000
Total				**17,000**

$$\text{Base Index: } \frac{17,000}{25,915} \times n = 200$$

$$n = 304.88$$

Exhibit 4 ● Improving Performance

Treatment of material "Methyl Isobutyl Ketone":

	Tons	X	TWF	X	MFP =	Community Welfare Impact Units	
						Period 1	Period 2
A	10		100		4→2	4,000	2,000

Source reduction of material "Calcium Carbonate"

B	10,000→6000	X	1	X	1	10,000	6,000

Recycling of material "Lead"

C	1	X	1,000	X	3→1	3,000	1,000
						17,000	9,000

Period 2 Production: 24,656 tons

Period 2 Index:

$$\frac{9,000}{24,656} \times 304.88 = 111$$

Notes

1. SPCC stands for "statistical process control chart," a total quality management tool. IPI's managers joked that they "spoke SPCC" because of the company's emphasis on quality tools.

2. The Toxics Release Inventory is a publicly available database maintained by EPA. At the time, it listed releases of approximately 300 chemicals (subsequently increased to 600) by manufacturing facilities in the U.S. based on annual facility reports.

3. The Toxic Substances Control Act Inventory is an inventory of existing chemicals in commerce maintained by EPA.

4. IPI's Information Services group developed a simple Lotus spreadsheet program that performed these calculations automatically.

36

Oil in the Ecuadorean Rainforest

**Christopher A. Cummings,
Barbara L. Marcus,
R. Edward Freeman,
and Jason Linday**

Ecuador's Amazon region is considered to be one of the greatest areas of biodiversity in the world, serving as home to over 22,000 plant and animal species. This biodiversity has great practical value (for example, raw materials for new drug development) as well as aesthetic value. This region is also the home of numerous indigenous peoples who depend on plant and animal abundance for their survival. This region, like many other tropical rainforest regions, is considered threatened. Economic and social pressures have led to the deforestation of 200 million hectares of the world's tropical rainforest in the past two decades.

In 1991, a consortium of foreign oil companies led by Conoco, Inc. has proposed to develop several oil fields in Ecuador's Amazon region. . . . The debate over the future of Ecuador's rainforest pits two compelling perspectives against one another. Conoco and the Ecuadorean government believe that the fields can be developed in an environmentally sensitive way, while environmental organizations, indigenous peoples' representatives, and multilateral lending institutions are all questioning the company's intent and the appropriate development strategy for the region.

●

Reprinted by permission of The Management Institute for Environment and Business, a program of the World Resources Institute.

BACKGROUND

The consortium . . . led by Conoco, Inc. has spent $90 million on exploration efforts in the area, known as Block 16, over the past four years and determined that the block has over 200 million barrels in reserves, 20% of Ecuador's total reserves. Conoco's proposed development plan would require an up-front investment of $600 million for drilling and production equipment, two parallel 160 km pipelines and a new 140 km road. Approximately $60 million, 10% of the total expected investment, is intended for environmental protection initiatives. Conoco has submitted this plan to Petroecuador, the state oil company that manages oil exploration and production, for approval.

Conoco's plans for development in Block 16 have been questioned. Past development efforts by Petroecuador and foreign oil companies have damaged forest and water resources, and resulted in the colonization of rainforest areas. The government has yet to establish comprehensive environmental guidelines on oil exploration and extraction activities.

Block 16 borders Yasuni National Park, an area which numerous ecologists claim is one of the most biologically diverse regions on earth. The block also is located within the traditional territory of the Waorani, an indigenous Indian tribe. Environmental and indigenous peoples groups are pressuring the government to halt future development in the region. In order to meet its financial obligations to Conoco, Petroecuador has solicited the World Bank for a $100 million loan. Indigenous and environmental groups have demanded that the loan be reconsidered and that no further development in rainforests be allowed until various demands have been met.

Block 16 has emerged as the focus of a major international debate over the parameters of sustainable development, and all of the stakeholder parties are facing difficult questions.

THE STAKEHOLDERS

Several stakeholders have emerged within the debate over Block 16:

Conoco, Inc.

Conoco, the $15.9 billion subsidiary of E.I. du Pont de Nemours and Company, is interested in developing Block 16. The company has spent three years exploring Block 16 and together with its development partners has spent $90 million. The company firmly believes that the block can be developed without damaging the area's natural resources or indigenous communities. The company is aware that several companies in similar situations have terminated operations or been slowed by battles with local groups.

The Waorani

The Waorani, nomadic, isolated groups of hunters and farmers, live within the boundaries of Block 16. The Waorani have halted the operations of other companies in the region, have called for a moratorium on exploration and production in the region, and desire legal rights to "their" land.

The Ecuadorean Government

The government depends on oil revenues for 50% of the country's foreign exchange and 60% of its annual budget. But past oil practices have devastated areas with important natural resources, and the government is under pressure from multilateral institutions and environmental groups to improve management of its natural resources and to cede land rights to indigenous peoples.

The Natural Resources Defense Council (NRDC)

Based in New York, NRDC is an international environmental advocacy organization with a staff of 150 lawyers and scientists. NRDC is concerned that continued development of rainforest regions and poor environmental stewardship will eliminate Ecuador's natural resources and have a severe impact on indigenous tribes.

Fundación Natura

Ecuador's leading environmental group, Natura has worked for a decade to promote environmental education, establish national parks and train park personnel. Natura is concerned that Yasuni National Park, the primary focus of its efforts, will be forever changed by oil production.

The World Bank

The world's leading lending institution for development projects, the World Bank has come under fire from environmental advocates for supporting projects with negative environmental impacts. The organization is considering a $100 million loan to finance Ecuador's oil operations.

Tierra Viva

One of Ecuador's radical environmental groups, Tierra Viva is opposed to any new development in rainforest land. The group represents young environmentalists and has held a protest against Conoco's development plans in Quito, the nation's capital.

STAKEHOLDER DIALOGUE

In November of 1990, Conoco convened a meeting of the stakeholders in Quito to share information and develop an agenda for discussion. The meeting generated an extensive list of options to ensure that development of Block 16 would not jeopardize Yasuni or the Waorani.

It is now January of 1991, and Conoco has convened a second meeting in an effort to develop a comprehensive plan and ensure unanimous support for its proposal. The company has proposed an environmental management plan which includes four major areas: drilling techniques, preventing colonization, pipeline management and park management.[1] Specific actions are detailed below:

Drilling Techniques

- Utilize diagonal drilling techniques, which entail drilling at various angles from a small number of wells as opposed to vertically from many. This practice could reduce deforestation at Conoco's proposed initial 500,000 acre production block to 1,000 hectares—a 90% reduction by industry standards in the region.[2]

- Reinject toxic formation water produced in oil drilling back into the ground. Reinjection would eliminate the typical industry practice of diverting formation water to unlined collection pits, which frequently spill into nearby rivers and streams and adversely affect groundwater supplies. Reinjection also improves oil flow by filling underground voids. To date, only the Atlantic Richfield Company (ARCO) has engaged in this practice in Ecuador.[3]

- Allow stakeholders to audit Conoco's operations and fund their ongoing involvement in the management of Block 16.[4]

Preventing Colonization

- Create and manage a road-monitoring system in order to prevent colonization and agricultural conversion of new lands. Many environmentalists believe that colonization is the greatest threat to the ecosystem and indigenous populations. To date, only Petro-Canada has set up such a system—it is working with the Ecuadorean Army to control settlement.[5]

- Do not construct a bridge to new areas. In Block 16, the Napo River acts as a natural barrier to colonization in and around the block. Barges will be used to transport employees and all supplies, so that park rangers can prevent would-be colonists from using the road to enter Yasuni National Park.[6]

- Disallow any contact between Conoco employees and the Waorani. In the past, oil companies have spread disease and, through gifts and trading, made native populations dependent on western goods.[7]

Pipeline Management

- Bury the pipeline, which would minimize the threat of oil spills and help to reduce the size of the road needed. In the past, flooding and earthquakes have severely damaged the Trans-Ecuadorean pipeline (above-ground), resulting in spills estimated at over 10 million gallons.[8]

- Minimize road construction and take measures to minimize deforestation and silt run-off. Helicopters can be used to transport materials for the pipeline. While roads are not necessary for pipeline construction, they are seen as necessary for on-going maintenance.[9]

Park Management

- Avoid production drilling in the portion of Block 16 that overlaps with Yasuni National Park.[10]
- Create an environmental management plan for Yasuni National Park with relevant stakeholders. Fund government management of the park and training for rangers.
- Use drilling areas as outposts for scientific research teams.[11]

Other options for consideration may include:

- Reinject natural gas into the ground in order to store it for later use or regulate its combustion to minimize emissions. Natural gas, a valuable energy resource, is a by-product of oil extraction. However, oil companies typically burn this gas with open flames, without regard for emissions.[12]

- Provide the Waorani with meaningful title to their lands, giving them profit-sharing opportunities through leasing.[13]
- Work with the Waorani to establish needed services, such as schools and health clinics.[14]
- Disallow fishing, hunting, or trapping by Conoco employees.[15]
- Inoculate indigenous people to help minimize the spread of disease.[16]

A PRIMER

Ecuador is located on the northwestern coast of South America between Columbia to the north and Peru to the south. The country's landscape comprises of three distinct regions running from north to south: the *Costa* region, by far the most populous and urbanized region, which runs along Ecuador's coastal zone; the *Sierra* region, where the Andean mountains stretch through the middle of the country; and the *Oriente* region, home to the country's rainforests and oil reserves. The country is roughly 284,000 square kilometers, about the size of Colorado. . . .

For much of the twentieth century, Ecuador's government has alternated between democratic rule and military dictatorship. Ecuador's large number of political parties made it difficult for one group to gain widespread support. Strong military regimes of the 1960s and 1970s gave way to democratic rule in 1979.

ECUADOR'S POPULATION

Ecuador has been inhabited for thousands of years by a large indigenous population with a variety of cultures and languages. The Incas entered the region from neighboring lands and the Spanish from the coast. Ecuador's current population is composed in large part of descendants of marriages between Spanish and Indian ancestors. Over 50% of the population is under the age of 20, and the World Bank estimates that the population will double within the next 25 years. Native peoples make up about one-third of the country's 10.3 million people.

The World Bank estimates that 85 to 100 thousand native peoples inhabit the Amazon region and have retained relatively autonomous and traditional lifestyles.[17] . . . Indigenous peoples live in all of the major regions of the country but are highly concentrated in the eastern, less-densely populated portion of the country.

People of the Oriente

Six main native groups inhabit Ecuador's Oriente region. The Quicha (40,000), Shuar (35,000), and Achuar (2,000) mainly inhabit the southern regions. They were the first to encounter envoys from Ecuadorean society and have adapted to it, adopting many marketplace practices such as cattle ranching and farming. The Quicha have had the greatest financial success and have moved north into new lands to expand their operations. The Quicha and the Shuar are the primary advocates of indigenous rights within the region.

The northern Amazon natives—the Cofan (350–400), Siona-Secoya (400–500), and Waorani (850–900)—are much fewer in number and have had only sporadic contact with outsiders. The Cofan, which anthropologists believe once numbered near 15,000, have been decimated by the encroachment of Ecuador's western society and oil operations. Their traditional lands have been consumed by oil roads, storage facilities and settlers. Oil pollution of surrounding regions, foreign diseases, and handouts from oil companies altered their way of life and left them dependent on foreign companies. The Siona-Secoya have had contact with settlers and palm plantation workers for many years but have managed to maintain a way of life relatively separate from these neighboring people.

The Waorani are the most secluded of the indigenous groups. The Waorani traditionally lived in small groups of extended families and isolated themselves deep within the rainforest regions, mainly in the area now designated as Yasuni National Park. Their livelihood and culture depends on hunting, farming, fishing and food collecting. Earliest interactions between the Waorani and oil companies were violent. When Royal Dutch/Shell personnel began exploring the Oriente in the 1940s, the Waorani killed hundreds of workers and looted the camps. In 1968, after years of appeals from the Summer Institute of Linguistics, four groups of Waorani (the Guequetairi, Piyamoiri, Baihuairi, and Huepeiri) moved into the Reserva Waorani, a 1,600 square kilometer protectorate southwest of their traditional lands. Approximately 700 Waorani live in the reserve.

The remaining 100–150 Waorani occupy lands within Yasuni National Park and continue to resist contact from outsiders, including the government and foreign companies. Despite their wishes, increased interest in the region has expanded their contact with outsiders. Over the years, missionary groups have entered the region offering spiritual guidance, education, and health services. Today, the region's natural resources draw scientists, environmentalists, and tourists to the national parks and wildlife refuges. The Tagairi Waorani, the most isolated and only hostile group of Waorani, gained attention in 1987 when they ritualistically killed two missionaries sent by oil companies to establish contact. The consortium temporarily suspended operations. Rumors abound that oil representatives killed Tagae, this group's leader, in 1989.

According to the World Bank, the Waorani face "special problems because of their smaller size and greater dependency upon forest resources (wildlife, fish, gathered products, etc.)."[18] Oil spills in water sources, disruptions of wildlife habitat, and colonization threaten their livelihood. Viral infections, brought in by outsiders, are a major cause of death among the Waorani.

ECUADOR'S NATURAL RESOURCES

Beginning with Charles Darwin's research in the Galapagos Islands, Ecuador has long been recognized for its wealth of natural resources. The country is home to some of the most biologically diverse rainforests in the world as well as significant oil reserves.

Biological Diversity

Ecuador contains 25% of all species found in Latin America and the Caribbean. The country contains between 20,000 and 25,000 recognized plant species; North America as a whole contains 17,000 plant species. Ecuador is also home to over 2,400 terrestrial vertebrate species, compared with less than 1,400 similar species found in the continental United States.[19] Ecuador's

Oriente region houses the western tip of the Amazon Basin, which scientists deem the world's largest and most important rainforest. . . . The Oriente, which is only one-fifth the size of the Brazilian Amazon, contains 70% of all the species found in the Brazilian region.[20]

Officially created in 1979, Yasuni National Park stands out among Ecuador's protected areas. The park protects nearly 700,000 hectares of tropical rainforest, wetlands, lakes and rivers.[21] Home to an estimated 600 species of birds, 500 species of fish, 500 species of flowering plants and 120 species of mammals, the park is listed among the top "conservation priorities" of several leading environmental groups, such as Conservation International and The Nature Conservancy.[22] In 1989, the United Nations Man and the Biosphere Program designated the park a U.N. Biosphere due to its biological importance. U.N. Biospheres receive international support for monitoring, but a Yasuni monitoring system has not yet been developed.

Oil Reserves

Oil mining began in Ecuador in 1909 when the state government contracted several British and Italian companies to search for underground oil, providing the state with a percentage of the profits from any discoveries. In the 1930s, a predecessor of British Petroleum began pumping operations on the Santa Elena peninsula, on the southern coast. Though production volumes were small by industry standards, enough was being pumped by British Petroleum that exports from Ecuador outpaced domestic consumption by about four to one.

There was periodic exploration in the country's Oriente region, located in the heart of the Amazon jungle. Although various experts believed that the region was potentially the world's most valuable petroleum reserve, infant technologies and rugged terrain precluded explo-

ration success. In the late 1960s and early 1970s, a Texaco–Gulf Oil Company consortium found five commercially attractive fields which still account for the majority of Ecuador's production. By 1972, the Texaco consortium had completed a 498 km Trans-Ecuadorean Pipeline, which transfers oil from the Oriente region through refining and processing stations in Quito to the port city of Esmeraldas, at a cost of $150 million.

Ecuador's oil production grew from 3,700 barrels per day (b/d) in 1971 to 208,800 b/d in 1973. The country became a member of the Organization of Petroleum Exporting Countries (OPEC) and the second largest oil producer in Latin America. By the late 1970s, 36 foreign companies were prospecting in 10 million hectares in the Oriente region.

Ecuador's military government established a state oil company—now called Petroleos del Ecuador or Petroecuador—and reclaimed two-thirds of the Texaco-Gulf concessions. It boosted its production royalties, levied taxes on foreign corporations, and slashed the size of foreign companies' concessions. Petroecuador forced Gulf to pull out of Ecuador and took over its partnership with Texaco.

Based on optimistic expectations of oil revenues in the mid and late 1970s, the government borrowed heavily from foreign countries for Petroecuador's activities, industry diversification, social programs, and the government's own burgeoning bureaucracy. But falling prices brought on a cash shortfall, and the government was unable to make its required payments on several occasions.

Oil remained the government's major financing tool. However, the rate of extraction quickly sent net reserves plummeting, and state-run exploration efforts failed to stem the reserve loss. By 1981, only five companies were exploring 6,000 hectares.

ECUADOR'S DEVELOPMENT

Population Pressures

Due to population growth, environmental degradation and drought conditions, Ecuadoreans began to migrate out of the rural areas of the country's Costa and Sierra regions.[23] Ecuador's 1978 Ley de Colonizacion de la Region Amazonica established development and settlement in the Oriente as a national priority. Indian groups see gaining legal title to lands as the only means to protect themselves from colonization and to preserve their way of life. Pressure from groups in the region has strained relations with the Ecuadorean government.

Under current law, the lands occupied by indigenous communities are classified as *tierras baldias,* or unoccupied lands, and are subject to state ownership and regulation. The Ecuadorean Institute for Agrarian Reform and Land Settlement is supposed to set aside lands traditionally occupied by indigenous communities, but these peoples can obtain legal title to the land only if they organize themselves in cooperatives such as settler populations. As of 1990, only 24 of 78 Quicha communities and 83 of 265 Shuar communities had gained titles to their lands.

Native populations have increasingly organized themselves into regional indigenous federations in order to reaffirm native culture and pursue land rights. In 1980, the Confederacion de Nacionalidades Indigenas de la Amazonia Ecuadoriana (CONFENIAE) formed to represent the natives of the region. Eight local federations with representatives from over 960 Amazonian communities compose the group's membership. The group has stressed the importance of "conservation and rational development of the resources of the Amazon Region."[24] CONFENIAE is dominated by the Quicha and the Shuar, and certain Waorani groups are not parties to the organization.

Economic Pressures

The country's economy is based mainly on agriculture and oil production. In 1970, bananas accounted for nearly 47% of total export revenues; coffee and cacao followed. But dramatic increases in oil production volumes of the early 1970s catapulted petroleum to the top of the country's export charts, and price shocks in the early and late 1970s compounded oil's importance.

Year	U.S.$/Barrel	% of Total Export Revenue
1972	2.50	19
1974	13.70	60

Between 1972 and 1982, the government generated $7.4 billion in oil revenues, which allowed it to expand its operations and invest in new industries and transportation infrastructure. Government expenditures grew by 9.6% and gross domestic product by 9.1% annually over the same period. The country's oil revenues and untapped reserves were used to attract loans from banks in developed countries to further develop the oil industry Foreign debt spiraled upward from $600 million in 1973 to $6.3 billion in 1983. Government efforts to diversify the economy proved unsuccessful.

One observer stated, "In the 1980s, recession among Ecuador's trading partners, rising interest rates, and falling oil prices crippled Ecuador's economy."[25] Oil prices fell from a peak of $45/barrel in the late 1970s to $15/barrel by the mid-1980s. By 1987, Ecuador's total external debt had reached $9.6 billion, split evenly between multilateral development institutions and commercial banks. The government engaged in debt renegotiations throughout most of the 1980s. Payments were temporarily suspended after a 1987 earthquake severely ruptured the Trans-Ecuadorean pipeline and halted oil production.

Oil production has raised average incomes 500% since the 1960s and currently provides over 50% of the country's foreign exchange and 60% of the government's yearly budget. Ecuador's annual economic growth rate is 2.8% and per capita GNP is $980.[26] By 1990, total outstanding debt was $12.4 billion, 120% of GNP.

Efforts to Increase Oil Production

By 1982, after 10 years of unsuccessful exploration by Petroecuador and Texaco, the country's reserves had fallen far short of production levels. The government took steps to revive foreign interest in exploration and development in an effort to stem losses in its reserves and minimize its financial exposure. The government designed new legislation to allow foreign oil companies to undertake exploration activities under service/risk contracts.

Under the service/risk approach, foreign companies bid to explore particular geographic regions and negotiate contracts with Petroecuador. Contracts detail the service that the foreign company will provide. The risk of exploration is borne entirely by foreign companies. If no commercially-attractive reserves are found, the foreign company loses its investment.

If commercially attractive reserves are found, the Ecuadorean government reimburses the foreign company in crude or cash for investments and production costs. The foreign companies can then negotiate a 20-year production contract with Petroecuador. The government collects royalties based on production levels, as well as taxes.

Since 1985, six bidding rounds have resulted in thirteen new contracts. Thirty companies have undertaken exploration activities at a total investment of $400 million. Ten of the exploration blocks are located in the Oriente region and four are located in state parks or biological reserves. State officials hope that current development efforts will enable Ecuador to

increase its reserves by 1 billion barrels, but "the results have been disappointing, with around 250 million barrels discovered."[27]

After the 1987 earthquake, emergency loans from the World Bank and assistance from Colombia kept some oil flowing, but not before major export revenues had been lost.

By 1990, Ecuador produced nearly 300,000 b/d or 110 million barrels per year. Ninety-nine percent of the country's daily output came from the Oriente region; most of these fields were in decline.[28] The U.S. Central Intelligence Agency estimates that the country's maximum sustainable production capacity is 330,000 b/d.[29] Petroecuador recently completed expansion of the pipeline's capacity, which can now transport 325,000 b/d. Domestic consumption, buoyed by a growing population, has risen 11% per year, causing exports to fall to approximately 50% of production. Experts predict that, if new fields are not developed, Ecuador will have no oil exports by the end of the century. Government officials are contemplating dropping out of OPEC.

OIL IN THE RAINFOREST

Oil exploration and development in Ecuador has come into conflict with the protection and conservation of the rainforest. Oil development supersedes the protection of natural resources in law and in deed. Special laws govern oil production—any minerals below the surface of the land are the property of the sovereign state, and can be exploited at Petroecuador's will. Oil production is currently underway in the Cuyabeno Wildlife Reserve and Limoncocha Biological Reserve. Production techniques and development patterns impact the whole of Ecuador's Amazon region and its national parks, including Yasuni:

Oil Pollution

The Trans-Ecuadorean pipeline has pumped 1.5 billion gallons of oil from the Oriente to Esmeraldas; it is estimated that over 10 million gallons have been spilled. A consultant to the Natural Resources Defense Council (NRDC) estimated that 4.3 million gallons of toxics were dumped every day into unlined waste pits.[30] According to Ecuador's Ministry of Energy and Mines, these pits overflow into nearby rivers and streams. Pipeline officials estimate that 210,000 gallons of oil have spilled into the watershed areas of four major rivers, destroying plant and animal life for hundreds of miles and jeopardizing local populations dependent on the land and its resources for their sustenance.

Petroecuador claims that such problems will not happen in the future. According to Luis Roeman, President of Petroecuador: "We developed these fields in a hurry. Because our prices were going down and exports were declining, and we need to repay our foreign debt. And I have to be very honest with you, we had money from the World Bank to develop these fields in a hurry. We probably were not very careful when it came to our problems . . . I think we ought to be very honest and say, 'yes, we've done things very bad.' And what we're trying to do now is to correct whatever damages we've done in the past. From now on we're not going to make those same mistakes."[31]

Deforestation

Exploration and development activities require clearing portions of land to undertake seismic testing and facilitate helicopter transportation. In an average block, the Atlantic Richfield Company reported that it cleared 355 acres and felled some 372,000 trees.[32] An independent commission estimated the total to be at least 7 times as much. These numbers rise significantly when a block moves from the exploration phase and into the development and production phase.

Colonization

Roads may be the greatest long-term threat to the landscape and its people. Data from the country's 1982 census indicate that 70% of the Oriente's population arrived after 1972, when oil extraction got underway. The Oriente's population growth rate is twice the national average. World Bank experts estimate that for each mile of new road built by the oil industry in the rainforest, 1,600 to 10,000 acres of land are colonized. Colonists clear the forest for farmland to grow cash crops such as coffee, *naranjilla,* and cacao. Land speculators, loggers, and ranchers typically follow. Experts are debating whether well-planned road building can control colonization.

NRDC had previously called on Texaco to establish a $50 million fund to finance environmental clean-ups within the region. The company stated that its practices were consistent with the rest of the industry, and admitted to no wrong-doing.

A 1990 World Bank study of Ecuador's Amazon region concluded that, if current trends continued, the country could expect the following:

- Irreversible loss of the region's renewable and non-renewable resources and of their potential to produce regional and national economic benefits;
- Diminishing returns of economic activities over time as the fragile resource base is depleted;
- Social conflicts between indigenous and migrant populations; and
- Eventually, reverse migration as people abandon the degraded Amazon region, thus contributing to even greater pressures in non-Amazon regions.[33]

ENVIRONMENTAL PROTECTION EFFORTS

Fundación Natura, Ecuador's leading environmental nonprofit organization, was founded in 1978. Since its inception, Natura has focused public attention on environmental conditions in the Oriente, which is experiencing deforestation at a rate of 2.3% per year. Although down from a rate of 3.4% in the early 1980s, the deforestation rate is "more and more shameful," according to Natura.[34] The group estimates that 320,000 acres of Ecuador's rainforests were destroyed by 1980 and the rest will be gone by 2035. The Oriente, Natura believes, will go the way of Ecuador's western region, where over 90% of the original forests have been lost and only 3.4% have been reforested.

In 1984, several individuals left Natura to form Tierra Viva, a more radical environmental organization. Tierra Viva has focused most of its attention on the Oriente and has identified oil development projects as the primary threat to the region. The group accuses the government of "working against the environment" and is opposed to any development within the Oriente.

The Ecuadorean government has recently undertaken several actions with regard to environmental protection:

- In 1989, the Subsecretario de Medio Ambiente (SMA), Ecuador's environment agency, was established. SMA has an annual budget of $10,000 and full-time staff of four. Oversight of the oil industry is a primary responsibility.

- In 1989, staff within the Ministry of Energy and Mines began to design a comprehensive set of guidelines for oil development in the country. After several months of work, this staff was instructed to stop its work. As a substitute, eleven major oil companies, Petroecuador, and Fundación Natura signed an Act of Commitment (voluntary agreement) with the Ministry of Energy and Mines in August of 1990. The main element of the two-year accord is a commitment by the companies "to ensure the rational management of oil

activities and to undertake environmental impact studies."[35]

Fernando Santos, former minister of the Department of Energy and Mines, is not confident that environmental laws or voluntary agreements will have any impact: "I see an attitude of hypocrisy. If Texaco is guilty of causing harm to the environment, Petroecuador is 10 times worse. For the new companies, they have been very strict, demanding guarantees that the environment will be protected. I can assure you that Petroecuador will laugh at this rule. They operate under no rule of environmental protection."[36]

In April of 1990, the government altered the boundaries of Yasuni National Park. See Exhibit 1. Prior to the changes, Block 16, a major oil development site, was entirely within Yasuni. Afterward, Yasuni and Block 16 overlap only in a small area that is not planned for development. The scientific community was outraged at the government's actions. A draft management plan for Yasuni, developed by an American environmental group and the government and financed by Conoco, designated up to 50% of the park for industrial use. Tierra Viva and others have sharply criticized the plan for its pro-development bent.

In October 1990, the Ecuadorean Tribunal of Constitutional Guarantees ruled that new oil development within park boundaries was illegal, but that existing concessions could continue. Later that month, the Tribunal reversed its earlier decision, stating that new development was permissible.[37] Indigenous peoples were instructed not to "impede or obstruct" oil or mining activities on those lands. Currently, nine oil fields are in operation in the Cuyabeno Wildlife Reserve, located north of Yasuni, and several blocks which overlap with national park land are slated for exploration. Shortly after the Tribunal's ruling, the government instituted a $100,000 environmental tax on each company

Exhibit 1

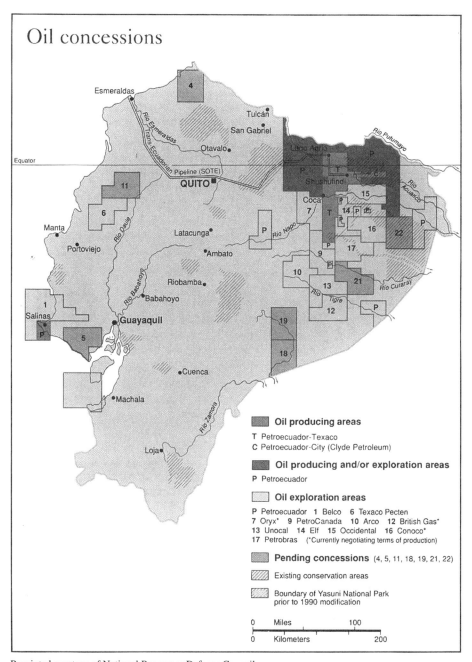

Reprinted courtesy of National Resources Defense Council.

involved in oil exploration to fund the clean-up of past environmental damages.

BLOCK 16

Block 16, 160 miles southeast of Quito in the heart of the Oriente, is the most promising of the contracts negotiated since 1982. The various economic and environmental pressures Ecuador's policy makers must face are all relevant to the proposed development of this region.

In 1986, a consortium led by Conoco, Inc. entered into a contract with the Ecuadorean government to conduct oil exploration in Block 16. These efforts have yielded five commercially attractive fields with estimated reserves of 200 million barrels, 20% of Ecuador's proven reserves. Conoco and Petroecuador believe Block 16 will support 45,000 b/d for 20 years. No further exploration work is scheduled until Conoco receives official approval for its development plans.

The oil extracted from the Oriente region is relatively heavy and very viscous. This type of oil is considered inferior to Brent North Sea crude and sells for approximately $4 per barrel less. The average long-term price for Ecuador's oil has been estimated at $15 per barrel.[38]

To date, the Conoco-led consortium has invested $90 million in the exploration of Block 16. Conoco's exploration activities have been disrupted by Waorani tribesmen on two occasions. During their first "raid," unarmed Waorani warriors entered the Conoco camp, stopped operations, and took a chainsaw upon their departure; during the second, they came armed with shotguns and automatic rifles and left with another chainsaw. Ecuadorean conservationists speculate that these men are not the same as those responsible for the death of the Catholic missionaries in 1987.

The company's proposed development plan would require an up-front investment of $600 million for production equipment, two parallel 160 km pipelines and a 140 km road. The Conoco plan states that the environmental impacts will be low to moderate and will be reversible. . . .

Conoco's development plans call for $60 million for environmental protection initiatives. The company originally allocated this percentage to its plans because, in the words of Alex Chapman, manager of environmental projects in Ecuador, "If we designed for a low standard and then later had to upgrade to higher standards, costs could be excessive."[39] One challenge that Conoco faces is ensuring that this level of investment is supported by Petroecuador. Petroecuador ultimately will pay the sum under the service/risk contract structure. Conoco managers included the following environmental investments and initiatives in its original development proposal to Petroecuador:

- Reinject formation water and other wastes.
- Engage in directional drilling in a number of areas.
- Use synthetic materials, rather than felled trees, for new road areas.
- Construct four "police stations" along the new roads to protect Yasuni National Park.[40]

Conoco expects that environmentally sound production will raise its operating and maintenance costs by approximately 15%.

The government has designated Block 16 land as a new addition to the Waorani protectorate, but with the explicit mandate that the group cannot "impede or obstruct" oil or mining activities. James Yost, an anthropologist later hired as a consultant to Conoco, has warned Conoco that further loss of land will result in harm to the Waorani—"deculturation and ethnocide."[41]

Petroecuador needs cash to meet the financial obligations of the service/risk contract it has with Conoco. The World Bank is considering a $100 million loan to Petroecuador, which could total $450 million with co-financing from other sources. Petroecuador's most recent loan from the World Bank required the creation of an environmental management program for the Oriente and the pipeline. Petroecuador has not yet fulfilled this requirement.

CONFENIAE has attacked the World Bank for considering the loan. CONFENIAE has issued demands that "must be met" before any further actions are taken in Block 16. Among them, the organization wants guaranteed land rights for Indians, including the Waorani, and a 10-year moratorium on oil exploration and production within the Oriente. . . .

Local groups are concerned that revenues from oil generation are not helping the people of Ecuador. In the words of Ecuadorean ecologist Eduardo Asanza: "Ecuador is a poor country and we need the oil, but I have lived here for fifteen years and have seen this area grow poorer and poorer. Now when I go to Lago Agrio [a town located near a large oil field], I wonder, how can those people survive? We were all told that the oil would help the country, but sometimes we wonder, 'Who is being helped?'"[42]

Notes

1. Ann Blumberg, "How Conoco is Working to Minimize Damage to Ecuador's Rain Forest," *Business International,* June 23, 1990.

2. Ibid.

3. James Brooke, "New Effort Would Test Possible Coexistence of Oil and Rain Forest," *New York Times,* February 26,1991.

4. Robert F. Kennedy, "Amazon Sabotage," *Washington Post,* August 24,1992.

5. Brooke, op cit.

6. Blumberg, op cit.

7. Brooke, op cit.

8. Ibid.

9. Ibid.

10. Douglas Southgate, "The Economics of Pollution Control in Eastern Ecuador," *Ecodecision,* June 1992.

11. Brooke, op cit.

12. Judith Kimerling with the Natural Resources Defense Council, *Amazon Crude* (New York: NRDC, 1991).

13. Martha M. Hamilton, "Sierra Club, Law Firm Allege Oil Firm Misdeeds in Ecuador," *Washington Post,* May 16, 1991,

14. Brooke, op cit.

15. Ibid.

16. Southgate, op cit.

17. James F. Hicks, *Ecuador's Amazon Region: Development Issues and Options,* World Bank Discussion Paper #75 (Washington, DC: World Bank Publications, 1990).

18. Ibid.

19. Ibid.

20. World Resources Institute, *The 1992 Information Please Environmental Almanac* (Boston: Houghton Mifflin Company, 1992).

21. James D. Nations, "Road Construction and Oil Production in Ecuador's Yasuni National Park," author's files, May 1988.

22. Brooke, op cit.

23. Hicks, op cit.

24. Ibid.

25. Kimerling, op cit.

26. World Bank, *World Development Report 1992: Development and the Environment* (Oxford, England: Oxford University Press, 1992).

27. Christopher Brogan, "Struggle to Replace Reserves," *Petroleum Economist,* July 1991.

28. Christopher Brogan, "Concern over Export Capacity," *Petroleum Economist,* July 1990.

29. "Ecuador boosts E&D to stem reserves slide," *Oil & Gas Journal,* 1990.

30. Kimerling, op cit.

31.   National Public Radio, "Vanishing Homeland: Ecuador, Amazon, and Oil," Morning Edition, January 13, 1992.

32.   Kimerling, op cit; Joe Kane, "With Spears from All Sides," *The New Yorker,* September 27, 1993.

33.   Hicks, op cit.

34.   Leslie Ware, "Sucres of Cecropias?" *Audubon,* January 1985.

35.   Brogan, "Struggle to Replace Reserves," op cit.

36.   National Public Radio, op cit.

37.   Dianne Dumanoski, "Probe of Oil Firms Asked in Reversal of Amazon Drilling Curb," *The Boston Globe,* May 16, 1991; Martha M. Hamilton, "Sierra Club, Law Firm Allege Oil Firm Misdeeds in Ecuador," *Washington Post,* May 16, 1991; "Oil Companies Pressured Ecuador on Amazon Project, Sierra Club Charges," *Platt's Oilgram News,* May 15, 1991.

38.   Douglas Southgate and Morris Whitaker, *Economic Progress and the Environment: One Developing Country's Policy Crisis* (New York: Oxford University Press, 1994).

39.   Susan E. A. Hall, "Conoco's Green' Oil Strategy," (Cambridge, MA: Harvard Business School, 1992), Case # 9-394-001.

40.   Brooke, op cit.

41.   Kane, op cit.

42.   Kimerling, op cit.

37

Cost Accounting and Hazardous Wastes at Specialty Glass, Inc.
Christopher H. Stinson

1. THE COMPANY, ITS PRODUCTS, AND MARKETS

Specialty Glass is a privately-owned company that manufactures about 30 percent of the world's supply of specialty sheet glass (i.e., colored sheet glass for stained-glass windows or lamps). Specialty is a high-volume, low-margin producer of specialty sheet glass with about $12 million annual sales. A majority (50–60 percent) of their sales are to the stained glass market (e.g., arts and crafts shops, stained glass artists, etc.). The remaining sales are to overseas manufacturers of specialty lighting who receive the shipped glass, produce lighting products, and ship the finished products back to the United States. Although there are other manufacturers of specialty sheet glass in North America, Specialty (with 160 employees) is substantially larger than any of these competitors (typically with 5–6 employees each).

Specialty uses both daytanks (where melting, cooking, and usage take place in a 24-hour cycle) and continuous furnaces (where molten glass is removed at the same rate that raw materials are added); the latter process produces glass that withstands more stress than other sheet glass. Continuous furnaces require large amounts of electricity; this is affordable for Specialty because of the relatively low price for electricity in the Pacific Northwest. Continuous furnaces also require a substantial investment in equipment. These high upfront and operating costs keeps many of Specialty's smaller competitors from investing in similar equipment, and gives Specialty a competitive advantage in producing this glass. Apparently, the limited size of the worldwide market keeps better capitalized firms from entering this market.

2. MANUFACTURING PROCESS FOR SPECIALTY SHEET GLASS

Specialty manufactures its specialty glass on a batch basis in a plant built in 1979. For each production run, the precursors of glass (sand, soda ash, and limestone) and coloring chemicals are mixed together. Because some of the colorants are hazardous, they are mixed with the cullet in a closed weighing room. The colorants are mixed with a measured volume of glass cullet and put into an electric furnace. Furnace smoke (as well as weighing room dust) is ventilated into a baghouse (i.e., a room separated from the plant by a series of fabric filters that help separate solid particulates from the air).

After the furnace melts the glass and oxidizes the colorants, the new sheet glass is formed, cooled, and removed from the furnace. If the

Acknowledgments and Disclaimer. This case is based on material collected for *Green Ledgers: Case Studies in Corporate Environmental Accounting,* a 1995 publication of the World Resources Institute (Washington, D.C.) edited by Daryl Ditz, Janet Ranganathan, and R. Darryl Banks. The author gratefully acknowledges the support of the World Resources Institute as well as editorial suggestions from Daryl Ditz and Janet Ranganathan. The information presented in this MEB case is intended only to stimulate classroom discussion; this case is not intended to identify specific management practices as either desirable or undesirable.

glass is broken during cooling or subsequent handling, it is crushed into cullet. Sometimes this cullet is recycled through the furnace; however, it is not always possible to reuse cullet (e.g., the original mix may have included some chemicals that changed composition when they were heated).

Specialty's continuous manufacturing process mixes "fines" (i.e., fine ash collected from cloth filters in the baghouse) from the different glasses. Specialty Glass generates about 15,300 pounds of "fines" annually as well as an additional 2,700 pounds of other hazardous waste each year. Specialty pays approximately $3,500/ton (i.e., $32,500/year) to dispose of the fines and other hazardous waste.

After manufacture, the finished glass is cut into desired dimensions and packed for shipping. Because the glass must be well protected during shipping, about one-tenth of Specialty's product cost is for packaging. Any remaining glass fragments are crushed into cullet; the cullet is either recycled internally or sold.

3. ENVIRONMENTAL ISSUES FACING SPECIALTY GLASS

Cadmium oxide and other pigments used in the manufacture of yellow, orange, and red glass are highly toxic, hazardous chemicals. For the past ninety years, both glaze and glass producers have searched (unsuccessfully, to date) for alternative, less toxic pigments. Specialty Glass is one of only two U.S. manufacturers still making ruby-red glass; because of environmental concerns, the manufacture of this red glass is prohibited in Europe. Consequently, individuals building new churches in Florida or new mosques in North Africa purchase red glass for their stained-glass windows from Specialty.

The coloring chemicals are the primary source of the environmental issues—hazardous waste disposal and air emissions—facing Specialty Glass. For example, increasingly restrictive regulations on the manufacture of cadmium

oxide (which is used in the manufacture of ruby-red glass) will probably lead to the disappearance of this product in the near future. Asarco (in Tacoma, Washington) had been Specialty Glass's biggest supplier of cadmium oxide but they have discontinued this product; other manufacturers are apparently also considering discontinuing the manufacture of cadmium oxide. Alternatively, some manufacturers are moving their cadmium production out of the United States where they will melt the cadmium into glass, crush the glass, and ship the crushed glass back to their U.S. customers.

A news item from *Greenwire* (November 27, 1995, Vol. 5, No. 144) describes one of the many human-health consequences of cadmium exposure.

> High concentrations of cadmium may be responsible for increased levels of kidney disease in residents living along the Jinzu River in Japan's Toyama prefecture, according to a new study by the Toyama Medical and Pharmaceutical U. The Mitsui Mining and Smelting Co. in 1968 released cadmium into the Jinzu River, causing at least 181 Toyama prefecture residents to suffer from the "excruciatingly painful" Itai Itai disease. The Itai Itai outbreak "ranks as the second worst pollution related disease" in Japan, after the Minamata mercury poisoning episode. In 1984 and 1995, the researchers tested the urine of 111 women in five cadmium-contaminated areas and 17 women in a noncontaminated area. All were born between 1914–29 and gave birth when cadmium poisoning in the region became more severe. In 1995, 63.1% of the women showed signs of a kidney disorder, compared with 43.2% in 1984.

Air Emissions.   In 1990 and 1991, state environmental regulators became concerned with the "visible plume" of smoke from Specialty's stack. Specialty Glass installed emission controls that eliminated the "visible" component of their air emissions. However, by 1992, Specialty Glass's technical staff realized that their operations would be limited by additional regulatory constraints regarding air emissions. In the extreme, their company might be closed down and their jobs (in a relatively small, specialized industry) might disappear. Currently, Specialty faces the same regulations as non-specialty glass manufacturers (i.e., limits on the particulates in air emissions without regard for their toxicity). However, more restrictive emission requirements of cadmium were pending from the Puget Sound Air Quality Control Board (PSAQCB). In anticipation of these new regulations, Specialty Glass started sampling the air emissions from their smokestacks.

The stack sampling showed that Specialty was still emitting measurable amounts of cadmium into the atmosphere. In response to these results, Specialty installed a "bag house" on the furnace; in a bag house, most toxic particulates from the weighing room and furnace are recaptured and not emitted into the atmosphere. Currently, the bag house captures 99.7 percent of the material previously emitted into the air. This is currently the "best available technology" but this does not ensure future compliance if more advanced technologies are developed in the future. *Hazardous \Wastes.* Hazardous solid wastes are produced when cadmium burns off during the manufacturing process and is captured as ash in the stack. Hazardous wastes are also generated from spilling and wastage that ends up on the plant floor. However, not all glass breakage becomes hazardous waste. For example, Specialty's white glass cullet is sold to a marble manufacturer who makes "industrial marbles" for mixing the paint stored inside cans of spray paint.

Until mid-1993, Specialty had been shipping their cadmium wastes to an Oregon landfill.

However, this landfill recently closed its gates to all cadmium wastes. Now, Specialty has these wastes trucked to a waste processor in Arkansas. Specialty has the alternative of mixing the ash from their stacks with melted glass, thereby creating a glass-encased waste that would not allow diffusion or leaching of any contained hazardous materials. However, because this would be a "treatment" of hazardous wastes (under RCRA and associated federal regulations), Specialty Glass would have to apply for permission to operate as a Treatment, Storage, and Disposal (TSD) Facility; this application process requires a lengthy and expensive regulatory review. Furthermore, despite the fact that Specialty's glass engineers are certain that the glass-encased waste would be stable, there is no guarantee that the procedure would receive regulatory approval. Currently, Specialty does take their floor sweepings and melt them into glass which is then crushed and sold for use in roads and driveways; because these glass pellets are sold, they are not a hazardous "waste."

4. HOW SPECIALTY GLASS PRICES THEIR DIFFERENT PRODUCTS.

Speciality Glass charges roughly the same price for its different products (i.e., different colors of sheet glass). This price is based on the average cost of input materials and labor that are common to all their products as well as a proportional share of Specialty's overhead. Some colors of glass are priced higher than other colors because the higher-priced products have higher direct manufacturing costs. For example, some coloring pigments are more volatile than others; these less stable pigments require more pigment per square foot of finished glass as well as more labor during production (i.e., both direct-material and direct-labor costs are higher for the higher-priced products).